The Pinochet File

A Declassified Dossier on Atrocity and Accountability

PETER KORNBLUH

NEW YORK
LONDON

First published in the United States by The New Press, New York, 2003
This paperback edition published by The New Press, 2013
Distributed by Perseus Distribution

ISBN 978-1-59558-912-5 (pbk.)

LIBRARY OF CONGRESS CATALOGING-IN-PUBLICATION DATA

Kornbluh, Peter.
The Pinochet file: a declassified dossier on atrocity and accountability / Peter Kornbluh.
p. cm.
Includes bibliographical references.
ISBN 1-56584-586-2 (hc.)
1. Pinochet Ugarte, Augusto. 2. Chile–History–1970–973–Sources.
3. Chile–History–1973–1988–Sources. 4. Chile–History–1988–Sources. 5. Human rights–Chile–History–20th century–Sources. 6. State-sponsored terrorism–Chile–History–20th century–Sources. 7. Subversive activities–Chile–History–20th century–Sources. 8. United States. Central Intelligence Agency–Sources. 9. Chile–Relations–United States–Sources. 10. United States–Relations–Chile–Sources. I. Title.
F3101.P56K67 2003
983.06'5–dc21

2003050956

The New Press publishes books that promote and enrich public discussion and understanding of the issues vital to our democracy and to a more equitable world. These books are made possible by the enthusiasm of our readers; the support of a committed group of donors, large and small; the collaboration of our many partners in the independent media and the not-for-profit sector; booksellers, who often hand-sell New Press books; librarians; and above all by our authors.

www.thenewpress.com

Composition by Westchester Book Composition

Printed in the United States of America

2 4 6 8 10 9 7 5 3 1

GABRIELA VEGA

Peter Kornbluh directs the Chile Documentation Project at the National Security Archive. His books include *The Bay of Pigs Declassified*, *The Iran-Contra Scandal* (with Malcolm Byrne), and *The Cuban Missile Crisis, 1962* (with Laurence Chang). He lives in Washington, D.C.

Also by Peter Kornbluh

BOOKS

Talking to Castro: The Hidden History of U.S.-Cuban Diplomacy (with William LeoGrande, forthcoming in 2014)

Pinochet: El Archivo Secreto

Los EEUU y El Derrocamiento De Allende

Bay of Pigs Declassified: The Secret CIA Report on the Invasion of Cuba

The Iran-Contra Scandal: The Declassified History (with Malcolm Byrne)

The Cuban Missile Crisis, 1962 (with Lawrence Chang)

Low Intensity Warfare: Counterinsurgency, Proinsurgency, and Antiterrorism in the Eighties (with Michael Klare)

Nicaragua: The Price of Intervention

DOCUMENT COLLECTIONS

Chile and the United States: U.S. Policy Toward Democracy, Dictatorship, and Human Rights, 1970–1990

The Cuban Missile Crisis Revisited: An International Collection of Documents, from the Bay of Pigs to the Brink of Nuclear War

The Iran-Contra Affair: The Making of a Scandal, 1983–1988 (with Malcolm Byrne)

Nicaragua: The Making of U.S. Policy, 1978–1990

Contents

IN MY MEMORY

To my father, Hy Kornbluh, this book is dedicated. He taught me, through parental patience as well as his social and political commitment, the simple meaning of human decency in a world of many ills and evils that could not be ignored—as he made sure I understood. To him I owe the construct of conscience and the sense of common community that has enabled this work from the first page to the last.

Introduction: History and Accountability

It is not a part of American history that we are proud of.
—Secretary of State Colin Powell, responding to a question on the morality of the U.S. role in Chile, February 20, 2003

Just before midnight on October 16, 1998, two Scotland Yard officials slipped through the halls of an elite private clinic in London and secured the room in which former Chilean dictator, General Augusto Pinochet, was recovering from back surgery. With English efficiency, they disarmed his private bodyguards, disconnected the phones, posted eight policemen outside the door, and then proceeded to serve Pinochet with a warrant from INTERPOL. Within minutes, British authorities accomplished what the Chilean courts had refused to do since the end of his military regime in 1990—they placed Pinochet under arrest for crimes against humanity.

General Pinochet, whose name became synonymous with gross violations of human rights during his seventeen-year dictatorship, spent 504 days under house arrest in London. Only aggressive diplomatic intervention by Chile's civilian government, pressured by the *Pinochetistas* in the Chilean military, and an adroit propaganda campaign waged by his lawyers, kept him from being extradited to Spain to stand trial for offenses ranging from torture to terrorism. After sixteen months in detention, the British government released the eighty-four-year-old general on what it termed "humanitarian grounds." When he returned to his homeland, however, he was stripped of his immunity from prosecution, indicted, and interrogated. At one point Pinochet even faced the ignominious prospect of being fingerprinted and posing for a mug shot. Initially, the Chilean courts ruled that due to age-related dementia Pinochet could not be put on trial for the abuses committed under his military reign; at the time of his death, however, Pinochet faced multiple indictments.

Pinochet evaded punishment. But the saga of the "Pinochet Case" remains a historic milestone in the pursuit of accountability over atrocity. His arrest marked a long-awaited vindication for not only Pinochet's victims, but the victims of repression everywhere, as well as a turning point in the use of international law to pursue their repressors. It will forever be remembered as a transformational moment for the human rights movement, and a landmark event in both Chile and the United States of America.

For the cause of human rights, the drama of Pinochet's detention has established a precedent for the globalization of justice. Now that the Pinochet case has empowered the concept of universal jurisdiction—the ability of any state to hold gross violators accountable to international codes of justice—tyrants will no longer be able to leave their homelands and feel secure from the reach of international law. For Chile, Pinochet's arrest ended his ability to repress his nation's collective memory of the horrors of his rule, and restrain his victims from seeking legal accountability for the crimes committed during his regime. Although Pinochet eluded justice, he did not escape judgment. Moreover, a number of his top military men have been indicted, arrested, and imprisoned since his arrest.

As Chileans continue to resurrect and redress their bloody and buried past, in Washington Pinochet's arrest has also led to a massive exhumation of secret U.S. government archives. The declassified Pinochet files not only renewed international interest in the history of his regime; they have refocused public attention on the United States's own responsibility for the denouement of democracy and the rise of dictatorship in Chile.

The Other 9/11

For almost three decades, September 11 marked a day of infamy for Chileans, Latin Americans, and the world community—a day when Chilean air force jets attacked La Moneda palace in Santiago as the prelude to the vicious coup that brought Pinochet to power. In the aftermath of "9/11," 2001, it is more likely to be remembered for the shocking terrorist attack on the World Trade Center and the Pentagon. With that horror, the United States and Chile now share "that dreadful date," as writer Ariel Dorfman has eloquently described it, "again a Tuesday, once again an 11th of September filled with death."

But the histories of the United States and Chile are joined by far more than the coincidence of Osama bin Laden's timing. Washington has played a pivotal role in Chile's traumatic past. Beginning in the early 1960s, U.S. policy makers initiated more than a decade of efforts to control Chile's political life, culminating in a massive covert effort to "bring down," as Richard Nixon and members of his cabinet candidly discussed, the duly elected Popular Unity government of Salvador Allende. Within hours of realizing that goal on September 11, 1973, the White House began transmitting secret messages welcoming General Pinochet to power and expressing a "desire to cooperate with the military Junta and to assist in any appropriate way." Until September 1976, when Pinochet sent a team of assassins to commit an act of international terrorism in Washington, D.C., Secretary of State Henry Kissinger steadfastly maintained a posture of avid support for the Pinochet regime. The assassination of Orlando Letelier and Ronni Moffitt on the streets of the nation's capital would dominate U.S.-Chilean relations for the next decade, until the dictatorship began to unravel under growing popular pressure in Chile, and the United States fully and finally abandoned its one-time anticommunist ally. U.S. policy had an impact in changing not only the composition of Chile's government in 1973 but also the course of its violent future during the next seventeen years.

If U.S. policy has had a major influence on events in Chile, those events have returned to influence the political discourse of the United States—and indeed the world. The country that Chilean poet Pablo Neruda described as a "long petal of sea, wine and snow" holds a special place in the hearts and minds of the international community. Since the early 1960s, Chile has attracted international attention for a number of utopian political projects and economic and social experiments. In 1964, Chile became a designated "showcase" for the Alliance for Progress—a U.S. effort to stave off revolutionary movements in Latin America by bolstering centrist, middle-class, Christian Democratic political parties. But with the election of Salvador Allende on September 4, 1970, Chile became the first Latin American nation to democratically elect a socialist president. The *Via Chilena*—peaceful road to socialist reform—captured the imagination of progressive forces around the globe, while provoking the consternation of imperial-minded U.S. policy makers. "We set the limits of diversity," Kissinger was heard to tell his staff as the United States initiated a series of covert operations against Allende, which "at a minimum will either insure his failure," according to a SECRET Kissinger proposal to Nixon, "and at a maximum might lead to situations where his collapse or overthrow later may be more feasible."

The sharp contrast between the peaceful nature of Allende's program for change, and the violent coup that left him dead and Chile's long-standing democratic institutions destroyed, truly shocked the world. The Pinochet regime's dictatorial bent, and abysmal human rights record quickly became a universal political and humanitarian issue. Revelations of CIA involvement in Allende's overthrow, and Washington's unabashed embrace of the Junta raised Chile's worldwide profile even further, to a point where U.S. policy makers could no longer ignore the condemnation. "Chile has taken on Spain's image in the 1940s as a symbol of right-wing tyranny," an aide reported to Kissinger in one SECRET briefing paper. "Like it or not, we are identified with the regime's origins and hence charged with some responsibility for its actions." "Chile," the U.S. embassy noted in a 1974 strategy paper stamped SECRET,

> has become something of a cause celebre in both the Western and Communist worlds. What happens in Chile is thus a matter of rather special significance to the United States. Distant and small though it is, Chile has long been viewed universally as a demonstration area for economic and social experimentation. Now it is in a sense in the front line of world ideological conflict.

In the United States, Chile joined Vietnam on the front line of the national conflict over the corruption of American values in the making and exercise of U.S. foreign policy. During the mid-1970s, events in Chile generated a major debate on human rights, covert action, and the proper place for both in America's conduct abroad. The Kissingerian disregard for Pinochet's mounting atrocities appalled the public and prompted Congress to pass precedent-setting legislation curtailing foreign aid to his regime, and to mandate a human rights criteria for all U.S. economic and military assistance. At the same time, revelations of the CIA's covert campaign to block Allende's election and then destabilize his democratically elected government generated a series of sensational intelligence scandals forcing the country for the first time, according to the late Senator Frank Church, "to debate and decide the merits of future use of covert action as an instrument of U.S. foreign policy."

Indeed, Chile became the catalyst for the first public hearing ever held on covert action. Senator Church's Senate Select Committee to Study Government Operations with Respect to Intelligence Activities—known as the Church Committee—conducted the first major Congressional investigation into clandestine operations and published the first case studies, *Covert Action in Chile, 1963–1973*, and *Alleged Assassination Plots Involving Foreign Leaders*, detailing those operations abroad. Once revealed, the U.S. government's covert campaign in Chile led to the exposure of other foreign policy excesses, scandals, and corruptions.

The findings of the Church Committee, and the public revulsion of Washington's ongoing association with Pinochet's brutality, prompted a widespread movement to return U.S foreign policy to the moral precepts of American society. "Chile is just the latest example for a lot of people in this country of the United States not being true to its values," one internal State Department memo conceded in June 1975. The debate around U.S. misconduct in Chile, as Richard Harris wrote in *The New Yorker* magazine in 1979, raised the fundamental question: "How did we become such a nation?"

That question remains relevant to the worldwide debate over the exercise of U.S. power in the twenty-first century. Indeed, a historical review of U.S.-Chilean relations raises many of the same contentious issues the American people, and the international community, confronted as the Bush administration launched its war on Iraq: preemptive strikes, regime change, unilateral aggression, international terrorism, political assassination, sovereignty, and the deaths of innocents. After so many years, Chile remains the ultimate case study of morality—the lack of it—in the making of U.S. foreign policy. "With respect to . . . Chile in the 1970s," as Secretary of State Colin Powell conceded when asked how the United States could consider itself morally superior to Iraq when Washington had backed the overthrow of Chilean democracy, "it is not a part of American history that we are proud of."

Chile Declassified

For all of Chile's importance and notoriety in the ongoing debate over U.S. foreign policy, the historical record has remained largely hidden from public scrutiny. The covert operations, murders, scandals, cover-ups, and controversies over human rights violations—all generated massive amounts of top-secret documentation. But only a handful of the hundreds of documents reviewed by the Senate Committee staff in the mid-1970s were actually declassified. Legal proceedings against former CIA director Richard Helms for lying to Congress on covert operations in Chile, and civil lawsuits brought by the families of Pinochet's most famous victims, Charles Horman, Orlando Letelier, and Ronni Karpen Moffitt, yielded references to thousands of records on U.S. relations with the Pinochet regime at the height of its repression; but the U.S. government refused to release most of those. The documents the government did declassify were so heavily censored—many completely blacked out except for their title and date—as to render them useless for judicial or historical evaluation.

Pinochet's arrest in London renewed national and international interest in the vast secret U.S. archives on Chile. Those records—CIA intelligence reports, State Department cables, Defense Department analysis, NSC memoranda, among other documents—were known to contain extraordinarily detailed coverage of Pinochet's atrocities, the inner workings of his internal repression and acts of international terrorism, as well as Washington's policies toward his regime. U.S. documentation would provide a wealth of evidence to prosecute Pinochet and his subordinates—if only the Clinton administration could be persuaded to declassify thousands of files containing tens of thousands of pages of secret information compiled during Chile's military dictatorship.

The Clinton White House had already pioneered a process of declassifying U.S. documentation to advance the cause of human rights. During his first term, President Clinton authorized major declassifications on El Salvador, Honduras, and Guatemala in response to scandals over U.S. misconduct and repression in those countries. On Chile, the administration faced a chorus of strong and poignant voices from the families of Pinochet's American victims, as well as pressure from Congress to release evidence that would assist Spain's efforts to bring Pinochet to justice. Both publicly and privately, human rights and right-to-know groups including my organization, the National Security Archive, lobbied administration officials to declassify documents in the name of human rights, justice, and history.

For a variety of political reasons, the Clinton administration resisted any policy initiative or gesture that would aid Spain's unprecedented application of universal jurisdiction to Pinochet's crimes. Doing nothing, however, would be perceived as protecting the vilest of Latin American dictators in recent history. Eventually, the administration agreed to conduct a "Chile Declassification Project"—not to provide documents to Spain but for the benefit of Chilean and American citizens. The declassification review, the State Department announced in February 1999, would "respond to the expressed wishes" of Congress and the families of Pinochet's American victims, and encourage "a consensus within Chile on reinvigorating its truth and reconciliation process."

To its credit, the Clinton administration pulled, prodded, and pushed the secrecy system into divulging significant amounts of information. Under the leadership of Secretary Madeleine Albright, the State Department appreciated the need for thorough declassification to advance human rights and historical honesty; the National Archives (in charge of presidential papers), the NSC,

Pentagon, and Justice Department in descending degrees also cooperated in the project. But the "securocrats" in the CIA—the agency with the most revealing documentation to offer, but also the most secrets to hide—proved to be particularly recalcitrant. For months, Agency officials sought to withhold any document demonstrating covert U.S. involvement in the death of democracy and rise of dictatorship in Chile. A special amendment to the Intelligence Act in 1999 required the Agency to produce a written report for Capitol Hill on its covert operations, *CIA Activities in Chile*. But only significant public pressure—from human rights groups, key members of Congress, and dedicated officials inside the executive branch including President Clinton himself—forced the CIA to partially open its secret files on covert American ties to the violence of the coup and, in its aftermath, to the military and secret police institutions that systematically carried out Pinochet's abuses.

The Chile Declassification Project yielded some 2,200 CIA records. In addition, approximately 3,800 White House, National Security Council, Pentagon, and FBI records were released, along with 18,000 State Department documents that shed considerable light on Pinochet's seventeen-year dictatorship as well as U.S. policies and actions in Chile between 1970 and 1990. In all, the Declassification Project produced 24,000 never-before-seen documents—the largest discretionary executive branch release of records on any country or foreign policy issue.

These documents provide a chronicle of twenty dramatic and dense years of American policy and operations in Chile, as well as a comprehensive chronology of Pinochet's rampant repression. Stamped TOP SECRET/SENSITIVE, EYES ONLY, NODIS [no distribution to other agencies] NOFORN, [No Foreign Distribution], and ROGER CHANNEL [high urgency, restricted dissemination], among other classification categories, they include White House memoranda of conversation [memcons] recording the private commentary of U.S. presidents and their aides; decision directives and briefing papers prepared for Richard Nixon, Gerald Ford, Jimmy Carter, and Ronald Reagan; minutes of covert-action strategy meetings chaired by Henry Kissinger; high-level intelligence reports based on informants inside the Pinochet regime; and hundreds of heavily redacted but still revealing CIA Directorate of Operations communications with agents in its Santiago Station that detail massive covert action to change the course of Chilean history.

Indeed, the documents contain new information on virtually every major issue, episode, and scandal that pockmark this controversial era. They cover events such as: Project FUBELT, the CIA's covert action to block Salvador Allende from becoming president of Chile in the fall of 1970; the assassination of Chilean commander-in-chief René Schneider; U.S. strategy and operations to destabilize the Allende government; the degree of American support for the coup; the postcoup executions of American citizens; the origins and operations of Pinochet's secret police, DINA; CIA ties to DINA chieftain Manuel Contreras; Operation Condor; the terrorist car-bombing of Orlando Letelier and Ronni Moffitt in Washington, D.C.; the murder by burning of Washington resident Rodrigo Rojas; and Pinochet's final efforts to thwart a transition to civilian rule. Many of the documents name names, revealing atrocities and exposing those who perpetrated them. These records have been, and are being, used to advance judicial investigations into the human rights atrocities of Pinochet's military and to hold regime officials accountable for their crimes.

They are also being used to rewrite the history books on the U.S. role in Chile. For students of this history, the declassified documents offer an opportunity to be a fly on the wall as presidents, national security advisers, CIA directors, and secretaries of state debated crucial decisions and issued nation-changing orders. They also allow the reader to observe the minute-by-minute, day-by-day process of how those orders were implemented in Chile. A comparison between what was said and done in secret and the official statements, testimonials, and memoirs reveals, in stunning detail, the mendacity that accompanied U.S. policy.

The documents also permit a reexamination of many if not all of the outstanding questions that haunt this history. Questions such as:

- What role did the United States actually play in the violent September 11, 1973, coup that brought Augusto Pinochet to power?
- What motivated President Nixon and his National Security Adviser Henry Kissinger to authorize and oversee a campaign to overthrow and undermine Chilean democracy?
- What support did the CIA covertly provide to help the Pinochet regime consolidate? What assistance did the CIA give to the murderous secret police, DINA?
- Were U.S. officials negligent, or possibly complicit, in the execution of Charles Horman, an American citizen detained by the Chilean military following the coup whose case became the subject of the Hollywood movie, *Missing*?
- What did U.S. intelligence know about Operation Condor, the Chilean-led network of Southern Cone secret police agencies that organized international acts of state-sponsored terrorism to eliminate critics of their regimes?

- Could U.S. officials have detected and deterred the September 21, 1976, car-bombing that killed Orlando Letelier and Ronni Karpen Moffitt—the most egregious act of international terrorism committed in Washington, D.C. before the September 11, 2001, attack on the Pentagon?
- And, in the end, what role did Washington play in the denouement of General Pinochet's dictatorship?

The Pinochet File

This book is an effort to revisit the complex and controversial history of U.S. policy toward democracy and dictatorship in Chile. The secret files declassified pursuant to Pinochet's arrest constitute a trove of new evidence that goes well beyond what the Church Committee reported in the mid-1970s on U.S. efforts to destabilize Chile's democratically elected government. CIA memoranda with titles such as "Chile: Initial Post Coup Support," and "Western Hemisphere Division Project Renewals for FY 1975," shed considerable light on the long hidden history of secret U.S. efforts to support the incipient military Junta. Intelligence reporting on the regime's machinery of repression provides a clear chronology of what Washington knew and when it knew it regarding General Pinochet's campaign of terror—both inside Chile and abroad. And the declassified record reveals, in rather extraordinary detail, what U.S. officials did and did not do when confronted with that knowledge.

Drawing on the abundance of information contained in the declassified documents, *The Pinochet File* provides an investigative narrative to advance a history that remains disputed to this day. At the same time, the book is an attempt to tell the story of the United States and Chile through a representative selection of documents, drawn from the long paper trail left by multiple U.S. offices and agencies, from the White House to the CIA Santiago Station. Distilling a full history into a compilation of one hundred or so reproduced records is, admittedly, impossible; for reasons of space, I have been forced to select relatively short documents and in some cases only partially reproduce them. Dozens of key documents that could not be included are quoted at length in the text. Full versions of abbreviated records published in this book, along with additional germane documentation, can be accessed on the National Security Archive's Web site, www.nsarchive.org. Ambitious readers who want to explore the broader universe of declassified documents on Chile can consult the Department of State Web site—www.state.gov—for the full collection of 24,000 U.S. records declassified under the Chile Declassification Project.

Documents are essential to the reconstruction of history, but they do not always tell the whole story. Still classified records—and there are many on Chile—may contain additional or even contradictory information; moreover elements of these events may not have been recorded on paper. Where possible, I have attempted to supplement and clarify the information in the documents through interviews with the retired U.S. foreign policy makers who wrote or read them, among them former assistant secretaries of state for Inter-American affairs, NSC senior advisers on Latin America, several ambassadors and numerous State Department, NSC, Justice Department, and intelligence officials. I have also sought to determine what information remains hidden under the blackened sections of key documents. In a number of cases—designated in the text by information inserted within parenthesis—material blacked out in one document could be gleaned from another. There are still secrets being kept on Chile, to be sure; but today there are fewer of them.

That the secrecy surrounding Chile and U.S. relations with Pinochet has been maintained for so long reflects both the controversial nature of this past, as well as its continuing relevance to the ongoing and future debate over American intervention abroad and the moral foundations of U.S. foreign policy. The declassified documents highlighted in the pages that follow are, in essence, a dossier of atrocity and accountability, addressing not only the general and his regime, but also the shameful record of U.S. support for bloodshed and dictatorship. "One goal of the project," states the White House statement that accompanied the final release of thousands of once-secret papers, "is to put the original documents before the public so that it may judge for itself the extent to which U.S. actions undercut the cause of democracy and human rights in Chile." This book, hopefully, can contribute to rendering that judgment.

1

Project FUBELT: "Formula for Chaos"

Carnage could be considerable and prolonged, i.e. civil war. . . . You have asked us to provoke chaos in Chile . . . we provide you with formula for chaos which is unlikely to be bloodless. To dissimulate U.S. involvement will clearly be impossible.

—TOP SECRET CIA Santiago Station cable, October 10, 1970

On September 15, 1970, in a fifteen-minute meeting between 3:25 and 3:40 P.M., President Richard Nixon ordered the CIA to initiate a massive covert intervention in Chile. The goal: to block Chilean President-elect Salvador Allende from taking and holding office. Allende was a well-known and popular politician in Chile; the 1970 campaign constituted his fourth run for the presidency. He was "one of the most astute politicians and parliamentarians in a nation whose favorite pastime is kaffeeklatsch politics," noted one secret CIA analysis. His victory on September 4, in a free and fair—if narrow—election, marked the first time in the twentieth century that a "socialist parliamentarian," as Allende referred to himself, had been democratically voted into office in the Western Hemisphere.

During a White House meeting with Henry Kissinger, Attorney General John Mitchell, and CIA Director Richard Helms, Nixon issued explicit instructions to foment a coup that would prevent Allende from being inaugurated on November 4, or subsequently bring down his new administration. Handwritten notes, taken by the CIA director, recorded Nixon's directive:

- 1 in 10 chance perhaps, but save Chile!
- worth spending
- not concerned risks involved
- no involvement of embassy

- $10,000,000 available, more if necessary
- full-time job—best men we have
- game plan
- make economy scream
- 48 hours for plan of action

Helm's summary would become the first record of an American president ordering the overthrow of a democratically elected government. (Doc 1)

The CIA moved quickly to implement the president's instructions. In a meeting the next day with top officials of the Agency's covert operations division, Helms told his aides that "President Nixon had decided that an Allende regime in Chile was not acceptable to the United States" and had "asked the Agency to prevent Allende from coming to power or to unseat him." (Doc 2) Under the supervision of CIA deputy director of plans, Thomas Karamessines, and Western Hemisphere division chief, William Broe, a "Special Task Force" with two operational units—one focused exclusively on the Chilean military headed by veteran covert operative David Atlee Phillips, and the second devoted to the "political/constitutional route" to blocking Allende—was immediately established and activated. By 8:30 A.M. on September 17, 1970, the new Chile Task Force had produced its first "Situation Report" complete with an organizational chart and a list of "possibilities" to "stimulate unrest and other occurrences to force military action." (Doc 3)

To provide a presidential cachet for the Task Force, later that day Kissinger obtained Nixon's signed authorization to create a "mechanism" to "work fast and in secrecy" and "make decisions, send out directives, keep tabs on things . . . coordinate activities, and plan implementing actions."[1] In an afternoon meeting on September 18, Kissinger received an initial briefing from DCI Helms on the status of what would become one of the CIA's most infamous covert operations. By then, CIA headquarters had dispatched a special covert agent to Santiago to deliver secret instructions to the Station chief on the new operation, code-named Project FUBELT.[2] And the CIA's Chile Task Force had already produced "Situation Report #2" proclaiming: "there is a coup possibility now in the wind."

Genesis of a Coup Policy

Nixon's bald directive on Chile was neither unparalleled nor unprecedented. Throughout the nineteenth and early twentieth-century history of U.S. policy toward Latin America, presidents frequently authorized overt military efforts to remove governments deemed undesirable to U.S. economic and political interests. After the signing of the United Nations charter in 1948, which highlighted nonintervention and respect for national sovereignty, the White House made ever-greater use of the newly created Central Intelligence Agency to assert U.S. hegemonic designs. Under Dwight Eisenhower, the CIA launched a set of covert paramilitary operations to terminate the Guatemalan government of Jacobo Arbenz; both Eisenhower and John F. Kennedy gave green lights to clandestine action to undermine Fidel Castro in Cuba. It was the Kennedy administration that first initiated covert operations in Chile—to block the election of Salvador Allende.

Allende first attracted Washington's attention when his socialist coalition, then known as the Frente de Accion Popular (FRAP), narrowly lost the 1958 election to the right-wing Partido Nacional, led by Jorge Alessandri. The Alessandri government, noted a report prepared by the Agency for International Development's (AID) predecessor, the International Cooperation Administration, had "five years in which to prove to the electorate that their medicine is the best medicine. Failure almost automatically ensures a marked swing to the left."

But in the aftermath of the 1959 revolution in Cuba, the Kennedy administration recognized that Washington's traditional support for small oligarchic political parties, such as the Partido Nacional, was far more likely to enhance the strength of the Latin American left, rather than weaken it. Fostering reformist, centrist political parties to be what Kennedy called "a viable alternative" to leftist revolutionary movements became a key goal. "The problem for U.S. policy is to do what it can to hasten the middle-class revolution," Kennedy's aide Arthur Schlesinger Jr. wrote to the president in a March 10, 1961, report that would become an argument for the Alliance for Progress. "If the possessing classes of Latin America made the middle-class revolution impossible, they will make a 'workers-and-peasants' revolution inevitable."

In Chile, the Partido Democrata-Christiano (PDC) led by Eduardo Frei appeared tailor-made as a model for that "middle-class" revolution. Overruling aides who wanted to continue support for Alessandri, Kennedy arranged for Frei, and another centrist leader, Radomiro Tomic, to have a secret backdoor visit to the White House in early 1962. The purpose of the visit was to allow the president to evaluate these new Chilean leaders personally, and, as one report noted, "decide to whom to give covert aid in the coming election."[3]

The CIA's two-volume internal history of clandestine support for the Christian Democrats titled *The Chilean Election Operation of 1964—A Case History 1961–1964* remains highly classified. It is known to contain information, however, on covert operations that started in 1961—through the establishment of assets in the small centrist political parties and in key labor, media, student, and peasant organizations, and the creation of pivotal propaganda mechanisms—and escalated into massive secret funding of Frei's 1964 campaign. In April 1962, the 5412 Panel Special Group, as the then high-level interagency team that oversaw covert operations was named, approved CIA proposals to "carry out a program of covert financial assistance" to the Christian Democrats.[4] Between then and the election, the CIA funneled some $4 million into Chile to help get Frei elected, including $2.6 million in direct funds to underwrite more than half of his campaign budget. In order to enhance Frei's image as a moderate centrist, the CIA also covertly funded a group of center-right political parties.

In addition to direct political funding, the agency conducted fifteen other major operations in Chile, among them the covert creation and support for numerous civic organizations to influence and mobilize key voting sectors. The biggest operation, however, was a massive $3 million anti-Allende propaganda campaign. The Church Committee report, *Covert Action in Chile 1963–1973*, described the breadth of these operations:

> Extensive use was made of the press, radio, films, pamphlets, posters, leaflets, direct mailings, paper streamers, and wall paintings. It was a "scare campaign" that relied heavily on images of Soviet tanks and Cuban firing squads and was directed especially to women. Hundreds of thousands of copies of the anticommunist pastoral letter of Pope Pius XI were distributed by Christian Democratic organizations. . . . "Disinformation" and "black propaganda"—material which purported to originate from another source, such as the Chilean Communist Party—were used as well.[5]

In the several months before the September 1964 election, these operations reached a crescendo of activity. One CIA propaganda group, for example, was distributing 3,000 anticommunist political posters and producing twenty-four radio news spots day, as well as twenty-six weekly news commentaries—all directed at turning Chilean voters away from Allende and toward Eduardo Frei. The CIA, as the Church Committee report noted, regarded this propaganda campaign "as the most effective activity undertaken by the U.S. on behalf of the Christian Democratic candidates."

"All polls favor Eduardo Frei over Salvador Allende," Secretary of State Dean Rusk reported in a recently declassified "TOP SECRET—EXCLUSIVE DISTRIBUTION" memorandum for President Lyndon Johnson dated August 14, 1964, three weeks before the election:

> We are making a *major covert effort* to *reduce chances* of Chile being the first American country to elect *an avowed Marxist president.* Our well-concealed program embraces special economic assistance to assure stability, aid to the armed forces and police to maintain order, and political action and propaganda tied closely to Frei's campaign. [emphasis in original]

The CIA would subsequently credit these covert operations with helping Frei to an overwhelming 57 percent majority victory on September 4, 1964—a margin unheard of in Chile's typical three-way presidential races.

With Frei's election, the Johnson administration declared Chile "a showcase for the Alliance for Progress." But Washington faced the same dilemma it had faced in 1958—if Frei's policies failed to sustain social and economic development Chilean voters would turn to Allende's leftist coalition in the 1970 election. The U.S., therefore, embarked on a massive program of economic, military, and covert political assistance.

Almost overnight, Chile became the leading recipient of U.S. aid in Latin America. Between 1962 and 1970, this country of only ten million people received over 1.2 billion dollars in economic grants and loans—an astronomical amount for that era. In addition, AID pressured major U.S. corporations, particularly the two copper giants, Anaconda and Kennecott, which dominated the Chilean economy, to modernize and expand their investments and operations. Since Frei's main appeal to many Chilean voters was his policy of "Chileanization"—partial nationalization of the copper industry—the U.S. government offered the corporations what Ambassador Edward Korry called "a sweetheart deal," providing "political risk insurance" for investments and assets in Chile. Meant to mobilize private capital in uncertain investment climates, the program was first administered through AID, and later a new quasi-governmental organization called the Overseas Private Investment Corporation (OPIC). In 1969, OPIC's $400 million of political risk coverage in Chile not only dwarfed its programs in all other nations, but far exceeded its actual holdings. The program created a further U.S. political and economic incentive to block the appeal of an Allende candidacy in 1970.

U.S. military assistance programs also dramatically increased during the 1960s. Although Chile faced no internal or external security threat, military aid totaled $91 million between 1962 and 1970—a clear effort to establish closer ties to the Chilean generals. A Congressional survey of security assistance programs in Latin America determined that such assistance to Chile was "political and economic in nature, rather than simply military."[6]

And the CIA continued its covert intervention through political action and propaganda operations. Between 1965 and 1970, the Agency spent $2 million on some twenty projects designed to enhance the Christian Democrats and undermine Allende's political coalition. In February 1965, for example, the Agency was authorized to spend $175,000 on direct funding of select candidates in the March Congressional elections; nine CIA-backed candidates were elected, and thirteen FRAP candidates the CIA had targeted for defeat lost. In July 1968, $350,000 was approved for influencing the 1969 congressional elections; ten of twelve CIA-selected candidates won. The Santiago Station also provided surreptitious funding to Frei's party for two years following his election, and developed assets in his cabinet, as well as within the military. Funds were provided to church organizations and pro-U.S. labor agencies. New media assets were developed, including those who "placed CIA-inspired editorials almost daily in *El Mercurio*," according to the Church Committee report. The propaganda mechanisms developed during the 1960s, in particular, put the CIA in a strong position to influence the three-way 1970 presidential campaign, which pitted Allende's new coalition, Unidad Popular (UP) against former president Jorge Alessandri, and Radomiro Tomic of the Christian Democrat party.

By 1970, the United States had a major political and economic stake in preventing Allende from becoming Chile's president. Indeed, his accession to that office would signify the abject failure of a protracted and concerted U.S. policy to undermine his socialist appeal. Indeed, the ten-year history of U.S. overt and covert actions and investments in Chile did far more than simply set a precedent for President Nixon's decision to foment a coup against Allende; it created what Ambassador Korry called a "fiduciary responsibility"—an imperial sense of obligation and entitlement—to overturn the democratic decision of the Chilean electorate. As Korry put it: The question was "not saying 'whether,' but 'how' and 'when' the U.S. would intervene."[7]

"Extreme Option": Coup Contingencies

In his memoirs, Henry Kissinger identified Chilean millionaire, owner and publisher of *El Mercurio* and distributor for the Pepisco Co., Agustín Edwards, as the catalyst of Richard Nixon's September 15 orders for a coup. "By then Nixon had taken a personal role," he writes in *White House Years*. "He had been triggered into action on September 14 by Agustín Edwards, the publisher of *El Mercurio*, the most respected Chilean daily newspaper, who had come to Washington to warn of the consequences of an Allende takeover. Edwards was staying at the house of Don Kendall, the chief executive officer of Pepsi-Cola, who by chance was bringing his father to see Nixon that very day."

Through Kendall, who was one of Nixon's closest friends and biggest contributors, Edwards played a role in focusing the president's angry attention on Allende. On the morning of September 15, Edwards met with Kissinger and Attorney General Mitchell for breakfast and briefed them on the threat Allende posed to his and other pro-American business interests. On Kissinger's instructions, Helms had also met with Edwards in a downtown Washington hotel. In a deposition before the Church Committee—still classified after more than twenty-eight years—Helms stated that it was his impression "that the President called this [September 15] meeting [to order a coup] because of Edwards presence in Washington and what he heard from Kendall about what Edwards was saying about conditions in Chile and what was happening there."[8]

But the declassified record demonstrates that the White House, CIA, State Department, and the Pentagon had already been preparing and evaluating coup contingencies for weeks before Nixon issued his directive. As early as August 5, a full month before the election, Assistant Secretary of State John Crimmins sent Ambassador Korry a secret "eyes only" cable regarding contingency options in the event of Allende's election. "As you can see," it read, "there are three options in September:"

> We want you also to consider a fourth which we are treating separately with very restricted redistribution. This option would be the overthrow or prevention of the inauguration. We would like to have your views on
> A. Prospects of Chilean military and police who would take action to overthrow Allende. . . .
> B. Which elements of the military and police might try and overthrow.
> C. Prospects for success of military and police who try and overthrow Allende or prevent his inauguration.
> D. The importance of U.S. attitude to initiate or success of such an operation.[9]

Korry's response, partially declassified thirty years later, provided a remarkably detailed analysis of the various election scenarios, U.S. options, and expectations. His thirteen-page cable identified all the key elements that would figure in the forthcoming covert efforts to stop Allende: the key time frame between the September 4 election and the October 24 congressional ratification of the winner when a military coup would be possible; the impediment of the strong constitutionalist position of Chilean commander-in-chief General René Schneider, which Korry called the "Schneider Doctrine of Nonintervention;" and the identification of retired General Roberto Viaux as the military figure most predisposed to move against Allende.[10]

This secret inquiry into the potential for a military coup came as the intelligence community was concluding a "review of U.S. policy and strategy in the event of an Allende victory" for the White House. On Kissinger's orders, CIA, State, and Defense Department analysts conducted a major study into the implications for the United States. The intelligence assessment they produced in mid-August was called National Security Study Memorandum 97. "Regarding threats to U.S. interests," NSSM 97 stated clearly, "we conclude that:"

> 1. The U.S. has no vital national interests within Chile. There would, however, be tangible economic losses.
> 2. The world military balance of power would not be significantly altered by an Allende government.
> 3. An Allende victory would, however, create considerable political and psychological costs:
>
> a. Hemispheric cohesion would be threatened by the challenge that an Allende government would pose to the OAS, and by the reactions that it would create in other countries. We do not see, however, any likely threat to the peace of the region.
> b. An Allende victory would represent a definite psychological setback to the U.S. and a definite psychological advance for the Marxist idea.[11]

"In examining the potential threat posed by Allende," the review for Kissinger added, "it is important to bear in mind that some of the problems foreseen for the United States in the event of his election are likely to arise no matter who becomes Chile's next president."

NSSM 97 concluded that an Allende election carried no military, strategic or regional threat to U.S. interests in security and stability. But the report contained a previously undisclosed "covert annex." A secret CIA supplement titled "Extreme Option—Overthrow Allende," addressed the assumptions, advantages, and disadvantages of attempting to foster a military coup. "This option assumes that every effort would be made to ensure that the role of the United States was not revealed, and so would require that the action be effected through Chilean institutions, Chileans and third-country nationals," states the secret position paper drafted by the Agency on August 11. The advantages were clear: "Successful U.S. involvement with a Chilean military coup would almost certainly permanently relieve us of the possibility of an Allende government in Chile."

But there were clear disadvantages as well. The most important, according to this analysis, was that

> There is almost no way to evaluate the likelihood that such an attempt would be successful even were it made. An unsuccessful attempt, involving as it probably would revelation of U.S. participation, would have grave consequences for our relations with Chile, in the hemisphere, in the United States and elsewhere in the world.[12]

Even if the coup did succeed, these analysts noted in a prescient observation, there was another drawback: "Were the overthrow effort to be successful, and even were U.S. participation to remain covert—which we cannot assure—the United States would become a hostage to the elements we backed in the overthrow and would probably be cut off for years from most other political forces in the country."[13]

But almost every member of the embassy and intelligence community shared the opinion that fostering a coup in Chile in the fall of 1970 was a nearly impossible, diplomatically dangerous, and undesirable operation. At the September 8 meeting of the high-level national security team known as the 40 Committee that oversaw covert operations, Kissinger and CIA director Helms confronted the State Department argument that a more effective approach would be to focus on rebuilding the Christian Democratic Party for the 1976 Chilean election. The minutes of the meeting record Helms's acknowledgement "that there was no positive assurance of success [of a coup] because of the apolitical history of the military in Chile" but, in any case, "a military *golpe* against Allende would have little chance of success unless undertaken soon." Kissinger also voiced his "considerable skepticism that once Allende is in the presidency there w[ould] be anyone capable of organizing any real counterforce against him." He requested "a cold blooded assessment of . . . the pros and cons and prospects involved should a Chilean military coup be organized now with U.S. assistance." (Doc 4)

Ambassador Korry's response was quick and unequivocal. On September 12 he cabled the State Department:

> We believe it now clear that Chilean military will not, repeat not move to prevent accession barring unlikely situation of national chaos and widespread violence. . . . What we are saying in this "cold-blooded assessment" is that opportunities for further significant U.S.G. action with the Chilean military are nonexistent. (Doc 5)

On September 25, Korry again cabled Kissinger to reiterate, "I am convinced we cannot provoke [a coup] and that we should not run the risks simply to have another Bay of Pigs."

CIA Chief of Station in Santiago, Henry Hecksher, who used the code name "Felix," provided an equally negative assessment. On September 9, six days before Nixon's decision, Hecksher received a special cable from the CIA's head of the Western Hemisphere William Broe that demonstrates the CIA's early preparation, apparently with White House urging, for plotting a coup. "The only prospect with any chance of success whatsoever is a military *golpe* either before or immediately after Allende's assumption of power," Broe advised. He instructed the CIA Station to undertake "the operational task of establishing those direct contacts with the Chilean military which are required to evaluate possibilities and, at least equally important, could be used to stimulate a *golpe* if and when a decision were made to do so." (Doc 6) The Chief of Station immediately began to implement this order but his reports back to headquarters contained multiple caveats on the difficulties in accomplishing this mission. "Forget about black operations and propagandistic conditioning of Armed Forces. They barely read," Hecksher cabled Langley on September 23. "Bear in mind that parameter of action is exceedingly narrow and available options are quite limited."[14] "I had left no doubt in the minds of my colleagues and superiors," Hecksher would later secretly testify before the Church Committee, "that I did not consider any kind of intervention in those constitutional processes desirable."

In Washington, other officials presented even more comprehensive arguments against the Nixon-Kissinger course of covert action in Chile. In late September, a member of the CIA's Directorate of Operations assessed the Cold War conventional wisdom that U.S. officials had applied to Chile. Far from being a pawn of the Communists, he argued, "Allende will be hard for the Communist Party and for Moscow to control." Moreover, Allende was "no blind follower of Fidel Castro nor do they and their followers agree on everything by any means." Covert operations to stop Allende from becoming president, this analyst predicted, would "be worse than useless:

> Any indication that we are behind a legal mickey mouse or some hard-nosed play will exacerbate relations even further with the new government. I am afraid that we will be repeating the errors we made in 1959 and 1960 when we drove Fidel Castro in the Soviet camp. If successful for the moment in denying the UP its candidate, we would bring upon ourselves a much more dangerous civil war in Chile . . . and a much worse image throughout Latin America and the world.[15]

Similar arguments were on Henry Kissinger's desk even before Nixon gave his order to foment a coup. In the late evening of September 4, the day of Allende's election, Kissinger's top aide on Latin America, Viron Vaky, sent him a TOP-SECRET cable arguing that "it is far from given that wisdom would call for covert action programs; the consequences could be disastrous. The cost-benefit-risk ratio is not favorable." On September 14, Vaky presented Kissinger with a SECRET/SENSITIVE memorandum summarizing a CIA position paper on Chile along with analytical comment, conclusions, and recommendations. "Military action is impossible," Vaky reported. "We have no capability to motivate or instigate a coup," he wrote, and "any covert effort to stimulate a military takeover is a nonstarter." Success in blocking Allende would lead to possible "widespread violence and even insurrection," requiring an escalating U.S. involvement in Chile to prop up a substitute government; failure could strengthen and radicalize Allende's forces, and "would be this administration's Bay of Pigs."

Somewhat more courageously, Vaky questioned whether the dangers of an Allende government outweighed the dangers and risks of the probable chain of events Washington would set in motion through covert intervention. He provided this answer:

> What we propose is patently a violation of our own principles and policy tenets. Moralism aside, this has practical operational consequences. . . . If these principles have any meaning, we normally depart from them only to meet the gravest threat to us, e.g. to our survival. Is Allende a mortal threat to the U.S.? It is hard to argue this.[16]

Track I and Track II

In Chile, Latin America, and Washington, Salvador Allende's election on September 4 was a momentous event. His victory set off a frantic, virtually minute-by-minute reaction within the Nixon administration. On election day Ambassador Edward Korry sent no fewer than eighteen updates on the vote count. Those were followed by dozens of lengthy, verbose cables—known in the Department as "Korrygrams" for their unique language and rather undiplomatic opinions—to Washington, blaming the "bumbling, disorganized, naïve, and impotent" character of the centrist Christian Democrats, and the "myopia of arrogant stupidity" of Chile's right-wing upper class for allowing Allende to win. "Leadership depends upon, if I may use Spanish, *cabeza, corazon,* and *cojones* (brains, heart, and balls)," Korry wrote disparagingly in a September 5 cable titled "Allende Wins." "In Chile they counted upon *chachara* (chatter)."

Over the next several weeks, the ambassador sent a constant series of SECRET/NOFORN cables with such titles as "No Hopes for Chile" and "Some Hope for Chile." A number of his field reports identified what Korry skeptically called "the Rube Goldberg contraption," or "an undercover organizational operation" to "constitutionally" block Allende from being ratified by the Chilean Congress on October 24. Through covert political means, the Chilean Congress would be induced to ratify the runner-up candidate, Jorge Alessandri, on October 24; he would then renounce the presidency and initiate new elections in which the outgoing Christian Democrat president Eduardo Frei could run again, and presumably defeat Allende. This scheme was the initial blueprint for what the CIA called "Track I"—the "parliamentary solution." Track II became the internal designation for operations in the aftermath of Nixon's September 15 order to foment, by whatever means possible, a military coup.

The origins of Track I date back to June 18, 1970, when Ambassador Korry proposed that the 40 Committee allocate a contingency slush fund of $250,000 to bribe members of the Chilean Congress as "Phase II" of a $360,000 "spoiling operation" against Allende. If no candidate won a majority on September 4, the Chilean Congress would vote to ratify the winner—normally the candidate with the most votes—on October 24. Allende's UP party controlled some eighty-two votes in Congress; to win he would need nineteen additional votes controlled by the Christian Democrats, and could conceivably be ratified even if he were the runner-up. Korry's concern was to assure that the U.S. controlled enough votes among the Christian Democrats to block Allende. The money was approved, but distribution was tabled until after the election.[17]

On September 14, the 40 Committee authorized Korry to spend the $250,000 for "covert support of projects which Frei or his trusted team deem important." However, the embassy and the CIA soon realized that the potential for exposure made bribery operations too risky—one leak would provoke an anti-American backlash throughout Chile's nationalist political system. The bribery plan was abandoned, but the U.S. continued to covertly pressure the military and the Christian Democrats to orchestrate the so-called "Frei reelection gambit." Within days of Allende's election, Ambassador Korry was meeting with Chilean general Camilo Valenzuela to promote a plan whereby the runner-up, Alessandri, would be ratified; he would form a military cabinet and resign; and the military would oversee new elections between Frei and Allende. But this plan also considered "a nonstarter" after the CIA determined that there was no way to siphon off enough Congressional votes to ratify Alessandri.

By mid-September the embassy and the CIA were pursuing a scheme that amounted to little more than a Frei-authorized military coup. This plan called for Frei to order the (1) resignation of his cabinet; (2) formation of a new cabinet composed entirely of military figures; (3) appointment of an acting president; and (4) Frei's departure from Chile, leaving the country under effective military control. "The success of such a coup," one CIA status report stated, "would ultimately depend on Frei's total commitment to follow through."

Therein lay the main problem for the success of Track I—Frei's wavering unwillingness to betray Chile's long-standing tradition of civil, constitutional rule. Korry, who met secretly with Frei and his intermediary, Defense Minister Ricardo Ossa, gravitated between lauding the president as the "one and only one hope for Chile," and disparaging him as a man "with no pants on." At the CIA, David Atlee Phillips captured the problematic possibilities of a coup plot based on the voluntarism of Chile's respected president to sacrifice his country's sacred democratic traditions. "The first and fundamental task," he wrote in a September 21 cable to the Station, "is to induce Frei to take action which will produce desired results:"

> After this we get fuzzy since we have no clear understanding of what we wish Frei to do other than lead the military coup himself, something we can hardly expect of this too gentle soul. We can wistfully aspire to have him act in a manner which will not only exacerbate climate for a coup but which will actively precipitate it.

According to the declassified "Report on CIA Chilean Task Force Activities," the CIA "mobilized an interlocking political action and propaganda campaign designed to goad and entice Frei" into setting this coup plan in motion. The most superficial of these operations ranged from planting false articles in newspapers around the world stating that the Communists planned "to destroy Frei as an individual and political leader after Allende [took] office"—and then having Frei directly informed of such stories—to orchestrating a series of telegrams to his wife from fictitious women's groups in other Latin American nations beseeching her to help save the region from the horrors of communism. (One CIA cable on Track I, dated October 9, reported that "among influences moving Frei to adopt stronger course is 'sudden change in character of Mrs. Frei.' ") Far more sinister and violent operations designed to "influence Frei's frame of mind" were conducted in tangent with Track II coup plotting.

The historical distinction between Track I and Track II—that the first favored a constitutional approach and the second focused on a military coup to block Allende—is inaccurate. Track I quickly evolved to focus on a military takeover as well—what the CIA's deputy director for covert operations (DDP) Tom Karamessines called "a quiet and hopefully nonviolent military coup." In a September 21 cable covering both Tracks I and II, the CIA Task Force director informed the chief of Station in Santiago that the "purpose of exercise is to prevent Allende assumption of power. Parliamentary legerdemain has been discarded. Military solution is objective."

The main difference between the two approaches was that Track I required Frei's participation and involved Ambassador Korry's efforts to pressure the Chilean president to give a green light to the Chilean military. Track II focused on identifying any Chilean military officer, active duty or retired, willing to lead a violent *putsch*, and providing whatever incentive, rationale, direction, coordination, equipment, and funding necessary to provoke a successful overthrow of Chilean democracy. The Track II component of Project FUBELT was highly compartmentalized; most members of the 40 Committee were not aware of its existence. (Following 40 Committee meetings, Kissinger would meet with a much smaller group of CIA and NSC officials knowledgeable of FUBELT.) On Nixon's orders, Ambassador Korry and his staff were excluded from knowledge and participation in this set of operations.[18]

Track II operations began with Broe's September 9 cable to Hecksher, and accelerated with Nixon's September 15 mandate. The Chile Task Force, which also coordinated Track I, immediately set up a special communications channel with the chief of Station. Additional agents were dispatched to Santiago, according to "Project FUBELT Situation Report #1" to "augment the Station strength." DDP Karamessines, WH/C Broe, and Task Force Chief David Atlee Phillips began meeting every day; the Task Force kept a daily log of activity, and filed frequent situation reports on the status of the Chile operations.[19] Under "constant, constant, just constant pressure . . . from the White House," according to CIA officials, Karamessines periodically briefed Kissinger and his deputy Alexander Haig on the progress of fomenting a military coup in Chile.

CIA pursued a basic three-step plan: (1) identify, contact, and collect intelligence on coup-minded officers; (2) inform them that the U.S. was committed to "full support in coup" short of sending the marines; and (3) foster the creation of "a coup climate by propaganda, disinformation and terrorist activities" to provide a stimulus and pretext for the military to move.

Even before Nixon's coup directive, the chief of Station had begun to contact select members of the Chilean military. But the Station had limited access and no close relations within the officer corps. (The second "Situation Report" on Track II refers to a CIA inquiry to all its covert operatives for anyone with prior contacts among the Chilean military.) Indeed, at the initiation of Project FUBELT, the CIA had only two "assets"—paid agents—in the Chilean military. For that reason, the Agency recruited the services of the Defense Intelligence Agency (DIA) military attaché in Chile, Colonel Paul Wimert, who, according to a Task Force Report "enjoyed unusually close, frank, and confidential relationships" with potential coup plotters. On September 29, Wimert received a secret message from the DIA acting director, Lt. Gen. Jamie Philpott, sent via the CIA's Chile Task Force, ordering him to "work closely with the CIA chief . . . in contacting and advising the principal military figures who might play a decisive role in any move which might, eventually, deny the presidency to Allende. Do not, repeat not, advise the Ambassador," Wimert was instructed.[20]

The CIA also mobilized a small elite unit of four special agents—known as "false flaggers," or the "illegal team." These operatives, "chosen for their ability to assume non-U.S. nationality," according to internal CIA summaries of Track II, operated under extreme deep cover, posing as Spanish-speaking Latin Americans; their use was intended for "those contacts with the highest risk potential, that is, those individuals whose credentials, reliability, and security quotient were unproven and unknown"—to safeguard against exposure. "Headquarters proposed establishing small staff of false-flag officers in Santiago to handle high risk target-of-opportunity activities," records the September 28 entry in the CIA's daily log on Track II.

Together, Hecksher, Wimert, and the false-flag officers made some two-dozen contacts with Chilean military and police officials from late September to late October. The message passed to all of them was that the United States intended to cut military assistance to Chile unless they moved against Allende, and that the U.S. desired, and would actively support, a coup. As the CIA Task Force instructed Wimert to tell key Chilean generals: "High authority in Washington has authorized you to offer material support short of armed intervention to Chilean armed forces in any endeavors they may undertake to prevent the election of Allende on October 24, his inauguration on 4 November, or his subsequent overthrow."

Initially, the CIA targeted several active duty officers, among them Brig. Gen. Camilo Valenzuela, commander of the Santiago barracks, air force General Joaquin Garciá, and a high commander of Chile's police forces, the Carabineros, believed to be General Vicente Huerta as likely coup leaders. They also evaluated the potential of retired General Arturo Marshall, a fanatical extremist dedicated to terrorism that included bombings in Santiago and the actual assassination of Allende. But, in the Station's opinion, the "only military leader of national stature [who] appears committed to denying Allende the presidency by force" was Roberto Viaux, a disgruntled commander who had attempted a takeover in 1969 against Frei.[21]

Yet coup plotting remained problematic. General Viaux was retired after his unsuccessful coup attempt and therefore commanded no actual troops; one high-level CIA source discounted him as a "man who could lead a coup attempt that fails with resulting carnage." General Marshall, who the CIA met with and passed funds to, was quickly deemed too unstable and contact was dropped "because of his extremist tendencies," according to CIA reporting. And the active-duty officers were immobilized by their own commander in chief, General René Schneider, who had publicly stated his position in support of a constitutional transfer of power. "While Frei has been exploring with the military the possibilities for intervening, and realizes that General Schneider is the major stumbling block," noted a CIA special situation report dated October 2, "he has not yet been able to muster the courage to neutralize Schneider or send him out of the country." Frei, David Atlee Phillips complained in a cable to the Santiago Station the same day, "is waiting for the military to depose him. However, the constitutionalist-minded Chilean military are waiting for Frei to give them instructions to stage a coup. Thus, they are in a stalemate." In another cable three days later, the Task Force director predicted "only economic chaos or serious civil disorder is likely to alter the military posture."

"Flashpoint for Action": Creating a Coup Climate

To implement President Nixon's order to foment a coup, the CIA faced what Director Helms described as "the impossible" challenges of forcing President Frei to move against the democratic structures of his own nation, "neutralizing," if necessary, Chile's respected commander-in-chief, General Schneider, and overcoming what agency records called "the apolitical, constitutional-oriented inertia of the Chilean military." Moreover, there existed no reason, no justification, nor even a pretext for the military to move to block Allende's Popular Unity coalition from taking office. In reality, the vast majority of Chileans were at peace with the outcome of their political process. "There is now no peg for a military move," as the Station reported on September 29, "in face of the complete calm prevailing throughout the country."

In the most sinister set of operations related to Tracks I and II, the CIA, with the help of the embassy and the White House, actively set out to change tranquility into turmoil in order to foster a "coup climate" in Chile. The objective was to instigate such socioeconomic crisis and upheaval that Frei and/or the military would be prompted to act. "We conclude that it is our task to create such a climate climaxing with a solid pretext that will force the military and the president to take some action in the desired direction," Broe and Phillips informed the Santiago Station on September 28 in a cable that provides a covert blueprint for how the CIA intended to foment a coup in Chile. (Doc 7) "We should direct our attention in a systematic fashion to the three main and interlinked thrusts of a program designed to: (a) force Frei to act or go; (b) create an atmosphere in which he or others can act successfully; (c) assist in creating the flashpoint for action."

The three "thrusts" for the "creation of coup climate" consisted of "economic warfare," "political warfare," and "psychological warfare." If successful in "heightening tension" through those three sets of operations, the CIA strategists suggested, a pretext for a coup would somehow present itself—"the one act that will force massive Communist reaction and/or public outrage," as Broe and Phillips hoped and predicted. "We can be looking for the opportunity and when the time comes spark it."

From the first day of Project FUBELT, real and threatened economic pressure were considered key components of coup strategy—"to make the economy scream," in Nixon's now famous words. Situation Report # 1, for example, called for the CIA to "begin immediately to determine just what economic pressure tactics can be employed." In a special cable to Kissinger, who was traveling with the president in Europe in early October, Richard Helms noted that "a suddenly disastrous economic situation would be the most logical pretext for a military move," and that "the only practical way to create the tense atmosphere in which Frei could muster the courage to act is to see to it that the Chilean economy, precarious enough since the election, takes a drastic turn for the worse." According to Helms: "At least a mini-crisis is required."

Both CIA and State Department officials enlisted the support and help of U.S. businesses with interests in Chile. In late September, Korry convened an embassy meeting with a large group of corporate representatives to discuss the situation. He also met with a Frei intermediary, Defense Minister Ossa, and passed a dramatic warning: "Not a nut or bolt will be allowed to reach Chile under Allende. We shall do all within our power to condemn Chile and the Chilean to utmost deprivation and poverty. . . . hence, for Frei to believe that there will be much of an alternative to utter misery, such as seeing Chile muddle through, would be strictly illusionary."

In a discussion with one unidentified official, Korry discussed a series of hostile economic steps that might contribute to a rapid slowdown in the economy and provoke a military reaction. On September 24, Korry cabled Washington with a number of ideas and proposals: starting rumors of imminent rationing to create a "run on food stocks;" asking U.S. banks to suddenly halt renewal of credit to Chile; getting "U.S. companies here to foot-drag to maximum possible . . . hold off on orders, on deliveries of spare parts"; spreading false information that Chilean building and loan associations were near bankruptcy, and pressing several major U.S. corporations to declare publicly that they were closing down their Chilean operations. Korry followed up on September 25 with an additional list of recommendations that included putting pressure on the U.S. mining giant, Anaconda Copper, to take a hard line on an ongoing miners strike; circulating propaganda that an Allende government would seek to block "technical and managerial talent" from leaving Chile, spurring an exodus of such personnel now; pressuring Ford Motor Co. to pull out of Chile, and Bank of America to close its doors, which in Korry's opinion, "would provide sharp blow to Chilean banking circles and dry up one source of credit."[22]

High-level State Department officials did meet with corporate executives at Ford and Bank of America to enlist their support. The CIA, in turn, stepped up its collaboration with the most anti-Allende of U.S. corporations—the International Telephone and Telegraph Co. ITT had holdings of $153 million in Chile—it owned the telephone company, two Sheraton hotels, and Standard Electric among other properties—making it the third largest American conglomerate in that nation. Certainly ITT was the most interventionist. In mid-July, weeks before Allende's election, ITT board member and former CIA director John McCone had placed a call to his successor, Richard Helms, and suggested ongoing communications and collaboration between ITT and the CIA to undermine Allende's candidacy. A series of high-level meetings ensured, according to leaked corporate papers, including a meeting on September 11 between McCone, Helms, and Kissinger during which ITT offered $1 million "for the purpose of assisting any [U.S.] government plan . . . to stop Allende."[23] On September 29, the CIA's William Broe met with ITT senior vice president Edward Gerrity to "explore the feasibility of possible actions to apply some economic pressure on Chile." While the CIA has not released its memorandum of conversation on this meeting—one of some forty contacts between highest-level CIA and ITT officials on Chile in 1970 and 1971—Gerrity's report to company CEO Harold Geneen stated that the CIA official had presented a plan "aimed at inducing economic collapse" in Chile.[24] In a phone call to Geneen the same day, the CIA supervisor of Project FUBELT, Tom Karamessines, covered the same issues.

As part of the campaign of economic pressure, the CIA also pushed for direct pressure against other major countries with strong economic ties to Chile. On the eve of President Nixon's meeting in London with British Prime Minister Edward Heath, Helms sent a cable to Kissinger concerning "the [British] role in the Chilean economic scene." A TOP SECRET/SENSITIVE memorandum of conversation captured Nixon telling Heath on October 3 "he wanted the British to give no encouragement to the idea that this [Allende] government might prove acceptable until the die is cast." As Nixon added, "he hoped the British would suspend loans and other matters of this kind."[25] At the meeting of the 40 Committee on October 6, Kissinger noted that "higher authority" had been "advising heads of state in Europe of the absolute undesirability of an Allende regime in Chile."

By early October, the Nixon administration had taken a number of steps to destabilize Chile's economy. In the financial sector, one pending export-import bank loan was deferred; the bank had been secretly instructed to downgrade Chile's credit rating to restrict further credit transactions. A major loan for cattle farming was delayed. All new Inter-American Development Bank loans would be deferred. Bank of America had agreed to restrict additional credit lines. Further discussions with executives at ITT to coordinate and pressure other U.S. companies to limit their operations in Chile were planned.[26]

Political warfare, in the form of propaganda placements and mobilization of CIA-controlled organization and assets also accelerated. The CIA effort was intended to isolate Allende's Popular Unity coalition by directing and financing negative statements by political and civic leaders, anti-Allende rallies, and hostile media, through CIA-owned or -supported newspapers, radio stations, and television assets. In addition, the Station was also directed to conduct multiple "black propaganda" operations—planting false but provocative information about Allende's plans in the press and inside the military. In early October, for example, the Station was told to create and plant fictitious intelligence reports on how Chile's intelligence services would "be reorganized along the Soviet/Cuban mold thus creating the structure for a police state."

"The key is the psych war within Chile," CIA officials stressed. "We cannot endeavor to ignite the world if Chile itself is a placid lake. The fuel for the fire must come from within Chile. Therefore, the Station should employ every stratagem, every ploy, however bizarre, to create this internal resistance." (Doc 7) The tactics of CIA-instigated psychological warfare ranged from the superfluous to the sinister. On October 7, Phillips and Broe directed the Station to "begin at once a rumor campaign, based whenever possible on tangible peg, which will help create this [coup] climate. Suggest you assign false flag officers task of getting out to bars and planting at least three rumors each day for next ten days. Believe Station can provide this grist for rumor mill easily."[27] In another, and far more sinister, cable dated the same day the Station was ordered to consider instigating "terrorist" activities that might provoke Allende's followers.

Almost all references to the use of terrorism have been redacted from the declassified CIA records, but they do contain enough information to show that terrorist acts were part of the effort to create a coup climate. The Task Force Daily logs show that the Agency was monitoring and providing small amounts of funding for the actions of a neofascist group, Patria y Libertad. An October 6 CIA status report noted that the Station had contacted "a representative of an anticommunist group intent on organizing terrorist activities"—a reference to a false-flagger meeting with retired General Arturo Marshall—and "this group is allegedly counting on the leadership of General Viaux." The daily log for October 10 noted that Viaux "intends to increase the level of terrorism in Santiago over the weekend. The objective of this activity is to provoke the UP into retaliatory violence and public disorder." (Doc 8)

Ironically, the most forceful advocate against plotting with Viaux and other Chilean military officials was the U.S. ambassador. On October 6 Korry heard about military coup plotting through his own sources and once again ordered Hecksher and Wimert to stay away from all Chilean military figures. "I am appalled to discover that there is liaison for [deleted] coup plotting," he angrily cabled Kissinger. "The military will not carry out a coup to put Viaux in power. Nor is there a public mood that would provide a moral justification for a coup. . . . In sum, I think any attempt on our part actively to encourage a coup could lead us to a Bay of Pigs failure." An abortive coup, Korry warned, "would be an unrelieved disaster for the U.S. . . . and do the gravest harm to U.S. interests throughout Latin America if not beyond."

In Washington, Korry's advice was ignored, and Kissinger immediately overruled the ambassador's orders to the CIA. At the 40 Committee meeting of October 6, Kissinger directed that Korry's instructions to cease all contacts with the Chilean military be "rescinded forthwith."

At the same October 6 meeting, Kissinger pressed the CIA to instigate the coup. He pointed out that "there were only eighteen days left and that some drastic action was called for to shock the Chileans into action." His pressure resulted in a sharply worded Chile Task Force directive to the Station the next day. This unique cable, signed for emphasis by the DCI, Richard Helms, ordered the Station to "sponsor a military move" using "all available assets and stratagems" to create a coup climate. "Every hour counts," the cable stated; "all other considerations are secondary." "Contact the military and let them know the USG wants a military solution," the instructions read, "and that we will support them now and later." (Doc 9)

Under extreme pressure to come up with a "shock" to instigate upheaval, the CIA Station arrived at what it called "the only viable solution for blocking Allende"—the "Viaux solution," a military action by retired general Roberto Viaux. Viaux's value to the CIA as a coup catalyst was apparent to the agency at the start of Project FUBELT; in the very first situation report on September 16, the Task Force noted that one way to "stimulate unrest" would be to "determine whether General Viaux [could be] induced to take action which would cause Communist reaction and in turn force military hand." A viable Viaux plan could also become leverage to push Frei to "seize the bull by the horns and act," asserted one CIA proposal; Frei would be told that "a Viaux coup would only produce a massive bloodbath" and "though preferable to Allende, would be a tragedy for Chile."

Through a foreign intermediary, the CIA first contacted Viaux on October 5. A second, more substantive contact was then made through a member of the false-flagger team. The Track II daily log for October 9 stated that a "false flag staffer was instructed to contact General Viaux. This officer will offer Viaux moral, financial, and material (arms) support in behalf of an unidentified U.S. group."

Two of the four-member "false-flag" team who served as a liaison with Viaux and his group can now be identified as Anthony Sforza and Bruce MacMasters. MacMasters was based out of the CIA's Mexico City Station; Sforza was a legendary deep cover agent who had spent twenty years operating throughout Latin America, Europe, and Asia pretending to be a Mafia-connected smuggler and using the alias Henry J. Sloman; he had also been working in Mexico City on a top-secret CIA operation against Fidel Castro's regime in Cuba known by the code name JKLANCE. MacMasters entered Chile using a false passport from Colombia. In his half-dozen contacts with Viaux and his men, according to a still classified CIA memorandum, he introduced himself as "a Colombian businessman," and told them he was "representing American business interests such as the Ford Foundation, the Rockefeller Foundation, and other unidentified business groups." Sforza passed himself off as an Argentine with connections to Latin American business.

In his initial meetings with the Viaux conspirators, Sforza obtained details on their needs and military strategy. Among the equipment the retired general requested was riot control and crowd dispersal weapons and immediate U.S. assistance after the new regime was installed. "Viaux expects some

10,000 casualties in Santiago area before leftist mobs are put down," the false flagger reported to Hecksher. In his analysis, the Station chief predicted the evolution of events that Viaux's coup effort would set in motion:

> He can split armed forces, with certain army units siding with him and others rallying around Schneider, i.e. Allende. Militant effectives of Unidad Popular will side with loyalist troops. Strength estimates as to opposing camps speculative to warrant serious effort. Fencesitters will watch tide of battle before engaging themselves on either side. Carnage could be considerable and prolonged, i.e. civil war.

"You have asked us to provoke chaos in Chile," Hecksher's cable concluded. "Thru Viaux solution, we provide you with formula for chaos which is unlikely to be bloodless."[28]

The Assassination of General Schneider

It was Ambassador Korry who first pointed out on September 21, 1970 that to block Allende's ascension to the presidency, "General Schneider would have to be neutralized, by displacement if necessary." The commander in chief, and his "Schneider Doctrine" of nonintervention in Chilean politics, constituted "the main barrier to all plans for the military to take over the government," according to CIA reporting. "What does Viaux plan to do to neutralize the Alto Mando [High Command]? What is to keep Schneider from making statement in early hours which will freeze those military leaders who might otherwise join Viaux?" CIA headquarters cabled the Station on October 13. In another cable, Broe and Phillips queried Hecksher on how to "remove" General Schneider: "anything we or Station can do to effect the removal of Schneider? We know this [is a] rhetorical question but want to inspire thought on both ends on this matter."[29]

The answer was to kidnap him. On October 7, the U.S. military attaché, Colonel Wimert, first discussed this idea with members of Chile's war academy, a military institution headed by General Alfredo Canales who would become an active coup plotter. On October 8, the CIA Station chief also discussed the possibility of Schneider's "abduction" with a high-ranking member of Chile's Carabinero police. The false flaggers, Sforza and MacMasters, had discussions with the Viaux group about a kidnap plot. On October 13, a Viaux representative called to report that an "attempt will be made to remove General Schneider within the next forty-eight hours" in order to precipitate a coup.

On paper, the plan to kidnap Schneider appeared to potentially kill numerous birds with one stone. It removed the most powerful opponent of a *golpe* from the top military post; that post would then be filled with a military figure sympathetic to a coup; the kidnapping would be blamed on leftist extremists, undermining Allende's integrity; and the ensuing public outrage would create the "coup climate" and the justification the CIA had been seeking for a military takeover. The problem confronting the CIA was whether Viaux actually had the ability to pull off a kidnapping and a military *putsch*.

In the early meetings with Viaux, he demanded that the false flaggers—appropriately referred to as "sponsors" in the cable traffic—establish their bona fides by air-dropping weapons to his group and providing the plotters with "life and physical disability policies immediately," as the Santiago Station reported. (In a second meeting on October 10, Viaux requested "five blank policies up to $50,000 U.S. currency and twenty other policies up to $25,000.") Headquarters responded that an arms drop was risky, particularly given the lack of knowledge of Viaux's capabilities. The Task Force ordered Hecksher to have a false flagger "recontact Viaux and offer him . . . sufficient funds to impress Viaux with bona fides. Money is to buy arms, bribe arsenal commanders to provide arms, or to acquire them in any fashion he can." Broe and Phillips also directed the Station to gather intelligence on "whether Viaux coup has any chance of success on its own or whether could trigger larger coup."[30]

On October 11, a member of the "illegal" team, Anthony Sforza, met with Viaux and his group several times. That evening, Sforza conferred with MacMasters in the bar of the Hotel Carrera—a meeting the CIA considered a major security breach because the false-flag agents were not supposed to be seen together. The next day, Sforza departed Santiago for CIA headquarters in Langley, Virginia, for a "debriefing" with Broe and Phillips on the renegade general's capabilities and demands. "We have debriefed [Sforza]. Believe it imperative that Viaux be recontacted ASAP, by another false flagger"—MacMasters took over Sforza's contacts after he left—the task force directors cabled on October 13th. The airdrops and "paralyzing gas" Viaux had requested could not be furnished, but the "sponsors" could pledge $250,000 for insurance purposes. Headquarters suggested that the Station "keep Viaux movement financially lubricated" while the CIA tried to coordinate his activities with other coup plotters.[31]

"The prospects for a coup may have improved significantly in the last twenty-four hours," states the October 14 task force log on Track II. "Last week General Viaux appeared to be the only military leader committed to blocking Allende. Now we are beginning to see signs of increased coup activity from other military quarters." Intelligence gathering indicated that military units in Concepcion and Valdivia "were ready to move against the government." And CIA contacts with high-level active-duty military officers, among them navy Adm. Hugo Tirado, army Gen. Alfredo Canales, and Brig. Gen. Camilo Valenzuela were yielding signals of a willingness to move. In a discussion that Henry Hecksher described as "uninhibited" and in "complete candor" with one such official, the Station chief passed on U.S. intelligence on the ability of Allende's supporters to resist—they "could not hold out for more than sixteen hours"—and assured the Chilean military commander that after the coup

> the U.S.G. would promptly transact with military Junta . . . we would be most comprehending. Obviously we could not allow armed forces to deteriorate and prompt measures would be taken to modernize its plant. Military should not worry about image they present abroad and ignore lament of public opinion in democratic nations.

With active-duty officers now involved in coup plotting, the CIA Task Force became concerned that Viaux might move precipitously, and undercut chances for a successful military operation. "It became evident," the CIA Task Force postmortem on Track II noted, "that Viaux did not have the organization or support to carry out a successful coup, but might trigger prematurely an action that would spoil the better chances of doing so from within the active military itself."

Faced with a tactical decision on whether to try to get Viaux to hold off until active-duty officers were ready, the CIA came under renewed pressure to act from the highest authority in the U.S. government. In a secret White House meeting with Karamessines and Kissinger between 10:59 and 11:09 A.M. on October 13—the same day Viaux had told agents in Chile that Schneider would be kidnapped within forty-eight hours—President Nixon explicitly reissued his orders to block Allende from becoming president. As Karamessines recalled the meeting, the "president went out of his way to impress all of those there with his conviction that it was absolutely essential that the election of Mr. Allende to the presidency be thwarted." As they were leaving the Oval Office, Karamessines later testified, "the president took [me] aside to reiterate the message."[32]

Two days later, Nixon passed the same message to Ambassador Edward Korry who had been recalled to Washington for consultations. "That son of a bitch, that son of a bitch," the ambassador recalls the president swearing while striking his fist against his open palm as Korry and Kissinger entered the Oval Office at 12:54 P.M. on October 15. When Nixon saw the perplexed expression on Korry's face, he exclaimed: "Not you, Mr. Ambassador. It's that son of a bitch Allende. We're going to smash him." For the duration of the twenty-one-minute meeting, Korry (who remained unaware of the president's orders to the CIA on Track II) shared his evaluation with Nixon and Kissinger that Allende's ratification was a fait accompli, and that any covert effort to foment a military coup would backfire on U.S. international interests. "Mr. President," as Korry remembers giving advice Nixon did not want to hear, "I tell it like it is."[33]

Several hours later, at 4:30 P.M., Kissinger met with Karamessines at the White House for an update on Project FUBELT. In preparation for the meeting, the CIA's senior officer on Track II drafted a memorandum on the "Probable Reaction to an Unsuccessful Viaux Coup," focusing on the implications for the United States (which would be blamed), the radicalization of a future Allende government, and the decreased "prospects for a postinaugural coup." (Doc 10) He told Kissinger that "Viaux did not have more than [a] one chance in twenty—perhaps less—to launch a successful coup." According to minutes of the meeting, Kissinger and Karamessines reviewed together the repercussions of a failed coup and decided "that the Agency must get a message to Viaux warning him against any precipitate action."

Later, after the details of the Schneider operation and Track II were publicly revealed, Kissinger would repeatedly claim that he "turned off" all coup plotting at this October 15 meeting. In his still classified testimony before the Church Committee on August 12, 1975, Kissinger asserted that after that meeting "In my mind, Track II was finished." In his memoirs, *Years of Renewal*, he wrote "On October 15, I called off Track II before it was ever implemented."

But the detailed declassified documents relating to the October 15 meeting do not record any directive to terminate Track II; rather, according to the meeting minutes, Kissinger approved "the decision to de-fuse the Viaux coup plot, *at least temporarily*," (emphasis added). He authorized a message to Viaux stating: "preserve your assets . . . The time will come when you with all your friends can do something. You will continue to have our support." The memorandum of conversation of the October 15, 1970, meeting contained Kissinger's instructions to Karamessines "to preserve Agency assets in Chile, working clandestinely and securely to maintain the capability for Agency operations against Allende in the future." (Doc 11) Finally, the meeting concluded on

> Dr. Kissinger's note that the Agency should continue keeping the pressure on every Allende weak spot in sight—now, after the 24th of Oc-

> tober, after 5 November, and into the future until such time as new marching orders are given. Mr. Karamessines stated that the Agency would comply.

Far from turning off Track II, Kissinger's marching orders were to continue the covert pressure "on every Allende weak spot"—up to the Congressional ratification and inauguration, and thereafter. In a cable the next day to the Santiago Station, Karamessines transmitted this reaffirmed mandate. "[FUBELT] policy, objectives, and actions were reviewed at high USG level afternoon 15 October. Conclusions, which are to be your operational guide, follow:"

> It is firm and continuing policy that Allende be overthrown by a coup. It would be much preferable to have this transpire prior to 24 October but efforts in this regard will continue vigorously beyond this date. We are to continue to generate maximum pressure toward this end utilizing every appropriate resource. It is imperative that these actions be implemented clandestinely and securely so that the USG and American hand be well hidden. (Doc 12)

The cable ordered the Station to pass a message to Viaux—using the exact language that was worked out with Kissinger. The Station was to encourage him to "amplify his planning" and "join forces with other coup plotters." Headquarters ordered Hecksher to

> Review all your present and possibly new activities to include propaganda, black operations, surfacing of intelligence or disinformation, personal contacts, or anything else your imagination can conjure which will permit you to continue to press forward toward our [FUBELT] objective.

Beyond Viaux's problematic prospects, the CIA had briefed Kissinger on the activities of several active-duty military officers, including Admiral Tirado and General Canales, who were also engaged in coup plotting. But although Kissinger ordered the Agency to keep the pressure on, he emerged from his October 15 meetings with both Karamessines and Korry pessimistic that the CIA would be able to block Allende's accession to the presidency. At 5:58 that evening, according to President Nixon's Oval Office logs, Kissinger called to tell him that the CIA's main coup gambit was not viable. Kissinger's "telcons"—transcripts of his telephone conversations—record him as informing the president that because of the risks the Viaux plot would not succeed,

"I turned it off. Nothing would be worse than an abortive coup."[34] Three days later, on October 18, Kissinger sent a comprehensive seven-page action memorandum to Nixon, "Subject: Chile—Immediate Operational Issues," broaching the broad and specific policy decisions necessary for undermining an Allende government. "Our capacity to engineer Allende's overthrow quickly has been demonstrated to be sharply limited," Kissinger wrote in an oblique reference to Project FUBELT "It now appears certain that Allende will be elected President of Chile in the October 24 Congressional run-off elections:" Kissinger's SECRET/SENSITIVE memo recommended the president and NSC consider a longer-term "adversary strategy" and "action program" as soon as Nixon's schedule permitted.[35]

Ironically, at the very moment Kissinger and Nixon began to strategize on how to overthrow a post-inaugural Allende government, the CIA's efforts to foment a preemptive strike finally seemed to be yielding results. "At last, the military is pulling itself together in an effort to deny Allende the presidency," noted a CIA "special situation report" on October 19. "Apparently a number of senior military leaders (General Valenzuela [deleted names of other coconspirators]) have joined together and have agreed to move against the government."

By then, a full-fledged coup conspiracy led by General Valenzuela in collaboration with Admiral Tirado and retired General Viaux, had taken shape. On October 17, at a late-evening clandestine meeting with U.S. military attaché Paul Wimert, two of Valenzuela's deputies requested that "[Wimert] arrange [to] furnish them with eight to ten tear gas grenades," according to a CIA cable. "Within forty-eight hours they need three 45-caliber machine guns ('grease guns') with 500 rounds ammo each." When a CIA false flagger met with Viaux's group on October 18 to "de-fuse" their plotting, the Agency operative was told that the plan to kidnap Schneider was going forward the next night as the "first link" in a "chain of events." In a separate conversation at 10:30 P.M. that evening, Valenzuela told Wimert that Viaux was "knowledgeable of [the] operation" and briefed the U.S. military attaché on the progression of events that would bring the military to power.

On the evening of October 19, Valenzuela advised, General Schneider would attend an army VIP "stag party" at the house of the commander-in-chief of the army on Presidente Errazuriz Street. As Schneider left the party he would be kidnapped. Schneider's abduction would begin the following progression of events to establish an anti-Allende military regime:

1. After arriving at the house, Schneider would be abducted.
2. He would be taken to a waiting airplane and flown to Argentina.
3. Valenzuela would announce that Schneider had "disappeared."

4. The military would blame the kidnapping on leftists and would "institute a search for Schneider in all of Chile, using this search as a pretext to raid Communist-controlled poblaciones [neighborhoods]."
5. The military command would be shuffled to put coup plotters in positions of power.
6. Frei would resign and leave Chile.
7. A new military Junta would "be installed" headed by Admiral Hugo Tirado.
8. The Junta would dissolve Congress. (Doc 13)

To kidnap Schneider, Valenzuela said, the plotters would need to pay $50,000 to an unidentified team of abductors—money that the CIA Station subsequently authorized Wimert to provide.

The October 19 kidnapping attempt failed. Schneider's police security detail at the party was supposed to withdraw, allowing the kidnappers to act, but did not do so; instead of leaving in his official Mercedes, Schneider took his personal car and the abduction team "became nervous due to inexperience," the Station cabled. On October 20, Wimert's military contact reported that another kidnapping attempt was now underway. Schneider was to be intercepted while leaving the Ministry of Defense during rush hour. But the kidnappers got stuck in traffic and lost sight of his car.[36] Headquarters requested that the station "continue to assure Valenzuela and the others with whom he has been in contact that USG support for anti-Allende action continues."

Late the next day, the six submachine guns and ammunition arrived via the embassy's diplomatic pouch—specially wrapped and falsely labeled to disguise what they were from State Department officials. (Doc 14) It took the Station almost twenty-four hours to arrange a clandestine transfer. At 2:00 A.M. on October 22, Colonel Wimert drove to a desolate spot in Santiago to deliver the weapons to a Chilean army officer waiting in his vehicle.

Only hours later, at 8:00 A.M., Schneider's chauffer-driven car was deliberately struck and stopped by a jeep as he drove to military headquarters in Santiago. Five individuals then surrounded his car; one used a sledgehammer to break in the rear window. Schneider was shot three times at close range. Despite emergency open-heart surgery, he died on the morning of October 25.[37]

The CIA's initial reaction to the shooting is reflected in the cold-blooded cable traffic between the Station and headquarters. Hecksher transmitted a report indicating some uncertainty about who was actually responsible but offering hope that the conditions were now propitious for a coup. "We know that Gen. Valenzuela was involved . . . but cannot prove or disprove that execution of attempt against Schneider was entrusted to elements linked with

Viaux," he wrote. "All we can say is that attempt against Schneider is affording armed forces one last opportunity to prevent Allende's election. . . ." After briefing DCI Richard Helms, the Task Force directors Broe and Phillips sent back a cable of commendation: "The Station has done excellent job of guiding Chileans to point today where a military solution is at least an option for them. COS [and others involved] are commended for accomplishing this under extremely difficult and delicate circumstances." (Doc 15)

"Valenzuela's group coup plan has been put into action," CIA Task Force analysts noted in a pair of "Special Reports" on the "Machine Gun Assault on General Schneider." The Task Force analysts optimistically asserted that "the die has been cast," and the coup plotters had "gone beyond the point of no return." If Allende assumed power the role of the military in the Schneider operation would become known, according to this analysis. Therefore, the coup plotters had only two options: "try and force Frei to resign or they can attempt to assassinate Allende!"[38] "With only twenty-four hours remaining before the Congressional run-off, a coup climate exists in Chile," proclaimed one of the final task force situation reports on Track II dated October 23. In the CIA's estimation, all the elements to complete Project FUBELT had fallen into place:

> Schneider has been removed, a state of emergency has been declared, General Prats has replaced General Schneider, radicals have been arrested, and General Valenzuela has assumed control of Santiago Province. [deleted] Although the plotters may have second thoughts about a coup, they nonetheless are irrevocably committed to executing the plot—even if Frei refuses to resign—since it can be assumed that their plotting would eventually surface under an Allende government. Hence they have no alternative but to move ahead. The state of emergency and the establishment of martial law have significantly improved the plotters [sic] position: *a coup climate now prevails in Chile.* [emphasis added]

Covering up the U.S. Role

On October 24, 1970, the Chilean Congress overwhelmingly ratified Salvador Allende as president. The vote count was 153, which included all seventy-four Christian Democrat Senators and Congressmen, to thirty-seven votes from the Nationalist Party delegates for runner-up Jorge Allesandri. Far from fostering a coup climate, the Schneider shooting produced an overwhelming public and political repudiation of violence and a clear reaffirmation of Chile's civil, constitutional tradition. The CIA's self-serving predictions of an obligatory Allende assassination or military move to take power proved to be quite incorrect.

For several days, Agency reports bemoaned that fact that "there are no indications that Valenzuela or Viaux's group are planning a coup before 3 November"—the date of Allende's inauguration. But most of the CIA's official attention after the assassination focused on a "security review" of FUBELT to ascertain its vulnerabilities to exposure. The declassified record shows considerable concern about news articles on the Schneider operation, based on sources inside the coup plotters' camps, that appeared in the *Washington Post* and Latin American press, including an extremely detailed and accurate expose in *Prensa Latina* published in Havana, Cuba. As conspirators, including Viaux, were identified and arrested, the CIA conducted a detailed assessment of the dozens of contacts and communications between the false flaggers, Wimert, Station personnel, the embassy, and Chilean coup plotters from late September and late October. The Task Force produced comprehensive chronological lists on "Contacts with Chilean Military," "Individuals Witting of Coup Attempt and Degree of Knowledge," and "Station Feelers and Contacts with Viaux Group"—in order to anticipate and evaluate potential trouble spots and leaks.[39]

Two key problems concerned the CIA: first, that Viaux "may not want to be fall guy" for the killing and could implicate the U.S. One of the false flaggers, the Station determined, had given Viaux a written message that could potentially prove a U.S. role. Second and more importantly, a Chilean military officer still had the CIA machine guns, and ammunition that Colonel Wimert had given him—apparently hidden in his house. On October 29, headquarters requested that Wimert "manage to regain possession of material." But the Chilean official resisted, arguing that the guns might be useful in the future. He promised, according to one CIA memorandum of conversation, "to take special care in hiding hardware and remove telltale indicators of origin such as fingerprints." On November 5, Broe sent another cable reiterating the concern that U.S.-supplied "hardware could ultimately be discovered." This led Wimert to forcefully retrieve the weapons. "This equipment was subsequently returned to the Station," a CIA report cryptically concluded. Wimert also recalled that he was forced to pistol-whip General Valenzuela into returning the $50,000 supplied to pay the kidnappers.[40] To dispose of the guns, as Wimert would later admit, he and Hecksher "drove seventy miles west, to the resort town of Vina del Mar, and threw the weapons into the Pacific Ocean."

In addition to destroying evidence, CIA Station officials received orders to lie in response to any allegations of involvement, even to other U.S. officials. If any "points of compromise" of the CIA's secret role in the Schneider assassination surfaced in the press or through the Chilean government's investigation, headquarters warned in an October 28 cable reflecting the anxiety in Washington, "absolute denial will be the order of the day even with Ambassador and other embassy colleagues."[41] According to Broe and Phillips, the CIA's "position will be stonewall all the way."

The stonewall strategy succeeded for four years—until investigative reporter Seymour Hersh broke the story of Track II and CIA efforts to destabilize the Allende government on the front page of the *New York Times* in September 1974. The revelations created an immediate political scandal. As the U.S. Senate launched a major investigation into CIA covert action in Chile, both the White House and the CIA defined their damage-control positions. The White House would claim ignorance; the CIA would claim to be following orders. Both would argue that they had disassociated the United States from the Viaux group prior to the Schneider assassination and therefore Washington was blameless.

In an August 12, 1975 closed-door deposition, Secretary Kissinger presented his story that he had told the CIA to "stand down" on Project FUBELT, shutting off coup plotting on October 15, 1970—a week prior to the Schneider shooting. Moreover, he asserted, "we never received another report on the subject." After October 15, he claimed, "Track II was dead as far as my office was concerned."[42] Kissinger, according to the Church Committee report, also "testified that he was informed of no coup plan which began with the abduction of General Schneider." Asked specifically by Senator Gary Hart to clarify whether he had prior knowledge of the kidnapping plot against General Schneider, Kissinger was emphatic in his disavowal: "I said I did not know."[43]

But just nine weeks prior to his testimony before the Senate committee, in the privacy of the Oval Office, Kissinger acknowledged to President Ford that he had been briefed on the kidnapping plan and claimed that was the reason he turned off the Viaux plot. According to the SECRET/NODIS/XGDS memorandum of their conversation, the two were discussing Senator Church's investigation of U.S.-sponsored assassination plots:

> *President:* I am concerned at Church trying to sensationalize by focusing on the assassinations. From what I am told, we made some clumsy attempts. From what I see, if he pushes it, it could make Kennedy look bad. But at the same time, it is so clumsy it makes CIA look bad. [. . .]
> *Kissinger:* I think if everything were known, Kennedy and Johnson did far more than Nixon did. . . . Not since I have been here has there been

> anything even thought of. *There was the killing of the Chilean chief of staff, but we had dissociated from that group when we heard they were plotting to kidnap him.* [emphasis added][44]

Contrary to his testimony that his office considered Track II "dead" and received no post–October 15 reports on coup-plotting activities, Kissinger's office was kept informed of the flurry of events between October 18 and 22. The cables from CIA headquarters to the Station repeatedly referred to the need for information since "we must be prepared to advise higher echelons." Indeed, on October 19, between 3:30 P.M. and 4:30 P.M., Karamessines went to the White House to update Kissinger's deputy, General Haig, whose job was to rapidly pass such information to the national security adviser.[45] That morning the CIA deputy director had received a detailed intelligence report from the Santiago Station outlining General Valenzuela's comprehensive plan—starting with the Schneider kidnapping scheduled for that very evening—for a coup. (See Doc 13) In secret testimony before the Church Committee, Karamessines noted that he would have shared this information with Kissinger "very promptly, if for no other reason than that we didn't have all that much promising news to report to the White House." Haig apparently asked to be quickly informed of any developments. In a cable to Santiago that night, the CIA's Chile Task Force requested that the Station provide a status report on "whatever events may have occurred night 19 October," and whether "ref action was aborted, postponed, or whatever." The cable noted that "Station will understand that HQS must respond during morning 20 Oct. to queries from higher levels"—the traditional reference to Kissinger's office.

At 4:00 P.M. on October 22, eight hours after General Schneider was shot, Karamessines's calendar shows he met again with Haig at the White House. No records of this meeting and the briefing Haig likely gave to Kissinger have been declassified. But the meeting was clearly to discuss the Schneider shooting and its impact on coup plotting.

The argument that Kissinger presented to protect the White House cast the CIA as a veritable rogue elephant, operating without authorization as the Nixon-ordered Project FUBELT culminated in a flurry of coup plotting and criminality during the week of October 15–22. The CIA, citing meetings with, and instructions from, both the president and his national security adviser, understood its clandestine operations to have the full backing of the White House. The fact remained, however, that Washington had been covertly involved in a shocking act of political assassination abroad—the Chilean equivalent of John F. Kennedy's assassination.

To distance itself from any culpability for this crime of state, the Agency drafted a series of nuanced, self-serving, postmortems about the Schneider killing. A secret overview titled "The Assassination of General René Schneider" and written as the Senate investigation into Track II began, claimed that the murder was "totally unplanned and unforeseen." Unplanned perhaps but certainly not unforeseen, the declassified records demonstrate. On two occasions the CIA's coup conspirators raised the possibility that Schneider might be killed. During a conversation between Hecksher and a high-ranking official in the Carabineros on October 8, according to the memorandum of conversation, they analyzed "available means to remove" General Schneider. "Abduction attempt might lead to bloodshed," they concluded, and as the military official presciently predicted, "Schneider's accidental death would rally army firmly behind flag of constitutionalism." In a meeting with a false-flag officer on October 16, a representative of Viaux's group asked for "sponsor's opinion about plan [to] import five Puerto Ricans to carry out kidnapping of Schneider." He "explained Viaux group did not like killing and that kidnapping might result in violence."

In a secret October 1974 briefing paper, titled "Special Mandate from the President on Chile," the CIA attempted to rewrite FUBELT history, forcefully asserted that "the Viaux group, acting independently" had killed Schneider. "To sum up, the tragic death of General Schneider resulted from a unilateral kidnap attempt taken on the initiative of the Viaux group despite and against the advice of an Agency representative." This argument ignored the fact, well-documented in the CIA's own records, that Viaux was not acting independently or unilaterally, but clearly as a co-conspirator with Valenzuela who had the unreserved support of the CIA—support that included $50,000 to pay the kidnap team Viaux had hired.[46] CIA documents written at the time of the shooting repeatedly referred to the assault as part of the "Valenzuela's group coup plan."

Viaux had accepted the CIA's advice to "join forces with other coup planners so that they may act in concert." The final coup plot called for Viaux to handle the abduction, using a small group of extreme right-wing civilians so that the crime could not be traced to the Chilean armed forces; in the aftermath of the kidnapping, Valenzuela, Admiral Tirado, and the active-duty military officers were supposed to take over the government. The initial kidnap attempt on October 19, Chilean court records show, had been Valenzuela's idea and a collaborative effort—Valenzuela would make sure the guests stayed inside when Schneider left, and Viaux's henchmen would pursue Schneider when he departed. A Chilean jury determined that the same group that attempted the kidnapping on October 19—part of the plan that

Valenzuela had described in detail to Colonel Wimert to be paid for by $50,000 in CIA funds—had shot Schneider on October 22. Both Viaux and Valenzuela were subsequently convicted of conspiracy to cause a coup.

To absolve itself from accountability for what has come to be one of the most famous acts of political assassination in the history of U.S. covert operations, the CIA diligently fostered the impression before the Church Committee that all contact with Viaux's forces had ceased after October 18, when the Agency attempted to "de-fuse" his plotting—four days *before* the shooting. But key documents withheld from Senate investigators reveal multiple CIA contacts with Viaux's group *after* the shooting, as well as covert efforts to abet a conspiracy to obstruct justice and hide the U.S. role in this crime.

More than twenty-five years after the Senate select committee published its report on *Alleged Assassination Plots Involving Foreign Leaders*, the CIA was forced to declassify a cable that showed that a "Viaux rep" had contacted the CIA in Santiago on October 24 with requests "that the group wants to see fulfilled 'based on your promises.' " Among them: "financial aid in resettling those of the group who have been identified with the conspiracy and who will have to leave Chile." Based on the concern that Viaux might "inculpate" Washington, the Agency had an incentive to help. In early November, according to a declassified November 9 cable from the Station, the CIA received intelligence that Viaux had "deposited detailed record of his activities . . . in safe custody abroad," and advised that "all bets are off if [Viaux] has to fight for his life." In a subsequent meeting at Langley headquarters, CIA false flagger Bruce MacMaster noted that several members of the Viaux gang were in prison and "there is a serious concern that one of these people now jailed in Chile will possibly implicate CIA in the action taken against Schneider." In a still classified memorandum of the conversation, MacMaster stated that he had recently met with a member of Viaux's group who was "seeking a large amount of money—somewhere in the neighborhood of $250,000 for the purpose of providing support for the families of the members of the group." According to MacMaster, the CIA "could probably get away with paying around $10,000 for the support of each family." (Doc 16)

The CIA did, in fact, pay "hush" money to those directly responsible for the Schneider assassination—and then covered up that secret payment up for thirty years. In a short paragraph, buried in a September 2000 report to Congress on *CIA Activities in Chile*, the Agency conceded that

> In November 1970 a member of the Viaux group who avoided capture recontacted the Agency and requested financial assistance on behalf of the group. Although the agency had no obligation to the group because it acted on its own, in an effort to keep previous contact secret, maintain

the good will of the group and for humanitarian reasons, $35,000 was passed."[47]

At the time of the Schneider assassination, only a handful of high U.S. officials and CIA operatives knew that this atrocity was set in motion by an explicit presidential directive for covert action to undermine Chilean democracy. Unwitting of how and why General Schneider had come to be shot, the State Department recommended to Kissinger that President Nixon send a condolence message to Chile's outgoing president Eduardo Frei. (Doc 17) "Dear Mr. President," reads the text of the most ironic document to be generated by Project FUBELT:

> The shocking attempt on the life of General Schneider is a stain on the pages of contemporary history. I would like you to know of my sorrow that this repugnant event has occurred in your country. . . .
>
> Sincerely,
>
> Richard Nixon

DOCUMENT 1. CIA, Richard Helms Handwritten Notes, "Meeting with the President on Chile at 1525," September 15, 1970.

~~SECRET~~

MEETING WITH PRESIDENT
ON CHILE AT 1525 SEPT 15, '70
PRESENT: JOHN MITCHELL, HENRY KISSINGER

1 in 10 chance perhaps, but save Chile!
worth spending
not concerned risks involved
no involvement of embassy
$10,000,000 available, more if necessary
full-time job — best men we have
game plan
make the economy scream
48 hours for plan of action

[illegible]

MEETING WITH THE PRESIDENT
ON CHILE
1525, 15 SEPTEMBER 1970 — PRESENT WERE: JOHN MITCHELL AND HENRY KISSINGER

~~SECRET~~

DOCUMENT 2. CIA, Memorandum, "Genesis of Project FUBELT, September 16, 1970.

16 September 1970

MEMORANDUM FOR THE RECORD

SUBJECT: Genesis of Project FUBELT

1. On this date the Director called a meeting in connection with the Chilean situation. Present in addition to the Director were General Cushman, DDCI; Col. White, ExDir-Compt; Thomas Karamessines, DDP; Cord Meyer, ADDP; William V. Broe, Chief WH Division; [redacted] Deputy Chief, WH Division, [redacted] Chief, Covert Action, WH Division; [redacted] Chief, WH/4.

2. The Director told the group that President Nixon had decided that an Allende regime in Chile was not acceptable to the United States.. The President asked the Agency to prevent Allende from coming to power or to unseat him. The President authorized ten million dollars for this purpose, if needed. Further, The Agency is to carry out this mission without coordination with the Departments of State or Defense.

3. During the meeting it was decided that Mr. Thomas Karamessines, DDP, would have overall responsibility for this project. He would be assisted by a special task force set up for this purpose in the Western Hemisphere Division. The Chief of the task force would be Mr. David Phillips, [redacted]

4. Col. White was asked by the Director to make all necessary support arrangements in connection with the project.

5. The Director said he had been asked by Dr. Henry Kissinger, Assistant to the President for National Security Affairs, to meet with him on Friday, 18 September to give him the Agency's views on how this mission could be accomplished.

(Signed) William V. Broe

William V. Broe
Chief
Western Hemisphere Division

DOCUMENT 3. CIA, **SECRET** Report, "[Deleted] Situation Report # 1," September 17, 1970.

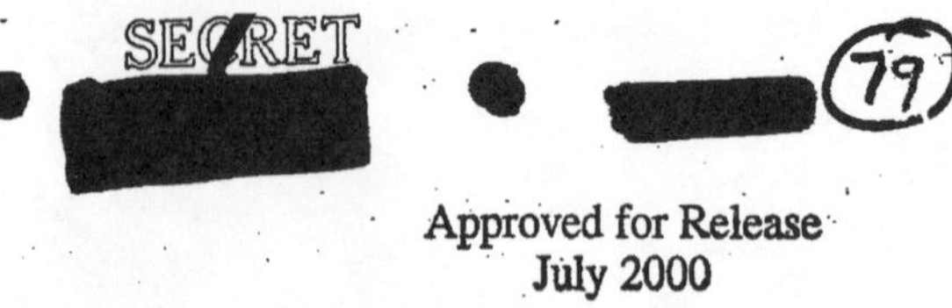

[redacted] ituation Report # 1

The following actions have been taken as of 0830 hours 17 September 1970:

A. Organizationally:

(1) Two special operational units will be in being in Hqs by close of business 17 September. (These are as shown in the attached chart.) Both units will operate under the cover of the [redacted] 40 Committee approval of 14 September for political action and the probing for military possibilities to thwart Allende.

(2) [redacted] are being recalled and should be in Washington by morning 18 September: David Phillips [redacted] to be Chief and Deputy Chief o[redacted] should also be at Hqs. the same morning thus enabling us to devote the weekend to preparation of the initial operational plan.

(3) We are assignin[redacted] as Executive Officer to th[redacted] unit. [redacted] has had extensive experience in crash endeavors of this sort and recently headed [redacted]

SECRET

SECRET

(4) We plan to supplement this group with and who will conduct special recruitment and other direct approaches - they all have "false flag" experience. Other officers who will be assigned to the unit are: will concentrate on matters.

(5

(6) will arrive in Santiago on mid-day, to augment the Station strength. We have also acted on the Ambassador's request for a offering him have experience, long exposure to are quick and top-notch officers.

SECRET

(7) Space for a minimum of [redacted] people in the [redacted] unit has been prepared contiguous to the WH front office. The original [redacted] group has also been augmented by adding [redacted] on military matters, who will remain at present quarters on the [redacted] This unit will continue full time to provide support to the 40 Committee program.

(8) Our search for Staff Officer contacts out of the past which may be of use now continues. We initially intend to send [redacted]

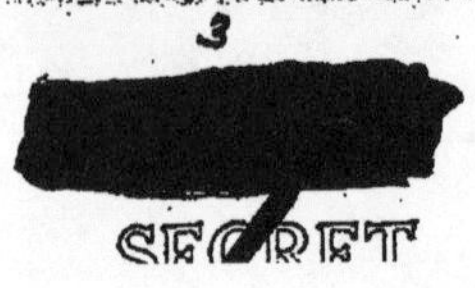

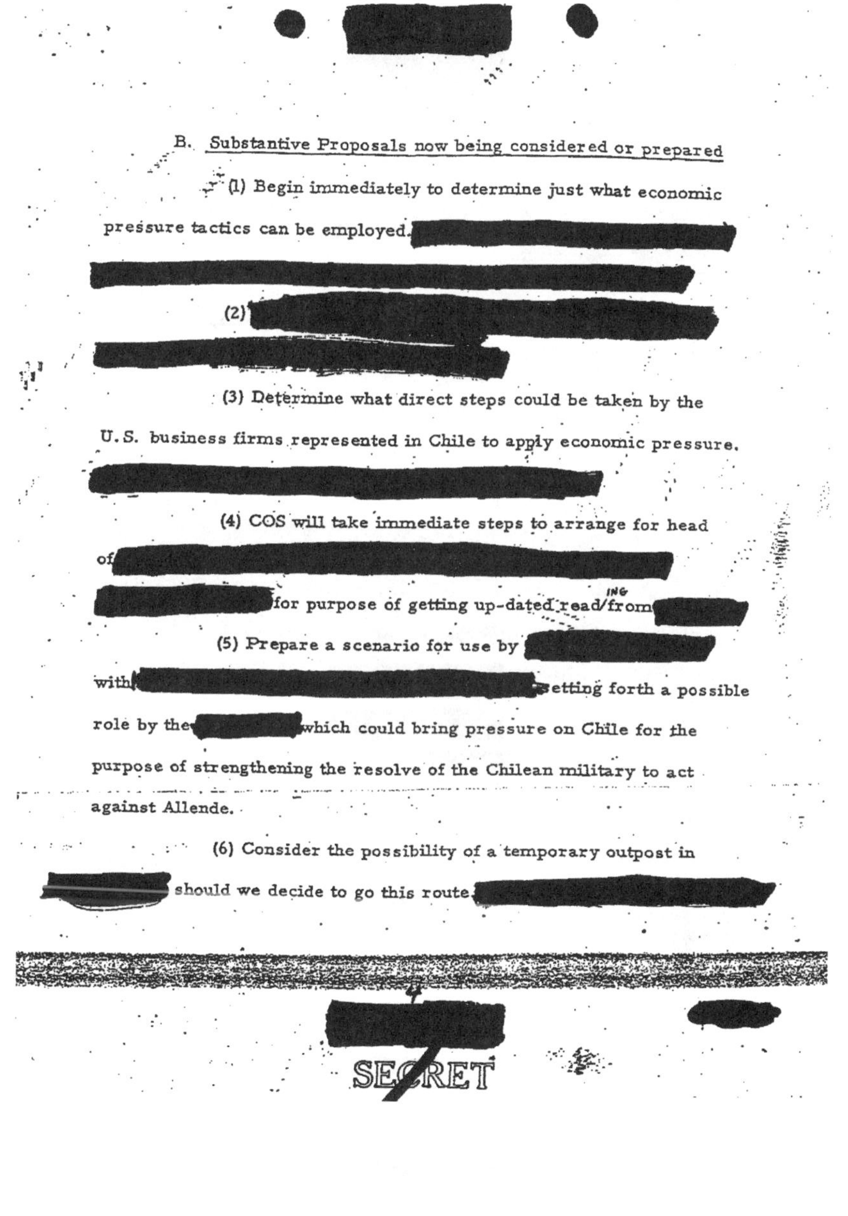

B. Substantive Proposals now being considered or prepared

(1) Begin immediately to determine just what economic pressure tactics can be employed.

(2)

(3) Determine what direct steps could be taken by the U.S. business firms represented in Chile to apply economic pressure.

(4) COS will take immediate steps to arrange for head of for purpose of getting up-dated read/from

(5) Prepare a scenario for use by with setting forth a possible role by the which could bring pressure on Chile for the purpose of strengthening the resolve of the Chilean military to act against Allende.

(6) Consider the possibility of a temporary outpost in should we decide to go this route.

SECRET

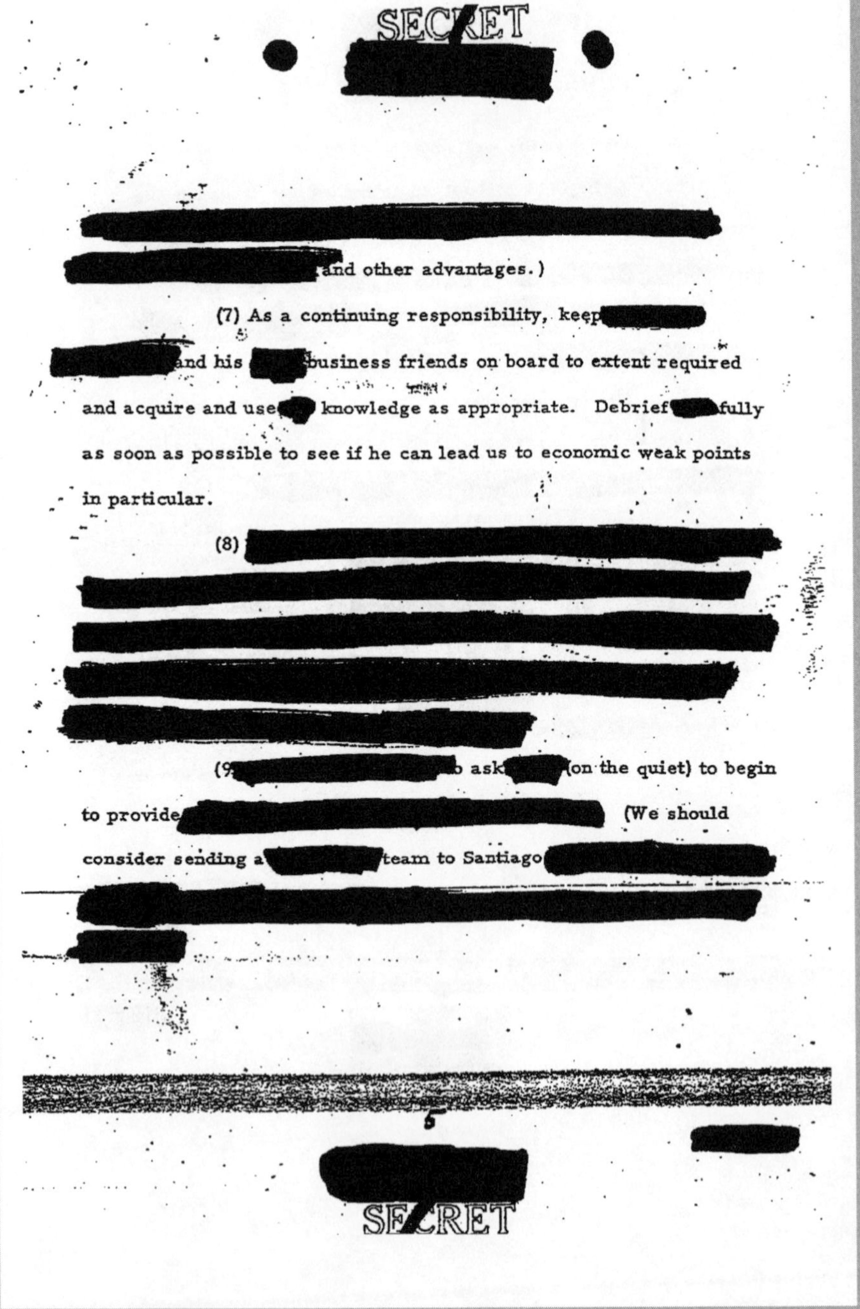

SECRET

and other advantages.)

(7) As a continuing responsibility, keep and his business friends on board to extent required and acquire and use knowledge as appropriate. Debrief fully as soon as possible to see if he can lead us to economic weak points in particular.

(8)

(9 o ask (on the quiet) to begin to provide (We should consider sending a team to Santiago

5

SECRET

SECRET

C. Specific possibilities for future study

1. [redacted]

(a) Review list of contacts in [redacted] for possible use in propaganda and for action programs inside or outside of Chile.

(b) Review list of past, existing, or possible contacts in [redacted] in Chile to determine possibility for propaganda or action use.

2. Stimulate unrest and other occurrences to force military action:

(a) Approach [redacted] to make statement in favor of Alessandri, [redacted]

(b) [redacted]

(c) Determine whether General Viaux [redacted] ~~induced to take action which would cause Communist reaction~~ and in turn force military hand.

SECRET

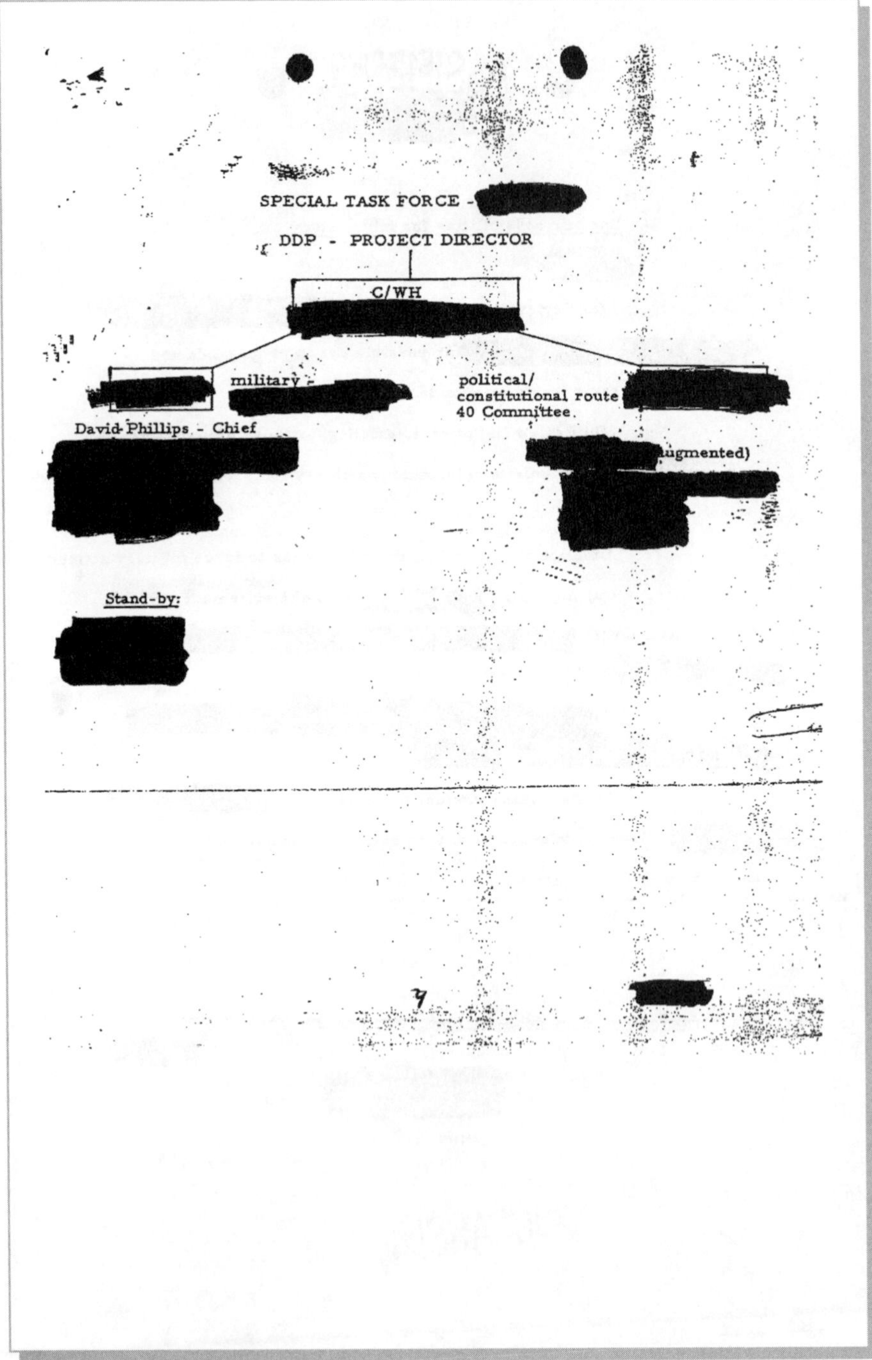

SPECIAL TASK FORCE -

DDP - PROJECT DIRECTOR

C/WH

military -

political/
constitutional route
40 Committee.

David Phillips - Chief

ugmented)

Stand-by:

7

DOCUMENT 4. NSC, **SECRET** Meeting Minutes, "Minutes of the Meeting of the 40 Committee, 8 September 1970," September 9, 1970.

9 September 1970

MEMORANDUM FOR THE RECORD

SUBJECT: Minutes of the Meeting of the 40 Committee, 8 September 1970

PRESENT: Mr. Kissinger, Mr. Mitchell, Mr. Packard, Mr. Johnson, Admiral Moorer, and Mr. Helms

Mr. Charles A. Meyer, Mr. Viron P. Vaky, Mr. William McAfee, Mr. Thomas Karamessines, and Mr. William Broe were also present.

Chile

a. The Chairman opened the meeting with a reference to Ambassador Korry's excellent cable of 7 September 1970 and asked for an analysis of where prospects now stand for taking any kind of action which might successfully preclude Allende assuming the presidency of Chile following his garnering of a plurality of the popular vote in the elections on 4 September.

b. Mr. Broe summarized the situation and highlighted some of the points in Ambassador Korry's cable. He noted that Korry is attempting to maintain flexibility and that there is some, but not much, fluidity in the situation. He pointed out that Frei is an essential cog to success in any action, congressional or military, to frustrate an Allende take-over and that Ambassador Korry is very pessimistic about the prospects of Frei doing much more than deploring Allende's electoral victory. He concluded that it is still too early to decide on a given course of action and suggested that the Embassy and CIA field elements be requested during the next week to probe all possible aspects of feasible actions and forward recommendations as to what might be done.

c. In the lively discussion which followed, there was general agreement that more time to assess the situation was essential. It was also agreed that there is now little likelihood of success in the previously proposed operation to influence the 24 October congressional run-off election against Allende.

d. Mr. Helms, noting that congressional action against Allende was not likely to succeed, offered his personal observation that once Allende is in office it is predictable that the Chilean opposition to him will disintegrate and collapse rapidly. He expressed the view that Allende will quickly neutralize the military and police after which there will be no effective rallying point for opposition against him. Without advocating it as a course of action, he observed that a military golpe

NSC DECLASSIFICATION REVIEW [E.O. 12958]
/X/ Release in full
by L.Salvetti Date 7/28/2000

PAGE 2 OF 2

-2-

against Allende would have little chance of success unless undertaken soon. He stated that even then there is no positive assurance of success because of the apolitical history of the military in Chile and the presence of Allende supporters in various military elements.

e. Mr. Packard was also strongly of the view that any effective military action to prevent Allende from assuming the presidency would have to occur in the very near future. He expressed the hope that the Chilean military leaders would undertake such action soon on their own initiative.

f. Messrs. Johnson and Meyer pointed out that if Allende's election is frustrated by a military take-over, there is a strong likelihood that his supporters would take to the streets and plunge the country into full-scale civil war. They felt that Allende was possibly the lesser of two evils. They suggested that Frei should be strongly counseled to start immediately building an effective political opposition for the future before important individuals who would constitute that opposition might decide to leave the country.

g. The Chairman and Mr. Mitchell expressed considerable skepticism that once Allende is in the presidency there will be anyone capable of organizing any real counterforce against him.

h. In accord with the agreement of those present, the Chairman directed that the Embassy be immediately requested for a cold-blooded assessment of:

(1) the pros and cons and problems and prospects involved should a Chilean military coup be organized now with U.S. assistance, and

(2) the pros and cons and problems and prospects involved in organizing an effective future Chilean opposition to Allende.

i. The Chairman stated that these assessments and recommendations should be available in time for 40 Committee consideration in a meeting to be convened on 14 September.

Frank M. Chapin

Frank M. Chapin

Distribution
Mr. Mitchell
Mr. Packard
Mr. Johnson
Admiral Moorer
Mr. Helms

UNCLASSIFIED

DOCUMENT 5. U.S. Embassy, **SECRET** Cable, "Ambassador's Response to Request for Analysis of Military Option in Present Chilean Situation," September 12, 1970 (pages 1, 2).

UNCLASSIFIED
SECRET

9-12-70

Chile Project (#S199900030)
U.S. Department of State
Release____ Excise ✓ Deny____
Declassify: In Part ✓ In Full____
Exemption(s) B-1

12 SEPTEMBER 1970

(MA025)

MEMORANDUM

SUBJECT: AMBASSADOR'S RESPONSE TO REQUEST FOR ANALYSIS OF MILITARY OPTION IN PRESENT CHILEAN SITUATION

1. WE BELIEVE IT NOW CLEAR THAT CHILEAN MILITARY WILL NOT REPEAT NOT MOVE TO PREVENT ALLENDE'S ACCESSION, BARRING UNLIKELY SITUATION OF NATIONAL CHAOS AND WIDESPREAD VIOLENCE. ALL INFO AVAILABLE TO US INDICATES THAT ARMED FORCES' CHIEFS ARE UNPREPARED GO BEYOND SEEKING MINIMAL "GUARANTEES" FROM ALLENDE WHICH IN THEIR VIEW WOULD PROTECT EXISTING RANK STRUCTURE AND PREVENT POLITICIZING OF MILITARY. (WE REGARD SUCH GUARANTEES AS VIRTUALLY WORTHLESS OVER THE LONG HAUL.)

2. OUR OWN MILITARY PEOPLE HAVE HAD FAIRLY EXTENSIVE CONTACTS WITH THEIR CHILEAN COLLEAGUES DURING LAST FEW DAYS. THEY ARE UNANIMOUS IN REJECTING POSSIBILITY OF MEANINGFUL MILITARY INTERVENTION IN POLITICAL SITUATION PRIOR TO OCTOBER 24 CONGRESSIONAL ELECTION OF PRESIDENT. THERE IS APPARENTLY SOME TALK AMONG SOME OFFICERS OF DOING SOMETHING AFTER THAT DATE IF ALLENDE IS ELECTED. IN OUR JUDGEMENT SUCH MUTTERINGS ARE NOT TO BE TAKEN SERIOUSLY.

3. YOU WILL HAVE SEEN FROM OUR RECENT REPORTING THAT THE ALESSANDRI-TO NEW ELECTIONS-TO FREI FORMULA HAS ACQUIRED NEW LIFE. WE CANNOT YET BE OPTIMISTIC; WE BELIEVE THAT THE SCHEME MIGHT JUST POSSIBLY WORK IF INTENSE PRESSURES ON PDC BUILD UP (DISINTEGRATING ECONOMIC SITUATION, SPREADING FEAR AROUSED BY PREMATURE COMMUNIST MOVES, ETC.) AND IF FREI SUCCEEDS IN WHAT IS BEGINNING TO LOOK LIKE AN ALL-OUT EFFORT.

4. MILITARY IN THEIR CURRENT AND CUSTOMARY STATE OF FLABBY IRRESOLUTION HAVE NO PART TO PLAY IN THIS SCENARIO UNTIL THE FINAL ACT. WHATEVER THE OUTCOME OF ANY DISCUSSIONS WITH ALLENDE WHICH MAY TAKE PLACE, WE FORESEE NO SIGNIFICANT, SUSTAINED PRESSURE FROM THAT

UNCLASSIFIED
SECRET

(3)

81D121

- 2 -

QUARTER ON FREI AND PDC. WE HAVE TO ACCEPT FACT THAT THIS MILITARY ESTABLISHMENT SIMPLY LACKS COHESION AND POLITICAL PURPOSE; ITS ONLY REAL UNIFYING INSTINCT IS TO SURVIVE SO AS TO ENJOY MINOR PRIVILEGES (CARS, HOUSES, PENSIONS AND THE LIKE) AND DAZZLE PARADE-GROUND AUDIENCES. FEARS IN THE ARMED FORCES OF WHAT A MARXIST REGIME WILL MEAN FOR THE INSTITUTION--AND THEY DO EXIST--CAN ALL TOO EASILY BE TRANQUILIZED BY ALLENDE APPEALS TO THESE PETTY SELF-INTERESTS, ACCOMPANIED BY THE HOLLOW GUARANTEES TO WHICH WE HAVE REFERRED. IN ALL FAIRNESS, WE MUST ADD THAT MILITARY ARE ALSO AFFLICTED BY NIGHTMARE OF CONFRONTATION IN THE STREETS WITH "POPULAR FORCES" AND ARE UNWILLING OR UNABLE TO CONSIDER HOW THEY MIGHT PRE-EMPT OR CONTAIN SUCH FORCES. UNLESS BACKED BY UNAMBIGUOUS CONSTITUTIONAL AND LEGAL AUTHORITY, THEY WOULD SHRINK FROM PROSPECT OF HAVING TO SHOOT CIVILIANS AND OTHERS PROVOKING WHAT THEY SEE AS POSSIBLE CIVIL WAR. ARMED FORCES ARE SO DISORGANIZED AND INEXPERIENCED IN THERE MATTERS AS TO MAKE IMPOSSIBLE THE KIND OF QUICK BLOODLESS MILITARY INTERVENTION (INCLUDING PRIOR ROUNDUP OF LEFTIST LEADERS) WE ARE FAMILIAR WITH IN OTHER LATIN AMERICAN COUNTRIES.

Part of "positive track" Frei

5. AS STATED, HOWEVER, MILITARY WOULD HAVE A VITAL PART TO PLAY ON OCTOBER 24-25 IF SCENARIO WERE TO UNFOLD FAVORABLY. TROOPS IN THE BACKGROUND PREPARED TO MAINTAIN ORDER IN SANTIAGO, AND TO ENSURE THAT THE CONSTITUTIONAL WILL OF THE CONGRESS PREVAILED, WOULD BE NECESSARY. IT IS OUR JUDGEMENT THAT FREI AGAIN IS THE KEY TO THIS PROBLEM. THE COMMANDERS CAN BE EXPECTED TO OBEY HIS ORDERS, AND WE THINK IT LIKELY THAT THE TROOPS, DESPITE SOME MARXIST PENETRATION, WILL OBEY THEIRS. IT SEEMS TO US, THEN, THAT THE SUCCESS OF SUCH AN ENTERPRISE IN ALL ITS ASPECTS MUST DEPEND ON THE PRESIDENT'S WILL AND SKILLS--PERSONAL QUALITIES ON WHICH EXPERIENCE COUNSELS WE CANNOT PIN MORE THAN MODEST HOPES.

Frei Frei

6. WHAT WE ARE SAYING IN THIS "COLD-BLOODED ASSESSMENT" IS THAT OPPORTUNITIES FOR FURTHER SIGNIFICANT USG ACTION WITH THE CHILEAN MILITARY ARE NONEXISTENT. THEY ALREADY KNOW THEY HAVE OUR BLESSING FOR ANY SERIOUS MOVE AGAINST ALLENDE, AND WE CAN MANAGE TO REPEAT THE MESSAGE IF CIRCUMSTANCES SHOULD SO DICTATE. BUT THIS IS AS FAR AS WE CAN PRUDENTLY OR REASONABLY GO.

Question

81D121 2L

DOCUMENT 6. CIA, **SECRET** Cable from Headquarters [Initial Orders to Explore a Military Golpe], September 9, 1970 (page 1).

MESSAGE FORM
TOTAL COPIES: 9

SECRET

ROUTING AND/OR INITIALS - SEEN BY

63

Deputy Chief, WHD

9 September 1970

FILE SECRETARIAT DISSEMINATION

INDEX NO INDEX RETURN TO ______ BRANCH

(classification) (date and time filed) (elite) (reference number) (pica)

09 SEP 70

CITE DIRECTOR

PRIORITY SANTIAGO

Declassified and
Approved for Release
July 2000

1. IT IS REASONABLY CLEAR, IN EXPLORING AVENUES TO PREVENT AN ALLENDE GOVERNMENT FROM EXERCISING POWER, THAT (A) THE POLITICAL/CONSTITUTIONAL ROUTE IN ANY FORM IS A NON-STARTER AND (B) THE ONLY PROSPECT WITH ANY CHANCE OF SUCCESS WHATSOEVER IS A MILITARY GOLPE EITHER BEFORE OR IMMEDIATELY AFTER ALLENDE'S ASSUMPTION OF POWER. THIS CABLE IS ADDRESSED TO THE OPERATIONAL TASK OF ESTABLISHING THOSE DIRECT CONTACTS WITH THE CHILEAN MILITARY WHICH ARE REQUIRED TO EVALUATE POSSIBILITIES AND, AT LEAST EQUALLY IMPORTANT, COULD BE USED TO STIMULATE A GOLPE IF AND WHEN A DECISION WERE MADE TO DO SO.

(Continued.....)

RELEASING OFFICER COORDINATING OFFICERS AUTHENTICATING OFFICE

SECRET

REPRODUCTION BY OTHER THAN THE ISSUING OFFICE IS PROHIBITED

DOCUMENT 7. CIA, **SECRET** Cable from Headquarters [Blueprint for Fomenting a Coup Climate], September 27, 1970 (pages 1–7).

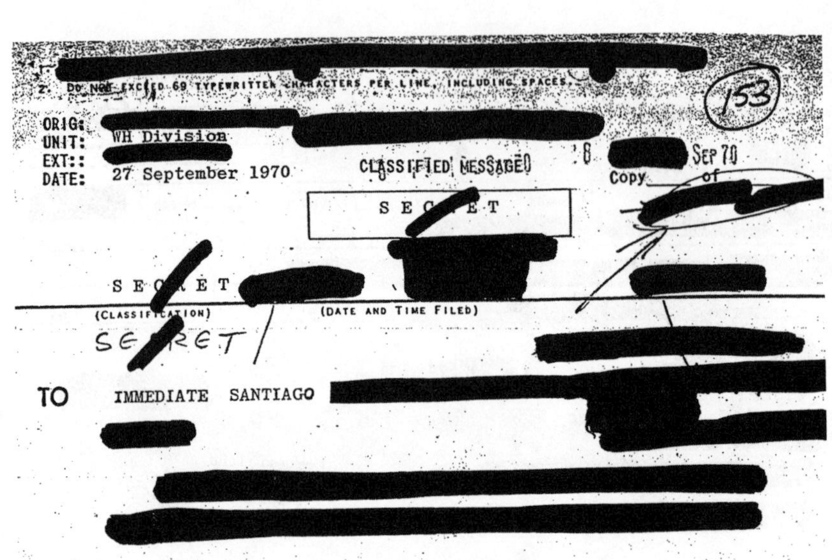

2. DO NOT EXCEED 69 TYPEWRITTEN CHARACTERS PER LINE, INCLUDING SPACES.

153

ORIG:
UNIT: WH Division
EXT::
DATE: 27 September 1970

CLASSIFIED MESSAGE

SEP 70

Copy of

SECRET

SECRET

(CLASSIFICATION) (DATE AND TIME FILED)

SECRET

TO IMMEDIATE SANTIAGO

I. PHILOSOPHY

WE ACCEPT AS AXIOM THAT FREI MUST EITHER MANAGE THE COUP ACTIVELY, OR GO, IF IT IS TO SUCCEED. WE ACCEPT AS HYPOTHESIS THAT FREI PROBABLY WILL NOT MOVE. WE POSTULATE THAT FREI'S ABILITY TO MOVE AND TO A LESSER EXTENT HIS WILLINGNESS, IS INTERRELATED TO THE CREATION OF A CLIMATE IN WHICH SUCH A MOVE CAN TAKE PLACE SUCCESSFULLY. WE CONCLUDE THAT IT IS OUR TASK TO CREATE SUCH A CLIMATE CLIMAXING WITH A SOLID PRETEXT THAT WILL FORCE THE MILITARY AND THE PRESIDENT TO TAKE SOME ACTION IN THE DESIRED DIRECTION.

Approved for Release
July 2000

CONTINUED ...

COORDINATING OFFICERS

129

RELEASING OFFICER

SECRET

AUTHENTICATING OFFICER

FORM 3205

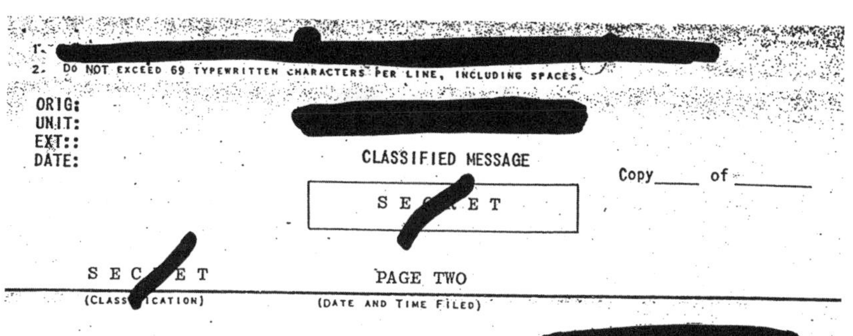
1.
2. DO NOT EXCEED 69 TYPEWRITTEN CHARACTERS PER LINE, INCLUDING SPACES.
ORIG:
UNIT:
EXT:
DATE:
CLASSIFIED MESSAGE
Copy____ of______

S E C R E T

S E C R E T (CLASSIFICATION) PAGE TWO (DATE AND TIME FILED)

TO

II. SITUATION

AS OF THIS DATE A NUMBER OF ACTIONS HAVE BEEN PLACED IN TRAIN TO SENSITIZE THE EXTERNAL WORLD TO THE THREAT ALLENDE POSES. THIS IS A NECESSARY FIRST STEP TOWARD MOVING TO MORE VITAL PRESSURE POINTS SUCH AS THE ACCEPTANCE OF THE FAILURE OF THE POLITICAL SOLUTION AND THE NEED FOR THE MILITARY ONE. THIS EFFORT IS IN ITS FIRST STAGES. WE WERE MOST PLEASED TO NOTE THE PROGRAM FOR [redacted] WHICH IS A CONCRETE MOVE TOWARD MOBILIZING INTERNAL RESISTANCE TO ALLENDE. WE BELIEVE THAT THE EXTERNAL EFFORT, WHICH IS BY NATURE COMPLEMENTARY, IS USELESS UNLESS WE CAN SPARK INTERNAL RESISTANCE.

III. TASKS

IT THEREFORE FOLLOWS THAT WE SHOULD DIRECT OUR ATTENTION IN A SYSTEMATIC FASHION TO THE THREE MAIN AND INTERLINKED THRUSTS OF A PROGRAM DESIGNED TO: A) FORCE FREI TO ACT OR GO; B) CREATE AN ATMOSPHERE IN WHICH HE OR OTHERS CAN ACT SUCCESSFULLY;

CONTINUED . . .

COORDINATING OFFICERS
RELEASING OFFICER
S E C R E T
AUTHENTICATING OFFICER

1
2 DO NOT EXCEED 69 TYPEWRITTEN CHARACTERS PER LINE, INCLUDING SPACES.

ORIG:
UNIT:
EXT::
DATE:

CLASSIFIED MESSAGE

Copy____ of________

SECRET

SECRET (CLASSIFICATION)

PAGE THREE (DATE AND TIME FILED)

TO

C) ASSIST IN CREATING THE PRETEXT OR FLASH POINT FOR ACTION.

IV. CREATION OF COUP CLIMATE

A) ECONOMIC WARFARE

MOST OF THE WORK HERE MUST BE DONE BY CHILEAN AND

THE AMBASSADOR, WELL WITHIN HIS GUIDELINES, CAN BE OF POWERFUL ASSISTANCE IN THIS EFFORT.

B) POLITICAL WARFARE

IT IS ESSENTIAL THAT ALLENDE RECEIVE THE SMALLEST NUMBER OF VOTES AT THE 24 OCTOBER SESSION OF CONGRESS AND THAT LONG BEFORE THEN IT APPEARS THAT HE HAS MINIMUM POLITICAL SUPPORT.

CONTINUED . .

COORDINATING OFFICERS

RELEASING OFFICER

SECRET

AUTHENTICATING OFFICER

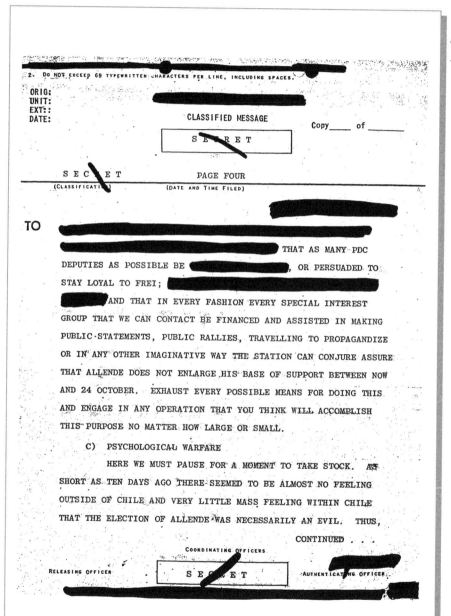

2. DO NOT EXCEED 69 TYPEWRITTEN CHARACTERS PER LINE, INCLUDING SPACES.

ORIG:
UNIT:
EXT:
DATE:

CLASSIFIED MESSAGE

Copy____ of _______

SECRET

SECRET (CLASSIFICATION) PAGE FOUR (DATE AND TIME FILED)

TO

THAT AS MANY PDC DEPUTIES AS POSSIBLE BE [redacted], OR PERSUADED TO STAY LOYAL TO FREI; [redacted] AND THAT IN EVERY FASHION EVERY SPECIAL INTEREST GROUP THAT WE CAN CONTACT BE FINANCED AND ASSISTED IN MAKING PUBLIC STATEMENTS, PUBLIC RALLIES, TRAVELLING TO PROPAGANDIZE OR IN ANY OTHER IMAGINATIVE WAY THE STATION CAN CONJURE ASSURE THAT ALLENDE DOES NOT ENLARGE HIS BASE OF SUPPORT BETWEEN NOW AND 24 OCTOBER. EXHAUST EVERY POSSIBLE MEANS FOR DOING THIS AND ENGAGE IN ANY OPERATION THAT YOU THINK WILL ACCOMPLISH THIS PURPOSE NO MATTER HOW LARGE OR SMALL.

C) PSYCHOLOGICAL WARFARE

HERE WE MUST PAUSE FOR A MOMENT TO TAKE STOCK. AS SHORT AS TEN DAYS AGO THERE SEEMED TO BE ALMOST NO FEELING OUTSIDE OF CHILE AND VERY LITTLE MASS FEELING WITHIN CHILE THAT THE ELECTION OF ALLENDE WAS NECESSARILY AN EVIL. THUS,

CONTINUED . . .

COORDINATING OFFICERS

RELEASING OFFICER SECRET AUTHENTICATING OFFICER

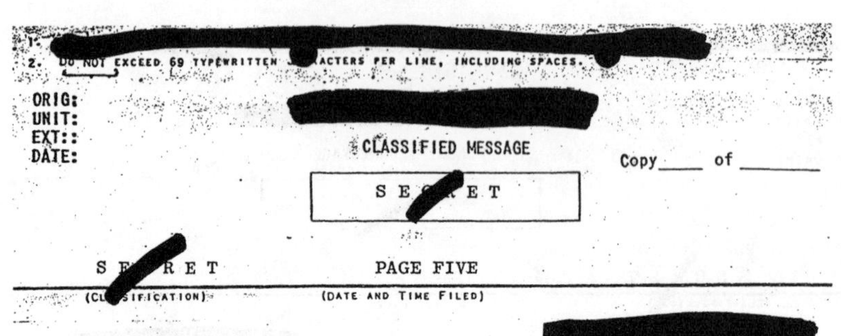

2. DO NOT EXCEED 69 TYPEWRITTEN [redacted]ACTERS PER LINE, INCLUDING SPACES.

ORIG:
UNIT:
EXT::
DATE:

CLASSIFIED MESSAGE

Copy____ of ________

SECRET

SECRET PAGE FIVE

(CLASSIFICATION) (DATE AND TIME FILED)

TO IT MAY BE DIFFICULT TO INSTANTLY MOVE INTO A HARD LINE ABOUT A MILITARY COUP. WE MUST BEGIN TO GRADUALLY CREATE A CLIMATE IN WHICH THIS CONCLUSION BECOMES INEVITABLE. THUS WE FORESEE A FOUR-STAGE CAMPAIGN: (1) SENSITIZE FEELING WITHIN AND WITHOUT CHILE THAT ELECTION OF ALLENDE IS A NEFARIOUS DEVELOPMENT FOR CHILE, LATIN AMERICA, AND THE WORLD. WE ARE WELL ALONG ON THIS OBJECTIVE OUTSIDE CHILE BUT ARE STILL IN DOUBT AS TO THE PSYCHOLOGICAL TEMPERATURE ON THIS POINT WITHIN CHILE. WE ARE TALKING ABOUT MASS PUBLIC FEELING AS OPPOSED TO THE PRIVATE FEELINGS OF FREI, THE PN AND OTHER ELITE; (2) CREATE THE CONVICTION THAT ALLENDE MUST BE STOPPED; WE ARE WORKING ON THAT PREMISE FOR THE BALANCE OF THIS WEEK TOGETHER WITH POINT 3; (3) DISCREDIT PARLIAMENTARY SOLUTION AS UNWORKABLE. WE FORESEE A MASSIVE EFFORT IN THIS DIRECTION DURING THE WEEK OF 5 OCTOBER; (4) SURFACE INELUCTABLE CONCLUSION THAT MILITARY COUP IS THE ONLY ANSWER. THIS TO CARRY FORWARD UNTIL IT TAKES PLACE. TIME IS SHORT AND WE MUST TELESCOPE SOME OF THE PHASES

CONTINUED . . .

COORDINATING OFFICERS

RELEASING OFFICER SECRET AUTHENTICATING OFFICER

FORM 3205

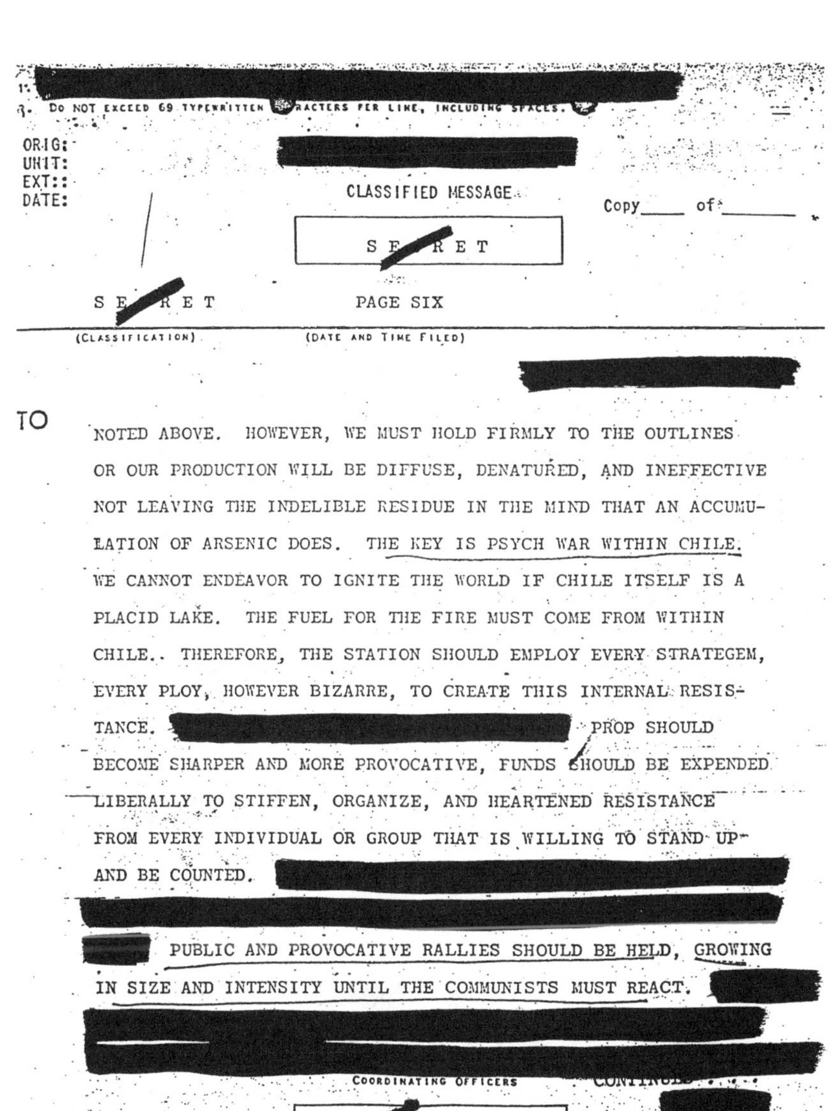

DO NOT EXCEED 69 TYPEWRITTEN CHARACTERS PER LINE, INCLUDING SPACES.

ORIG:
UNIT:
EXT:
DATE:

CLASSIFIED MESSAGE

Copy____ of______

SECRET

SECRET PAGE SIX

(CLASSIFICATION) (DATE AND TIME FILED)

TO

NOTED ABOVE. HOWEVER, WE MUST HOLD FIRMLY TO THE OUTLINES OR OUR PRODUCTION WILL BE DIFFUSE, DENATURED, AND INEFFECTIVE NOT LEAVING THE INDELIBLE RESIDUE IN THE MIND THAT AN ACCUMULATION OF ARSENIC DOES. THE KEY IS PSYCH WAR WITHIN CHILE. WE CANNOT ENDEAVOR TO IGNITE THE WORLD IF CHILE ITSELF IS A PLACID LAKE. THE FUEL FOR THE FIRE MUST COME FROM WITHIN CHILE. THEREFORE, THE STATION SHOULD EMPLOY EVERY STRATEGEM, EVERY PLOY, HOWEVER BIZARRE, TO CREATE THIS INTERNAL RESISTANCE. PROP SHOULD BECOME SHARPER AND MORE PROVOCATIVE, FUNDS SHOULD BE EXPENDED LIBERALLY TO STIFFEN, ORGANIZE, AND HEARTENED RESISTANCE FROM EVERY INDIVIDUAL OR GROUP THAT IS WILLING TO STAND UP AND BE COUNTED.

PUBLIC AND PROVOCATIVE RALLIES SHOULD BE HELD, GROWING IN SIZE AND INTENSITY UNTIL THE COMMUNISTS MUST REACT.

COORDINATING OFFICERS CONTINUED

RELEASING OFFICER SECRET AUTHENTICATING OFFICER

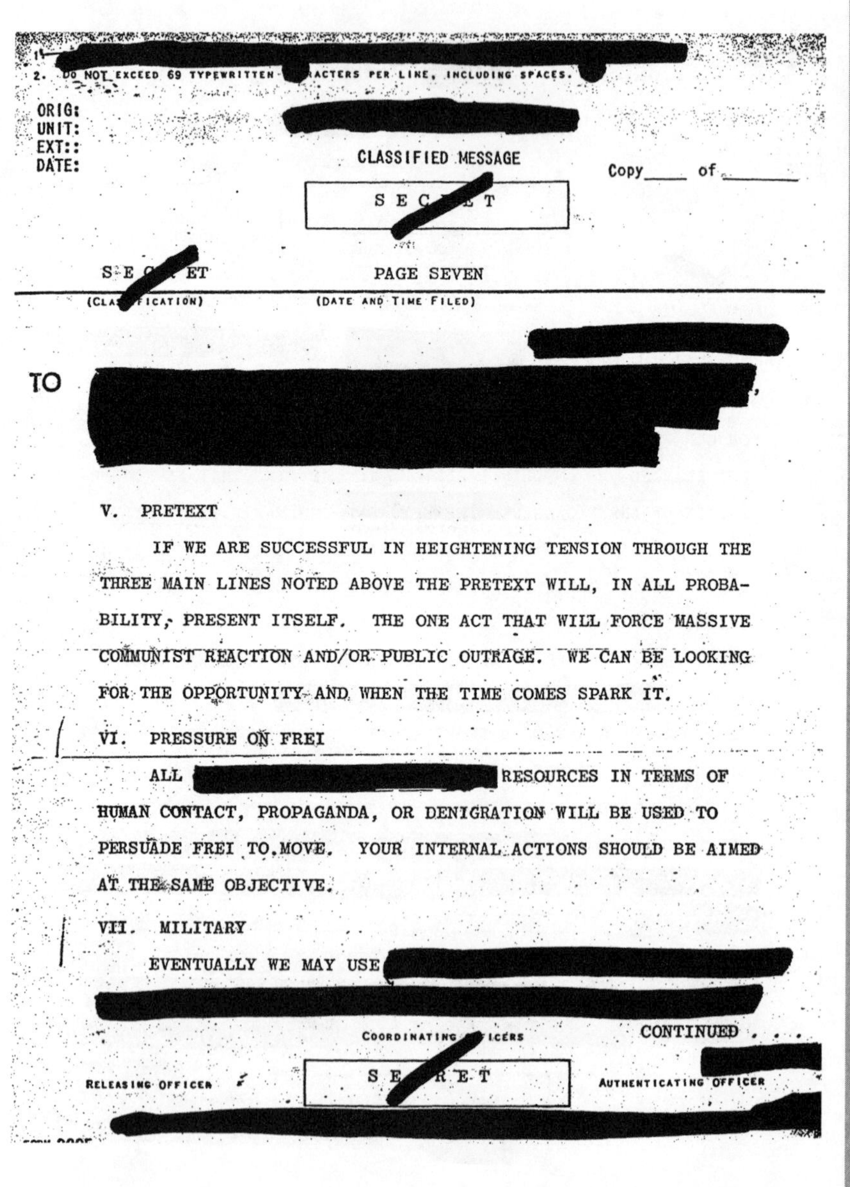

1. [redacted]
2. DO NOT EXCEED 69 TYPEWRITTEN [redacted] ACTERS PER LINE, INCLUDING SPACES.

ORIG:
UNIT:
EXT::
DATE:

CLASSIFIED MESSAGE

Copy____ of_______

SECRET

SECRET (CLASSIFICATION)   PAGE SEVEN (DATE AND TIME FILED)

TO [redacted]

V. PRETEXT

IF WE ARE SUCCESSFUL IN HEIGHTENING TENSION THROUGH THE THREE MAIN LINES NOTED ABOVE THE PRETEXT WILL, IN ALL PROBABILITY, PRESENT ITSELF. THE ONE ACT THAT WILL FORCE MASSIVE COMMUNIST REACTION AND/OR PUBLIC OUTRAGE. WE CAN BE LOOKING FOR THE OPPORTUNITY AND WHEN THE TIME COMES SPARK IT.

VI. PRESSURE ON FREI

ALL [redacted] RESOURCES IN TERMS OF HUMAN CONTACT, PROPAGANDA, OR DENIGRATION WILL BE USED TO PERSUADE FREI TO MOVE. YOUR INTERNAL ACTIONS SHOULD BE AIMED AT THE SAME OBJECTIVE.

VII. MILITARY

EVENTUALLY WE MAY USE [redacted]

CONTINUED . . .

RELEASING OFFICER   COORDINATING OFFICERS   AUTHENTICATING OFFICER

SECRET

DOCUMENT 8. CIA, **SECRET** Status Report, "Track II," October 10, 1970.

10 October 1970

Track II

1. Station "false flag" officer contacted General Viaux who claimed that he had suspended his coup planned for this weekend until he talked with our officer. Viaux requested that we make an airdrop to establish our bona fides.

2. [redacted]

3. [redacted] told the Chief of Station that he believes there is no chance of military intervention directed by the Army High Command.

4. COS met with [redacted] who said that he had talked with General Viaux, and as a consequence is convinced that Viaux has no military support.

5. General Viaux intends to increase the level of terrorism in Santiago over the weekend. The objective of this activity is to provoke the UP into retaliatory violence and public disorders.

ACCOMPLISHMENTS:

The COS and [redacted] have passed the word to the highest levels of the Chilean military that the USG is willing to support any military move to deny Allende the Presidency. Yesterday the COS held exploratory conversations with [redacted] who was very pessimistic about the possibility for military intervention, and a false flag staffer met with General Viaux who requested an air drop of weapons to help him launch a coup.

SITUATION:

Although the Military High Command is aware of our desire and willingness to help block Allende, they remain reluctant to act. At the present time only one military leader of national stature, General Viaux, appears committed to denying Allende the Presidency by force, and it is not clear how much support this retired General will be able to muster for a coup attempt.

Declassified and
Approved for Release
July 2000

DOCUMENT 9. CIA, **SECRET** Cable [Urgent Directive from Director Helms to Stimulate a Military Solution], October 7, 1970 (pages 1, 2).

NOT EXCEED 69 TYPEWRITTEN [CHAR]ACTERS PER LINE, INCLUDING SPACES.

David A. Phillips

WHD

E: 7 Oct 70

CLASSIFIED MESSAGE

Copy ____ of ____

SECRET

(CLASSIFICATION) (DATE AND TIME FILED)

TO IMMEDIATE SANTIAGO

Approved for Release
July 2000

1. INSTRUCTS YOU TO CONTACT THE MILITARY AND LET THEM KNOW USG WANTS A MILITARY SOLUTION, AND THAT WE WILL SUPPORT THEM NOW AND LATER.

2.

3. REQUIRES THAT YOU USE ALL AVAILABLE ASSETS AND STRATAGEMS INCLUDING THE RUMOR-MILL TO CREATE AT LEAST SOME SORT OF COUP CLIMATE. IF MAJOR REACTION BY THE LEFT CANNOT BE PROVOKED, THIS EFFORT TO BE TOPPED

COORDINATING OFFICERS

CONTINUED...

RELEASING OFFICER

SECRET

AUTHENTICATING OFFICER

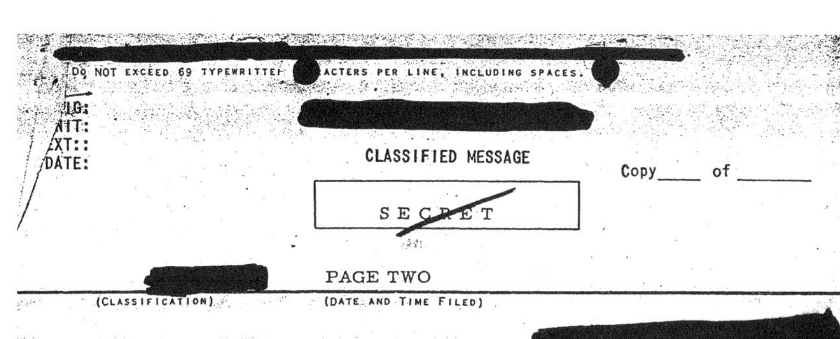

DO NOT EXCEED 69 TYPEWRITTEN CHARACTERS PER LINE, INCLUDING SPACES.

ORIG:
UNIT:
EXT::
DATE:

CLASSIFIED MESSAGE

Copy ____ of ______

SECRET

PAGE TWO

(CLASSIFICATION) (DATE AND TIME FILED)

TO WHICH CAN BE USED BY MILITARY AS PRETEXT.

4. ARE YOUR INSTRUCTIONS FOR ACTION BETWEEN NOW AND 24 OCTOBER. ALL OTHER CONSIDERATIONS ARE SECONDARY, AND YOU SHOULD NOT LET ANY OTHER ACTIVITY BY YOU AND YOUR OFFICERS VITIATE THIS THREE-PRONGED TASK. EVERY HOUR COUNTS. DO NOT CONCERN YOURSELF NOW WITH PDC, FREI, VITAL CENTER, AND PN.

5. YOUR EFFORTS TO PREPARE FOR FUTURE WHILE NECESSARY SHOULD BE CONSIDERED SECOND PRIORITY (WE ARE APPROVING YOUR SPONSORSHIP OF DIVISIVE TACTICS IN UP BY IN SEPARATE MESSAGE).

6. IN SUM, WE WANT YOU TO SPONSOR A MILITARY MOVE WHICH CAN TAKE PLACE, TO THE EXTENT POSSIBLE, IN A CLIMATE OF ECONOMIC AND POLITICAL UNCERTAINTY. WORK TO THAT END WITH REFERENCES AS YOUR CHARTER.

END OF MESSAGE

CONTINUED...

COORDINATING OFFICERS

RELEASING OFFICER SECRET AUTHEN...ER

FORM 220E

DOCUMENT 10. CIA, **SECRET** Report, "The Coup that Failed: The Effects on Allende and his Political Posture, With Special Emphasis on his Stance Before U.S. Positions, Moderate or Tough," October 15, 1970.

SECRET/

KEEP ATTACHMENT

3/13

15 October 1970

SUBJECT: The Coup That Failed: The Effects on Allende and his Political Posture, With Special Emphasis on his Stance Before U.S. Positions, Moderate or Tough

I. Probable Reaction to an Unsuccessful Viaux Coup.

A. Should General Roberto Viaux launch an unsuccessful military coup to deny Allende the Chilean presidency, the results could range from a quick snuffing out of his rebellious candle to a flaming civil war situation. But certain basic assumptions are valid without definition of the degree or circumstance of failure.

(1) Allende would be forced to proclaim U.S. sponsorship of the coup attempt. He would be under considerable international pressure from anti-American elements abroad to denounce the movement as American-inspired. Consequently, U.S. prestige in Chile, Latin America, and the free world would be diminished.

(2) The Communist power-base would increase significantly. They would have the excuse to move quickly into control of what they considered power points, especially press, radio and television.

(3) Allende would attempt to consolidate his position within the military, thereby decreasing the prospects for a post-inaugural coup.

(4) Allende would exploit this situation by pressuring the political opposition (PDC, PN) to support his nationalization program.

(5) Allende would call for an advance in any timetable of expropriation and would significantly increase his public attacks against the military and the U.S.

B. Even if Allende's long-range strategy is to achieve the aims of his program through a moderate approach, the combination

SECRET

233

of the above factors might force Allende to adopt a demagogic and nationalistic posture in the early days of his presidency.

II. Allende's Probable Reaction to a Moderate U.S. Posture

A. Allende may find it difficult but not impossible to carry out a long-range program which could be bruited as reasonable and moderate.

B. Allende would find a moderate U.S. posture a fertile atmosphere for carrying out a nationalistic program with ties to the West, especially in keeping his copper in the dollar markets and resisting pressures to drastically reduce (or break) diplomatic relations with the U.S.

C. Allende might be able to take a more independent stance in resisting the Soviets and Cubans.

III. Allende's Probable Reaction to a Tough U.S. Posture

A. Allende would find it extremely difficult to adopt a reasonable and moderate program for Chile. He would have a reduced capability to impede the rapid political expansion of Communists and leftists.

B. Allende's attempts to maintain dollar markets would not be significantly reduced by a tough U.S. stance. But internal pressure to greatly reduce diplomatic relations with the U.S. would be given added impetus.

C. The most probable effect of a tough U.S. position would be the acceleration of Allende's and Chile's move toward the Communist camp.

SECRET

DOCUMENT 11. CIA, **SECRET** Memorandum of Conversation, "Dr. Kissinger, Mr. Karamessines, Gen. Haig at the White House—15 October 1970," October 15, 1970.

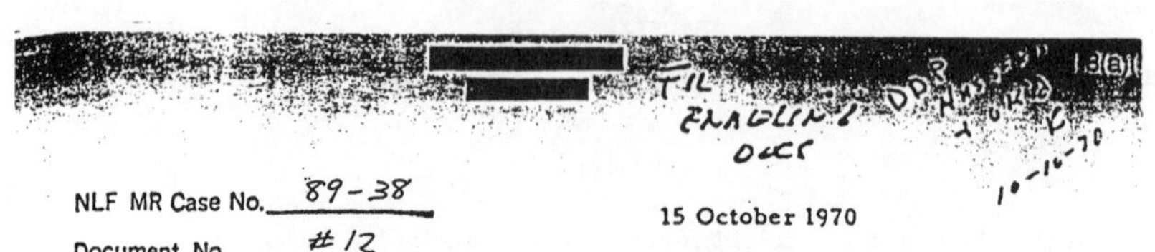

NLF MR Case No. 89-38

Document No. #12

15 October 1970

MEMORANDUM OF CONVERSATION:

Dr. Kissinger, Mr. Karamessines, Gen. Haig at the White House - 15 October 1970

1.3(a)(4)

2. Then Mr. Karamessines provided a run-down on Viaux, the Canales meeting with Tirado, the latter's new position (after Porta was relieved of command "for health reasons") and, in some detail, the general situation in Chile from the coup possibility viewpoint.

3. A certain amount of information was available to us concerning Viaux's alleged support throughout the Chilean military. We had assessed Viaux's claims carefully, basing our analysis on good intelligence from a number of sources. Our conclusion was clear: Viaux did not have more than one chance in twenty - perhaps less - to launch a successful coup.

4. The unfortunate repercussions, in Chile and internationally, of an unsuccessful coup were discussed. Dr. Kissinger ticked off

1.3(a

his list of these negative possibilities. His items were remarkably similar to the ones Mr. Karamessines had prepared.

5. It was decided by those present that the Agency must get a message to Viaux warning him against any precipitate action. In essence our message was to state: "We have reviewed your plans, and based on your information and ours, we come to the conclusion that your plans for a coup at this time cannot succeed. Failing, they may reduce your capabilities for the future. Preserve your assets. We will stay in touch. The time will come when you with all your other friends can do something. You will continue to have our support".

6. After the decision to de-fuse the Viaux coup plot, at least temporarily, Dr. Kissinger instructed Mr. Karamessines to preserve Agency assets in Chile, working clandestinely and securely to maintain the capability for Agency operations against Allende in the future.

7. Dr. Kissinger discussed his desire that the word of our encouragement to the Chilean military in recent weeks be kept as secret as possible. Mr. Karamessines stated emphatically that we had been doing everything possible in this connection, including the use of false flag officers, car meetings and every conceivable precaution. But we and others had done a great deal of talking recently with a number of persons. For example, Ambassador Korry's wideranging discussions with numerous people urging a coup "cannot be put back into the bottle". [redacted] (Dr. Kissinger requested that copy of the message be sent to him on 16 October.) 1.3(a)(4

8. The meeting concluded on Dr. Kissinger's note that the Agency should continue keeping the pressure on every Allende weak spot in sight - now, after the 24th of October, after 5 November, and into the future until such time as new marching orders are given. Mr. Karamessines stated that the Agency would comply.

DOCUMENT 12. CIA, **SECRET** Cable from Headquarters [Firm and Continuing Policy that Allende be Overthrown by a Coup], October 16, 1970.

1. RESTRICTED-HANDLING MESSAGES [redacted]T BE DELIVERED DIRECTLY TO SPECIAL S[redacted]AL CENTER.
2. DO NOT EXCEED 69 TYPEWRITTEN [redacted]ARACTERS PER LINE, INCLUDING SPACES.

(327)

Declassified and Approved for Release July 2000

ORIG: [redacted]
UNIT:
EXT:
DATE: 16 October 1970

RESTRICTED HANDLING

CLASSIFIED MESSAGE

SECRET

Copy____ of ______

LESNA ENABLING DOCUMENTS

(CLASSIFICATION) (DATE AND TIME FILED)

TO [redacted] 422

CITE HEADQUARTERS 802

IMMEDIATE SANTIAGO (EYES ONLY [redacted]
[redacted]

16 14 08Z OCT 70

1. [redacted] POLICY, OBJECTIVES, AND ACTIONS WERE REVIEWED AT HIGH USG LEVEL AFTERNOON 15 OCTOBER. CONCLUSIONS, WHICH ARE TO BE YOUR OPERATIONAL GUIDE, FOLLOW:

2. IT IS FIRM AND CONTINUING POLICY THAT ALLENDE BE OVERTHROWN BY A COUP. IT WOULD BE MUCH PREFERABLE TO HAVE THIS TRANSPIRE PRIOR TO 24 OCTOBER, BUT EFFORTS IN THIS REGARD WILL CONTINUE VIGOROUSLY BEYOND THIS DATE. WE ARE TO CONTINUE TO GENERATE MAXIMUM PRESSURE TOWARD THIS END UTILIZING EVERY APPROPRIATE RESOURCE. IT IS IMPERATIVE THAT THESE ACTIONS BE IMPLEMENTED CLANDESTINELY AND SECURELY SO THAT THE USG AND AMERICAN HAND BE WELL HIDDEN. WHILE THIS IMPOSES UPON US A HIGH DEGREE OF SELECTIVITY IN MAKING MILITARY CONTACTS AND DICTATES

238

COORDINATING OFFICERS

....CONTINUED....

RELEASING OFFICER

SECRET

AUTHENTICATING OFFICER [redacted]

GROUP 1

1: RESTRICTED-HANDLING MESSAGES [redacted]T BE DELIVERED DIRECTLY TO SPECIAL S[redacted]AL CENTER.
2.- DO NOT EXCEED 69 TYPEWRITTEN [redacted]ARACTERS PER LINE, INCLUDING SPACES.

ORIG:
UNIT:
EXT::
DATE:

RESTRICTED HANDLING

CLASSIFIED MESSAGE

Copy____ of ______

SECRET

(CLASSIFICATION) (DATE AND TIME FILED)

PAGE TWO CITE HEADQUARTERS

TO

THAT THESE CONTACTS BE MADE IN THE MOST SECURE MANNER. IT DEFINITELY DOES NOT PRECLUDE CONTACTS SUCH AS REPORTED IN SANTIAGO 544 WHICH WAS A MASTERFUL PIECE OF WORK.

3. AFTER THE MOST CAREFUL CONSIDERATION IT WAS DETERMINED THAT A VIAUX COUP ATTEMPT CARRIED OUT BY HIM ALONE WITH THE FORCES NOW AT HIS DISPOSAL WOULD FAIL. THUS, IT WOULD BE COUNTERPRODUCTIVE TO OUR [redacted] OBJECTIVES. IT WAS DECIDED THAT [redacted] GET A MESSAGE TO VIAUX WARNING HIM AGAINST PRECIPITATE ACTION. IN ESSENCE OUR MESSAGE IS TO STATE, "WE HAVE REVIEWED YOUR PLANS, AND BASED ON YOUR INFORMATION AND OURS, WE COME TO THE CONCLUSION THAT YOUR PLANS FOR A COUP AT THIS TIME CANNOT SUCCEED. FAILING, THEY MAY REDUCE YOUR CAPABILITIES FOR THE FUTURE. PRESERVE YOUR ASSETS. WE WILL STAY IN TOUCH. THE TIME WILL COME

COORDINATING OFFICERS

....CONTINUED....

RELEASING OFFICER

SECRET

AUTHENTICATING OFFICER

THIS FORM FOR USE BY AUTHORIZED RESTRICTED HANDLING MESSAGE USERS ONLY.

PAGE 3 OF 4

1. RESTRICTED-HANDLING MESSAGES [redacted]T BE DELIVERED DIRECTLY TO SPECIAL S[redacted]AL CENTER.
2. DO NOT EXCEED 69 TYPEWRITTEN [redacted]ARACTERS PER LINE, INCLUDING SPACES.

ORIG: [redacted]
UNIT:
EXT::
DATE:

RESTRICTED HANDLING

CLASSIFIED MESSAGE

Copy____ of________

SECRET

(CLASSIFICATION) (DATE AND TIME FILED)

SECRET PAGE THREE CITE HEADQUARTERS

TO

WHEN YOU TOGETHER WITH ALL YOUR OTHER FRIENDS CAN DO SOMETHING. YOU WILL CONTINUE TO HAVE OUR SUPPORT." YOU ARE REQUESTED TO DELIVER THE MESSAGE TO VIAUX ESSENTIALLY AS NOTED ABOVE. OUR OBJECTIVES ARE AS FOLLOWS: (A) TO ADVISE HIM OF OUR OPINION AND DISCOURAGE HIM FROM ACTING ALONE; (B) CONTINUE TO ENCOURAGE HIM TO AMPLIFY HIS PLANNING; (C) ENCOURAGE HIM TO JOIN FORCES WITH OTHER COUP PLANNERS SO THAT THEY MAY ACT IN CONCERT EITHER BEFORE OR AFTER 24 OCTOBER. (N.B. SIX GAS MASKS AND SIX CS CANNISTERS ARE BEING CARRIED TO SANTIAGO BY SPECIAL [redacted] COURIER ETD WASHINGTON 1100 HOURS 16 OCTOBER.)

4. THERE IS GREAT AND CONTINUING INTEREST IN THE ACTIVITIES OF TIRADO, CANALES, VALENZUELA ET AL AND WE WISH THEM OPTIMUM GOOD FORTUNE.

5. THE ABOVE IS YOUR OPERATING GUIDANCE. NO OTHER

....CONTINUED....

COORDINATING OFFICERS

RELEASING OFFICER

SECRET

AUTHENTICATING OFFICER

THIS FORM FOR USE BY AUTHORIZED RESTRICTED HANDLING MESSAGE USERS ONLY

1. RESTRICTED HANDLING MESSAGES [redacted]T BE DELIVERED DIRECTLY TO SPECIAL S[redacted]AL CENTER.
2. DO NOT EXCEED 69 TYPEWRITTEN [redacted]ARACTERS PER LINE, INCLUDING SPACES.

ORIG: [redacted]
UNIT:
EXT::
DATE:

RESTRICTED HANDLING

CLASSIFIED MESSAGE

Copy____ of ______

SE[redacted]ET

(CLASSIFICATION) (DATE AND TIME FILED)

SECRET PAGE FOUR CITE HEADQUARTERS

TO

POLICY GUIDANCE YOU MAY RECEIVE FROM [redacted] OR ITS MAXIMUM EXPONENT IN SANTIAGO, ON HIS RETURN, ARE TO SWAY YOU FROM YOUR COURSE.

6. PLEASE REVIEW ALL YOUR PRESENT AND POSSIBLY NEW ACTIVITIES TO INCLUDE PROPAGANDA, BLACK OPERATIONS, SURFACING OF INTELLIGENCE OR DISINFORMATION, PERSONAL CONTACTS, OR ANYTHING ELSE YOUR IMAGINATION CAN CONJURE WHICH WILL PERMIT YOU TO CONTINUE TO PRESS FORWARD TOWARD OUR [redacted] OBJECTIVE IN A SECURE MANNER.

END OF MESSAGE

WILLIAM V. BROE
C/WHD

RELEASING OFFICER

COORDINATING OFFICERS

DAVID A. PHILLIPS
C/WH/TFR

AUTHENTICATING OFFICER

SE[redacted]RET

DOCUMENT 13. CIA, **SECRET** Cable from Santiago Station [Report on Plan to Kidnap Gen. René Schneider and Initiate a Military Coup], October 19, 1970.

PAGE 1 OF 4

347

4

19 [redacted]

Approved for Release
July 2000

SECRET 19 [redacted] OCT 70 CITE SANTIAGO [redacted]

IMMEDIATE [redacted]

[redacted]

1. FOLL IS CHRONOLOGY OF EVENTS ON 18 OCTOBER.

2. [redacted] PICKED UP [redacted] AT [redacted] HOURS [redacted] [redacted] WHERE [redacted] AND [redacted] WERE WAITING. [redacted] TURNED OVER 2 PACKAGES (TEAR GAS AND GAS MASKS) TO [redacted] [redacted] JOINED OTHER TWO CHILEANS IN THEIR VEHICLE AND LEFT SITE. [redacted] RETURNED TO [redacted] WHERE GENERAL CAMILO VALANZUELA HAD IN MEANWHILE CALLED TO SAY THAT HE WOULD BE VISITING [redacted] AT 2230 HOURS.

3. VALENZUELA ARRIVED PUCTUALLY. REMINDED [redacted] OF LAST TALK WHEN HE HAD PROMISED TO ALERT [redacted] WHEN ARMY READY TO ACT. THIS NOW THE CASE. FOLL WAS PLAN:

A. GENERAL SCHNEIDER INVITED TO STAG PARTY AT ARMY VIP HOUSE EVENING 19 OCTOBER AT 2130 HOURS.

B. WHEN ARRIVING AT VIP HOUSE, SCHNEIDER WILL BE ABDUCTED.

C. SCHNEIDER WILL BE TAKEN TO WAITING AIRPLANE AND FLOWN TO [redacted]

[redacted]

4

PAGE 2 SANTIAGO S E R E T

D. VALENZUELA WILL ANNOUNCE TO ASSEMBLED GENERALS THAT SCHNEIDER HAD DISAPPEARED AND THAT GENERAL CARLOS PRATS TO SUCCEED SCHNEIDER AS CINC PROTEM.

E. TO KEEP CARABINEROS AWAY FROM VIP HOUSE AREA TO INSURE THAT ABDUCTION WILL NOT BE INTERFERED WITH.

F. ON 20 OCTOBER CABINET WILL RESIGN. ONLY ZALDIVAR (FINANCE) AND FIGUEROA (ECONOMY) WILL STAY.

G. ALL OTHER CABINET POSTERS WILL BE GIVEN TO MEMBERS OF ARMED FORCES AND POLICE.

H. GENERAL SCHAFFHAUSER, CHIEF OF STAFF OF ARMY, WILL BE APOINTED MINISTER OF PUBLIC WORKS.

I. GENERAL URBINA WILL BE RELIEVED OF COMMAND OF SECOND DIVISION IN SANTIAGO AND APPOINTED CHIEF OF STAFF VICE SCHAFFHAUSER.

J. ON 21 OCTOBER, FREI WILL RENOUNCE PRESIDENCY AND LEAVE CHILE

K. ON 22 OCTOBER, MILITARY JUNTA HEADED BY

PAGE 3 SANTIAGO S E R E T

 ILL BE INSTALLED

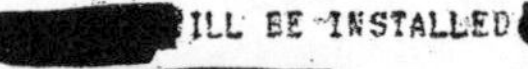

L. CAPTAIN RAUL LOPEZ WILL BE APPOINTED CINC NAVY WHICH AUTOMATICALLY RESULTS IN RETIREMENT OF ALL ADMIRALS.

M. GENERALS HUERTA AND VALENZUELA WILL STAY IN THEIR PRESENT POSITIONS.

N. GENERAL JOAQUIN GARCIA WILL BE APPOINTED CINC AIR FORCE.

M. JUNTA WILL DISSOLVE CONGRESS (VALENZUELA COMMENTED THAT THIS WOULD BE MILITARY'S ONLY UNCONSTITUTIONAL ACT).

4. GENERAL VIAUX KNOWLEDGEABLE OF ABOVE OPERATION BUT NOT DIRECTLY INVOLVED. HE HAS BEEN SENT TO VINA TO STAY WITH PROMINENT PHYSICIAN. WILL BE SEEN IN PUBLIC PLACES DURING 19 AND 20 OCTOBER TO DEMONSTRATE FACT THAT ABOVE OPERATION NOT HIS DOING. WILL BE ALLOWED TO RETURN TO SANTIAGO AT END OF WEEK.

5. MILITARY WILL NOT ADMIT INVOLVEMENT IN SCHNEIDER'S ABDUCTION WHICH IS TO BE BLAMED ON LEFTISTS. ALMOST IMMEDIATELY, CARABINEROS WILL INSTITUTE SEARCH FOR SCHENEIDER IN ALL OF

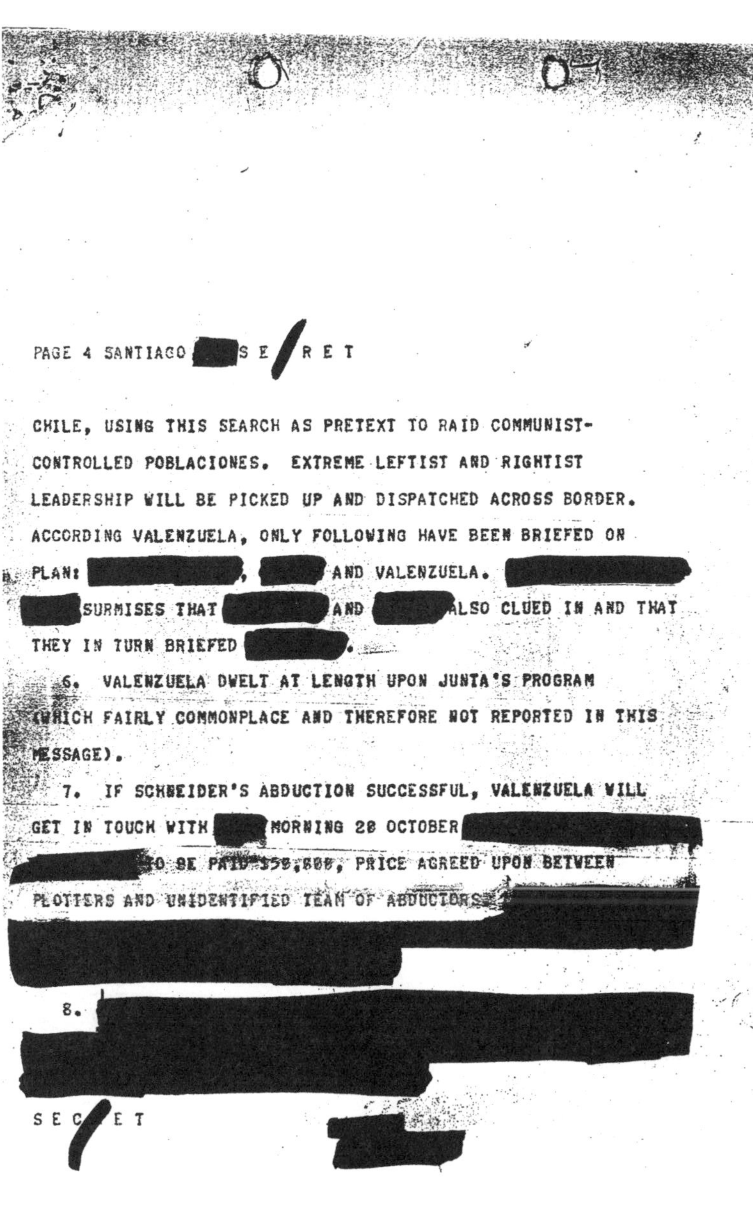

4

PAGE 4 SANTIAGO [redacted] SE/RET

CHILE, USING THIS SEARCH AS PRETEXT TO RAID COMMUNIST-CONTROLLED POBLACIONES. EXTREME LEFTIST AND RIGHTIST LEADERSHIP WILL BE PICKED UP AND DISPATCHED ACROSS BORDER. ACCORDING VALENZUELA, ONLY FOLLOWING HAVE BEEN BRIEFED ON PLAN: [redacted], [redacted] AND VALENZUELA. [redacted] SURMISES THAT [redacted] AND [redacted] ALSO CLUED IN AND THAT THEY IN TURN BRIEFED [redacted].

6. VALENZUELA DWELT AT LENGTH UPON JUNTA'S PROGRAM (WHICH FAIRLY COMMONPLACE AND THEREFORE NOT REPORTED IN THIS MESSAGE).

7. IF SCHNEIDER'S ABDUCTION SUCCESSFUL, VALENZUELA WILL GET IN TOUCH WITH [redacted] MORNING 20 OCTOBER [redacted] TO BE PAID 50,000, PRICE AGREED UPON BETWEEN PLOTTERS AND UNIDENTIFIED TEAM OF ABDUCTORS. [redacted]

8. [redacted]

SEC/ET

DOCUMENT 14. CIA, **SECRET** Cable from Headquarters [Submachine Guns Being Sent to Station for Kidnapping Plot], October 18, 1970.

1. RESTRICTED HANDLING MESSAGE MUST BE DELIVERED DIRECTLY TO SPECIAL SIGNAL CENTER.
2. DO NOT EXCEED 69 TYPEWRITTEN CHARACTERS PER LINE, INCLUDING SPACES.

334

RUESNA-2FF4

ORIG:
UNIT: WH/TFR
EXT:
DATE: 18 October 1970

RESTRICTED HANDLING

CLASSIFIED MESSAGE

Copy ___ of ___

SECRET

MILITARY

(CLASSIFICATION) (DATE AND TIME FILED)

18 23 11z Oct 70 CITE HEADQUARTERS - 856

431

TO IMMEDIATE SANTIAGO (EYES ONLY

REF: SANTIAGO 562

SUB-MACHINE GUNS AND AMMO BEING SENT BY REGULAR COURIER LEAVING WASHINGTON 0700 HOURS 19 OCTOBER DUE ARRIVE SANTIAGO LATE EVENING 20 OCTOBER OR EARLY MORNING 21 OCTOBER. PREFERRED USE REGULAR COURIER TO AVOID BRINGING UNDUE ATTENTION TO OP.

END OF MESSAGE

Declassified and
Approved for Release
July 2000

257

WILLIAM V. BROE
C/WHD

COORDINATING OFFICERS

DAVID A. PHILLIPS
C/WH/TFR

AUTHENTICATING

DOCUMENT 15. CIA, **SECRET** Cable from Task Force Director [Commendation for Schneider Shooting], October 23, 1970 (page 1).

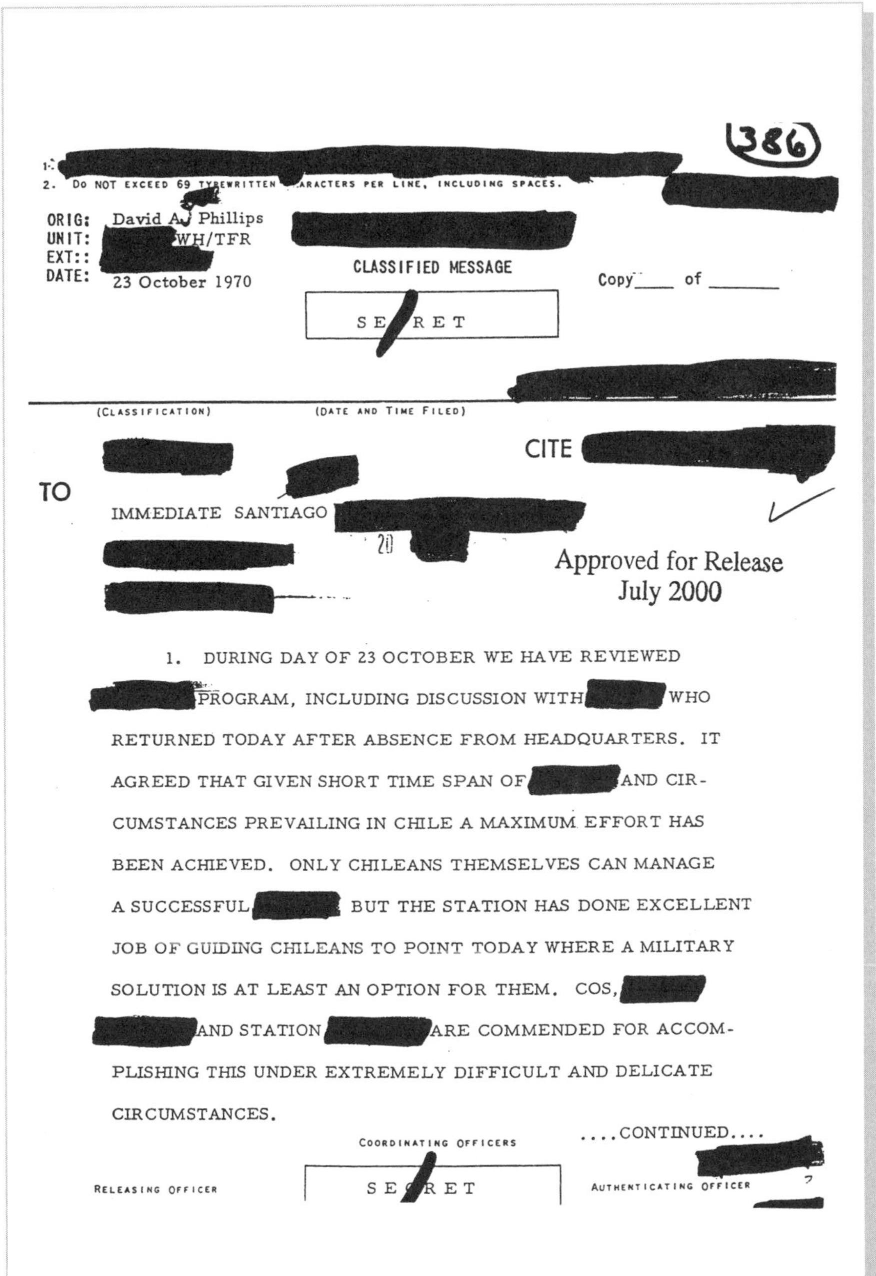

(386)

1.
2. DO NOT EXCEED 69 TYPEWRITTEN CHARACTERS PER LINE, INCLUDING SPACES.

ORIG: David A. Phillips
UNIT: WH/TFR
EXT::
DATE: 23 October 1970

CLASSIFIED MESSAGE

Copy ____ of ______

SECRET

(CLASSIFICATION) (DATE AND TIME FILED)

CITE

TO

IMMEDIATE SANTIAGO

Approved for Release
July 2000

1. DURING DAY OF 23 OCTOBER WE HAVE REVIEWED [redacted] PROGRAM, INCLUDING DISCUSSION WITH [redacted] WHO RETURNED TODAY AFTER ABSENCE FROM HEADQUARTERS. IT AGREED THAT GIVEN SHORT TIME SPAN OF [redacted] AND CIRCUMSTANCES PREVAILING IN CHILE A MAXIMUM EFFORT HAS BEEN ACHIEVED. ONLY CHILEANS THEMSELVES CAN MANAGE A SUCCESSFUL [redacted] BUT THE STATION HAS DONE EXCELLENT JOB OF GUIDING CHILEANS TO POINT TODAY WHERE A MILITARY SOLUTION IS AT LEAST AN OPTION FOR THEM. COS, [redacted] [redacted] AND STATION [redacted] ARE COMMENDED FOR ACCOMPLISHING THIS UNDER EXTREMELY DIFFICULT AND DELICATE CIRCUMSTANCES.

....CONTINUED....

COORDINATING OFFICERS

RELEASING OFFICER SECRET AUTHENTICATING OFFICER

DOCUMENT 16. CIA, **SECRET** Memorandum from John Horton on Conversation with False Flagger, "Conversation with Bruce MacMaster–Chile Operations," February 18, 1971.

18 February 1971

MEMORANDUM FOR: Chief, Western Hemisphere Division

FROM : Chief, WH/1

SUBJECT : Conversation with Bruce MacMaster--Chile Operations

1. Because of the nature of the following information I feel that it is incumbent on me to inform you of a conversation which I had with Mr. MacMaster concerning his involvement in a sensitive Chilean operation. As part of a commentary by Mr. MacMaster on certain events which took place in Mexico City, all of which I have reported to you in previous memoranda, the following specific references to actions concerning events in Chile are hereby reported.

2. Mr. MacMaster said that in his travel to Santiago, Chile, in September of 1970 he had met Henry J. SLOMAN at the bar of a local hotel. According to MacMaster, the meeting was unavoidable since SLOMAN was arriving and he was departing the area and they were both involved as part of the same operation. Several items of interest including the grand bargains attainable in Santiago were discussed by SLOMAN and MacMaster. The main subject and the ramifications surrounding it I wish to call to your attention now is difficult to pinpoint in exact terms of time. However, it is clear that this subject was discussed by SLOMAN with MacMaster some time after the events I will relate to you took place. In one sequence, it is probable that MacMaster is reflecting on a conversation with an unnamed Chilean which presumably took place within the last fortnight.

SECRET, EYES ONLY

3. To begin at the beginning, MacMaster told me on 16 February 1971 that he was sent on a mission to Chile to recruit certain individuals for an action designed to cause difficulty for the Allende political forces in Chile. MacMaster said that he had met with three or four individuals whom I gather were Chilean military since he identified the key contact of this group as Brigadier General Roberto Viaux Marambio, former Commander of Army Regent No. 1 in Antofagasta and former First Army Division Commander in the Chilean Armed Forces. Further, MacMaster stated that he ostensibly was representing American business interests such as the Ford Foundation, the Rockefeller Foundation and other unidentified business groups. MacMaster introduced himself as a Columbian businessman with ties to the aforementioned American business institutions. He did not go into any particular detail as to what his representations were designed to accomplish but said that the goal of his mission was to help create a situation which would encourage the Chilean military to activate a military take-over of the Chilean Government. He said that part of the theme he expressed to the group representatives he met with was that as a representative of American business interests he was most anxious to see the continuance of democratić institutions in Chile. In other words, should the Allende forces assume governmental control in Chile, the forces of democracy would suffer a severe if not permanent defeat.

4. Mr. MacMaster said that SLOMAN also met with members of the same Chilean military group mentioned above and represented himself as an Argentine with close ties to Latin American business interests. In referring to much later contact in the United States with a representative of the military group, Mr. MacMaster said that this individual referred to SLOMAN as either a representative of the CIA or of the Mafia or possibly both. Mr. MacMaster then said that the action against General Scheinder designed to create the climate to allow the military to effect a Golpe did not accomplish the desired objective. He mentioned the planned employment of a group of individuals of probable military make-up who were to kidnap General Scheinder using mace or chloroform which in turn was supposed to create a situation and thus set the stage for the military to act. MacMaster referred to a second group of right-wing students who also were under the control of Viaux who became involved in the action against Scheinder. According to Mr. MacMaster it appears that the student group was responsible for the machine-gun attack on General Scheinder.

SECRET, EYES ONLY

5. Mr. MacMaster said that at the moment three or four or possibly five members of the Viaux group are now in prison in Chile and that he believes there is serious concern that one of these people now jailed in Chile will possibly implicate CIA in the action taken against Schneider. MacMaster said that an individual from this group met him recently and is seeking a large amount of money--somewhere in the neighborhood of $250,000 for the purpose of providing support for the families of the members of the group jailed by the Allende Government in Chile. Mr. MacMaster said that we could probably get away with paying around $10,000 for the support of each family.

6. The foregoing account coupled with the statements, one by John Horton regarding the possible necessity of psychiatric treatment for MacMaster, the other by Paul Harwood which suggests that the role played by MacMaster in Chile may have an affect on how MacMaster views the Agency and events associated with the Agency, could conceivably have serious implications for the Agency.

7. Once again, it is most difficult for me to judge the validity of the information contained in this memorandum. One thing is clear from this and previous memoranda, that there exists an animosity between MacMaster and SLOMAN which needs careful watching to prevent a serious situation from developing.

DOCUMENT 17. Department of State, Memorandum for Henry Kissinger, "Message to Chilean President Frei on Attempted Assassination of Army Commander," October 22, 1970.

22995

DEPARTMENT OF STATE

Washington, D.C. 20520

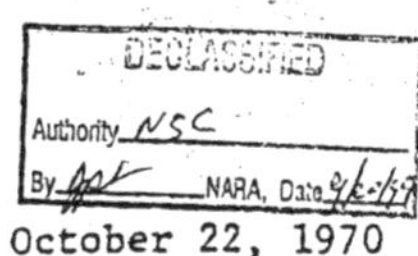

S/S 14291

~~CONFIDENTIAL~~

October 22, 1970

MEMORANDUM FOR MR. HENRY A. KISSINGER
THE WHITE HOUSE

SUBJECT: Message to Chilean President Frei on Attempted Assassination of Army Commander

General Rene Schneider, Commander of the Chilean Army, is in serious condition as a result of bullet wounds inflicted by unknown assailants early October 22 in Santiago.

The Department recommends that the President send to President Frei of Chile a message along the lines of the enclosed suggested message.

If White House approves, we will have our Embassy in Santiago deliver the message.

Theodore L. Eliot, Jr.
Executive Secretary

Enclosure:

Suggested message

~~CONFIDENTIAL~~
~~Group 3~~
~~Downgraded at 12-year intervals;~~
~~not automatically declassified.~~

LIMITED OFFICIAL USE

DEPARTMENT OF STATE

Suggested Reply

Dear Mr. President:

The shocking attempt on the life of General Schneider is a stain on the pages of contemporary history. I would like you to know of my sorrow that this repugnant event has occurred in your country, and would ask you to extend to General Schneider and his family my sympathy and best wishes for speedy recovery.

Sincerely,

Richard Nixon

2

Destabilizing Democracy: The United States and the Allende Government

Our main concern in Chile is the prospect that he [Allende] can consolidate himself and the picture projected to the world will be his success.
—Richard Nixon on why the U.S. had to "bring down" Allende, November 1970

Within two days of Salvador Allende's inauguration, President Nixon convened his entire National Security Council to discuss ways to "bring about his downfall." "We want to do it right and bring him down," Secretary of State William Rogers declared at the November 6, 1970, NSC meeting on Chile. The Secretary of Defense, Melvin Laird, agreed: "We have to do everything we can to hurt [Allende] and bring him down."

The SECRET/SENSITIVE memorandum of conversation of this cabinet meeting—a pivotal document withheld from the Church Committee on the grounds of "executive privilege" and kept secret for thirty years—records the unyielding White House commitment to undermine Chilean democracy, as well as the reason for it. "Our main concern in Chile is the prospect that he [Allende] can consolidate himself and the picture projected to the world will be his success," stated Nixon, providing the only candid explanation of his policy to prevent the democratic election of a socialist from becoming a model for Latin America and elsewhere. "No impression should be permitted in Latin America that they can get away with this, that it's safe to go this way. All over the world it's too much the fashion to kick us around," the president continued. "We cannot fail to show our displeasure." (Doc 1)

After the failure of Project FUBELT, U.S. policy makers adjusted their strategy; but the goal of bringing Allende down remained. Rather than a small group of covert operatives trying to stimulate a military move in a short period of time, most of the U.S. government would now be involved in a long-term, expanded effort to destabilize the Chilean government—economically, politically, and militarily. "The question," as Kissinger's talking points for the NSC meeting called for him to say, "is whether there are actions we can take ourselves to intensify Allende's problems so that at a minimum he may fail or be forced to limit his aims, and at a maximum might create conditions in which a collapse or overthrow may be feasible."[1] If forceful action was not taken, as Kissinger implied to Nixon's scheduler when he requested an hour to brief the president before the National Security Council members met, Chile "could end up being the worst failure in our administration—'our Cuba' by 1972."

Kissinger's pressure on Nixon to take a hard-line policy posture on Allende is revealed in an eight-page White House briefing paper titled "NSC Meeting, November 6," and classified SECRET/SENSITIVE. "The election of Allende as president of Chile poses for us one of the most serious challenges ever faced in this hemisphere," Kissinger dramatically emphasized to Nixon. "Your decision as to what to do about it may be the most historic and difficult foreign affairs decision you will make this year." Allende had been president of Chile for less than 48 hours, but a preemptive U.S. strike was necessary. Chile posed "some very serious threats" to U.S. interests, Kissinger informed Nixon—among them "U.S. investments (totaling some one billion dollars)" that could be lost. More important was what Kissinger called the "insidious" "model effect" of Allende's democratic election:

> The example of a successful elected Marxist government in Chile would surely have an impact on—and even precedent value for—other parts of the world, especially in Italy; the imitative spread of similar phenomena elsewhere would in turn significantly affect the world balance and our own position in it. (Doc 2)

Notwithstanding this danger, Kissinger warned, the State Department believed that Washington had no choice but to coexist with Allende because he was the legitimately elected leader of Chile and U.S. measures to oppose him would cause serious diplomatic damage to America's image abroad. Nixon would have to overrule this position. "It is essential that you make it crystal clear where you stand on this issue" at the NSC meeting, Kissinger counseled: "If all concerned do not understand that you want Allende opposed as strongly as we can, the result will be a steady drift toward the *modus vivendi* approach."

The clear position of Kissinger and Nixon, and indeed the very purpose of the November 6 NSC meeting, stands in sharp contrast with the many public representations that the president and his men would later make about the benign nature of the U.S. approach toward Chile during the Allende years. Only a few months after ordering massive efforts to undermine Allende's administration, Nixon falsely asserted in his 1971 State of the Union address that "we are prepared to have the kind of relationship with the Chilean government that it is prepared to have with us." Four years after recommending a program of action against Allende that "might lead to . . . his collapse or overthrow," Kissinger testified before the Senate Foreign Relations Committee in September 1974 that "the intent of the United States was not to destabilize or to subvert [Allende] but to keep in being [opposition] political parties. . . . Our concern was with the election of 1976 and not at all with a coup in 1973 about which we knew nothing and [with] which we had nothing to do. . . ." In an unprecedented presidential acknowledgement of a CIA covert operation, President Gerald Ford would argue that the United States had acted to preserve Chilean democracy. "The effort that was made in this case," he told the press, "was to help assist the preservation of opposition newspapers and electronic media and to preserve opposition political parties."

This was, submitted President Ford in one of the most famous statements made regarding U.S. intervention against Allende, "in the best interests of the people of Chile and certainly in our best interests."

Cool But Correct: National Security Decision Memorandum 93

"We will be very cool and very correct, but doing those things which will be a real message to Allende and others," Nixon informed his aides on November 6. Presenting U.S. policy as detached diplomatic accommodation of the Popular Unity government while pursuing direct hostile actions designed to make it collapse, was a deliberate, conscious decision made at the highest levels of the White House. In the wake of the Schneider fiasco and Allende's inauguration, as Henry Kissinger explained to the National Security Council, a high-level policy review had produced several options for U.S. policy: (1) to seek a modus vivendi with the Allende government; (2) implement an overt, hostile policy; or (3) "adopt what is in fact a hostile posture but not from an overt stance, that is, to move in hostility from a low-key posture." A modus vivendi was out of the question; Kissinger had already secretly lobbied Nixon against that option prior to the meeting.[2] But a posture of overt hostility would be problematic. "Events in Chile," Kissinger told the NSC members, according to his talking points, were "taking a form which makes them extremely difficult to deal with or offset":

a. Allende was elected legally and constitutionally. Therefore, he has legitimacy as far as Chileans and most of the world is concerned;

there is nothing we can do to deny him legitimacy or claim he does not have it as a tactic for weakening him.

b. He is unlikely to move things along lines which would permit us easily to marshal international or hemisphere censure of him . . . he will project Chile as an 'independent' socialist country, not as a 'communist government' or a Soviet puppet.

c. We ourselves have traditionally espoused the principles of self-determination; we have stressed our opposition to the concept of intervention in foreign affairs. It would therefore be costly for us to act in ways that appear to violate those principles.[3]

For that reason, Kissinger urged, and Nixon approved, Option 3, which in innocuous bureaucratic language stated: "Maintain an outwardly correct posture, but making clear our opposition to the emergence of a Communist government in South America; act positively to retain the initiative vis-à-vis the Allende government." A "cool but correct" posture masking continuing efforts to subvert the Chilean government, Nixon determined, would guide U.S. policy against Allende.

"The merit of the non-overt course," as Kissinger had told the president, "is that while it also utilizes the same kinds of pressure and hostility it promises to increase their effectiveness by avoiding the risks inherent in public hostility." Those risks, U.S. policy makers understood, included discrediting Washington among its principle allies in Europe and Latin America as well as serving "Allende's purpose of rallying the Chilean people around him in the face of the 'foreign devil,' " as one briefing paper prepared for Kissinger stated. In a special "briefing paper" for Secretary of State Rogers, the Bureau of Inter-American Affairs argued that were Washington to openly violate its announced policy of "respect for the outcome of democratic elections" it would

> Reduce our credibility throughout the world . . . increase nationalism directed against us . . . be used by the Allende Government to consolidate its position with the Chilean people and to gain influence in the rest of the hemisphere . . . and move the Allende Government to seek even closer relations with the USSR than it might have initially contemplated.[4]

U.S. strategy for a broad range of low-profile pressures against Allende's government was laid out, at least partially, in National Security Decision Memorandum 93, "Policy toward Chile." In guarded bureaucratic language, the TOP SECRET/SENSITIVE/EYES ONLY directive—signed by Kissinger and distributed to CIA, State, Defense, the Joint Chiefs, and AID among other agencies—expressed the goal of U.S. policy: within "the context of a publicly cool and correct posture," the United States would "seek to maximize pressure on the Allende government to prevent its consolidation." (Doc 3) The measures identified in NSDM 93 reflected Washington's intent to isolate, weaken, and destabilize Chile until the country was ungovernable.

Among its other provisions, NSDM 93 called for "vigorous efforts" to rally other Latin American nations to join the United States in isolating and undermining Allende's sociopolitical experiment, with particular focus on Brazil and Argentina. As enticement, Nixon authorized "close relations with friendly military leaders in the hemisphere" who were considered allies against the left in the region—including the Chilean military.

NSDM 93 also identified a range of economic measures designed to continue U.S. efforts to "make the economy scream," as Nixon had previously ordered. The directive stated that "necessary action be taken" to: reduce and terminate current and future financing for U.S. exports and guarantees for corporate investment in Chile; lobby private investors to curtail economic activities; "bring maximum feasible influence" on the multilateral banks to cut their lending to Chile; and terminate bilateral economic aid programs. The NSDM also ordered a study from the Office of Emergency Preparedness on copper "stockpile disposal actions"—Nixon's idea to dump part of the U.S. copper holdings on the international market to quickly undermine the world price of copper, Chile's main natural resource. "I want something in a week on how we can sell from the stockpile," the president ordered Kissinger and others at the NSC meeting of November 6. "Cutting the stockpile would hurt Chile. This is very important. I want State and Defense and everyone to study it. It could be the most important thing we can do."[5]

The Invisible Blockade

U.S. efforts to isolate Chile and quietly curtail bilateral and multilateral economic support constituted an "invisible blockade" against a country whose economy was deeply dependent on financial, industrial, and commercial relations with the United States. U.S. businesses generated two-thirds of the $1.6 billion in foreign investment in Chile. Two major U.S. copper corporations, Anaconda and Kennecott, controlled 80 percent of the Chilean copper industry—an industry that accounted for some four-fifths of all export earnings. During the Frei years, Chile had run up almost $1 billion in debt to U.S. banks. Economic operations relied heavily on U.S. commercial credits to finance machinery and parts for key industries as well as Chilean trucking, buses, taxis, and planes.

For years U.S. officials, and their supporters in academia, blamed Allende's socialist programs and nationalization of U.S. businesses for the severe drop-off in bilateral and international financial support for Chile; there was no "invisible blockade," according to the disingenuous official histories, and Allende was responsible for his own demise. "It was the policies of the Allende government, its insistence on forcing the pace beyond what the traffic would bear much more than our policies," Henry Kissinger testified on Capital Hill one day after the coup, "that contributed to the economic chaos." But recently declassified NSC records on Chile show conclusively that the Nixon administration moved quickly, quietly and politically to shut down multilateral and bilateral aid to Chile—well before Allende had had any opportunity to implement his own economic policies or any question of Chile's creditworthiness had arisen.

At the Inter-American Development Bank (IDB), the White House acted "to effect the early departure of the incumbent chairman," who was deemed not sufficiently malleable, according to a secret memo written by Kissinger's deputy, Alexander Haig.[6] The White House also passed the message to the U.S. representative that he did not have instructions to vote for loans to Chile. A SECRET/NODIS "Status Report on U.S. Stance on IDB Lending to Chile"—prepared for Dr. Kissinger several weeks after Allende's inauguration—laid out the surreptitious credit cutoff:

> The U.S. Executive Director of the Inter-American Development Bank understands that he will remain uninstructed until further notice on pending loans to Chile. As . . . an affirmative vote by the U.S. is required for loan approval, this will effectively bar approval of the loans.

"We have instructed our representative to delay action on Chilean loans pending before the Inter-American Development Bank," Kissinger reported to Nixon in a mid-November, 1970, SECRET/SENSITIVE "Status Report on Chile." "We are seeking the cooperation of the IBRD [World Bank] to similarly delay loans to Chile."[7]

At the World Bank, U.S. officials worked behind the scenes to assure that Chile would be disqualified for a pending $21 million livestock-improvement credit, and for future loans. Since the United States did not have veto power at the World Bank, the State Department's Bureau of Inter-American Affairs prepared a series of questions for a Bank delegation to pose to authorities in Santiago—in an effort to show that Allende's economic platform did not meet criteria for credits. "The [U.S.] Executive Director will routinely and discreetly convey these questions to Bank staff members," another NSC "status report" for Kissinger noted, "as to insure adequate attention to them by the team visiting Chile and by other staff elements within the Bank, but without the hand of the U.S. Government showing in the process."

And at the Export-Import Bank and the Agency for International Development (AID) the NSC issued "classified instructions" to withhold "any new commitments of U.S. bilateral assistance to Chile, including AID loans, AID Investment Guarantees, and Eximbank loans and export guarantees." The Eximbank, which Chile relied on for credits to purchase major industrial equipment, spare parts, and other machinery critical for key industries, particularly copper mining, simply extended the reduction of credit status and loans it had implemented during Track II when Kissinger's office ordered the bank director to drop Chile's credit rating from a "B" to a "D" rating. A long-planned $21 million loan toward the purchase of Boeing jets to upgrade the national airline, LAN–Chile, became the first casualty of the EX-IM Bank's rating reduction. Since the "D" status influenced private U.S. banks, corporations, and private investors, as the Church Committee report pointed out, "it aggravated Chile's problem of attracting and retaining needed capital inflow through private foreign investment."[8]

By any evaluation, the cutoff of aid and credits to Chile was dramatic. In 1970, IDB loans approved before Allende's election totaled $46 million; following the election only two small loans for Chilean universities—totaling $2 million—were approved until after the military coup. The World Bank, which had provided $31 million in loans to the Frei government in 1969–1970, approved zero loans between 1971 and 1973. Bilateral U.S. assistance, administered through AID, reached $110 million between 1968 and 1970; from 1971 to 1973 that figure dropped to approximately $3 million. The U.S. Export-Import Bank, which provided some $280 million in commercial loans and credits between 1967 and 1970 to Chile, granted not a penny of financing or lending in 1971.[9]

Predictably, one sector of U.S. assistance rose during the Allende years—U.S. military sales and assistance. Training and other military aid programs doubled between 1971 and 1972 from $1 million to $2.3 million. Between 1967 and 1970, sales of U.S. military equipment totaled $6 million; between 1970 and 1973, that figure more than tripled to $19 million. "With regard to the *Chilean military* we are maintaining our military mission on a 'business as usual' basis," Kissinger wrote in a memorandum to Nixon, "in order to maintain maximum contacts with the Chilean military."[10]

Kissinger also reported to the president that "on the economic side" U.S. officials had "informed U.S. business and labor leaders of our discouraging view of developments in Chile." Since Chilean labor unions had a key role to play in agitating against Allende, on November 12, 1970, U.S. officials gave an "off-the-record briefing" to AFL-CIO president George Meany, presumably discussing whatever influence and support the powerful union organization could provide in Chile through its international affiliates and the

American Institute for Free Labor Development, which had collaborated closely with the CIA in anti-Allende operations during the 1960s. CIA officials continued to hold "luncheon meetings," and other secret rendezvous with high-level ITT executives even after press revelations on their covert collaboration against Allende sparked the first major Chile scandal in March 1972. And the Nixon administration attempted to assist U.S. copper corporations in their effort to obtain major compensation for nationalized mining facilities in Chile by linking adequate indemnification with the rescheduling of Chile's foreign debt payments.

At the personal direction of President Nixon, Washington sought to block Allende's ability to renegotiate the massive national debt inherited from the Christian Democrats. In mid-January 1972, Nixon became infuriated by a secret memorandum from Treasury Secretary John Connally, complaining that the State Department bureaucracy was not sufficiently supportive of "keeping the pressure on Chile" and was planning to allow Chile to renegotiate its debt with European nations. Treasury should be named to lead the delegation to the upcoming Paris talks, Connally demanded, to advance "our principal purpose . . . to get broad creditor support to isolate Chile." (Doc 4) In a margin notation, Nixon initialed his "RN" approval and scrawled "this is our policy." He immediately sent a TOP SECRET directive to Connally giving him presidential authority to represent the United States at the Paris talks. On the Chilean loan matter, the president ordered:

> Any suggestion, expressed or implied, that I favor U.S. support of an agreement to renegotiate the Chilean loan is in total contradiction to the views I have expressed on a number of occasions in various meetings on this matter. . . . I expect you to see that all agencies of the government strictly comply with my position.

With that presidential mandate, the U.S. took a hard-line position at the 1972 and 1973 Paris Club debt negotiations. Pressure was brought on major European creditor nations to join the U.S. in refusing to conclude a rescheduling of Chile's foreign debt. When the other European nations moved to renegotiate Chile's debt despite U.S. pressure, the Nixon administration broke ranks and refused to reschedule Chilean payments on more than $1 billion owed to U.S. government and private sector creditors.

The Nixon administration also attempted to isolate Allende's government diplomatically around the world. A SECRET/NODIS set of strategy papers, presented to Kissinger in early December 1970, reported on "USG consultation with selected Latin American governments . . . to promote their sharing of our concern over Chile." In his update to the president, Kissinger reported that "particular efforts are being made to consult with key countries such as Brazil and Argentina through both diplomatic and military channels." The White House also considered trying to expel Chile—à la Cuba—from the OAS. A twenty-six-page "Study of Options for U.S. Strategy Concerning Chile's Future Participation in the Organization of American States" seriously weighed the possibility of forcing the Chileans to withdraw or be ejected. But, the working group concluded, such tactics were "likely to boomerang," be "highly devisive . . . alienate many of our Latin American supporters" and undercut the "cool but correct" facade of U.S. policy.

Covert Destabilization

Economic strangulation and diplomatic isolation were two legs of a triad of destabilization measures under NSDM 93; the third—unidentified in the presidential directive because of its sensitivity—was CIA clandestine intervention. In a "covert annex" to a major NSC options paper on Chile developed as part of the NSDM process, the CIA submitted its initial blueprint to sabotage an Allende government in late October. At Kissinger's explicit prodding to broaden "the scope for covert operations," in mid-November the Agency drafted an eight-page "Covert Action Program for Chile"—along with a $7 million operational budget—"keyed to NSDM 93."[11]

For the CIA, a sitting Allende government provided a far broader target of opportunity than the brief transition period in the fall of 1970. A secret special report titled "Allende After the Inauguration" noted that "prospects for a military coup in the post-inaugural period" would significantly improve as Allende faced "tremendous administrative and governmental problems brought on by a continued economic decline and by an increase in political infighting within his coalition." A coup climate "will begin to materialize and the military would have justification for intervening. Thus," as the analysts predicted, "Allende's administration may be short lived."[12]

Toward that end, the CIA designed its covert operations to create and exacerbate economic, political, governmental, and military tensions "to divide and weaken Allende." The "Covert Action Program for Chile," submitted to Kissinger on November 17, was "directed at the Allende government, the Chilean Armed Forces, the non-Marxist opposition, the Chilean public, and other Latin American countries in an effort to maximize pressure on the Allende government." In a SECRET/SENSITIVE/EYES ONLY summary for President Nixon, his national security adviser outlined the "five principal elements" of the CIA's "Covert Action Program—Chile:"

1. Political action to divide and weaken the Allende coalition.
2. Maintaining and enlarging contacts in the Chilean military.
3. Providing support to non-Marxist opposition political groups and parties.
4. Assisting certain periodicals and using other media outlets in Chile which can speak out against the Allende government.
5. Using selected media outlets [in Latin America, Europe, and elsewhere] to play up Allende's subversion of the democratic process and involvement by Cuba and the Soviet Union in Chile. (Doc 5)

The CIA Western Hemisphere chief, William Broe, presented this covert program to the 40 Committee on November 19. Kissinger, sounding more like director of Central Intelligence than the National Security Adviser, attempted to micromanage the operation. Casting himself as a "devil's advocate," Kissinger pointed out that the CIA's political operations against Allende's coalition focused on supporting moderates. Since Allende was "holding himself out as a moderate," Kissinger asked, "why not support extremists?" This would enhance the position of the most extreme groups—presumably the militant Movimiento Izquierdista Revolucionario (MIR)—and, according to the talking points Kissinger carried with him to the meeting "disrupt Allende's game plan (i.e., maintain a moderate respectable image)." His talking points also called for Kissinger to emphasize that the goal of maintaining contacts and influence in the Chilean military was "not just for intelligence but for potential future action . . . obviously a very important element." When Broe stated that the CIA had acted on a practical proposal Kissinger had raised at the last 40 Committee deliberations—"that prompt steps be taken to procure escudos [Chilean currency] for possible future expenditures in Chile"—Kissinger questioned the amount of the fund.[13] "Mr. Kissinger referred to the proposed stockpile of [deleted amount] in escudos and commented that this did not seem to be a very large fund to have on hand if stringent currency controls should be imposed," states deleted section "d." of the heavily censored minutes of the November 19 meeting.[14] (Doc 6) He "raised this question because he did not wish the problem of a lack of operational funds in Chile to be used later as a justification for [CIA] not to be able to follow through on desirable actions."

Between 1970 and 1973 the CIA poured millions of dollars, and escudos, into extensive covert actions to undermine Allende. More than $3.5 million was funneled into opposition political parties and allied organizations—not only to influence municipal and congressional elections and but to "bolster and encourage opposition" to the Popular Unity government, as one CIA talking paper noted, and to incite major ongoing anti-Allende campaigns.

Station operatives conducted a $2 million propaganda program, concentrating on Chile's leading newspaper, *El Mercurio.* More than $1.5 million was passed to business, labor, civic, and paramilitary organizations organizing protests, demonstrations, and violent actions against Allende's administration. A penetration and psychological operations program to rebuild access and influence within the Fuerzas Armadas de Chile provided the CIA, the Defense Intelligence Agency, and Washington with close contacts among military coup plotters. Those contacts became increasingly important as U.S.-supported economic and political upheaval inevitably created the long-sought "coup climate" necessary for overthrowing Chile's elected government.

Political Operations

Since 1962, the Christian Democrat Party had been a leading recipient of CIA political operations in Chile as a beacon of democracy; after Allende's inauguration, the Agency poured covert funding into the party to transform it into a pro-coup force. On Ambassador Korry's recommendation, Kissinger summoned the 40 Committee to a special meeting on November 13 to approve funds—the amount remains classified—to be used to influence the party's political convention scheduled for early December. Washington's concern was not that Allende threatened the existence of the PDC; rather that the left-wing of the party, led by former foreign minister Gabriel Valdes, would win control away from the centrist faction and weaken what Kissinger's office believed was "the best potential source of organized opposition to the consolidation of the Allende Government." "As you know," Kissinger's aide Arnold Nachmanoff reported to him on November 12, Valdes "represents the group in the PDC that is prepared to accommodate to and cooperate with Allende." If it was "feasible to influence the PDC decision in favor of the Frei group," Nachmanoff wrote, "I would recommend approval of Korry's request."

Based on conversations with his sources within Frei's camp, Korry subsequently determined that "no funds and no actions are required" for the upcoming convention. But significant "foreign financing" would still be necessary. The party was twenty-five million escudos in debt from the 1970 campaign; it had "needs for 1971 operational expenses," Korry reported in a heavily redacted SECRET/EYES ONLY/SENSITIVE December 4 cable for the CIA's William Broe and Assistant Secretary Charles Meyer. Under still censored portions of the cable, the ambassador recommended that the CIA covertly help the PDC purchase a newspaper that would serve as a party oracle against Allende's government.[15]

In December 1970, the Santiago Station chief, Henry Hecksher, was recalled to Langley headquarters to develop plans for working with elements of the PDC. The CIA also sent agents to meet with a PDC representative "to explore in depth certain proposals and requests for substantial support." Similar meetings were held with representatives of Chile's right-wing Partido Nacional (PN). In late January 1971, the Agency presented a comprehensive fourteen-page proposal on "Financial Support of Chilean Opposition Parties for the April 1971 Elections and [media purchases]" to the 40 Committee for approval. The Agency requested $1,240,000 to covertly finance the campaigns of PDC and PN candidates, as well as those of the smaller Democratic Radical Party in the upcoming April 4 municipal elections. These elections "have a fundamental importance. . . . There is no doubt that a massive UP electoral victory will have significant repercussions not only in Chile but throughout Latin America," the CIA argued:

> When one considers Allende's superb political performance during the first two months of his administration, and the speed and effectiveness with which the UP has moved to implement the most popular aspects of its program, it becomes obvious that the UP goal of a popular electoral majority may be achieved in the April elections. Such a victory could encourage nascent popular unity movements elsewhere in the hemisphere as well as disheartening opposition and institutional forces inside Chile.

On January 28, Kissinger's 40 Committee authorized these operations. Shortly thereafter, the CIA funneled significant funds to all three parties, as well as sufficient monies for the PDC and PN to purchase their own newspaper and radio station to expand their anti-Allende campaigns. On March 22, May 20, May 26, July 6, and November 5, 1971, the 40 Committee authorized additional covert funds for the PDC and other opposition parties; on October 26, 1972, the CIA sought and received another $1,427,666 to covertly finance opposition campaigns and yet another appropriation of $175,000 was approved before the end of that year for a total of $1,602,666 in anticipation of the March 1973 Congressional election. And on August 20, 1973, another $1,000,000 was approved "to continue covert actions to strengthen opposition political parties and private sector organizations opposed to Allende's UP government."[16]

The Agency used hundreds of thousands of dollars of these appropriations to covertly fund the operations of private-sector organizations dedicated to undermining Allende's ability to govern. CIA officials would later testify that "financial support to the private sector was confined to specific activities . . . such as voter registration drives and a get-out-the vote campaign." In point of fact, as the CIA conceded to Congress in its September

2000 report, "CIA Activities in Chile," the Agency "provided assistance to militant right-wing groups to undermine the president and create a tense environment." A number of the organizations receiving CIA support—they included major associations of large and small businessmen and umbrella organizations of opposition groups—directly supported, and were closely allied with, key sectors fomenting economic and social upheaval, notably the truck owners and strikers that paralyzed Chile in 1973. The CIA has withheld documents on the truckers, including records from the Station that showed that one private-sector organization on the CIA payroll had passed $2,800 directly to the strikers. But, according to Senate investigators who did review some of these records, "it is clear that antigovernment strikers were actively supported by several of the private sector groups which received CIA funds."[17]

The CIA was well aware that "a substantial portion of the business community" was collaborating with groups dedicated to promoting violent disorder designed to "build a political atmosphere which would be propitious for a military coup." In an August 29, 1972, cable the Station reported on "efforts by Patria y Libertad and Business Leaders to Provoke a Coup." (During the Track II period, the CIA funneled $38,500 to Patria y Libertad, a self-proclaimed neo-fascist paramilitary group responsible for numerous acts of terrorism between 1970 and 1973; low-level covert funding continued through 1971.) P&L and a "large segment" of the business community, the Station cabled, "are undertaking actions to increase discontent and incidents of violence, especially in the Santiago area, in order to create an atmosphere in Chile which would be propitious for a military coup. The business leaders involved are trying to foment strikes and labor conflicts, while P&L will attempt to provoke incidents of violence." The collaboration of those organizations to foment disorder would continue until the coup finally took place.

The El Mercurio *Project*

The covert operation that, according to the CIA's own internal records, played "a significant role" in bringing about a coup was clandestine funding for the "*El Mercurio* project." Throughout the 1960s, the CIA poured funds into Chile's largest—and staunchly right-wing—newspaper, *El Mercurio*, putting reporters and editors on the payroll, writing articles and columns for placement and providing additional funds for operating expenses. After the paper's owner, Agustín Edwards came to Washington in September 1970 to lobby Nixon for action against Allende, the CIA used *El Mercurio* as a key outlet for a massive propaganda campaign as part of Track I and Track II.

Throughout Allende's aborted tenure, the paper continued an unyielding campaign, running countless virulent, inflammatory articles and editorials exhorting opposition against—and at times even calling for the overthrow of—the Popular Unity government. "*El Mercurio* continues strong opposition to regime," the CIA informed the White House in early 1971, "publishing attacks against Allende attempts to nationalize banks, violation of press freedom, and land seizures." While CIA intelligence reports documented that the Edwards media empire retained its independence during the Allende years, *El Mercurio* did face growing financial problems from its own mismanagement, credit, and cash-flow problems, as well as advertising cutbacks, newsprint shortages, and labor unrest for which the Edwards and the CIA blamed the Popular Unity government.

In September 1971, a representative of the Edwards media group requested "covert support totaling $1 million" from the CIA. The request prompted a significant internal debate among U.S. policy makers. In a SECRET options paper the CIA presented to Kissinger on September 8, the agency suggested that the newspaper faced an "economic squeeze" and passed on the position of *El Mercurio*'s proprietors that "the paper needs at least $1 million to survive for the next year or two." Washington had two "basic options:

A. *To provide extensive financing for the newspaper* with the understanding that this may not be sufficient to stop the Allende newsprint, or labor stoppages. This would involve an initial commitment of at least $700,000.
B. *Allow* El Mercurio *to go out of business* and arrange a maximum propaganda effort on the issue of freedom of the press. (Doc 7)

Option B was risky, the CIA advised, because "Allende might be able to counter that by demonstrating that it was *El Mercurio*'s financial ineptitude which resulted in its closing." The CIA Station chief and Ambassador Korry favored funding; others within the administration believed that $1 million was "a very expensive price to pay for a little extra time" if the paper was going to close anyway.

Indeed, when the members of the 40 Committee were polled, each had a different position. Kissinger's aide, Arnold Nachmanoff, argued "we should probably take both options and link them." The paper would receive $700,000 but the U.S. would "condition our support on an understanding that *El Mercurio* will launch an intensive public attack on the Allende Government's efforts to force them out of business." Attorney General John Mitchell, according to a summary of the discussion, felt "we should keep a strong voice alive but a weak one would not be worth it;" the Pentagon's representative, Adm. Thomas Moorer, stated "we were gambling with a loser and [the] expenditure [was] extravagant;" CIA director Richard Helms opined that "the prospects were not good either for the short or long term."[18]

Faced with a major disagreement regarding a specific anti-Allende operation, Kissinger simply decided to "take the matter to higher authority." On September 14, in a rare example of presidential micromanagement of a covert operation, Nixon personally authorized the $700,000—and more if necessary—in covert funds to *El Mercurio.* That evening, Kissinger called Helms to tell him that

> (a) the President had just approved the proposal for supporting *El Mercurio* in the amount of $700,000, and, (b) the President wished to see the paper kept going and the amount stipulated could be exceeded if it would usefully serve that purpose.

Per the president's decision, Helms authorized his Western Hemisphere division to "exceed the authorized $700,000 and go up to, and even over, $1,000,000 provided it was warranted to keep the paper going." (Doc 8) The initial $700,000 was sent immediately; in October, Kissinger personally authorized the additional $300,000.

Seven months later, the CIA requested that "an additional $965,000 be made available to *El Mercurio*"—a covert "tranche" that would bring total expenditures on the paper to $1.95 million in less than a year.[19] In a proposal prepared by the new head of the Western Hemisphere division, Theodore Shackley, the CIA argued that the decision to continue funding "must be based . . . on a value judgment of the importance of attempting to ensure the paper's continued existence for political purposes."[20] The paper was no longer on the verge of being shut down by the Allende government, but it was about to run out of credit. The new allotment, Kissinger was informed in a TOP SECRET memorandum, would be

> used to repay a loan, to cover monthly operating deficits through March 1973, and to provide for a contingency fund of [deleted amount] to meet emergency needs such as credit requirements, new taxes, and other bank debts which could come up on short notice.[21]

El Mercurio, according to the CIA argument advanced for this money, was "deemed essential" to help CIA-backed opposition candidates win the March 1973 Congressional election—a major electoral test of Allende's popularity. Now, as Kissinger aide William Jorden noted in a top secret White House "action" memorandum, the consensus was that "*El Mercurio* is important. It is a thorn in Allende's side. It does help give heart to the opposition forces." And if, in the end, the newspaper did "go down the drain," Jorden reminded Kissinger, "we have an excellent 'freedom of the press' issue to use there and in the Hemisphere."[22] On April 11, Kissinger's office approved the funds.

Additional secret monies flowed to *El Mercurio* through the CIA's main corporate collaborator in Chile—the ITT Corporation. A declassified May 15, 1972 memorandum of a conversation between CIA officer Jonathan Hanke and ITT official Hal Hendrix recorded a discussion about $100,000 bank deposits ITT was secretly making to Agustín Edwards. "He had told me money for the Edwards group went through a Swiss account," Hanke reported to his superiors.

Sustained by a massive influx of covert funding, the Edwards media empire became one of the most prominent actors in the downfall of Chilean democracy. Far from being a news outlet, *El Mercurio* positioned itself as a bullhorn of organized agitation against the government. In the summer of 1973, the CIA's Santiago Station identified *El Mercurio*, along with the paramilitary Patria y Libertad and militant elements of the Partido Nacional as the main private-sector organizations that "have set as their objective creation of conflict and confrontation which will lead to some sort of military intervention." The CIA's Western Hemisphere covert action division credited the paper with a singular contribution to creating a coup climate. In heavily redacted project renewal memoranda dated in January 1974, Agency officials stressed that continued funding was necessary to reward and sustain the propaganda outlets provided by *El Mercurio* because of its role in bringing down Allende:

> Prior to the coup the project's media outlets maintained a steady barrage of anti-government criticism, exploiting every possible point of friction between the government and the democratic opposition, and emphasizing the problems and conflicts which were developing between the government and the armed forces.[23]

In an admission that U.S. covert operations had directly contributed to the overthrow of Allende, the CIA asserted that the propaganda effort, in which *El Mercurio* was the dominant actor, "played a significant role in setting the stage for the military coup of 11 September 1973."

The Military Project

The Chilean military remained the "essential" player in Chile's future, according to assessments that CIA operatives in Chile repeatedly sent to Washington in one form or another. The Station placed tremendous emphasis on covert operations targeting the armed forces. For the first year following Allende's election, the CIA invested considerable time and effort rebuilding its asset network—decimated by arrests and purges of those involved in the Schneider killing—within the Chilean armed forces. The Station recruited a number of new agents inside the military with the goal of penetrating leading officer groups so that they could be in communication with real and potential coup leaders, assuming that "the [deleted] program's end objective, a military solution to the Chilean problem, must be sought within very carefully drawn guidelines." "We conceive our mission as one in which we work consciously and deliberately in the direction of a coup," the Station cabled in November 1971, a position that headquarters cautioned was subject to conducive circumstances. Given the dramatic failure of Track II, both Langley and the Station agreed that "there must be predisposition on the part of military to take initiative themselves, that artificially stimulated or ill-planned precipitous action would be counterproductive."[24]

By the fall of 1971, the CIA Station was conducting a "deception operation," designed to convince the Chilean generals that Allende was secretly plotting with Castro to undermine the army high command, in order to "arouse the military" to "move against [Allende] if necessary." By early 1972, the CIA was subsidizing an anti-Allende newsletter targeting the armed forces; and the Santiago Station began compiling arrest lists, installation targets, and other operational data necessary for coup contingency planning.

In August 1971, the Station began sending detailed lists of officers "strongly opposed to the present regime" back to Washington. The first concrete "Intelligence Information Special Report" on coup plotting, distributed to DCI Helms and to Kissinger, was dated on November 9 of that year. In "Preliminary Planning for an Eventual Military Move Against the Chilean Government," the CIA reported, "senior Army, Navy, and Carabinero officers have decided on the overthrow of the Chilean Government some time in the spring of 1972." By that time, the plotters expected, the Chilean economy would have deteriorated sufficiently to provoke a state of emergency during which the military could move. (Doc 9) In March 1972, the FBI sent Kissinger a "priority" intelligence report on various regiments, navy officers, majors and colonels who believed a coup "could become a reality in the near future." The brothers-in-law of General Roberto Viaux, the FBI informed Kissinger, were "actively engaged" in coordinating the anti-Allende activities of right-wing exiles throughout the Southern Cone nations and "desired to convey the foregoing information to the United States Government."[25]

Intelligence gathering on pro-coup Chilean military officers brought the CIA, inevitably, to General Augusto Pinochet. Although Pinochet signed onto the September 11, 1973, putsch only days before it took place, U.S.

intelligence had him on their radar screen of potential plotters as early as the summer of 1971. Drawing on an informant who attended a dinner party with Pinochet on August 5, the Station reported to headquarters that the general was a "mild, friendly, narrow-gauged military man who [is] totally immersed in new field of security, public order and political events and who clearly enjoyed feeling of being important." His wife, according to this intelligence report, was turning against the Allende government, and his son was married to a member of the National Party who hoped to "push Pinochet to effect [a] coup." But, the informant noted, other plotters assessed Pinochet as a person "who would not lead any coup." (Doc 10)

At the time, Pinochet was the commandant of the army's Santiago garrison; but he had also been given the position of Jefe de la Plaza in the capital city, making him responsible for emergency crowd control. "Seems he would have major functions in controlling any major military/civilian convulsion in Santiago," stated one of many index cards the CIA kept on Chilean military officers in September 1971; by March of the following year, the index card had been updated to indicate that Pinochet was "involved with coup preparations" of army chief of staff General Alfredo Canales, with whom the CIA had collaborated during Project FUBELT.

In various intelligence reports, Chilean military officers cast Pinochet as uncommitted and therefore unreliable—"Pinochet would favor but would want to close eyes to events" one asset told the CIA in Santiago. On September 27, 1972, however, a CIA informant inside Pinochet's camp reported that the general was "harboring second thoughts" about the necessity of overthrowing Allende. Pinochet now believed "that Allende must be forced to step down or be eliminated;" these were, in his words, the "only alternatives." When Pinochet traveled to Panama that month to negotiate the transfer of U.S. tanks to the Chilean army, "he felt he was very well treated," as a member of his entourage reported back to a CIA handler. And U.S. army officers at the Southern Command, according to this source, passed an important message along to Pinochet's delegation: the *"U.S. will support coup against Allende 'with whatever means necessary' when the time comes."* [emphasis added] (Doc 11)

As the CIA began issuing more strident reports on the likelihood of a military move, officials in Washington took up the issue of how and with what means to assist. In October 1972, a team of "appropriate CIA elements"—officials and analysts—gathered at Langley headquarters and "brainstormed the current Chilean situation from every conceivable angle," weighing "various courses of action . . . to accelerate current Chilean events leading toward a coup," as Shackley reported to the Senior Review Group (SRG) on October 17. The CIA group concluded, "no course of action which could be taken would help in a decisive manner to achieve the objective of removing Allende from power." At a State Department meeting "on Current Chilean Situation" later that day, CIA, NSC, and State Department officials evaluated what U.S. policy should be if coup plotters requested concrete assistance for overthrowing the Allende government, and/or assurances of post-coup U.S. support as a condition for undertaking the coup. As noted in a heavily censored memorandum for the record of this meeting, the SRG determined that because direct U.S. support for a military coup was not necessary for its success, the proffer of such assistance was not worth the inherent political risks. (Doc 12) According to the minutes of the meeting, "the group finally did agree on the following:

a. If and when the Chilean military decided to undertake a coup, they would not need U.S. Government assistance or support to do so successfully nor are they likely to seek such support. Further, given the Chilean military capabilities for an unaided coup, any U.S. intervention or assistance in the coup per se should be avoided.
b. [page and a half of text deleted that discussed whether the United States should provide assurances to Chilean coup plotters of assistance to a post-coup military government.][26]

The CIA-ITT Scandal

As Nixon administration officials weighed the degree to which Washington might directly aid and abet a coup, their caution was certainly influenced by the breaking of a major political scandal on U.S. intervention in Chile—the first of a series of covert operations scandals that would plague the CIA throughout the 1970s. On March 21, 1972, columnist Jack Anderson reported that "secret documents which escaped shredding by International Telephone and Telegraph show . . . that ITT dealt regularly with the Central Intelligence Agency and, at one point, considered triggering a military coup to head off Allende's election."[27] "These allegations are astonishing," the *Washington Post* exclaimed in a lead editorial the next day. "How could it be—if it is so—that in 1970 an American President could consider the possibility of acting to prevent the democratically elected president of a supposedly friendly country from taking office?" Unprecedented in their detail, the ITT records—twenty-four secret documents totaling seventy-nine pages of strategy papers, memoranda of conversations, and meeting notes—candidly charted the intrigue of covert corporate collaboration between the CIA, White House, and embassy officials to provoke economic chaos and subvert Chilean democracy in 1970 and early 1971.

In Chile, the revelations set off an explosion of nationalist indignation. The leaked documents bolstered a long-standing belief among the Chilean left of U.S. economic imperialism, and confirmed widespread suspicions of Washington's covert efforts to thwart the Chilean socialist experiment. Moreover, with the publication of the secret papers, the facade of the Nixon's administration's "cool but correct" diplomatic posture toward Chile was destroyed. The Allende government, which had been in extensive yearlong talks with ITT officials over the value and acquisition of the company's majority interests in the Compania de Telefonos de Chile, cancelled negotiations and announced that ITT's holdings would be expropriated through a vote of the Chilean Congress.

In the United States, the Anderson article set off the first of many congressional investigations into covert action in Chile—and eventually the whole history of CIA operations abroad. Forty-eight hours after its publication, the powerful chairman of the Senate Foreign Relations Committee, Senator William Fulbright, received a private memo from his top aide calling for a major inquiry. Anderson's articles, wrote Pat Holt

> indicate scandalous behavior by representatives of ITT and of the U.S. government as well. I do not think it suffices to have a denial, which we got yesterday, by the Secretary of State of improper government conduct. If we leave it at that, the Committee would well be accused of being party to a cover-up. Some further action by the Committee is called for.[28]

The next day, Senator Fulbright authorized the establishment of a special Subcommittee on Multinational Corporations, and named a then little-known senator from Idaho, Frank Church, as chairman. The subcommittee had a broad mission to investigate the activities and influence of multinational corporations on U.S. foreign policy; but Church also oversaw a separate, discrete, inquiry into ITT and the anti-Allende operations, which produced the first hearings on covert action in Chile and the first in-depth official report on the issue: *The International Telephone and Telegraph Company and Chile, 1970, 1971.*[29]

With this major breach of secrecy in the midst of ongoing covert intervention in Chile, the Nixon administration went into crisis control mode. The exposure of Track I—in which ITT had played an active role—and Track II were at stake, as well as the continuing covert efforts to subvert the elected Chilean government. The unraveling of the truth, as White House counsel John Dean would tell the CIA director, could be "rather explosive."

For two days, the State Department, CIA, and NSC withheld all public comment. During that time, as the declassified documents reveal, officials debated the wording of a deceptive denial of U.S. operations to block or overthrow Allende. The first Department draft stated the U.S. government had "weighed various contingencies" after Allende's election but "the government did not at that time and has not since worked for or sought the overthrow of the elected government of Chile." A second draft concluded with the statement "any ideas of thwarting Chilean constitutional processes during the election period during 1970 were firmly rejected by this Administration." A final draft, issued by the State Department spokesman Charles Bray at a press conference on March 23 subtly changed that language to read: "any ideas of thwarting Chilean constitutional processes following the election of 1970 were firmly rejected by this Administration."

"What about before the election?" was the first question asked at the March 23 press conference. Reporters bombarded Bray with demands for clarification on whether CIA operations as described in the ITT papers had taken place. They pursued the question of whether Ambassador Edward Korry—as cited in a "personal and confidential" September 28, 1970 ITT memorandum—had been given "the green light to move in the name of President Nixon . . . to do all possible short of a Dominican Republic-type action to keep Allende from taking power." Bray's responses ranged from evasion, to disinformation, to simply false information. "My principle purpose here today," he stated, "is to make it clear that the United States government did not engage in improper activities in Chile." A few minutes later Bray reiterated: "There were no improper activities in which the embassy, the mission in Santiago, our representatives in Chile engaged."[30]

President Nixon, who was personally involved in instigating the anti-Allende operations, kept closely informed of his administration's effort to contain the CIA-ITT scandal. A few hours after the press conference, he received a telephonic briefing from White House Press Secretary Ron Zeigler. Their conversation was recorded by the secret taping system in the Oval Office:

Zeigler: They [the State Department] denied it [U.S.-ITT involvement] but they were cautious on how they dealt with the Korry statement because they were afraid it might backfire.
Nixon: Why? What did Korry say?
Zeigler: Well, Korry said that he had received instructions to do anything short of a Dominican-type—alleged to have said that.
Nixon: Korry did?
Zeigler: Yeah.

Nixon: How the hell did that get out?
Zeigler: Well, Anderson got that from some source. Al Haig is sitting with me now.
Nixon: Well, he *was*—he [Korry] *was* instructed to. But he just failed, the son of a bitch. That was his main problem. He should have kept Allende from getting in.[31]

The initial Orwellian response to the CIA-ITT scandal set the stage for a protracted cover-up, made possible by a display of official mendacity virtually unparalleled in the annals of foreign policy. Outright deception—of the public, of Congress and even other sectors of the U.S. government—permeated the administration's effort to contain and conceal the facts of Track I and Track II. The CIA, State Department, and the NSC sought to obstruct the Senate Subcommittee on Multinational Corporations investigation. Cooperation was severely restricted; evidence was withheld; government and corporate witnesses committed perjury. In its commitment to hide the truth, and contain the inquiry, the administration even assisted ITT in defrauding the Overseas Private Investment Corporation (OPIC)—and by extension the U.S. taxpayer—in order to collect a $94 million political risk insurance claim for its expropriated Chilean properties.

ITT's investments in Chile were insured by OPIC for close to $100 million. But the OPIC insurance contract carried a clause excluding coverage "for expropriations resulting from 'provocation' by the Investor," except for "actions taken in compliance with a specific request' by the U.S.," as Assistant Secretary for Inter-American Affairs Charles Meyer warned in a SECRET/SENSITIVE/EYES ONLY memo. For OPIC's management, the disclosure of the ITT papers strongly suggested that the corporation's own covert actions had provoked expropriation of its telephone company in Chile.

Full disclosure of the Track I documentation would show that ITT had indeed "provoked" its own expropriation by engaging in illicit and illegal intervention in internal Chilean politics. The corporation had approached the CIA in July 1970 and offered a secret "election fund" to support the conservative candidate Jorge Alessandri; it had conducted its own covert political operations inside Chile, among them passing funds to Alessandri through a secret channel provided by the CIA; ITT had urged the embassy to be more aggressive in blocking Allende, and conspired with CIA officials to destabilize the economy and "stop Allende." After the elections, ITT officials had secretly funneled tens of thousands of dollars into a secret Swiss bank account for *El Mercurio* as part of a covert CIA propaganda operation. But the Nixon administration's effort to cover up the scandal precluded sharing any information with OPIC; and officials feared that if denied its claim, ITT would "turn on the USG" and argue that its covert involvement in Chile was undertaken at official request. "Our primary interests," as Meyer wrote, "are to avoid or to minimize disclosures that could severely compromise opposition forces in Chile and embarrass the Administration."

So, when OPIC requested that the State Department turn over "all reliable information available to the intelligence community on the activities of ITT which could constitute 'provocation,' " the State Department denied it had any. "We have carefully reviewed our files," stated the November 29, 1972, letter signed by Assistant Secretary Meyer, who had personally sent top secret cables to Ambassador Korry on meetings with ITT and other U.S. corporations during Track I. "We have no material that adds to the [routine] information we have already made available to you."

The CIA also misled OPIC by baldly deceiving officials about the nature and knowledge of Agency-ITT collaboration in Chile and denying the existence of relevant records. A subsequent file review conducted for the Agency's inspector general examined whether the agency had provided "adequate and correct information to the Overseas Private Investment Corporation for its use in considering the ITT claim." The documents showed that "the Agency's initial replies to OPIC queries about ITT activities were not correct, and those incorrect replies were allowed to stand for some time."[32]

On March 16, 1973, in a SECRET/EXDIS memorandum, "The Church Committee Hearings on Multinational Corporations: Chile-ITT," the State Department briefed Kissinger on the OPIC problem. "A central question is OPIC's decision whether to pay ITT's $92.5 million claim," the memo stated:

> OPIC management proposes to deny the claim on the grounds that ITT activities disclosed by the so-called "Anderson papers" were in breach of its contract and prejudiced OPIC's rights. The company presumably would resist such a finding in arbitration on the theory that it did nothing improper in Chile, that it rejected the suggestions allegedly made to it by USG officials or, alternatively, that anything it did was at the request of the USG. OPIC has scheduled a meeting of its Board of Directors for March 19 to take a final decision on the case.

After a series of corporate appeals—and perhaps subtle White House intervention—in January 1975 OPIC agreed to provide ITT $94 million in insurance compensation for its expropriated properties in Chile.

Senator Church's Subcommittee on Multinational Corporations suffered similar deceptions. "It is clear that the Agency did not provide the Church Subcommittee all relevant information," the CIA's own internal file review would later conclude. ". . . the Agency was not totally forthcoming." The State Department decided to withhold the file of cables between Korry and Washington—the same file it had told OPIC didn't exist. "We do not plan to release the cable file to the Committee," stated the secret March 16, 1973, memo to Kissinger from State Department Executive Secretary Theodore Eliot.

Both the CIA and the State Department did their utmost to limit the Senate subcommittee's ability to investigate the CIA-ITT collaboration. The State Department maneuvered to prevent the committee from calling Viron Vaky—Kissinger's NSC aide in the fall of 1970 who was privy to all the details of Track I and 40 Committee deliberations—to testify, threatening to invoke executive privilege. The CIA played hardball with the subcommittee's request that former Western Hemisphere chief William Broe become the first covert operative to testify before a Congressional panel, attempting to limit his testimony to written answers to questions on "the narrow topic of CIA's relations with ITT during the 1970 election period in Chile."

Ultimately, on March 27, Broe did testify in executive session. His testimony, Senator Church announced the next day, "enables the subcommittee to have before it a full and complete record." In fact, Broe, along with other key witnesses from CIA, State, and ITT deliberately misled the subcommittee—some to the point of bald mendacity. After a "careful review" in September 1974, chief of staff Jerome Levinson reported in a confidential memo to Senator Church that Broe's testimony that there was "no" U.S. policy to intervene in the 1970 Chilean election was only "technically shy of perjury." The CIA's own internal file review concluded "there is reason to believe that perjury [by various witnesses] was committed and that the Agency was aware of that fact."

Indeed, under the supervision of the Western Hemisphere chief, Theodore Shackley, the CIA conspired with ITT officers to deceive the Church Committee. In early May 1972, ITT senior vice president Raymond Brittenham traveled to Washington to discuss "with the Agency what ITT might say in the Senate hearings, what the Agency might say, etc.," according to one memorandum of conversation. Shackley, according to David Corn's biography, *Blond Ghost*, ordered his deputy Jonathan Hanke to meet with ITT operative Hal Hendrix for further discussions on withholding information. On May 11, 1972, Hanke picked Hendrix up on a street corner at 8:00 A.M. and "after driving around awhile we had breakfast at the Marriott Hotel in Rosalyn," Virginia, Hanke reported back. According to Hanke's summary of the meeting, Hendrix advised him on efforts by ITT executives to keep incriminating documents on the covert transfer of funds in Chile from falling into the hands of the Senate. "If they finally turn over the three sensitive documents to the committee," Hanke advised Shackley, "names of persons, banks, and funding mechanisms will be deleted."[33]

ITT officials, among them CEO Harold Geneen, senior vice president Edward Gerrity, and Southern Cone manager Robert Berellez, all deceived the subcommittee. Geneen claimed that ITT "did not take any steps to block the election of Salvador Allende." Gerrity claimed the $1 million that ITT had offered to the CIA to help block Allende was for "low-cost housing . . . a farming program." And Berellez repeatedly misled the Church subcommittee by denying any ITT contact with CIA officials in Chile.[34]

State Department lead witness Charles Meyer also lied to the subcommittee. Meyer, who was a key, if not particularly supportive, participant in 40 Committee deliberations during the Track I operations and who actively participated in decisions to clandestinely fund political parties and media groups in Chile to implement NSDM 93, told Senator Church under oath that

> The policy of the Government, Mr. Chairman, was that there would be no intervention in the political affairs of Chile. We were consistent in that we financed no candidates, no political parties before or after September 8, or September 4, rather . . . the policy of the United States was that Chile's problem was a Chilean problem to be settled by Chile.

Under questioning by Senator Charles Percy he continued

> Let me simply say, Senator Percy, and with pride, and I don't want to hammer on this, that the policy of the U.S. government, despite all of the electricity in the air at any given point, remained noninterventionist. We neither financed candidates nor financed parties nor financed Alessandri gambits. . . . Nor tried to precipitate economic chaos, and promoted neither civil nor military nor any other coup. The policy of Chile's future was Chile's.[35]

But the most egregious effort to deceive the Senate, and the American public, was undertaken by former CIA director Richard Helms—conceivably the most knowledgeable official on covert operations to destabilize Chile.[36] After a long career in the Agency, in November 1972 Nixon removed Helms as DCI.[37] The president then nominated him to be U.S. ambassador to Iran. On February 7, 1973, during desultory confirmation hearings before the Senate Foreign Relations Committee, Missouri Senator Stuart Symington, who was sympathetic to the CIA, asked Helms two questions: "Did you try in the Central Intelligence Agency to overthrow the government of Chile?"

and "Did you have any money passed to the opponents of Allende?" Helms answered "No, sir" to both questions. As the CIA itself would later admit, "some of the statements in Mr. Helms' testimony . . . seem not to be in full accord with the facts." Helms, as Multinational Subcommittee senior staff member Jerome Levinson reported to Senator Fulbright in a memo, stamped SECRET, "had been less than candid and there were several important questions which had not been raised." Levinson recommended recalling Helms because "the best way to get at the question of what really happened is through face-to-face questioning."[38]

Helms was called again, in executive session, before the full Committee on Foreign Relations on March 6, and swore "to tell the truth, the whole truth, and nothing but the truth." Senator Fulbright turned over questioning him to Senator Church, whose staff had prepared dozens of extremely specific questions. As it became evident that Helms would not be able to get away with his usual method of evasive responses, Levinson recalls, Senator Symington managed to abort the hearing—but not before Helms had feigned forgetfulness and issued blanket denials. The following exchange took place:

> *Senator Church:* Mr. Helms, did the CIA attempt at any time to prevent Salvador Allende Gossens from being elected President of Chile in 1970?
> *Helms:* No, sir.
> *Senator Church:* Now, following the election, and up to the time that the Congress of Chile cast its vote installing Allende as the new President, did the CIA attempt in any way to influence that vote?
> *Helms:* Which vote?
> *Senator Church:* The vote of the [Chilean] Congress.
> *Helms:* No, sir.

"Mr. Helms did not have to deceive us," Senator Church would later submit. "No one coerced him to commit perjury. He could have said 'no comment.' "

When the Chile scandal over revelations of Project FUBELT exploded in the press again in the fall of 1974, the Justice Department under President Ford was forced to open a major investigation into "possible charges of perjury and obstruction of justice" by Helms. The Carter administration inherited the controversial case, and to avoid further embarrassing revelations at trial about CIA covert intervention in Chile, made a deal for the most minimal plea possible. On October 31, 1977, Helms made history. He became the first CIA director ever to be indicted for a crime. The Justice Department charged him with a two-count misdemeanor that he "did refuse and fail to answer material questions" before the Senate subcommittee. He pleaded nolo contendere and was fined $2,000.

Helms had been caught, but neither punished nor chastened. "I wear this conviction like a badge of honor," he told the press as his CIA colleagues threw him a victory party and passed the hat to raise the amount of his fine. Lost amidst the Carter administration's rush to let Helms and the CIA off the hook was the importance and impact of his crime: Helms and other members of the Nixon administration had sustained a cover-up of covert operations at a very sensitive time in U.S. efforts to undermine the Allende government, successfully evading public scrutiny until well after the coup took place.[39]

Countdown Toward a Coup

A day after the Chilean military violently took power, State Department officials met to discuss press guidelines for Henry Kissinger on "how much advance notice we had on the coup." Assistant Secretary for Inter-American Affairs Jack Kubisch noted that one Chilean military official—General Pinochet himself, as it turns out—had told the embassy that the plotters had withheld from their U.S. supporters the exact date they would move against Allende. But Kubisch said he "doubted if Dr. Kissinger would use this information, for it would reveal our close contact with coup leaders."[40]

In the months leading up to the coup, the CIA and the Pentagon had extensive contacts with Chilean plotters through various assets and agents and at least three days' advance knowledge of a concrete date for a military takeover. Their communications derived from refocused covert operations targeting the military after the March 1973 Congressional elections in Chile. The dismal electoral outcome convinced many CIA officials that the political and propaganda operations had failed to achieve their goals, and that the Chilean military, as Agency documents suggested, was the final solution to the Popular Unity problem.

Until the spring of 1973, the political operations and propaganda generated by *El Mercurio*, and other CIA-funded media outlets, focused on a major political opposition campaign to decisively win the March 4 Congressional elections, when all of Chilean representatives and half of Chilean senators were up for reelection. The CIA's maximum goal was to gain a two-thirds majority for the opposition in order to be able to impeach Allende; its minimum goal was to prevent the Popular Unity from obtaining a clear majority of the electorate. Of the 3.6 million votes cast, the opposition polled 54.7 percent; the Popular Unity candidates garnered 43.4 percent, picking up two

Senate seats and six seats in the Congress. "Actions undertaken by CIA in the 1973 elections have made a contribution to slowing down the Socialization of Chile," proclaimed a "Briefing on Chile Elections" written at Langley headquarters.

The reality was quite different, as both CIA headquarters and the Santiago Station understood. In the first national test of its popularity since Allende took office, his Popular Unity government had actually increased its electoral strength—despite concerted CIA political action, a massive covert anti-Allende propaganda campaign, and a U.S.-directed socioeconomic destabilization program. "The UP program still appeals to a sizeable portion of the Chilean electorate," the Station lamented in one cable. The CIA now had to reassess its entire clandestine strategy in Chile. "Future options," headquarters cabled on March 6, "now being reviewed in light of disappointing election results, which will enable Allende and UP to push their program with renewed vigor and enthusiasm."

The Station, now under the direction of a new COS, Ray Warren, took a forceful position on what "future options" would be necessary. In a pivotal March 14 postmortem on the congressional elections, the CIA Station articulated plans to reinforce its focus on the military program. "We feel that during foreseeable future, Station should give emphasis to [covert] activity, to widen our contacts, knowledge, and capability in order to bring about one of following situations:"

> A. Consensus by leaders of armed forces (whether they remain in govt or not) of need to move against the regime. Station believes we should attempt induce as much of the military as possible, if not all, to take over and displace the Allende govt. . . .
>
> B. Secure and meaningful Station relationship with a serious military planning group. Should our re-study of the armed forces groups indicate that would-be plotters are in fact serious about their intentions and that they have the necessary capabilities, Station would wish to establish a single, secure channel with such elements for purposes of dialoguing and, once basic data on their collective capabilities is obtained, to seek HQS authorization to enter into an expanded . . . role.[41]

At the same time, the Station also reaffirmed the need to refocus attention on creating a coup climate—the long-standing goal of U.S. policy. "While the Station anticipates giving additional impetus to our [military] program"

> Other political power centers (political parties, business community, media) will play an essential support role in creating the political atmosphere which would allow us to accomplish objectives (A) or (B) above. Given the outcome of the election results, Station feels that creation of a renewed atmosphere of political unrest and controlled crisis must be achieved in order to stimulate serious consideration for intervention on part of the military.

The Station's gung-ho position, which clearly influenced its attitude and actions on the ground in Chile, was supported by a number of hard-liners within the Western Hemisphere directorate who pushed for a far more aggressive, violent approach—an approach that clearly did not count "saving democracy" in Chile as an objective. In a bald and blunt internal challenge to the strategy of pursuing political operations, on April 17 a group of CIA officers sent a memorandum to WH/C Shackley on "Policy objectives for Chile" calling for cutting covert support for the mainstream opposition parties. Such support "lulled" those parties into believing they could survive until the 1976 election. Moreover, if the CIA helped the opposition Christian Democrats win in 1976, the authors argued, it would be a "pyrhic victory" because the PDC would pursue leftist "communitarian policies."

Instead, the CIA should directly seek "to develop the conditions which would be conducive to military actions." This involved "large-scale support" to the terrorist elements in Chile, among them Patria y Libertad and the "militant elements of the National Party" over a fixed time frame—six to nine months—"during which time every effort would be made to promote economic chaos, escalate political tensions and induce a climate of desperation in which the PDC and the people generally come to desire military intervention. Ideally, it would succeed in inducing the military to take over the government completely."[42]

But the position of the Station and the hardliners at Langley was not shared by the State Department, nor by key senior CIA officials who feared the consequences of precipitous military action and believed in the prudence of caution given the ongoing congressional committee investigation into ITT and covert operations in Chile. There was disagreement on a number of fundamental and strategic questions:

- Could the Chilean military be counted on to act against Allende?
- Should the CIA be encouraging violent demonstrations through covert funding of militant groups before knowing for sure that the military would not move to put down the demonstrators?
- Given the current Congressional inquiry on the CIA in Chile, did

> the risks of exposure outweigh potential gains of working directly with the militant private sector and the Chilean military to sponsor a coup?[43]

These questions were discussed repeatedly as the process of formulating the Agency's Fiscal Year 1974 proposals and budget for covert action became grounds for a significant internal debate—kept secret for twenty-seven years—over the strategic nuances of U.S. intervention in Chile.

The State Department, led by a new Assistant Secretary for Inter-American Affairs, Jack Kubisch, opposed the Station's desire to foment a coup, through direct support for the Chilean military or collaboration with extremist private-sector groups. Along with Ambassador Nathaniel Davis, who replaced Edward Korry in mid-1971, Kubisch preferred to concentrate covert action on an opposition victory in the 1976 elections. In addition, CIA officers at headquarters, such as former Chile Task Force director David Atlee Phillips—who would return to Chile operations as the new chief of the Western Hemisphere Division in June—well remembered the Schneider fiasco, and remained skeptical of the Chilean military's commitment to a coup. Cables from headquarters to Santiago reflected their uncertainty over whether the Chilean military would be more likely to move against the government than to move against street demonstrators and strikers that the Station wanted to support. Promoting "large-scale protests such as a strike," cautioned a March 6 cable from Langley, "should be avoided, as should any action which might provoke military reaction against the opposition." In a March 31, 1973 budget proposal, "Covert Action Options for Chile—FY 1974," headquarters argued that

> Although we should keep all options open, including a possible future coup, we should recognize that the ingredients for a successful coup are unlikely to materialize regardless of the amount of money expended, and thus we should avoid encouraging the private sector to initiate action likely to produce either an abortive coup or a bloody civil war. We should make it clear that we will not support a coup attempt unless it becomes clear that such a coup would have the support of most of the Armed Forces as well as the CODE [Chilean opposition democratic] parties, including the PDC.

On May 1, Langley sent a cable to chief of Station Warren stating "we wish to defer any consideration of action program designed to stimulate military intervention until we have more definite evidence that military is prepared to move and that opposition, including PDC, would support a coup attempt." The Chief of Station responded with a request that headquarters postpone its request for FY 1974 funding until the proposal could be redrafted to reflect current Chilean realities. "The most militant parts of the opposition," including CIA-supported organizations such as *El Mercurio* and the National Party, the Station reported, were mobilizing to foment a coup:

> The planning focus and action of all the opposition forces is on the period immediately ahead rather than on 1976. If we are to maximize our influence and help the opposition in the way it needs help, we should work within this trend rather than try to oppose and counter it by trying to get the opposition as a whole to focus on the distant and tenuous goal of 1976. In sum, we believe the orientation and focus of our operational effort should be on military intervention.

On April 10, the Western Hemisphere division did secure the approval from CIA director James Schlesinger for "accelerated efforts against the military target." These covert actions, according to a May 7 memorandum to Schlesinger from WH division chief Theodore Shackley, were "designed to better monitor any coup plotting and to bring our influence to bear on key military commanders so that they might play a decisive role on the side of the coup forces when and if the Chilean military decides on its own to act against Allende." (Doc 13) Headquarters authorized the Santiago Station "to move ahead against military target in terms of developing additional sources," and promised to seek appropriations for an expanded military program when "we have much more solid evidence that military is prepared to act and has reasonable chance of succeeding."[44]

The Chilean high command provided evidence that the military was not yet ready to act on June 29, when several rogue units of the Chilean armed forces deployed to take over the presidential palace known as La Moneda. In his secret "Sit Rep # 1" for President Nixon, Kissinger reported that Chilean army units had "launched an attempted coup against the government of Salvadore Allende." (Doc 14) Later that day, Kissinger sent Nixon another memo, "Attempted Chilean Rebellion Ends," noting that "the coup attempt was an isolated and poorly coordinated effort," and that the leaders of all three branches of the military "remained loyal to the government." (Doc 15) The failed coup attempt reinforced the hand of cautious U.S. policy makers who opposed a more activist CIA role to directly support the Chilean military.

This ongoing internal debate led to a delay in approval for the CIA's FY 1974 covert action budget as the CIA and the State Department worked out compromises on how funding authorizations would be used in

Chile. Finally, on August 20, the 40 Committee authorized, via telephone, $1 million for clandestine funding to opposition political parties and private-sector organizations—but designated a "contingency fund" for the private-sector operations that could only be spent with approval from Ambassador Davis. Within three days, the Station was pressing for approval to use the money to sustain strikes and street demonstrations as well as to orchestrate a takeover from within—pushing the military to take key positions in Allende's cabinet where they could wield the power of state and reduce him to a "figurehead" president. "Events are moving very fast and military attitudes are likely to be decisive at this moment," the Station cabled on August 24. "It is a time when significant events or pressures could effect [Allende's] future."

In Washington the next day, CIA director William Colby sent a memo to Kissinger, submitting the Station's arguments—word-for-word—and requesting authorization to move forward with the funds. The memo, "Proposed Covert Financial Support of Chilean Private Sector," used language designed to assuage State Department sensitivities. "The Santiago Station would not be working directly with the armed forces in an attempt to bring about a coup nor would its support to the overall opposition forces have this as its result," Colby submitted. But he added this caveat: "Realistically, of course, a coup could result from increased opposition pressure on the Allende government." (Doc 16)

By then, the CIA had multiple, and promising, reports of coup plotting. In mid-August, C/WHD Phillips had dispatched a veteran agent to Santiago to assess the situation. He cabled back that "in the past several weeks we have again received increased reporting of plotting and have seen a variety of dates listed for possible coup attempt." One report noted that military plotters had chosen July 7 as the "target date" for another coup attempt, but the date was now being postponed because of the opposition of Commander in Chief Carlos Prats, as well as the difficulty in lining up "the key Army regiments in the Santiago area." According to the CIA source:

> Key problem for the military plotters is now how to overcome this vertical command impediment. One way would be for the plotting Army generals to meet with General Prats, advise him he no longer enjoyed the confidence of the Army high command, and thus remove him. The plotters' choice to replace Prats, at the time of the coup d'etat is to be attempted, is General Manuel Torres, commander of the fifth army division and the third ranking Army general. The plotters do not regard General Augusto Pinochet, who is the second most senior officer in the army, as a suitable replacement for Prats under such conditions.

In late July, the CIA reported that a coordinated coup plan was "near completion." The plotters were still dealing with the Prats problem. "The only way to remove Prats," the Station noted, "would appear to be by abduction or assassination. With the memory of the affair of the former Army Commander, René Schneider, ever present in their minds, it will be difficult for the plotters to bring themselves to carry out such an act."

The CIA also reported that the military was attempting to coordinate its takeover with the Truck Owners Federation, which was about to initiate a massive truckers strike. The violent strike, which paralyzed the country throughout the month of August, became a key factor in creating the coup climate the CIA had long sought in Chile. Other factors included the decision by the leadership of the Christian Democrats to abandon negotiations with the Popular Unity government and to work, instead, toward a military coup. In a CIA "progress report" dated in early July, the Station noted "there has been increasing acceptance of the part of PDC leaders that a military coup of intervention is probably essential to prevent a complete Marxist takeover in Chile. While PDC leaders do not openly concede that their political decisions and tactics are intended to create the circumstances to provoke military intervention, Station [covert] assets report that privately this is generally accepted political fact."[45] The Christian Democrat position, in turn, prompted the traditionally moderate Chilean Communist Party to conclude that political accommodation with the mainstream opposition was no longer feasible and to adopt a more militant position, creating deep divisions with Allende's own coalition. The military's hard-line refusal to accept Allende's offer of certain cabinet posts also accelerated political tensions. "The feeling that something must be done seems to be spreading," CIA headquarters observed in an analytical report on "Consequences of a Military Coup in Chile."

The resignation of Commander in Chief Carlos Prats in late August, after an intense public smear campaign led by *El Mercurio* and the Chilean right wing, eliminated the final obstacle for a successful coup. Like his predecessor, General Schneider, Prats had upheld the constitutional role of the Chilean military, blocking younger officers who wanted to intervene in Chile's political process. In an August 25 intelligence report stamped "TOP SECRET UMBRA," the Defense Intelligence Agency (DIA) noted that the departure of Prats "has removed the main factor mitigating against a coup." On August 31, U.S. military sources within the Chilean army were reporting that "the army is united behind a coup, and key Santiago regimental commanders have pledged their support. Efforts are said to be underway to complete coordination among the three services, but no date has been set for a coup attempt."

By then, the Chilean military had established a "special coordination team" made up of three representatives of each of the services and carefully selected right-wing civilians. In a series of secret meetings on September 1 and 2, this team presented a completed plan for overthrowing the Allende government to heads of the Chilean army, air force, and navy. The incipient Junta approved the plan and set September 10 as the target date for the coup. According to a review of coup plotting obtained by the CIA, the general who replaced Carlos Prats as commander in chief, General Augusto Pinochet, was "chosen to be head of the group" and would determine the hour for the coup to begin.[46]

On September 8, both the CIA and the DIA alerted Washington that a coup was imminent, and confirmed the date of September 10. A DIA intelligence summary stamped TOP SECRET UMBRA reported that "the three services have reportedly agreed to move against the government on 10 September, and civilian terrorist and right-wing groups will allegedly support the effort." (Doc 17) The CIA reported that the Chilean navy would "initiate a move to overthrow the government" at 8:30 A.M. on September 10th and that Pinochet "has said that the army will not oppose the navy's action."

On September 9, the Station updated its coup countdown. A member of the CIA's covert agent team in Santiago, Jack Devine, received a call from an asset who was fleeing the country. "It is going to happen on the eleventh," as Devine recalled the conversation. His report, distributed to Langley headquarters on September 10, stated:

> A coup attempt will be initiated on 11 September. All three branches of the Armed Forces and the Carabineros are involved in this action. A declaration will be read on Radio Agricultura at 7 A.M. on 11 September. The Carabineros have the responsibility of seizing President Salvador Allende.

According to Donald Winters, a CIA high-ranking agent in Chile at the time of the coup, "the understanding was they [the Chilean military] would do it when they were ready and at the final moment tell us it was going to happen."[47] On the eve of the putsch, however, at least one sector of the coup plotters became nervous about what would happen if fighting became protracted and the takeover did not go as planned. On the night of September 10, as the military quietly assumed positions to violently take power the next day, a "key officer of [the] Chilean military group planning to overthrow President Allende," as CIA headquarters described him, contacted a U.S. official—it remains unclear whether it was a CIA, defense or embassy officer—and "asked if the U.S. government would come to the aid of the Chilean military if the situation became difficult." The officer was assured that his question "would promptly be made known to Washington," according to a highly classified memo sent by David Atlee Phillips to Henry Kissinger on September 11, as the coup was in progress. (Doc 18)

At the time of the coup, both the State Department and the CIA were making contingency plans for U.S. assistance if the military move appeared to be failing. On September 7, Assistant Secretary Kubisch reported to State and CIA officers that high-level department officials had discussed Chile and determined the following: "If there should be a coup attempt, which appears likely to be successful and satisfactory from our standpoint, we will stand off;" but "if there should be a coup, which might be viewed as favorable but which appears in danger of failure we may want a capability for influencing the situation." Kubisch tasked the CIA to "give this problem attention."[48]

That issue proved to be irrelevant. "Chile's coup d'état was close to perfect," Lt. Col. Patrick Ryan, head of the U.S. military group in Valparaiso, reported in a "Sitrep" to Washington. By 8:00 A.M. on September 11, the Chilean navy had secured the port town of Valparaiso, and announced that the Popular Unity government was being overthrown. In Santiago, Carabinero forces were supposed to detain President Allende at his residence, but he managed to make his way to La Moneda, Chile's White House, and began broadcasting radio messages for "workers and students" to come "and defend your government against the armed forces." As army tanks surrounded La Moneda firing on its walls, Hunter jets launched a pinpoint rocket attack on Allende's offices at around noon, killing many of his guards. Another aerial strafing attack accompanied the military's ground effort to take the inner courtyard of the Moneda at 1:30 P.M.

During the fighting, the military repeatedly demanded that President Allende surrender, and made a perfunctory offer to fly him and his family out of the country. In a now famous audiotape of General Pinochet issuing instructions to his troops via radio communications on September 11, he is heard to laugh and swear "that plane will never land." Forecasting the savagery of his regime, Pinochet added: "Kill the bitch and you eliminate the litter." Salvador Allende was found dead from gunshot wounds in his inner office around 2:00 P.M.[49] At 2:30 P.M., the armed forces radio network broadcast an announcement that La Moneda had "surrendered" and that the entire country was under military control.

International reaction to the coup was immediate, widespread, and overwhelmingly condemnatory. Numerous governments denounced the military takeover; massive protests were held throughout Latin America. Inevitably, finger-pointing was directed at the U.S. government. In his confirmation hearings as secretary of state—only one day after the coup—Kissinger was peppered with questions about CIA involvement. The Agency "was in a very minor way involved in 1970 and since then we have absolutely stayed away from any coups," Kissinger responded. "Our efforts in Chile were to strengthen the democratic political parties and give them a basis for winning the election in 1976."

"Preservation of Chilean democracy" summed up the official line, spun after the fact, to obfuscate U.S. intervention against the Allende government. On September 13, CIA Director Colby sent Kissinger a secret two-page overview of "CIA Covert Action Program in Chile since 1970," meant to provide guidance on the questions concerning the Agency's role. (Doc 19) "U.S. policy has been to maintain maximum covert pressure to prevent the Allende regime's consolidation," the memo stated candidly. After a selective review of the political, media and private-sector covert operations, Colby concluded: "while the agency was instrumental in enabling opposition political parties and media to survive and to maintain their dynamic resistance to the Allende regime, the CIA played no direct role in the events which led to the establishment of a new military government."

By the most narrow definition of "direct role"—providing planning, equipment, strategic support, and guarantees—the CIA does not appear to have been involved in the violent actions of the Chilean military on September 11, 1973. The Nixon White House sought, supported, and embraced the coup, but the political risks of direct engagement simply outweighed any actual necessity for its success. The Chilean military, however, had no doubts about the U.S. position. "We were not in on planning," recalled CIA operative Donald Winters. "But our contacts with the military let them know where we stood—that was we were not terribly happy with [the Allende] government." The CIA and other sectors of the U.S. government, moreover, were directly involved in operations designed to create a "coup climate" in which the overthrow of Chilean democracy could and would take place. Colby's memo appeared to omit the CIA's military deception project, the covert black propaganda efforts to sow dissent within the Popular Unity coalition, the support to extremist elements such as Patria y Libertad, and the inflammatory achievements of the *El Mercurio* project, which agency records credited with playing "a significant role in setting the stage" for the coup—let alone the destabilizing impact of the invisible economic blockade. The argument that these operations were intended to preserve Chile's democratic institutions was a public relations ploy, contradicted by the weight of the historical record. Indeed, the massive support that the CIA provided to the ostensible leading representatives of Chilean democracy—the Christian Democrats, the National Party, and *El Mercurio*—facilitated their transformation into leading actors in, and key supporters of, the Chilean military's violent termination of Chile's democratic processes.

"You may also recall discussion of a Track Two in late 1970—which has *not* been included in this summary," Colby wrote to Kissinger on the routing slip of his September 13 memorandum. Fundamental to the Chilean generals' understanding of Washington's support was the knowledge that the CIA had sought to directly instigate a coup three years earlier. "Track II never really ended," as Thomas Karamessines, the top CIA official in charge of covert operations against Allende, testified in 1975. "What we were told to do was to continue our efforts. Stay alert, and to do what we could to contribute to the eventual achievements and of the objectives and purposes of Track II. I am sure that the seeds that were laid in that effort in 1970 had their impact in 1973. I do not have any question about that in my mind."[50]

"Our policy on Allende worked very well," Assistant Secretary Kubisch commented to Kissinger on the day following the coup. Indeed, in September of 1973 the Nixon administration had achieved Kissinger's goal, enunciated in the fall of 1970, to create conditions which could lead to Allende's collapse or overthrow. At the first meeting of the Washington Special Actions Group, held on the morning of September 12 to discuss how to assist the new military regime in Chile, Kissinger joked that "the President is worried that we might want to send someone to Allende's funeral. I said that I didn't believe we were considering that." "No," an aide responded, "not unless you want to go."

On September 16, President Nixon called Kissinger for an update; their conversation was recorded by Kissinger's secret taping system. "The Chilean thing is getting consolidated," Kissinger reported, "and of course the newspapers are bleating because a pro-Communist government has been overthrown." Nixon and Kissinger commiserated over the fact that they wouldn't get laudatory credit in the media for Allende's demise. "In the Eisenhower period," Kissinger stated, referring back to the CIA's covert overthrow of Jacobo Arbenz in Guatemala, "we would be heroes."

The two then candidly discussed the U.S. role. "Well we didn't—as you know—our hand doesn't show on this one though," the president noted. "We didn't do it," Kissinger responded, referring to the issue of a direct involvement in the coup itself. "I mean we helped them. [Omitted word] created the conditions as great as possible." "That is right," the president agreed.[51]

DOCUMENT 1. The White House, **SECRET** Memorandum of Conversation, "NSC Meeting—Chile (NSSM 97)," November 6, 1970.

MEMORANDUM

THE WHITE HOUSE

WASHINGTON

~~SECRET/SENSITIVE/XGDS~~

MEMORANDUM OF CONVERSATION - NSC MEETING - CHILE (NSSM 97)

PARTICIPANTS:
The President
The Vice President
Secretary of State William P. Rogers
Secretary of Defense Melvin Laird
Director of Emergency Preparedness George A. Lincoln
Attorney General John N. Mitchell
General William Westmoreland, Acting Chairman, Joint Chiefs of Staff
Director of Central Intelligence Richard Helms
Under Secretary of State John N. Irwin II
Deputy Assistant Secretary of State Robert A. Hurwitch
Assistant to the President for National Security Affairs Henry A. Kissinger
General Alexander M. Haig, NSC Staff
Mr. Arnold Nachmanoff, NSC Staff
Col. Richard T. Kennedy, NSC Staff

PLACE: The Cabinet Room

DATE & TIME: Friday - November 6, 1970
9:40 a.m.

The President opened the meeting by asking Director Helms to brief.

Director Helms read from the briefing paper which is attached at Tab A. The President interrupted to review what Director Helms said about the makeup of the Allende Cabinet. [See page 9] He wished to emphasize the degree to which the Cabinet ministries were controlled by Marxists.

The President then asked Dr. Kissinger to brief.

Dr. Kissinger: All of the agencies are agreed that Allende will try to create a socialist State. As for our response to this, the SRG came up with four options. But really basically it amounts to two choices: (1) seek a modus vivendi with the Allende Government, or (2) adopt a posture of overt and frank hostility. In between is a third possibility: adopt what is in fact a hostile posture but not from an overt stance, that is, to move in hostility from a low-key posture.

~~SECRET/SENSITIVE/XGDS~~

DECLASSIFIED
Authority State, CIA, DOS, NSC
By ___ NARA, Date ___

11/6/70
76A

A modus vivendi has the risk that he will consolidate his position and then move ahead against us. A posture of overt hostility gives strength to his appeal of nationalism and may not work anyway. As for in between -- the problem is that he will know we are working against him and he can expose us anyway even though we maintain a correct and cool posture.

All of these options have advantages and disadvantages. There is no clear choice.

Secretary Rogers: Dr. Kissinger has spelled it out well. There is general agreement that he will move quickly to bring his program into effect and consolidate his position. We are also in agreement that it is not necessary to make a final decision now.

Private business and the Latin American countries believe that we have done the right things up to now. If we have to be hostile, we want to do it right and bring him down. A stance of public hostility would give us trouble in Latin America. We can put an economic squeeze on him. He has requested a debt rescheduling soon -- we can be tough. We can bring his downfall perhaps without being counterproductive.

The Christian Democratic Foreign Minister thinks we are doing the right thing. He sees two possibilities: that his economic troubles will generate significant public dissatisfaction, or second, that his difficulties will become so great that there will be military moves against him. I think the U.S. militar should keep in contact with their Chilean colleagues and try to strengthen our position in Chile.

We have severe limitations on what we can do. A strong public posture will only strengthen his hand. We must make each decision in the future carefully in a way that harms him most but without too much of a public posture which would only be counterproductive.

Secretary Laird: I agree with Bill Rogers. We have to do everything we can to hurt him and bring him down, but we must retain an outward posture that is correct. We must take hard actions but not publicize them. We must increase our military contacts. We must put pressure on him economically. He is in the weakest position now that he will be in; we want to prevent his consolidation.

Moorer [to Rogers]: What is the reaction of the Congress?

Secretary Rogers: There is very little, but if he consolidates his position the criticism will build up. Attitudes are therefore favorable to our policy.

Moorer: What would be the reaction if he resorts to expropriation later, after we have given more aid?

Secretary Rogers: We shouldn't give any more credit guarantees. We should do everything we can to show hostility without publicizing it.

Vice President: China and USSR are watching our approach to Argentina. If we show undue interest before anything happens; for example if we sell F-4s to Argentina, it could trigger massive support to Chile from the USSR and China. We should act principally inside Chile.

Director Lincoln: Copper accounts for 80% of Chile's exports. They are expanding production rapidly. Other producers (Zambia, Australia, etc.) are also going up in production. So there could be a price decline in the future, with an adverse economic impact in Chile. They blame us. We have a stockpile. If we are adopting a hostile posture, maybe we have to increase the stockpile or alternatively to sell if the market eases in the future.

The President: I want something in a week on how we can sell from the stockpile. Now we can do it. Cutting the stockpile would hurt Chile and also save on the budg

Director Lincoln: We'll do this. We've been studying this on a priority basis.

The President: This is very important -- will it hurt anyone else? I want State and Defense and everyone to study it. It could be the most important thing we can do.

Director Lincoln: The law says we can't sell from the stockpile unless we do it to stabilize the price. The copper price is down in the world market. We've already sold 50 million tons before the prices dropped.

Secretary Rogers: Can we help others build up their production, to help our friends?

The President: We should do this if we can.

Director Lincoln: If we sell anything too fast it will destabilize the price. Most things don't sell fast.

Mr. Irwin: The problem is how to bring about his downfall. I would question our capability to do it. Internal forces in Chile are the only way. The question is how best to influence the internal forces to create the conditions for change. He will need to consolidate his position and probably he will move slowly for the sake of respectability as he moves. It will be soon that dissatisfaction begins. As he tries to consolidate he will inevitably have strains. If we move too quickly in opposition to him we will help him consolidate quickly. As we move to consider specific issues either overt or covert, we should be hostile only if we can be sure it will have a significant effect on the internal forces there in a way that will hurt Allende and prevent his consolidation. This may mean we may have to do things we would not want to do -- it depends on the effects on the internal situation in Chile. Graham Martin would like to see us move along as we have.

The President: It is all a matter of degree. If Chile moves as we expect and is able to get away with it -- our public posture is important here -- it gives courage to others who are sitting on the fence in Latin America. Let's not think about what the really democratic countries in Latin America say -- the game is in Brazil and Argentina. We could have moves under the surface which bring over time the same thing.

I will never agree with the policy of downgrading the military in Latin America. They are power centers subject to our influence. The others (the intellectuals) are not subject to our influence. We want to give them some help. Brazil and Argentina particularly. Build them up with consultation. I want Defense to move on this. We'll go for more in the budget if necessary.

Our main concern in Chile is the prospect that he can consolidate himself and the picture projected to the world will be his success. A publicly correct approach is right. Privately we must get the message to Allende and others that we oppose him. I want to see more of them; Brazil has more people than France or England combined. If we let the potential leaders in South America think they can move like Chile and have it both ways, we will be in trouble. I want to work on this and on the military relations -- put in more money. On the economic side we want give him cold Turkey. Make sure that EXIM and the international organizations toughen up. If Allende can make it with Russian and Chinese help, so be it -- but we do not want it to be with our help, either real or apparent.

We'll be very cool and very correct, but doing those things which will be a real message to Allende and others.

This is not the same as Europe -- with Tito and Ceaucescu -- where we have to get along and no change is possible. Latin America is not gone, and we want to keep it. Our Cuban policy must not be changed. It costs the Russians a lot; we want it to continue to cost. Chile is gone too -- he isn't going to mellow. Don't have any illusions -- he won't change. If there is any way we can hurt him whether by government or private business -- I want them to know our policy is negative. There should be no guarantees. Cut back existing guarantees if it's possible.

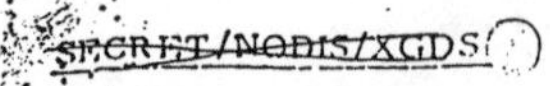

No impression should be permitted in Latin America that they can get away with this, that it's safe to go this way. All over the world it's too much the fashion to kick us around. We are not sensitive but our reactions must be coldly proper. We cannot fail to show our displeasure. We can't put up with "Give Americans hell but pray they don't go away." There must be times when we should and must react, not because we want to hurt them but to show we can't be kicked around.

The new Latin politicians are a new breed. They use anti-Americanism to get power and then they try to cozy up. Maybe it would be different if they thought we wouldn't be there.

We must be proper on the surface with Allende, but otherwise we will be tough. He is not going to change; only self-interest will affect him.

DOCUMENT 2. The White House **SECRET** Memorandum for the President, "NSC Meeting, November 6—Chile," November 5, 1970.

MEMORANDUM

THE WHITE HOUSE

WASHINGTON

SECRET/SENSITIVE

November 5, 1970

MEMORANDUM FOR THE PRESIDENT

FROM: Henry A. Kissinger

SUBJECT: NSC Meeting, November 6 -- Chile

This meeting will consider the question of what strategy we should adopt to deal with an Allende Government in Chile.

A. DIMENSIONS OF THE PROBLEM

The election of Allende as President of Chile poses for us one of the most serious challenges ever faced in this hemisphere. Your decision as to what to do about it may be the most historic and difficult foreign affairs decision you will have to make this year, for what happens in Chile over the next six to twelve months will have ramifications that will go far beyond just US-Chilean relations. They will have an effect on what happens in the rest of Latin America and the developing world; on what our future position will be in the hemisphere; and on the larger world picture, including our relations with the USSR. They will even affect our own conception of what our role in the world is.

Allende is a tough, dedicated Marxist. He comes to power with a profound anti-US bias. The Communist and Socialist parties form the core of the political coalition that is his power base. Everyone agrees that Allende will purposefully seek:

-- to establish a socialist, Marxist state in Chile;

-- to eliminate US influence from Chile and the hemisphere;

-- to establish close relations and linkages with the USSR, Cuba and other Socialist countries.

The consolidation of Allende in power in Chile, therefore, would pose some very serious threats to our interests and position in the hemisphere, and would affect developments and our relations to them elsewhere in the world:

-- US investments (totaling some one billion dollars) may be lost, at least in part; Chile may default on debts (about $1.5 billion) owed the US Government and private US banks.

SECRET/SENSITIVE

-- Chile would probably become a leader of opposition to us in the inter-American system, a source of disruption in the hemisphere, and a focal point of support for subversion in the rest of Latin America.

-- It would become part of the Soviet/Socialist world, not only philosophically but in terms of power dynamics; and it might constitute a support base and entry point for expansion of Soviet and Cuban presence and activity in the region.

-- The example of a successful elected Marxist government in Chile would surely have an impact on--and even precedent value for--other parts of the world, especially in Italy; the imitative spread of similar phenomena elsewhere would in turn significantly affect the world balance and our own position in it.

While events in Chile pose these potentially very adverse consequences for us, they are taking a form which makes them extremely difficult for us to deal with or offset, and which in fact poses some very painful dilemmas for us:

a. Allende was elected legally, the first Marxist government ever to come to power by free elections. He has legitimacy in the eyes of Chileans and most of the world; there is nothing we can do to deny him that legitimacy or claim he does not have it.

b. We are strongly on record in support of self-determination and respect for free election; you are firmly on record for non-intervention in the internal affairs of this hemisphere and of accepting nations "as they are." It would therefore be very costly for us to act in ways that appear to violate those principles, and Latin Americans and others in the world will view our policy as a test of the credibility of our rhetoric.

On the other hand, our failure to react to this situation risks being perceived in Latin America and in Europe as indifference or impotence in the face of clearly adverse developments in a region long considered our sphere of influence.

c. Allende's government is likely to move along lines that will make it very difficult to marshal international or hemisphere censure of him--he is most likely to appear as an "independent" socialist country rather than a Soviet satellite or "Communist government."

Yet a Titoist government in Latin America would be far more dangerous to us than it is in Europe, precisely because it can move against our policies and interests more easily and ambiguously and because its "model" effect can be insidious.

A. Dimensions of the Problem (continued)

Allende starts with some significant weaknesses in his position:

-- There are tensions in his supporting coalition.

-- There is strong if diffuse resistance in Chilean society to moving to a Marxist or totalitarian state.

-- There is suspicion of Allende in the military.

-- There are serious economic problems and constraints.

To meet this situation, Allende's immediate "game plan" is clearly to avoid pressure and coalescing of opposition prematurely, and to keep his opponents within Chile fragmented so that he can neutralize them one by one as he is able. To this end, he will seek to:

-- be internationally respectable;

-- move cautiously and pragmatically;

-- avoid immediate confrontations with us; and

-- move slowly in formalizing relations with Cuba and other Socialist countries.

There is disagreement among the agencies as to precisely how successful Allende will be in overcoming his problems and weaknesses, or how inevitable it really is that he will follow the course described or that the threats noted will materialize.

But the weight of the assessments is that Allende and the forces that have come to power with him do have the skill, the means and the capacity to maintain and consolidate themselves in power, provided they can play things their way. Logic would certainly argue that he will have the motivation to pursue purposefully aims he has after all held for some 25 years. Since he has an admittedly profound anti-US and anti-capitalist bias, his policies are bound to constitute serious problems for us if he has any degree of ability to implement them.

B. THE BASIC ISSUE

What all of this boils down to is a fundamental dilemma and issue:

a. Do we wait and try to protect our interests in the context of dealing with Allende because:

-- we believe we cannot do anything about him anyway;

-- he may not develop into the threat we fear or may mellow in time;

-- we do not want to risk turning nationalism against us and damaging our image, credibility and position in the world;

AND thereby risk letting Allende consolidate himself and his ties with Cuba and the USSR, so that a year or two from now when he has established his base he can move more strongly against us, and then we really will be unable to do anything about it or reverse the process. Allende would in effect use us to gain legitimacy and then turn on us on some economic issue and thereby caste us in the role of "Yankee imperialist" on an issue of his choice.

OR

b. Do we decide to do something to prevent him from consolidating himself now when we know he is weaker than he will ever be and when he obviously fears our pressure and hostility, because:

-- we can be reasonably sure he is dedicated to opposing us;

-- he will be able to consolidate himself and then be able to counter us in increasingly intense ways; and

-- to the extent he consolidates himself and links to the USSR and Cuba the trend of events and dynamics will be irreversible.

AND thereby risk:

-- giving him the nationalistic issue as a weapon to entrench himself;

-- damaging our credibility in the eyes of the rest of the world as interventionist;

-- turning nationalism and latent fear of US domination in the rest of Latin America into violent and intense opposition to us; and

-- perhaps failing to prevent his consolidation anyway.

C. OUR CHOICES

There are deep and fundamental differences among the agencies on this basic issue. They manifest themselves in essentially three possible approaches:

1. The Modus Vivendi Strategy:

This school of thought, which is essentially State's position, argues that we really do not have the capability of preventing Allende from consolidating himself or forcing his failure; that the main course of events in Chile will be determined primarily by the Allende government and its reactions to the internal situation; and that the best thing we can do in these circumstances is maintain our relationship and our presence in Chile so that over the long haul we may be able to foster and influencing domestic trends favorable to our interests. In this view actions to exert pressure on Allende or to isolate Chile will not only be ineffective, but will only accelerate adverse developments in Chile and limit our capacity to have any influence on the long-range trend.

In this view the risks that Allende will consolidate himself and the long-range consequences therefrom are less dangerous to us than the immediate probable reaction to attempts to oppose Allende. It's perception of Allende's long-term development is essentially optimistic and benign. Implicit is the argument that it is not certain he can overcome his internal weaknesses, that he may pragmatically limit this opposition to us, and that if he turns into another Tito that would not be bad since we deal with other governments of this kind anyway.

2. The Hostile Approach:

DOD, CIA and some State people, on the other hand, argue that it is patent that Allende is our enemy, that he will move counter to us just as soon and as strongly as he feels he can; and that when his hostility is manifest to us it will be because he has consolidated his power and then it really will be too late to do very much--the process is irreversible. In this view, therefore, we should try to prevent him from consolidating now when he is at his weakest.

Implicit in this school of thought is the assumption that we can affect events, and that the risks of stirring up criticism to our position elsewhere are less dangerous to us than the long-term consolidation of a Marxist government in Chile.

2. The Hostile Approach (continued)

Within this approach there are in turn two schools of thought:

a. Overt Hostility.

This view argues that we should not delay putting pressure on Allende and therefore should not wait to react to his moves with counter-punches. It considers the dangers of making our hostility public or of initiating the fight less important than making unambiguously clear what our position is and where we stand. It assumes that Allende does not really need our hostility to help consolidate himself, because if he did he would confront us now. Instead he appears to fear our hostility.

This approach therefore would call for (1) initiating punitive measures, such as terminating aid or economic embargo; (2) making every effort to rally international support of this position; and (3) declaring and publicizing our concern and hostility.

b. Non-overt Pressure, Cold, Correct Approach.

This approach concurs in the view that pressure should be placed on Allende now and that we should oppose him. But it argues that how we package that pressure and opposition is crucial and may make the difference between effectiveness and ineffectiveness. It argues that an image of the US initiating punitive measures will permit Allende to marshal domestic support and international sympathy on the one hand, and make it difficult for us to obtain international cooperation on the other. It further argues that it is the effect of pressure not the posture of hostility that hurts Allende; the latter gives him tactical opportunities to blunt the impact of our opposition.

Implicit in this approach is the judgment that how unambiguous our public position is and making a public record are all less important in the long run than maximizing our pressure and minimizing risks to our position in the rest of the world.

This approach therefore calls for essentially the same range of pressures as the previous one, but would use them quietly and covertly; on the surface our posture would be correct, but cold. Any public manifestation or statement of hostility would be geared to his actions to avoid giving him the advantage of arguing he is the aggrieved party.

D. ASSESSMENTS

As noted, the basic issue is whether we are to wait and try to adjust or act now to oppose.

The great weakness in the modus vivendi approach is that:

-- it gives Allende the strategic initiative;

-- it plays into his game plan and almost insures that he will consolidate himself;

-- if he does consolidate himself, he will have even more freedom to act against us after a period of our acceptance of him than if we had opposed him all along;

-- there are no apparent reasons or available intelligence to justify a benign or optimistic view of an Allende regime over the long term. In fact, as noted, an "independent" rational socialist state linked to Cuba and the USSR can be even more dangerous for our long-term interests than a very radical regime.

There is nothing in this strategy that promises to deter or prevent adverse anti-U.S. actions when and if Chile wants to pursue them -- and there are far more compelling reasons to believe that he will when he feels he is established than that he will not.

The main question with the hostile approach is whether we can effectively prevent Allende from consolidating his power. There is at least some prospect that we can. But the argument can be made that even if we did not succeed -- provided we did not damage ourselves too severely in the process -- we could hardly be worse off than letting him entrench himself; that there is in fact some virtue in posturing ourselves in a position of opposition as a means of at least containing him and improving our chance of inducing others to help us contain him later if we have to.

In my judgment the dangers of doing nothing are greater than the risks we run in trying to do something, especially since we have flexibility in tailoring our efforts to minimize those risks.

I recommend, therefore that you make a decision that we will oppose Allende as strongly as we can and do all we can to keep him from consolidating power, taking care to package those efforts in a style that gives us the appearance of reacting to his moves.

E. THE NSC MEETING

Contrary to your usual practice of not making a decision at NSC meetings, it is essential that you make it crystal clear where you stand on this issue at today's meeting. If all concerned do not understand that you want Allende opposed as strongly as we can, the result will be a steady drift toward the modus vivendi approach. This is primarily a question of priorities and nuance. The emphasis resulting from today's meeting must be on opposing Allende and preventing his consolidating power and not on minimizing risks.

I recommend that after your opening remarks you call on Dick Helms to give you a briefing on the situation and what we might expect. I would then outline the main issues and options along the above lines, after which you could call on Secretaries Rogers and Laird for their views and observations. Your Talking Points, which are appended, are written along these lines.

Also included in your book are:

-- A State/DOD options paper.

-- An analytical summary of that options paper.

DOCUMENT 3. National Security Council, **TOP SECRET** National Security Decision Memorandum 93, "Policy Towards Chile," November 9, 1970.

NATIONAL SECURITY COUNCIL
WASHINGTON, D.C. 20506

TOP SECRET/SENSITIVE/EYES ONLY UNCL

November 9, 1970

National Security Decision Memorandum 93

TO: Secretary of State
Secretary of Defense
Director, Office of Emergency Preparedness
Director of Central Intelligence

SUBJECT: Policy Towards Chile

Following the discussion at the meeting of the National Security Council on November 6, 1970, the President has decided that the basis for our policy toward Chile will be the concept underlying Option C of the Interagency paper submitted November 3, 1970 by the Department of State for the consideration of the National Security Council as outlined in the guidelines set forth below.

The President has decided that (1) the public posture of the United States will be correct but cool, to avoid giving the Allende government a basis on which to rally domestic and international support for consolidation of the regime; but that (2) the United States will seek to maximize pressures on the Allende government to prevent its consolidation and limit its ability to implement policies contrary to U.S. and hemisphere interests.

Specifically, the President has directed that within the context of a publicly cool and correct posture toward Chile:

-- vigorous efforts be undertaken to assure that other governments in Latin America understand fully that the U.S. opposes consolidation of a communist state in Chile hostile to the interests of the United States and other hemisphere nations, and to the extent possible encourage them to adopt a similar posture.

-- close consultation be established with key governments in Latin America, particularly Brazil and Argentina, to coordinate efforts to oppose Chilean moves which may be contrary to our mutual interests; in pursuit of this objective, efforts should be increased to establish and maintain close relations with friendly military leaders in the hemisphere.

TOP SECRET/SENSITIVE/EYES ONLY UNCLAS

-- necessary actions be taken to:

a. exclude, to the extent possible, further financing assistance or guarantees for U.S. private investment in Chile, including those related to the Investment Guarantee Program or the operations of the Export-Import Bank;

b. determine the extent to which existing guarantees and financing arrangements can be terminated or reduced;

c. bring maximum feasible influence to bear in international financial institutions to limit credit or other financing assistance to Chile (in this connection, efforts should be made to coordinate with and gain maximum support for this policy from other friendly nations, particularly those in Latin America, with the objective of lessening unilateral U.S. exposure); and

d. assure that U.S. private business interests having investments or operations in Chile are made aware of the concern with which the U.S. Government views the Government of Chile and the restrictive nature of the policies which the U.S. Government intends to follow.

-- no new bilateral economic aid commitments be undertaken with the Government of Chile (programs of a humanitarian or private social agency character will be considered on a case by case basis); existing commitments will be fulfilled but ways in which, if the U.S. desires to do so, they could be reduced, delayed or terminated should be examined.

The President has directed that the Director of the Office of Emergency Preparedness prepare a study which sets forth the implications of possible developments in world copper markets, stockpile disposal actions and other factors as they may affect the marketing of Chilean copper and our relationships with Chile.

The President also has directed that the Senior Review Group meet monthly or more frequently as necessary to consider specific policy issues within the framework of this general posture, to report actions which have been taken, and to present to him further specific policy questions which may require his decision. To facilitate this process the President has directed the establishment of an Ad Hoc Interagency Working Group, comprising representatives of the Secretaries of State and Defense, the Director of Central Intelligence, and the President's Assistant for National Security Affairs, and chaired by the representative of the Secretary of State, to prepare options for specific courses of action and related action plans for the consideration of the Senior Review Group and to coordinate implementation of approved courses of action.

Henry A. Kissinger

cc: Secretary of the Treasury
Administrator, A. I. D.
Director, Office of Management and Budget
Chairman, Joint Chiefs of Staff

DOCUMENT 4. Treasury Department, John Connally to President Nixon, **SECRET** "Memorandum for the President," January 15, 1972 (initialed and annotated by Richard Nixon).

Authority E.O. 12958
By RW NARA Date 7-26-02

00525

THE SECRETARY OF THE TREASURY
WASHINGTON

SECRET JAN 1 5 1972

MEMORANDUM FOR THE PRESIDENT

It is my understanding that you have made it very clear that we should keep maximum pressure on Chile.

They have recently stopped repaying their debts to the U. S. Government and reportedly most other creditors. A meeting of creditor nations has been called for early February in Paris to discuss this.

In my view the U. S. objective at this meeting is to get the other creditors to line up behind the U. S. position. If they were to go off and negotiate with Chile separately our leverage could be reduced substantially.

However, we have good reason to believe that far from keeping the pressure on Chile, they have now been led to believe we have already agreed to a renegotiation of their debts. (If there is any doubt on this point, I have top secret information to show you.) As I understand it, this is not our intention and our principal purpose is to get broad creditor support to isolate Chile.

Since this matter falls within the Treasury purview, I strongly urge that Treasury be named to head the U. S. delegation to Paris to insure that we fully protect our economic interests and keep the pressure on Chile.

There will be a Senior Review Group meeting of the NSC to discuss this issue shortly.

John Connally

Totally against my instructions

This is our policy

approved RN

DOCUMENT 5. National Security Council, Henry Kissinger to President Nixon, **SECRET** "Covert Action Program—Chile," November 25, 1970.

(un-log)

UNCLASSIFIED

SECRET/SENSITIVE/EYES ONLY

INFORMATION

MEMORANDUM FOR THE PRESIDENT

FROM: Henry A. Kissinger

SUBJECT: Covert Action Program -- CHILE

In addition to the actions outlined in my memorandum of November 25 (subject: Status Report on Chile), the 40 Committee has been reviewing a covert action program keyed to the overall policy towards Chile which you established at the NSC Meeting on November 5. The program has five principal elements:

1. Political action to divide and weaken the Allende coalition;

2. Maintaining and enlarging contacts in the Chilean military;

3. Providing support to non-Marxist opposition political groups and parties;

4. Assisting certain periodicals and using other media outlets in Chile which can speak out against the Allende Government; and

5. Using selected media outlets [redacted] 25x(1) [redacted] to play up Allende's subversion of the democratic process and involvement by Cuba and the Soviet Union in Chile.

The Committee approved development of the general plan proposed by CIA and a contingency budget, but will review each specific operation on a periodic basis.

Nachmanoff/vmr 11-25-70 SECRET/SENSITIVE/EYES ONLY

UNCLASSIFIED

DOCUMENT 6. National Security Council, **TOP SECRET** Meeting Minutes, "Minutes of the Meeting of the 40 Committee, 19 November 1970/Chile-Covert Action Program," December 10, 1970.

10 December 1970

MEMORANDUM FOR THE RECORD

SUBJECT: Minutes of the Meeting of the 40 Committee, 19 November 1970

PRESENT: Mr. Kissinger, Mr. Mitchell, Mr. Packard, Mr. Johnson, Admiral Moorer, and General Cushman.

Messrs. John Irwin, Charles A. Meyer, William Broe, Arnold Nachmanoff, and Wymberley Coerr were present for Item 1.

Colonel Richard T. Kennedy and Mr. Thomas Karamessines were present for the entire meeting.

1. <u>Chile</u> - <u>Covert Action Program</u>

a. <u>Mr. Kissinger</u> commented that the first item on the agenda was Chile and asked the CIA to provide a briefing on the proposals outlined in the paper dated 17 November 1970.

b. <u>Mr. Broe</u> stated that, essentially, the program consisted of a number of political actions designed to divide and weaken the Allende government:

(1) [redacted] has requested CIA financial support for [redacted] effort to form a political bloc capable of stopping the Communist Party from eventually gaining complete control of the UP. 25x(1)

(2) Increased efforts are being made to develop intelligence showing specific vulnerabilities or tensions within the UP [redacted] 25x(1)

(3) Various subtle efforts are being made to take advantage of Allende's weaknesses and sensitivity to direct criticism [redacted]

-2-

(4) Also being explored is the desirability of stimulating and assisting

But it is recognized that such action could have negative results in the loss of competent opposition leadership within Chile during a crucial period.

25x(1)

(5) Contacts are being maintained and, where possible, enlarged within the Chilean military forces.

(6) Special briefings are being provided

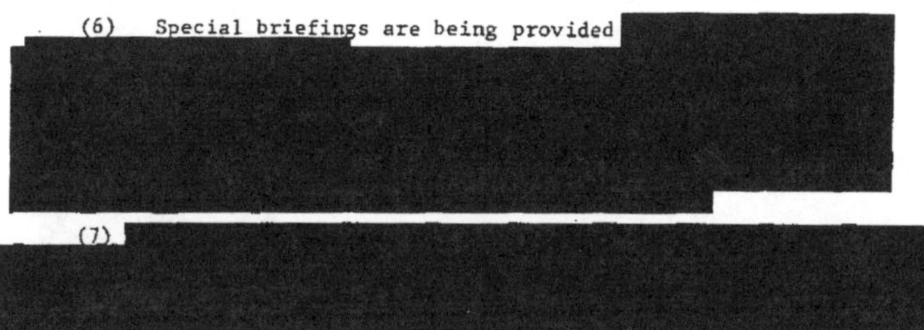

25x(1)

(7)

(8) Since the Democratic Radical Party (PDR) seems to be finished politically, Frei's PDC and the National Party (PN) and their media are the only sources of serious political opposition.

25x(1)

The forthcoming PDC Junta and the upcoming senatorial by-elections and the municipal elections should be of help in identifying potential opposition leadership.

25x(1)

(9) While some support is now being provided it is recognized this could be short-lived in event of a government crackdown. Therefore, serious consideration is being given to

(10)

25x(1)

-3-

(11) [redacted] 25x(1)

(12) The estimate for funding the above proposed CIA covert action program for Chile is [redacted]

c. Mr. Broe requested Committee approval in principle for the foregoing program including specifically funds for the [redacted] continued funding of [redacted] and the general support provided in the periodical and media field. He stated that future specific proposals will be submitted for Committee approval on such expensive items as [redacted] should further study and developments make such actions seem feasible and desirable. 25x(1)

d. Mr. Kissinger referred to the proposed stockpile [redacted] 25x(1)

e. Mr. Broe responded that CIA was confident that it could work out [redacted] 25x(1)

f. Mr. Kissinger stated that he raised this question because he did not wish the problem of a lack of operational funds in Chile to be used later as a justification for not being able to follow through on desirable actions.

g. [redacted] 25x(1)

h. [redacted] 25x(1)

i. Mr. Broe [redacted] 25x(1)

j. Mr. Irwin asked if the capability really exists to carry out the proposed CIA program or if it is just good general planning. He also questioned just how helpful it would really be to [redacted] in order to weaken the effectiveness of the government [redacted] 25x(1)

-4-

k. Mr. Broe pointed out that some of the activities involving [redacted] With regard to [redacted] he agreed that this is a most difficult question to decide and clearly one which needs further study. 25x(1)

l. Mr. Kissinger, in the role of the devil's advocate, pointed out that the proposed CIA program was aimed at supporting moderates. Since Allende is holding himself out as a moderate, he asked why not support extremists.

m. Mr. Broe answered that the overall objective is to sow dissension within the coalition of parties and individuals supporting Allende, so anything might be done on a selective basis where it appears advantageous to this end.

n. Mr. Kissinger polled the members, all of whom agreed in principle with the CIA program as submitted with the understanding that additional specific proposals involving large expenditures would be presented to the Committee as developed.

o. Mr. Mitchell suggested that the Committee be kept regularly informed on progress and developments under the program.

p. Mr. Kissinger agreed and called for a monthly progress report, or in the alternative, a report on covert action developments for the 40 Committee principals only following each Senior Review Group (SRG) meeting convened for the purpose of discussing Chile.

25x(1)

DOCUMENT 7. National Security Council, **SECRET** Action Memorandum for Henry Kissinger, "40 Committee Meeting, September 9, 1971—Chile," September 8, 1971.

MEMORANDUM

[Outside System]

NATIONAL SECURITY COUNCIL

ACTION
8 September 1971

UNCLASSIFIED

SECRET/SENSITIVE/EYES ONLY

MEMORANDUM FOR: DR. KISSINGER

FROM: ARNOLD NACHMANOFF

SUBJECT: 40 Committee Meeting, September 9, 1971 -- CHILE

[redacted] 25x(1)

The 40 Committee meeting is scheduled to consider a request [redacted] of El Mercurio (the largest independent newspaper in Chile) for covert support totalling $1 million. [redacted] 25x(1) [redacted] and will be prepared to brief on this subject if you wish to take it up after the Chile discussion. If not, this can be covered at the next 40 Committee meeting, scheduled for September 15.

CHILE

The CIA paper on the El Mercurio proposal (tabbed) reports on the increasing pressure which the Allende Government is bringing to bear against El Mercurio. The economic squeez on the newspaper is made possible by the increasing governmental control over finance and business in Chile. [redacted] 25x(1) [redacted] the paper needs at least $1 million to survive for the next year or two. The pressure for an immediate decision comes from the fact that an opportunity has presented [redacted]

The basic options posed in the CIA paper are:

A. To provide extensive financing for the newspaper with the understanding that this may not be sufficient to stop the Allende Government from closing the paper anyway (e.g., through control of newsprint, or labor stoppages). This would involve an initial commitment of at least $700,000.

SECRET/SENSITIVE/EYES ONLY

UNCLASSIFIED

NSC DECLASSIFICATION REVIEW [E.O. 12958]
/X/ Exempt in part and redact as shown
by L.Salvetti Date 9/14/2000

60

SECRET/SENSITIVE/EYES ONLY - 2 -

B. Allow El Mercurio to go out of business and arrange a maximum propaganda effort on the issue of freedom of the press. Allende might be able to counter that by demonstrating that it was El Mercurio's financial ineptitude which resulted in its closing.

Ambassador Korry and the Station Chief recommend the first option. Their position is that we have a great interest in maintaining an opposition voice in Chile and that without it, the political opposition would be seriously weakened. Allende's intense efforts to destroy El Mercurio indicate that he probably regards it as a significant barrier to his internal political strategy. On the negative side, however, $1 million would be a very expensive price to pay for a little extra time if we conclude that Allende intends and has the capability to close down the newspaper anyway.

Option B would obviously be less costly and might force Allende to a confrontation on the press freedom issue before he really is prepared. [redacted] 25x(1)

My judgment is that we should probably take both options and link them. I believe we should go ahead with the $700,000 deal, understanding full well that : (a) this may buy only a very limited amount of time for El Mercurio, and (b) that we are not making a commitment to continue to bail out El Mercurio in the future. Moreover, we should condition our support on an understanding that El Mercurio will launch an intensive public attack on the Allende Government's efforts to force them out of business-- [redacted] 25x(1) The U. S. Government, of course, should not get into a public shouting match on this issue, [redacted] It seems to me that this course would keep the opposition voice alive for awhile and force Allende either to back down or risk intensive criticism on the press freedom issue. If he chooses the latter course, it should be helpful to us in diverting and perhaps even undercutting some of his support on the copper compensation which will probably reach a climax in the next couple of months.

Your Talking Points pursue this line of reasoning.

SECRET/SENSITIVE/EYES ONLY

UNCLASSIFIED

DOCUMENT 8. CIA, **SECRET** "Memorandum, "Authorization for 'El Mercurio' Support," September 30, 1971.

(1294)

SECRET

30 SEP 1971

MEMORANDUM FOR THE RECORD

SUBJECT: Authorization for "El Mercurio" Support

1. On the evening of 14 September 1971, the DCI notified the DD/P that he had received a call from Dr. Henry Kissinger in which the latter indicated that (a) the President had just approved the proposal for supporting "El Mercurio" in the amount of $700,000, and, (b) the President wished to see the paper kept going and the amount stipulated could be exceeded if it would usefully serve that purpose. The DCI said, on the strength of that, he felt that we could exceed the authorized $700,000 and go up to, and even over, $1,000,000 provided it was warranted to keep the paper going.

2. On 20 September 1971, at the close of a meeting on another matter, the Chief, WHD queried the DCI on the nature of the authorization and the DCI reiterated, essentially, the points noted in paragraph 1 above.

Signed William V. Broe

William V. Broe
Chief
Western Hemisphere Division

Declassified and
Approved for Release
July 2000

SECRET

DOCUMENT 9. CIA, **SECRET** Intelligence Information Special Report, "Preliminary Planning for an Eventual Military Move Against the Chilean Government," November 9, 1971 (page 1).

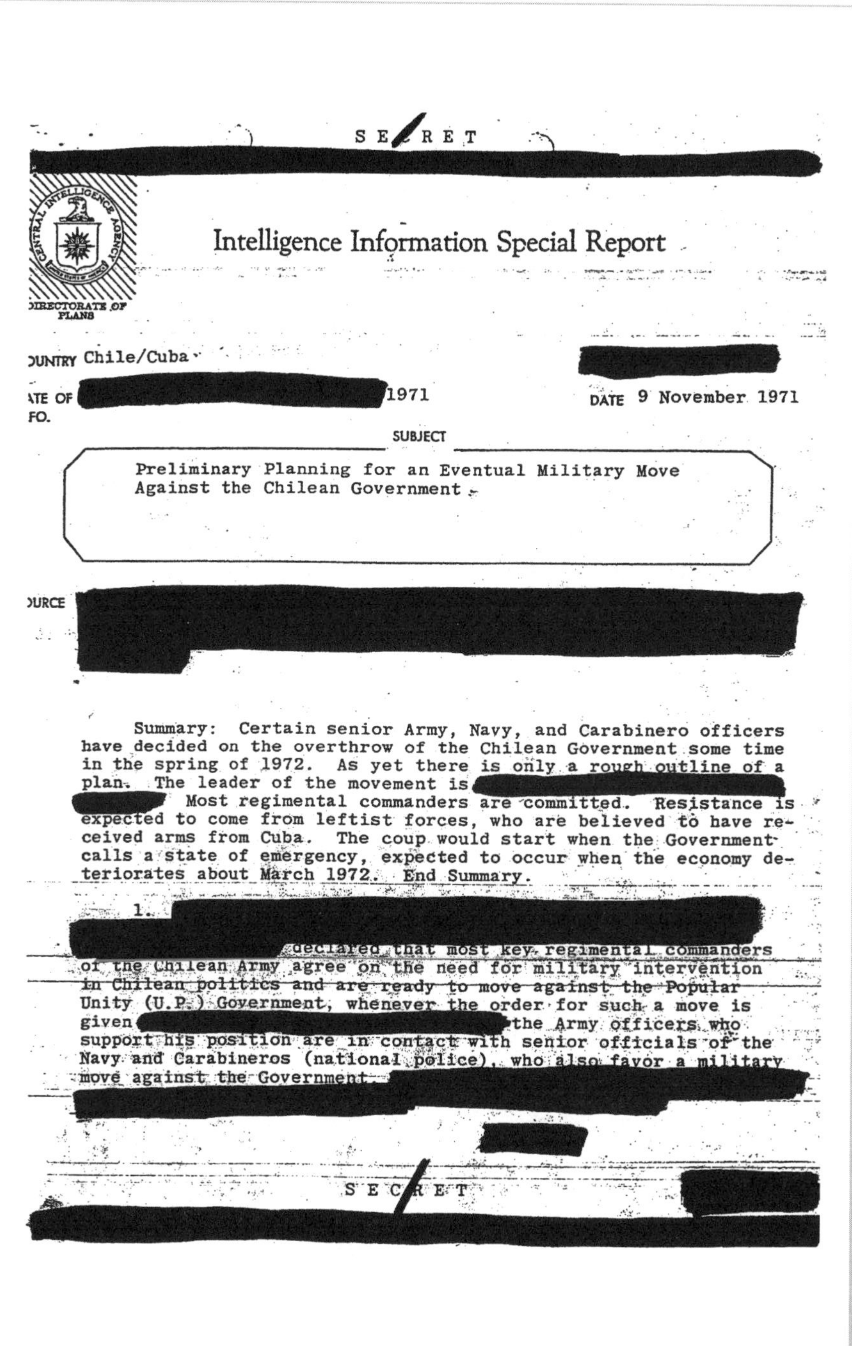

SECRET

Intelligence Information Special Report

DIRECTORATE OF PLANS

COUNTRY Chile/Cuba

DATE OF INFO. [redacted] 1971

DATE 9 November 1971

SUBJECT

Preliminary Planning for an Eventual Military Move Against the Chilean Government

SOURCE [redacted]

Summary: Certain senior Army, Navy, and Carabinero officers have decided on the overthrow of the Chilean Government some time in the spring of 1972. As yet there is only a rough outline of a plan. The leader of the movement is [redacted] Most regimental commanders are committed. Resistance is expected to come from leftist forces, who are believed to have received arms from Cuba. The coup would start when the Government calls a state of emergency, expected to occur when the economy deteriorates about March 1972. End Summary.

1. [redacted] declared that most key regimental commanders of the Chilean Army agree on the need for military intervention in Chilean politics and are ready to move against the Popular Unity (U.P.) Government, whenever the order for such a move is given [redacted] the Army officers who support his position are in contact with senior officials of the Navy and Carabineros (national police), who also favor a military move against the Government [redacted]

SECRET

DOCUMENT 10. CIA, **SECRET** Cable [Dinner with General Pinochet], August 6, 1971.

PAGE 1 OF 2

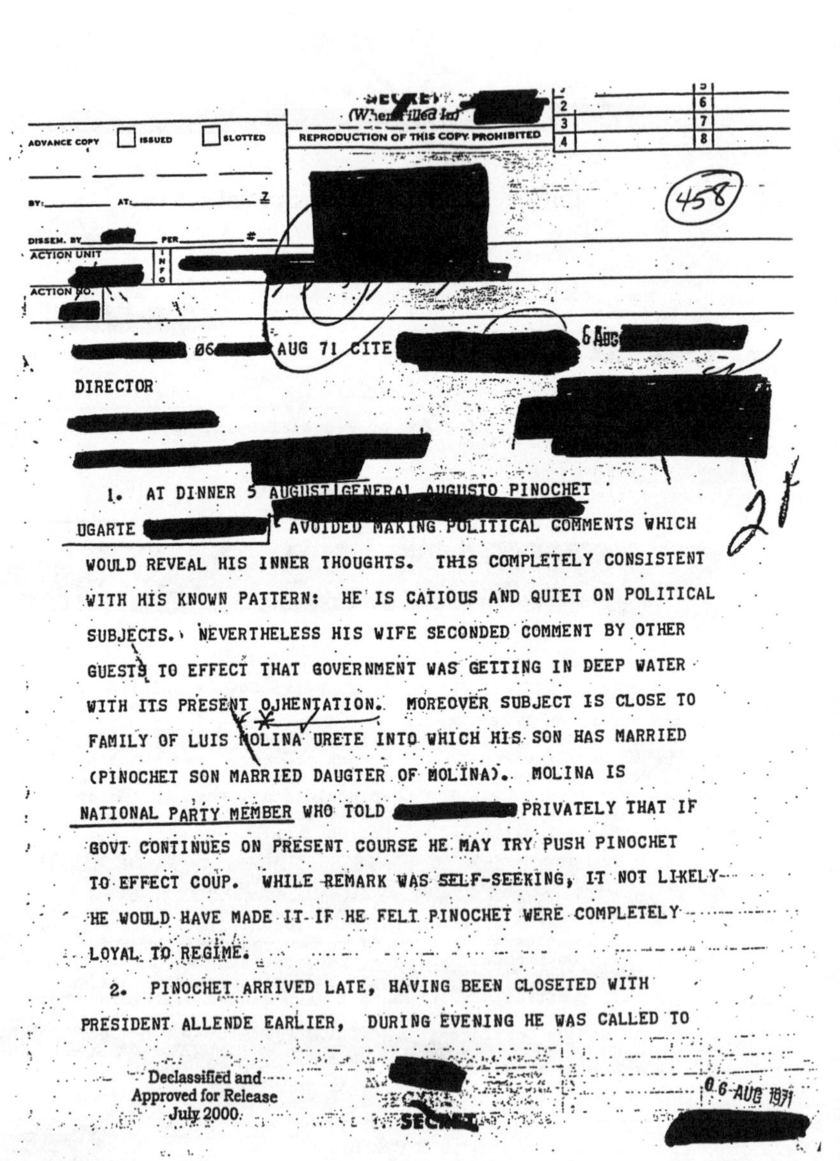

SECRET
(When Filled In)
REPRODUCTION OF THIS COPY PROHIBITED

ADVANCE COPY ISSUED SLOTTED

BY: AT: Z

DISSEM. BY PER #

ACTION UNIT

ACTION NO.

458

06 AUG 71 CITE

DIRECTOR

1. AT DINNER 5 AUGUST GENERAL AUGUSTO PINOCHET UGARTE AVOIDED MAKING POLITICAL COMMENTS WHICH WOULD REVEAL HIS INNER THOUGHTS. THIS COMPLETELY CONSISTENT WITH HIS KNOWN PATTERN: HE IS CATIOUS AND QUIET ON POLITICAL SUBJECTS. NEVERTHELESS HIS WIFE SECONDED COMMENT BY OTHER GUESTS TO EFFECT THAT GOVERNMENT WAS GETTING IN DEEP WATER WITH ITS PRESENT OJHENTATION. MOREOVER SUBJECT IS CLOSE TO FAMILY OF LUIS MOLINA URETE INTO WHICH HIS SON HAS MARRIED (PINOCHET SON MARRIED DAUGTER OF MOLINA). MOLINA IS NATIONAL PARTY MEMBER WHO TOLD PRIVATELY THAT IF GOVT CONTINUES ON PRESENT COURSE HE MAY TRY PUSH PINOCHET TO EFFECT COUP. WHILE REMARK WAS SELF-SEEKING, IT NOT LIKELY HE WOULD HAVE MADE IT IF HE FELT PINOCHET WERE COMPLETELY LOYAL TO REGIME.

2. PINOCHET ARRIVED LATE, HAVING BEEN CLOSETED WITH PRESIDENT ALLENDE EARLIER, DURING EVENING HE WAS CALLED TO

Declassified and Approved for Release July 2000

SECRET

06 AUG 1971

(When Filled In) [redacted]

COPY ☐ ISSUED ☐ SLOTTED

REPRODUCTION OF THIS COPY PROHIBITED

AT: Z

PER

UNIT INFO [redacted]

NO.

PAGE 2 [redacted]

PHONE HALF DOZEN TIMES TO GET REPORTS ON SITUATION IN CITY, STATUS OF PDC MEETING DOWNTOWN, ETC. IT WAS QUITE CLEAR THAT AS JEFE DE LA PLAZA HE IS NOT CEREMONIAL FIGURE. PINOCHET APPEARED TO BE MILD, FREINDLY, NARROW-GUAGED MILITARY MAN WHO TOTALLY IMMERSED IN NEW FIELD OF SECURITY, PUBLIC ORDER AND POLITICAL EVENTS AND WHO CLEARLY ENJOYED FEELING OF BEING IMPORTANT.

3. [redacted]

4. IN CONNECTION WITH [redacted] DOES NOT CONSIDER PINOCHET TO BE PRO-PDC OR TO BE BEHOLDEN TO PDC.

[redacted]

ACCORDING TO [redacted], COMITE REVOLCIONARIO ASSESSES SUBJECT AS PERSON WHO COULD POSSIBLY BE NEUTRALIZED BY CONSPIRATORIAL GROUP BUT WHO WOULD NOT LEAD ANY COUP.

6. [redacted]

SECRET

DOCUMENT 11. CIA, **SECRET** Cable [General Pinochet's Views on Allende], September 27, 1972.

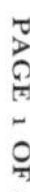

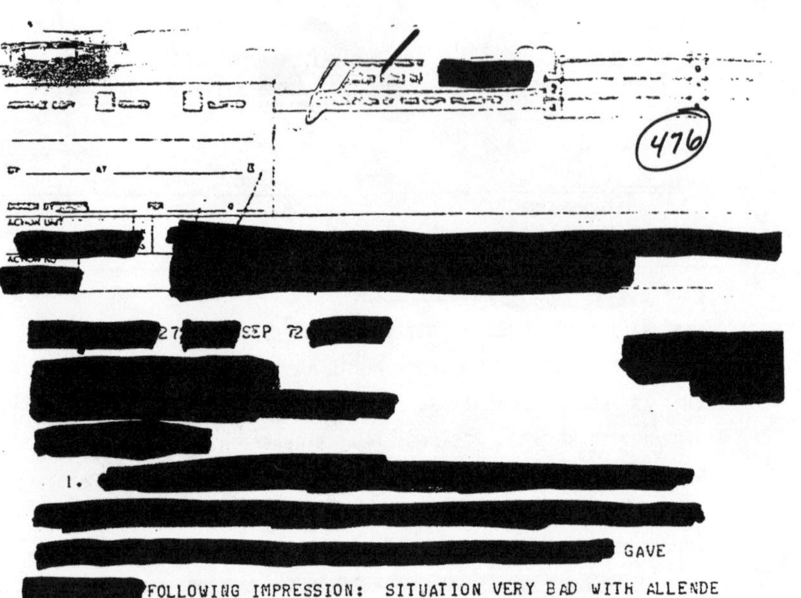

27 SEP 72

1. GAVE FOLLOWING IMPRESSION: SITUATION VERY BAD WITH ALLENDE INCAPABLE OF MAINTAINING CONTROL OR RUNNING GOVT. NO COUP PLANS AFOOT, BUT ALL BELIEVE OVERTHROW ATTEMPT CAN DEVELOP SOON. YOUNG OFFICERS PARTICULARLY DISCONTENTED WITH HIGH COMMAND COMPLIANCE WITH ALLENDE POLICIES.

2. PINOCHET, PREVIOUSLY THE STRICT CONSTITUTIONALIST, RELUCTANTLY ADMITTED HE NOW HARBORING SECOND THOUGHTS: THAT ALLENDE MUST BE FORCED TO STEP DOWN OR BE ELIMINATED ("ONLY ALTERNATIVES"). PINOCHET (WHO PRATS MAN) BELIEVES PRATS LEADING CANDIDATE TO HEAD NEW GOVT BUT ADMITS THAT IF COUP IS LED BY YOUNGER OFFICERS (FAR OUT POSSIBILITY), PRATS WON'T HAVE CHANCE BECAUSE HE TOO CLOSELY IDENTIFIED WITH ALLENDE.

3. ALLENDE CONTINUES TO PRESSURE HIGH COMMAND TO BUY SOVIET

Declassified and
Approved for Release
July 2000

SECRET (When Filled In)

ADVANCE COPY ☐ ISSUED ☐ SLOTTED

REPRODUCTION OF THIS COPY PROHIBITED

BY: AT: Z

DISSEM BY PER #

ACTION UNIT

ACTION NO.

PAGE 2

MILITARY EQUIPMENT, BUT SENIOR OFFICERS RESISTING SUCCESSFULLY. ARMY DOES NOT WANT NEW LINE OF WEAPONS NOR PRESENCE OF SOVIET ADVISERS OR TECHNICIANS. MOST ARMY WILLING ACCEPT WOULD BE ANTI-AIRCRAFT WEAPONS OR GENERAL LOGISTIC ITEMS. PINOCHET WAS IN PANAMA BEFORE COMING MEXICO TO NEGOTIATE PURCHASE OF TANKS FROM U.S. GOVT. HE FELT HE WAS VERY WELL TREATED AND CAME AWAY BELIEVING U.S. WILL SUPPLY TANKS AFTER ALL. (WHILE IN PANAMA, TALKED WITH MORE JUNIOR U.S. ARMY OFFICERS HE KNEW FROM DAYS AT SCHOOL OF AMERICAS AND WAS TOLD U.S. WILL SUPPORT COUP AGAINST ALLENDE "WITH WHATEVER MEANS NECESSARY" WHEN TIME COMES.)

DOCUMENT 12. CIA, **SECRET** Meeting Minutes, "Meeting on Current Chilean Situation at Department of State, 1630–1830, 17 October 1972," October 18, 1972 (pages 1–3).

PAGE 1 OF 3

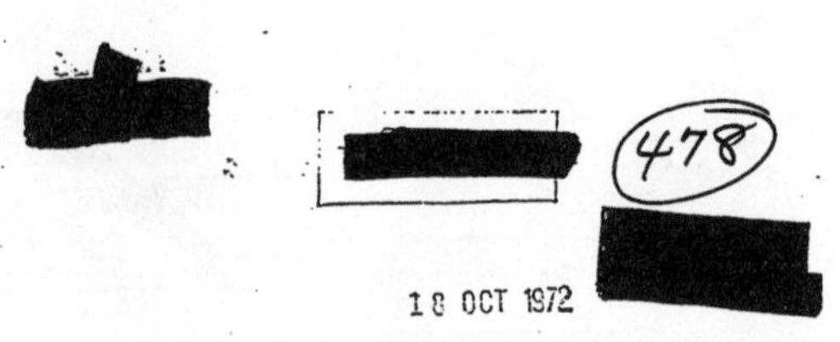

478

18 OCT 1972

MEMORANDUM FOR THE RECORD

SUBJECT : Meeting on Current Chilean Situation at Department of State, 1630-1830, 17 October 1972

ATTENDEES: Assistant Secretary of State for Inter-American Affairs Charles A. Meyer
Deputy Assistant Secretary of State for Inter-American Affairs John H. Crimmins
Mr. William J. Jorden, Senior Staff Member of the National Security Council
Mr. John W. Fisher, Director of Bolivian/Chilean Affairs, Department of State
Mr. James R. Gardner, Chief, Operations Policy Staff, Department of State
[redacted] Chief, WH Division
[redacted]

1. Mr. Meyer's purpose in calling the meeting was to consider as a contingency, what the U.S. Government's response should be if the opposition to Allende were to approach the Embassy [redacted] Santiago with a request for (a) support in toppling the Allende Government, or (b) an assurance of post-coup support as a prior condition for undertaking a coup, or, (c) U.S. Government commitment to post-coup support for a coup already arranged and decided upon. Since time would probably be a factor in responding to any such request, the Department of State felt it was necessary to have at least some preliminary discussion of the problems and options involved in this type of contingency.

2. [redacted] noted that, earlier in the day, appropriate CIA elements had brainstormed the current Chilean situation from every conceivable angle. This had resulted in the conclusion that the most likely outcome in the current crisis was that a coup would

C-7

Declassified and Approved for Release

18

not develop within the next few days. This conclusion was based on the estimate that the country would have to suffer a little more under Allende before the kind of consensus which would provoke the military into deciding on a coup would be reached among the main elements of the opposition -- that is, the military, the political parties, and the private sector. It was stressed that up to 17 October, there had been absolutely no indication that General Carlos Prats, the Chilean Army Commander-in-Chief, was ready to do anything except maintain law and order and, in the process, support the constitutional Allende government. The point was also made that it was fairly obvious that the opposition political parties were reluctantly caught up in this wave of strikes and other actions against the government; essentially they started out supporting the strikes in order to preserve their credentials in the opposition. The private sector, in instigating the strikes which led to the current situation, had, and have, no clear goals but felt this was the only way to create a situation in which the military and the political sectors would be forced to consider a coup against the Allende regime. [redacted] concluded his assessment by stating that it is, of course, always possible that some action which could not be reasonably anticipated might take place and act as a catalyst for moving the military into a coup effort. As an example of this type of unforeseen occurrence he mentioned a clash between the security forces and students in which a number of students were killed. Short of that, however, the coup probabilities seemed quite low at this juncture. [redacted] noted that in the course of the CIA brainstorming session, various courses of action had been examined to see if it were in the net interests of the United States to accelerate current Chilean events leading toward a coup. The conclusion was that no course of action which could be taken would help in a decisive manner to achieve the objective of removing Allende from power.

3. It was conceded by all that, in the final analysis, the Chilean military were the key to any coup that might develop now or in the future. [redacted]

6. The group finally did agree on the following:

a. If and when the Chilean military decided to undertake a coup, they would not need U.S. Government assistance or support to do so successfully nor are they likely to seek such support. Further, given the Chilean military capabilities for an unaided coup, any U.S. intervention or assistance in the coup *per se* should be avoided.

b.

DOCUMENT 13. CIA, **SECRET** Memorandum from Theodore Shackley to James Schlesinger, **SECRET**, "The Agency's Covert Action Program in Chile," May 8, 1973.

SECRET/

8 MAY 1973

MEMORANDUM FOR: Director of Central Intelligence

VIA : Deputy Director for Operations

FROM : Chief, Western Hemisphere Division

SUBJECT : The Agency's Covert Action Program in Chile

Attached is a paper outlining Agency covert action involvement in Chile since 1970. The WH Division is presently in the process of implementing the Director's decision of 10 April 1973 which calls for financial assistance to the anti-Allende opposition at above the FY 1973 level ($1,000,000), as well as for accelerated efforts against the military target. The latter is designed to better monitor any coup plotting and to bring our influence to bear on key military commanders so that they might play a decisive role on the side of the coup forces when and if the Chilean military decides on its own to act against Allende.

Western Hemisphere Division

Attachment
As Stated Above

cc: DDCI

DDO/WH/ (7 May 1973)

Distribution:
Orig & 1 - DDI
1 - DDCI
1 - Executive Reg.
1 - DDO
1 - ADDO
2 - C/WHD
1 -
1 -

SECRET

Declassified and
Approved for Release
July 2000

DOCUMENT 14. National Security Council, Henry Kissinger to President Nixon, **SECRET**, Situation Report, "Attempted Coup in Chile," June 29, 1973.

Sit Rep #-1

~~SECRET/SENSITIVE~~

INFORMATION
June 29, 1973

MEMORANDUM FOR: THE PRESIDENT

FROM: HENRY A. KISSINGER

SUBJECT: Attempted Coup in Chile

Chilean Army units are reported to have launched an attempted coup against the government of Salvadore Allende this morning. Army troops supported by four tanks (presumably from the 1st Armored Division) moved against the Presidential Palace at 9:00 a.m. Carabinero (police) guarding the palace exchanged shots with the coup forces. An unconfirmed report says the coup forces have taken over the palace. Witnesses claimed to have seen five persons dead on the streets at the palace.

Allende was not yet in his office at the time. He has made a broadcast to the people from his home denouncing the coup and asking the people to come to the defense of the Government. He warned them against moving into the scene of the fighting, however. He also claimed that loyal Army units were either moving to the defense of the palace or standing by for orders to move. This contradicts other reporting that includes two of the units Allende mentioned as being part of the coup forces.

There are no indications yet of any participation by Navy or Air Force units or personnel. They had been reported as taking an active part in coup planning in recent weeks.

The Chilean Trade Union Confederation (controlled by the Socialists and Communists) has called on its workers to seize industrial plants and to take steps to mobilize to defend the government.

~~SECRET/SENSITIVE~~

DECLASSIFIED
Authority NSC
By NARA, Date

Retyped:nm:6/29/73

DOCUMENT 15. National Security Council, Henry Kissinger to President Nixon, **SECRET**, Situation Report, "Attempted Chilean Rebellion Ends," June 29, 1973.

~~SECRET/SENSITIVE (XGDS-3)~~

INFORMATION
June 29, 1973

MEMORANDUM FOR: THE PRESIDENT

FROM: HENRY A. KISSINGER

SUBJECT: Attempted Chilean Rebellion Ends

Loyalist troops have apparently crushed the rebellion of some Chilean Army units against the government of Salvador Allende. Our Embassy reports that President Allende, accompanied by Army Commander-in-Chief Prats, arrived at the Presidential Palace shortly before noon and that pro-government crowds were mobbing the Palace square, singing the National anthem and shouting for the President. Rebellious troops were leaving the area unarmed and with hands up. The tanks which attacked the Palace this morning have withdrawn. The fighting between loyalists and rebels lasted some three hours and left a number of dead and wounded.

The Under Secretary of Interior had announced earlier that Allende has ordered a state of emergency throughout the country.

All indications are that the coup attempt was an isolated and poorly coordinated effort. Most of the military leaders, including the commanders-in-chief of all three branches of the Armed Forces, remained loyal to the government.

~~SECRET/SENSITIVE (XGDS-3)~~

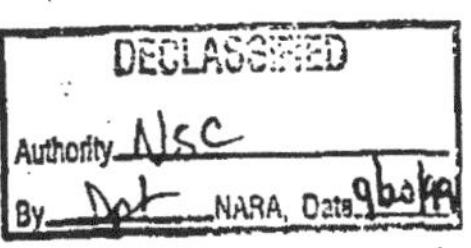

DOCUMENT 16. CIA, Memorandum from William Colby, "Proposed Covert Financial Support of Chilean Private Sector," August 25, 1973.

(1422)

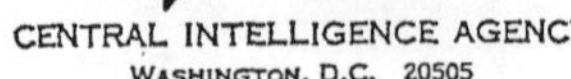

CENTRAL INTELLIGENCE AGENCY
WASHINGTON, D.C. 20505

25 AUG 1973

MEMORANDUM FOR: The Assistant to the President for National Security Affairs
Mr. Jack B. Kubisch
Assistant Secretary of State for Inter-American Affairs

VIA: Mr. William J. Jorden
Senior Staff Member
National Security Council

SUBJECT: Proposed Covert Financial Support of Chilean Private Sector

1. On 20 August 1973, the 40 Committee approved the expenditure of $1,000,000 through June 1974 for support to the Chilean opposition political parties and the private sector. [redacted] The 40 Committee specified in its approval that the contingency fund [redacted] allocated to the private sector could only be spent with Ambassador Davis' approval.

2. Chile continues in a state of crisis and the pressures on President Allende and his government are increasing. Allende and his forces appear to be on the defensive, fearing a military coup and unsure of their ability to deal effectively with it if it comes. It is a crucial period in the revolutionary process being pursued by the Allende government. While the key to the situation undoubtedly lies with the military, the left and Allende, the opposition pressure is an essential element of the picture and encourages the military in its resistance to Allende and the left.

Classified by signer. Exempt from General Declassification Schedule of E. O. 11652. Exemption Category 5B (2). Impossible to determine date of automatic declassification.

Declassified and Approved for Release July 2000

3. Given this situation, the CIA Chief of Station in Santiago on 24 August recommended that covert financial support be given to the opposition, beginning with a [redacted] to the private sector, in order to keep the pressure on Allende and sustain some of the present strikes. The Chief of Station discussed his recommendation with Ambassador Davis with the latter indicating that he could not endorse his proposal, particularly support to the private sector, because such a course of action could lead to a de facto U.S. Government commitment to a coup which was a policy issue that only Washington could decide. The Ambassador did agree that soundings should be made in Washington on this matter.

4. The Santiago Station would not be working directly with the armed forces in an attempt to bring about a coup nor would its support to the overall opposition forces have this as its objective. Realistically, of course, a coup could result from increased opposition pressure on the Allende government. However, the broad concensus of the opposition appears to have the massive entrance of the military into the Allende government with real power as its present objective.

/s/ W. E. Colby
W. E. Colby

DOCUMENT 17. Defense Intelligence Agency, **TOP SECRET** UMBRA Report, "Chile," September 8, 1973.

UNCLASSIFIED ~~TOP SECRET UMBRA~~

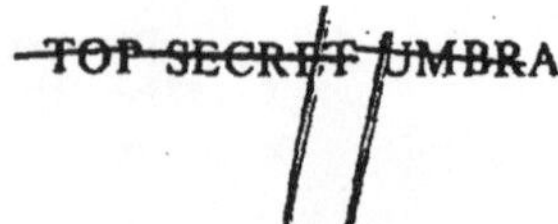

CHILE

THE MILITARY MAY ATTEMPT A COUP AGAINST THE ALLENDE GOVERNMENT ON 10 SEPTEMBER. MEANWHILE, OPPOSITION PARTIES ARE CALLING FOR ALLENDE'S RESIGNATION AND THE IMPEACHMENT OF HIS CABINET.

The three services have reportedly agreed to move against the government on 10 September, and civilian terrorist and right-wing groups will allegedly support the effort with a campaign to block roads and disrupt possible government resistance. The military's final decision may have resulted from President Allende's refusal to accept the resignation of Navy Commander Adm Raul Montero, even after Vice Adm Jose Merino presented him with an ultimatum during a meeting on the 7th. There are indications that some armed forces units wanted to move as early as the 8th but were dissuaded by higher-ranking officers who stressed the need for a coordinated effort, which they said could not possibly be put together until 10 September.

The coup appears to have the support of all the service commanders, a situation that Allende had been able to avoid over the past year. The President is reportedly aware that resistance by his supporters is futile and that any effort to oppose the military could result in heavy casualties. The National Police, who also feel that a coup is imminent, have reportedly been in contact with army plotters and have agreed not to resist the military if a coup is attempted.

Should no coup develop, however, Allende is still faced with further political troubles. In the wake of this week's demonstrations and resulting violence, the political opposition has hardened its stance against the Allende government. Moderate

Declassified with redactions by DIA

(Continued)

UNCLASSIFIED ~~TOP SECRET UMBRA~~

UNCLASSIFIED ~~TOP SECRET UMBRA~~

Christian Democrats have solidified their charges against the Cabinet and are proceeding with impeachment action despite the President's declaration that such an act is illegal. They have also thrown full support behind a nationwide strike and are encouraging workers already on strike to continue. The rightist National Party has gone one step further and is demanding Allende's resignation for incompetence.

PREPARED BY: Western Area Division (DI-5)
SOURCES:
DAO Santiago 604 and 605 7 Sep 73 ~~(S/NFD)~~
Emb Santiago 4056 7 Sep 73 ~~(C)~~
LATEST INFO: 7 Sep 73

DOCUMENT 18. CIA, **SECRET** Memorandum from David A. Phillips to Henry Kissinger, "Possible Request for U.S. Government Aid from Key Officer of Chilean Military Group Planning to Overthrow President Allende," September 11, 1973.

1427

SECRET/[redacted]

CENTRAL INTELLIGENCE AGENCY
DOCUMENT RECEIPT

NOTICE TO RECIPIENT
Sign and Return as Shown on Reverse Side

COURIER REC. NO.: | DATE SENT:

SENDER OF DOCUMENT(S): DDO/WHD | ROOM: [redacted] | BLDG.: HQS | DATE DOCUMENT(S) SENT: 11 September 1973

DESCRIPTION OF DOCUMENT(S) SENT

CIA NO.	DOCUMENT DATE	COPIES	DOCUMENT TITLE	ATTACHMENTS	CLASS
			Possible Request for U.S. Government Aid from Key Officer of Chilean Military Group Planning to Overthrow President Allende SECRET/[redacted] 1 cy		

RECIPIENT

ADDRESS OF RECIPIENT:
Mr. William J. Jorden
Senior Member, NSC
Room 380
Executive Office Building

SIGNATURE (ACKNOWLEDGING RECEIPT OF ABOVE DOCUMENT(S)):

OFFICE: | DATE OF RECEIPT:

FORM 12-61 615 USE PREVIOUS EDITIONS (33)

SECRET/[redacted]

SECRET/[redacted]

OPTIONAL FORM NO. 10

UNITED STATES GOVERNMENT

Memorandum

TO : Senior Member
National Security Council
Mr. William J. Jorden

DATE: 11 September 1973

FROM : Mr. David A. Phillips

SUBJECT: Possible Request for U.S. Government Aid from Key Officer of Chilean Military Group Planning to Overthrow President Allende

We are forwarding for your information the attached memorandum on a possible request for U.S. Government aid from a key officer of the Chilean military group planning to overthrow President Allende.

[redacted]

SECRET/[redacted]

Declassified and Approved for Release July 2000

CENTRAL INTELLIGENCE AGENCY
WASHINGTON, D.C. 20505

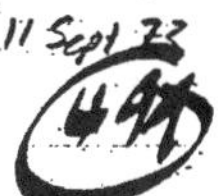

MEMORANDUM FOR: The Assistant to the President for National Security Affairs
Mr. Jack B. Kubisch
Assistant Secretary of State for Inter-American Affairs

VIA: Mr. William J. Jorden
Senior Staff Member
National Security Council

SUBJECT: Possible Request for U.S. Government Aid from Key Officer of Chilean Military Group Planning to Overthrow President Allende

1. Late 10 September 1973 [redacted], contacted an officer [redacted] and advised that early 11 September 1973 a significant part of the Chilean military planned to move to overthrow President Allende. He then asked if the U.S. Government would come to the aid of the Chilean military if the situation became difficult. He did not further explain exactly what he desired from the U.S. Government.

2. In response to [redacted] query, the [redacted] officer said that he could not comment on the matter, that the planned action against President Allende was a Chilean operation, and he could only promise that [redacted] question would promptly be made known to Washington.

3. [redacted]

Approved for Release
July 2000

DOCUMENT 19. CIA, **SECRET** Memorandum from William Colby to Henry Kissinger, "CIA's Covert Action Program in Chile Since 1970," September 13, 1973.

1430

CENTRAL INTELLIGENCE AGENCY
DOCUMENT RECEIPT

NOTICE TO RECIPIENT
Sig. nd Return as Shown on Reverse Side

COURIER NO. | DATE SENT

SENDER OF DOCUMENT(S): DDO/WHD
ROOM: [redacted]
BLDG.: HQS
DATE DOCUMENT(S) SENT: 13 September 1973

DESCRIPTION OF DOCUMENT(S) SENT

CIA NO.	DOCUMENT DATE	COPIES	DOCUMENT TITLE (IN BRIEF)	ATTACHMENTS	CLASS
	CIA's Covert Action Program in Chile Since 1970				
	SECRET/[redacted] 1 cy				

RECIPIENT

ADDRESS OF RECIPIENT:
Dr. Henry A. Kissinger
The Assistant to the President
for National Security Affairs
The White House

SIGNATURE (ACKNOWLEDGING RECEIPT OF ABOVE DOCUMENT(S))

OFFICE | DATE OF RECEIPT

(33)

MEMORANDUM FOR: HAK

You may also recall discussion of a Track Two in late 1970 - which has not been included in this summary.

[redacted]

Declassified and
Approved for Release
July 2000

(DATE) [redacted]

FORM NO. 101 REPLACES FORM 10-101
1 AUG 54 WHICH MAY BE USED.

NO. N173411

DATE

TO: Dr. Henry A. Kissinger
The Assistant to the President
for National Security Affairs
The White House

TYPE OF MATERIAL
ENVELOPE (S)
PACKAGE (S)
OTHER

ORIGINATOR: DO NOT COMPLETE THIS COPY BELOW THIS LINE. REMOVE THIS COPY IF LOG DATA IS TO BE ADDED ON COPIES 2 AND 3. INSERT ONLY THIS COPY IN THE WINDOW POCKET, OR ATTACH SECURELY TO ENVELOPE OR PACKAGE WITHOUT A WINDOW POCKET.

SIGNATURE OF RECIPIENT (NOT INITIALS) | DATE AND TIME OF RECEIPT

COURIER'S RECEIPT 1

FORM 6-60 240 USE PREVIOUS EDITIONS (24-25)

COURIER RECEIPT AND LOG RECORD

CENTRAL INTELLIGENCE AGENCY
WASHINGTON, D.C. 20505

MEMORANDUM FOR: Dr. Henry A. Kissinger
The Assistant to the President
for National Security Affairs

SUBJECT: CIA's Covert Action Program
in Chile Since 1970

1. This Agency did not conduct covert action operations in support of either of the two democratic candidates who opposed Salvador Allende in the 1970 presidential election. Our role in the election was limited to an effort to denigrate Allende and his Popular Unity (UP) coalition during the campaign. Since Allende's inauguration, U.S. policy has been to maintain maximum covert pressure to prevent the Allende regime's consolidation. Under this policy the 40 Committee has approved since January 1971 financial support totaling $6,476,166 for Chilean political parties, media, and private sector organizations opposed to the Allende regime. The attachment provides a summary of the amounts approved by the Committee and the purposes for which these funds were used.

2. Funds [redacted] channeled to opposition forces in Chile through our Santiago Station enabled the three opposition political parties -- Christian Democratic Party (PDC), National Party (PN) and Democratic Radical Party (PDR) -- to improve their internal organizations [redacted] to compete successfully in a number of congressional by-elections. [redacted] These congressional elections were considered by both the UP and the opposition as a form of plebiscite to determine whether or not the government had a popular mandate to continue the implementation of its revolutionary program [redacted]

[redacted]

SECRET

SECRET

-2-

[redacted] Limited support was also made available to private sector organizations, but because some of these groups began to try to provoke a military coup, our funding was confined to specific activities in support of the opposition coalition in the March congressional elections.

3. After the March 1973 elections, it became increasingly apparent that three years of political polarization had strained the fabric of Chilean society to the breaking point. Various U.S. policy options were considered, and on 20 August 1973 the 40 Committee approved an additional $1,000,000 to support opposition political parties and private sector organizations through June 1974; support to the private sector, however, was made contingent on the concurrence of Ambassador Davis and the Department of State. Since this concurrence was not given, no support was provided to the private sector, whose initiative in launching and maintaining a series of crippling strikes was instrumental in provoking the military coup of 11 September 1973. Thus, while the Agency was instrumental in enabling opposition political parties and media to survive and to maintain their dynamic resistance to the Allende regime, the CIA played no direct role in the events which led to the establishment of the new military government.

W. E. Colby
Director

Attachment:
Summary of 40 Committee Approvals

3

Pinochet in Power: Building a Regime of Repression

There are three sources of power in Chile: Pinochet, God, and DINA.
—Chilean intelligence officer to the U.S. defense attaché,
February 6, 1974

The advent of the Pinochet regime was both violent and vicious. In the days following the coup, the military's bloodshed was so widespread that the CIA's own sources could not accurately tally the casualties. "Thus far," the Station reported on September 20, "4,000 deaths have resulted from the 11 September 1973 coup action and subsequent clean-up operations." Four days later the Station cabled estimates of civilian "death figures from 2,000 to 10,000." The new military government admitted to only 244 killed but the U.S. intelligence community knew that number was false. "These figures will not be recorded and, therefore, there will never be an accurate tally of the total deaths," the CIA Station advised on the rampage of repression that followed the military takeover. "Only the Junta members will have a really clear idea of the correct death figures, which they will probably keep secret."[1]

In late October, the CIA did obtain a "highly sensitive" summary on post-coup repression prepared for the new military Junta. The document became the basis for a special secret briefing paper titled "Chilean Executions" prepared for Secretary of State Henry Kissinger.[2] (Doc 1) In the six weeks following the coup, according to the report, the military had massacred approximately 1,500 civilians. Of those, some 320–360 were summarily executed by firing squads while in custody or shot on sight in the street.

The summary estimated that more than 13,500 Chilean citizens had been quickly rounded up through raids and mass arrests aimed at officials of the deposed Popular Unity government, political activists, labor unions, factory workers, and shantytown dwellers. They were being held at approximately twenty detention camps scattered throughout the nation, "only a few [of which]," the CIA reported, "are known to the general public."[3] By far the largest and most infamous known sites were two converted sports arenas—the National Stadium and the smaller Chile Stadium in Santiago. According to statistics compiled in the secret report for the new Junta, a total of 7,612 prisoners were processed through the National Stadium between September 11 and October 20.[4] (Doc 2) All were held incommunicado; many subjected to intense interrogation in locker rooms and luxury skyboxes that the military had transformed into torture chambers.

After savage abuse, numerous prisoners were executed, their bodies buried in secret graves, thrown in the Mapocho River, dropped into the ocean, or dumped at night on city streets. The acclaimed Chilean folk singer, Victor Jara, met such a fate after being imprisoned at the Chile Stadium. His body, discovered in a dirty canal "with his hands and face extremely disfigured, had forty-four bullet holes," according to an inquiry conducted by the Chilean National Commission on Truth and Reconciliation in 1990.[5] Two American citizens, Charles Horman and Frank Teruggi, seized by military squads at their homes following the coup and detained at the National Stadium, were similarly executed.[6]

During a ruthless seventeen-year dictatorship, the Chilean military would be responsible for the murder, disappearance and death by torture of some 3,197 citizens—with thousands more subjected to savage abuses such as torture, arbitrary incarceration, forced exile, and other forms of state-sponsored terror.[7] The majority of the killings and disappearances took place during the first several years of the regime, as it consolidated and institutionalized its repressive rule. Within weeks of the coup, Pinochet created a secret police force empowered to eliminate any and all enemies of his regime. The Junta quickly banned all political activities, closed Congress, suspended political parties, nullified electoral roles, took over the universities, and shut down all but the most right-wing, pro-putsch media outlets in a clear effort to impose a military dictatorship. "Severe repression is planned," the CIA Station bluntly reported on September 21. "There is no indication whatever that the military plans any early relinquishment of full political power in Chile."

Pinochet Ascends

Augusto Pinochet was the last general to sign onto the coup; but after September 11 he quickly positioned himself as Chile's preeminent leader. Originally, the military Junta—formed from heads of the army, air force, navy, and Carabineros—was intended to be a commission of equals, with a rotating presidency. Pursuant to protocol, the Junta named Pinochet, the oldest member and head of the army, as its first chief. "I was elected [Junta president] because I am the oldest," as Pinochet told the press shortly after the coup. But, "after awhile, Admiral Merino will be, then General Leigh, and so on. I am not an ambitious man," he added. "I would not want to seem to be a usurper of power."[8]

In fact, Pinochet moved methodically to distinguish himself from the rest of the Junta and usurp powers the coup plotters had intended to share. His dual role as army commander in chief and head of the Junta afforded him a base of institutional support and concentration of force that he wielded to an autocratic advantage. With the army behind him, Pinochet soon discarded the rotation concept. By June 1974, he had pressured the other Junta members into signing Decree Law 527 naming him "Supreme Chief of the Nation." On December 18, 1974, he assumed the mantle of "President of the Republic"—a title he held until January 1990 when his dictatorship ended.[9]

Both the U.S. intelligence community and the State Department appeared to underestimate Pinochet's individual ruthlessness.[10] A secret post-coup Defense Intelligence Agency Biographic Data report characterized the Chilean general as

> quiet; mild-mannered; very businesslike. Very honest, hard working, dedicated. A devoted, tolerant husband and father; lives very modestly. Drinks scotch and pisco sours; smokes cigarettes; likes parties. (Doc 3)

In an October 12, 1973 cable to Washington, Ambassador Nathaniel Davis described a "gracious and eloquent" private conversation with the budding dictator. "If the Junta government fails, Chile's tragedy [would] be permanent," Pinochet told Davis, seeking U.S. economic and military assistance. When Davis pointed out that human rights issues—the Horman and Teruggi murders high on the list—were already creating political problems, Pinochet responded: "the Chilean government shares fully [your] concern for human rights, and is doing its best to prevent violations and loss of life."[11] (Doc 4)

Only three days after this conversation, Pinochet set in motion a series of massacres that came to be known as "the Caravan of Death." He dispatched General Sergio Arellano Stark, a coup leader and chief enforcer of the new regime, to "expedite" justice in the cases of political prisoners—regional representatives of the Popular Unity government, mayors, police chiefs, prominent trade unionists, and civic leaders—in the northern provinces. Between October 16 and October 19, Stark and a death squad of five officers[12] traveled to the provincial centers of La Serena, Copiapo, Antofagasta, and Calama in a Puma helicopter. During each stop, Stark identified prisoners, most of who had turned themselves in after an official summons. They were removed from their cells, taken away, brutalized, bayoneted and shot. In La Serena: fifteen dead; in Copiapo, sixteen. In Antofagasta, fourteen taken from their cells and executed in the middle of the night; in Calama the next day, twenty-six prisoners shot and stabbed.[13] Over four days, the Caravan left a death trail of sixty-eight individuals. Most of the victims were unceremoniously thrown into common graves; their families denied permission to bury them. Fourteen bodies were never recovered and are considered among the first groups of "desaparecidos" at the hands of the new military regime.

U.S. intelligence knew of these massacres, but reported on them only in vague and incomplete terms. In its biographic report on General Arellano, the DIA noted that he was "considered close to Gen. Pinochet" and part of the "hard line in months after the Sept. 1973 coup because of his summary executions of leftists." The CIA Station generously described Stark's operations as part of a campaign to "neutralize extremists"—although most victims of the Caravan of Death were upstanding civic officials and well-known members of their communities. "The military will continue to act against any person taking belligerent action against law and order," according to a heavily redacted October 25 CIA intelligence report on Pinochet's harsh measures:

> As an example of this type of action General Sergio Arellano gave instructions during a recent trip to the South of Chile, to deal harshly with extremists. As a result of these instructions, six extremists who had been captured were executed. Arellano gave the same instructions in the North and already 15 have been executed there.

Stark himself was acting on instructions. Indeed, more than any other atrocity during his reign, witnesses and evidence tied Pinochet directly to this massacre. When the provincial military commander in charge of the Antofagasta region, General Joaquín Lagos (who was not told of the delegation's true mission) confronted General Arellano and denounced this "monstrous and cowardly crime," Arellano showed him a document signed by Pinochet designating him the *oficial delegado*—official delegate—to "review and accelerate" the judicial process on political prisoners in the north. When Lagos complained directly to Pinochet, he was summoned to Santiago on November 1. After turning in a report attributing dozens of deaths to "the delegate of the Army Commander-in-Chief [General Arellano]," Pinochet sent his assistant to give Lagos the following order: rewrite the report eliminating all references to Arellano's involvement.[14]

As an act of official savagery, these mass executions clearly defined the character of the regime Augusto Pinochet intended to establish. The Caravan of Death reflected a decision at the highest level of the Junta to take vengeance on even nonviolent, civilian supporters of democratic governance. At the same time, it appeared designed to weed out "soft" commanders such as General Lagos—who was forced into retirement within a few months—and dramatically reconstitute Chile's traditionally law-abiding, constitutionalist officer corps for fighting a dirty war. "The official and extraordinary character of this delegation's journey to the north and its degree of authority—from the commander in chief—coupled with what it left in its wake in the form of executions without trial and the blatant impunity with which it operated," as the Commission on Truth and Reconciliation noted, could "only have given officers of the armed forces and the police one signal: there was only one command structure, and it was going to be used with severity."[15]

The Directorate of National Intelligence (DINA)

The murderous mission and message of the Caravan of Death portended the creation of a Chilean secret police agency, DINA. In some respects, DINA represented the institutionalization of the Caravan—a roving instrument of repression, accountable only to Pinochet, intended to eliminate enemies of the state, circumvent civil, legal norms, and strike fear into the populace and less aggressive military services. Initial personnel derived from the caravan team. General Arellano Stark, as the U.S. intelligence learned, was appointed to an elite military commission "tasked by General Pinochet" with preparing a plan for the reorganization of Chile's intelligence agencies that resulted in DINA's creation.[16] Four members of his Caravan death squad were transferred to the new intelligence agency after it was secretly authorized. One, Colonel Pedro Espinoza, quickly became DINA's deputy director, overseeing repressive operations inside the country and acts of international terrorism abroad. A second member, Armando Fernández Larios, played a key role in DINA's most infamous external operation—the Washington, D.C. assassination of Orlando Letelier and Ronni Moffitt. Aside from Augusto Pinochet himself, DINA would become the main pillar of power for the military dictatorship—and its most representative and enduring symbol.

DINA was officially created by Junta decree no. 521 on June 14, 1974. The new law described it as a "specialized agency which can provide systematic processed information . . . in the areas of National Security and Development." Eight published articles of the decree mandated "a military agency of a professional technical nature," composed of personnel from the armed forces, and when necessary, civilian officials. Three final sections remained secret—articles 9, 10, and 11—that provided DINA with its repressive powers to conduct raids, arrests, and secret detentions. U.S. intelligence recognized that the decree provided a statutory foundation for "a Gestapo-type police force" intended to supplant the intelligence units of each branch of the Chilean armed forces. "Taken at face value," the U.S. naval attaché, Gerald Breschta, reported to the DIA, the decree granted

> sweeping investigative powers to the DIRECTOR-DINA. In addition, and equally significant, there are no apparent restrictions to the intelligence operations that the Director can initiate. In total, the law provides legal/official blessing to an organization that is already fully active, and represents a potentially damaging blow to the efforts of the service intelligence organizations to consolidate and enhance their positions.[17]

By the time it was officially constituted, DINA had been operating as a brutal secret police agency for more than six months. Its origins dated back to a "DINA Commission" created after the coup and led by Lt. Col. Juan Manuel Contreras Sepúlveda, a mid-level army administrator with close personal ties to General Pinochet. With Pinochet's blessing, on November 12, 1973, Contreras presented the directors of intelligence for the army, navy, air force, and Carabineros with a blueprint for establishing a national intelligence directorate. Some military officials foresaw DINA as a personal vehicle to enhance Pinochet's power at their expense, but Contreras's plan was quickly approved.[18] On November 17, as the CIA later reported, Pinochet quietly authorized the formal creation of this new secret police force.

DINA was intended to centralize both the gathering of intelligence and the dispensing of repression—operations then being conducted by the individual services. The air force's Servicio de Intelligencia de la Fuerza Aerea, SIFA, became renowned for torture and disappearances. The navy had its Servicio de Intelligencia Naval—SIN. The army ran SIM, the Military Intelligence Service, and DINE, the Directorate of Army Intelligence; the national police had SICAR, the Police Intelligence Service. In late 1973, the services created CECIFA, the Armed Forces Counterintelligence Center, in an effort to coordinate and strengthen their own operations; in 1975, they initiated a "joint command" to track down and eliminate members of the Chilean Communist Party. But while committing countless atrocities, the activities of these agencies paled in comparison to DINA, which, between 1974 and 1977, became the reigning intelligence service engaged in political repression.

DINA began operations as a unit hidden within the National Executive Secretariat for Detainees (SENDET)—a new administrative bureaucracy created in December 1973 ostensibly to handle the mass of civilians being rounded up and held by the new military regime under the state of siege. Portrayed as a mechanism to provide "regular, permanent and coordinated attention" to the plight of thousands of imprisoned Chileans, in reality SENDET provided clandestine cover for DINA, which operated as its so-called "intelligence department." This department, according to the decree establishing SENDET, would

> have as its responsibilities the fixing of norms for interrogations or re-interrogations of the detained; determining the degree of danger (which they pose for the nation); maintaining a permanent coordination with the Intelligence Branches of the Armed Forces, Carabineros and Investigaciones, with the object of exchanging and maintaining current information which they are able to give about the detained.[19]

From the start, DINA became notorious for its brutality, even among the other violent intelligence units in the Chilean armed forces. Agents not only coordinated and conducted interrogations, but also carried out systematic clandestine raids and arrests, while building a network of secret detention and torture centers to extract information from supporters of the former Allende government, terminate and disappear them. In late January 1974, the CIA reported that DINA was committing "incidents which have been the source of embarrassment to the ministry of defense" including secret detentions that the ministry was unaware of and had denied. "[A]s originally predicted," the U.S. defense attaché Col. William Hon reported back to Washington, "it seems as though [DINA] is developing into a KGB-type organization." The rival services were referring to DINA as "the monster," Hon cabled again on February 5, 1974, "reflecting their apprehension about its growing power and size."[20]

At that point, DINA had an estimated 700 agents and officials drawn from ranks of the police, army, and the paramilitary legions of the civilian neo-fascist group Patria y Libertad; by April 1975, it had, in the peculiar parlance of DIA reporting, "blossomed to approximately 2,000 regular members" with an additional force of 2,100 civilian personnel deployed throughout the nation. With funds approved by Pinochet, in 1975 DINA constructed a new twenty-four-story headquarters at the end of Belgrado Street in Santiago to house its massive expansion.

The agency's mission went beyond decimating the left in Chile. DINA also infiltrated a network of spies inside the military government to insure full loyalty to the Pinochet regime, as well as posted its own agents in policy positions to influence the direction the regime took. Operating at every level of the regime served to enhance DINA's power of repression, which Contreras implemented extrajudicially, circumventing the courts and ignoring the legal rules and regulations. "No judge in any court or any minister in the government is going to question the matter further if DINA says they are handling [it]," one source told Hon in early February 1974.[21] The CIA characterized DINA as "an all service (military gendarmerie) intelligence organization," but with Pinochet's blessing, it would become essentially a government-within-a-government. "There are three sources of power in Chile," the informant told Col. Hon: "Pinochet, God, and DINA."[22]

Large as it was, the secret police personnel, organizational structure, resources, and operations remained largely unknown to the Chilean public. They were, however, known to U.S. intelligence. The CIA began collaborating with DINA soon after it was covertly created.[23] The DIA routinely reported on DINA's continuing institutionalization. In June 1975, a high-level source handed an officer of the U.S. Military Group—the unit of American officers at the embassy known as the MilGroup—a comprehensive organizational diagram on Chile's "largest and most influential intelligence organization." (Doc 5) The structural chart showed a vast apparatus, with numerous operational divisions both inside and outside the country. Key "brigades" included: the Metropolitan Intelligence Brigade—known as BIM—which conducted all raids, arrests, and detentions in Santiago; the Economic Brigade "responsible for field operations related to the monitoring of public and private sector business/economic activities;" and the "Citizens Brigade" of informers throughout the country. The diagram also identified a "*secreta*"—a secret brigade close to the director whose function remains unknown.

Col. Contreras devised and supervised all these operations. In late 1973, Pinochet handpicked him as DINA director; U.S. intelligence dated his appointment on February 24, 1974. Contreras had no formal military background in the field of intelligence; he had spent much of his career as a professor and administrator at Chile's military engineering academies. (From September 1966 to September 1967 he attended the U.S. Army Career Officers School at Ft. Belvoir, Virginia, ostensibly taking engineering courses.) But his U.S. Department of Defense biographic report recorded that he had taught a course on "strategy and intelligence" at the Chilean Army War College in the mid-1960s, where then Lieutenant Colonel Pinochet was deputy commandant. The two apparently established a close friendship that enabled Contreras to become Pinochet's closest advisor and ally after the military coup.

A DIA biographic assessment would describe Contreras this way:

> Strong character, with intense loyalty to President Pinochet. Apparent designer, and certainly implementer, of hard line policy. . . . A very intelligent, observing officer with a keen sense of humor. . . . Strongly

> anti-Communist and anti-Marxist to the point that he envisions leftist plots behind every action which seems to him to be counter to Chilean best interests. . . . Extremely capable performer, who is intensely disliked by many, both superiors and peers, because of his ruthless means employed by DINA. While he has ability to achieve higher positions, he will advance only with the personal support of President Pinochet, and could be expected to fall from any position of responsibility without this support.[24]

At the time of the coup, Contreras headed the Military Engineer School at Tejas Verdes, near the port town of San Antonio about sixty miles from Santiago. On September 11, he transformed the engineering school into a detention center known as prison camp no. 2, which became the prototype DINA torture-execution facility.[25] His early success in extracting confessions and disposing of victims helped to catapult Contreras over the military hierarchy to become Pinochet's intelligence chieftain and confident, while providing him with a reputation for viciousness that he institutionalized through the DINA.

Under Contreras's command, DINA became notorious for three defined types of gross human rights violations: a web of secret detention camps, the systematic and inhuman practice of torture, and the disappearances of hundreds of Chileans.

In addition to Tejas Verdes, DINA operated at least a dozen other secret detention and torture facilities in Santiago and throughout the country.[26] These included:

- **Villa Grimaldi**—a walled estate built in 1835 and located in a residential section of the Santiago foothills, which served as the headquarters of BIM, DINA's metropolitan brigade. As DINA's most important facility in the capital, Villa Grimaldi—known within the military as the Terranova barracks—operated around the clock, with hooded prisoners being trucked into the camp at all hours of the night and day, to be abused by rotating shifts of torturers. Victims were housed in small wooden rooms, some no bigger than closets. In a small water tower on the property, DINA guards constructed ten cramped spaces where prisoners were kept after torture but prior to execution. The "tower" proved to be a final station for many who disappeared at the hands of BIM agents.[27]
- **The Discoteque/La Venda Sexy**—a house located on Calle Iran in Santiago served as another DINA torture center. Its name derived from prisoner reports that music was played continuously while var-

ious types of abuses took place and that DINA agents used sexual torture as their preferred form of repression at this facility. Many victims were then disappeared.

- **Londres No. 38**—a facility housed in the former Socialist Party headquarters in the Santiago region. DINA maintained up to sixty prisoners at a time here, before transferring them to harsher camps.
- **Cuatro Alamos**—in a section of the Tres Alamos prison in downtown Santiago, DINA secretly controlled a series of holding cells for prisoners, many of them awaiting transfer from one torture camp to another.
- **Colonia Dignidad**—one of the most secretive facilities used by DINA outside of Santiago, Colonia Dignidad was a cultlike German enclave started by ex-Luftwafte officials from Nazi Germany, located in the Parral province in southern Chile. DINA's regional intelligence brigade operated out of a house owned by the Colonia in Parral. According to the Rettig Commission, "a certain number of people apprehended by DINA were really taken to Colonia Dignidad, held prisoner there for some time, and some of them subjected to torture."

All of these facilities shared a similar modus operandi: blindfolded victims were brought to them after being snatched in their homes or on the street by plainclothed agents in DINA's signature unmarked Ford Falcons. Prisoners were severely abused. One Chilean military officer told the U.S. defense attaché that DINA used a system of interrogation "straight out of the Spanish Inquisition." Each facility specialized in particular forms of torture. At Londres No. 38, for example, DINA agents often rounded up a prisoner's family members and sexually abused them with the prisoner present in order to extract information. Villa Grimaldi was known for its "Chile rooms"—wooden isolation compartments so small that prisoners could not kneel nor lay down.

Other forms of torture were commonly used at all DINA facilities. The Report of the Chilean National Commission on Truth and Reconciliation catalogued the horrific methods favored by DINA practicioners to obtain "intelligence" from prisoners:

- **The Grill:** prisoners would be tied to a metal bedspring and electrical current applied to sensitive body parts, including sexual organs.
- **La Parilla:** a bar on which victims were suspended by the wrists or by wrists and knees for long periods of time. While suspended, victims received electric shocks, and beatings.

- **The Submarine:** forced immersion in a vat of urine and excrement, or frigid water.
- **The Dry Submarine:** use of a cloth bag roped around the head to bring victims to the point of suffocation. This practice was often accompanied with burning victims with cigarettes to accelerate loss of air.
- **Beatings:** administered with gun butts, fists, and chains. In one technique, called "the telephone," according to a survivor, the torturer "slammed his open hands hard and rhythmically against the ears of the victim" leaving the prisoner deaf.[28]

In some camps, routine sadism was taken to extremes. At Villa Grimaldi, recalcitrant prisoners were dragged to a parking lot; DINA agents then used a car or truck to run over and crush their legs. Prisoners there recalled one young man who was beaten with chains and left to die slowly from internal injuries. Rape was also a reoccurring form of abuse. DINA officers subjected female prisoners to grotesque forms of sexual torture that included insertion of rodents and, as tactfully described in the Commission report, "unnatural acts involving dogs."

Few prisoners who were severely tortured lived to provide evidence of these atrocities. DINA agents murdered hundreds of victims. Many of them remain *disaparecidos*—disappeared. Approximately 1,100 Chileans—and one U.S. citizen—vanished during the seventeen-year Pinochet dictatorship—the majority of them at the hands of DINA. Some were killed and buried in secret graves; others were airlifted in a helicopter and thrown into the ocean by DINA agents "after first cutting their stomach open with a knife to keep the bodies from floating," states the Rettig Commission report. Making victims simply disappear was a particularly cruel method of terrorizing the opposition, inflicting psychological injuries on surviving family members, while avoiding legal constraints and evidence of responsibility and criminal accountability.[29]

But many families and human rights workers in Chile did hold the military regime and its secret police accountable, as did the international community. DINA's involvement in secret detention, torture, and disappearances drew strong and continuous condemnation from around the world. "The Pinochet regime moves across the world scene like a metal duck in a shooting gallery," CIA analysts lamented in a top-secret report titled, "Chile: Running the Gauntlet," dated in early 1976. "Its assailants have plenty of ammunition based on the excesses accompanying Salvador Allende's overthrow and the alleged abuses that still mark Chile's security and detention practices."[30] Contreras, rather than Pinochet, became a lightening rod for criticism. U.S. intelligence analysts declared him "the number one obstacle" to the improvement of human rights in Chile. During a private meeting with CIA officials, Assistant Secretary of State for Inter-American Affairs William D. Rogers told his colleagues privately what no U.S. official would state publicly: The DINA chieftain had become "the most notorious symbol of repression in Chile."[31]

Pinochet and DINA

The June 1974 decree that established DINA stated clearly that it would be "a military agency . . . directly subordinate to the government Junta." Pinochet would propagate this myth for years. "I could never say that I was actually running DINA," Pinochet argued in his last interview while detained in London. "[They] were under the orders, under the supervision of all of the Junta, the four members of the Junta."[32]

In fact, the Junta never supervised DINA operations, and from its inception to its closure, Contreras took orders only from Pinochet himself. "The DINA," as the U.S. defense attaché reported only several weeks after it was formed, "is directly subordinate to Junta President Pinochet."[33] Another DIA report dated in April 1975 reiterated: "Col. Contreras has reported exclusively to, and received orders only from President Pinochet." Two years later, a CIA report on DINA's responsibility for "the recent increase in torture, illegal detentions, and unexplained 'disappearances,' " stated that "Contreras answers directly to the President, and it is unlikely that he would act without the knowledge and approval of his superior." (Doc 6)

Pinochet exercised sole control over DINA because it provided him with much of his ability to consolidate his authority. Not only did Contreras's agents severely repress any opposition from the left; DINA also spied on and intimidated anyone who dared to disagree with Pinochet from within his own military. When the head of the Armed Forces Counterintelligence Center (CECIFA), Lt. Com. Raul Monsalve complained about DINA's operations and Contreras's relation with Pinochet, other high military officials warned him to "moderate" his objections or "face the possibility that DINA personnel would fabricate an incident which would destroy his career and get him out of their way," witnesses told U.S. officials. Such threats were made, and carried out, repeatedly during DINA's tenure. "One of Pinochet's major sources of power is the National Directorate of Intelligence (DINA), an organization whose principal mission is internal security but which is extending its influence to ever-growing areas of activity," the U.S. embassy cabled the

State Department in mid-1975. "DINA reports directly to Pinochet and is ultimately controlled by him alone."[34]

Pinochet not only controlled DINA, he empowered its rapid expansion at the expense of other sectors of the military. He gave Contreras carte blanche in establishing personnel levels at the DINA and backed him as he drew agents and staff away from the other services while forcing them to foot the payroll bills. In January 1975, Contreras drafted, and Pinochet signed, an order giving DINA sole responsibility for persecuting the MIR, the regime's number-one counterinsurgency target. Pinochet also ordered the air force intelligence unit, which Contreras considered a particular rival, to disband and turn over its operations to DINA.

As international complaints about Chile's gross violations of human rights escalated, Pinochet used them in an Orwellian effort to broaden DINA's power. In September 1975, the CIA Station learned that Pinochet had "conducted a personnel investigation into human rights practices and violations by the armed forces" and determined that prisoners held by some of the intelligence units were being abused. He then ordered the interior and defense ministers "to issue a secret decree to the heads of all the services clearly stating the authorization and procedures for detentions throughout the country."

Purportedly intended to improve Chile's human rights record, Pinochet's secret decree in fact bestowed maximum latitude on the main agency responsible for the majority of atrocities. The September 22 order, obtained by CIA operatives, established DINA as the sole agency responsible for detentions, exempting it from obligation to report its activities to the courts or the other military services:

> The directorate of national intelligence, DINA is authorized to conduct detentions of persons suspected of subversion or political activity throughout the country. In any case in the Santiago area in which the armed forces, carabineros or the [deleted] in the course of their patrol duties detain individuals engaged in subversive activity, the detainees must be immediately turned over to DINA. . . . DINA will act as the Central coordinator for all detention decrees.[35]

DINA's monolithic growth created intense rivalries and strains within the regime as other members of the military sought to assert their influence on Chile's future. Threatened by Contreras's power, and expressing concern about DINA's "barbaric" practices, a number of military officers sought out CIA and Defense Department officials and shared stories of efforts to persuade Pinochet to reign in DINA operations. In April 1975, several army officers tried "to convince the president that DINA should be subject to the direction and control of a National Security Council type of authority rather than just the presidency," the DIA reported. "To date, the president has not received these suggestions with enthusiasm."

Even U.S. military officers began to express concern about the implications of DINA's power. In comments attached to a detailed intelligence report on DINA's expansion, U.S. defense attaché, Capt. J.R. Switzer, described DINA's development as "a particularly disturbing phenomenon":

> The apprehension of many senior Chilean military authorities regarding the possibility of DINA becoming a modern day Gestapo may very well be coming to fruition: DINA's autonomous authority is great, and increasing. Junta members are apparently unable to influence President Pinochet's decisions concerning DINA activities in any way. Regarding DINA organization, policies and operations Colonel Contreras' authority is near absolute—subject only to an unlikely Presidential veto. (Doc 7)

Until the end of 1975, the U.S. MilGroup viewed this phenomenon as evidence that Contreras had taken control—over Pinochet himself. "With the rapid growth of DINA into almost every aspect of the government, this office at times felt that the organization and its leaders had gotten out of hand and that the tail might be wagging the dog in Chile," the defense attaché cabled Washington. But during a dinner party with "a very senior DINA official"—perhaps Contreras himself—the U.S. air force attaché in Santiago, Lt. Col. Lawrence Corcoran, gathered intelligence on Pinochet's personal involvement in the operations of his secret police. Contreras met Pinochet every morning at 7:30 A.M., and privately briefed him on "the coming events and status of existing DINA activities," this official informed Corcoran. "The president issues instructions on DINA; is aware of its activities; *and in fact heads it.*" (Emphasis added.)

"Brigada Exterior": The External Section

As DINA advanced its effort at wiping out all opposition to the regime, Pinochet and Contreras decided to expand Chile's secret police functions. DINA's mission would not be limited to internal security but would build an extraterritorial operational capability to neutralize threats from abroad—particularly the vocal international solidarity and human-rights network that focused worldwide attention on Pinochet's atrocities. The organizational diagram of DINA, obtained by U.S. intelligence, listed a "Brigada Exterior." This section, a Chilean source reported, was made up of "DINA operatives who conduct traditional intelligence operations in foreign countries." (See Doc 5)

The Exterior Brigade, however, did not conduct "traditional" operations. Instead of gathering intelligence on the military capabilities and attitudes of potentially hostile governments posing national security threats, the DINA's foreign branch focused on three main missions: forging alliances with other secret police forces, as well as violent anticommunist and neo-fascist groups, in the Southern Cone, United States, and Europe; tracking Pinochet's critics abroad, and organizing acts of international terrorism against prominent exiles. (See Chapter 6) To spy on exile movements and activities, DINA posted agents and assets in Chilean embassies around the world, and among the personnel serving the national airline, as well as at international airports, including those in New York. Drawing on the CIA's organizational model, Contreras ordered the creation of DINA stations abroad to facilitate these operations, with agents operating under civilian, rather than military, cover.

In the spring of 1974, DINA established its first station in Buenos Aires. There, according to the Rettig Commission report, Chilean agents engaged in the "investigation, surveillance, apprehension, and even elimination of opposition Chileans who had taken refuge [in Argentina]." Subsequently, an undercover agent was based at the Chilean embassy in Madrid, Spain with responsibility for Western Europe. Contreras also tried to insert DINA representatives in France, England, and West Germany to help track the movements of exiled Chilean politicians and more militant groups working across the continent. In 1976, DINA, in collaboration with the secret police services in Argentina and Uruguay, apparently attempted to open a station in Miami, Florida.[36]

In their contacts and secret calls, DINA agents used a code name, "Luis Gutierrez," to refer to the international division. The division had a unique communications and computer system, separate from the rest of the directorate. Army Maj. Raúl Iturriaga Neumann oversaw the operations of Brigada Exterior, although Contreras exercised close control of this special unit through his deputy, Pedro Espinoza. The Brigade drew its staff from Chilean military personnel, and recruited a number of civilians from the ranks of violent rightist groups such Patria y Libertad.

But the most famous member of DINA's foreign branch was not Chilean: he was an American, born in Waterloo, Iowa, named Michael Vernon Townley. Townley was the son of a Ford Motor Company overseas manager. He had moved with his family to Chile at age fourteen and, only four years later, married a twenty-six-year old Chilean woman, Inés Mariana Callejas, with three small children. His first job in Chile in the early 1960s was an encyclopedia salesman. In 1967, Townley and his family moved to Miami, Florida where he became both familiar and friendly with the hard-line, and often violent, anti-Castro Cuban exile community. After Salvador Allende was elected in Chile in September 1970, Townley's anticommunist Cuban friends urged him to contact the CIA and return to Chile to play an undercover role in efforts to undermine the new Chilean government.[37]

As he prepared to return to Chile, Townley did approach the CIA in December 1970 to offer his services as a covert asset against the Allende government. Two months later, according to records of the Agency's Office of Security, the Directorate of Operations (DO) requested "preliminary security approval to use Mr. Townley in an operational capacity." It is not clear how, or if, the CIA employed Townley over the next year, but on December 21, 1971, the DO alerted the Office of Security that the Station had cancelled its interest in him as an agent.[38]

By then Townley was a fixture at the Santiago embassy—an "embassy barnacle" as one diplomat characterized him. (Townley's handwritten name, telephone number, and address at 1454 Oxford St. appear on the inside flap of one 1971 embassy telephone directory.) He spent considerable time hanging out with various U.S. attachés and officials—Frederick Purdy, David Stebbing, Jeffrey Davidow among them—passing on information about his anti-Allende activities.

He had stories to share. Townley was now an operative with Patria y Libertad (PL), the avowedly pro-fascist paramilitary group that modeled itself after Hitler's Brownshirts. He headed a commando unit responsible for bombings and acts of economic sabotage using Molotov cocktails. Townley also applied his self-taught skills as an electronics expert to design electronic surveillance equipment that allowed Patria y Libertad to intercept radio transmissions between Allende, his guards and party officials—tapes of which were then provided to the U.S. embassy. He became renowned in the extremist opposition community for building and deploying mobile radio transmitters and illicit, anti-Allende television stations. When the government tried to scramble those transmissions, Townley led a PL raid in March 1973 to disable a jamming device at a TV station in the city of Concepcion. During the operation, Townley gagged and hog-tied a homeless man who was using the station as shelter. He was found dead of asphyxiation the next day. Now a fugitive, Townley fled Chile to Miami.

Wanted for murder in Chile, Townley simply waited until the Allende government had been overthrown to return to his adopted country and rejoin his colleagues from Patria y Libertad to celebrate their anticommunist victory.

On October 3, he obtained a fake Florida driver's license under the alias Kenneth Enyart. On October 5, he received a new U.S. passport using that name. Five weeks after the coup, Townley flew back to Santiago.

Before leaving Miami, however, he met with an old friend from the U.S. embassy, David Stebbing, and provided him with significant information. In a letter to the State Department's Chile desk officer, Stebbing provided a debriefing of Townley that covered coup plotting, Patria y Libertad, and the murder in Concepcion. Prior to the coup, Townley reported, "an assassination squad had been formed by Chilean exiles" to kill up to twenty-five members of Allende's government.

> If there had been no intervening coup, they would have acted in October. The plan was for 6 or 8 people to enter Chile no more than 2 or 3 days before the target date and to pick off as many of their unbodyguarded targets as possible within a space of 3 or 4 hours.

Now that the coup had been completed Patria y Libertad members were "showing up as key officials or advisors throughout the new government," Townley advised. "Many of his friends are not at all bothered by the term 'Fascist,' " Stebbing reported. "Mike" expected to return to Chile within a few days, and "will probably be in contact with the embassy again." As Stebbing presciently predicted, "he may someday be in trouble again."

Indeed, Townley returned to Santiago and immediately resumed his quest to work with the United States as an operative or informant. Embassy files record numerous contacts between him and U.S. personnel. Aware that Townley was a fugitive in the Concepcion murder case, the American consul, Fred Purdy, nevertheless welcomed him back and provided him with a new, clean, passport in his real name. In December 1973, Townley called attaché Jeffrey Davidow to report that he was "working with the same Patria y Libertad types he knew prior to the coup, and that the group is accepting assignments from military intelligence." Townley told Davidow that he was "eager to establish an intelligence relationship with the embassy." In a biographic memorandum drafted in June 1974, Davidow described Townley as an "AMCIT [American citizen] with rather unsavory past with crypto-fascist Chilean groups . . . suggest keeping him at arms length."[39] But just two months later another embassy officer, Michael Lyons, accepted a dinner invitation with Townley and his wife, Ines, and reported that the expatriate American was still interested in being a "conduit for information" for the United States.

By then, Townley was a DINA agent. In the late spring of 1974, Contreras's deputy, Col. Pedro Espinoza, recruited him into the service of the secret police; within several months Contreras had provided Townley with an alias, Juan Andres Wilson, a large home to use as a base, and a four-member team for operations.[40] As a committed, rabid, anticommunist U.S. citizen, Townley provided DINA with multiple skills and opportunities. "My husband was [not] an imitation James Bond," his wife would write in a lengthy handwritten account of Townley's DINA career:

> But I certainly can state that DINA found his knowledge of electronics, English, and purchasing extremely useful. Add to that the fact that as an American he had free access to the United States at any moment without having the need for hard-to-get visas. My husband, moreover, had qualities that made him especially effective in the intelligence community: a bright mind, an incredible memory, and a fail-safe determination and loyalty. And he was absolutely convinced that the military government and Señor Pinochet were the best things that ever could have happened to Chile.[41]

Townley became the Brigada Exterior's leading assassin. In September 1974 he carried out his first major mission—the cold-blooded car bomb attack that killed former Chilean commander in chief Carlos Prats and his wife in Buenos Aires. In the spring of 1975, his DINA superiors sent him to Mexico City in a failed effort to blow up a convention center filled with exiled former members of the Allende government. That September, he arranged an assassination plot in Rome, Italy, that left the exiled leader of the Christian Democratic party, Bernardo Leighton, and his wife critically wounded. And in September 1976, he organized and implemented DINA's most infamous operation: the car bomb assassination of former Chilean minister Orlando Letelier and his American colleague, Ronni Karpen Moffitt in downtown Washington, D.C. Although his name was not known at the time, in the mid-1970s Michael Townley ranked among the world's most active—and dangerous—international terrorists.

Project Andrea

From the laboratory basement of his DINA-owned mansion in the Lo Curro district of Santiago, Townley directed another top-secret DINA operation with tremendous terrorist potential: the creation of a biological weapon of mass destruction. Code-named "ANDREA," the project reflected the Pinochet regime's desire to possess a secret weapon that could be used in the event of war against Chile's neighbors, Peru or Argentina. Townley, and a team of chemists, developed, manufactured, and stored a nerve gas with the scientific name *Isopropylmethylphosophonofluoridate*—commonly known as Sarin.

Sarin is extremely lethal. Even a few drops can bring the quick and painful death of hundreds of people; a military delivery system would kill thousands. The gas, according to an FBI memorandum on Project ANDREA distributed by then director William Webster, "vaporizes on being exposed to the atmosphere, producing droplets that enter the body through the skin or lungs to interdict the neurochemistry that permits the respiratory muscles to function." The Japanese cult Aum Shinrikyo used Sarin in the Tokyo subway gas attack that killed twelve people and wounded 500 in March 1995. The Bush administration also believed Sarin to be part of Saddam Hussein's alleged arsenal of chemical warfare weapons in Iraq.

Townley's mission, as Taylor Branch and Eugene Propper wrote in their book *Labyrinth*, was to "develop a weapon that [would] be extremely lethal to large masses of people but whose effects c[ould] be localized within a relatively small area."[42] After studying the chemical work of German scientists during operations in Europe in the summer of 1975, Townley procured laboratory equipment and compounds from a British chemical engineering company, Gallenkamp; he also purchased a large microwave oven and rented gas storage canisters in Miami. The equipment was paid for out of a special DINA account, under the fictitious company Prosin Ltd., at the Southeast First National Bank in Miami, Florida.

By the time of the mission to kill Letelier in Washington, D.C., DINA had manufactured significant amounts of Sarin and Townley was working on a military delivery system that would allow the gas to be deployed in a wartime setting. But he had also opened his nerve gas laboratory to representatives of the Cuban National Movement, a violent anti-Castro organization that collaborated in various DINA assassination missions including the Letelier bombing. The CNM members, as Townley later told his FBI interrogators, "requested that the Cuban Nationalist Movement be furnished a supply of nerve gas to utilize in their terrorist activities." (Doc 8)[43]

Townley himself considered the possibility that Sarin could be utilized in a terrorist mission. In preparation for the assassination of Orlando Letelier, he took a small quantity of the nerve gas, put it into a Chanel No. 5 perfume bottle and transported it aboard a LAN-Chile flight to the United States. As Townley would later admit, he considered the possibility that a female DINA agent could get close enough to Letelier to deploy the gas, or that he could toss the Chanel bottle into Letelier's car at a stop sign or red light. Once in Washington, however, he resorted to his signature weapon—a car bomb—and eventually returned the gas to a secure DINA storage facility in Santiago.[44]

The National Center for Information (CNI)

The Letelier mission, while accomplishing Contreras's objectives, brought about DINA's dissolution. The shadow cast over Chile's military as an institution strengthened the hand of the Contreras's enemies in the high command to the point where they convinced General Pinochet to dissolve DINA and reorganize the intelligence service. On August 13, 1977, the Junta issued decree law No. 1876 abolishing DINA, citing the need to restructure "in accord with present circumstances the functions of an agency created during a situation of internal conflict that has now been surpassed." A second decree, No. 1878, issued the same day, established the National Center for Information, CNI, and authorized it to take over DINA's staff, properties, and budgets. Whereas DINA reported to Pinochet, U.S. military intelligence advised in a cable, "DINA Dissolved," the CNI supposedly would report to the Ministry of Interior and would not have the power of arrest and detention of its predecessor. (Doc 9) But Contreras remained as director, meaning that this change in the structure of the secret police was in name only.

Between August and November, Chilean intelligence agents at Contreras's direction conducted a string of bombings, robberies, kidnappings, and killings, all of which the CNI blamed on "extremists." In fact, as U.S. intelligence quickly reported, Chilean military agents were attempting to orchestrate a climate of chaos and terrorism, to exaggerate the leftist threat. In one coordinated operation, the Chilean secret police blew up two suspected safe houses, killing several people, and then blamed the explosions on the left. "Arrests and prosecutions would 'take months,' " one Chilean official explained to the U.S. military attaché, but "an explosion would produce speedy justice."[45]

In early November, high-ranking military commanders met with Pinochet again and demanded that Contreras be relieved of his duties as CNI director. Chile's international image on human rights, they argued, would never improve as long as he remained. On November 4, Pinochet abruptly removed Contreras—he was promoted from colonel to brigadier general and given a post at the Army Engineering School—and appointed one of DINA's critics, General Odlanier Mena, as new CNI director. According to a CIA intelligence report filed on November 9, Pinochet realized "that as long as the leadership of the CNI remains basically the same as its predecessor organization, DINA, many critics of the Chilean government will insist that no real change has taken place." CIA informants claimed that Contreras was "completely shocked" at his ouster. One source compared Contreras, once the most feared and loathed individual in Chile, to "a cuckolded husband who is the last to realize his wife was being unfaithful."[46]

According to the Defense Intelligence Agency, General Mena would "probably improve Chile's claims of housecleaning within the security community." But CNI proved to be qualitatively, if not quantitatively, as repressive as its predecessor. The levels of political killings abated between 1978 and 1980, but as organized protests against the regime escalated so did CNI's acts of repression. CNI agents would eventually be charged in several of the most gruesome atrocities committed toward the end of the dictatorship, including the killing of trade union leader Tucapel Jimenez in February 1982 and the decapitation murders of three Chilean professors in March 1985. Between 1978 and 1985, the Chilean Commission on Truth and Reconciliation estimated, fatal human rights violations committed by the regime totaled 160 people. "Most of them are attributed to the CNI."[47]

DOCUMENT 1. Department of State, **SECRET** Memorandum for Henry Kissinger, "Chilean Executions," and "Fact Sheet-Human Rights in Chile," November 27, 1973.

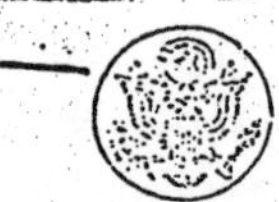

DEPARTMENT OF STATE

BRIEFING MEMORANDUM

S/S

7321744

SECRET - NODIS

TO: The Secretary

FROM: ARA - Jack B. Kubisch

Chilean Executions

You requested by cable from Tokyo a report on this subject.

-- On October 24 the Junta announced that summary, on-the-spot executions would no longer be carried out and that persons caught in the act of resisting the government would henceforth be held for military courts. Since that date 17 executions following military trials have been announced. Publicly acknowledged executions, both summary and in compliance with court martial sentences, now total approximately 100, with an additional 40 prisoners shot while "trying to escape". An internal, confidential report prepared for the Junta puts the number of executions for the period September 11-30 at 320. The latter figure is probably a more accurate indication of the extent of this practice.

-- Our best estimate is that the military and police units in the field are generally complying with the order to desist from summary executions. At least the rather frequent use of random violence that marked the operations of these units in the early post-coup days has clearly abated for the time being. However, there are no indications as yet of a disposition to forego executions after military trial.

-- The Chilean leaders justify these executions as entirely legal in the application of martial law

SECRET - NODIS
XGDS

under what they have declared to be a "state of siege in time of war". Their code of military justice permits death by firing squad for a range of offenses, including treason, armed resistance, illegal possession of arms and auto theft. Sentences handed down by military tribunals during a state of siege are not reviewable by civilian courts.

The purpose of the executions is in part to discourage by example those who seek to organize armed opposition to the Junta. The Chilean military, persuaded to some degree by years of Communist Party propaganda, expected to be confronted by heavy resistance when they overthrew Allende. Fear of civil war was an important factor in their decision to employ a heavy hand from the outset. Also present is a puritanical, crusading spirit -- a determination to cleanse and rejuvenate Chile. (A number of those executed seem to have been petty criminals.)

The Junta now has more confidence in the security situation and more awareness of the pressure of international opinion. It may be a hopeful sign that the Junta continues to stall on bringing to trial former cabinet ministers and other prominent Marxists -- people the military initially had every intention of standing up before firing squads. How the military leaders proceed in this area from now on will be influenced to some degree by outside opinion, and particularly by ours, but the major consideration will continue to be their assessment of the security situation.

At Tab A is a Chile situation report and at Tab B a fact sheet on human rights in Chile.

Attachments:

Tab A - Situation Report
Tab B - Fact Sheet

SECRET - NODIS
XGDS
Drafted: ARA:HWShlaudeman:mph
Ext. 23542:11/16/73

FACT SH[illegible] -- HUMAN RIGHTS IN CHILE
(Prepared November 15, 1973)

Figures without asterisk are from public sources.

Total arrested in Chile since September 11	13,500*
Arrested originally and held in National Stadium in Santiago	7-8,000
Released from Stadium	6,500
Presently held in Stadium	0
Detained in Santiago jails	550
Detained outside Santiago	2,000
Estimated number serving sentence or pending trial	1,500*
Executions acknowledged	100 (approx)
Executions according to intelligence source	320*
Number killed attempting to escape military custody	40
American citizens detained (27 detainees had been released by October 17)	0
American citizens dead since coup	2
Safeconducts issued to asylees in Embassies	1,791
Safeconducts issued to others	3,100
Safeconduct requests not yet acted upon	408
Departed from Chile (Chileans and foreigners)	2,000 (approx)
Foreigners registered with UNHCR for permanent resettlement	
In safe havens (refugee camps, etc.)	820
At home (possibly some under house arrest)	824
In diplomatic missions	172
In GOC detention centers	203
Total number still in foreign Embassies	N.A. (368 a/o mid-Oct
Total dead: According to Chilean authorities	600 (approx)
According to Barnes article in October 8 Newsweek	2,796
According to October 21 Washington Post article on CIA Director Colby's statement to Congressional Committee	2-3,000
Recent SRF source estimate	1,500*

SECRET

DOCUMENT 2. CIA, **SECRET** Intelligence Report [Executions in Chile Since the Coup], October 27, 1973.

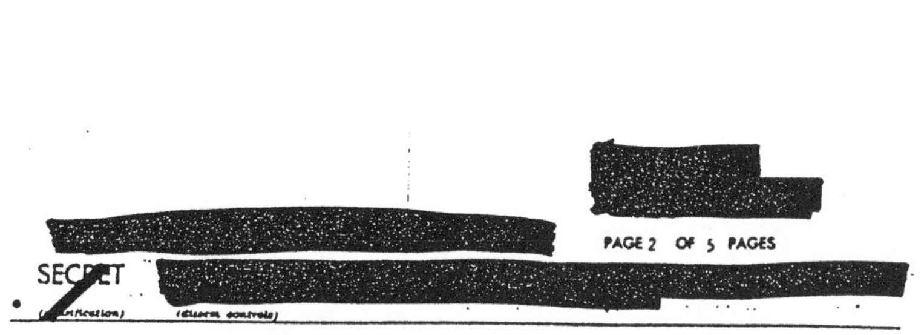

PAGE 2 OF 5 PAGES

SECRET

(classification) (dissem controls)

1.5.(C)

1. ACCORDING TO [redacted] HIGHLY SENSTIVE FIGURES PREPARED FOR THE JUNTA INDICATE THAT A TOTAL OF 1,020 DEATHS OF CIVILIANS AND ARMED FORCES PERSONNEL OCCURRED DURING THE PERIOD 11 THROUGH 30 SEPTEMBER 1973 AS THE RESULT OF THE 11 SEPTEMBER COUP. DURING THIS PERIOD IN SANTIAGO, 22 MEMBERS OF THE ARMED FORCES AND 624 CIVILIANS DIED AS A RESULT OF MILITARY ACTIONS. IN ADDITION, A TOTAL OF 240 CIVILIANS WERE EITHER EXECUTED BY FIRING SQUADS AFTER SUMMARY MILITARY TRIALS OR EXECUTED ON THE SPOT FOR ARMED RESISTANCE AGAINST MILITARY FORCES. DURING THE SAME PERIOD OUTSIDE OF SANTIAGO, AT TOTAL OF EIGHT ARMED FORCES MEN WERE KILLED; 46 CIVILIANS WERE KILLED DURING MILITARY ACTIONS; AND 80 CIVILIANS WERE EITHER EXECUTED ON THE SPOT OR KILLED BY FIRING SQUADS AFTER MILITARY TRIALS. [redacted] COMMENT: THESE FIGURES DO NOT REFLECT THE NUMBER OF CARABINEROS (UNIFORMED NATIONAL POLICE) KILLED DURING THIS TIME PERIOD NOR DO THE FIGURES REFLECT THE EXECUTION OF KNOWN CRIMINALS AND DELINQUENTS BY THE DEPARTMENT OF IN-

S E C R E T

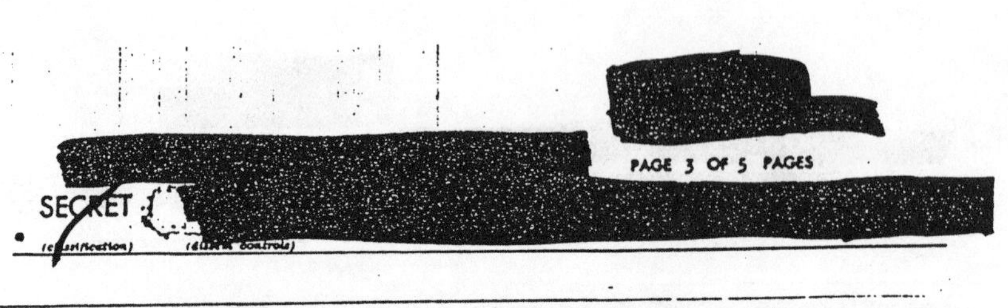
PAGE 3 OF 5 PAGES

SECRET

(classification) (dissem controls)

VESTIGATIONS (DI, CHILEAN CIVIL POLICE), BECAUSE FIGURES ARE NOT BEING KEPT ON THESE LATTER CATEGORIES. [redacted] COMMENT:

A. [redacted] D AN UNOFFICIAL ESTIMATE THAT ABOUT 1,600 CIVILIAN DEATHS OCCURRED BETWEEN 11 SEPTEMBER AND 10 OCTOBER, WITH NO ESTIMATE OF MILITARY AND POLICE CASUALTIES. IT IS NOT KNOWN IF THE 1,600 FIGURE INCLUDED COMMON CRIMINALS. ALSO, IT IS IMPORTANT TO NOTE THE DIFFERENCE IN TIME PERIODS COVERED IN THESE TWO REPORTS. 1.5 (c)

B. ON [redacted] OCTOBER, [redacted] THAT AT HIGH LEVELS IN THE JUNTA GOVERNMENT THERE IS A REALIZATION THAT THE OFFICIAL DEATH FIGURES WILL HAVE TO BE RAISED, BECAUSE THE PUBLIC DOES NOT BELIEVE THE FIGURE (ABOUT 600) USUALLY QUOTED BY THE GOVERNMENT. IF A DECISION IS MADE TO RAISE THE NUMBER, IT WILL BE PLACED AT SLIGHTLY OVER 1000. THE MOST ACCURATE NUMBER, HOWEVER, IS APPROXIMATELY 1,500.) 1.5 (c)

2. [redacted] BETWEEN 11 SEPTEMBER

SECRET

313

PAGE 4 OF 5 PAGES
SECRET
(classification) (dissem controls)

AND 10 OCTOBER A TOTAL OF 13,500 PRISONERS HAD BEEN REGISTERED AS DETAINED BY THE ARMED FORCES, CARABINEROS AND THE DI THROUGHOUT THE COUNTRY. AS OF 10 OCTOBER A TOTAL OF 2,300 PRISONERS WERE BEING HELD IN ARMED FORCES DETENTION CENTERS THROUGHOUT CHILE, BUT NOT INCLUDING SANTIAGO. 680 PRISONERS HAD BEEN SENTENCED UNDER THE MILITARY JUSTICE SYSTEM AND WERE SERVING TERMS IN PRISON CAMPS. IN ADDITION, A TOTAL OF 2,360 PRISONERS WERE BEING HELD IN CARABINERO AND DI FACILITIES WHILE THEIR CASES WERE BEING TRIED. A TOTAL OF 360 COMMON CRIMINALS HAD ALSO BEEN DETAINED, TRIED AND SENTENCED BETWEEN 11 SEPTEMBER AND 10 OCTOBER.

3. [redacted] THAT AS OF 20 OCTOBER, A TOTAL OF 7,812 PRISONERS HAD BEEN PROCESSED THROUGH THE DETENTION CENTER AT THE NATIONAL STADIUM IN SANTIAGO. OF THIS NUMBER, 2,112 HAD BEEN GIVEN UNCONDITIONAL LIBERTY AND HAD NO FURTHER CHARGES AGAINST THEM; 2,408 HAD BEEN PLACED IN CONDITIONAL LIBERTY AND CONTINUED UNDER INVESTIGATION; 1,840 INDIVIDUALS CHARGED WITH MINOR CRIMES HAD BEEN PLACED IN LIBERTY FOLLOWING PAYMENT OF A BAIL; 522 DETAINEES HAD BEEN SENT TO PUBLIC JAILS AFTER MILITARY TRIALS; AND 680 HAD BEEN SENT TO PRISON CAMPS CONTROLLED BY THE ARMED FORCES. AN ADDITIONAL 250 CASES WERE PENDING. ONCE THE

1.5 (c)

SECRET

PAGE 4 OF 4

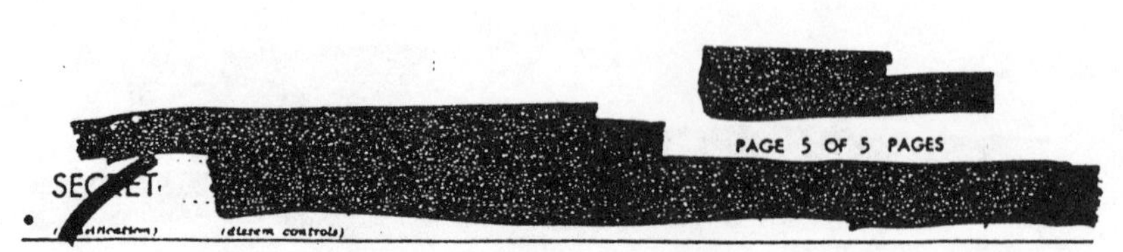
PAGE 5 OF 5 PAGES

SECRET

(classification) (dissem controls)

NATIONAL STADIUM IS CLOSED AS A DETENTION CENTER. ALL FUTURE DETAINEES ARE TO BE SENT TO CARABINERO AND DI FACILITIES FOR PROCESSING AND CONTROL. [redacted] COMMENT: THE GOVERNMENT HAS ANNOUNCED THAT THE NATIONAL STADIUM IS BEING CLEARED OF PRISONERS TO ALLOW TIME FOR PREPARATIONS FOR THE WORLD CUP SOCCER MATCH BETWEEN CHILE AND THE USSR TO BE HELD THERE IN LATE NOVEMBER.)

4. THE ARMED FORCES IS ADMINISTERING OVER 20 DETENTION SITES THROUGHOUT THE COUNTRY. OF THIS NUMBER ONLY A FEW, SUCH AS DAWSON ISLAND, ARE KNOWN TO THE GENERAL PUBLIC.

5.

1.5 (c)

SECRET

DOCUMENT 3. Defense Intelligence Agency, **SECRET** Biographic Data on General Augusto Pinochet, January 1975.

UNCLASSIFIED

~~SECRET~~

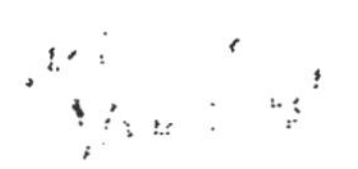

BIOGRAPHIC DATA

CHILE
Gen Augusto PINOCHET Ugarte
January 1975

(U) NAME: Gen Augusto Pinochet Ugarte (pee-noh-CHET), Army.

(U) POSITION: President (chief of state since 12 Sept 1973; position officially named President of the Government Junta, 12 Sept 1973-June 1974; Supreme Chief of the Nation and Head of the Executive Branch June-Dec 1974; President since 18 Dec 1974); and Commander in Chief of the Army (since 24 Aug 1973).

(U) 1973

~~(S/NFD)~~ SIGNIFICANCE: Gen Pinochet, an intelligent, ambitious, professionally competent and experienced Infantry officer, is widely admired and respected by fellow officers. He became President and the strongest member of the Government Junta (composed of the four service commanders) following the 11 Sept 1973 military coup, the first in Chile since 1931, which overthrew the government of Marxist-Socialist Salvador Allende Gossens (President, 1970-1973). In June 1974, the Junta structure changed and Pinochet became head of the executive branch of the government, while continuing as head of the Junta, which became the legislative branch. Gen Pinochet would have preferred that the Armed Forces, and particularly the Army, remain in their traditional role as a professional, apolitical force that does not involve itself with partisan politics. The deteriorating economic and political situation, however, forced Pinochet reluctantly to join in the military intervention. The Junta abolished Congress and all political parties but claims to be moving towards a return to democracy. It is most concerned with rebuilding Chile, especially the economy; obtaining foreign arms purchases and making other preparations against the threat of war with Peru; and improving Chile's world image regarding human rights.

~~(S/NFD)~~ POLITICS:

~~(C/NFD)~~ International: Anti-Communist and anti-Cuban, Gen Pinochet has always spoken favorably of, and desires to keep close ties with, the United States. He has twice travelled to the U.S. He favors the acquisition of U.S. equipment and the training of Chilean military personnel in U.S. service schools. He shares the common concern of most Chilean Army officers over the threat of a possible invasion of Chile by Peru. Pinochet has served as an Instructor at the Ecuadorean Army War College and has travelled to Mexico and the Canal Zone.

UNCLASSIFIED

CLASSIFIED BY DI
EXEMPT FROM GENERAL DECLASSIFICATION SCHEDULE OF EXECUTIVE ORDER 11652
EXEMPTION CATEGORY 2
DECLASSIFY ON 31 Dec 2005

NO FOREIGN DISSEM
~~SECRET~~

Declassified by DIA

UNCLASSIFIED

~~SECRET~~

CHILE
Gen Augusto PINOCHET Ugarte
January 1975

~~(S/NFD)~~ Internal: Gen Pinochet is conservative in his political thinking. It is believed that he remained basically apolitical during the administration of President Allende, viewing the government as legally and constitutionally elected. Pinochet enjoyed the complete confidence of Eduardo Frei Montalva (President, 1964-1970).

~~(C/NFD)~~ PERSONAL DATA:

(U) Birth: 25 Nov 1915 in Valparaíso, Chile.

~~(C/NFD)~~) Family: Wife, Lucía Hieriart Rodríguez de Pinochet (born about 1926; of French ancestry; Roman Catholic; married about 1943; charming, attractive; socially at ease; family is very close; has long been interested in and directed a Catholic assistance program for illegitimate children; in 1973 allegedly strongly denounced the then Army Commander in Chief, Carlos Prats González, for his "lackey" relationship with President Allende). Children (5): Lucía (f), born about 1944 (married; is an infant-welfare specialist); Augusto (m), born about 1946 (a military officer); María Verónica (f), born about 1950 (married; is a computer programmer); Marco Antonio (m), born about 1957; Jacqueline Marie (f), born about 1959. One daughter lived with her husband, an engineer, in Panama.

~~(C/NFD)~~) Description: Caucasian. Large build (5'10", 180 lbs): dark brown hair, green eyes, oval face; fair complexion; has a mustache; wears glasses for reading; quiet; mild-mannered; very businesslike. Very honest, hard working, dedicated. A devoted, tolerant husband and father; lives very modestly. Drinks scotch and pisco sours; smokes cigarettes; likes parties. Sports interests are fencing, boxing, and horseback riding. Member of Geographic Society of Chile. He is well known as a military geographer and has authored three geography books, at least one of which is used as a secondary-school textbook. Enjoys discussing world military problems and would respond to a frank, man-to-man approach.

(U) Languages: Native Spanish, some French and English.

(U) Religion: Roman Catholic.

(U) Decorations: Colombian Order of Merit General José María Córdoba. Ecuadorean Abdón Calderon Star (Gold). Peruvian Military Order of Ayacucho. Chilean Military Star of the Armed Forces (Grand Star for Military Merit, for 30 years' service); Goddess Minerva Medal; Minerva Medal.

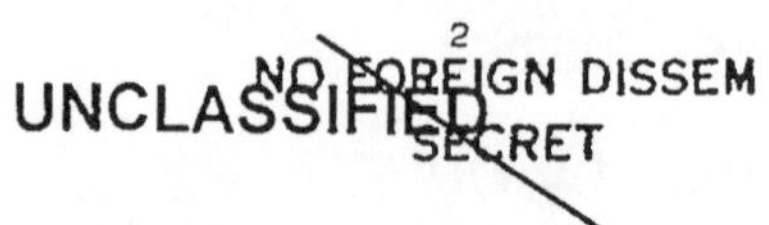

UNCLASSIFIED

~~SECRET~~

CHILE
Gen Augusto PINOCHET Ugarte
January 1975

(U) *CIVIL EDUCATION*: Secondary school presumably in Chile. Attended courses on judicial and social sciences at the University of Chile for 2 years (dates not known).

(U) CAREER:

1933-1937	-Cadet, Military Academy, Santiago, Mar 1933-Jan 1937. Commissioned Probationary 2d Lt in Infantry, 1 Jan 1937.
1937-1938	-Assigned to 6th "Chacabuco" Infantry Regiment. Promoted to 2d Lt, 1937; to 1st Lt, 1938.
1939	-Assigned to 2d "Maipo" Infantry Regiment.
1940-1941	-Student, Infantry School, San Bernardo.
1942-1946	-Instructor, Army War College, Santiago. Promoted to Capt, 1946.
1947	-Assigned to 5th "Carampangue" Infantry Regiment, Iquique.
1948	-Government Delegate to the Schwager Coal Mines (merged with Lota Coal Mines in 1963), located near Concepción.
1948	-Assigned to 9th Infantry Regiment.
1949-1951	-Student, Command and General Staff Course, Army War College.
1952	-Assigned to the Military Academy. Promoted to Maj, 1952.
1953	-Operations Officer, 4th "Rancagua" Infantry Regiment, Arica.
1954	-Instructor, Army War College.
1955	-Aide to Subsecretary for Army, Ministry of National Defense.
1956-1959	-Instructor, Military Geography, Ecuadorean Army War College, Quito.
1960	-Staff Officer, Headquarters, 1st Infantry Division, Antofagasta. Promoted to Lt Col, 23 Jan 1960.
1961-1963	-Commander, 7th "Esmeralda" Infantry Regiment, Antofagasta.
1964-1968	-Deputy Commandant, Chilean Army War College, Jan 1964-Jan 1968. *Member, orientation tour of U.S. and Canal* Zone, Jan-Feb 1965. Promoted to Col, 23 Jan 1966.
1968	-Chief of Staff, 2d Army Division, Santiago. Official visit to U.S. and Canal Zone, Jan-Feb. Promoted to Brig Gen, 31 Dec 1968.
1969-1971	-Commander, 6th Army Division, Iquique. Promoted to Maj Gen, 30 Dec 1970.
1971-1972	-Commander, Santiago Garrison, Mar 1971-Jan 1972.
1972-1973	-Chief of the Army General Staff, Jan 1972-Aug 1973. Concurrently served as Acting Commander in Chief of the Army, Nov 1972-Mar 1973, Apr-June 1973, and Aug 1973. Official visit to Mexico for Independence Day celebrations and to the Canal Zone, Sept 1972.

NO ~~FOREIGN~~ DISSEM

~~SECRET~~

UNCLASSIFIED

DOCUMENT 4. U.S. Embassy, Cable, "Conversation with Pinochet," October 12, 1973.

O 122330Z OCT 73
FM AMEMBASSY SANTIAGO
TO SECSTATE WASHDC IMMEDIATE 6158

[redacted] SANTIAGO 4992

Chile Project (#S199900006)
U.S. Department of State
✓ Release ___ Excise ___ Deny ✓ Decla
Exemption(s) ___

EO 11652: GDS
TAGS: CI, PINT
SUBJ: CONVERSATION WITH PINOCHET

1. AT COLOMBUS DAY RECEPTION TODAY JUNTA PRESIDENT PINOCHET SAID HE WOULD LIKE A QUIET MOMENT TO TALK - SO I WENT BY HIS OFFICE AT 7 P.M. TONIGHT.

2. PINOCHET WAS GRACIOUS AND ELOQUENT IN EXPRESSING DISAPPOINTMENT AT MY TRANSFER. HE SAID CHILE GREATLY NEEDED OUR HELP, BOTH ECONOMIC AND MILITARY ASSISTANCE. HE ADDED THAT IF THE JUNTA GOVERNMENT FAILS, CHILE'S TRAGEDY WILL BE PERMANENT. I TOOK THE OCCASION TO POINT OUT THAT POLITICAL PROBLEMS WE ARE ENCOUNTERING AT THIS TIME. A DISCUSSION OF THE KENNEDY AMENDMENT, TERUGGI AND HORMAN CASES, AND THE HUMAN RIGHTS PROBLEM ENSUED. PINOCHET INDICATED THAT THE CHILEAN GOVERNMENT SHARES FULLY OUR CONCERN FOR HUMAN RIGHTS, AND IS DOING ITS BEST TO PREVENT VIOLATIONS AND LOSS OF LIKE. HE ADDED THAT THIS IS NOT EASY, AS THE LEFT EXTREMISTS CONTINUE TO ATTACK OFFICERS AND SOLDIERS, ENGAGE IN SNIPING AND ATTEMPT ACTS OF SABOTAGE. HALF OF THE EXTREMISTS' ARMS, PINOCHET SAID, ARE STILL AVAILABLE TO THEM, AND MOTOR AND BAZOOKA FACTORIES AND ALL MATTER OF OTHER ILLICIT ARMS MANUFACTURING CONTINUE TO BE UNCOVERED. IF THE ARMY SHOULD LET THIS PROBLEM GET OUT OF HAND, THE RESULT WOULD BE FAR GREATER BLOODSHED THAN CHILE IS PRESENTLY EXPERIENCING. IF THE LEFT EXTREMISTS HAD HAD THEIR WAY, AND HAD CARRIED OUT THEIR OWN AUTOGOLPE PLAN,

[redacted]

[redacted]

PAGE 02 SANTIA 04992 122347Z

THERE WOULD HAVE BEEN A MILLION DEAD. NEVERTHLESS, CHILE SHARES OUR CONCERN
AND IS DOING ITS BEST. (THE FOREGOING CONVERSATION WAS

CLEARLY UNDERSTOOD BY PINOCHET TO BE PRIVATE AND IN CONFIDENCE).

3. I REITERATED ASSURANCES OF THE GOOD WILL OF THE USG AND OUR DESIRE TO BE HELPFUL. I NOTED THAT WE HAD SOME PROBLEMS WHICH WOULD OBLIGE US TO DEFER CONSIDERATION OF CHILEAN REQUESTS IN SOME AREAS. SO FAR AS ECONOMIC AND MILITARY AID ARE CONCERNED, I SAID WE WOULD WANT TO WAIT BEFORE ADDRESSING THIS QUESTION UNTIL THE KENNEDY AMENDMENT WAS CLARIFIED THROUGH A SENATE-HOUSE CONFERENCE. REGARDING COPPER, PINOCHET SAID CHILE REALIZES IT SHOULD PAY COMPENSATION. HE ADDED, HOWEVER, THAT CHILE IS BROKE, AND WILL NEED SOME HELP GETTING ON ITS FEET IF IT IS TO BE ABLE TO MEET THESE AND OTHER OBLIGATIONS. HE ASSERTED THAT A LARGE PART OF SOVIET AND EASTER EUROPEAN AID HAD BEEN "A FRAUD", AS CHILE HAD HAD TO PAY FOR IT IN COPPER.

4. IN CONCLUSION PINOCHET SAID HE WOULD LIKE TO GET TOGETHER AGAIN AFTER HUERTA'S RETURN, WHEN HUERTA AND THE JUNTA HAD HAD THE OPPORTUNITY TO SORT OUT THE RESULTS OF HUERTA'S U.S. TRIP.
DAVIS

[redacted]

DOCUMENT 5. Defense Intelligence Agency, Report, "Organization Diagram of the Directorate of National Intelligence (DINA)," June 17, 1975.

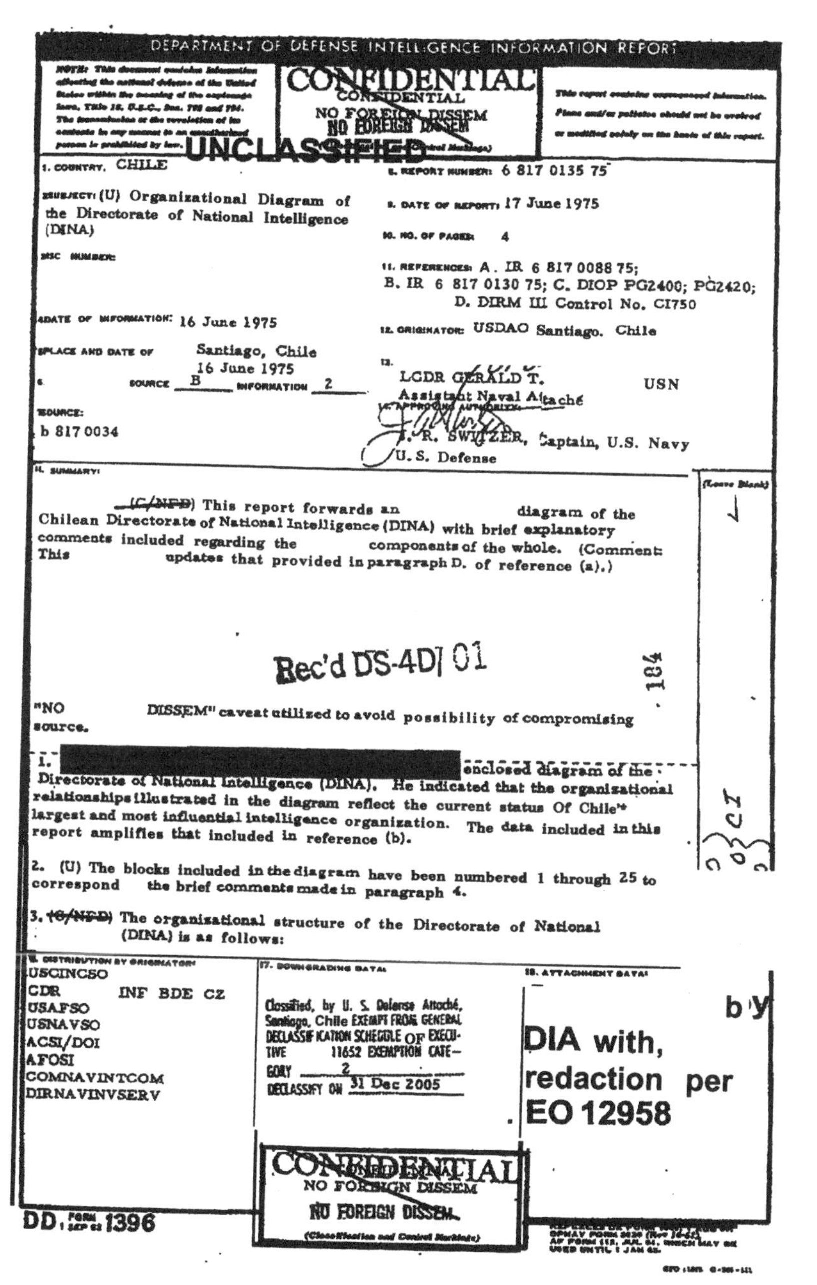

DEPARTMENT OF DEFENSE INTELLIGENCE INFORMATION REPORT

NOTE: This document contains information affecting the national defense of the United States within the meaning of the espionage laws, Title 18, U.S.C., Sec. 793 and 794. The transmission or the revelation of its contents in any manner to an unauthorized person is prohibited by law.

CONFIDENTIAL
CONFIDENTIAL
NO FOREIGN DISSEM
NO FOREIGN DISSEM
UNCLASSIFIED

This report contains unprocessed information. Plans and/or policies should not be evolved or modified solely on the basis of this report.

1. COUNTRY: CHILE

SUBJECT: (U) Organizational Diagram of the Directorate of National Intelligence (DINA)

REPORT NUMBER: 6 817 0135 75

DATE OF REPORT: 17 June 1975

NO. OF PAGES: 4

REFERENCES: A. IR 6 817 0088 75; B. IR 6 817 0130 75; C. DIOP PG2400; PG2420; D. DIRM III Control No. CI750

DATE OF INFORMATION: 16 June 1975

ORIGINATOR: USDAO Santiago, Chile

PLACE AND DATE OF: Santiago, Chile 16 June 1975

SOURCE B INFORMATION 2

LCDR GERALD T. USN
Assistant Naval Attaché

APPROVING AUTHORITY:
J. R. SWITZER, Captain, U.S. Navy
U.S. Defense

SOURCE:
b 817 0034

SUMMARY:

~~(C/NFD)~~ This report forwards an diagram of the Chilean Directorate of National Intelligence (DINA) with brief explanatory comments included regarding the components of the whole. (Comment: This updates that provided in paragraph D. of reference (a).)

Rec'd DS-4D] 01

"NO DISSEM" caveat utilized to avoid possibility of compromising source.

1. [redacted] enclosed diagram of the Directorate of National Intelligence (DINA). He indicated that the organizational relationships illustrated in the diagram reflect the current status Of Chile's largest and most influential intelligence organization. The data included in this report amplifies that included in reference (b).

2. (U) The blocks included in the diagram have been numbered 1 through 25 to correspond the brief comments made in paragraph 4.

3. ~~(C/NFD)~~ The organizational structure of the Directorate of National (DINA) is as follows:

DISTRIBUTION BY ORIGINATOR:
USCINCSO
CDR INF BDE CZ
USAFSO
USNAVSO
ACSI/DOI
AFOSI
COMNAVINTCOM
DIRNAVINVSERV

DOWNGRADING DATA:
Classified, by U. S. Defense Attaché, Santiago, Chile EXEMPT FROM GENERAL DECLASSIFICATION SCHEDULE OF EXECUTIVE 11652 EXEMPTION CATEGORY 2
DECLASSIFY ON 31 Dec 2005

ATTACHMENT DATA:

by DIA with, redaction per EO 12958

CONFIDENTIAL
NO FOREIGN DISSEM
NO FOREIGN DISSEM
(Classification and Control Markings)

DD FORM 1 SEP 62 1396

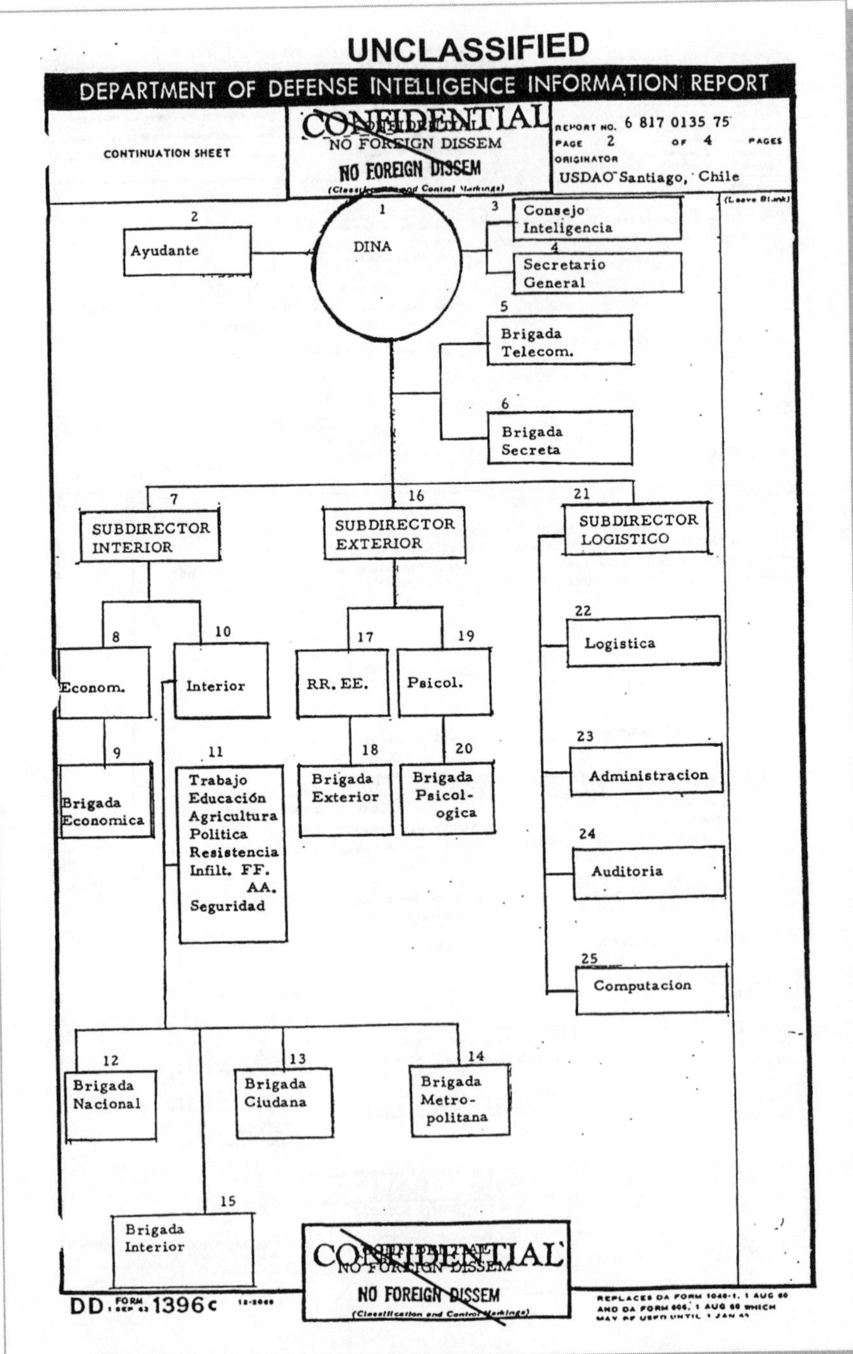
UNCLASSIFIED

DEPARTMENT OF DEFENSE INTELLIGENCE INFORMATION REPORT

CONTINUATION SHEET

CONFIDENTIAL
NO FOREIGN DISSEM
NO FOREIGN DISSEM
(Classification and Control Markings)

REPORT NO. 6 817 0135 75
PAGE 2 OF 4 PAGES
ORIGINATOR
USDAO Santiago, Chile

(Leave Blank)

DD FORM 1 SEP 63 1396c

CONFIDENTIAL
NO FOREIGN DISSEM
NO FOREIGN DISSEM
(Classification and Control Markings)

REPLACES DA FORM 1048-1, 1 AUG 60 AND DA FORM 806, 1 AUG 60 WHICH MAY BE USED UNTIL 1 JAN 63

DEPARTMENT OF DEFENSE INTELLIGENCE INFORMATION REPORT

UNCLASSIFIED
CONTINUATION SHEET

CONFIDENTIAL
CONFIDENTIAL
NO FOREIGN DISSEM
NO FOREIGN DISSEM
(Classification and Control Markings)

REPORT NO. 6 817 0135 75
PAGE 3 OF 4 PAGES
ORIGINATOR
USDAO Santiago, Chile

(Leave Blank)

4. ~~(C/NFD)~~

1. Director of DINA

2. Aide to the Director

3. Intelligence Committee - called into being by the Director to discuss specific intelligence problems or operations. Membership varies depending on the nature of the problem under discussion

4. General Secretary for administrative matters within the Director's office

5. Telecommunications Brigade - manages record correspondence distribution and filing and controls distribution of electronic sensors

6. Secret Brigade - function unknown

7. Subdirector of the Interior - responsible for intelligence operations within Chile

8. Economic Section - responsible for monitoring the activities of public and private business/economic interests to insure compliance with government economic policy

9. Economic Brigade - responsible for field operations related to the monitoring of public and private sector business/economic activities

10. Interior Section - responsible for combating real or perceived internal subversion

11. Interior Sub-sections - place special emphasis on subversive activities within the fields of Labor, Education, Agriculture, Political Activity, Resistance, Infiltration of the Armed Forces and Internal Security

12. National Brigade - field operatives who are full time DINA employees both military and civilian who usually work outside of Santiago

13. Citizen's Brigade - civilians, some of which work full or part time without pay, or part time with pay. They usually act as informers. They normally work outside of Santiago.

14. Metropolitan Brigade - Full and part time DINA operatives working only in Santiago

15. Interior Brigade - mobile units that deploy from Santiago to outlying areas

16. Subdirector of the Exterior - responsible for intelligence operations outside of Chile.

17. Foreign Relations Section - plans traditional intelligence operations to be conducted outside of Chile

18. Exterior Brigade - DINA operatives who conduct traditional intelligence operations in foreign countries

CONFIDENTIAL
CONFIDENTIAL
NO FOREIGN DISSEM
NO FOREIGN DISSEM
(Classification and Control Markings)

DD FORM 1 SEP 62 1396c 12-2040

REPLACES DA FORM 1048-1, 1 AUG 60 AND DA FORM 608, 1 AUG 60 WHICH MAY BE USED UNTIL 1 JAN 63.

PAGE 4 OF 4

DEPARTMENT OF DEFENSE INTELLIGENCE INFORMATION REPORT

UNCLASSIFIED CONFIDENTIAL
CONTINUATION SHEET
NO FOREIGN DISSEM
NO FOREIGN DISSEM
(Classification and Control Markings)

REPORT NO. 6 817 0135 75
PAGE 4 OF 4 PAGES
ORIGINATOR
USDAO Santiago, Chile

(Leave Blank)

19. Psychological Section - plans psychological operations to be conducted outside of Chile (such as influencing the information published by foreign media)

20. Psychological Brigade - DINA operatives who conduct psychological operations in foreign countries (not necessarily different than the operatives discussed in item 19)

21. Subdirector for Logistics - responsible for ensuring that DINA logistical requirements are satisfied

22. Logistics Section - maintains physical control of an provides for supplies used by DINA

23. Administrative Section - provides administrative services to all sections and subsections within the DINA

24. Legal Section - provides legal services and advice to DINA plans and policy makers

25. Computer Section - provides computer services (such as biographic records)

COMMENT: ~~(C/NFD)~~ This report is the third in a series initiated by reference (b), and tends to confirm the continuing institutionalization of the Directorate of National Intelligence.

DD FORM 1 SEP 62 1396c 12-2040

CONFIDENTIAL
NO FOREIGN DISSEM
NO FOREIGN DISSEM
(Classification and Control Markings)

REPLACES DA FORM 1048-1, 1 AUG 60 AND DA FORM 806, 1 AUG 60 WHICH MAY BE USED UNTIL 1 JAN 63.

DOCUMENT 6. CIA, **SECRET** Report, "Chile: Violations of Human Rights," May 24, 1977 (Page 1).

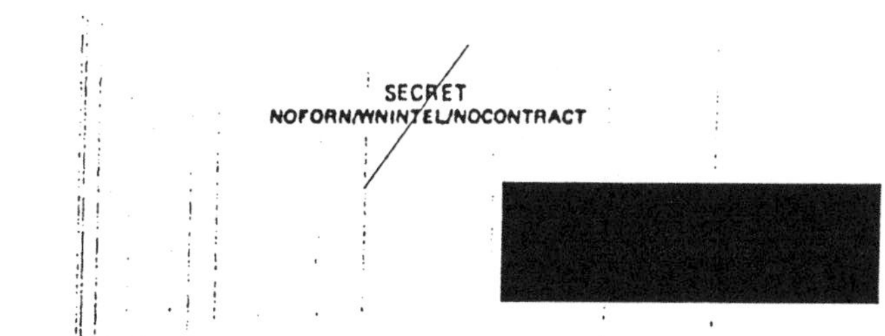

SECRET
NOFORN/WNINTEL/NOCONTRACT

Chile: Violations of Human Rights

Reports of gross violations of human rights in Chile, which had nearly ceased earlier this year, are again on the rise. [redacted] the Pinochet government is reverting to the practices that have jeopardized its international standing since the 1973 coup. 1.5C

This backsliding comes at a particularly bad time for Chile, since apparent improvement in the human rights situation was helping improve its image abroad. Critics will now have additional ammunition for their attacks on the Chilean regime and their appeals to boycott it.

Chile's National Intelligence Directorate is apparently behind the recent increase in torture, illegal detentions, and unexplained "disappearances." The Directorate's chief, Colonel Manuel Contreras, is a close confidant of Pinochet, who acclaimed the organization in a recent press interview for its "decisive role" in bringing extremism under control. Contreras answers directly to the President, and it is unlikely that he would act without the knowledge and approval of his superior.

Colonel Manuel Contreras

[redacted]
24 May 1977

1

SECRET

DOCUMENT 7. Defense Intelligence Agency, Report, "Directorate of National Intelligence (DINA) Expands Operations and Facilities," April 15, 1975.

PAGE 1 OF 3

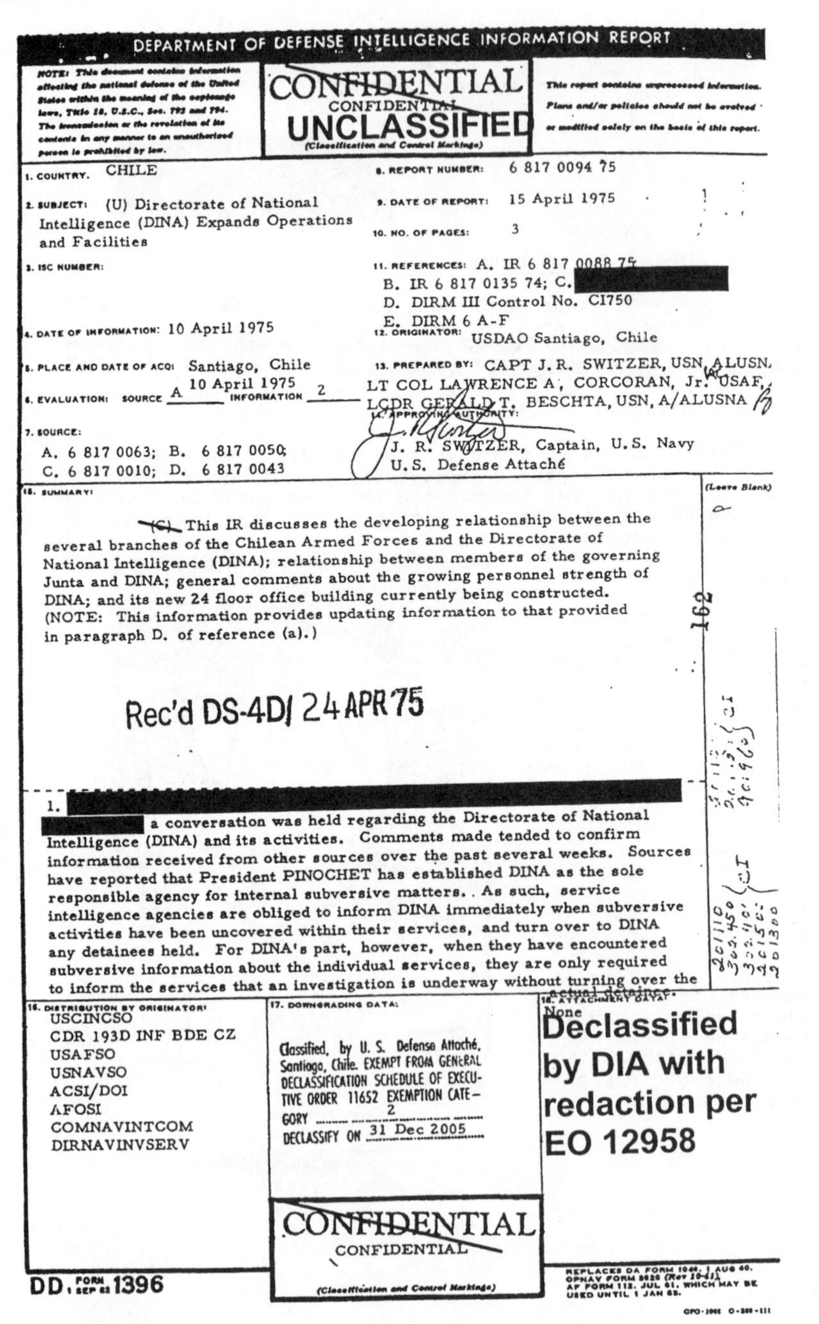

DEPARTMENT OF DEFENSE INTELLIGENCE INFORMATION REPORT

NOTE: This document contains information affecting the national defense of the United States within the meaning of the espionage laws, Title 18, U.S.C., Sec. 793 and 794. The transmission or the revelation of its contents in any manner to an unauthorized person is prohibited by law.

~~CONFIDENTIAL~~ CONFIDENTIAL UNCLASSIFIED (Classification and Control Markings)

This report contains unprocessed information. Plans and/or policies should not be evolved or modified solely on the basis of this report.

1. COUNTRY: CHILE
2. SUBJECT: (U) Directorate of National Intelligence (DINA) Expands Operations and Facilities
3. ISC NUMBER:
4. DATE OF INFORMATION: 10 April 1975
5. PLACE AND DATE OF ACQ: Santiago, Chile 10 April 1975
6. EVALUATION: SOURCE A INFORMATION 2
7. SOURCE: A. 6 817 0063; B. 6 817 0050; C. 6 817 0010; D. 6 817 0043
8. REPORT NUMBER: 6 817 0094 75
9. DATE OF REPORT: 15 April 1975
10. NO. OF PAGES: 3
11. REFERENCES: A. IR 6 817 0088 75 B. IR 6 817 0135 74; C. [redacted] D. DIRM III Control No. CI750 E. DIRM 6 A-F
12. ORIGINATOR: USDAO Santiago, Chile
13. PREPARED BY: CAPT J. R. SWITZER, USN, ALUSN, LT COL LAWRENCE A. CORCORAN, Jr. USAF, LCDR GERALD T. BESCHTA, USN, A/ALUSNA
14. APPROVING AUTHORITY: J. R. SWITZER, Captain, U.S. Navy U.S. Defense Attaché

15. SUMMARY:

~~(C)~~ This IR discusses the developing relationship between the several branches of the Chilean Armed Forces and the Directorate of National Intelligence (DINA); relationship between members of the governing Junta and DINA; general comments about the growing personnel strength of DINA; and its new 24 floor office building currently being constructed. (NOTE: This information provides updating information to that provided in paragraph D. of reference (a).)

Rec'd DS-4D/ 24 APR 75

1. [redacted] a conversation was held regarding the Directorate of National Intelligence (DINA) and its activities. Comments made tended to confirm information received from other sources over the past several weeks. Sources have reported that President PINOCHET has established DINA as the sole responsible agency for internal subversive matters. As such, service intelligence agencies are obliged to inform DINA immediately when subversive activities have been uncovered within their services, and turn over to DINA any detainees held. For DINA's part, however, when they have encountered subversive information about the individual services, they are only required to inform the services that an investigation is underway without turning over the actual detainee.

16. DISTRIBUTION BY ORIGINATOR: USCINCSO, CDR 193D INF BDE CZ, USAFSO, USNAVSO, ACSI/DOI, AFOSI, COMNAVINTCOM, DIRNAVINVSERV

17. DOWNGRADING DATA: Classified by U.S. Defense Attaché, Santiago, Chile. EXEMPT FROM GENERAL DECLASSIFICATION SCHEDULE OF EXECUTIVE ORDER 11652 EXEMPTION CATEGORY 2 DECLASSIFY ON 31 Dec 2005

18. ATTACHMENT DATA: None

Declassified by DIA with redaction per EO 12958

~~CONFIDENTIAL~~ CONFIDENTIAL (Classification and Control Markings)

DD FORM 1 SEP 62 1396

REPLACES DA FORM 1046, 1 AUG 60, OPNAV FORM 3820 (Rev 10-61), AF FORM 112, JUL 61, WHICH MAY BE USED UNTIL 1 JAN 63.

DEPARTMENT OF DEFENSE INTELLIGENCE INFORMATION REPORT

CONTINUATION SHEET

~~CONFIDENTIAL~~ CONFIDENTIAL ~~UNCLASSIFIED~~

(Classification and Control Markings)

REPORT NO. 6 817 0094 75
PAGE 2 OF 3 PAGES
ORIGINATOR-
USDAO Santiago, Chile

(Leave Blank)

2. ~~(C)~~ Additionally, the original DINA personnel manning level of 1500 persons has blossomed to approximately 2000 regular members (the great majority of which are active duty military personnel), augmented by some 2100 additional civilian personnel located throughout the country, that work on an on-call basis (most part time but some full time). The 2100 civilians (only some of which are paid for their services) constitute a subordinate unit to DINA named BRIGADA INTELIGENCIA CIUDANA (Citizens Intelligence Brigade). During operations, members of this civilian unit work in company with regular DINA operatives if arrests are to be made. Apparently President PINOCHET has given the DINA Director, Colonel Juan Manuel CONTRERAS Sepulveda, a free hand in establishing personnel requirements for DINA. An example given by source A. indicated that in late 1974, DINA tasked Navy to provide an additional 40 female/clerical personnel to their rolls. When the Navy indicated their lack of personnel assets, DINA independently contracted 40 civilian females to work for their organization, and subsequently assigned pay and housing responsibilities to the Navy. This rather high-handed measure reportedly received the approval of President PINOCHET, and the Navy has had to accept the situation (with no evident complaint being voiced by Admiral MERINO). Attempts by service intelligence agencies to check DINA's growth have been effectively countered by Colonel CONTRERAS. The Navy, in an attempt to place a responsible and loyal officer in the position of Deputy Director of DINA has found that the chosen man, Captain Rolando GARCIA LeBlanc has apparently turned his allegiance to DINA instead of the Navy. The Air Force, in an attempt to diminish the authority of DINA tried to have its previous Deputy Director, Colonel Mario JAHN Barrera removed. Colonel JAHN refused to leave his position, and in a showdown with CINC of the Air Force, retained his position as a DINA Deputy Director. The end result was that DINA now has one Director, and two Deputy Directors.

3. ~~(C)~~ The relationship between DINA and the several branches of the armed forces vary considerably. The NAVY has adopted a rather pragmatic attitude, recognizing that they have neither the monetary, material nor personnel assets to conduct the widespread anti-subversion activities that characterize DINA operations. As a result, they seldomfind themselves with conflicting interests vis a vis DINA (the personnel situation discussed above representing an exception). Usually, when DINA uncovers subversive activities within the Naval community, they advise Navy Intelligence who then is kept abreast of the DINA operation. The CARABINEROS have a working relationship with DINA very similar to that of the Navy for the same reasons. However, ARMY/DINA relations have been considerably less cordial. Army Intelligence, headed by a general officer and operating with an impressive budget has been most reluctant to "knuckle under" to the wishes of DINA, headed by an Army Colonel. Army Intelligence Chief General MENA (and General POLLONI before him) is consistently irritated by the abrasive attitude of Colonel CONTRERAS, and resents the expansion of DINA operations into what are considered Army domains. He, and several other flag officers of the various services, are quite concerned about the "barbaric" tactics employed during some DINA operations. Much of the blame is attributed to poorly trained DINA agents operating under inadequate supervision. The AIR FORCE, like the Army, has strained relations with DINA. Air Force Intelligence was antagonized during the first days of 1975 when the total responsibility for anti-MIR operations was given to DINA by order of President PINOCHET (drafted by Colonel CONTRERAS). The Air Force center of anti-subversive activities located at the Air Force War Academy was disestablished and all duties previously under Air Force cognizance have been transferred to DINA. The Air Force Director of Counterintelligence, Colonel OTAIZA was

~~CONFIDENTIAL~~

~~CONFIDENTIAL~~

DD FORM 1 SEP 62 1396c

REPLACES DA FORM 1046-1, 1 AUG 60 AND DA FORM 606, 1 AUG 60 WHICH

DEPARTMENT OF DEFENSE INTELLIGENCE INFORMATION REPORT

CONTINUATION SHEET

~~CONFIDENTIAL~~ ~~CONFIDENTIAL~~ UNCLASSIFIED
(Classification and Control Markings)

REPORT NO. 6 817 0094 75
PAGE 3 OF 3 PAGES
ORIGINATOR USDAO Santiago, Chile

(Leave Blank

was given a secondary position under the Director of Air Force Intelligence.

4. ~~(C)~~ Junta relations with DINA have changed considerably since the early days of the intelligence organizations establishment. When Colonel CONTRERAS was building DINA, he was quick to ensure that the rapport between himself and the Junta was maintained at a high level. It was during the early days that the Colonel was calling for considerable support from the various services in the form of personnel assets. But since the promulgation of Decree Law No. 521, officially establishing DINA as the national intelligence arm of the government (ref (b) refers), Colonel CONTRERAS has reported exclusively to, and received orders only from President PINOCHET. A facade of politeness is maintained with the other three members of the Junta, but their opinions and/or advice is neither sought nor desired by DINA's Director. This situation has prompted several Army officers to try and convince the President that DINA should be subject to the direction and control of a National Security Council type of authority rather than just the Presidency (ref (c) refers). To date, the President has not received these suggestions with enthusiasm. The original concept that DINA would be an intelligence body to support all of the Junta members no longer exists.

5. ~~(C)~~ When DINA was first setting-up operations, their headquarters were located in three houses on Belgrado Street in Santiago (near the intersection of Vicuña McKenna and Rancagua). Presently, however, they have been authorized funds by the President, and are building a 24 story building at the end of Belgrado Street to serve as their national headquarters. The expected completion date of this new headquarters is as yet unknown.

COMMENT: ~~(C)~~ DINA's current pattern of growth is not consistent with any form of democratic control or management of its activities. The apprehensions of many senior Chilean military authorities regarding the possibility of DINA becoming a modern day Gestapo may very well be coming to fruition. DINA's autonomous authority is great, and increasing. Junta members are apparently unable to influence President PINOCHET's decisions concerning DINA activities in any way. Regarding DINA organization, policies and operations, Colonel CONTRERAS' authority is near absolute - subject only to an unlikely Presidential veto. DINA's development is a particularly disturbing phenomenon in view of the Chilean government's desire to enhance their international image. Any advantage gained by humanitarian practices can easily be offset by terror tactics (even if on a relatively small scale) on the part of poorly trained and supervised DINA operatives.

~~CONFIDENTIAL~~
~~CONFIDENTIAL~~

DD FORM 1 SEP 65 1396c 12-2069 REPLACES DA FORM 1048-1, 1 AUG 60

DOCUMENT 8. FBI, Memorandum from William Webster [Project Andrea—Chile's Nerve Gas Program], December 9, 1981.

U.S. Department of Justice

Federal Bureau of Investigation

Office of the Director

Washington, D.C. 20535

Date: December 9, 1981

To: Administrator
Federal Aviation Administration
800 Independence Avenue, SW
Washington, D. C. 20591

From: William H. Webster
Director

Subject: GUILLERMO NOVO SAMPOL; ALVIN ROSS DIAZ; VIRGILIO PABLO PAZ ROMERO; JOSE DIONISIO SUAREZ ESQUIVEL; IGNACIO ROBERTO NOVO SAMPOL; MICHAEL VERNON TOWNLEY; JUAN MANUEL CONTRERAS SEPULVEDA; ARMANDO FERNANDEZ LARIOS; PEDRO ESPINOSA BRAVO; VICTIMS - ORLANDO LETELIER; RONNI KARPEN MOFFITT; PROTECTION OF FOREIGN OFFICIALS - MURDER; EXPLOSIVES AND INCENDIARY DEVICES; CONSPIRACY; OBSTRUCTION OF JUSTICE; PERJURY

Enclosed for each recipient are two copies of a self-explanatory memorandum which contains information concerning the manufacture and projected utilization of nerve gas by components of the Chilean Government. The enclosed memorandum discloses that the nerve gas, which had been manufactured by DINA, the Chilean Intelligence Service, was transported to the United States during September, 1976, by DINA agent Michael Vernon Townley in connection with the assassination of Orlando Letelier. The nerve gas was not used in the Letelier assassination and, according to Townley, it was returned to Chile.

1 - Managing Director
Civil Aeronautics Board - Enclosure
1 - Assistant Secretary of State
for Latin American Affairs - Enclosure
1 - Assistant Attorney General
Criminal Division - Enclosure
1 - Director of Central Intelligence
Central Intelligence Agency - Enclosure
1 - Director, Defense Intelligence Agency - Enclosure
1 - Director, U. S. Secret Service - Enclosure
1 - Honorable Charles Ruff, U. S. Attorney, Washington, D.C.
Attention: Mr. E. Lawrence Barcella
Major Crimes Unit - Enclosure

FBI/DC

U.S. Department of Justice

Federal Bureau of Investigation

Office of the Director

Washington, D.C. 20535

December 9, 1981

GUILLERMO NOVO SAMPOL; ALVIN ROSS DIAZ; VIRGILIO PABLO PAZ ROMERO; JOSE DIONISIO SUAREZ ESQUIVEL; IGNACIO ROBERTO NOVO SAMPOL; MICHAEL VERNON TOWNLEY; JUAN MANUEL CONTRERAS SEPULVEDA; ARMANDO FERNANDEZ LARIOS; PEDRO ESPINOSA BRAVO; VICTIMS - ORLANDO LETELIER; RONNI KARPEN MOFFITT;
PROTECTION OF FOREIGN OFFICIALS - MURDER; EXPLOSIVES AND INCENDIARY DEVICES; CONSPIRACY; OBSTRUCTION OF JUSTICE, PERJURY

Eugene M. Propper, the former Chief United States Prosecutor in the Letelier assassination, and author Taylor Branch are collaborating in writing a book detailing the United States investigation of captioned matter, which book is to be published in early 1982. In connection with extensive research to develop material for their book, Propper and Branch interviewed numerous individuals connected with captioned matter, including former officials of DINA, the Chilean Intelligence Service. They traveled extensively and Branch visited several foreign countries, including Chile. Propper and Branch advised that they secured a number of

This document contains neither recommendations nor conclusions of the FBI. It is the property of the FBI, and is loaned to your agency; it and its contents are not to be distributed outside your agency."

FBI/DOJ

letters which were sent from the United States by self-admitted DINA agent Michael Vernon Townley to his DINA "cut-out" Gustavo Etchepare in Chile. According to Propper and Branch, Townley made references in several of his letters to a highly secret DINA undertaking known as "Project Andrea." Propper and Branch advised that in his letters, Townley expressed concern that the United States Government would ascertain details of "Project Andrea," which would be highly embarrassing to the Chilean Government. Propper and Branch indicated that Townley also expressed apprehension that the United States Government would be able to determine details related to "Project Andrea" through the GallenKamp Company in London, England, and through companies in Miami, Florida, that sold a microwave oven to Townley and rented a number of gas storage cylinders to Townley. Propper and Branch also indicated that Townley, in his letters, expressed concern that the United States Government would be able to ascertain details concerning "Project Andrea" through an individual in Miami, Florida, identified as Sam McIntoch, who sold Townley unidentified electronic components bearing the brand name "Sierra." Propper and Branch reported that Townley's father, J. Vernon Townley, also assisted his son and Etchepare in liquidating outstanding bills in the respective amounts of 350 pounds sterling, $525.00, $160.00 and $325.00 to the GallenKamp Company, the company which sold the microwave oven to Townley and the company which rented the gas storage cylinders to Townley and to Sam McIntoch. Propper and Branch noted that Townley also expressed concern in his letters that the Federal Bureau of Investigation would trace payments to the aforementioned companies and McIntoch through a checking account in the name of Prosin Limited at the Southeast First National Bank, Miami, Florida, which Townley utilized in connection with his official DINA responsibilities.

According to Propper and Branch, "Project Andrea" involved the manufacture of nerve gas by DINA, which was to be utilized against Argentina and Peru in the event of hostilities between these countries and Chile. Propper and Branch advised that Townley, acting as a DINA agent, manufactured and stored a quantity of nerve gas at a laboratory located at Townley's residence in Santiago, Chile, during 1975 and 1976 and utilized chemicals purchased through the GallenKamp Company, the microwave oven and the rented gas cylinders in the process. Propper and Branch advised that Townley created a substance known as isopropylmethylphosopho-nofluoridate, a clear liquid organophosphate commonly known as sarin, which vaporizes on being exposed to the atmosphere, producing droplets that enter the body through the skin or lungs to interdict the neurochemistry that permits the respiratory muscles to function. Propper and Branch advised that Eugenio Berrios, a chemical engineer who was known by his DINA code name "Hermes," worked with Townley and also was involved in a parallel project on behalf of the Chilean Army for the manufacture of the same nerve gas. Propper and Branch advised that when Townley traveled to the United States in September, 1976, via LAN-Chile on his mission to assassinate Orlando Letelier, he carried a quantity of the nerve gas with him on board the aircraft in his shirt pocket in a Chanel No. 5 perfume atomizer. Propper and Branch advised that Townley was considering the utilization of this nerve gas to assassinate Letelier, but decided against using this method. Propper and Branch advised that, according to Townley, Guillermo Novo Sampol and Virgilio Pablo Paz Romero, leaders of the Cuban Nationalist Movement, an anti-Castro terrorist organization, who assisted Townley in the planning and execution of the assassination of Orlando Letelier, were aware of Townley's possession of the nerve gas in the United States and also had witnessed the preparation of the nerve gas at Townley's laboratory at his residence in Santiago, Chile, during the period April, 1976, through June, 1976, when both Novo and Paz visited Townley in Chile.

According to Propper and Branch, the following LAN-Chile personnel assisted Townley and DINA in transporting materials between Chile and the United States:

Ronnie Berger	Bernardo Lacasia
Alejandro Fornes	Ronnie Lowery
Eugenio Herrera	Pocho Acevedo
Guillermo Neira	Jorge Nordenflycht

Subsequent to the receipt of the above information from Propper and Branch, arrangements were made to have Townley brought to Federal Bureau of Investigation Headquarters from the place of his incarceration in a Federal penitentiary, where he was interviewed by Special Agents of the Federal Bureau of Investigation. Townley confirmed Propper's and Branch's information regarding the manufacture and intended use of the nerve gas by the Chilean Government. Townley, however, denied that he personally carried the nerve gas with him from Chile to the United States on a LAN-Chile aircraft. Townley claimed to have had the nerve gas sent from Chile to the United States through LAN-Chile flight personnel who were unaware that they were transporting nerve gas. Townley did confirm that the nerve gas was transported to the United States by LAN-Chile flight personnel in a Chanel No. 5 perfume atomizer. Townley advised that Novo and Paz requested that the Cuban Nationalist Movement be furnished a supply of nerve gas to utilize in their terrorist activities; however, Townley claimed that because of the unstable nature of Novo and Paz and other members of the Cuban Nationalist Movement, he refused their request. Townley advised that he insured that the nerve gas transported to the United States by LAN-Chile flight personnel was returned to Chile to the custody of DINA by the same method.

DOCUMENT 9. Defense Intelligence Agency, Cable, "DINA Dissolved," August 13, 1977.

UNCLASSIFIED

DEPARTMENT OF DEFENSE
JOINT CHIEFS OF STAFF
MESSAGE CENTER

VZCZCMLT641SCP056 ~~C O N F I D E N T I A L~~ ZYUW
MULT 4930

ACTION

INFO: CJCS(04) DJS(01) J3(14) J4(08) J5(07) SAGA(04) J3:NMCC
J3:JRC USRMCLO(01) SECDEF(10) ASD:ISA(10) ASD:PA(03) DDRE(02)
ARPA(06) AE(01) DIA(195) ASD:PA&E(03) IADB(01) NSC(01) MRAL(02) (
(273)

TRANSIT/132158Z/132200Z/000:02GRP0545
DE RUEKJCS #3607 2252200
ZNY CCCCC
RULYSCC T USS ALAMO USS ANCHORAGE USS CAYUGA USS SCHENECTADY
RULYSCC T USS JOHN F KENNEDY USS NEW ORLEANS USS RANGER
RULYSCC T USS CONSTELLATION USS CORAL SEA USS BLUE RIDGE
RULYSCC T USS ST LOUIS USS DWIGHT D EISENHOWER USS MIDWAY
RULYSCC T USS JUNEAU USS KITTY HAWK
RULYSCC T USS ENTERPRISE USS MOUNT WHITNEY USS TUSCALOOSA
RULYSCC T USS PT DEFIANCE USS SARATOGA USS TARAWA
RULYSCC T CTG77PT6 CTG76PT4 CTG76PT5 CTG79PT4 CTG77PT5 CTG77PT9
RULYSCC T CTG77PT3 CTG79PT5 CTG79PT1 CTG62PT1 CTU79PT4PT1
RULYSCC T AIRANTISUBRON THREE SEVEN
RULYSCC T HELANTISUBRON LIGHT THREE ONE
RULYSCC T COMCRUDESGRU TWO
RULYSCC T HELANTISUBRON TWO
RULYSCC T FITRON ONE
R 132158Z AUG 77 ZEX
FM DIA WASHINGTON DC
TO DIACURINTEL
AIG 7011
BT
~~C O N F I D E N T I A L NOFORN~~ 4930
FROM DN-2G

SUBJ: DIA DEFENSE INTELLIGENCE NOTICE (DIN) (U)

DIADIN 225-6A - (AS OF: 1620 EDT 13 AUG 77)

CHILE: DINA DISSOLVED. (U)

1. ~~(C/NOFORN)~~ THE GOVERNMENT OF CHILE HAS ABOLISHED ITS DEPARTMENT OF NATIONAL INTELLIGENCE (DINA) EFFECTIVE 6

PAGE 1 ~~C O N F I D E N T I A L~~ 00000001

Declassified by DIA

UNCLASSIFIED

UNCLASSIFIED

DEPARTMENT OF DEFENSE
JOINT CHIEFS OF STAFF
MESSAGE CENTER

PAGE 2 ~~CONFIDENTIAL~~ 4930

AUGUST. DINA WAS IN EFFECT A POLITICAL POLICE FORCE OPERATING UNDER THE DIRECT CONTROL OF THE PRESIDENT. IT WAS RESPONSIBLE FOR THE ARREST, INTERROGATION, AND DETENTION OF LARGE NUMBERS OF ANTI-JUNTA ELEMENTS IN THE MONTHS FOLLOWING THE COUP AGAINST THE ALLENDE GOVERNMENT AND HAD BEEN THE SUBJECT OF WIDESPREAD INTERNATIONAL CRITICISM FOR HUMAN RIGHTS VIOLATIONS.

2. ~~(C/NOFORN)~~ A NEW ENTITY, THE NATIONAL INFORMATION CENTER (CNI), HAS BEEN CREATED BY THE JUNTA AND PLACED UNDER THE CONTROL OF THE MINISTRY OF THE INTERIOR. THE CNI WILL INHERIT DINA'S INTELLIGENCE COLLECTION FUNCTION AND WILL PROBABLY ABSORB MUCH OF THE DISSOLVED AGENCY'S PERSONNEL RESOURCES. UNLIKE ITS PREDECESSOR, HOWEVER, THE CNI WILL NOT HAVE THE POWER OF ARREST AND DETENTION. THOSE FUNCTIONS, ACCORDING TO CHILEAN OFFICIALS, WILL NOW BE TURNED OVER TO THE JUDICIAL POLICE AND THE CARABINIEROS, BOTH CONVENTIONAL LAW ENFORCEMENT AGENCIES UNDER THE MINISTRY OF DEFENSE.

3. ~~(C/NOFORN)~~ THROUGH THE REPRESSIVE MEASURES OF ITS SECURITY SERVICES, THE JUNTA GOVERNMENT OF CHILE HAS ELIMINATED VIRTUALLY ALL POTENTIAL CHALLENGES TO ITS RULE. THE DISSOLUTION OF DINA DOES NOT LESSEN THE GOVERNMENT'S CAPABILITY TO CONTINUE TO SUPPRESS POLITICAL OPPOSITION, ALTHOUGH THE SEPARATION OF THE ARREST AND INTELLIGENCE COLLECTION FUNCTIONS DOES INDICATE A MORE BUREAUCRATIC AND PERHAPS MEASURED APPROACH FOR RESPONDING TO PERCEIVED SUBVERSIVE THREATS. MOREOVER, THE SECURITY REORGANIZATION DOES DEMONSTRATE THE GOVERNMENT'S SENSITITIVITY TO INTERNATIONAL CRITICISM AND A DESIRE TO IMPROVE ITS IMAGE, ESPECIALLY WITH THE US -- FACTORS WHICH COULD PORTEND AT LEAST SOME IMPROVEMENT IN THE HUMAN RIGHTS CONDITIONS IN CHILE.

PREPARED BY: [redacted] ALERT CENTER
(GDS-31 DEC 83)
BT
#3607
ANNOTES
CSB

UNCLASSIFIED

PAGE 2 ~~CONFIDENTIAL~~ 00000001

NNNN
132200Z

4

Consolidating Dictatorship: The United States and the Pinochet Regime

A documented case can be made for the proposition that the current regime in Chile is militaristic, fascistic, tyrannical and murderous.

—Internal State Department Dissent Memo, February 1974

In the United States, as you know, we are sympathetic with what you are trying to do here. . . . We want to help, not undermine you.

—Henry Kissinger speaking privately to Augusto Pinochet, June 8, 1976

The USG wishes to make clear its desire to cooperate with the military Junta and to assist in any appropriate way," states a classified cable from the White House Situation Room dated September 13, 1973. "We welcome General Pinochet's expression of Junta desire for strengthening ties between Chile and U.S." (Doc 1) With that secret message, the Nixon administration officially embraced the bloody coup d'état in Chile. The White House directed Ambassador Nathaniel Davis to convey this position to Pinochet "at earliest possible opportunity." Davis cabled back the next day: "Pinochet expressed most sincere appreciation and said he would like to keep privately in touch."

Publicly, the White House portrayed its posture towards the coup as one of neutrality. "We took the decision that we would not say anything that indicated either support or opposition—that we would avoid what we had done in Brazil in 1964 where we rushed out by recognizing the government," Kissinger explained to the Senate Foreign Relations Committee during his confirmation hearing as secretary of state on September 17. But privately, according to the declassified cable traffic, U.S. officials were assuring Chile's military rulers of Washington's full endorsement of their violent move to take power. With bodies overflowing from morgues, domestic and international condemnation of the bloodshed, strong criticism from the U.S. Congress, and widespread charges of covert U.S. involvement in the coup, the Nixon White House decided to cover up its warm welcome and avoid open identification with Chile's new military regime.

Initially, the Nixon administration communicated with Pinochet through an embassy intermediary, the U.S. MilGroup officer, Col. Carlos Urrutia. At midday on September 12, Urrutia secretly met with Pinochet and received a briefing on the status of mopping-up operations, and the Junta's political plans, as well as Chile's need for U.S. economic and military assistance. The two also discussed the "delicacy of matter of contact" and a delay in Washington's formal recognition of the new regime. Urrutia then reported their conversation back to Ambassador Davis. Pinochet, as Davis cabled the White House Situation Room, "showed understanding and was relaxed about the matter of recognition and volunteered that obviously we should not be the first to recognize."[1]

Indeed, Washington waited two weeks until more than a dozen other nations had formally recognized the military Junta before quietly extending recognition to the Pinochet regime on September 24. "We strongly believe domestic and international considerations make this very brief delay highly advisable in overall interests of new GOC [government of Chile] as in our own," a cable from Kissinger and his NSC deputy Brent Scowcroft explained to Davis as he prepared for a furtive "nonofficial" meeting with the regime's foreign minister one week after the coup. "In the meantime, we want GOC to know of our strongest desire to cooperate closely and establish firm basis for cordial and most constructive relationship." (Doc 2)

In the immediate aftermath of the coup, close cooperation took the form of behind-the-scenes diplomatic support, as well as a sympathetic stance on aid useful for continuing acts of repression. On September 14, the U.S. delegation to the United Nations strongly recommended that the new Chilean government dispatch a "representative of stature, presence and alertness to New York without delay" to present a persuasive justification for the overthrow of Allende and counter harsh criticism leveled by the Soviets and Cubans. U.S. officials at the UN worked closely with Chilean diplomats to cast the coup in the most positive light. Back in Santiago, Ambassador Davis lobbied members of the new Junta on "enlisting" the help of the Christian Democrats "with this problem of foreign image." This idea eventually led to a tour of Latin America and Europe by prominent members of Chile's Christian Democratic Party to present a public justification for the coup—a tour secretly financed by the CIA.

On September 15, the U.S. air force attaché was approached by the head of logistics for the Chilean air force who requested the U.S. immediately provide 1,000 flares to be used "for illumination purposes in military operations against extremist groups," as well as 1,000 steel helmets for soldiers. "I believe it is advisable to accommodate this request—discreetly if possible," Ambassador Davis cabled Washington.[2] In another cable the same day, he argued that providing the equipment would be a key signal of support: "The new Chilean government is obviously operating under great strains, and is counting friends in this moment. Negative from us could have serious repercussions and set pattern of attitudes we should probably be willing to take some risks to avoid."[3] Two weeks later, Davis alerted the State Department that the Chilean military had requested a U.S. "detention center advisor" and needed technical support as well as portable tents and housing as they scouting new locations for the eventual transfer of thousands of prisoners from the National Stadium. The ambassador recognized that "sending of advisor to aid in establishment of detention camps provides obvious political problems," but he recommended Washington send temporary housing equipment without specifying its usage. "Dept. may wish to consider feasibility of material assistance in form of tents, blankets etc.," Davis recommended, "which need not be publicly and specifically earmarked for prisoners."[4]

From the outset, Washington confronted the political pressures of aligning U.S. foreign policy with a ruthless regime. As major media outlets such as the *New York Times* reported death tolls in the thousands, Nixon administration officials faced increasingly tough questioning from both the press and Congress. "In some of these Congressional hearings, I've been asked: 'How many people have been killed? Is it true the rumors that we hear?' " Assistant Secretary Kubisch confided to Kissinger during an October 1 staff meeting. But the new secretary of state made his position clear. The U.S. would not defend atrocities by the new regime, but "we should not support moves against them by seeming to disassociate ourselves from the Chileans." As he admonished: "I think we should understand our policy—that however unpleasant they act, this government is better for us than Allende was."[5]

Helping the Regime Consolidate: Overt Assistance

The Nixon administration mobilized quickly to help the Chilean military consolidate its rule. Within one day of the coup, the WSAG—an interagency task force known as the Washington Special Actions Group—met to begin preparing assessments on "anticipated short, medium and long term Chilean assistance requirements," according to a SECRET/NODIS briefing memorandum prepared for Kissinger. The CIA immediately began gathering intelligence on Chile's currency reserves and debt obligations. Within a week of the coup, action programs were readied on meeting Chile's economic, monetary, and military necessities. On September 20, Kissinger chaired a meeting of the WSAG where the decision was made to instruct Ambassador Davis "to talk to the Junta . . . to inform them of our goodwill . . . of our intention to recognize and when; when the emergency food supplies will be delivered; and authorizing the Ambassador to discuss, with Junta, Chile's middle and long-term economic needs." (Doc 3)

Almost overnight, Washington reopened the spigot of bilateral and multilateral economic assistance to Santiago. In every category of direct and indirect bilateral and multilateral economic and military assistance to Chile, U.S. aid rose dramatically following the coup—marking the end of the "invisible blockade" Nixon and Kissinger had used to undermine the Allende government. "It is quite apparent that Chile is going to need considerable aid," Assistant Secretary Kubisch declared to Congress on September 29, "and if it adopts a sensible government, I would expect that aid to be given."

On October 6, the U.S. Department of Agriculture granted the Pinochet regime $24 million in commodity credits for the purchase of wheat to help alleviate food shortages—credits that had been previously denied to the Allende government; in November, another such credit was authorized. "On November 14, we announced our second CCC credit to Chile—$24 million for feed corn," Kissinger's aides informed him—in a secret situation report attached to the classified memorandum, "Chilean Executions," alerting him to hundreds of murders by the regime during its first weeks in power.

Those commodity credits were supplemented by dramatic allocations from AID's Food for Peace Program—known as P.L 480 Title 1 and 2. During the first three years of the military government, Chile received $132 million in Food for Peace grants, as compared to $14.7 million during the three years before the coup. Pinochet's Chile not only received far greater amounts of U.S. assistance than the Allende government; the military regime obtained remarkable preferential treatment over all other countries in Latin America. In fiscal years 1975 and 1976, Chile received 80 percent of all Title I Food for Peace assistance to Latin America, even though the country contained only 3 percent of the region's population. "On PL 480, I understand Chile is getting two-thirds of the total for Latin America," Kissinger told Foreign Minister Patricio Carvajal during a September 29, 1975 meeting.[6] During the same time period, Chile received over $30 million from AID in housing guarantees, compared to only $4 million of such grants AID dispersed among the rest of Central and South America.[7]

Freed from U.S. obstruction at the multilateral lending institutions, the

World Bank and the IDB both reopened their loans programs in Chile. IDB loans between 1971 and 1973 totaled $11.6 million. During the first three years of Pinochet's rule, that figure rose to $237.8 million. The World Bank, which had provided zero credit to the Allende government, authorized $66.5 million from 1974 to 1976. When Pinochet's ambassador to Washington, Manuel Trucco, complained to Kissinger and Assistant Secretary for Inter-American Affairs William Rogers that "with the World Bank we are experiencing certain delays," Rogers assured him that Chile "should have no problem. We are leaning hard on the bureaucracy."[8]

The multilateral bank loans obtained with U.S pressure totaled "hundreds of millions," Ambassador David Popper wrote to Rogers in late July 1975. In addition, there was "the hundreds of millions we have saved for Chile through our part in debt rescheduling arrangements." Having actively discouraged any debt negotiations during Allende the United States encouraged repeated rescheduling under Pinochet. "We spearheaded the Paris Club debt rescheduling," noted one secret memo sent to Rogers. In 1975, the U.S. agreed to reschedule nearly $100 million Chile owed to U.S. banks.

U.S. policy was to "maintain and strengthen" the new Pinochet regime, according to declassified State Department records. Indeed, Washington's largesse allowed the Junta to quickly overcome the food shortages that had plagued Chile during Allende, stabilize the economy, and curry favor with the middle and upper classes—all of which contributed to its consolidation of power. The United States had provided "absolutely vital assistance to the Chileans," Ambassador Popper noted in a major policy review paper in July 1975. "The Chileans are fully aware of it, and are quick to express their appreciation."[9]

Washington's economic largesse freed up foreign exchange for the acquisition of armaments. Once in power, the Chilean military went on a buying binge, reaching agreement with the U.S. to expedite delivery of arms ordered before the coup and on more than $100 million in new weapons and spare parts. The Chileans sought M-60 tanks and F5 supersonic fighter aircraft, as well as complex air defense systems, TOW missiles, and various types of munitions. They also ordered equipment that could be directly deployed for repression—armored personnel carriers, recoilless rifles, jeeps, trucks, antiriot gear, and communication systems. The Chileans requested, but were forced to withdraw, an application for $12 million in foreign military sales credits for "counterinsurgency gear to outfit twenty-three special counterinsurgency 'basic units.' "[10] But on December 28, 1973, the State Department began authorizing export licenses for commercial sale of lethal equipment, including 2,500 M-16 rifles, 1,600 submachine guns, and 2.2 million rounds of ammunition that the Chilean's paid for with cash. Within three years of taking power, Pinochet's Chile had established itself as the fifth largest customer in the world—behind such major-league buyers as Israel, Saudi Arabia, Jordan, and Iran—of U.S. military hardware.[11]

Helping the Regime Consolidate: Covert Assistance

Clandestine U.S. support also helped Pinochet establish his violent grip on power. The CIA's Santiago Station, with many connections to the military and civilian groups now behind the Junta, was well-situated to offer critical aid; covert action projects being run against Chile's elected government prior to September 11, could be extended and reconfigured to contribute to consolidation of the new military regime. In the aftermath of September 11, the CIA initiated what cables referred to as an "effort to make new govt strong and effective."[12] That included amending covert political and propaganda operations, and developing new "agents of influence" and assets within Chile's post-coup power structures. The Station also established close relations with Pinochet's new security services, providing organizational training and support for DINA after it began operations in late 1973.

At the time of the coup, the Santiago Station was heavily staffed with numerous veteran officers and a roster of new agents sent in the late summer of 1973. They included: Chief of Station Raymond Warren, who lived at 952 America Vespucio St., and operated under the cover of embassy political officer; deputy COS Donald Winters, who also posed as an embassy officer and resided at 1275 Tobalaba, and John Devine, an operative who handled the CIA's media and propaganda operations in Chile.[13] Two other CIA agents, John Hall and James Anderson, operated as vice-consuls in the consulate, where, incredibly, they handled cases of U.S. citizens disappeared, detained, and abused by the Chilean military following the coup.

In the aftermath of September 11, the CIA Station quickly offered material assistance to the regime. But the barrage of accusations of Agency involvement in the military takeover prompted Langley headquarters to delay direct aid. "Regret [deleted] has already discussed this matter with Junta," Western Hemisphere Division chief David Atlee Phillips cabled Santiago on October 3. "Agency operational activities in Chile are now prime target for Congressional investigations and we expect questioning to continue for some time, especially in view of increasing news coverage hostile to the repressive measures being adopted by Junta." The CIA, Phillips added, "must provide honest answers to questions regarding current OPS activities and thus cannot assist Junta."[14]

Instead, the CIA focused on helping the Junta improve its bloody image abroad, and popularity at home. On September 19, Ambassador Davis approved a Station request to finance the purchase of what David Atlee Phillips described as a "small network" of media outlets that would be instrumental "in mounting a propaganda campaign to popularize the Junta's programs;"[15] two CIA collaborators helped the Junta draft a *White Book of the Change of Government in Chile*—a public relations publication that was widely distributed to the press and political figures in the United States and other nations.[16] And the CIA continued to covertly underwrite its most important asset, the *El Mercurio* newspaper empire, as it became the leading voice of pro-regime propaganda in Chile, regularly maximizing the military's "reforms" while minimized reporting on repression.

Prior to the coup, the CIA's fiscal year 1974 propaganda project budget for Chile, authorized what the CIA called "a steady barrage of antigovernment criticism" against Allende to exploit "every possible point of friction." That budget approved covert funding for *El Mercurio* and its "propaganda mechanisms" through April 1974. Following the coup, however, the Santiago Station and the Western Hemisphere division determined an extension was necessary—a "high" additional subsidy through the end of June to allow the military regime's key oracle a smooth transition off the clandestine U.S. dole. Covert funding was "essential to maintaining the trust and continued collaboration of the [assets] and through them, to maintain our capability for influencing the Junta and molding Chilean public opinion," according to a staff report opposing a deadline for terminating the propaganda project.[17] This project had not only "played a significant role in setting the stage for the military coup," David Atlee Phillips reminded his superiors in a January 9, 1974 memorandum, it was essential to advance national and international propaganda efforts in support of the Pinochet regime: "Since the coup, these media outlets have supported the new military government," he wrote:

> They have tried to present the Junta in the most positive light for the Chilean public and to assist foreign journalists in Chile to obtain facts about the local situation. . . . The project is therefore essential in enabling the Station to mold Chilean public opinion in support of the new government. (Doc 4)

Faced with State Department pressure to wrap up its pre-coup covert projects, the CIA's Western Hemisphere division sought—and obtained—an additional $176,000 to "give this multifaceted propaganda mechanism the opportunity to locate alternative funding sources," and assure that CIA propaganda assets had an incentive to continue working with the Station. The additional funds helped cushion the blow for Agustín Edwards's media empire as years of covert U.S. financing were finally phased out. In late February 1974, agents from the CIA Station met with *El Mercurio* representatives and informed them that post-coup circumstances "made it impossible for us to continue to subsidize [deleted] media outlets and that we wished to divest ourselves of any responsibility for them." The Chileans were told that at the end of the fiscal year, "all subsidy support . . . would cease." For these long-standing Chilean media assets, the CIA Station chief reported back in a secret March 1, 1974 cable to Phillips, "this news came as a shock and disappointment."

Through its political action programs, the CIA also covertly promoted the image of the new regime. In October 1973, the Station secretly financed an international tour by a group of prominent Christian Democrats to justify the military overthrow. The trip, which lasted more than a month, included party leaders such as Enrique Krauss, Pedro Jesus Rodriguez, Juan de Dios Carmona, and Juan Hamilton.[18] "The party arrived at a plan for sending a 'truth squad' to a number of Latin American and European capitals to explain the background of the Chilean military coup and the PDC's association with, and support of, the Junta in this situation," the CIA's directorate of operations advised in a secret memorandum for the Kissinger-chaired 40 Committee. "Unfortunately, the PDC has not had the time to recover from the financial drought of the Allende period; therefore," according to the CIA memo, covert funding was necessary.

Post-coup covert support for the Christian Democrats, and other political action projects became subject to a lengthy, and rather extraordinary debate among high-ranking U.S. officials in the CIA and Department of State. At the time of the coup, only $13,000 of the $1 million in covert funds authorized on August 20 by the 40 Committee for political-action operations had been dispensed by the Santiago Station; initially, the CIA and Ambassador Davis believed they still had authority to distribute the rest—even after the events of September 11. But in Washington, CIA and State Department officials determined that the August 20 authorization was "a dead letter." The "situation has changed so drastically since 20 August 40 Committee approval that we must start anew," as Langley headquarters cabled the CIA Station on September 21. Ongoing projects would be reviewed and reconsidered and post-coup expenditures would have to be approved again by the 40 Committee. In early October, the CIA presented its first appeal for "Initial Post-Coup Support" to the 40 Committee. (Doc 5)

On October 15, the 40 Committee did approve interim funding for the propaganda projects to improve the Junta's image. The CIA then moved to renew and amend the subsidies for the political parties it had supported to bring down Allende. On December 26, the Agency proposed to reconfigure the FY 1974 budget to support the National Party—described as "the government's party"—to $580,666. The PN, according to the CIA proposal, "feels that if it succeeds in becoming the government's standard-bearer it will not need further U.S. Government financial support."

The CIA also proposed to renew covert funding for the Partido Democrata-Cristiano, including payments promised before the coup, along with a clandestine subsidy—"surge funding"—to allow the near-bankrupt party to pay its bills in the year following the coup. In late November, the Agency sought to adjust the FY 1974 budget for the PDC political-action program to $685,150 and requested $160,000 to underwrite the party from December 1973 through April 1974.[19] Facing State Department resistance to continuing political-action projects in Chile, several weeks later the CIA submitted a SECRET/SENSITIVE proposal for the 40 Committee titled "Request for [$160,000] for Chilean Christian Democratic Party," asking for at least three months' worth of financing, and a "terminal payment" that would allow the Christian Democrat Party to meet its payroll in early 1974 and wean itself away from twelve long years of covert U.S. support.[20]

The debate over this $160,000 proposal at the highest levels of Kissinger's State Department reflected U.S. determination to back a brutal military regime over even minimal support for the party that had represented Washington's greatest hope for Chilean democracy since John F. Kennedy's Alliance for Progress. Now that Allende was dead, the rationale for covert action to "preserve Chile's democratic institutions" no longer seemed important to U.S. policy makers—even as the regime that overthrew him was systematically dismantling those very institutions.

Only one State Department official—a Bureau of Intelligence and Research analyst named James Gardner, who served as a liaison to the CIA on covert operations—seemed to grasp the stark hypocrisy in the U.S. posture. "A documented case can be made for the proposition that the current regime in Chile is militaristic, fascistic, tyrannical and murderous," Gardner wrote in a February 1974 secret memo in an effort to convince his superiors at INR to support covert assistance to the PDC in Chile:

> At the same time I think a case can be made for the proposition that the PDC is a sturdily democratic political organization, perhaps the only one in Latin America. The financial cost we are asked to pay to make it perhaps possible for this party to survive is small. . . . The projected assistance would seek only to strengthen an element in Chilean society that might be able to moderate the excesses of this regime. I cannot really believe that our acceptance of the Junta must involve passive identification with its more grotesque aberrations.

Gardner cited a historical reason as well:

> With the exception of our past aid to democratic elements in Chile, I am unfamiliar with any case in which our [covert] intervention has had any effect but to favor conservative or reactionary elements. We have never worked against the right, no matter how extreme it has been. If we refuse to assist the PDC in Chile . . . we will have preserved unbroken a record in which I would take some pleasure in seeing at least one flaw, especially if our interests were thereby served.[21]

Other U.S. officials endorsed minimal covert assistance to the PDC, but for different reasons. At a meeting with the CIA in November 1973, Deputy Assistant Secretary Harry Shlaudeman took the position that a covert subsidy would enable the PDC to support the new regime, but "should be extended with the clear understanding that after such and such a date the party would be over." If aid were terminated now, he conceded, "we would be causing ourselves trouble, for it would look as if we had been interested simply in knocking off Allende." The CIA, for its part, advanced the cogent position that support the PDC was necessary for it to compete politically against leftist parties if and when Pinochet returned power to civilian rule. Otherwise, "an abrupt cessation of U.S. Government financial support would strain the PDC's already depleted resources before it had a chance to find alternative sources," the CIA noted, "and, probably of greater import, would adversely affect the U.S. Government's relationship with the party."[22] And Ambassador Popper weighed in with the argument that support for the Christian Democrats was a way to *help* the Junta. Covert funding, he cabled "would assist in influencing the PDC in the direction of strengthening its policy of maintaining correct relations with the Junta, support of constructive Junta goals, and avoiding at all costs an open break with the government."[23]

But Kissinger's top aides worried that Pinochet would view as an insult any CIA covert support for political forces that the regime intended to suppress. For the first time in more than a decade of massive covert intervention, U.S. officials voiced concern that Washington could be accused of "meddling" in Chile's internal affairs. At a November 23 ARA-CIA meeting, Assistant Secretary Kubisch voiced his opposition "in principle" to covert political operations, particularly since "we now have a different situation in Chile." The SECRET meeting minutes recorded his position:

> The question now was whether, given the abrupt change in Chile and in the security situation there, it was really essential to fine tune a political situation simply to be a moderating influence and to help the opposition stay alive. He found it difficult to see a persuasive case that we should do so. His feelings were sharpened by the problems that

seemed to be emerging between the Junta and the PDC, and by the fact that the Secretary had made it clear that the change in regime in Chile was much in our interest and that we should do all we could to help the Junta succeed. In view of the Secretary's remarks, he would not be comfortable recommending assistance to any element in Chile that was not completely identified with the Junta. (Doc 6)

What would happen if the Junta discovered that the U.S. was still clandestinely supporting democratic parties? According to Kubisch, "they naturally would ask what the hell we were doing," he told his colleagues on November 23. "If we could say our program had ended with the overthrow of Allende," he concluded, "our position would be sound." In a cable from CIA headquarters to Santiago reporting on the meeting, CIA officials complained that Kubisch "kept raising serious problem specter if Junta discovered we were funding PDC," and requested that the Station send "any new or particularly compelling arguments in favor of proposal since we will obviously need best possible ammunition."

Without resolution, the internal debate between the CIA and the State Department over secret funding for the Christian Democrats extended well into the spring of 1974. On April 4, the head of the Bureau of Intelligence and Research, William Hyland, wrote a memorandum opposing what he called "a messy affair . . . driven by bureaucratic-clandestine momentum." Kissinger should be told, Hyland argued, that any payments to the PDC would be "exposing ourselves to Congressional reactions for continued 'meddling' in Chile." Moreover, he added, "I don't quite understand why we continue to support a political party that is, in effect, in opposition to the government, which I presume we now support." After former Chilean president Eduardo Frei raised the sensitive issue of the covert funding with Ambassador Popper during an April 18 meeting, however, the embassy sent a special cable—through CIA channels—appealing for reimbursement of funds the PDC had spent "during the climactic days of the civilian opposition struggle against the Allende Government." Popper argued that "it is in our interest to maintain a minimally satisfactory relationship with the PDC, and to avoid the imputation of bad faith. We have been put on notice," he added, "that our failure to meet the [deleted] obligation will result in deterioration of our present contacts."[24]

The ambassador's advocacy led to a compromise: Since the CIA had pledged financing to the PDC before the coup and the party had made commitments based on that pledge, the CIA would make a final, secret payment—adjusted for inflation—to cover pre-coup PDC commitments made between July 1 and September 10. If asked by the U.S. Congress or the Chilean Junta,

U.S. officials could then claim no clandestine political operations following the coup. "With the understanding that it would mark the end of our covert assistance to the PDC, I believe we should approve the payment of the [$50,000]," Assistant Secretary Kubisch recommended to Kissinger's deputy, Joseph Sisco, on May 7. In a June 11 SECRET/SENSITIVE/EYES ONLY action memorandum titled "Termination of the Chile Account"—marked "outside system" to hide it from the NSC bureacracy—Kissinger's office approved the "State/CIA compromise" for clandestine commitments made before the coup in Chile. (Doc 7) On June 24, the 40 Committee authorized this final payment.[25]

Officially, the CIA's twelve-year covert action program to underwrite the Christian Democrats ended on June 30, 1974, with the CIA implementing "liquidation plans" to close down safe houses, bank accounts, and other covert mechanisms of this funding operation. So too did the clandestine operations in support of other political parties such as Partido Nacional, the Democratic Radical Party, and the Radical Party of the Left. By the end of June, the Agency had also formally terminated its "covert action propaganda activity" built around *El Mercurio*—considered to be its most successful and influential covert action project in Chile in support of the military takeover.

With the Pinochet regime firmly in place, the CIA now reconfigured its role in Chile. The Santiago Station's "operational and budgetary emphasis shifted from covert action operations to one which was predominantly non-CA oriented," as internal CIA records described the transformation after the coup. By the summer of 1974, the CIA's operations focused on "liaison relationships" with Chile's security services, particularly the secret police force—the Directorate of National Intelligence, DINA.

The CIA and DINA

"After the coup, the CIA renewed liaison relations with the Chilean government's security and intelligence forces," noted the Church Committee in its report, *Covert Action in Chile, 1963–1973*. For more than two decades, that oblique sentence constituted the only official recognition of CIA support for DINA and the other intelligence units responsible for repression during the initial years of the regime. In its own September 2000 report, *Covert Activities in Chile*, the CIA slightly expanded the description of its "liaisons" with the Pinochet regime. "The CIA offered these services assistance in internal organization and training to combat subversion and terrorism from abroad." Covert assistance, as one intelligence officer elaborated, consisted of manuals, technical support, organizational methodology, and facility blueprints.[26] But covert ties to DINA extended beyond such basic assistance.

The CIA regards its "liaison" relations with foreign intelligence services among its most sacred of secrets; the details of its support for DINA remain highly classified. But it is clear that the CIA helped DINA become the dominant force it became during the early years of the dictatorship. Shortly after DINA was created, CIA Station chief Ray Warren promised Colonel Contreras planning, training, and organizational support.[27] To demonstrate the CIA's high-level commitment, the legendary deputy director of Central Intelligence, Gen. Vernon Walters, arrived in Santiago to confer with Pinochet over CIA assistance. Pinochet told Walters that he had "hand-picked Contreras to lead [DINA]." Contreras then received an invitation to come to Washington in the early spring of 1974.

On March 4, the CIA hosted a lengthy lunch meeting between Contreras, Walters, and officers of the CIA's Western Hemisphere division. A report on the session sent to the CIA Santiago Station totaled three pages recording the various elements of collaboration the CIA could supply; but years later the Agency would only declassify one paragraph in which CIA officials stressed to Contreras that they would provide training and support, but not for "any activities which might be construed as 'internal political repression.' " (Doc 8) In August of 1974, according to Contreras, a team of eight CIA specialists arrived in Santiago to train DINA officers. How long they stayed, and the substance of their training mission remains top secret.

The CIA assisted DINA even though officials understood the distinction between support for fighting external subversion and internal repression to be a false one. In documents reviewed by the Church Committee but never declassified, Agency officials acknowledged that "while most of CIA's support to the various Chilean forces would be designed to assist them in controlling subversion from abroad, the support could be adaptable to the control of internal subversion as well."[28] More than once, U.S. officials raised the specter of DINA's escalating human rights atrocities and expressed concerns that the CIA could be accused of contributing to DINA's repression. "The policy community and CIA," the Agency's own review, *Covert Activities in Chile*, determined, "recognized that the relationships opened the CIA to possible identification with the liaison services' internal operations involving human rights abuses but determined that the contact was necessary for CIA's mission."

In pursuit of that "mission," CIA agents maintained close communications with Contreras while he was DINA chieftain between 1974 and 1977. The Agency characterized this relationship as "correct" but "not cordial and smooth." But State Department and embassy officials interpreted his relations with the CIA differently. According to U.S. embassy political officer John Tipton, the Agency and DINA "were in a close relationship"—particularly after a new Station chief, Stuart Burton, arrived in the spring of 1974 to replace Ray Warren. "Burton and Contreras used to go on Sunday picnics together with their families," Tipton told journalist Lucy Komisar in an interview. The closeness of their relations, he remembered, "permeated the whole CIA Station."[29] In Washington, the memoranda from the State Department's Chile desk also noted the close ties between Contreras and Deputy Director Gen. Walters. "Colonel Manuel Contreras considers himself a bosom buddy of the general," the desk officer reported.

Pinochet and Contreras utilized these ties whenever they could. When the political controversy over Pinochet's human rights record escalated in July 1975 after the regime abruptly cancelled the visit of the United Nations Human Rights Commission (UNHRC), Pinochet authorized Contreras to approach chief of Station Burton for permission to meet with CIA deputy director Vernon Walters in Washington, D.C. The message Contreras conveyed was that "General Pinochet wishes that Gen. Walters receive an emissary for the purpose of learning Chile's position on the human rights issue for passage to Secretary Kissinger," a cable from Burton to headquarters noted. The trip would have to be top secret; as Ambassador Popper told Burton "if there were publicity, [it] could be counterproductive:

> [Amb. Popper] recognizes value in maintaining good relations with President Pinochet, who should not be led to believe we are rebuffing his efforts to communicate with us. Therefore, thinks it would be worthwhile if General Walters could give Contreras a little time to allow latter to unburden himself on human rights and, thus, let leadership let off steam. (Doc 9)

Secretary Kissinger was briefed that "the investigator," as aides referred to Contreras, intended to travel to Washington. At the White House, Kissinger's national security deputy, Brent Scowcroft, signed off on the visit.

On the Saturday morning of July 5, Contreras secretly met with Walters at a CIA office at Fort Myer in Arlington, Virginia. He provided the CIA deputy director with a DINA dossier on the five members of the UNHRC purporting to demonstrate that they were "definitely leftists and biased in their views," according to one debriefing of the meeting, and said he "wanted senior members of the United States government to know this."[30] In a subsequent memo to Scowcroft reporting on Contreras's visit, Walters noted that Pinochet had sought "understanding" for the decision to block the UNHRC, as well as a pledge "of U.S. support against any effort in the United

Nations to expel Chile." Perhaps more importantly, Walters reported that Contreras raised the issue of how to circumvent Congressional sanctions on U.S. military equipment: "Chileans know they cannot get direct aid because of Congressional opposition. Wonder if there is any way they could get it indirectly via Spain, Brazil, or the Republic of Korea."[31]

Contreras spent another four days in the States before returning to Santiago on July 9—much to the relief of State Department officials. In the CIA-ARA meeting on July 11, Assistant Secretary Rogers expressed his concern that the DINA chieftain had been noticed attending a Washington dinner party. Contreras, Rogers declared, was "notorious" for his repression; his mission to meet with the CIA deputy director "would be dynamic if it came out."

Yet only several weeks later, this "notorious" individual was back in Washington, meeting again with General Walters, and running diplomatic and political interference for the Pinochet regime against the international and congressional chorus of condemnation on the regime's human rights record. On August 23, Contreras traveled to New York to confer with Chile's UN mission, ostensibly to brief them on Pinochet's strategy for defusing the uproar over the human rights commission, and to quietly lobby Secretary-General Kurt Waldheim to come to Chile or send a select delegation in place of the working group. The main purpose of the meetings in New York, it appeared however, was to consult on the advisability of Pinochet traveling to the UN to defend Chile himself.

On August 24, Contreras returned to Washington. He met first with the State Department's Chile desk officer, Rudy Fimbres, and assured him that the regime soon would liberalize its internal security practices. According to a four-page memcon of the meeting, Contreras argued that the Pinochet regime was simply misunderstood. "He recognized Chile's image abroad was negative," Fimbres reported. "While much of this was the result of Communist activity, he thought there were sincere and moderate leaders in the U.S. who had not had a chance to appreciate the positive accomplishments of the Pinochet government."[32] On Fimbres's recommendation Contreras met with the office of one of Pinochet's leading critics, Rep. Donald Fraser. "There is no torture," he told them, "and there wasn't much before."[33]

On August 25, Contreras again met with General Walters—this time at Langley headquarters for lunch. "The luncheon will be essentially for protocol purposes," a memo to DCI William Colby stated. "Private discussions will be held between the DDCI and Colonel Contreras after lunch when Colonel Contreras will explain recent measures taken by the Chilean Government to improve its image on the civil rights issue [deleted]." (Doc 10) Before the meeting, CIA and State Department officials met to discuss "Colonel Contreras's Current Visit to the U.S." They agreed on a set of talking points—"Chile and Human Rights"—for Gen. Walters to invoke during the meeting. But there is no evidence that Walters used them and all information regarding why Walters would meet with Contreras in Washington twice in the space of seven weeks remains classified.[34]

At that time, the CIA was guarding its darkest, and best-kept secret in its relations with Contreras: the DINA chieftain was a paid CIA asset. In the late spring of 1975, as the CIA was reporting that Contreras bore the responsibility for much of the Pinochet regime's ongoing human rights atrocities, Santiago Station Chief Stuart Burton began lobbying to put him on the CIA payroll. "In May and June 1975," the CIA acknowledged years later, "elements within the CIA recommended establishing a paid relationship with Contreras to obtain intelligence based on his unique position and access to Pinochet."

Besides access to Pinochet, the Agency had another reason for putting Contreras on the payroll. "There was one particular operation on which the CIA sought his help," a former intelligence officer recalled.[35] The Station had set up secret bank accounts to surreptitiously pass funds to Contreras for collaborative projects. "Speaking of accounts," as DINA operative Michael Townley wrote in a private letter to a Chilean colleague, "Mamo [Contreras] has at least one, if not more, current accounts, open together with the CIA. Accounts that are used to reimburse the Service for work done for the CIA or together with them."[36] Contreras maintained two bank accounts at the Riggs Bank in Washington D.C.—a personal account and a "DINA service account" under the fictitious company Benito Vilar Construction, Townley told the FBI. In one secret account, the CIA deposited a still-classified sum as a payment for Contreras in the mid-summer of 1975.[37] Records from the Riggs Bank show that on July 21, 1975, a $6,000 deposit was made to Contreras's personal account in Washington—"from an unknown source."[38]

The Santiago Station expected to make such deposits on a monthly basis, but at CIA headquarters, Ray Warren, the head of the Western Hemisphere division (and Burton's predecessor in Chile), abrogated this agent-asset arrangement. At the time Contreras was placed on the payroll, DINA's involvement in disappearing hundreds of Chileans had become an international human rights scandal; State Department officials were known to be concerned over Agency's contacts with Chilean intelligence. Moreover, the CIA was, in the summer of 1975, coming under intense Congressional scrutiny for its covert involvement in Chile. When the contractual paperwork on Contreras arrived on his desk, Warren recalled in a later conversation with a U.S. diplomat, "I said, 'Oh my god, this guy is going to haunt us' and cut it off."[39] Burton received orders to inform Contreras that he "was not popular" in

Washington and headquarters had rejected making him a full-time covert asset. Payment, therefore, would be "one-time" only.[40]

CIA Scandals and Investigations

On July 14 and 15, 1975, around the same time CIA headquarters and the Santiago Station were placing Manuel Contreras on their covert payroll, Director of Central Intelligence William Colby was called to testify in closed session before a special Senate panel—the Select Committee to Study Government Operations with Respect to Intelligence Activities, led by Senator Frank Church. Colby was questioned extensively about former President Nixon's orders to foment a coup in Chile in 1970, Track II, and the assassination of General René Schneider. His responses—Colby denied the CIA was involved in an assassination plot, but admitted it had attempted to foster a coup in Chile—were promptly leaked to the *New York Times*. "It was all very discouraging," the CIA's liaison to ARA, George Lauder told Assistant Secretary Rogers about the disclosures. "The CIA had to protect its sources." More importantly, Rogers angrily responded, the State Department "had to protect the (expletive deleted) hemisphere. A price would be paid for the leak. The CIA had got out of the assassination charges by saying it had taken part in a coup attempt." From a diplomatic perspective, Rogers continued, "the confession of having planned a coup d'etat had been almost as bad as an assassination. Diplomatically it was terribly damaging. It was the most explicit admission yet."[41]

This was the second time Colby's secret testimony about Chile had created a major uproar when his revelations spilled into the press. On April 22, 1974, the CIA director appeared in executive session before the House Armed Services Committee for a briefing on clandestine operations the CIA had conducted in Chile between 1970–1973. "The Agency activities in Chile," Colby indicated according to a summary of his testimony, "were viewed as a prototype, or laboratory experiment; to test the techniques of heavy financial investment in efforts to discredit and bring down a government."[42]

Such admissions appeared to significantly contradict sworn denials by high-ranking officials, among them Kissinger and former DCI Richard Helms, that the CIA had attempted to undermine Allende. When Massachusetts Representative Michael Harrington read a classified transcript in July, he realized that U.S. officials had grossly deceived Congress during the ITT-CIA hearings the year before. He immediately contacted the Chairmen of the Senate Foreign Relations and Subcommittee on Multinational Corporations, J. William Fulbright and Frank Church, but they were reluctant to revisit the Chile scandal. The congressmen "asked what I thought he should do," Church's staff director Jerome Levinson recalled in an unpublished memoir. Levinson recommended that Harrington "give it one more try through established channels. I suggested he send a letter to Fulbright detailing the basis for his concerns and requesting a special inquiry." Harrington took that advice. Congress and the American people, he concluded in his letter summarizing Colby's testimony, "have a right to learn what was done in our name in Chile."

A copy of Harrington's letter, of course, landed on Levinson's desk. In a report to Senator Church, stamped CONFIDENTIAL, Levinson summarized Colby's revelations:

> (a) the Nixon administration authorized more than $8 million for covert activities by the agency in Chile between 1970 and 1973 "in an effort to make it impossible for President Salvador Allende Gossens to govern," and (b) that all these activities were specifically authorized by the Forty Committee, the Interdepartmental Group, chaired by Secretary of State Kissinger, which authorizes CIA clandestine activities. The goal of the clandestine activities was to "destabilize" the Allende government; it was considered a "test of using heavy cash payments to bring down a government viewed as antagonistic to the U.S."

Colby's testimony, Levinson argued, provided key evidence of lying by high U.S. officials during several Congressional hearings in 1973. "It appears that Secretary of State Kissinger deceived the [Foreign Relations] Committee during the course of his confirmation hearing with respect to the extent and object of the CIA's activities in Chile," Levinson wrote. Richard Helms "committed perjury."[43]

Levinson took one additional step to call attention to the revelations in Colby's still-secret testimony. In early September, after lunch with Seymour Hersh at Jean-Pierre's, a swanky French restaurant in downtown Washington, D.C., he quietly provided a copy of the Harrington letter to the intrepid *New York Times* investigative reporter. The leak set in motion the biggest scandal on covert operations ever to hit the intelligence community.

On September 8, 1974, the *New York Times* published Hersh's front-page story, CIA CHIEF TELLS HOUSE OF 8 MILLION CAMPAIGN AGAINST ALLENDE IN '70–'73. The article detailed both the Chile operations and their cover-up by Nixon administration officials. Gerald Ford, who had assumed the presidency only six weeks earlier, read the article and discussed it with Kissinger the following morning. "I saw the Chile story," Ford said. "Are there any repercussions?" According to a secret-sensitive memorandum of conversation, Kissinger responded: "Not really."

In fact, the story and a series of follow-ups written by Hersh, had significant repercussions—for the Ford administration, Kissinger, the CIA, and the conduct of covert operations abroad. Hersh's revelations on Chile, coupled with further disclosures of CIA involvement in assassination plots against foreign leaders, and "Operation Chaos," a domestic spying and disruption program against antiwar groups, set off a major political scandal. The scandal, in turn, led to the first major congressional inquiry into abuses of executive branch power, the misconduct of the intelligence community and the presidential use of clandestine warfare as a foreign policy weapon. Following the scandals of Watergate and the collapse of Saigon, as Kissinger would concede in his memoir, *Years of Renewal*, the Hersh articles "had the effect of a burning match in a gasoline depot."[44]

The uproar over Hersh's September 8 article was immediate. Senate and House leaders denounced the executive branch for misconduct abroad and gross deception at home. Amidst a barrage of criticism, Ford convened his cabinet to discuss what he called "the Chile deal" and defend the CIA. "We need a CIA and we need covert operations," Ford told his top advisors before calling on Kissinger to "give the details." In his briefing, Kissinger claimed that the U.S. was only defending democracy. He omitted any discussion of Track II and mendaciously denied that the U.S. had waged an economic destabilization campaign against Allende. "There might have been proclivity for economic warfare," he said, "but the issue never came up. What happened was the result of [Allende's] mismanagement and his nationalization and expropriations." Decisions relating to Chile "were made in accordance with the law," Ford asserted. "I wanted you all to have the story." (Doc 11)

That was the position the president took publicly. In a historic press conference on September 16 (devoted largely to his controversial pardon of Richard Nixon) Ford became the first U.S. president to acknowledge, and defend, covert operations against a democratically elected government—operations designed to be "plausibly denied." Is it the policy of your administration to attempt to destabilize the governments of other democracies?, a reporter asked the president. "I think this is a very important question," President Ford responded:

> Now in this particular case, as I understand it, and there is no doubt in my mind, our government had no involvement whatsoever in the Allende coup. To my knowledge, nobody has charged that. The facts are we had no involvement in any way whatsoever in the coup itself.
>
> In a period of time, three or four years ago, there was an effort being

> made by the Allende government to destroy opposition news media, both the writing press as well as the electronic press, and to destroy opposition political parties.
>
> The effort that was made in this case was to help and assist the preservation of opposition newspapers and electronic media and to preserve opposition political parties.
>
> I think this is in the best interest of the people in Chile, and certainly in our best interest.

CIA officials knew the president's statements were inaccurate, and alerted the White House. In a subsequent "eyes only" memorandum, White House counsel Jack Marsh advised Ford that his response was "not fully consistent with the facts because all of the facts had not been made known to you."[45]

Presidential spin on the Chile operations did nothing to halt public and congressional outrage over revelations of CIA misconduct. In early January, when CBS news correspondent Daniel Schorr broke the story of CIA efforts to assassinate foreign leaders such as Fidel Castro, Patrice Lumumba, and René Schneider, the intelligence scandal escalated dramatically. "What is happening is worse than in the days of McCarthy," Kissinger complained to Ford in an emergency meeting early Saturday morning on January 4. "Helms said all these stories are just the tip of the iceberg. If they come out blood will flow," Kissinger advised. "The Chilean thing," he continued referring to the Schneider killing, "that is not in any report. That is sort of blackmail on me."[46]

At the January 4 meeting, Ford and his advisors agreed that he would announce the creation of a blue-ribbon Commission on CIA Activities, to be chaired by Vice President Nelson Rockefeller—as a way to head off the threat of an independent Congressional inquiry. But on January 27, the Senate voted 82–4 to establish a special Committee to Study Government Operations with Respect to Intelligence Activities, which subsequently became known as the Church Committee. On February 19, the House also voted to initiate a panel of inquiry into "CIA transgressions," headed by New York Representative Otis Pike.

The Ford administration saw these investigations, in Kissinger's words, as "an assault on the intelligence community" and "the substance of American foreign policy" in the turbulent mid-1970s. "After all the country had been through," he wrote in his memoirs, "a full scale public investigation into the entire range of the nation's intelligence activities was a worrisome prospect in the existing morbid atmosphere."[47] At the State Department, Assistant Secretary Rogers recommended against "official acknowledgement" of covert operations against Allende, which would "destroy people and institutions important to Chile and to us" as well as damage respect for the United States in the entire hemisphere. In a secret memo to Kissinger, Rogers voiced his opposition to covert action as "bad principle and bad practice" but warned: "we should expect the gravest consequences to our Latin American relations for years to come if these matters are now to be laid bare."[48]

Led by Kissinger, the Ford administration adopted a policy of strategic stonewalling with the Congressional panels. U.S. officials disdainfully resisted cooperation with the Pike Committee staff, who Colby characterized as a "ragtag, immature, and publicity seeking . . . bunch of children who were out to seize the most sensational high ground they could." Kissinger claimed executive privilege on State Department documents. When informed that the Committees were seeking cable traffic relating to Chile dated between 1964 and 1970 Kissinger told his aides "no," according to a secret transcript of his July 14, 1975, staff meeting. "We have to tell the committee straight out that we're not going to—?," one deputy asked. "No," Kissinger replied. "You shift it to the White House and let the White House refuse it—and I'll see to it that the White House refuses it."[49] At one point, the Pike Committee issued three contempt-of-Congress citations against the secretary of state for refusing to turn over records.

The House inquiry was plagued by controversy and conflict; the Senate Committee met with greater success. For several months, the White House, CIA, and State Department delayed response to multiple requests for records, claiming to be understaffed. In truth, "the White House told us not to cooperate," Colby would remember. "They just didn't want to turn over documents." Eventually the committee staff worked out an agreement over access to censored versions of CIA records and the White House turned over some, but not all, of the thousands of documents needed for the Senate investigation. This transition "from intransigence to cooperation," as Church's staff officer, Loch Johnson, described it, "moved with the pace of a glacier."[50]

As the Church Committee inquiry culminated in the fall of 1975, the White House took further steps to obstruct its work, and protect and conceal the controversial covert history the Senate investigation had uncovered. On October 31, President Ford sent a strongly worded letter to all members of the committee demanding that their report on five assassination plots—in Cuba, the Congo, the Dominican Republic, Vietnam, and Chile—remain classified to protect national security; and the administration began a concerted lobbying effort in the Senate to block release of the report. The next day, Ford initialed a secret presidential order to oppose the select committee's plans to hold an open hearing on covert operations in Chile on the grounds that it would "establish a precedent that would be seized on by the Congress in the future to hold additional open hearings on covert action," and "would have a shattering effect on the willingness of foreign political parties and individuals to cooperate with the U.S. in the future on such operations."[51]

The Church Committee managed to circumvent these executive branch roadblocks. On November 20, after an acrimonious and unresolved debate in a rare closed session of the Senate over approving the committee's findings, Senator Church simply released *Alleged Assassination Plots Involving Foreign Leaders* to the press. At the time, the report represented the most comprehensive exposé of the dark and seamy side of U.S. foreign policy operations ever published. On December 4, the committee released a second, dramatic case study, *Covert Action in Chile, 1963–1973*, detailing a decade of clandestine CIA intervention to control Chilean politics, prevent Allende from becoming president, and undermine his government after he was elected.

Finally, over White House and CIA objections, the committee did convene the first public hearing ever held on covert operations. The hearings focused on Chile as an "example of the full range of covert action," Senator Church explained in his opening remarks, which "permits the committee, the Senate, and the country to debate and decide the merits of future use of covert action as an instrument of U.S. foreign policy." The select committee had taken "this unusual step," Senator Church noted, "because the committee believes the American people must know and be able to judge what was undertaken by their government in Chile. The nature and extent of the American role in the overthrow of a democratically elected Chilean government are matters for deep and continuing public concern," he concluded. "This record must be set straight."[52]

The Chile Syndrome

The scandal over covert operations to undermine Chilean democracy, coupled with the Nixon-Ford administration's embrace of Pinochet's violent regime, contributed to a dramatic national reevaluation of U.S. foreign policy. For the first time, CIA intervention became subject to public debate over the propriety of such practices—a debate that would endure and influence U.S. operations in countries from Angola to Nicaragua to Iraq in the last quarter of the twentieth century. Moreover, Pinochet's atrocities with Washington's ongoing assistance, mobilized church and solidarity groups who transformed human rights into a movement, and a potent political issue on Capitol Hill. The "Chile syndrome"—supplementing the Vietnam syndrome of national reticence to U.S. military intervention in distant lands—reflected growing public demand that U.S. foreign policy return to the moral precepts of American society. "The issue [of Chile] arose in America at the worst possible time," Kissinger would complain in his memoirs. "In the aftermath of Vietnam and during Watergate, the idea that we had to earn the right to conduct foreign policy by moral purity—that we could prevail through righteousness rather than power—had an inevitable attraction."[53]

In spite of Kissinger's objections—indeed, because of them—Chile became the battleground for the first major fight between the executive branch and Congress over human rights and U.S. foreign policy. Between 1974 and 1976, Congress passed a wave of precedent-setting human rights legislation in an effort to directly or indirectly block the Ford administration's support for Pinochet—laws that institutionalized human rights as a component of U.S. bilateral relations with other nations. In the House of Representatives, a number of congressmen, among them Donald Fraser, who chaired the first hearings on human rights issues, Michael Harrington, Tom Harkin, Toby Moffett, and George Miller, took the lead in exposing Chilean atrocities, while sponsoring pioneering laws to penalize Pinochet, and other governments that violated the rights of their citizens. The Senate, led by Edward Kennedy, James Abourezk, and George McGovern, repeatedly called Kissinger and his aides to task for their support for the regime, and moved to curtail both economic and military assistance to Chile.

Senator Kennedy must be credited with being the most outspoken congressional critic of Pinochet and U.S. assistance to his regime. Soon after the coup, Kennedy condemned the

> continued silence of the government of the United States which has not issued a single public expression of remorse over the military coup which toppled a democratically elected government, or over the deaths, beatings, brutality, and repression which have occurred in that land.

Kennedy convened the first Senate hearings on Chile only seventeen days after the coup took place. On October 2, 1973, he offered a "sense of Congress" resolution urging the president to "deny economic or military assistance, other than humanitarian aid, until he finds that the Government of Chile is protecting the human rights of all individuals, Chilean and foreign." In December 1974, Kennedy successfully obtained a $25 million cap on economic aid to Chile in the foreign assistance appropriations bill, which the Ford administration simply ignored; at the same time, Kennedy also sponsored the first limits on U.S. military aid and training to the Chilean Junta. In July 1976, Congress passed the far more comprehensive Kennedy amendment, banning all military assistance, credits, and cash sales of weapons to

Chile—marking the first time Congress had terminated military aid to another government because of human rights abuses.

Congress also passed the "Harkin amendment"—model legislation tying U.S. economic assistance to the human rights record of other governments. The amendment, attached to the 1975 International Development and Food Assistance Act, was sponsored by then Iowa Congressman—now Senator—Tom Harkin. The new law mandated a cutoff of economic assistance to any country that engaged in a consistent pattern of gross violations of human rights. Chile was the original target of the bill, recalls Joseph Eldridge of the Washington Office on Latin America, who along with Edward Snyder of the Friends Committee on National Legislation drafted its language. The Ford administration ignored this law also, but the Harkin amendment established human rights as a legal criterion in U.S. foreign policy.

Congressionally imposed restrictions hampered U.S.-Chilean relations, creating consternation in both Washington and Santiago. "The United States will one day understand that Chile is a true friend, probably the best, and perhaps the only true friend in the Hemisphere," Pinochet complained to Ambassador Popper after Congress passed the first restrictions on military assistance. "Chile is a better friend of the United States than the U.S. is of Chile."[54] The sanctions on military acquisitions hurt the Junta's reputation with younger officers; moreover, the regime's growing international isolation threatened its economic relations with the Western world. As the Pinochet regime came under increasing international criticism and pressure, it cast about for a way to improve its despotic image in the United States while continuing its repression. Pinochet initiated a covert propaganda and lobbying operation in the United States.

The regime's main effort to influence the media and Congress was conducted through an illicit, and illegal, program—most likely run by DINA. This campaign, organized by a fictitious "public committee" called the American-Chilean Council (ACC) between March 1975 and December 1978, was the brainchild of prominent conservative columnist William Buckley, and a veteran lobbyist for right-wing causes, Marvin Liebman. "For the sake of future Chilean-American relations, it is vital that Chile's case be put forward to the American people," Liebman wrote in a secret letter to Buckley after both were approached by Chile's UN ambassador for help. "The one way of doing this—as I know from many years of experience—is by a carefully planned program of international propaganda, and, when required, the mobilization of public action."

The ACC's propaganda program consisted of paying an unregistered lobbyist, L. Francis Bouchey, to "counter communist charges about human rights abuses in Chile"; publishing a series of pamphlets designed to portray the Allende government as an agent of the USSR,[55] and a biweekly information review on Chile to key congressional offices, interest groups, and policy actors; and financing trips by conservative pundits to Santiago.

Private donations from concerned U.S. citizens paid for these activities—or so the ACC claimed in its literature. In fact, the Pinochet regime was the "true foreign principal," according to Justice Department records, funneling hundreds of thousands of dollars secretly through an agent in Chile's United Nations mission in New York to Marvin Liebman's Madison Ave. office to underwrite the ACC's operations. The U.S. Justice Department eventually shut down these operations, charging that Liebman was acting as an unregistered foreign agent for Pinochet. The ACC, according to the Justice Department, was engaged "in a secret and illegal propaganda campaign aimed at making congressmen, journalists, academics and the American public more sympathetic to Chile's military dictatorship."[56]

Human Rights: The Internal Debate

While the Pinochet regime illegally lobbied Congress, the Ford administration adopted an *obedezco-pero-no-cumplo*—obey but don't comply—posture toward economic and military aid restrictions.[57] The administration ignored the FY 1975 ceiling of $25 million to Chile and sent over $112 million in food, materials, and credits; to exceed the cap the following year, AID lawyers provided policy makers with a contorted redefinition of the phrase *made available* in the FY 1976 legislation. The administration also chose to ignore the intent of the Harkin amendment. "The Department of State believes a serious question exists as to whether Chile is a 'country which engages in a consistent pattern of gross violations of human rights,' " Kissinger wrote to Congressman Fraser in April 1976, despite dozens of memos and reports from his aides on the Pinochet regime's systematic, ongoing atrocities.

Inside the executive branch, Secretary Kissinger personally led the effort to circumvent congressional restrictions and sustain aid to the Junta. In a December 3, 1974 meeting at the White House, he broached the issue directly with President Ford. "If we cut off arms, the military government will fall. They are lousy, but we just can't do things like this." On December 20, Kissinger again raised the issue with the president. "The Chilean aid cut is disastrous," as notes taken by White House aide Brent Scowcroft recorded Kissinger's argument. "I want to do everything possible to get arms for Chile."[58]

In meeting after meeting with his staff, Kissinger forcefully made the same point. Throughout December 1974, as Senator Kennedy's first effort to curtail U.S. military assistance to the Junta advanced through Congress, Kissinger berated his deputies for capitulating to the legislative branch, being soft on the human rights issue, and undermining the future of U.S. foreign policy. "Kennedy has the ball and is going to try and run with it," one aide, Carl Maw, informed the secretary on December 3. "The whole thing is on this silly human rights question." Kissinger responded: "If we don't stand with what our interest is, and if every time we get tackled we get compromised or call something a compromise, that's the same as yielding and we are in deep trouble." On December 20, he angrily reminded his aides: "We've got to go to the mat on things of national interest. What else are we here for? You can't throw a country to Kennedy just because it satisfies some ego trip that he's got." The Kissinger lecture continued: "My position is that I don't yield to Congress on matters of principle. . . . I don't tolerate the Department making these concessions."

In the highly revealing secret transcripts of his daily briefing with his assistant secretaries and regional officers, the secretary of state underscored several themes: first, that the Pinochet regime was being unfairly penalized. During the December 3 staff meeting, Kissinger repeatedly challenged Assistant Secretary Rogers on this point:

> *Secretary Kissinger:* I'd like to know whether the human rights problem in Chile is that much worse than in other countries in Latin America or whether their primary crime is to have replaced Allende and whether people are now getting penalized, having gotten rid of an anti-American government. Is it worse than in other Latin American countries?
> *Mr. Rogers:* Yes.
> *Secretary Kissinger:* Well, I think the consequences could be very serious, if we cut them off from military aide.

Kissinger returned again to this argument several minutes later:

> *Secretary Kissinger:* The worse crime of this government is that it's pro-American in the eyes of many of these supporters of these cutoffs. Is this government worse than the Allende government? Is human rights more severely threatened by this government than Allende?
> *Mr. Rogers:* Well, I can't say that, Mr. Secretary. In terms of freedom of association, Allende didn't close down the opposition party. In terms of freedom of the press, Allende didn't close down all the newspapers.

Kissinger also argued, repeatedly, that cutting off arms to Chile's military regime might lead it to collapse, be overthrown, or worse, seek to acquire weapons from China or the Middle East. "Am I wrong that this sort of thing is likely to finish off that government," he asked during his December 3 meeting. "And if the army winds up totally demoralized, that will affect amongst those out of office the whole future of politics. If it becomes clear that the army can [n]ever move again, the left will become immeasurably strengthened; am I wrong?" On December 20 he snapped at Rogers: "You know the only possible outcome of this can be an extreme left-wing government in Chile or driving the Chilean government sort of toward the Arabs . . . or the Chinese."[59]

But his greatest concern was that if Congress succeeded in Chile, it would be emboldened to apply human rights criteria to other nations. "If it happens in Chile, now," Kissinger complained during a December 23 meeting with his key deputies, "then it will be Korea next year. There isn't going to be any end to it. And . . . we are going to wind up in an unbelievable precarious position, in which no country can afford to tie up with us."[60] This was the "fundamental problem," Kissinger said. "It is a problem of the whole foreign policy that is being pulled apart, pulling out thread by thread, under one pretext or another. And it is an absurd argument to say Chile doesn't make a difference. . . ."

To William D. Rogers fell the unenviable task of explaining the political realities of the human rights movement to Kissinger. When the secretary denounced the legislated cuts in military aid to Chile as "insane," Rogers shared this assessment:

> It is insane. But Mr. Secretary, it does reflect an extraordinary strong feeling amongst the Congress, as you well know. You can go to the mat on it now if you want to. And I predict you will have a hell of a fight on your hands come January. . . . There are a lot of Democrats on the Hill this coming session who want to go the mat on the issue of human rights and want to make a fight about it. It is very hard to make a national interest argument on Chile. . . . [T]he human rights issue has caught the imagination up on the Hill, as you well know, Mr. Secretary, and amongst the American people.

"My diagnosis of the reason they stuck it [to] the department in this case," Rogers continued, "is that they didn't think we were sincere on the human rights issue."[61]

Indeed, the Ford administration's approach to Congress and the Chilean regime demonstrated an abysmal lack of sincerity on human rights. Rather than diplomatically employ the human rights legislation to press the Chileans to halt abuses, the administration appeared to commiserate with the Chileans. "The executive branch, from President Ford down, ha[s] consistently opposed restrictive legislation with regard to Chile," Ambassador Popper told

Pinochet in January 1975. "Both the Department of State and the embassy had exerted every effort to assist Chile in this area" and "we would work to change the restrictive legislation."[62] In his closed meetings with Chilean officials, Kissinger seemed to spend more time disparaging his staff's concerns for human rights than criticizing the regime for its atrocities. "I read the briefing paper for this meeting and it was nothing but Human Rights," Kissinger confided privately to Chilean foreign minister Patricio Carvajal during one meeting in 1975. "The State Department is made up of people who have a vocation for the ministry. Because there are not enough churches for them, they went into the Department of State."[63] During another meeting Kissinger told Carvajal, "I hold the strong view that human rights are not appropriate in a foreign policy context." Washington, Kissinger stated, "did not intend to harass Chile on this matter."[64]

A growing number of mid-level State Department officials recognized the folly of Kissinger's attitude towards Pinochet's atrocities. Washington's embrace of the regime had not only failed to ease repression in Chile; it was costly to U.S. national interests, creating divisions with Western allies, jeopardizing Congressional cooperation on other foreign assistance programs, and damaging America's moral leadership in the Third World. Befriending Pinochet had become a major liability. A defense of human rights, these officers argued, should be elevated to a prime objective of U.S. foreign policy, and a primary U.S. national interest. Increasingly, these officials made their voices heard in a heated internal debate over changing course in Chile.

The diverging positions in this debate became evident during the drafting of the Embassy's Country Analysis and Strategy Paper on Chile. The report, signed by Ambassador Popper and submitted on May 18, 1975, reflected Kissinger's position: "United States interest can best be served by maintaining and strengthening the present government in Chile. In conventional political and economic terms it is after all a highly friendly government." On human rights, Popper wrote, the U.S. would make its "preferences" known, and "encourage" and "offer incentives" for the military to end abuses. But the CASP report rejected "direct pressure tactics" which, Popper submitted, would contribute to the "siege mentality" in the regime.[65]

Ambassador Popper's position prompted a near mutiny within the embassy. Four embassy officers—senior political officer John Tipton, political officers Robert Steven and Michael Lyons, and labor attaché Arthur Nixon—drafted and signed a five-page "dissent" to the CASP report titled "U.S. Policy Toward Chile—An Alternative." In the first clear internal challenge to Kissinger's positive posture toward Pinochet, these embassy officers argued that "this policy of friendly persuasion has not worked" and proposed "a course of action, including tangible measures, which has the best chance of furthering

U.S. interests while at the same time causing real changes in the GOC's behavior." The human rights issue, according to their cogent critique, was paramount in U.S.-Chilean relations.

> In Chile at this time, it is and should be the dominant factor. There are no other U.S. interests in Chile, individually or collectively, which outweigh it. Further, the cost to the U.S. of continued identification as the principal supporter of the present GOC significantly outweighs the benefits received.
>
> To continue our present support for the GOC in the face of its continued serious human rights violations is to squander Executive Branch capital and credibility with Congress over a relatively unimportant issue when much more important ones are at stake. Further, by acting as a GOC advocate and protector in international fora and in representations to other governments we are expending our influence and effectiveness with our traditional friends and world allies over an issue of relatively little vital importance to us.

In an explicit rejection of Ambassador Popper and Kissinger's position, the embassy officers recommended: "that it should be U.S. policy to inform the GOC that we will take no new initiatives to assist Chile politically, economically, or militarily unless and until its human rights practices have reached an acceptable standard." (Doc 12)

In a series of interagency group meetings on future relations with the Pinochet regime, the Kissinger-Popper position prevailed. But there was still "disarray in Chile policy," as NSC aide Stephen Low titled a memorandum to Kissinger's White House deputy General Scowcroft.[66] Increasingly, the political fallout of ongoing assistance to the regime was affecting other bureaus and agencies in the State Department and Pentagon, adding to internal bureaucratic opposition. Pinochet's abrupt cancellation of the United Nations Human Rights Committee Working Group—a transparent attempt to cover up its atrocities—on July 5, strengthened the hand of critics of U.S. policy toward Chile, including those inside the U.S. government. Through the summer and fall of 1975, the internal debate continued, with the division among policy makers, diplomats, and desk officers growing more strident.

As the Bureau of Inter-American Affairs prepared for a major meeting about Chile in July, Ambassador Popper submitted a defense of the status quo—a twenty-six-page overview of "The Situation in Chile and the Prospects for U.S. Policy," framing the options of carrot vs. stick on the human rights issue. The human rights issue, he implied, had received more attention than warranted; in terms of U.S. national interests, Popper suggested, the human rights problem "is secondary, achieving its present importance principally because of its effect on our maneuverability in other areas." The ambassador opposed a high-level démarche to the regime and argued that the U.S. should simply "continue our general stance of disapproval."

At the Policy Planning office in ARA, Popper's arguments inspired analyst Richard Bloomfield to draft one of the bluntest and most candid documents ever written by an official on U.S. policy and human rights in Chile. "How would the Junta ever get the impression the USG 'disapproves'?" he asked in a two-page paper to Assistant Secretary Rogers. (Doc 13) "As the old saying goes, actions speak louder than words." In his memorandum, Bloomfield listed U.S. actions in support of the regime:

- We are solicitous about Chile's debt problem and deploy our diplomacy to promote a debt rescheduling.
- We use our influence in the IFIS [International Financial Institutions] to assure that Chilean loans are not held up.
- We vote against or abstain on resolutions in international organizations that condemn the GOC's human rights record.
- We assure the GOC that we want to sell it arms and that we regret congressional restrictions.

Bloomfield rejected the premise, put forth by Popper and Kissinger, that without U.S. backing the Pinochet regime would fall and some type of hostile leftist government would reemerge. "The need to 'live with' the absence of human rights in Chile in order to prevent the re-emergence of a hostile government is, in my mind, a distinctly secondary consideration," he wrote. The self-inflicted wounds to U.S. policy, however, were primary considerations. Both domestically and internationally, Washington's support for Pinochet had so damaged the image of the United States government as to undermine the credibility of the U.S government. "In the eyes of the world at large, we are closely associated with this Junta, ergo with fascists and torturers," Bloomfield asserted. "It is one more reason why much of the youth of the country is alienated from their government and its foreign policy. Chile is just the latest example for a lot of people in this country of the United States not being true to its values."

Kissinger and Pinochet

Growing public, congressional, and internal department pressure led to a bizarre and unexpected scene—Henry Kissinger giving a major international address on human rights in Santiago, Chile. His now famous June 1976 trip was part of a Latin American tour, a priority of his assistant secretary for inter-American affairs, William D. Rogers. Initially, it had been scheduled for February 1975, but the demands of the secretary's shuttle diplomacy in the Middle East forced a two-month postponement; then, in April the collapse of Saigon and chaotic end of the Vietnam War led to the cancellation of the planned trip. A year later, when the Organization of American States (OAS) scheduled its general assembly meeting in Santiago for June 1976, Kissinger agreed to attend. His high-profile visit, as Rogers understood, could meet several goals at once: calling attention to the Latin American region; mollifying Latin American governments who felt ignored, and addressing congressional skepticism about the State Department's interest in human rights.

At the top of the OAS agenda was the new, and highly critical, Inter-American Commission on Human Rights report on the Pinochet regime's atrocities. "The right of physical liberty of the person . . . continues to be frequently ignored by the Government of Chile," the ICHR report stated. "While decrees are being issued for the purpose of tranquilizing or confusing world opinion, the practice of arbitrary jailings and persecutions and tortures continue up to the present." Kissinger did not intend to focus his participation at the OAS on the human rights issue, but Assistant Secretary Rogers and the embassy convinced him that there was no way to avoid it. "For the Secretary to come to Chile without raising the human rights issue would generate criticism on a scale that effectively closes out the non-involvement option," deputy chief of mission Thomas Boyatt cabled Washington on April 21. Moreover, Boyatt argued: "no U.S. official of the Secretary's stature has visited Chile since the coup, nor does another visit at such a level appear likely during the present GOC's tenure. The Secretary will be listened to, and his visit offers the best opportunity we are likely to have to obtain significant improvements of human rights practices in Chile."[67] For that reason, the embassy recommended Kissinger hold a private meeting with Pinochet.

In terms of diplomatic strategy, Ambassador Popper's office counseled that only a direct, tough, message on human rights would get through. "Pinochet is so narrow-minded and convinced of his righteousness that it takes sledgehammer blows to all his attention to some unpleasant facts of life," Boyatt noted. "Pinochet's anti-communism is evangelical and self-righteous," Ambassador David Popper reiterated in an biographic, "about-the-man" cable intended to introduce Kissinger to the psychology of the individual he would face. "The traditional norms of diplomatic phraseology can be lost on the president. He needs direct treatment, and clear and specific statements. If we deal in platitudes Pinochet will never understand what is bothering us nor react to our recommendations."[68]

In preparation for the meeting, two weeks before the trip Assistant Secretary Rogers provided the key briefing paper—"Overall Objectives for Your Visit to Santiago"—to Kissinger. "When you do see [Pinochet]," Rogers submitted, "your objectives will be to make clear that:"

- The problem of human rights in Chile is central, not only to the Congress and the public but for our relations as a whole.
- We are well aware that there is an international propaganda campaign, and we discount it.
- But the problem . . . is not propaganda; a "public relations" response will not work.
- Basic steps to improve human rights practices would be in Chile's own interest and in ours.

The task, Rogers continued was "to convince the Chileans of the rudimentary facts of life, which they have not accepted from anyone else but may believe from you." Kissinger needed to make Pinochet understand that "only basic change in human-rights practices is likely to block efforts to:"

- Embargo the military pipeline.
- Prohibit future military sales.
- Reduce or cut off concessional wheat sales and housing guarantees.
- Cut off loans by international banks.

Similar to Franco's Spain in the 1940s, Chile had become "a symbol of right-wing tyranny," Rogers advised the secretary. "Like it or not, we are identified with the regime's origins and hence charged with some responsibility for its actions. This accents our strong interest in getting the GOC to pursue acceptable human-rights practices."[69]

In his memoirs, *Years of Renewal*, Kissinger described how he followed this advice, pushing the themes of democracy and human rights at a noontime meeting on June 8 in General Pinochet's presidential office. "A considerable amount of time in my dialogue with Pinochet was devoted to human rights," Kissinger recounted. "I outlined the main points of my speech to the OAS," he wrote. Quoting what he had told Pinochet, Kissinger continued: "Pinochet needed to understand that human rights were"

> a problem which complicates our relationships. . . . I am going to speak about human rights this afternoon in the General Assembly. I delayed my statement until I could talk to you. I wanted you to understand my position. We want to deal in moral persuasion, not legal sanctions.[70]

But Kissinger's public account is in sharp contrast with the text of the secret memorandum of conversation with Pinochet that reveals no effort at "moral persuasion," no mention of democracy, and only minimal concern expressed on human rights. As the declassified transcript indicates, Kissinger's intent was to brief Pinochet in advance on the speech and let him know that it was intended to appease the U.S. Congress rather than directed at Chile. "I can do no less without producing a reaction in the U.S. which would lead to legislative restrictions," Kissinger told Pinochet after outlining several points in the speech. (Doc 14) But he stressed: "*The speech is not aimed at Chile. I wanted to tell you about this.* My evaluation is that you are a victim of all left-wing groups around the world and that your greatest sin was that you overthrew a government which was going communist." (Emphasis added.)

In his selective rendition in *Years of Renewal*, Kissinger noted Pinochet's complaint that the United States "had a punitive system for its friends." "I returned to my underlying theme that any major help from us would realistically depend on progress on human rights," Kissinger wrote of his response. In fact, according to the secret transcript, Kissinger responded by commiserating with Pinochet over Congressional pressures on human rights and reassuring him of Washington's support. "There is merit to what you say. It is a curious time. It is unfortunate. We have been through Viet Nam and Watergate," Kissinger confided to Pinochet. "We welcomed the overthrow of the Communist-inclined government here. We are not out to weaken your position."

Kissinger did briefly raise the human rights issue, in the context of removing "the weapons in the arms of our enemies"—a reference to the U.S. Congress. "It would really help if you would let us know the measures you are taking in the human rights field," he said, immediately adding: "None of this is said with the hope of undermining your government. I want you to succeed. And I want to retain the possibility of aid."

The urging of the secretary's top aides to press the Chileans for "basic changes" in their human rights practices went unheeded. Moreover, throughout the meeting, Kissinger ignored the embassy's warning not to cloud his limited message on human rights with platitudes. "In the United States, as you know, we are sympathetic with what you are trying to do here," Kissinger told Pinochet at the outset. "We wish your government well." And toward the end of their conversation, he reiterated the Ford administration's support for Chile's military regime: "We want to help, not undermine you. You did a great service to the West in overthrowing Allende."

DOCUMENT 1. Department of State, Cable, "USG Attitude Toward Junta," September 13, 1973.

SENSITIVE

PAGE 51 SITUATION(S) MESSAGE(S) LISTING DATE 09/25/73//26

SITUATION: CHILE
SUBJECT CATAGORY: COUP

MESSAGE / ANNOTATION:

MESSAGE:
IMMEDIATE
O 131718Z SEP 73
FM SECSTATE WASHDC

TO AMEMBASSY SANTIAGO IMMEDIATE 3693

~~S E C R E T~~ STATE 182051

EXDIS
E.O.
TAGS:

SUBJECT: USG ATTITUDE TOWARD JUNTA

REF : SANTIAGO 4154
REF : SANTIAGO 4154
?. IE WELCOME GENERAL PINOCHET'S EXPRESSION OF JUNTA
1. WE WELCOME GENERAL PINOCHET'S EXPRESSION OF JUNTA DESIRE FOR STRENGTHENED TIES BETWEEN CHILE AND U.S. YOU ARE REQUESTED TO CONVEY AT EARLIEST POSSIBLE OPPORTUNITY INFORMAL RESPONSE TO GENERAL PINOCHET ALONG FOLLOWING LINES AND BY WHATEVER PRIVATE MEANS YOU DEEM MOST APPROPRIATE.

2. THE USG WISHES MAKE CLEAR ITS DESIRE TO COOPERATE WITH THE MILITARY JUNTA AND TO ASSIST IN ANY APPROPRIATE WAY. WE AGREE THAT IT IS BEST INITIALLY TO AVOID TOO MUCH PUBLIC IDENTIFICATION BETWEEN US. IN MEANTIME WE WILL BE PLEASED TO MAINTAIN PRIVATE UNOFFICIAL CONTACTS AS THE JUNTA MAY DESIRE. WE WILL HAVE RESPONSES TO OTHER POINTS AISED BY GENERAL PINOCHET AT AN EARLY DATE. RUSH

BT

PSN1027671 DTG:131718 TOR:2561739

DECLASSIFIED SENSITIVE

DOCUMENT 2. Department of State, Cable, "Continuation of Relations with GOC and Request for Flares and Helmets," September 18, 1973.

SENSITIVE

PAGE 264 SITUATION(S) MESSAGE(S) LISTING DATE 09/25/73//268

SITUATION: CHILE
SUBJECT CATAGORY: COUP

MESSAGE / ANNOTATION:

MESSAGE:
IMMEDIATE
O 180153Z SEP 73 ZFF4
FM SECSTATE WASHDC

TO AMEMBASSY SANTIAGO NIACT IMMEDIATE 3760

~~S E C R E T~~ STATE 185004

EXDIS
E.O. 11652: GDS
TAGS: CI, PINS, PINT

SUBJECT: CONTINUATION OF RELATIONS WITH GOC AND REQUEST FOR FLARES AND HELMETS

REF: (A) SANTIAGO 5617: (B) STATE 184139 (C) SANTIAGO 4304 (D) SANTIAGO 4328
FOR AMBASSADOR

1. YOU SHOULD CONVEY FOLLOWING MESSAGE INFORMALLY ASAP TO GOC -- IN A PRIVATE MEETING WITH ADMIRAL HUERTA, IF YOU DEEM IT APPROPRIATE.

2. USG WILL, OF COURSE, RESPOND AFFIRMATIVELY TO JUNTA'S NOTE RE CONTINUANCE OF RELATIONS. WE EXPECT THAT OUR RESPONSE WILL BE FORTHCOMING WITHIN THE NEXT FEW DAYS. IN MEANTIME, WE WANT GOC TO KNOW OF OUR STRONGEST DESIRE TO COOPERATE CLOSELY AND ESTABLISH FIRM BASIS FOR CORDIAL AND MOST CONSTRUCTIVE RELATIONSHIP. WE STRONGLY BELIEVE DOMESTIC AND INTERNATIONAL CONSIDERATIONS MAKE THIS VERY BRIEF DELAY HIGHLY ADVISABLE IN OVERALL INTERESTS OF NEW GOC AS WELL AS IN OUR OWN.

3. WITH RESPECT TO FLARES AND HELMETS, YOU MAY INFORM APPROPRIATE CHILEAN OFFICIAL THAT WE ARE ACTIVELY WORKING ON THE REQUEST AND WILL GIVE THEM A RESPONSE ASAP.

******* WHSR COMMENTS *******

HAK, SCOWCROFT, LL, JORDEN

PSN:031634 DTG:180153 TOR:261023O

SENSITIVE

DOCUMENT 3. Department of State, **SECRET** Meeting Minutes of the Washington Special Actions Group, "Chile," September 20, 1973.

UNCLASSIFIED

WASHINGTON SPECIAL ACTIONS GROUP MEETING

September 20, 1973

Time and Place: 3:05 p.m. - 3:49 p.m., White House Situation Room

Subject: Chile

Participants:

Chairman	Henry A. Kissinger	Treasury	William Simon Michael Bradfield
State	William Porter Jack Kubisch	OMB	Dolph Bridgewater
Defense	William Clements Robert Hill V/Adm. Ray Peet	NSC	B/Gen. Brent Scowcroft Richard Kennedy William Jorden Charles Cooper
JCS	Adm. John P. Weinel		James Barnum
CIA	William Nelson [redacted]		

50 U.S.C. § 403g (1994).

SUMMARY OF CONCLUSIONS

It was agreed that:

...recognition of the new government would be announced on Monday, 24 September 1973;

...Ambassador Davis is to talk to the junta on Friday, September 21, to inform them of our goodwill, our intention to recognize in the next few days, and about the delivery of medical supplies;

...a cable will be sent to Ambassador Davis telling him: of our intention to recognize and when; when the emergency food supplies will be delivered; and authorizing the Ambassador to discuss, with the junta, Chile's middle- and long-term economic needs;

...an economic team would not be sent to Chile until the junta requests one;

...the Chile Working Group will continue in operation.

SECRET/NODIS/XGDS

UNCLASSIFIED

DOCUMENT 4. CIA, **SECRET** Memorandum, "Project [Excised] Request for Amendment No. 1 for FY 1974," ca. January 1974 (page 1).

MEMORANDUM FOR: Associate Deputy Director for Operations

VIA: [Excised]

SUBJECT: Project [Excised] Request for Amendment No. 1 for FY 1974

1. [Excised], the Santiago Station's propaganda project, was renewed for FY 1974 for [Excised] on 4 April 1973. The project, which used a variety of propaganda mechanisms to inform the Chilean and foreign public of the Allende government's efforts to impose a Marxist totalitarian government, played a significant role in setting the stage for the military coup of 11 September 1973. Prior to the coup the project's media outlets maintained a steady barrage of anti-government criticism, exploiting every possible point of friction between the government and the democratic opposition, and emphasizing the problems and conflicts which were developing between the government and the armed forces. Since the coup, these media outlets have supported the new military government. They have tried to present the Junta in the most positive light for the Chilean public and to assist foreign journalists in Chile to obtain facts about the local situation. [Excised]

2. As a result of the overthrow of the Allende government, the [Excised] operation has had to adapt to the new situation, and has undergone some important changes. It was mutually agreed with the [Excised] to terminate a number of [Excised] activities [Excised]

[Excised]

DOCUMENT 5. CIA, **SECRET** Memorandum for William Colby, "Chile—Initial Post-Coup Support, October 9, 1973.

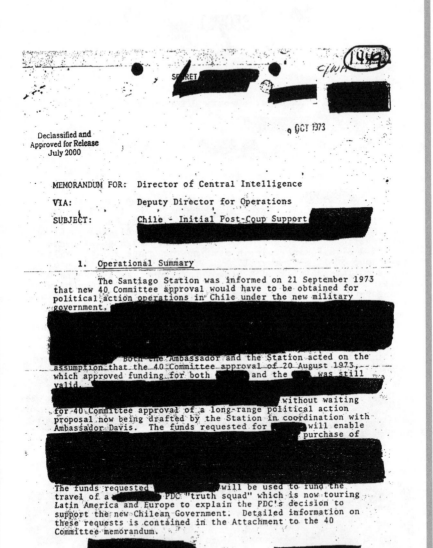

SECRET

C/WH 1449

9 OCT 1973

Declassified and Approved for Release July 2000

MEMORANDUM FOR: Director of Central Intelligence

VIA: Deputy Director for Operations

SUBJECT: Chile - Initial Post-Coup Support

1. Operational Summary

The Santiago Station was informed on 21 September 1973 that new 40 Committee approval would have to be obtained for political action operations in Chile under the new military government. Both the Ambassador and the Station acted on the assumption that the 40 Committee approval of 20 August 1973, which approved funding for both and the was still valid. without waiting for 40 Committee approval of a long-range political action proposal now being drafted by the Station in coordination with Ambassador Davis. The funds requested for will enable purchase of

The funds requested will be used to fund the travel of a PDC "truth squad" which is now touring Latin America and Europe to explain the PDC's decision to support the new Chilean Government. Detailed information on these requests is contained in the Attachment to the 40 Committee memorandum.

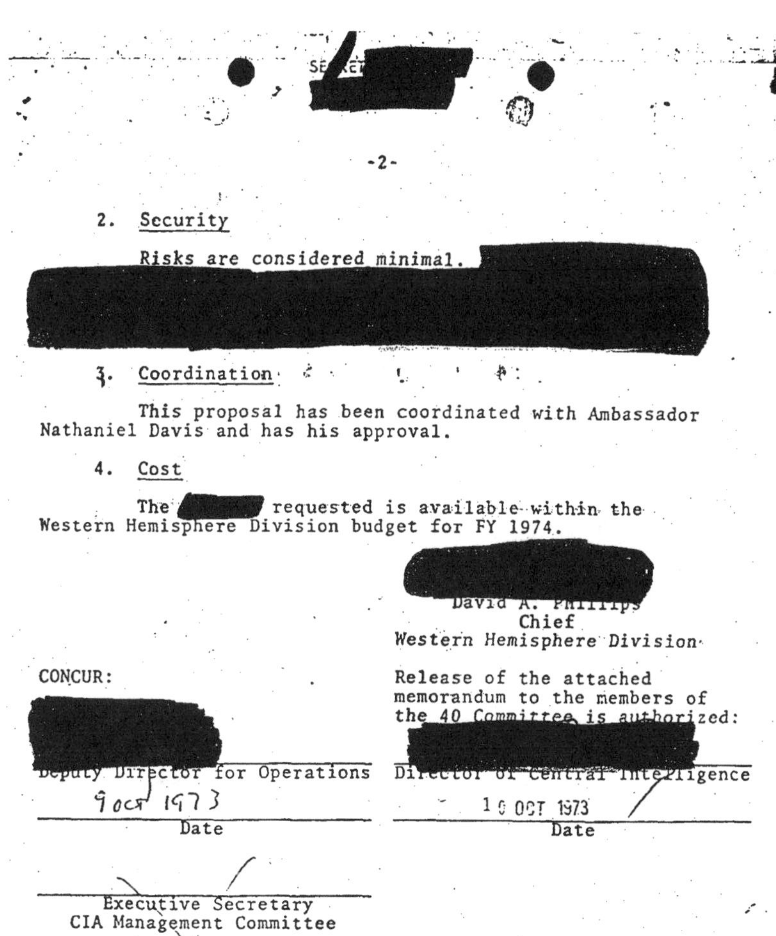

SECRET

-2-

2. Security

Risks are considered minimal.

3. Coordination

This proposal has been coordinated with Ambassador Nathaniel Davis and has his approval.

4. Cost

The requested is available within the Western Hemisphere Division budget for FY 1974.

David A. Phillips
Chief
Western Hemisphere Division

CONCUR:

Deputy Director for Operations

9 Oct 1973
Date

Release of the attached memorandum to the members of the 40 Committee is authorized:

Director of Central Intelligence

10 OCT 1973
Date

Executive Secretary
CIA Management Committee

Date

DOCUMENT 6. Department of State, Memorandum of Conversation, "ARA-CIA Weekly Meeting, 23 November 1973," November 27, 1973.

UNCLASSIFIED

EXCISE

P
B1

MEMORANDUM

November 27, 1973

TO : INR/DDC - Mr. William McAfee

FROM : INR/DDC - James R. Gardner

SUBJECT : ARA-CIA Weekly Meeting, 23 November 1973

PARTICIPANTS: ARA - Messrs. Kubisch, Shlaudeman and Bowdler (for latter half of meeting); CIA -[ ] and INR/DDC - James R. Gardner

Chile

Most of the discussion centered around the CIA proposal for giving covert assistance to the Chilean PDC and private sector organizations. The sum proposed is [ ] of which [ ] would go to the PDC, [ ] and another [ ] for contingencies. The purpose of the assistance, as explained in the CIA memorandum of proposal and by [ ] is to help the PDC and elements in the private sector bridge the radical change in the situation brought about by the Junta's overthrow of Allende.

Mr. Shlaudeman said that in his view the rationale for extending the assistance was a negative but real one. If we held off now we could be causing ourselves trouble, for it would look as if we had been interested simply in knocking off Allende. There was no question in his mind that a most important objective was for us to get out of political action in Chile once and for all. But the proposed program was a minimum one for a minimum time. He felt it should be extended with the clear understanding that after such and such a date the party would be over.

[ ] said that one problem was that reflected in the claim of the PDC that, if there were no PDC activity, the only ones that would benefit would be the Communists, since they would continue to operate and would continue to receive money.

Mr. Shlaudeman commented that this claim presumed a condition in Chile that was unlikely; that is, one in which the military would tolerate political activity by the Communists. Nonetheless, without

UNCLASSIFIED

the help of the PDC it was quite possible that the Junta would not be able to perform as an effective government, especially in the economic sphere. It needed the help of talented members of the PDC, although not necessarily that of the PDC itself. But a PDC break with the Junta, because of the effect it might have on individual dispositions to cooperate, could mean a breakdown in the effectiveness of the new government.

Mr. Kubisch said that, as we knew, he was in principle opposed to covert political operations:

(1) The political action possibilities available to us through CIA represented a means of influencing events and an instrument for action that should be used only if there were need.

(2) Given the evolution of events in the South American region in the last 25 years, and the increasing polarization in the region of contending political elements, and the history of our involvement in covert political and military action, we had to be extremely careful about using this instrument. In his view, we should employ it with the greatest reluctance and only when no other and better means were available. The damage to the US and to the USG were it to become known that we were engaged in covert operations could be very great, and across the board, in today's world. We have been hurt by publicity about covert programs. Therefore his initial stance would be one of strong skepticism when proposals for covert political action were raised. His preference was for none whatever in the hemisphere. It would be good if we could go for years without resorting to them, if such restraint would do us no harm. Therefore he would recommend use of such programs only if there were no other way to accomplish a vitally important end.

(3) He nevertheless wished to consider the present proposal carefully. The importance of Chile and the views of important US officials who were concurring in the proposal commanded our most careful attention. But his first reaction was clearly negative.

Mr. Kubisch then referred to the help that we had given to anti-Allende elements in the 1970 election and said that whatever it was we had done, we had done it to oppose Allende and we had not achieved our objectives. Our interests in Chile as a result of the 1970 elections came under direct and material threat. We now have a different situation in Chile. While it was understandable that we felt it necessary to oppose Allende in 1970, and to help his opposition once he was in office, the question now was whether, given the abrupt change in Chile and in the security situation there, it was really essential to fine tune a political situation simply to be a moderating influence and to help the opposition stay alive. He found it difficult to see a persuasive case that we should do so. His feelings was sharpened by the problems that seemed to be

emerging between the Junta and the PDC, and by the fact that the Secretary had made it clear that the change in regime in Chile was very much in our interest and that we should do all we could to help the Junta succeed. In view of the Secretary's remarks, he would not be comfortable recommending assistance to any element in Chile that was not completely identified with the Junta. It was not essential to the success of the Junta that the PDC survive as an entity. He mentioned in this regard the situation in Mexico and Brazil.

Mr. Shlaudeman said that the case of the PDC in Chile was to be distinguished from Brazil and Mexico since the PDC was a real party with a real base, and it was the only real surviving element in the political system. What we were talking about in this proposal was help only in a transitional term. It was perhaps correct to say that the survival of the PDC as a party was not important -- but what was important was that we not give the impression that we had no problems with a right wing dictatorship and that we had no interest in the survival of democracy in Chile after all that we had said over the years. He therefore still felt it would be best to tell the PDC that we would finance it for three to five months but that we were getting out of this kind of activity for good in very short order, that it was up to the PDC to put its house in order.

Mr. Shlaudeman said he was talking only about assistance to the PDC, he was against that part of the proposal that had to do with assistance to [ ]

Mr. Shlaudeman said that in his view, based on what he knew of the operations in Chile, the security risk would be minimal. The reaction of the junta if it found out about our assistance to the PDC would not be great if our aid went to the more conservative wing of the party and not to that represented by Tomic. Six or seven months from now, he said, the reaction would probably be somewhat sharper.

Mr. Kubisch asked what would happen if in January or February the Junta found out that we had made money available to the PDC. They naturally would ask what the hell we were doing, were we still intervening in Chile; still meddling? If we could say that our program had ended with the overthrow of Allende, our position would be sound, but if, on the other hand, we had to say that we had given a little to help the PDC over a transitional period, wouldn't the reaction be bad?

Mr. Shlaudeman said he really didn't think it would be.

Mr. Kubisch said that when Allende had been president, it was possible to make a case that his opposition should be supported. Now, however, the situation was much different, the right wing was in control. Were we perhaps not saying simply that the situation had gone too far the other way for our taste? In gross terms, when a major threat to US interest was involved, we should use means to correct the condition, no

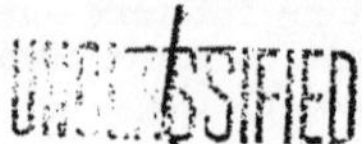

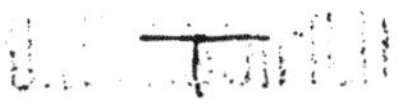

matter how extreme they might be. This was not such a case. Just because we did not like a government was no reason to intervene in their countries. He himself didn't like the Junta but he could not see it as a serious, extreme threat to our interests.

Mr. Shlaudeman said he agreed, but said that he was worried about the effects of a drastic, immeciate cut off right now, especially since we had been saying every since 1962 that our primary interest in Chile was the survival of democracy.

Mr. Kubisch responded that Chilean democracy had taken the country close to disaster. He felt that, attractive as an orderly disengagement would have been, the present circumstances did not make this the preferable option. There were a lot of things that we favored abroad, that we thought were good things, but simply because we felt that way was no reason to use covert action to see them realized, unless, as he had said before, our interests were actually gravely threatened.

Mr. Kubisch concluded the discussion by saying that he wished to think about the matter a little more, even though he saw little prospect that his mind would change. It was agreed that Mr. Shlaudeman would speak to Ambassador Davis if the latter might advance any considerations that had not be given sufficient attention.

NR

DOCUMENT 7. White House, **SECRET** Action Memorandum for Henry Kissinger, "Termination of Chile Account," June 11, 1974.

MEMORANDUM

THE WHITE HOUSE
WASHINGTON

SECRET/SENSITIVE/
EYES ONLY

OUTSIDE SYSTEM
ACTION

11 June 1974

MEMORANDUM FOR: SECRETARY KISSINGER

FROM: ROB ROY RATLIFF

SUBJECT: Termination of the Chile Account

Last August the 40 Committee approved a $1 million covert action program for Chile, but it never got started because less than a month later a coup changed the picture completely. This January, CIA submitted a request for [redacted] to [redacted] Christian Democratic Party (PDC) and provide the party operating funds for three months while the Agency sorted things out and determined if additional aid were warranted (TAB A). 25x(1)

Defense and JCS 40 Committee principals promptly approved the proposal, but State wrestled with it and after lengthy deliberation, including consultation with our Ambassador, State voted to approve compensation for commitments made before the coup up to [redacted] CIA participated in State's deliberations and says this is an acceptable resolution. These funds are available in CIA's budget for the current fiscal year which ends 30 June.

RECOMMENDATION:

That you approve the State/CIA compromise authorizing payment to the PDC of not more than [redacted] for commitments made before the coup in Chile.

APPROVE ______ DISAPPROVE______ OTHER______

Attachment:
TAB A

Concur:
Stephen Low
Richard Kennedy

NSC DECLASSIFICATION REVIEW [E.O. 12958]
/X/ Exempt in part and redact as shown
by L.Salvetti Date 9/14/2000

SECRET/SENSITIVE/EYES ONLY

110

DOCUMENT 8. CIA, **SECRET** Intelligence Memorandum [Col. Contreras Luncheon at CIA Headquarters], March 4, 1974 (page 1).

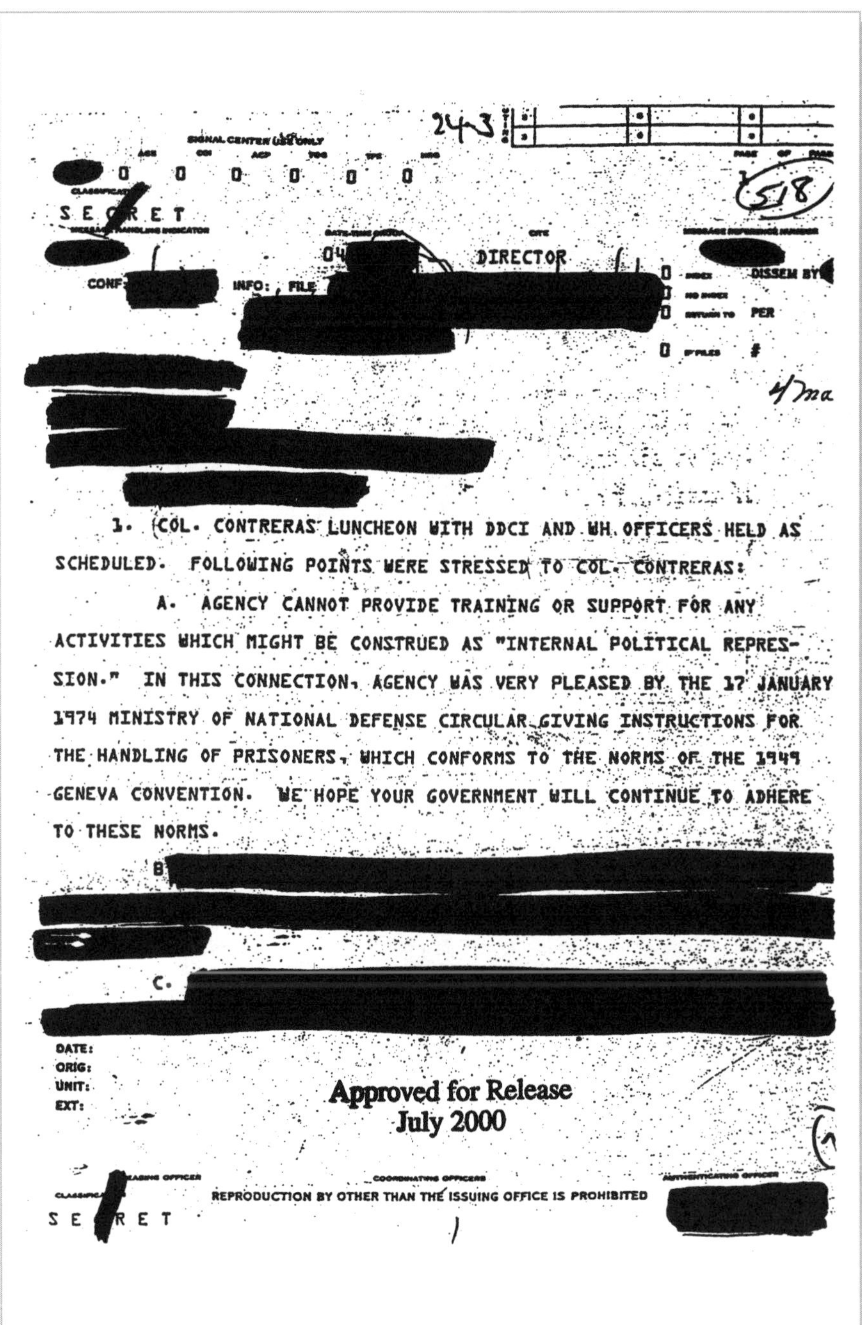

SIGNAL CENTER USE ONLY

SECRET

04 DIRECTOR

CONF: INFO: FILE

DISSEM BY

PER

1. COL. CONTRERAS LUNCHEON WITH DDCI AND WH OFFICERS HELD AS SCHEDULED. FOLLOWING POINTS WERE STRESSED TO COL. CONTRERAS:

A. AGENCY CANNOT PROVIDE TRAINING OR SUPPORT FOR ANY ACTIVITIES WHICH MIGHT BE CONSTRUED AS "INTERNAL POLITICAL REPRESSION." IN THIS CONNECTION, AGENCY WAS VERY PLEASED BY THE 17 JANUARY 1974 MINISTRY OF NATIONAL DEFENSE CIRCULAR GIVING INSTRUCTIONS FOR THE HANDLING OF PRISONERS, WHICH CONFORMS TO THE NORMS OF THE 1949 GENEVA CONVENTION. WE HOPE YOUR GOVERNMENT WILL CONTINUE TO ADHERE TO THESE NORMS.

B.

C.

DATE:
ORIG:
UNIT:
EXT:

Approved for Release
July 2000

REPRODUCTION BY OTHER THAN THE ISSUING OFFICE IS PROHIBITED

SECRET

DOCUMENT 9. CIA, **SECRET** Intelligence Memorandum [Pinochet Request for Contreras Meeting with Deputy Director Vernon Walters], ca. July 1, 1975.

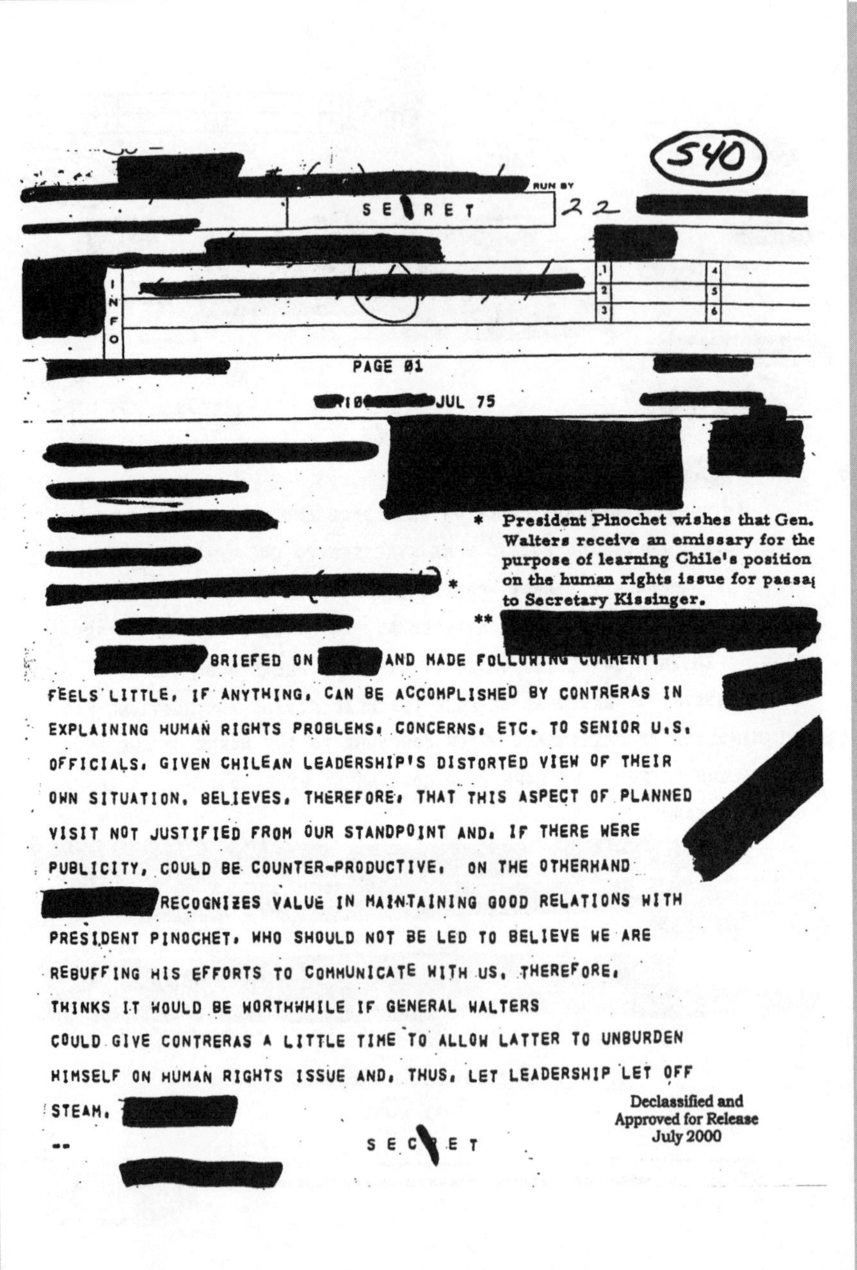

540

RUN BY

SECRET

22

INFO

PAGE 01

[redacted] JUL 75

* President Pinochet wishes that Gen. Walters receive an emissary for the purpose of learning Chile's position on the human rights issue for passa[ge] to Secretary Kissinger.

**

[redacted] BRIEFED ON [redacted] AND MADE FOLLOWING COMMENT:

FEELS LITTLE, IF ANYTHING, CAN BE ACCOMPLISHED BY CONTRERAS IN EXPLAINING HUMAN RIGHTS PROBLEMS, CONCERNS, ETC. TO SENIOR U.S. OFFICIALS, GIVEN CHILEAN LEADERSHIP'S DISTORTED VIEW OF THEIR OWN SITUATION. BELIEVES, THEREFORE, THAT THIS ASPECT OF PLANNED VISIT NOT JUSTIFIED FROM OUR STANDPOINT AND, IF THERE WERE PUBLICITY, COULD BE COUNTER-PRODUCTIVE. ON THE OTHERHAND [redacted] RECOGNIZES VALUE IN MAINTAINING GOOD RELATIONS WITH PRESIDENT PINOCHET, WHO SHOULD NOT BE LED TO BELIEVE WE ARE REBUFFING HIS EFFORTS TO COMMUNICATE WITH US. THEREFORE, THINKS IT WOULD BE WORTHWHILE IF GENERAL WALTERS COULD GIVE CONTRERAS A LITTLE TIME TO ALLOW LATTER TO UNBURDEN HIMSELF ON HUMAN RIGHTS ISSUE AND, THUS, LET LEADERSHIP LET OFF STEAM. [redacted]

--

SECRET

Declassified and Approved for Release July 2000

DOCUMENT 10. CIA, **SECRET** Memorandum for William Colby, "Juan Manuel Contreras Sepulveda Visit to Headquarters," August 23, 1975.

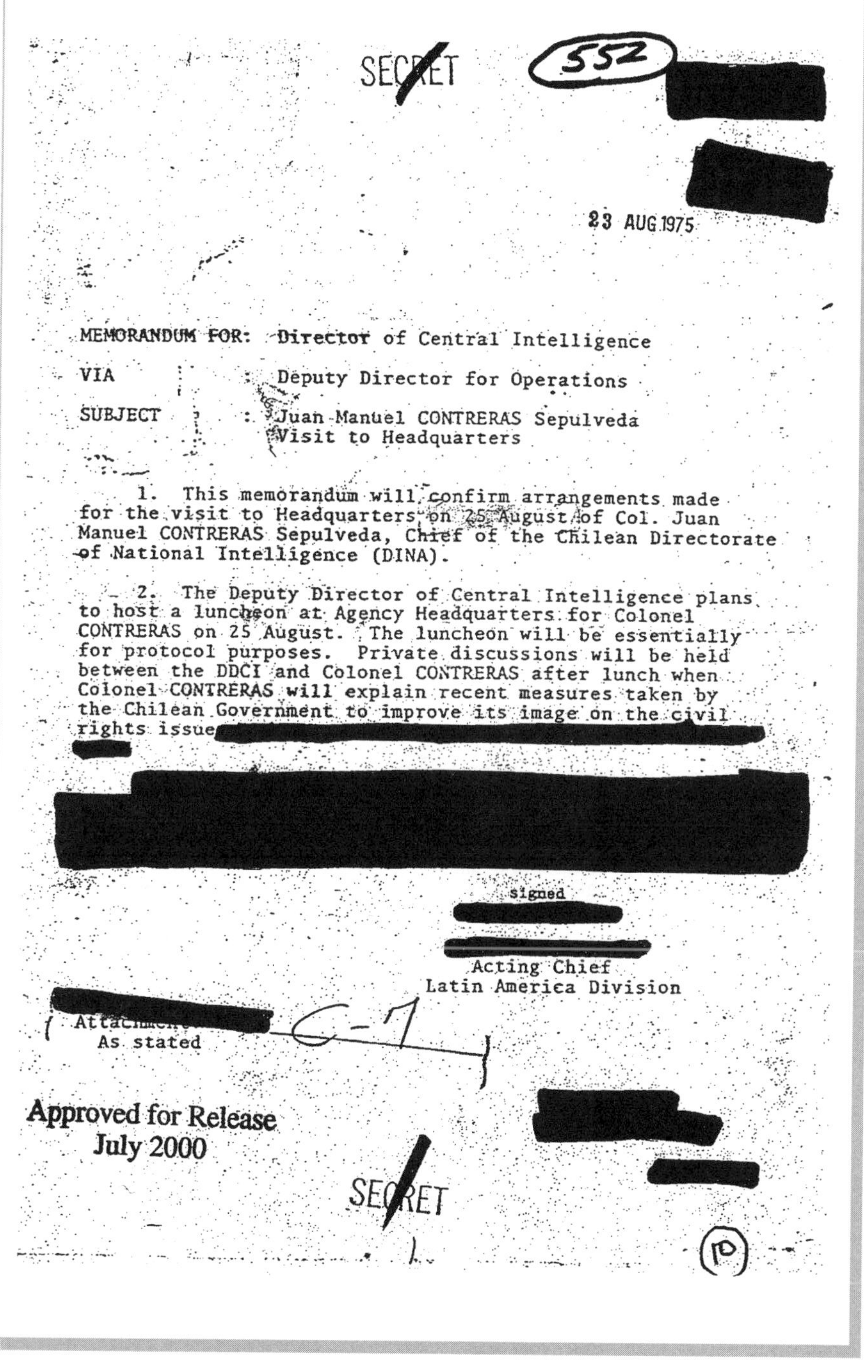

SECRET 552

23 AUG 1975

MEMORANDUM FOR: Director of Central Intelligence

VIA : Deputy Director for Operations

SUBJECT : Juan Manuel CONTRERAS Sepulveda Visit to Headquarters

1. This memorandum will confirm arrangements made for the visit to Headquarters on 25 August of Col. Juan Manuel CONTRERAS Sepulveda, Chief of the Chilean Directorate of National Intelligence (DINA).

2. The Deputy Director of Central Intelligence plans to host a luncheon at Agency Headquarters for Colonel CONTRERAS on 25 August. The luncheon will be essentially for protocol purposes. Private discussions will be held between the DDCI and Colonel CONTRERAS after lunch when Colonel CONTRERAS will explain recent measures taken by the Chilean Government to improve its image on the civil rights issue

Signed

Acting Chief
Latin America Division

Attachment
As stated

C-7

Approved for Release
July 2000

SECRET

(10)

DOCUMENT 11. White House, Memorandum of Conversation, "Cabinet Meeting, September 17, 1974–11:00 a.m." (pages 1, 2).

MEMORANDUM

THE WHITE HOUSE

WASHINGTON

~~SECRET~~

MEMORANDUM FOR THE RECORD

SUBJECT: Cabinet Meeting, September 17, 1974 - 11:00 a.m.

President: A number of news stories have appeared, and I commented last night on the Chile deal. It is my judgment, and I think that of every President, that the prime consideration is the national interest of the United States. We need a CIA and we need covert operations. This has been done since 1948.

Henry, could you give the details.

Kissinger: There are three aspects of the problem: What is the 40 Committee? What was the Chile situation? What did we do, overtly and covertly?

We face over the world threats to democratic institutions and we need covert action to deal with them. By their nature, we don't talk about these. So how do we deal with the leaks? Britain is certainly a democracy, yet a British paper couldn't print this stuff.

Every President has instituted safeguards. The 40 Committee has existed all this time. [redacted] Most projects are checked with the American Embassy involved. Projects are circulated, and if they are minor, they are signed off and go to the President for approval. The Assistant to the President doesn't decide; he presides as the representative of the President. If there is disagreement -- which happens rarely -- or if they are major matters, there is a meeting, and either a meeting is held or an options paper goes to the President. After six months there is automatic review of each program. The chairmen of the relevant committees are briefed.

Covert operations are those which can't be done in any other way. If they are leaked, we cannot conduct this policy. Not much is being done, but what is, is being done because they are important and can't be done in any other way.

~~SECRET~~

E.O. 12958
3.4(b)(1)
1.5(c)

NSC 3461

101 A

On Chile, the procedures were very regular, following those established under Truman.

One can argue that Allende wouldn't have won if we hadn't reduced the aid levels under Kennedy and Johnson.

What was the situation in Chile? In Chile, elections are won either by a popular majority or if there is no majority, an election in the Parliament. Allende got only 36% of the vote, and then proceeded to try to turn it into an irreversible dictatorial regime. On his left he had a group led from Cuba which accused him of not being extreme enough. This required that he concentrate on anti-US policies.

The effort of the 40 Committee was not to overthrow Allende but to preserve the democratic system for the 1976 elections. There was one famous newspaper they tried to put out of business, and they tried to throttle the opposition. Is this destabilizing? Sure, to a dictator.

The coup was produced by Allende's attempt to turn the regime into a Communist dictatorship, and the military eventually rebelled.

Last, there is the claim we waged economic warfare against Allende.

President Nixon did say we should be careful about aid to him, but the fact is that Allende nationalized American companies and defaulted on the obligation to give compensation. We did the minimum possible. We didn't give any new aid but continued what was in the pipeline, and PL 480, IDB loans, and humanitarian programs. The World Bank cut them off because they were in default.

E.O. 12958 3.4(b)(1) 1.5(c)

We did the same thing [redacted] There might have been proclivity for economic warfare, but the issue never came up. What happened was the result of his mismanagement and his nationalization and expropriations. Besides, we were cutting down on Chile and before 1970. He actually got more in multilateral aid than Frei.

Remember, he was an opponent of the U.S., and one can ask why shouldn't we oppose him?

President: I wanted you all to have the story. The decisions made were in accordance with the law. I think it is essential for the government to carry out certain covert activities. We will continue to carry them out.

DOCUMENT 12. Department of State, "FY 1976–77 Country Analysis and Strategy Paper for Chile, U.S. Policy Toward Chile—An Alternative," May 18, 1975.

DEPARTMENT OF STATE

AIRGRAM

Original to be Filed in __________ Decentralized Files.

FILE DESIGNATION

A-86

HANDLING INDICATOR

PRIORITY

TO : Department of State

E.O.11652: XGDS3

UNCLASSIFIED

TAGS: PFOR, US, CI

FROM : AmEmbassy SANTIAGO DATE: May 18, 1975

SUBJECT : FY 1976-77 CASP for Chile

REF :

Enclosed is this Mission's proposed Country Analysis and Strategy Paper for Chile for fiscal years 1976-1977.

POPPER

Enclosure: FY 1976-77 CASP

Chile Project (#S199900006)
U.S. Department of State
Release __ Excise __ Deny __ Declass
Exemption(s) ________

UNCLASSIFIED

FORM 10-64 DS-323

Drafted by:	Drafting Date:	Phone No.:	Contents and Classification Approved by:
POL:JBTipton:dm	5-16-75	243	DCM:HBThompson

Clearances:

UNCLASSIFIED 

Santiago A-86
Appendix
Page 35

US POLICY TOWARD CHILE -- AN ALTERNATIVE

Why an alternative proposal?

In last year's CASP (FY 75-76), this Mission concluded that it was in the U.S. interest to support this GOC, but recognized that human rights might be a problem. The recommended and approved policy was to try privately and quietly to persuade the GOC to improve its human rights practices, without threatening or imposing sanctions. This policy of friendly persuasion has not worked, and the GOC has not significantly modified its human rights practices.

Meanwhile, Congress, a substantial portion of U.S. public opinion, and the majority of the "free world" nations and international organizations have increasingly come to regard the GOC as an international pariah, largely because of its human rights practices. Some punitive actions have already been taken (e.g. the Congressional ban on military assistance to the GOC), and others are threatened (e.g. refusal by some countries to renegotiate the GOC's foreign debt).

Yet this year's CASP fails to take into account either the past failure of our efforts or the new situation. The key human rights recommendation is no different in any respect than the FY 75-76 CASP. There is no reason to believe that persuasion alone will be any more successful than it has been in the last year. Nowhere in the CASP is the recommendation further defined in terms of specific tools and concrete actions.

The alternative discussed below argues basically that the cost to the United States of continued support of the GOC now outweighs the benefits obtained therefrom. It proposes a course of action, including tangible measures, which has the best chance of furthering U.S. interests while at the same time causing real changes in the GOC's behavior.

Premises

1. As the FY 76-77 CASP now states, the military are and will be in control of Chile for at least the length of the CASP period. Withdrawal of U.S. political, economic, and military support will not cause the GOC to fall during the CASP period, nor most probably for the remainder of this decade.

2. The military leaders of Chile have lost their best chance to build the new and better society which they envision. In the political area, the military have failed to build a consensus, to broaden their political base, or to reconcile a bitterly divided nation, but instead have chosen to establish an authoritarian government intent upon imposing its will and its ideas. In the social area, in spite of a concern for the well-being of their fellow citizens and especially for the problems of the disadvantaged, they do not seem to know what to do or how to do it, and few concrete developments have taken place. In the economic area, the general thrust of their policies has been endorsed by many observers as having the potential for eventually achieving a strong and healthy economy, but the social cost at the moment is great and has the potential of alienating large segments of the population.

3. Yet the military government still remains sufficiently flexible and non-ideological to be able to change course and recoup some of its lost opportunities if it were motivated to do so.

4. At least in the human rights area, however, and probably others as well, as the CASP states, the GOC "will improve its human rights practices only slowly, usually in response to international pressure".

5. In the absence of that pressure, the GOC will continue doing what it is doing, i.e. failing to make meaningful changes in its human rights behavior. Continued U.S. support for the GOC, as proposed in the CASP, in effect, is support for an unacceptable status quo.

Issue

Is a status quo policy by the USG toward the GOC in the overall U.S. interest now and throughout the CASP period? The basic premise of this paper is that it is not.

Recommendation:

That it should be U.S. policy to inform the GOC that we will take no new initiatives to assist Chile politically, economically, or militarily unless and until its human rights practices have reached an acceptable standard. It should be made clear that existing commitments will be honored and economic and military assistance presently in the pipeline will be delivered. It should also be made clear that the GOC's human rights practices shall be deemed

UNCLASSIFIED 

Santiago A-86
Appendix
Page 37

"acceptable" only when there is a reasonable consensus to this effect of such impartial international bodies concerned with this area as the International Committee of the Red Cross, the OAS Human Rights Commission and the UN Human Rights Commission. Further, that this policy decision be publicly reported to the Congress in accordance with Section 32 of the Foreign Assistance Act of 1973 and Section 46 of the Foreign Assistance Act of 1974.

Reasons for Recommendation

1. As noted earlier, there is no reason to believe that persuasion in and of itself, as advocated in the CASP, will be any more successful in modifying GOC behavior than it has been in the past, even with the addition of the Congressionally-imposed ban on military assistance as a bargaining chip.

2. On the other hand, an immediate cutoff of all U.S. support, including pipeline assistance, and an immediate move into a "cool and correct" relationship with the GOC somewhat along the lines of U.S./Chile relations during the Allende period, could produce shock and confusion and increase the chances of GOC leaders withdrawing into an unproductive siege mentality.

3. The above recommendation is a more measured approach and provides the GOC time to react in an orderly fashion during which pipeline aid and other U.S. assistance is continuing.

4. It also provides the most effective incentive to the GOC to improve its human rights behavior and to make other desirable changes in its practices, especially in the area of establishing a more open society and reviving democratic political institutions.

5. U.S. foreign policy spokesmen have stated that the human rights question is only one factor in U.S. relations with any given country. In Chile at this time, it is and should be the dominant factor. There are no other U.S. interests in Chile, individually or collectively, which outweigh it. Further, the cost to the U.S. of continued identification as the principal supporter of the present GOC significantly outweighs the benefits received. This point requires further elaboration.

UNCLASSIFIED

DOCUMENT 13. Department of State, Memorandum, "Ambassador Popper's Policy Paper," July 11, 1975.

PAGE 1 OF 2

First Ring Hon

UNCLASSIFIED DECAPTIONED R J D Z203

July 11, 1975

TO: ARA:Mr. William D. Rogers
APA:Ambassador Hewson Ryan

FROM: ARA/PLC:Richard J. Bloomfield

SUBJ: Ambassador Popper's Policy Paper.

The Ambassador characterizes our present stance as one of "disapproval" (p. 20 and p. 21). But the image is otherwise, at least as far as the Executive Branch is concerned:

-- We are solicitous about Chile's debt problem and deploy our diplomacy to promote a debt rescheduling.

-- We use our influence in the IFIS to assure that Chilean loans are not held up.

-- We vote against or abstain on resolutions in international organizations that condemn the GOC's human rights record.

-- We assure the GOC that we want to sell it arms and that we regret Congressional restrictions.

How would the Junta ever get the impression that the USG "disapproves"? As the old saying goes, actions speak louder than words.

The Ambassador says that any stronger signs of our (read Executive Branch) disapproval would not improve the human rights situation (which I am willing to concede). Conclusion: We must provide economic and military assistance; in fact by page 25, we are worrying about our responsibilities for making the Junta's economic program a success. Why? Because "preventing the re-emergence of a Chilean Government essentially hostile to us (p. 22) is our chief interest and the human rights problem is secondary."

This argument overlooks the possibility that the human rights problem in Chile may not be "secondary" but may be a major U.S. interest in the present domestic and international context. In the minds of the world at

UNCLASSIFIED

UNCLASSIFIED

-2-

large, we are closely associated with this junta, ergo with fascists and torturers. This is the way it is perceived by a vocal and increasingly numerous element in Congress whose support we need for other aspects of our Latin American policy (e.g. Panama) and, indeed, for our foreign policy in general. It is one more reason why much of the youth of the country is alienated from their government and its foreign policy. Chile is just the latest example for a lot of people in this country of the United States not being true to its values.

This is not the emotionalism of a bleeding heart. The Secretary himself has said that no foreign policy will be successful if it is carried in the minds of a few and the hearts of none. Our current Chile policy comes perilously close to fitting that description.

The need to "live with" the absence of human rights in Chile in order to prevent the re-emergence of a hostile government is, to my mind, a distinctly secondary consideration. We survived a hostile government in Chile in the recent past. It is really a bizarre world when the globe's greatest superpower has to worry about the hostility of the dagger-pointed-at-the-heart-of-Antartica.

The specific objectives in human rights that Ambassador Popper sets out on page 21 are fine. The problem is that we will not achieve them without turning the screws harder and taking the risks that entails.

cc: Ambassador Popper
c/o Mr. Karkashian:ARA/BC

ARA/PLC:RJBloomfield/ahm
7/11/75:x29492

DOCUMENT 14. Department of State, **SECRET** Memorandum of Conversation between Henry Kissinger and Augusto Pinochet, "U.S.-Chilean Relations," June 8, 1976.

SECRET/NODIS

DEPARTMENT OF STATE

Memorandum of Conversation

DATE: June 8, 1976
TIME: 12:00 noon
PLACE: Santiago, Chile (President Pinochet's Office)

SUBJECT: U.S.-Chilean Relations

PARTICIPANTS: Chile

Augusto Pinochet, President
Patricio Carvajal, Foreign Minister
Manuel Trucco, Ambassador to United States
Ricardo Claro, OAS/GA Conference Coordinator for Chilean Government

United States

The Secretary
William D. Rogers, Assistant Secretary for Inter-American Affairs
Anthony Hervas (Interpreter)

DISTRIBUTION:

The Secretary: This is a beautiful building. The conference is well organized. Are you meeting with all the delegations?

Pinochet: Yes. Two or three a day. I want to tell you we are grateful that you have come to the conference.

The Secretary: It is an honor. I was touched by the popular reception when I arrived. I have a strong feeling of friendship in Chile.

Pinochet: This is a country of warm-hearted people, who love liberty. This is the reason they did not accept Communism when the Communists attempted to take over the country. It is a long term

ARA:WDRogers:cjs
(Drafting Office and Officer)

FORM DS-1254 2-65

SECRET/NODIS
XGDS

struggle we are a part of. It is a further stage of the same conflict which erupted into the Spanish Civil War. And we note the fact that though the Spaniards tried to stop Communism 40 years ago, it is springing up again in Spain.

The Secretary: We had the Spanish King recently, and I discussed that very issue with him.

Pinochet: I have always been against Communism. During the Viet-Nam War, I met with some of your military and made clear to them my anti-Communism, and told them I hoped they could bring about its defeat.

The Secretary: In Viet-Nam, we defeated ourselves through our internal divisions. There is a world-wide propaganda campaign by the Communists.

Pinochet: Chile is suffering from that propaganda effort. Unfortunately, we do not have the millions needed for counter propaganda.

The Secretary: I must say your spokesman (Sergio Diez) was very effective in this morning's General Assembly session in explaining your position. In the United States, as you know, we are sympathetic with what you are trying to do here. I think that the previous government was headed toward Communism. We wish your government well. At the same time, we face massive domestic problems, in all branches of the government, especially Congress, but also in the Executive, over the issue of human rights. As you know, Congress is now debating further restraints on aid to Chile. We are opposed. But basically we don't want to intervene in your domestic affairs. We can't be precise in our proposals about what you should do. But this is a problem which complicates our relationships and the efforts of those who are friends of

-3-

Chile. I am going to speak about human rights this afternoon in the General Assembly. I delayed my statement until I could talk to you. I wanted you to understand my position. We want to deal in moral persuasion, not by legal sanctions. It is for this reason that we oppose the Kennedy Amendment.

In my statement, I will treat human rights in general terms, and human rights in a world context. I will refer in two paragraphs to the report on Chile of the OAS Human Rights Commission. I will say that the human rights issue has impaired relations between the U.S. and Chile. This is partly the result of Congressional actions. I will add that I hope you will shortly remove those obstacles.

I will also call attention to the Cuba report and to the hypocrisy of some who call attention to human rights as a means of intervening in governments. I can do no less, without producing a reaction in the U.S. which would lead to legislative restrictions. The speech is not aimed at Chile. I wanted to tell you about this. My evaluation is that you are a victim of all left-wing groups around the world, and that your greatest sin was that you overthrew a government which was going Communist. But we have a practical problem we have to take into account, without bringing about pressures incompatible with your dignity, and at the same time which does not lead to U.S. laws which will undermine our relationship.

It would really help if you would let us know the measures you are taking in the human rights field. None of this is said with the hope of undermining your government. I want you to succeed and I want to retain the possibility of aid.

SECRET/NODIS

-4-

If we defeat the Kennedy amendment, -- I don't know if you listen in on my phone, but if you do you have just heard me issue instructions to Washington to make an all-out effort to do just that -- if we defeat it, we will deliver the F-5E's as we agreed to do. We held up for a while in others to avoid providing additional ammunition to our enemies.

Pinochet: We are returning to institutionalization step by step. But we are constantly being attacked by the Christian Democratics. They have a strong voice in Washington. Not the people in the Pentagon, but they do get through to Congress. Gabriel Valdez has access. Also Letelier.

The Secretary: I have not seen a Christian Democrat for years.

Pinochet: Also Tomic, and others I don't recall. Letelier has access to the Congress. We know they are giving false information. You see, we have no experience in government. We are worried about our image. In a few days we will publish the constitutional article on human rights, and also another setting up the Council of State. There are a number of efforts we are making to move to institutionalization. In the economic area, we have paid our debts, after the renegotiation. We are paying $700 million in debts with interest this year. We have made land reforms. And we are taking other constitutional measures. We have freed most detained prisoners. There have been 60 more just recently. In September 11, 1974, I challenged the Soviets to set free their prisoners. But they haven't done so, while we have only 400 people who are now detained. On international relations, we are doing well. In the case of Bolivia, we have extended our good will. It all depends now on Peru.

SECRET/NODIS

The Secretary: I have the impression that Peru is not very sympathetic.

Pinochet: You are right. Peru does not wish to see the idea proposed.

The Secretary: Peru told me they would get no port out of the arrangement.

Pinochet: Peru is arming. Peru is trying to buy a carrier from the British for $160 million. It is also building four torpedo boats in Europe. Peru is breaking the arms balance in the South Pacific. It has 600 tanks from the Soviet Union. We are doing what we can to sustain ourselves in case of an emergency.

The Secretary: What are you doing?

Pinochet: We are largely modifying old armaments, fixing junked units. We are a people with energy. We have no Indians.

The Secretary: I gather Chile generally wins its wars.

Pinochet: We have never lost a war. We are a proud people. On the human rights front, we are slowly making progress. We are now down to 400. We have freed more. And we are also changing some sentences so that the prisoners can be eligible for leaving.

The Secretary: If you could group the releases, instead of 20 a week, have a bigger program of releases, that would be better for the psychological impact of the releases. What I mean is not that you should delay, but that you should group the releases. But, to return to the military aid question, I really don't know how it will go tomorrow in the Senate.

Trucco: The Buchanan amendment is workable.

The Secretary: I repeat that if the House version succeeds, then we will send the planes.

Trucco: (Discusses the technical aspects of the 1975, 1976 and 1977 legislation.)

Trucco: The problem is now in the Senate, for the FY 1977 bill. Fraser has already had his amendment passed by the House.

The Secretary: I understand. We have our position on that. My statement and our position are designed to allow us to say to the Congress that we are talking to the Chilean government and therefore Congress need not act. We had the choice whether I should come or not. We thought it better for Chile if I came. My statement is not offensive to Chile. Ninety-five percent of what I say is applicable to all the governments of the Hemisphere. It includes things your own people have said.

Trucco: That's true. We are strongly in favor of strengthening the OAS Commission.

The Secretary: We are not asking the OAS to endorse anything. I have talked with other delegations. We want an outcome which is not deeply embarrassing to you. But as friends, I must tell you that we face a situation in the United States where we must be able to point to events here in Chile, or we will be defeated. As Angola demonstrates, Congress is in a mood of destructiveness. We were in a good position in Angola. We thought Angola could become the Viet-Nam of Cuba. This would have occurred if Cuba had begun to sustain 20 casualities a week. Cuba could not have stood that for long. We had the forces for that. Congress stopped us. But I am persuaded that the Executive, whoever is elected, will be stronger after the election.

Pinochet: How does the US see the problem between Chile and Peru?

SECRET/NODIS

-7-

The Secretary:	(after a pause) We would not like to see a conflict. Much depends on who begins it.
Pinochet:	The question is really how to prevent the beginning.
The Secretary:	The American people would ask who is advancing on whom.
Pinochet:	But you know what's going on here. You see it with your satellites.
The Secretary:	Well, I can assure you that if you take Lima, you will have little U.S. support.
Pinochet:	We did it once, a hundred years ago. It would be difficult now, in view of the present balance of forces.
The Secretary:	If Peru attacked, this would be a serious matter for a country armed with Soviet equipment. It would be serious. Clearly we would oppose it diplomatically. But it all depends, beyond that. It is not easy to generate support for U.S. military action these days.
Pinochet:	We must fight with our own arms?
The Secretary:	I distinguish between preferences and probabilities. It depends how it happens. If there is naked aggression, that means greater, more general resistance.
Pinochet:	Assume the worst, that is to say, that Chile is the aggressor. Peru defends itself, and then attacks us. What happens?
The Secretary:	It's not that easy. We will know who the aggressor is. If you are not the aggressor, then you will have support. But aggression does not resolve international disputes. One side can stage an incident. But generally we will know who the aggressor is.

SECRET/NODIS

Carvajal: In the case of Bolivia, if we give Bolivia some territory, Bolivian territory might be guaranteed by the American states.

The Secretary: I have supported Bolivia in its aspirations to the sea, but de la Flor is not happy about it.

Carvajal: If we gave some territory to Bolivia, and then permitted Peru to the use the port, Peru would get everything it needs.

The Secretary: It is my feeling Peru will not accept.

Pinochet: I am concerned very much by the Peruvian situation. Circumstances might produce aggression by Peru. Why are they buying tanks? They have heavy artillery, 155's. Peru is more inclined to Russia than the U.S. Russia supports their people 100%. We are behind you. You are the leader. But you have a punitive system for your friends.

The Secretary: There is merit in what you say. It is a curious time in the U.S.

Pinochet: We solved the problem of the large transnational enterprises. We renegotiated the expropriations, and demonstrated our good faith by making prompt payments on the indebtedness.

The Secretary: It is unfortunate. We have been through Viet-Nam and Watergate. We have to wait until the elections. We welcomed the overthrow of the Communist-inclined government here. We are not out to weaken your position. On foreign aggression, it would be a grave situation if one were attacked. That would constitute a direct threat to the inter-American system.

Carvajal: There is massive Cuban influenc in Peru. Many Cubans are there. The Per vians may

be pushed. And what happens to the thousands of Cuban soldiers now in Africa, when they are no longer needed there.

The Secretary: If there are Cuban troops involved in a Peruvian attack, then the problem is easy. We will not permit a Cuban military force of 5,000 Cubans in Peru.

Carvajal: They now have a system, where the Peruvians enter in groups of 20, but the Peruvian registry registers only 1.

The Secretary: The Cubans are not good soliders.

Carvajal: But there is the danger of irresponsible attack.

Claro: I have sources in Peru. There is, I am told, a real chance that Cuba could airlift troops to Peru.

The Secretary: This would change the situation, and the question then is easy. We will not permit Cuba another military adventure. A war between Peru and Chile would be a complex thing, but a war between Cuba and Chile or others, we would not be indifferent.

Claro: Your planners were down here in 1974. They did not believe that there was a Cuba threat. The Soviets use Cuba for aggression, I argued. Angola has since confirmed this.

The Secretary: We will not tolerate another Cuban military move. After the election, we will have massive trouble if they are not out of Angola. Secondly, I also feel stronger that we can't accept coexistence and ideological subversion. We have the conditions now for a more realistic policy. It would help you if you had some human rights progress, which could be announced in packages. The most important are the constitutional guarantees. The precise

SECRET/NODIS

-10-

numbers of prisoners is subordinate. Right to habeas corpus is also important. And if you could give us advanced information of your human rights efforts, we could use this. As to the Christian Democrats, we are not using them. I haven't seen one since 1969. We want to remove the weapons in the arms of our enemies. It is a phenomenon that we deal with special severity with our friends. I want to see our relations and friendship improve. I encouraged the OAS to have its General Assembly here. I knew it would add prestige to Chile. I came for that reason. We have suggestions. We want to help, not undermine you. You did a great service to the West in overthrowing Allende. Otherwise Chile would have followed Cuba. Then there would have been no human rights or a Human Rights Commission.

Trucco: We provided the General Assembly the answers to some of the Secretary's suggestions. What will be missing will be our explanation of the coming constitutional acts.

The Secretary: Can you do those while the OAS is here?

Pinochet: We have wanted to avoid doing anything while the OAS is here, since it then looks as though we did it to dampen OAS pressure. We might be able to in 30 days.

The Secretary: If we can, we are prepared to say we have the impression that the constitutional act is helpful.

Pinochet: I discussed it in my inaugural speech.

SECRET/NODIS

5

American Casualties

[The assistant secretary] raised this subject [of murdered Americans] in the context of the need to be careful to keep relatively small issues in our relationship from making our cooperation more difficult.

—memorandum of conversation between Assistant Secretary of State Jack Kubisch and Junta Foreign Minister Ismael Huerta, February 1974

On June 8, 1976, the very day that Henry Kissinger commended General Pinochet for his "service" to the West, a Chilean intelligence officer met with reporters from CBS News and the *Washington Post* and told them about the regime's post-coup execution of an American citizen. The meeting took place in a small, dark room in the Italian embassy where the officer, Rafael Gonzalez, had sought asylum in an attempt to leave Chile. Speaking passable English, Gonzalez recounted to the journalists that a few days after the coup, he had been summoned to the ninth floor of the Army's Military Intelligence Service (SIM) building to translate during the interrogation of an American prisoner named Charles Horman. "I was told . . . this guy knew too much . . . Horman, you know," as Gonzalez recounted the conversation with his superior, General Augusto Lutz, "and that he was supposed to disappear." According to a transcript of the recorded interview, Gonzalez added that he believed an American agent was in the room during Horman's interrogation—based on "the way that he behaves, his dressing, the shoes, you know and everything." "I wouldn't say the trigger was pulled by the CIA," he told the reporters. "But that the CIA was mixed up in this . . . yes. It was the Chileans that get [rid] of him, but the CIA was behind that."[1]

Twenty-seven years later, Gonzalez would be arrested and charged with being an "accomplice to homicide" in the death of Charles Horman. In January

2004 he would recant his story about an American being present during Horman's interrogation. But in 1976, Gonzalez's dramatic accusations transformed Charles Horman into the most famous American victim of the Pinochet regime; his case eventually became the subject of an Oscar-winning Hollywood movie, *Missing*. The film starred Jack Lemmon as Charles's father and Sissy Spacek as his wife; it portrayed his family's painful search for him in Santiago through an obstacle course of callous U.S. officials and a pro-coup U.S. policy.[2]

Horman was, however, the first of four U.S. citizens to be murdered by Chilean military. Another American, Frank Teruggi, also was seized by security forces at his home in Santiago nine days after the coup, and, like Horman, taken to the National Stadium where he was interrogated and executed. In January 1985, a military patrol detained a University of Pennsylvania mathematics professor named Boris Weisfeiler while he was hiking in southern Chile; Weisfeiler subsequently disappeared. In Washington D.C., Ronni Karpen Moffitt was killed in September 1976 by a car bomb planted by agents of the Chilean secret police, becoming an American casualty of the Pinochet regime's most infamous act of international terrorism. Years after they were committed, each of these horrific crimes would remain unresolved. Each would be defined by blatant cover-ups on the part of the Pinochet regime—and the concealment of evidence, negligence and/or simple disinterest on the part of the U.S. government.

Charles Horman

When Rafael Gonzalez's allegations about Charles Horman appeared in the *Washington Post*, they generated yet another scandal of potential U.S. misconduct—the premeditated murder of an American citizen, with alleged U.S. collusion, by a military actively influenced, and supported by the Nixon-Ford White House. For almost three years, the Pinochet regime had insisted that "extremists" of the left impersonating the military had murdered Horman, as well as Teruggi, to embarrass the new Junta. Even though the embassy had abundant evidence that this explanation was false, the U.S. government adopted and promoted such specious pronouncements. Only days after Chilean authorities privately conceded to his father that Charles had been shot in the National Stadium, a State Department spokeswoman told the press that Horman might have been killed by left-wing groups masquerading as soldiers—"really wicked people who would kill him just to make the military look bad."[3] Now, these revelations generated renewed demands from Horman's family for a complete accounting—his family filed a wrongful death lawsuit and legal demands for release of all relevant records—as well as a slew of angry letters from Capitol Hill, and public allegations of an official cover-up. "It now appears," stated a *Washington Post* editorial on June 27, 1976, that "American diplomats withheld from Mr. Horman's family crucial information about the circumstances of his death."

The U.S. government did withhold substantive information from the family—before June 1976, and for more than twenty years thereafter. Following the Gonzalez revelations, two State Department Latin American bureau officers did a cursory file review and quickly discovered a litany of liability: during his family's desperate search for him in Santiago after the coup, U.S. officials had failed to inform them that a credible source had told the embassy within days of his execution that Horman had been murdered in the National Stadium, and that they had undertaken no substantive actions in response to this information. Instead, U.S. officials passed on specious rumors that Charles was in hiding, or was making his way out of the country through a leftist "clandestine pipeline." Unbeknownst to the family, at least one of the U.S. consulate officials providing this information, James Anderson, was a CIA agent operating under diplomatic cover. The embassy never informed the family that the Chilean military seemed to have ready intelligence on Horman and Teruggi's leftist activities, and that U.S. officials had failed to pursue the question of how, and from where, the regime had obtained such information.

Indeed, the U.S. government's oft-repeated claims to be actively investigating the Horman-Teruggi murders were misleading, the State Department officials concluded. "We keep telling the families and the press that we are diligently pursuing every lead, doing everything to develop the circumstances surrounding the deaths of these Americans," the Chile desk officer Rudy Fimbres reported in a memorandum to Assistant Secretary for Inter-American Affairs, Harry Shlaudeman. "This is overdrawn."[4]

In their preliminary review of the files, mid-level ARA officials concluded that the Chilean military had executed Horman and that there was a possibility that U.S. intelligence agents in Chile had played some role in his death. "This case remains bothersome," three officers reported in a secret memorandum to Shlaudeman "Subject: Charles Horman Case" on August 25, 1976. "The connotations for the Executive are not good. In the Hill, academic community, the press, and the Horman family the intimations are of negligence on our part, or worse, complicity in Horman's death." Based on the files, they wrote, "we are persuaded that:"

> —The GOC sought Horman and felt threatened enough to order his immediate execution. The GOC might have believed this American could be killed without negative fall-out from the USG.
>
> There is some circumstantial evidence to suggest:

> —U.S. intelligence may have played an unfortunate part in Horman's death. At best, it was limited to providing or confirming information that helped motivate his murder by the GOC. At worst, U.S. intelligence was aware the GOC saw Horman in a rather serious light and U.S. officials did nothing to discourage the logical outcome of GOC paranoia.

The State Department deliberately hid these conclusions from the family. No U.S. official briefed the Hormans at the time; and when this pivotal document was first declassified in early 1980 pursuant to the family's lawsuit against U.S. officials, its content was completely censored. (Doc 1) Then, when the State Department declassified the document again in 1982 as part of continuing legal efforts around the Horman case, that specific section was blacked out, along with all other references to the CIA, on the grounds of "State Secrets" and "Executive Privilege."[5] (Doc 2) Only seventeen years later, in October 1999 when the Clinton administration released this memo intact among thousands of other documents relating to the United States and Chile, did the Horman family finally learn that, in 1976, at least a few U.S. officials had shared their suspicion of a possible role by U.S. covert operatives in Charles's murder. (Doc 3)

Charles Horman, along with Frank Teruggi, became two of an estimated 2,800 U.S. citizens caught in the cross fire of the Chilean coup. About half the Americans in Chile were part of the business and diplomatic community and supported the coup; but many others were graduate students, like Teruggi, who had come to do research on Chile's social revolution, or social activists like Charles and Joyce Horman who wanted to experience the Allende experiment firsthand. When the new Junta labeled them, and hundreds of others who had come from abroad to Chile during the Allende years as "foreign extremists" and began rounding them up en masse, they received little sympathy from the Nixon administration, whose paramount goal was to embrace the new regime, and avoid attracting attention to its bloodletting.

Top U.S. officials in Washington were well-aware that foreigners were being targeted for repression. On September 20, Kissinger chaired a meeting of the Washington Special Actions Group in the White House Situation Room to establish a date for U.S. recognition of the new regime and arrange emergency assistance. According to the secret minutes of the meeting, Assistant Secretary Jack Kubisch briefed Kissinger on the desperate situation of foreigners trying to get out of Chile:

> Most are third-country nationals who fled their own countries and got caught up in this thing. The government's holding about 5,000 in the stadium. They have been very candid about this. They intend to treat them in accordance with military courts. If innocent, they will be free to [go]. If guilty, the Junta intends to deal with them harshly.[6]

"There are few Americans caught up in it," Kubisch informed the secretary. The memorandum of conversation does not record any further discussion of their situation before officials turned to evaluating a Chilean military request for 1,000 flares and helmets to use in mopping-up operations.

The embassy "engaged in an all-out effort to ensure the welfare of... Americans in Chile," the State Department would submit to Congress in December 1973. But while other countries, most notably France, Sweden, the Netherlands, Belgium, and Venezuela flung open their embassy doors to provide refuge for their citizens and aggressively sought to secure their safety if they were detained, the United States did neither. A special investigation conducted by the U.S. General Accounting Office titled "An Assessment of Selected U.S. Embassy-Consular Efforts to Assist and Protect Americans Overseas During Crisis and Emergencies" concluded that the U.S. embassy and consulate buildings in Santiago had been specifically designed and equipped to house up to 450 persons for a three-day period in order to be responsive to a situation exactly like the Chilean coup. But requests for refuge were denied on the grounds that "the facilities were not adequate to permit them to stay overnight." U.S. officials also dragged their feet on aggressively interceding with Chile's new military authorities to protect detained U.S. citizens from abuse, failing to adhere to the Vienna Convention on consular relations by waiting to formally protest and demand their security until adverse media coverage forced them to do so. "In Chile," GAO investigators concluded:

> Prompt and effective protests by high-level U.S. officials on behalf of arrested and detained Americans in accordance with the international Vienna Convention on Consular Relations, were not always made.... Formal written protests were made only in response to press publicity and Congressional interest.

Some twenty-nine U.S. citizens were arrested and jailed in the days following the coup and at least fifteen imprisoned at the main detention-torture-execution center, the National Stadium. One, a Methodist priest named Joseph Doherty, was detained along with another Methodist, Francis Flynn, on September 16 and spent eleven horrific days there. On September 19, Doherty, who kept a detailed journal recording the beatings, torture and murders taking place around him, asked a Dutch embassy official who had gained access to prisoners to contact the U.S. consul "as neither of us had heard from them."[7] But Doherty did not have any contact with the U.S. consul, Frederick Purdy, until September 26 when he, Flynn and six other U.S. citizens were finally released into the custody of U.S. officials. "Mr. Purdy informed us that the condition of our release was that we had to leave the country," the Methodist pastor recorded in his journal. "Mr. Purdy informed us that if we did not accept this condition we could go back into the Stadium at which time the United States consulate would not be responsible for us."

Charles Horman, detained on the evening of September 17 and reportedly executed on or around September 20, was one of those Americans "caught up" in the coup. His friends described him as "a highly intelligent, liberal, mild-mannered, gentle individual." As a thirty-one-year old Phi Beta Kappa graduate of Harvard University, he had come to Santiago with his new wife Joyce in the late fall of 1972 to try his hand at writing and filmmaking. During the last year of his life, Charles, along with Frank Teruggi, worked as an editor of a small news service known as the North American Information Sources—which clipped, translated, and distributed U.S. news articles on Chile through a small progressive pamphlet called *FIN*. He also produced animated children's cartoons and was writing a book on the Allende government's effort to transform Chilean political society. According to his wife, at the time of the coup he was investigating the October 1970 assassination of General René Schneider.

The mysterious circumstances of his murder amidst the bloodshed of the Chilean coup have been catalogued in Thomas Hauser's compelling book, *The Execution of Charles Horman: An American Sacrifice*. On September 11, 1973, Horman happened to be visiting the scenic seaside town of Viña del Mar with Terry Simon, a vacationing family friend from New York. They found themselves trapped at their hotel, without access to news, phones or transportation back to Santiago. In search of other Americans with information, they met a U.S. navy engineer named Arthur Creter. "I'm here with the United States navy," he informed them. "We came down to do a job and it's done."[8]

Horman and Simon also met one of Creter's supervisors, Lt. Col. Patrick Ryan, deputy chief of the United States Naval Mission in Valparaiso, and one of the U.S. military attachés most ardently supportive of the coup. They pressed him for information on the coup and on the possibility of getting back to Santiago. "I was approached by subject couple who identified themselves as American tourists and requested, at that time essentially a SITREP [situation report]," Ryan wrote in an October 5, 1973, summary of his contacts with Horman. "I gave them what info I considered appropriate, promised to keep them posted and also to lend them money if their stay in Viña proved lengthy. I also directed them not to leave the hotel."[9]

The two were forced to stay at the hotel for four days, until Lieutenant Colonel Ryan arranged for them to be transported back to Santiago with the head of the U.S. military group, Captain Ray Davis (one of the only U.S. officials with clearance to travel freely in Chile in the aftermath of the coup). At the embassy, Davis told them that the United States had no provisions for getting Americans out of the country. When Horman and Simon returned to the embassy on the afternoon of September 17 in an effort to secure safe passage out of the country for themselves and Joyce, they experienced a rude brush-off from a secretary. She told them it was "not our job" to help Americans leave Chile and that they would have to go to the U.S. consulate a mile away. By then it was late afternoon and Charles determined he should return home to avoid being caught out after curfew; so Simon met alone with a consulate official. As she recalled, that official also informed her they would have to wait till the borders opened and that "we're not responsible for people who want to leave, and I have no information about the necessary procedures."[10]

Horman arrived at his home on Vicuna MacKenna street around 5:00 P.M.[11] (His wife was not home; caught by the curfew, Joyce was forced to spend a terrifying night outside in the cold, huddled in a doorway across town.) A summary State Department report records what happened:

> According to the neighbors, between 1600 and 1700 on September 17, a private non-military truck came to 4126 Vicuna MacKenna. Ten to 15 men in Chilean Army uniforms led by a man wearing Captain's or Lieutenant's insignia got out, tried the gate and, finding it locked, jumped the fence and broke the lock. They entered the house, removed Horman and a box of books and papers from the house, and loaded them on the truck. At about 2300 the same day, the same truck and two other trucks returned to 4126 Vicuna MacKenna, carried out some suitcases and a large box from the house, loaded them on the trucks and departed towards downtown Santiago.

From the outset there was overwhelming evidence that Charles had been detained and placed under interrogation by SIM, the Chilean Army Intelligence Service headed by General Augusto Lutz. A witness from the neighborhood had seen the truck carry Charles toward the National Stadium.[12] At 8:00 A.M. the next morning, a former neighbor of Horman's received a call from a military intelligence officer who stated that "SIM had detained a gringo with a beard," according to the State Department report. She was also asked if she "knew that the gringo worked in pictures, and if she was aware that the gringo was a leftist extremist."[13] A second call was placed to the house of a Horman friend, Warwick Armstrong, stating that an American who "makes films" had asked Armstrong to speak on his behalf and ordered him to proceed to a local police station.

From reports on both phone calls, the U.S. embassy learned of Horman's detention and the SIM inquiries on September 18.[14] A chronology on the Horman case kept by the U.S. Consul, Fred Purdy, recorded that on

> *18 September*—Consulate received report of Horman's detention from one of its local employees one of whose relatives know Horman. Few details given.
>
> —Later also received call from Mr. Armstrong, also telling that Horman missing since late 17 September when reportedly detained by military.[15]

On September 19, Joyce met with one of Purdy's CIA consulate deputies, John Hall, and informed him that her home had been ransacked, and her husband taken away by the military. He queried her on what type of information the soldiers might have found at the Horman residence, and she described to him her husband's research on General Schneider's assassination.[16] Later that day, Terry Simon called the head of the U.S. MilGroup, Captain Davis, and asked him for help in locating Charles. Over the next several days, both consulate and U.S. military officials made a series of informal inquiries to the Chilean police and military and intelligence offices; all denied detaining or holding Horman. Purdy went several times to the National Stadium to check the lists of detainees but "Horman's name did not appear as such or under any of several variants," Ambassador Nathaniel Davis cabled on September 25. "Embassy continues try locate him and all other amcits [American citizens] with full resources at its disposal."

Yet, the very next day Ambassador Davis refused Joyce Horman's plea to escalate the profile of U.S. efforts to find Charles by personally visiting the stadium. "She asked him to go to the Stadium with her," noted a report by the head of the U.S. MilGroup who attended the meeting.[17] "He declined and provided rationale for the negative response." According to Joyce Horman's recollection, Ambassador Davis told her, "We really can't do that. If we ask special favors of the ruling forces, everyone else will want them too. That might damage our relations with the new government."[18]

Inside the embassy, some U.S. officials had already concluded that Charles Horman was dead. "People were being killed in those days," Vice Consul Dale Shaffer recalled. "We thought Horman was dead," the head of the AID mission, Judd Kessler remembered. "We had asked the Chileans to tell us where he was and they hadn't, so we figured they were probably stalling to cover up." On or around September 30, a Chilean source named Enrique Sandoval informed Kessler that, in fact, Horman had been executed in the National Stadium.

Sandoval, a Ministry of Education official under the Allende government who had been briefly imprisoned in the Estadio Chile after the coup, met with Kessler twice. During the first meeting, around September 23, Kessler sought information on human rights atrocities, and told Sandoval that two Americans, Horman and Teruggi, were among the missing. Several days later, as Kessler recounted in a memo to the Chile desk officer on July 19, 1976, "I spoke with Sandoval again at which time he told me that someone he knew in the Chilean military had said that Horman had been in the National Stadium and either 'that he had been killed there,' or 'was dead.' " Kessler wrote no formal memorandum about this conversation; instead he informally passed it on to the chief consular officer, Fred Purdy during a hallway conversation in the U.S. embassy.[19] "I'll bet that's right," as Kessler remembers Purdy's response.[20] The consul general, whose job is the welfare of U.S. citizens, took no steps to follow up; inexplicably, Purdy neglected to pursue the leads Sandoval's story and his sources appeared to offer, failed to protest to the Chilean authorities, and withheld this information from Joyce Horman, and Charles's father when he flew from New York on October 5 to search for his son.

By the time Ed Horman arrived in Santiago, Frank Teruggi's body had been discovered at the morgue—not by the embassy, but by an American friend who insisted on looking for him there. The government of Chile claimed Teruggi had been picked up for curfew violations, taken to the National Stadium, released the next day and later found shot in the street. On October 3, the Foreign Ministry provided a virtually identical statement to the embassy on Horman: he had been detained at the National Stadium on September 20 for violations of curfew but released on September 21 "for lacking of merit to any charges against him," and the military was "checking into his whereabouts."[21] These events gave U.S. officials ever more reason to discount the regime's denials regarding the Horman case. In a meeting with Edmund Horman the day he arrived, however, Ambassador Davis never mentioned the regime's acknowledgement that his son had been in the stadium; instead the ambassador reiterated all of the Chilean military's disclaimers and then offered a theory that lent credence to them. "Davis said that the embassy feeling was that Charles probably was in hiding," as Horman recorded the commentary.[22]

Between October 5 and October 18 Ed and Joyce Horman conducted a poignant and desperate search for Charles. For two weeks they and, at Ed's demand, the embassy, pursued a set of inquiries that U.S. officials had failed to undertake: investigating detention centers other than the National Stadium; checking all foreign embassies where Charles might have sought asylum; a fingerprint check on all unidentified bodies at the morgue; issuing a press release to all Chilean newspapers; and publication of a reward for information leading to the whereabouts of Charles Horman. (When Ed requested that the CIA Station also be directed to utilize its resources to find Charles, however, Ambassador Davis sternly, and mendaciously, denied that any such thing existed in Chile.) Ed and Joyce traversed Santiago, searching hospitals and refugee centers, meeting anyone who might be helpful, and enduring useless questioning by low-level Chilean officials going through the motions of an investigation. With the embassy's help, they gained access to the inside of the stadium where, using a microphone, they called for Charles to come forward—a dramatic and wrenching scene depicted in the film *Missing.*

In the late afternoon of October 16, Purdy invited them to the embassy to meet with vice-consul/CIA Station operative James Anderson and a British journalist named Timothy Ross. Ross informed them he had a contact who claimed that Charles was "alive and well," and making his way through an underground "escape pipeline;" he was now in northern Chile and would soon be out of the country. At the end of the meeting, "following instructions from the ambassador," Anderson took Ed Horman aside and told him, "if you put any credence on this information you may wish to consider that any continuing embassy pressure in this case may be double-edged."[23]

The bizarre, unlikely, and contradictory nature of Ross's information—witnesses had seen Horman taken away by the military; military intelligence officials had clearly interrogated him and called his neighbors and friends the next day; and he had been missing for an entire month without a single communication—appeared to be lost on the embassy officials who found Ross credible enough to subject the Hormans to this meeting. The very next day, during a visit at the Ford Foundation's Santiago office, Ed Horman received a far more believable account of his son's fate: Charles "had been shot to death in the National Stadium on or before September 20." Although third-hand, this information rang true: it had been provided to a Foundation staffer, Lowell Jarvis, by an official in the Canadian embassy in Santiago who was close to a Chilean who, in turn, had obtained this information from high-ranking Chilean military sources.

Unbeknownst to the Hormans at the time, the source of this information was Enrique Sandoval, who had shared the identical story with the U.S. embassy almost three weeks earlier. In an effort to leave Chile and seek refuge for his family in Canada, Sandoval contacted the first secretary of the Canadian embassy, Mark Dolguin,[24] for assistance in early October, and told him the same thing he had told AID official Judd Kessler at the end of September. Then, Purdy had ignored this information; but now that Ed Horman pressed him to verify it, the embassy took less than twenty-four hours to confirm that Charles Horman was dead. In a terse cable to Washington, "subj: Deaths; Charles E. Horman," Ambassador Davis reported that

> Embassy informed afternoon October 18, 1973 that previously unidentified male body which delivered to morgue on September 18, 1973 and given autopsy number 2663 had been identified through fingerprints as being that of Charles E. Horman. Unidentified body delivered to Santiago Cemetery on October 3 and apparently interred thereafter. Cause of death was bullet wound. (Doc 4)

The cable concluded that "Embassy advising wife and father."

When they returned to New York City, an angry and grieving Edmund Horman and his daughter-in-law both wrote highly negative reports on their experience in Santiago to the chairman of the Senate Foreign Relations Committee, William Fulbright. The embassy's handling of his son's case, Ed Horman charged in his letter, had been derelict:

> The American Embassy did *nothing* to verify the evidence which had been placed in their hands on September 18th and which proved to be the key to the truth. From October 5th to the very end, their "efforts" produced no results beyond their repeated statements that they had contacted the Chilean government right up to General Pinochet, and had been told that the Chileans knew nothing about Charles or his whereabouts.

"I do not know the reason underlying the negligence, inaction and failure of the American Embassy," Horman concluded. "Whether it was incompetence, indifference or something worse, I find it shocking, outrageous and, perhaps, obscene."

In the search for a missing American the embassy indeed produced no information beyond what the military Junta decided to tell them. Initially, embassy officials made multiple, informal and low-level inquiries and visits—to police stations, the National Stadium, army military intelligence, and regime officials—and readily accepted repeated denials that the Chilean military was responsible for his disappearance. "Since we had received denials from military intelligence that they had any knowledge of Horman, we had seen no reason to follow this point further," as Purdy explained why he didn't actively pursue persuasive evidence that Horman was under the control of the Army's Military Intelligence Service.[25] One week after Horman's seizure, Washington requested a more substantive search. "Given Congressional and other high level interest in this case," Kissinger's office cabled the embassy on September 24, "would appreciate Embassy redoubling its efforts locate Horman, including possibility he may be detained by Chilean authorities." Only then did Ambassador Davis elevate the case to the level of a bilateral issue by discussing it with the regime's foreign minister, and other ministry officials. "I raised Teruggi and Horman cases, pointing out public relations implications of any continuance of the present situation where circumstances of their disappearances remain unexplained," Davis reported to Washington on a September 27 meeting with Chile's new ambassador to the United States. "It would be helpful if the GOC were able to clear up the mysteries involved in the cases of the two missing or deceased Amcits," Davis told a high foreign ministry official on October 3.[26] During a meeting with Pinochet himself on October 12 to discuss substantive U.S. assistance to the new regime, Davis alluded to the "political problems we are encountering"—among them the Kennedy amendment and the Horman-Teruggi cases.

Washington chose not to exercise the considerable leverage, influence, and power it had at its disposal. At a time when the Nixon administration was laying the groundwork for formal recognition of the new regime, expediting tens of millions of dollars in emergency economic assistance to Chile, and covertly assisting the formation of its intelligence apparatus, U.S. policy makers led by Secretary of State Kissinger refrained from linking avid support to satisfactory action, resolution, and justice in these cases. Only in the wake of adverse media coverage and Congressional outrage over the handling of the Horman case, did department officials prod their Chilean counterparts to address the murders of two Americans. Assistant Secretary for Inter-American Affairs Jack Kubisch reflected the administration's attitude when, during a February 1974 meeting with Junta Foreign Minister Ismael Huerta, he broached the Horman and Teruggi cases. "Kubisch raised this subject," according to a memorandum of the conversation, "in the context of the need to be careful to keep relatively small issues in our relationship from making our cooperation more difficult."[27]

Congress, not the executive branch, finally used U.S. assistance to leverage Chilean military cooperation in the Horman case. When the Hormans left Chile on October 20, they asked for the prompt repatriation of Charles's remains. "Our purpose," as Ed Horman would remind the State Department, "was to verify identity, determine time and method of death, [and] find any evidence of torture."[28] As the U.S. government feigned impotence for five months the Pinochet regime stalled on relinquishing the body—rendering impossible any autopsy that could tie the Chilean military to Horman's death.[29] In early March 1974, at a time when the Chilean navy was seeking TOW missiles from the U.S., the powerful senator from New York, Jacob Javits, moved to block further shipments of military equipment to Chile until the remains were returned. Almost immediately a Chilean counterintelligence official informed the U.S. MilGroup that "he had authority to effect the return," according to Department summary of the case.[30] "We had to send him fast out of here because Senator Javits said that he will not approve [military equipment] in the Congress," Rafael Gonzalez recalled to the U.S. reporters in his June 1976 interview. On March 21, Gonzalez went to the U.S. consulate and asked James Anderson—the embassy officer who, Gonzalez stated, had a "dual role" in Chile as a consulate and CIA official—to accompany him to the general cemetery to locate and remove Horman's body. Gonzalez stated quite clearly why he had been picked for this assignment: "I could ID . . . identify Horman when he was dead because I saw him alive."

One more obstacle, and one more example of official U.S. callousness, remained: obtaining payment from the Horman family for sending the body—in a slatted wooden crate—back to the United States. On March 22, the State Department began repeatedly calling and cabling Horman's parents and widow for a deposit to cover the costs of transshipment. On March 23, 1974, a telegram signed by Kissinger arrived at the home of Horman's parents:

> In order for the American embassy in Santiago to arrange shipment you will recall that a deposit of nine hundred dollars (900) is required to cover the estimated cost for preparation of the remains and transportation to New York City. . . . Funds and instructions should be sent to the Office of Special Consular Services, Department of State. Please accept our deepest condolences in this tragic affair. Kissinger (Doc 5)

Four days later, his widow received a cablegram advising her that "to date we have received neither instructions nor funds to cover the estimated costs" and "urgently need . . . a deposit of dols 900 to cover estimated expenses."

The State Department warned her of the possibility that "if instructions are not soon received the Government of Chile will order remains re-interred for health reasons." In a phone call the next day, a bureaucrat from the Consular Services Office gave her until the morning of March 30 to wire the money. Such official determination and pressure, from the family's perspective, contrasted sharply with the State Department's restrained response to Charles's disappearance six months earlier. "I pointed out," Ed Horman would tell the consular official who called again to request the nine hundred dollars, "that if certain employees of the Department of State had displayed the same sense of urgency at the right time, my son might still be alive."[31]

Frank Teruggi

U.S. officials considered the murders of Charles Horman and Frank Teruggi to be "closely linked." As the only two Americans killed by the regime following the coup, their special cases bear numerous similarities. Both of them worked on the publication of the small radical magazine-newsletter called *FIN*. Both were seized at home by Chilean military personnel who ransacked their houses, carting away books and papers considered to be evidence of a pro-Allende inclination. Both were taken to the National Stadium where Chilean authorities attempted to cover up the fact they had been there by keeping their names off lists shown to U.S. embassy officials. One additional commonality, as an internal State Department summary noted, was that "the Junta clearly had or quickly acquired derogatory information on Horman and Teruggi and frequently mentioned it to Embassy personnel."

The main apparent difference in their cases was that unlike Horman, Teruggi had not crossed paths with U.S. military or intelligence officers. Horman's experience, particularly in Viña del Mar, raised the suspicion that U.S. personnel might have "fingered him" for the Chilean military but there was no evidence that Teruggi had ever been on the U.S. radar screen. At least that is what his family was led to believe for more than twenty-five years after his death.

At the time of the coup, Frank Teruggi was a twenty-four-year-old graduate student studying Chile's economic transition under the Allende government. In October of 1971, after graduating from the California Institute of Technology, he enrolled in the School of Political Economy at the University of Chile in Santiago. He lived at a group house at 2575 Hernan Cortes St., frequented by Chilean militants, along with his American roommate David Hathaway.

At approximately 9:00 P.M. on the evening of September 20, according to a one-page summary of his case titled "Deceased United States Citizen," a squad of Chilean Carabinero police arrested Teruggi and Hathaway at their home:

> Both were taken to the Escuela de Suboficiales "Macul" of the Carabineros where they were detained overnight and then taken the morning of September 21, 1973 to the National Stadium. No reason for the detention was given. A note from the Chilean Foreign Office dated October 3, 1973 stated that Mr. Teruggi had been arrested on September 20 for violation of curfew and had been released for lack of merit on September 21, 1973. . . . According to Mr. Hathaway, the afternoon of September 21 an officer separated Mr. Teruggi from the other U.S. citizens detainees based upon a list of names he was carrying. Mr. Teruggi was not seen alive again. (Doc 6)

Hathaway's Chilean fianceé, Irena Muñoz, was at the house and witnessed the arrest. In a debriefing with vice-consul/CIA operative James Anderson, she observed that a unit of 15–20 police agents arrived and spoke to a neighbor outside who denounced Teruggi and Hathaway as "foreigners." She also told Anderson that during a search of Teruggi's bedroom, the squad had found the complete works of Karl Marx and accused him of "contaminating his mind." The police took the literature and other materials, along with the two Americans.

The U.S. embassy learned of Teruggi's detention on September 24, when a close friend, Steve Volk, reported them detained and missing. A "Chronology of Information Relevant to Frank Randall Teruggi," put together by the State Department, suggested that Purdy was told by Chilean authorities later that day that Teruggi was "being held at the National Stadium"; and during a visit to the facility the next morning a volunteer humanitarian worker told Purdy that Teruggi's interrogation had been "completed." In the late afternoon of September 25, however, Purdy received a call from the general morgue stating "that body of Frank Randall Teruggi, born 14 March, 1949, in United States had been brought to morgue dead of bullet wounds on 22 September."[32] The consul took Teruggi's roommate, David Hathaway, to the morgue on September 27, the day after Hathaway's release from the stadium. Hathaway was forced to examine over 150 bodies lined up in rows; but he could not positively identify the corpse tagged with Teruggi's name. At this point, the State Department called Teruggi's family in Des Plaines, Illinois, and told his parents that there was some "confusion" about the fate of their son. Finally on October 2, Steve Volk made a positive identification.[33]

In diplomatic note number 15126, dated October 3, the Chilean Foreign

Office advised the embassy that Teruggi had been detained for curfew violations on September 20—a statement clearly contradicted by the facts—and released the next day for lack of evidence. How, then, did he die? "It is possible that Mr. Teruggi might have been wounded fatally by curfew control patrols or by civilian criminal elements," according to the diplomatic note, "and later recovered and taken to the morgue." During an October 15 meeting with the the U.S. Defense Attaché, Col. William Hon, the Chilean head of SIM, General Augusto Lutz, was far less diplomatic. "His theory," Hon reported in a memorandum of conversation, "is that Teruggi was picked up by his friends and ultimately disposed of."[34] As for Horman, Lutz theorized "that during this particular time of his disappearance groups of robbers or extremists dressed in soldier uniforms were making searches and robberies of houses known to be occupied by North-Americans and foreigners with the purpose of finding dollars or other saleable merchandise."

General Lutz also informed Hon that the Chilean military had obtained incriminating information on Teruggi's activities. "Gen. Lutz said they have knowledge that Teruggi was here in Chile to spread false rumors to the outside world relating to Chile and the situation."[35] This theme dominated the one and only substantive statement that Pinochet's military provided to the United States on the Horman and Teruggi cases. On October 30, General Lutz sent the U.S. defense attaché an unsigned memorandum on the "Antecedents [facts] on two North American citizens' Decease." (Doc 7) In "special deference to the American Embassy," the report stated, the Chilean Military Intelligence Service had "accurately investigated" the fate of Teruggi and Horman:

> Available information on both persons leads to the conclusion that they were involved in extreme leftist movements in our country, which they supported both materially and ideologically. It is necessary, furthermore, to indicate that available and well supported data evidence existence of an organization linked to North American residents in our country, with connections in the rest of the countries in the Continent and led from the U.S., which has undertaken an offensive campaign [against the Junta]. This situation is related with the citizens Horman and Teruggi since there are concrete reasons to believe that at least [Teruggi] belongs to said organization.

U.S. officials did not share these allegations of subversive activities with the Teruggi or Horman families at the time; but later a number of State Department officials focused on them as a possible lead in resolving these murders. Did such evidence exist? If so, where did the Chilean military get it? What was the basis for their conclusions? In a compilation of known evidence and unanswered questions put together by Bureau of Inter-American Affairs officers in the summer of 1976 called "Gleanings," the authors noted that "the October 30 memorandum from Army Intelligence to Colonel Hon may have been based on information provided by U.S. intelligence."

In the Horman case, that supposition derived from a statement by the key source, Enrique Sandoval, that his contact inside the Chilean military "had seen an abundant dossier on Horman's U.S. activities in the United States."[36] In the case of Teruggi, whose activities seemed to attract the regime's attention even more than Horman's, speculation came to focus on one top secret and closely guarded CIA document.

In March 1975, Teruggi's father, Frank Teruggi Sr., initiated a Freedom of Information Act request to the CIA for all documents relating to his son and his death. "Our representative in Santiago advises that there are no documents in his files pertaining to your son," the CIA responded in May. The Agency did, however, acknowledge that it found "a single document which pertains to your son" at Langley headquarters; this document could not, however, be declassified because of national security considerations. More than a year later, the CIA informed an ACLU lawyer representing the Teruggi family that "the document was furnished to representatives of this Agency by an intelligence service of a foreign country. [It] was not obtained from the Government of Chile or any other South American country. Also it contains no derogatory information on Frank Randall Teruggi and does not concern his death in September 1973."[37]

The document did, in fact, contain derogatory information on Teruggi and worse—the address of his home at 2575 Hernan Cortes in Santiago. In July 1972, one of West Germany's intelligence agencies provided a report to the CIA on their surveillance of an American living in Heidelberg who was allegedly engaged in activities to foster desertion and dissent among U.S. servicemen stationed in Europe. This individual published a series of underground newsletters and sought contributing writers and editors from other parts of the world. Through an informant, West German intelligence operatives obtained information that the name of Frank Teruggi, along with his address in Santiago, had been provided to this individual as "an important contact" to have in his newsletter network.[38]

The Germans also shared this information with the U.S. army's 66th Military Intelligence Group based in Munich. That unit forwarded a report to the FBI in October 1972. "According to information received by source, Teruggi is an American residing in Chile who is closely associated with the Chicago Area Group for the Liberation of the Americas," noted the FBI memorandum. (Doc 8) The FBI then opened a file—No. 10053422—subject: "FRANK TERUGGI SM-SUBVERSIVE and ordered its Chicago office to "conduct appropriate investigation to identify subject . . . and submit results of investigation in [a] form suitable for dissemination." (Doc 9) By December, agents were filing reports on his affiliations and attendance at conferences, while conducting background checks and interviews with former colleagues and acquaintances.

Routing information on the documents does not indicate that the FBI disseminated this information to Chile. The key question was, and remains, whether the CIA did so. When the Agency refused to declassify the document, the staff of the Senate Select Committee on Intelligence sought access to it; eventually they were shown a strategically censored copy. In a secret memo to the Directorate of Operation's South American division in November 1976, the CIA's legislative counsel noted that the staffers had posed the obvious question: "did CIA, or the service which originally obtained it, pass the document to [Chilean intelligence]; or to another Latin American intelligence service which might have passed it to [Chilean intelligence]?" The Directorate of Operations responded that it had conducted a "thorough check that fails to reveal any evidence that the Central Intelligence Agency released or passed the information on Frank Teruggi Jr . . . to any Latin American liaison service, including [Chile's]," according an internal CIA memorandum. Nevertheless, the Agency continued to withhold from release even a sanitized version of the German intelligence report and any of the routing sheets that would have accompanied it that would allow verification of this statement.

Pursuing the Truth

Until the Gonzalez allegations generated a new public and political uproar in mid-1976, the U.S. government took very little action to resolve the Horman and Teruggi murders. Under pressure from the families and Capitol Hill, the embassy submitted a series of mildly worded diplomatic notes listing unanswered questions and requested an inquiry to determine the circumstances of their deaths—requests the military regime ignored, obfuscated, or simply denied. In a July 24, 1974, letter to Congress on the Horman case, the State Department reported that "competent" authorities of the Chilean government "consider it highly probable that the death was due to the action of snipers or extremists using military uniforms" and that the United States was "unable to establish a legal basis for attributing an international wrong to the Chilean government for the death of Mr. Horman."[39] During the period when the United States had the most leverage in its bilateral relations with the Pinochet regime, it never once took the position that these Americans had been deliberately killed by the military, nor demanded that the regime identify, prosecute or extradite the commanding officers and personnel responsible.

Both families made an energetic attempt to keep the investigation alive. In February 1974, Teruggi's father, Frank Teruggi Sr., traveled to Santiago with a group called the Chicago Commission of Inquiry and met with U.S. embassy and Chilean military officials. "Is this case closed?," he pressed the new ambassador David Popper, during a meeting at the embassy. Declassified meeting minutes record their exchange:

> *Ambassador Popper:* we have repeatedly tried to determine the facts in this case and we will continue to do what we can to clear up these discrepancies. In all honesty I cannot be very optimistic about getting a fuller story at this date and after this lapse of time.
>
> *Mr. Teruggi:* . . . it is difficult for [my] family to understand how the USG can be helping the Government of Chile when they don't even answer our questions.

In the broad scheme of U.S.-Chilean relations, State Department officials made clear, resolving this murder was not a priority. Both the embassy, and the Bureau of Inter-American Affairs, as one internal memorandum noted in June 1974, "now indicate that they believe further pressure in this regard will be of no avail and merely further exacerbate bilateral relations for no benefit."

For twenty-five years neither the U.S. nor the Chilean governments provided any new evidence in the case relating to the circumstances of Frank Teruggi's death. Only one piece of noteworthy information emerged—from a source outside the United States. In November 1975, a Belgian government official named André Van Lancker provided a sworn affidavit to the U.S. consulate in Brussels relating to his harrowing imprisonment in the National Stadium from September 17 and November 8, 1973. Between September 20 and 22, 1973, he recalled, "I got knowledge of the attendance among us of a United States citizen, named Frank, a university man who had been arrested." During a brutal interrogation at the hands of uniformed police officers, Van Lancker was severely injured and taken to a hospital tent where Red Cross workers intervened to save his life. When he was returned to his cell, "fellow prisoners told me what happened to Mr. Frank:"

> The military took him for interrogation the same days as me i.e. about the 20th to the 23rd of September 1973 to the "caracol", a kind of corridor of the velodrome (the cycle-racing track next to the football

> stadium where personalities could not enter). An officer whose identification was "Alfa-1" or "Sigma-1," I do not remember anymore, was in charge of the interrogation where Frank was heavily tortured by blows and electricity shocks. Finally Frank was in such a bad condition that the officer commented that he (the officer) had gone too far and he shot him with a burst of machine gun—as used in such cases. Afterward, fellow prisoners told me the military commented among themselves, their fear of having troubles with the government of the U.S.A., [and] that is why they did not want to recognize Frank's presence in the stadium.

The scent of scandal from Rafael Gonzalez's account of the Horman murder brought renewed attention to both cases, and forced the State Department, at least temporarily, into a more activist mode. To obtain the truth of the Horman and Teruggi cases, the Chile desk officer Rudy Fimbres warned, a comprehensive "probe" would be required accessing evidence from the files of the U.S. intelligence agencies that likely knew more about the case than they admitted. The Chile desk was "unconvinced the total U.S role is honestly and accurately reflected in the records available to the [State] Department," he informed Assistant Secretary Harry Shlaudeman, who was known to be close to the CIA.[40] In August, Fimbres and his colleagues wrote to Shlaudeman, "we find it hard to believe that the Chileans did not check with [the CIA Station] regarding two detained Americans. . . ." [The CIA Station's] lack of candor with us on other matters only heightens our suspicions."[41]

Assistant Secretary Shlaudeman promised the Senate Foreign Relations Committee that the department would do "everything possible" to investigate the unresolved murders of Horman and Teruggi and determine whether any official had initiated, condoned or was negligent in Horman's detention and execution. Instead, Shlaudeman simply assigned one lone career diplomat, Frederick Smith Jr., who happened to be in Washington awaiting his next embassy posting, to do a "thorough examination" of department records. In the fall of 1976, Smith recalled, he spent several weeks sifting through files and drafting a detailed twenty-six-page report entitled "Death in Chile of Charles Horman."[42]

Like his colleagues, Smith understood that the answers to the mystery of Horman's fate were likely to be found elsewhere. "I see no other alternative if we want to satisfy ourselves—and others—that we have done all we can to determine the truth of the matter," he wrote in a cover memo to Shlaudeman, but to make a "high-level approach to the U.S. intelligence community." As Smith noted: "If one concludes—as I do—that the GOC was directly responsible for Horman's (and Teruggi's) death, it is difficult to believe that the GOC would have felt sufficiently secure in taking such drastic action against two American citizens without some reason, however unjustifiably inferred or inadvertently given, to believe that it could do so without substantial adverse consequences vis-à-vis the USG."[43] The final paragraph of his report recommended that

> high-level inquiries be made of intelligence agencies, particularly the CIA, to try to ascertain to what extent, if any, actions may have been taken or information may have been furnished, formally or informally, to representatives of the forces that now constitute the GOC, either before or immediately after the coup, that may have led the Junta to believe it could, without serious repercussions, kill Charles Horman and Frank Teruggi.

Neither declassified State Department nor CIA files indicate that any such "high-level" inquiry was ever undertaken. Unlike the Pentagon, which ordered a written debriefing of all U.S. military personnel who came in contact with Horman or were involved in efforts to find him, the CIA apparently did not officially question its key Station operatives—James Anderson, John Hall, Ray Warren, John Devine, and Donald Winters among others—about their contacts with Chilean military officials in the days following the coup, or any discussions they might have had regarding Americans in Chile. Nor do the documents reflect any information on what effort the Agency (which had the best contacts inside the Chilean military) made to ascertain what happened to Horman and Teruggi after they were detained. The lack of documentation suggests no such effort was made.

The State Department did pursue two avenues of inquiry: a new set of questions for Rafael Gonzalez including, as Smith wrote, "if he knows of any information (pre or post coup) provided by U.S. sources [to Chile] regarding Horman or Teruggi or other American citizens"; and an effort to find and question Enrique Sandoval, the original source of the information that Horman had been killed in the stadium. On August 2, 1976, Fimbres tracked down Sandoval in exile in Montreal, Canada. "He confirmed he told Judd Kessler that 'Horman was dead, and not to look for him alive,' " Fimbres reported to the U.S. embassy, but he would not reveal his source:

> I said I felt I must continue to pursue this line of inquiry because the information he provided had proven to be accurate. Better late than never. To his protestation that there was no point now in pursuing this matter, I explained that in simple justice to Horman's parents and in response to the many inquires regarding the circumstances of the deaths

> of the two Americans, we had vigorously to pursue every lead. He said he saw a threat in this. . . . He volunteered that his primary sources (sic) "uniformed persons," were in jail. He implied they would be at the mercy of Chilean security if it was revealed that that "they" had passed on to us information on Horman.

The State Department had concluded, quite correctly, that Sandoval's source was his brother, who they unfortuantely misidentified as "most likely Colonel Guillermo Sandoval Velasquez."[44] For this reason, Fimbres confessed to being confused at Sandoval's repeated references to multiple sources. "His use of the plural 'uniformed persons' is confusing," Fimbres wrote, "perhaps deliberately so. But more than once he implied throughout the conversation that he had more than one source."[45]

Indeed, Sandoval repeatedly tried to obfuscate where his information came from. In an interview with Hauser in 1976, he claimed he had three separate sources, among them a "close relative" serving inside the stadium and a military officer who said he was present when Horman was led away to be executed.[46] In a private meeting in Manhattan with Joyce Horman in January 1975, Sandoval confided that his source was a relative serving as a "military fiscal"—an army lawyer—inside the stadium.

Sandoval's sources represented the only direct witnesses able to identify those Chilean military officers responsible for murdering an American. But, having identified his informant as his brother, and now concerned about the personal security of this source, U.S. officials decided to abandon this avenue of inquiry. Any approach in Chile, as Fimbres and two colleagues wrote to Shlaudeman, would "have to be made with considerable discretion," and would be "terribly sensitive. We are skeptical that anything positive can be accomplished through this line of inquiry." (See Doc 3.) In his own final report to Shlaudeman in December, Frederick Smith also recommended against pursuing the Sandoval lead: "To do so might seriously endanger his source (his brother) and confirmation of Horman's presence at the National Stadium or other information we might obtain from him would seem at this point to be marginal to our main concern."[47] And U.S. ambassador to Santiago, David Popper, opposed pursuing Sandoval's source, or any other inquiry to identify Horman's killers. "The U.S. cannot conduct a full investigation on the territory of another sovereign nation," he wrote to Fimbres. "Somewhere along the line we will have to take the position that we have gone as far as we can."[48]

A Final Missed Opportunity

There would be one more example of U.S. government irresponsibility in the Horman case—publicly unknown until the declassification of documents in June 2000—extending the long pattern of official disinclination, and simple inability, to bring the most famous crime against an American citizen in Chile to legal and historical closure. On March 11, 1987, an informant with credible ties to the Chilean secret police appeared at the U.S. embassy and requested to speak to Ambassador Harry Barnes, or the deputy chief of mission, George Jones. Instead he was referred to a junior political officer, David Dreher. In this initial meeting the informant—his name remains deleted from declassified files—said he knew what had happened to Charles Horman and wanted to come clean. "He knows who ordered the killing of Horman and that some of these people are currently top officials," Dreher reported. "He says he will name names."[49]

The State Department's Southern Cone desk, headed by David Cox, characterized this information as "intriguing," but took a remarkably reserved position on pursuing it. "It occurs to us, just as it probably has to you, that this could be a setup, by the extreme left or the GOC," Cox informed Ambassador Barnes. Rather than recommend that the informant be turned over to a high-level officer or even the FBI, the department recommended handling him at a very low level. "You are the best judge on who should meet with him," Cox wrote, "but from our vantage point, it would seem best at this stage to treat this as a consular matter."

On April 20, the informant returned to the embassy and spent ninety minutes discussing Horman's fate, providing for the first time new names of Chilean military officers involved in his seizure and death. According to the story he related to Dreher,

> Horman was seized by Intelligence Units acting on information provided by [General Hugo] Salas, current CNI head. He was taken to the Escuela Militar and interrogated. From there he was transferred to the National Stadium for additional questioning. Documents seized from his residence indicated that Horman was an "extremist." He was therefore considered a foreigner/extremist and the order was given to execute him. [The informant] said that Horman spoke little Spanish and the troops that had him were unaware that he was an American. Instead, they thought that he was a Brazilian, Italian, etc . . . The record indicating that he was an American arrived at the stadium after the execution. He was forced to change clothes and then shot three times. The body was dumped on the streets to indicate he had been killed in

a confrontation. The news of his death got lost in the confusion of those days and later was suppressed as it was known that he was an American.[50]

The source stated that Horman was among "several hundred people perished at the stadium." The person "who made the decision on who was to die," he said, naming names, was Col. Pedro Espinoza, who soon joined the secret police, DINA.[51] "[He] does not feel that the embassy did very much to help the Horman family," Dreher reported in a cable that went to the White House Situation Room. "[He] was highly critical of the Consul General at the time and also of the Military group for not acting to help a fellow citizen. He also said that he was getting the impression that the Embassy still was not very interested."[52]

Indeed, the embassy's handling of this informant reflected the same ambivalence about aggressively pursuing the Horman case that had dominated U.S. officialdom from the start. Here was a potential witness to the controversial murder of an American citizen—the first to step forward since Rafael Gonzalez in 1976. Yet the State Department seemed more focused on his motivations than evaluating what evidence he had to offer. "I don't understand his motivation. Why after fourteen years has he finally decided to tell his story?" Dreher complained in the report on the second meeting. When the informant returned to the embassy for a third and pivotal meeting on April 24, he said that he felt his family was being threatened and "insisted" that he had to get out of Chile and get his family to the United States. "[Deleted name] could be part of a GOC plot to compromise Embassy officials," the embassy noted in a comprehensive summary of the informant meetings. "On the other hand he could be on the level and have useful information." [Doc 10]

How to respond? If the United Stated did nothing it could create "the worse case scenario," in Dreher's assessment: the informant could be killed under mysterious circumstances and "it becomes known that he came to us for help after giving us new information on the Horman case [and] our reaction was to take the information lightly and to deny him any protection or aid. The press would crucify us." But stalling him was no longer an option. "We are going to have to decide what to do with this guy."[53]

After internal discussions, embassy officials simply decided to turn the informant away. When he returned for the fourth time on April 27 seeking some form of asylum, the informant was told that "the U.S. would not grant his request: transportation for subject and family to the United States and some form of subsistence for an indefinite period of time." He then left.[54]

Eighteen days later, after conferring with the Justice Department and FBI, the State Department partially changed its mind. Now officials in Washington took the position that "the Department has a fundamental interest in determining circumstances of deaths abroad of U.S. citizens, even thirteen years after the fact." Moreover, "we would consider it a very serious matter if senior GOC officials had been aware of the circumstances of Horman's death and attempted to conceal this information from the USG and Horman's family." Even so, the State Department was unwilling to send an investigative team to Santiago to establish the informant's bona fides. Instead it instructed the embassy to tell the informant that

> Before we could consider the possibility of his travel to the United States, we would have to interview him more thoroughly. This cannot be done in Chile. If [informant] is willing to travel at his own expense to Montevideo, US officials stationed there will interview him and make a determination as to his credibility. [Informant] should understand the USG cannot offer him special assistance, financial or otherwise. . . . If we find [informant] is fully truthful after questioning in Montevideo, including polygraph test, we would be willing to consider the possibility of his subsequent travel to the United States.

This unattractive offer was never delivered, and the new information on the Horman case never pursued. The embassy had identified the informant and obtained biographic data on him—"we verified he was who he said he was," one internal memo noted—but U.S. officials professed to be unable to find him. "Although Emboff asked [informant] to keep in touch, he has made no further attempt to contact us," the embassy complained.[55] "For our part we have no means of contacting subject as he steadfastly refused to provide us with an address or telephone numbers," Ambassador Barnes cabled the department on June 17, 1987. Unsatisfied with the embassy's lack of effort, on July 14 the State Department ordered a "mission-wide effort," including the use of U.S. intelligence operatives, to recontact this individual. A month later, the embassy sent back a brief, and final, status report: "Post unable to locate [informant]."

Boris Weisfeiler

As the Santiago embassy waited for the Horman informant to reappear in June 1987, a second Chilean military source came forward with what secret cable traffic described as a "startling report" about the fate of another American—a missing hiker named Boris Weisfeiler. Weisfeiler, a Russian-born, forty-three-year old naturalized U.S. citizen and a professor of mathematics at Penn State, had disappeared while on a solo backpacking trip in southern Chile in early January 1985. After a perfunctory investigation, the Chilean government announced he was "presumed to have drowned" while trying to cross the rushing waters of the Nuble River in the Parral region 250 miles south of Santiago. Weisfeiler's backpack was found on the riverbank. But no remains were ever recovered.

The source, who called himself "Daniel," told a far darker story, which could "throw a whole new light on Weisfeiler's disappearance," the embassy reported. In early January 1985 he had been part of a seven-man Chilean army unit patrolling the perimeter of Colonia Dignidad, described in secret State Department records as "a secretive German immigrant settlement reportedly with neo-Nazi tendencies" located in the Andean foothills in the southeastern part of the country.[56] The colony collaborated closely with the Pinochet regime and was used as a secret torture/detention center; "Daniel" cited visits by the head of DINA, Manuel Contreras and Pinochet himself to its massive 37,000-acre wilderness enclave. Due to the security surrounding "La Dignidad," as it was known in the region, and its proximity to the Chilean-Argentine border, the army patrol had "standing orders" to arrest anyone found in the area.

His unit, he said, received a radio call from two army soldiers guarding a cableway near the intersection of the Nuble and the Los Sauces Rivers. "They had turned away an individual trying to make use of [the cableway]" to cross the river. The army patrol then set out in search of this suspected subversive and found a hiker "washing something in the river." In a taped confession, "Daniel" described what transpired:

> When we came to a place where there were two rivers, the patrol came across a man with a backpack, etc. He did not speak good Spanish and he did not offer any resistance. . . . Subject was told he should not have entered the area. In continuing the search of subject we found the following documents, based on which, the officer-in-charge classified subject as a Russian spy and a "Soviet." A further search of subject produced a US passport and a letter saying that he was a professor at a US university. We then took off his shoes, tied him up and took him into Colonia Dignidad where he was turned over to the Chief of Security for Colonia Dignidad.

In further interviews with embassy officers, this informant, who said he was now detailed to the CNI, provided excruciating details of the human rights abuses Weisfeiler was forced to endure—including a rudimentary map of where Weisfeiler was found, stripped, and interrogated that closely corresponded to maps drawn by consulate and private investigators in 1985. (Docs 11, 12) According to "Daniel's" account

> Weisfeiler was taken downstream about five kilometers and then stripped and searched more thoroughly. The commander of the patrol again accused Weisfeiler of being a spy and began to kick him, strike him with his gunbutt, and submerge his head in the river. At this point Weisfeiler began to shout his name . . . and also began to shout to contact the American embassy. At a guard shelter along the southern edge of the Colonia, they turned Weisfeiler over to the Colonia's chief of security. . . . The patrol's commander and the Colonia's security chief entered the Colonia and interrogated Weisfeiler for a period of some two hours. When the interrogation was over, the patrol's commander emerged and stated that the prisoner was neither a Russian nor a CIA spy, but a Jewish spy.

His conscience prompted "Daniel" to come forward with this account of Weisfeiler's fate, he told U.S. officials. He was talking now in hopes this information could be used immediately to locate the victim. "Daniel" said he had recently been in contact with a former member of his army patrol who was once again assigned to Colonia Dignidad and "had just seen Weisfeiler alive," the embassy reported: "Our source has information from an eyewitness that Weisfeiler was in the Colonia as late as early June, 1987."[57]

In June 2000, more than fifteen years after Weisfeiler's disappearance, the State Department declassified this thirteen-page summary report on debriefing this informant, "Case of Boris Weisfeiler, Colonia Dignidad, New Information," along with 436 other documents relating to his case. None of the Weisfeiler files had ever been provided to his family and, yet, numerous records contained extraordinary information on what the embassy knew and when it knew it. Some documents indicated that within the first year of Weisfeiler's reported disappearance, embassy officials received a tip that he had not drowned and was still alive. By April 1985, consulate officers suspected the involvement of Colonia Dignidad but made no effort to gain access to the enclave. After "Daniel" surfaced, according to the files, embassy officials took few immediate steps to escalate efforts to locate Weisfeiler. And although consular officials wanted to initiate an official judicial investigation to unravel the regime's cover-up, the State Department delayed a decision for a year and then refused to authorize minimal funding for legal fees.

From the start, the shadow of Charles Horman hung over the case of another vanished American. "I didn't want what happened in that movie

Missing to happen again," then Consul General Jayne Kobliska recalled.[58] When Penn State University reported that Weisfeiler had failed to return to teach the winter semester, the consulate moved expeditiously to look for him. On January 23, a day after the Carabineros informed the embassy that Weisfeiler's green backpack had been found on the bank of the Nuble River, a consular officer—conoff—named Edward Arrizabalaga traveled by car and horseback to the small riverside village of Los Mayos to retrace Weisfeiler's steps, interview the peasants who had seen him, and request a special investigation from the local authorities. In the first clue that something was amiss, the consular officer observed that the contents of the backpack were dry—"not wet nor moldy smelling," according to his handwritten notes—and showed no signs of ever having been in the water. Weisfeiler's passport, plane ticket, and a diary he always kept were also missing. Nevertheless, Arrizabalaga reported, "accidental death is in fact the most likely explanation for his disappearance."

Embassy investigators soon learned, however, that at the very moment that Weisfeiler disappeared a unit of the Carabinero police and an army patrol were tracking him as a suspected subversive. On January 4, Luis López, one of the peasants who had seen Weisfeiler hiking, reported him to local police as a "possible extremist." All residents, as the embassy summarized Lopez's initial account, "had orders to report the presence of all strangers in the area immediately to the carabineros":

> Luis López reported the presence of the stranger to the commander of the El Roble outpost, Sargeano 2nd class Jorge Cofre Vega. Following López's report the Carabineros apparently set off on horseback to search for the stranger. . . . According to the testimony of Sgt. Cofre the Carabineros were assisted in their search by a military patrol from an Army regiment based in Concepcion which happened to be in the area on the day of January 4, 1985. Luis López is the last person who reportedly saw Boris Weisfeiler.[59]

But when embassy officials returned to the region, they were unable to interview the Carabineros who participated in this search because they had all been reassigned and dispersed around the country. Sgt. Cofre Vega was suddenly retired and not available. The Chilean military refused to identify the members of the army patrol. There were "a number of indications," the embassy cabled Washington, that witnesses "were under considerable pressure from the Carabineros to confirm the official story and minimize independent contact with consular officers." In the fall of 1986, the key witness, Luis López, was found dead in what the embassy called "mysterious circumstances"—hung from the infrastructure of the river cableway not far from where Weisfeiler disappeared.[60]

This cover-up was particularly disconcerting because, within the first year of his disappearance, declassified records indicate the embassy had "one hint" that Weisfeiler had not, in fact, drowned. A contact, who remains unidentified, apparently approached embassy officer Lawrence Penn and "suggested W. was still alive," according to a cryptic memorandum, classified SECRET, and written probably in late 1985 by the deputy chief of mission, George Jones. Is there "any way to refresh, revive, update that one contact you had?" Jones wrote to Penn as the new ambassador, Harry Barnes, considered the official verdict of accidental drowning. "Amb. said that one thing that bothered him about closing the file on the case was that one hint that W. was alive."

The case was kept open, largely due to the personal outrage of the Consul General Jayne Kobliska, over the Chilean military's evasive responses to U.S. inquiries. In April 1985, Kobliska discovered that the embassy had been misinformed about the boundary line of the seventy-square-mile mountain enclave of Colonia Dignidad. In an EYES-ONLY memorandum, "Welfare/Whereabouts: Case of Boris Weisfeiler," Kobliska reported that "at the time of his disappearance Weisfeiler was either on or very near to the Colonia property" and recommended that this information be transferred to Washington via "secure telephone." After another year of U.S. "informal approaches" yielded nothing from Chilean military officials, she drafted a strongly worded memorandum to the new ambassador, Harry Barnes, demanding he take definitive measures to raise the profile of this case and obtain answers on Weisfeiler's fate. "Inaction is damaging," she advised. "The real danger in this case is that we will delay action until it is too late to either save Weisfeiler's life or to determine the true circumstances of this death." (Doc 13)[61] After yet another year of the Pinochet regime's evasive diplomatic exchanges, Kobliska again urged the ambassador to take a more forceful stand: "The Mickey Mousing around we've done on this case with this government is disgraceful," she wrote, "and though I think forcefulness should have been applied a long time ago, it wasn't."

In the late spring of 1987, as Kobliska prepared to return to a new post in Washington, she initiated a detailed status report on the Weisfeiler case. The fourteen-page review cited "important contradictions" in the evidence, as well as indications that the police had pressured witnesses to falsely claim they saw Weisfeiler's footprints where he allegedly entered the river and drowned. Weisfeiler was a semi-professional hiker—he had trekked alone in Siberia, Alaska, China, and Peru—but "no satisfactory answer has yet been given to the question of why an experienced backpacker such as Weisfeiler would attempt a river crossing in an obviously dangerous place," the report noted. One possible explanation cited by the embassy was that the backpack had been "placed in a location [near the river] in order to feign an accidental death."[62]

By the time this report was cabled to Washington at the end of June, embassy officials had begun to interview the informant known only as "Daniel" who explained that the army patrol had sent the backpack to CNI headquarters for analysis before it was replaced on the riverbank.[63] If true, his story "would throw a whole new light on the case, and call into question a substantial portion of the information previously received and reported concerning Weisfeiler's disappearance," the embassy cabled the Bureau of Inter-American Affairs. To be sure, "Daniel's" account was "bizarre." But it was also absolutely believable. "His story is so detailed and fits so well with what we know from many other sources of Weisfeiler's whereabouts, physical description, and what he was carrying, that it seems likely to us that source did in fact participate in Weisfeiler's arrest and delivery to the Colonia," according to the embassy officers that met him.[64]

The possibility that Weisfeiler was still alive posed "a dilemma":

> If Weisfeiler is in fact alive and a prisoner at the Colonia or anywhere else with the knowledge of the GOC, any investigation we undertake which comes to the GOC's attention runs the risk of his being killed to cover up the affair. On the other hand, to take no action could be equivalent to abandoning an American citizen trapped in the hands of persons for whom paranoid is one of the kinder adjectives.

This calculation, along with sheer bureaucratic inertia and the abject ambivalence of top department officials, paralyzed any aggressive steps to ascertain Weisfeiler's whereabouts and welfare. Consular officer Philip Antweiler did propose pursuing what he called seven "unturned stones" in the case. But "Daniel's" story resulted in no immediate and direct U.S. initiatives to resolve his disappearance.

In August 1987, the State Department informed the embassy that Washington "would favor reopening of a separate judicial investigation over any revival of administrative inquiries, which as embassy has reported, had failed to resolve discrepancies in case."[65] But "next steps" were left to embassy officials who continued to seek regime support for administrative inquiries. Approaches to the authorities, however, yielded only more stalling, obstruction, and empty promises for further review of the case. In January 1988, a consular officer did obtain permission to travel to Parral and interview the Carabinero officials who had originally searched for Weisfeiler. During that meeting, Sgt. Cofre Vega produced a list of names of members of the army unit that had also tracked the hiker. But not until August 1988, more than a year after "Daniel" had come forward, did the U.S. government formally request access to those soldiers who "may have important information concerning the chain of events surrounding Mr. Weisfeiler's disappearance."[66] In December, almost four years after Weisfeiler's disappearance, the Chilean Foreign Ministry finally responded that only the local tribunal, the San Carlos Court, could legally mandate such interrogations. The court, however, would act only if proper judicial proceedings were initiated and deemed legally warranted by new, compelling evidence.

The year 1989 marked the phaseout of the Pinochet regime. With Chile entering a lengthy transition to civilian rule, consulate officers considered hiring a lawyer and pursuing legal avenues for a full, court-sanctioned investigation into Weisfeiler's fate as a logical and promising next step. "Who knows what might turn up in the next few years, particularly with a new government and altered political climate," Consul General William Barkell wrote in a January 3 recommendation to approach Alfredo Etcheberry, the prominent Chilean attorney representing the United States in the Letelier-Moffitt proceedings.[67] Etcheberry had already done considerable pro bono work on the Weisfeiler case; he asked for a moderate fixed retainer of several thousand dollars to represent the U.S. consulate in seeking to reopen a judicial inquiry. In mid-March, the embassy cabled the State Department requesting "approval to obtain legal services to permit consular officers to perform duties relating to protection of U.S. nationals" and to "engage a knowledgeable local attorney . . . Alfredo Etcheberry."

Months went by with no response. On August 29, the embassy cabled Washington again noting that "in spite of numerous follow up attempts . . . we received no reply" other than "department is studying proposal." This renewed request also "disappeared into a black hole as have all the others," Barkell complained in an internal embassy communication dated in October 3. On October 6, he cabled the State Department legal office: "Given the sensitivity of this case, which has sparked Congressional interest, we cannot understand the delay in responding to our request." (Doc 14)

Only after the U.S. ambassador to Chile, Charles Gillespie, returned to Washington and personally raised the issue did the State Department finally respond. On November 20, in a cable signed by Secretary of State James Baker, the Department noted that the issue had finally been vetted. "[T]he department has no objection to the Post's employment of private local counsel to prepare and file with the appropriate court, a petition on behalf of the Embassy that requests the government of Chile to reopen the investigation." There was one caveat: the Department would not provide any money. “The cost of the legal services will [have to] be paid for with Post’s funds.”

The U.S. embassy’s inability to decide whether it could budget several thousand dollars to hire a lawyer prompted even more procrastination and inaction in the Weisfeiler case. On November 28, 1989, Barkell requested that the administration office “check to see if funds were available.” In December and January, he asked again, only to be told “it is being looked into.” Finally, in February 1990, more than a year after first proposing the plan to hire Etcheberry, Barkell formally submitted a memorandum, “Funding to Engage Attorney to Reopen Weisfeiler Case.” “I would very much appreciate a definitive answer,” he wrote. “If funds are available, I would like to get cracking and reopen the case.”

In the end, the embassy’s business and finance office determined there was no money in the budget. Barkell received a terse, one-sentence memo informing him: “At present time there are no funds available in Post allotments for this project.” (Doc 15)

A full decade later, on January 3, 2000, the Chilean courts agreed to open a judicial investigation into the case—not at the behest of the embassy, but through a legal petition filed by Boris Weisfeiler’s sister, Olga. The State Department files on the Weisfeiler case had not yet been declassified; but the family cited as new evidence a statement made by “Daniel” who resurfaced in October 1997. During a radio talk show on the subject of Colonia Dignidad, he called in and retold the story of the Weisfeiler abduction and transfer to the German enclave. The talk show host, Ricardo Israel, convinced “Daniel” to meet with him privately. During that meeting, the informant provided a handwritten unsigned report on what had happened to Weisfeiler that Israel gave to the Chilean press and to the U.S. Embassy. Ten years earlier, “Daniel” had reported that Weisfeiler might still be alive, held prisoner at Colonia Dignidad. Now he stated that Weisfeiler had been executed. “Later on, we found that this person, after being savagely interrogated, was made to kneel on the ground and was murdered with a shot to the nape of his neck.” The U.S. embassy, in transmitting a translation of “Daniel’s” report to the State Department, noted that it “considers the case open and unsolved.”(Doc 16)

As of mid-2003, Boris Weisfeiler remained the one U.S. citizen among 1,119 Chileans “disappeared” at the hands of the Pinochet regime. Charles Horman and Frank Teruggi were the two Americans among more than 3,100 Chilean murder victims, whose killers remained unidentified and at large. Their cases spanned the systemic, arbitrary, and brutal atrocities inflicted on Chilean society from the day of the military coup until the end of Pinochet era; they also called worldwide attention to the indifferent posture of the U.S. government toward the Pinochet regime's human rights crimes—even as those crimes claimed the lives of Americans. But the fate of a fourth U.S. citizen, Ronni Karpen Moffitt, represented an escalation of such atrocities beyond Chile's borders into a crime of a very different category: international terrorism.

DOCUMENT 1. Department of State, **SECRET** Memorandum, "Charles Horman Case," August 25, 1976 (completely censored version, page 1).

DEPARTMENT OF STATE

Washington, D.C.

August 25, 1976

UNCLASSIFIED

343

TO: ARA - Mr. Shlaudeman

THROUGH: ARA - Ambassador Ryan

FROM: ARA/BC - R.V. Fimbres/R.S. Driscoll/W.V. Robertson

SUBJECT: Charles Horman Case.

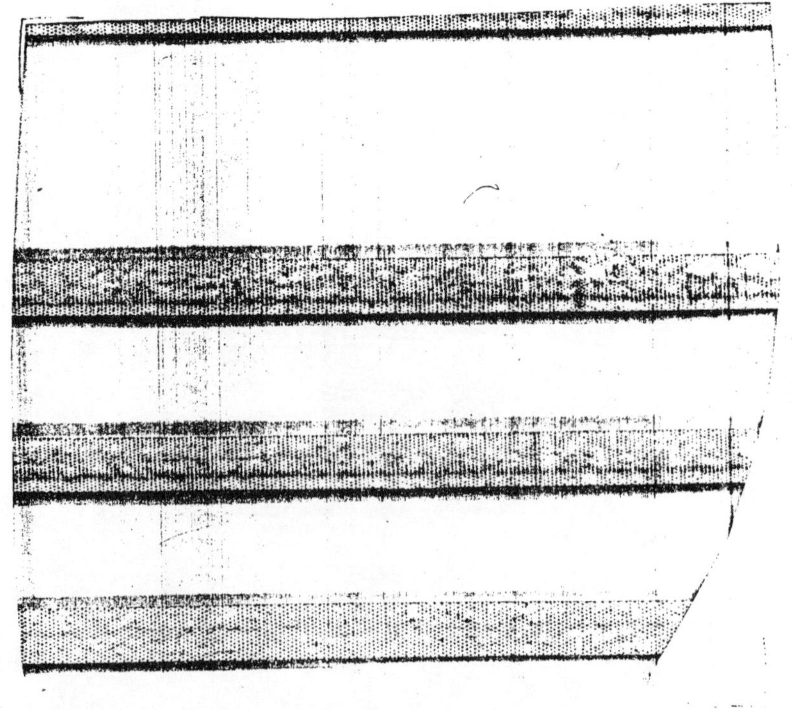

DOCUMENT 2. Department of State, **SECRET** Memorandum, "Charles Horman Case," August 25, 1976 (strategically censored version, pages 1, 2).

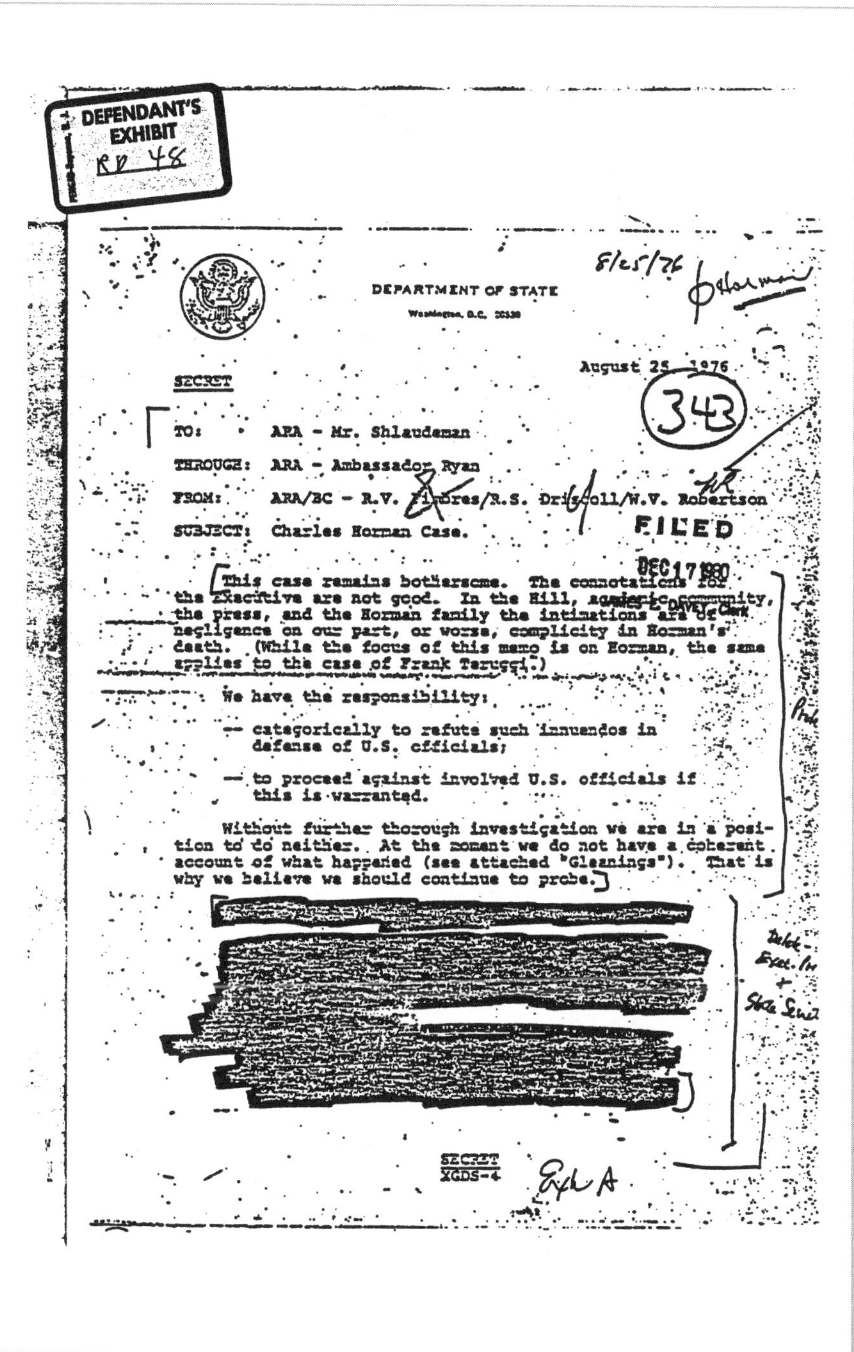

DEFENDANT'S EXHIBIT RD 48

8/25/76

DEPARTMENT OF STATE
Washington, D.C. 20520

SECRET

August 25, 1976

343

TO: ARA - Mr. Shlaudeman

THROUGH: ARA - Ambassador Ryan

FROM: ARA/BC - R.V. Fimbres/R.S. Driscoll/W.V. Robertson

SUBJECT: Charles Horman Case.

FILED DEC 17 1980

This case remains bothersome. The connotations for the Executive are not good. In the Hill, academic community, the press, and the Horman family the intimations are of negligence on our part, or worse, complicity in Horman's death. (While the focus of this memo is on Horman, the same applies to the case of Frank Teruggi.)

We have the responsibility:

-- categorically to refute such innuendos in defense of U.S. officials;

-- to proceed against involved U.S. officials if this is warranted.

Without further thorough investigation we are in a position to do neither. At the moment we do not have a coherent account of what happened (see attached "Gleanings"). That is why we believe we should continue to probe.

SECRET
XGDS-4

Exh A

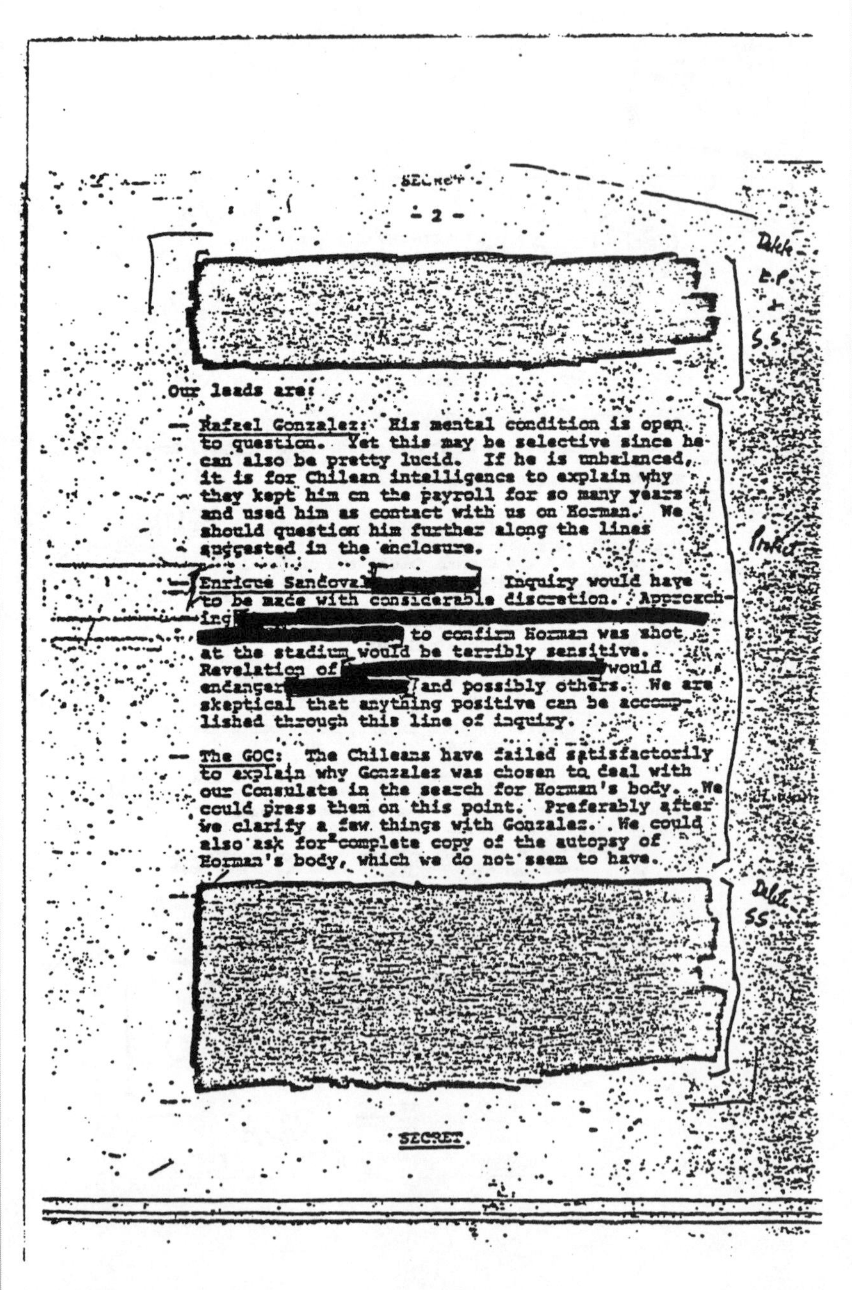
SECRET

- 2 -

Delete E.P. + S.S.

Our leads are:

— Rafael Gonzalez: His mental condition is open to question. Yet this may be selective since he can also be pretty lucid. If he is unbalanced, it is for Chilean intelligence to explain why they kept him on the payroll for so many years and used him as contact with us on Horman. We should question him further along the lines suggested in the enclosure.

— Enrique Sandoval [redacted] Inquiry would have to be made with considerable discretion. Approaching [redacted] to confirm Horman was shot at the stadium would be terribly sensitive. Revelation of [redacted] would endanger [redacted] and possibly others. We are skeptical that anything positive can be accomplished through this line of inquiry.

— The GOC: The Chileans have failed satisfactorily to explain why Gonzalez was chosen to deal with our Consulate in the search for Horman's body. We could press them on this point. Preferably after we clarify a few things with Gonzalez. We could also ask for complete copy of the autopsy of Horman's body, which we do not seem to have.

Protect

Delete SS.

SECRET.

DOCUMENT 3. Department of State, **SECRET** Memorandum, "Charles Horman Case," August 25, 1976 (uncensored version, pages 1, 2).

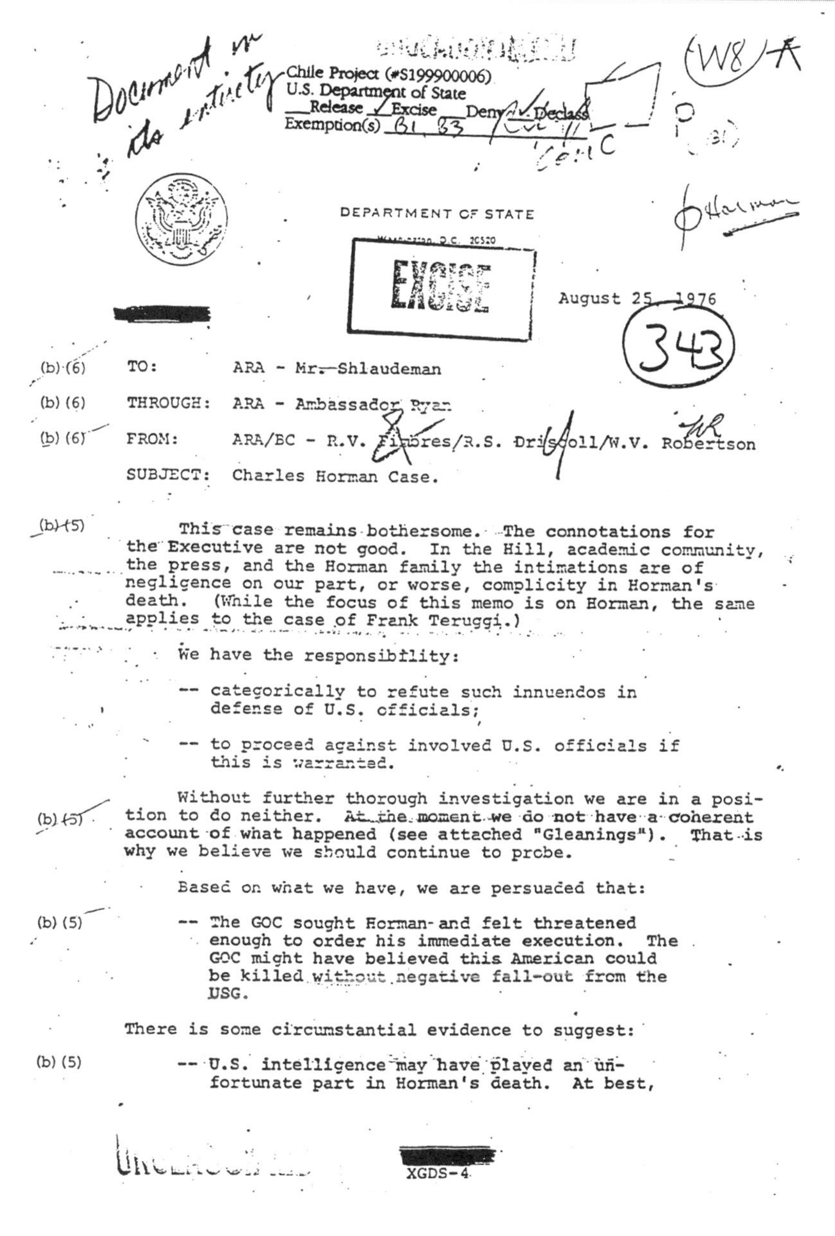

Document in its entirety

Chile Project (#S199900006)
U.S. Department of State
__Release ✓ Excise __Deny ✓ Declass
Exemption(s) B1 B3

(W8) A

343

DEPARTMENT OF STATE
Washington, D.C. 20520

EXCISE

August 25, 1976

(b) (6) TO: ARA - Mr. Shlaudeman

(b) (6) THROUGH: ARA - Ambassador Ryan

(b) (6) FROM: ARA/BC - R.V. Fimbres/R.S. Driscoll/W.V. Robertson

SUBJECT: Charles Horman Case.

(b) (5) This case remains bothersome. The connotations for the Executive are not good. In the Hill, academic community, the press, and the Horman family the intimations are of negligence on our part, or worse, complicity in Horman's death. (While the focus of this memo is on Horman, the same applies to the case of Frank Teruggi.)

We have the responsibility:

-- categorically to refute such innuendos in defense of U.S. officials;

-- to proceed against involved U.S. officials if this is warranted.

(b) (5) Without further thorough investigation we are in a position to do neither. At the moment we do not have a coherent account of what happened (see attached "Gleanings"). That is why we believe we should continue to probe.

Based on what we have, we are persuaded that:

(b) (5) -- The GOC sought Horman and felt threatened enough to order his immediate execution. The GOC might have believed this American could be killed without negative fall-out from the USG.

There is some circumstantial evidence to suggest:

(b) (5) -- U.S. intelligence may have played an unfortunate part in Horman's death. At best,

UNCLASSIFIED

XGDS-4

UNCLASSIFIED

- 2 -

(b)(5) it was limited to providing or confirming information that helped motivate his murder by the GOC. At worst, U.S. intelligence was aware the GOC saw Horman in a rather serious light and U.S. officials did nothing to discourage the logical outcome of GOC paranoia.

Our leads are:

(b)(5) -- Rafael Gonzalez: His mental condition is open to question. Yet this may be selective since he can also be pretty lucid. If he is unbalanced, it is for Chilean intelligence to explain why they kept him on the payroll for so many years and used him as contact with us on Horman. We should question him further along the lines suggested in the enclosure.

(b)(1) & (b)(6) -- Enrique Sandoval's brother: Inquiry would have to be made with considerable discretion. Approaching the brother (most likely, Colonel Guillermo Sandoval Velasquez) to confirm Horman was shot at the stadium would be terribly sensitive. Revelation of his indiscretion in 1973 would endanger the Colonel and possibly others. We are skeptical that anything positive can be accomplished through this line of inquiry.

(b)(5) -- The GOC: The Chileans have failed satisfactorily to explain why Gonzalez was chosen to deal with our Consulate in the search for Horman's body. We could press them on this point. Preferably after we clarify a few things with Gonzalez. We could also ask for a complete copy of the autopsy of Horman's body, which we do not seem to have.

(b)(1) & (b)(3) -- CIA: The Agency's comments on its relations with Gonzalez do not explain Gonzalez' knowledge of [ ] The [ ] needs further illumination no matter CIA disclaimers. Further, we find it hard to believe that the Chileans did not check with [ ] regarding two detained Americans when the GOC was checking with Horman's friends and neighbors regarding Horman's activities. [ ] lack of candor with us on other matters only heightens our suspicions. (B1) (B3)

UNCLASSIFIED

DOCUMENT 4. U.S. Embassy, Cable, "W/W Deaths; Charles E. Horman," October 18, 1973.

10/18/73

Department of State TELEC

(6)

LIMITED OFFICIAL USE

AN: D730089-1043

PAGE 01 SANTIA 05088 182010Z

55
ACTION SCS-03

INFO OCT-01 ARA-16 ISO-00 SCA-01 SSO-00 H-03 L-03 INR-10

INRE-00 CIAE-00 NSAE-00 (ISO) W
------------------------ 020512
O 181958Z OCT 73
FM AMEMBASSY SANTIAGO
TO SECSTATE WASHDC IMMEDIATE 6222

LIMITED OFFICIAL USE SANTIAGO 5088

E.O. 11652: N/A
TAGS: CDES, CI (HORMAN, CHARLES E.)
SUBJ: W/W DEATHS; CHARLES E. HORMAN
1. EMBASSY INFORMED AFTERNOON OCTOBER 18, 1973 THAT PREVIOUSLY UNIDENTIFIED MALE BODY WHICH DELIVERED TO MORGUE ON SEPTEMBER 18, 1973 AND GIVEN AUTOPSY NUMBER 2663 HAD BEEN IDENTIFIED THROUGH FINGERPRINTS AS BEING THAT OF CHARLES E. HORMAN. UNIDENTIFIED BODY DELIVERED TO SANTIAGO CEMETERY ON OCTOBER 3 AND APPARENTLY INTERRED THEREAFTER. CAUSE OF DEATH WAS BY BULLET WOUND. BODY HAD BEEN PICKED UP ON STREET BY MILITARY AND DELIVERED TO MORGUE.

2. EMBASSY SENDING NOTE TO FOREIGN OFFICE REQUESTING AUTOPSY REPORT AND EXHUMATION OF BODY.

3. EMBASSY ADVISING WIFE AND FATHER.
DAVIS

LIMITED OFFICIAL USE

DOCUMENT 5. Department of State, Cable, "Disposition of Horman Remains," March 23, 1974.

UNCLASSIFIED
n/a

Page: 1

EE22

R

ˉUNCLASSIFIED

.AGE 01 STATE 058819

42
ORIGIN SCSE-00

INFO OCT-01 ISO-00 /001 R

DRAFTED BY SCA/SCS/DCANDEY:EJH
APPROVED BY SCA/SCS/DCANDEY
--------------------- 069851

R 231453Z MAR 74
FM SECSTATE WASHDC
TO MR. AND MRS. EDMOND C. HORMAN
31 EAST 76TH STREET
NEW YORK NEW YORK TELEPHONE 212-744-2339

UNCLAS STATE 058819

E.O. 11652: N/A
TAGS: CDES, CI (HORMAN, CHARLES)
SUBJECT: DISPOSITION OF HORMAN REMAINS

THIS IS TO CONFIRM THE TELEPHONE CONVERSATION OF MARCH 21 BETWEEN MRS. HORMAN AND D.S. CANDEY OF THE DEPARTMENT ˈNFORMING YOU OF THE GOVERNMENT OF CHILI'S DECISION TO .PPROVE YOUR REQUEST FOR THE RELEASE OF THE REMAINS OF CHARLES HORMAN FOR RETURN TO THE U.S. IN ORDER FOR THE AMERICAN EMBASSY AT SANTIAGO TO ARRANGE SHIPMENT YOU WILL RECALL THAT A DEPOSIT OF NINE HUNDRED DOLLARS (900) IS REQUIRED TO COVER THE ESTIMATED COST FOR PREPARATION OF THE REMAINS AND TRANSPORTATION TO NEW YORK CITY. ADDITIONALLY, PLEASE PROVIDE THE NAME OF THE FUNERAL HOME WHERE YOU WANT THE REMAINS TO BE SHIPPED. FUNDS AND INSTRUCTIONS SHOULD BE SENT TO THE OFFICE OF SPECIAL CONSULAR SERVICES, DEPARTMENT OF STATE. PLEASE ACCEPT OUR DEEPEST CONDOLENCES IN THIS TRAGIC AFFAIR.

DIRECTOR, SPECIAL CONSULAR SERVICES
DEPARTMENT OF STATE
WASHINGTON, D.C. KISSINGER

UNCLASSIFIED

NNN

n/a
UNCLASSIFIED

Page:

DOCUMENT 6. Department of Defense, Report on Frank Teruggi, "Deceased United States Citizen," October 15, 1973.

AA236

Resume prepared approx. 15 Oct for use in discussions about case.

UNCLASSIFIED

SUBJECT: Deceased United States Citizen

Name: Frank Randall TERUGGI

DPOB: March 14, 1949 in Chicago, Illinois

Marital Status: Single

U.S. Passport: 81866047

Entered Chile: 1 October 1972 as a Resident Student

Address: Hernán Cortés 2575

Date of Death: Not known, but sometime between late afternoon September 21, 1973 and 22:15 hours on September 22, 1973.

Cause of Death: Multiple gunshot wounds on chest, neck and head.

Body Identified: By visual identification, dental comparison, and fingerprint data in the Gabinete de Identificación.

Details: TERUGGI was removed from his home along with another U.S. citizen, David Hathaway, at approximately 21:00 hours on September 20, 1973 by members of the Carabineros de Chile. Both were taken to the Escuela de Suboficiales "Macul" of the Carabineros where they were detained overnight and then taken the morning of September 21, 1973 to the National Stadium. No reason for the detention was given. A note from the Chilean Foreign Office dated October 3, 1973 stated that Mr. Teruggi had been arrested on September 20 for violation of curfew and had been released for lack of merit on September 21, 1973. Mr. Hathaway was not released along with Mr. Teruggi. According to Mr. Hathaway, the afternoon of September 21 an officer separated Mr. Teruggi from the other U.S. citizen detainees based upon a list of names he was carrying. Mr. Teruggi was not seen alive again. Mr. Teruggi did not sign a release from the National Stadium as was required of other persons released on the same date. According to records of the morgue, the body later identified as being that of Mr. Teruggi was brought to the morgue at 22:15 hours on September 22, 1973 by a soldier. There was no identification on the body. According to friends, Mr. Teruggi did not return to his residence after his reported release from the National Stadium on September 21, 1973.

UNCLASSIFIED

DOCUMENT 7. Department of Defense, Cover Memo and Chilean Military Report on Frank Teruggi and Charles Horman, October 30, 1973.

EMBASSY OF THE
UNITED STATES OF AMERICA

EXCISE

246
BB-85
P

Santiago, 2 November 1973.

MEMORANDUM FOR RECORDS

From: Col W.M. Hon, Defense Attache

Ref: Frank TERRUGI and Charles HORMAN.

On 18 October General Lutz told the undersigned that he was preparing a memorandum regarding the disappearance and death of Terrugi and Horman.

Since the above date the undersigned has repeatedly reminded General Lutz' office that the Embassy had not received the memorandum he promised. On 30 October I again called Comandante Herrera reminding him of General Lutz' promised memorandum and suggesting that it should be in our hands prior to the Ambassador's departure, 01 November. At 10:00, 31 October Comandante Herrera delivered to me a memorandum from General Lutz. This memorandum is not addressed to any particular agency and is unsigned. Copy is attached.

Copies have been provided DCM and Consul Fred Purdy.

CONSULATE OF THE UNITED STATES OF AMERICA
NOV 1973
SANTIAGO, CHILE

Chile Project (#S199900006)
U.S. Department of State
__Release ✓Excise __Deny __Declass
Exemption(s) B6

UNCLASSIFIED

TRANSLATION

MEMORANDUM

OCT 30, 1973

(Antecedents on two Northamerican citizens' decease)

A. BACKGROUND

1. American citizens FRANK RANDALL TERRUGI BOMBATCH and CHARLES HORMAN LAZAR, were accurately investigated by officials of the Military Intelligence Service, in order to establish cause of their death as a special deference to the American Embassy.

2. Available information on both persons leads to the conclussion that they were involved in extreme leftist movements in our country, which they supported both materially and ideologically.

3. It is necessary, furthermore, to indicate that available and well supported data evidence existence of an organization linked to Northamerican residents in our country, with connections in the rest of the countries in the Continent and led from the U.S., which has undertaken an offensive campaign tending to obtain the following fundamental objectives:

a. Help extremists and political leaders of the former government leave the country.

b. Carry out a campaign to discredit the Junta de Gobierno, intending through these actions, to impede economic or any other assistance from the U.S. to our country.

c. Discredit diplomatic procedures of the American Embassy in Chile, alleging that these have been weak and have permitted military action against Northamerican citizens residing in Chile.

This situation is related with the citizens HORMAN and TERRUGI, since there are concrete reasons to believe that at least the latter belongs to said organization.

4. On the participation of armed forces in the cases referred to, the following has been proved:

a. That FRANK TERRUGI was actually detained and taken to the National Stadium but subsequently he was set free and that his decease occurred while he was out of military or police control.

b. In the case of HORMAN, it has not been possible to prove the effectiveness of his detention by military or police forces, as no registration appears

-2-

on him in the pertaining Units, nor on any list of arrested people in any circumstances in the National Stadium.

c. To this respect, it can be stated that his classification during the investigations performed was "disappeared" and efforts to locate him were based on this fact.

d. Available information shows that Mr. Horman may have been detained by military personnel at his domicile located in what has been named "Bolt Vicuña Mackenna", but this situation is connected with elements that present an abnormal picture of the situation since these uniformed persons supposedly arrived in a civilian truck, without identifying themselves and without leaving any documentation on searchings, thus clearly trasgressing regulations in this respect.

5. In view of the above, action of the Service, which in all times contacted the parents and wife of Mr. Horman, was aimed at finding this citizen since he was classified as "disappeared". Thus, his decease was finally proved after accurate studies on identification by means of fingerprint tests and after finding that his corpse belonged to one of the non-identified persons turned into the Legal Medical Institute on 18 Sep 1973.

8. CONCLUSSIONS.

1. In accordance with the above data, it can be concluded that both American citizens died while out of military control.

2. It can also be concluded that during period 11 to 20 September, snipers and guerilla actions in Santiago had to be suppressed by force, during these actions it was verified that extremists fighting against civilians were responsible for killing people with weapons of a similar or equal caliber to those used by military forces, and therefore this fact must not be dismissed as a possible cause for death of both American citizens under reference.

3. Control on persons during those days, especially on people who had been detained, escape to the responsibility of Military Authorities and presumptions on any criminal action by these forces must be discarded, as they were under command of responsible officials with strict instructions in this respect.

SANTIAGO, 30 October 1973.

DOCUMENT 8. FBI, **SECRET** Intelligence Memorandum on Frank Teruggi, October 25, 1972.

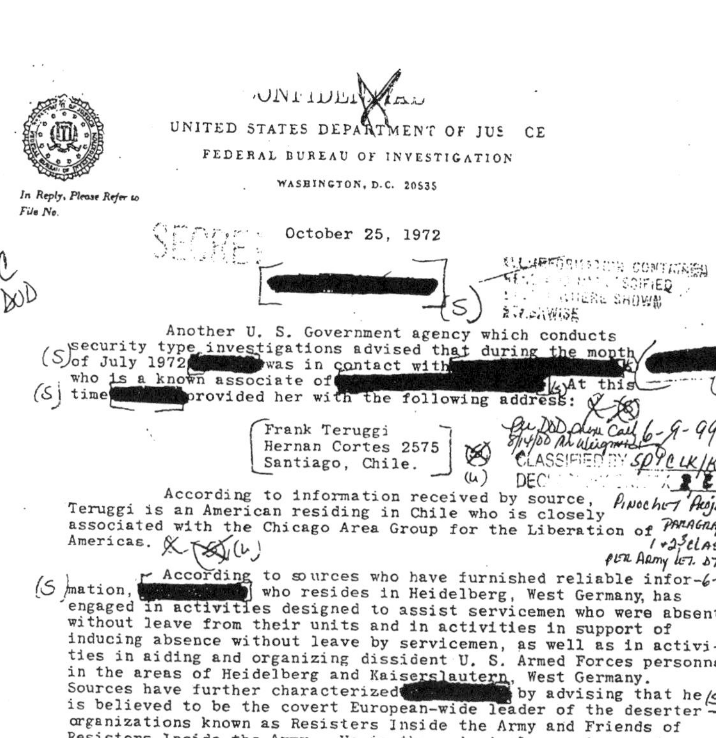

CONFIDENTIAL

UNITED STATES DEPARTMENT OF JUSTICE

FEDERAL BUREAU OF INVESTIGATION

WASHINGTON, D.C. 20535

In Reply, Please Refer to File No.

SECRET October 25, 1972

[redacted] (S)

Another U. S. Government agency which conducts security type investigations advised that during the month of July 1972 [redacted] was in contact with [redacted] who is a known associate of [redacted]. At this time [redacted] provided her with the following address:

Frank Teruggi
Hernan Cortes 2575
Santiago, Chile.

According to information received by source, Teruggi is an American residing in Chile who is closely associated with the Chicago Area Group for the Liberation of Americas.

According to sources who have furnished reliable information, [redacted] who resides in Heidelberg, West Germany, has engaged in activities designed to assist servicemen who were absent without leave from their units and in activities in support of inducing absence without leave by servicemen, as well as in activities in aiding and organizing dissident U. S. Armed Forces personnel in the areas of Heidelberg and Kaiserslautern, West Germany. Sources have further characterized [redacted] by advising that he is believed to be the covert European-wide leader of the deserter organizations known as Resisters Inside the Army and Friends of Resisters Inside the Army. He is the principal organizer and publisher of several anti-U. S. Military/Vietnam underground newspapers. He has a large following and a vast number of contacts with members of various leftist organizations throughout Europe and the Contenental United States.

This document contains neither recommendations nor conclusions of the FBI. It is the property of the FBI and is loaned to your agency; it and its contents are not to be distributed outside your agency nor duplicated within your agency.

Classified by another Government agency
Exempt for general declassification
Schedule of Executive Order 11652
Exemption category II
Automatically declassified on indefinite

WARNING NOTICE.
SENSITIVE SOURCES AND METHODS INVOLVED.

SPECIAL HANDLING REQUIRED.
Not Releasable to Foreign Nationals.

100-474363-

CONFIDENTIAL

0000030

DOCUMENT 9. FBI, **SECRET** Intelligence Memorandum, "Frank Teruggi," October 25, 1972.

OPTIONAL FORM NO. 10
MAY 1962 EDITION
GSA FPMR (41 CFR) 101-11.6
UNITED STATES GOVERNMENT

Memorandum SECRET

TO : ACTING DIRECTOR, FBI

DATE: 10/25/72

ALL INFORMATION CONTAINED HEREIN IS UNCLASSIFIED EXCEPT WHERE SHOWN OTHERWISE

FROM : LEGAT, BONN (100-2137) (P)

SUBJECT: FRANK TERUGGI
SM - Sub

CLASSIFIED BY SP-1 CLK/TPS
DECLASSIFY ON: 25X

Enclosed herewith are five copies of a self-explanatory LHM in which subject is mentioned.

Bureau is requested to review Bufiles and Identification Division records concerning subject, as well as the Chicago Area Group for the Liberation of Americas.

Chicago is requested to conduct appropriate investigation to identify subject as well as the Chicago Area Group for the Liberation of Americas and submit results of investigation in LHM form suitable for dissemination.

The U. S. Government agency mentioned in the LHM is the 66th Military Intelligence Group, Munich, West Germany, which furnished this information through the Office of Deputy Chief of Staff, Intelligence, Headquarters, U. S. Army Europe.

This information came from [redacted] The nature of this [redacted] however, should not be referred to outside the Bureau. (X) (S)

[redacted] is the subject of [redacted] (U)

5-Bureau (Encs. 5) ENCLOSURE
(1 - Foreign Liaison Desk)
(2 - Chicago)
1-Bonn
TMH:mm
(6)

100 -474363

MCT-14

NOV 22 1972

SECRET

Buy U.S. Savings Bonds Regularly on the Payroll Savings Plan

0000029

DOCUMENT 10. U.S. Embassy, Cable, "[Deleted name] Reports on GOC Involvement in Death of Charles Horman, Asks Embassy for Asylum and AID," April 28, 1987.

~~CONFIDENTIAL~~ HORMAN

WHITE HOUSE SITUATION ROOM

137

PAGE 01 OF 02

PRT: FLOWER
SIT: EOB VAX

<PREC> IMMEDIATE <CLAS> CONFIDENTIAL <DTG> 282129Z APR 87

FM AMEMBASSY SANTIAGO

TO RUEHC/SECSTATE WASHDC IMMEDIATE 1188

~~CONFIDENTIAL~~ SECTION 01 OF 03 SANTIAGO 03059
EXDIS
DEPT PLEASE PASS TO DEPTJUSTICE
DEPT FOR LEGAL ADVISOR KOZAK; FBI FOR SSA CORNICK
E.O. 12356: DECL:OADR
TAGS: PREL, PHUM, CI
SUBJ: REPORTS ON GOC INVOLVEMENT IN DEATH OF CHARLES HORMAN, ASKS EMBASSY FOR ASYLUM AND AID
REF: (A) SANTIAGO 2448 (EXDIS)

1. ~~CONFIDENTIAL~~ - ENTIRE TEXT.

>BEGIN SUMMARY>

2. SUMMARY: EMBOFF HAS HAD SEVERAL MEETINGS WITH ACCOUNT OF HORMAN'S DEATH CORRESPONDS WITH WHAT WE KNOW ABOUT THE CASE AND THE GOC ATTEMPT TO COVER UP THEIR INVOLVEMENT. INSISTS THAT HE IS IN VERY REAL DANGER FROM THE CNI (CHILEAN INTELLIGENCE) AND IS NOW SEEKING EMBASSY PROTECTION AND AID. HE HAS COMPARED HIS SITUATION TO THAT OF FERNANDEZ LARIOS AND WANTS TO GO TO THE U.S. FOR SAFETY. CLEARLY COULD BE PART OF A GOC PLOT TO COMPROMISE EMBASSY OFFICIALS, ESPECIALLY IN THE WAKE OF THE FERNANDEZ DEFECTION. ON THE OTHER HAND, HE COULD BE ON THE LEVEL AND HAVE USEFUL INFORMATION ABOUT COLONEL ESPINOZA, ONE OF THOSE UNDER INDICTMENT IN THE LETELIER CASE.

EMBASSY WOULD LIKE TO EXPLORE FURTHER WHAT MIGHT KNOW, BUT IT WOULD BE HELPFUL FIRST TO HAVE AN INDICATION FROM WASHINGTON AS TO WHETHER ANYTHING HE SAID IS NEW, OR POTENTIALLY USEFUL IN LETELIER CASE. END SUMMARY.
>END SUMMARY>

THE EMBASSY IN LATE FEBRUARY WHEN HE CALLED AND ASKED FOR AN APPOINTMENT WITH THE POLITICAL SECTION. HE SUBSEQUENTLY MET WITH A POLITICAL OFFICER ON MARCH 11, APRIL 20, AND APRIL 24. IN MID-MARCH HE ALSO MET WITH THE CONSUL GENERAL. HE RELATED THE FOLLOWING STORY.

4. HE IS ACCORDING TO HORMAN WAS DETAINED ON SEPTEMBER 18 BY A UNIT STATIONED AT THE MILITARY SCHOOL DURING A ROUTINE ACTION AGAINST A HOME REPUTED TO HOUSE EXTREMISTS. MATERIALS WERE FOUND AT THE HOUSE WHICH WERE CONSIDERED "EXTREMIST" IN CONTENT. HORMAN WAS INTERROGATED AT THE MILITARY SCHOOL AND THEN TRANSFERRED TO THE NATIONAL STADIUM FOR FURTHER QUESTIONING. HE WAS ORDERED SHOT AND KILLED THE EVENING OF SEPTEMBER 19. ACCORDING TO THE AUTHORITIES AT THE STADIUM DID NOT KNOW THAT HORMAN WAS AN AMERICAN SINCE HIS PAPERWORK ARRIVED AFTER HIS DEATH, AND HIS POOR KNOWLEDGE OF SPANISH MADE IT DIFFICULT FOR HIM TO UNDERSTAND AND ANSWER QUESTIONS. THEY ONLY KNEW THAT HE WAS A FOREIGNER AND AN "EXTREMIST". THE BODY WAS TAKEN FROM THE STADIUM AND LEFT AT A LOCATION TO CREATE THE IDEA THAT HE HAD BEEN KILLED IN A FIREFIGHT WITH THE MILITARY. HOWEVER, IN THE CONFUSED DAYS FOLLOWING THE COUP, AND AFTER IT WAS KNOWN THAT HE WAS AN AMERICAN, THE MILITARY SOUGHT TO HIDE THE FACT THAT HE WAS DEAD. CONFIRMED THAT HORMAN WAS REQUIRED TO CHANGE CLOTHES SHORTLY BEFORE HE WAS EXECUTED. ACCORDING TO PEDRO ESPINOZA WAS THE ONE AT THE STADIUM WHO APPROVED THE KILLING OF HORMAN. HE ADDED THAT SEVERAL HUNDRED WERE SHOT AT THE STADIUM BUT THAT MANY MORE WERE KILLED IN VALPARAISO, WHERE THE BODIES WERE DUMPED AT SEA.

5. WAS VERY CRITICAL OF THE ROLE OF EMBASSY OFFICERS IN THE DAYS FOLLOWING THE DEATH OF CHARLES HORMAN. HE SAID THAT EMBASSY OFFICERS SHOWED LITTLE INTEREST IN THE CASE AND DID NOT HELP THE FAMILY.
BT
#3059
BT
~~CONFIDENTIAL~~ SECTION 02 OF 03 SANTIAGO 03059
EXDIS
E.O. 12356: DECL:OADR
TAGS: PREL, PHUM, CI

IN RESPONSE TO A DIRECT QUESTION, SAID THAT, TO HIS KNOWLEDGE, NO U.S. OFFICIAL PLAYED ANY ROLE IN THE DEATH OF CHARLES HORMAN SINCE HE WAS DEAD BEFORE ANYONE IN THE EMBASSY WOULD HAVE KNOWN OF HIS DETENTION.

6. IN HIS EARLIER MEETINGS WITH EMBASSY OFFICIALS, INSISTED THAT HIS ONLY WISH WAS THAT THE TRUTH BE KNOWN. HOWEVER, HE LATER IMPLIED THAT HE WOULD HAVE TO LEAVE CHILE ONCE THE TRUTH WAS KNOWN THOUGH HE DENIED THAT MONEY WAS INVOLVED IN HIS MOTIVATION. DURING HIS MOST RECENT VISIT, HE BECAME VERY EMOTIONAL WHILE REPORTING THIS STORY AND STATED THAT THE EMBASSY WAS HIS ONLY HOPE AND THAT WE HAD TO HELP HIM. HE COMPARED HIS PLIGHT TO THAT OF FERNANDEZ LARIOS.

7. POST HAS BEEN HANDLING WITH GREAT CAUTION BECAUSE HE MAY BE A CNI PLANT WHOSE JOB

DECLASSIFIED
Authority FBI, State, CIA, NSC, DOJ
By KAH NARA, Date 6/15/00

~~CONFIDENTIAL~~

WHITE HOUSE SITUATION ROOM

PAGE 02 OF 02

IS TO COMPROMISE HIGH EMBASSY OFFICIALS AS REPORTED IN REFTEL. REPORTS OF SUCH AN ATTEMPT HAVE REACHED US AND THE GOC WRATH OVER THE DEFECTION OF FERNANDEZ LARIOS HAS PRESUMABLY ONLY WHETTED THE GOC DESIRE TO CATCH US IN THE ACT. THEREFORE, WE HAVE CONCLUDED THAT THERE IS A VERY REAL POSSIBILITY THAT [redacted] IS ATTEMPTING TO LURE US INTO A MISSTEP, SUCH AS A MEETING WITH THE AMBASSADOR OR A RECREATION OF THE FERNANDEZ LARIOS SCENARIO. WE HAVE NO DOUBT THAT HE IS WHO HE SAYS HE IS. HE HAS PROVIDED DOCUMENTARY PROOF OF THAT AND HIS INFORMATION ON THE NORMAN CASE AND HIS OWN PERSONAL HISTORY HAVE CHECKED OUT. OUR CURRENT CONCERN IS WHAT TO DO WITH HIM.

PRA 1; FOIA B-1 EO 12958 1.5c 3.4 b1&b3

-

8. AFTER THE FOREGOING WAS TYPED, [redacted] RETURNED TO THE EMBASSY ON APRIL 27, ACCOMPANIED BY [redacted]

PRA 1; FOIA B-1 EO 12958 1.5c 3.4 b1&b3

PRA 1; FOIA B-1 EO 12958 1.5c 3.4 b1&b3

-

THE UPSHOT OF ALL THIS WAS THAT HE WANTED THE U.S. GOVERNMENT TO GET HIM TO THE U.S. AS SOON AS POSSIBLE. DURING THE ENSUING DISCUSSION, IT WAS APPARENT THAT WHAT HE HAD IN MIND WAS SOMETHING SIMILAR TO THE DEAL STRUCK WITH FERNANDEZ LARIOS -- A HOTEL ROOM AND A NEW LIFE. HE REJECTED THE SUGGESTION THAT THE TWO CASES WERE DISSIMILAR. WHILE NEVER ACTUALLY REQUESTING ASYLUM, HE ARGUED THAT

WE WERE THE ONLY EMBASSY IN SANTIAGO THAT DID NOT GRANT ASYLUM.

-

9. EMBOFF SUGGESTED TO [redacted] THAT HE COULD, N THE INTERIM, OBTAIN CHILEAN LEGAL COUNSEL, PERHAPS THROUGH THE VICARIATE OF SOLIDARITY. FAILING THAT, HE COULD GO TO [redacted] REJECTED BOTH SUGGESTIONS OUT OF HAND, REINFORCING THE CONJECTURE THAT HIS

PRA 1; FOIA B-1 EO 12958 1.5c 3.4 b1&b3

BT
#3059
BT

~~CONFIDENTIAL~~ SECTION 03 OF 03 SANTIAGO 03059

EXDIS

E.O. 12356: DECL:OADR

TAGS: PREL, PHUM, CI

SUBJ: [redacted] REPORTS ON

PRIME MOTIVATION IS TO OBTAIN A VISA AND U.S. GOVERNMENT FINANCIAL ASSISTANCE. (FYI: IT IS WIDELY BELIEVED IN SANTIAGO THAT FERNANDEZ LARIOS RECEIVED A LARGE LUMP SUM PAYMENT IN RETURN FOR HIS TESTIMONY.)

PRA 1; FOIA B-1 EO 12958 1.5c 3.4 b1&b3

-

10. ACTION REQUESTED: POST LEANS TOWARD THE BELIEF THAT [redacted] IS LEGITIMATE RATHER THAN A CNI PLANT. WE DO NOT BELIEVE THAT HE IS IN ANY IMMINENT DANGER, NOTWITHSTANDING [redacted] HOWEVER,

PRA 1; FOIA B-1 EO 12958 1.5c 3.4 b1&b3

WE ARE UNABLE TO FULLY EVALUATE THE WORTH OF THE INFORMATION HE IS OFFERING. POST NEEDS TO KNOW IF THE DEPARTMENT CONSIDERS THE INFORMATION TO BE WORTHWHILE, NOT ONLY FOR ITS REVELATIONS ABOUT THE NORMAN CASE BUT ALSO FOR ITS CONNECTION TO INDIVIDUALS INVOLVED IN THE LETELIER CASE. WE CAUTION THAT THE THREAT OF ENTRAPMENT STILL EXISTS. POST WOULD APPRECIATE DEPARTMENT VIEW ASAP AS TO THE USEFULNESS OF MAINTAINING CONTACT WITH [redacted]

BARNES
BT
#3059

PRA 1; FOIA B-1 EO 12958 1.5c 3.4 b1&b3

DOCUMENT 11. U.S. Embassy, Map Drawn by U.S. Investigator on Disappearance of Boris Weisfeiler, ca. February 1985.

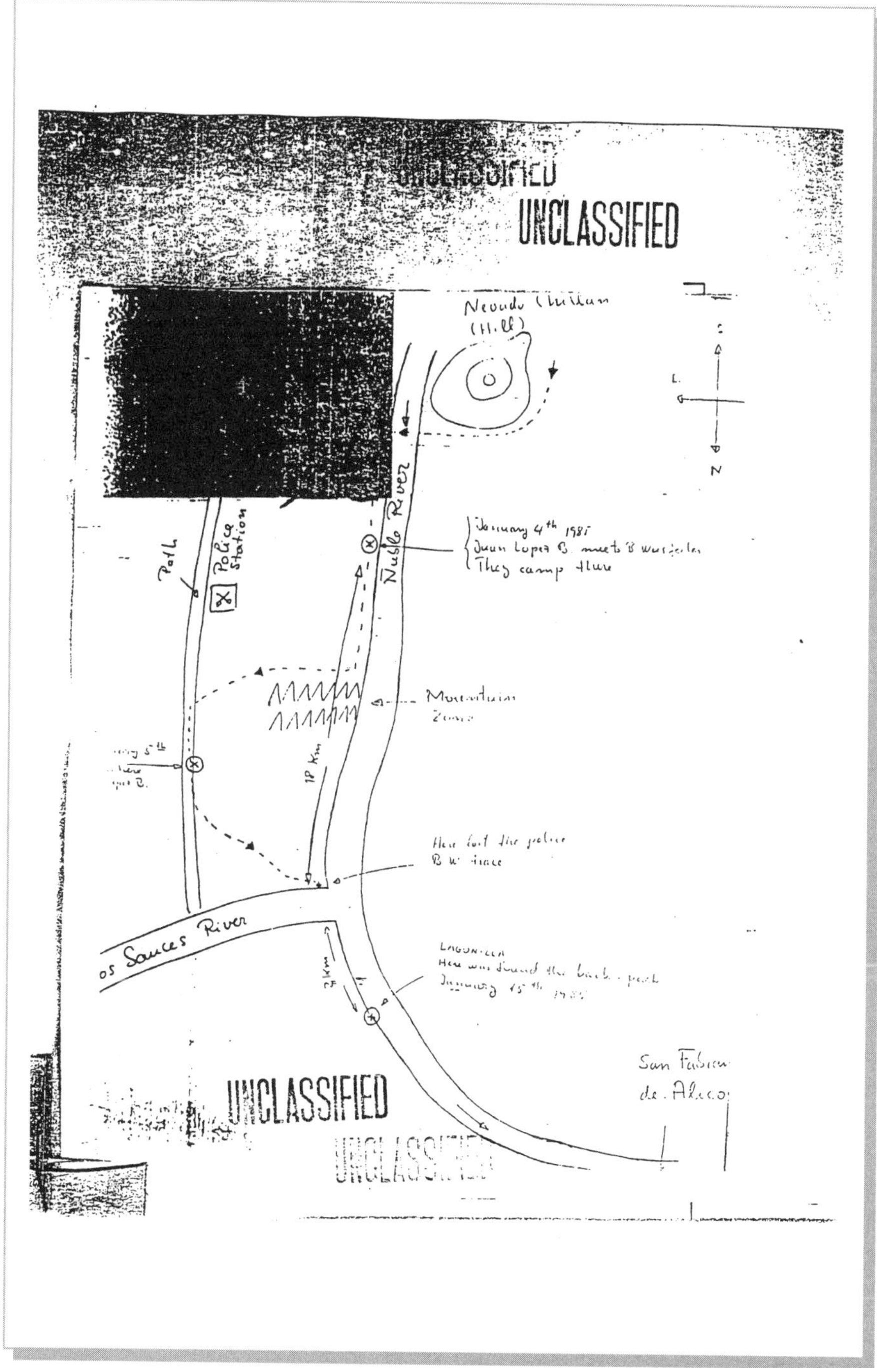

DOCUMENT 12. U.S. Embassy, Map Drawn by Chilean Informant, "Daniel," on Detention, Interrogation, and Transfer to Colonia Dignidad of Boris Weisfeiler, ca. June 1987.

UNCLASSIFIED

4/26/05 (SAØØ8V

Chile Project (#S199900030)
U.S. Department of State
Release X Excise_____ Deny_____
Declassify: In Part_____ In Full_____
Exemption(s)_____

R

12

LUGAR 1ER ENCUENTRO.

CHILLA.

SE DESNUDO AL PRISIONERO.

ENTRADA SUR.

DIGNIDAD.

DOCUMENT 13. U.S. Embassy, Memorandum from Consul General, "Case of Boris Weisfeiler," April 15, 1986.

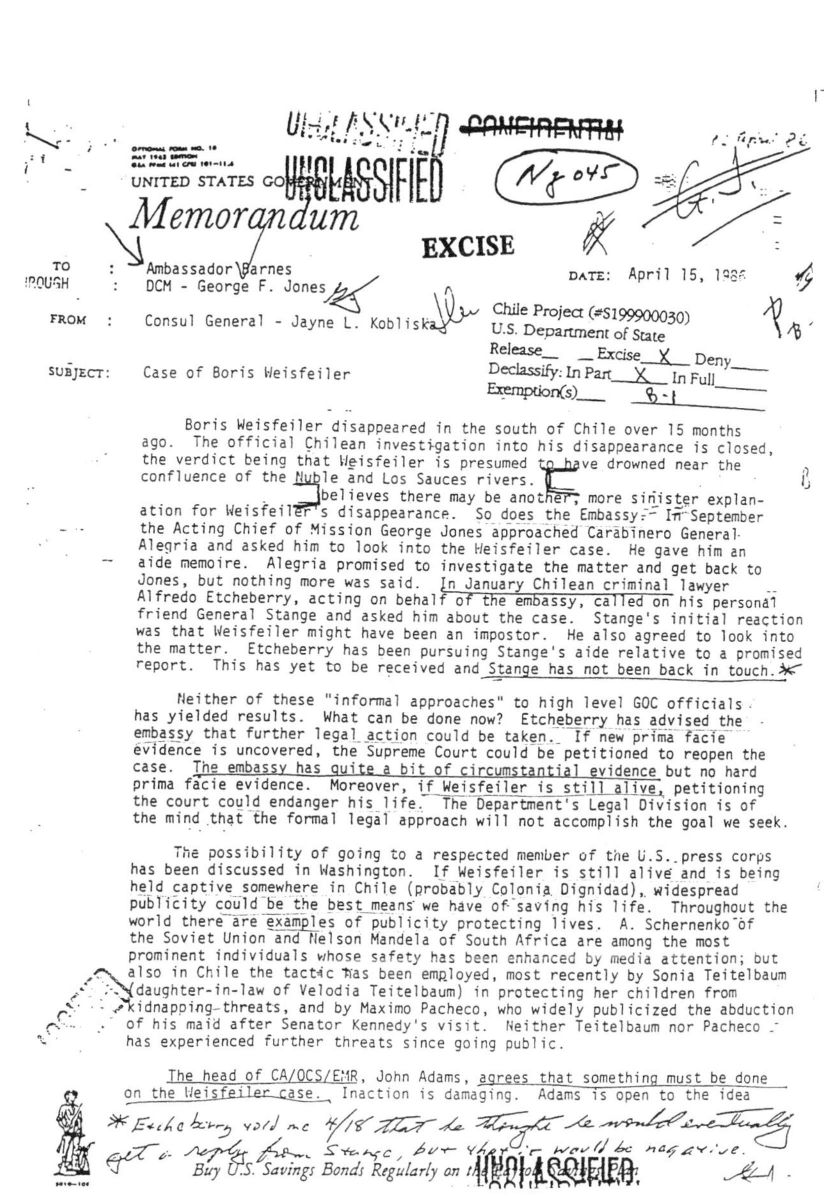

UNCLASSIFIED ~~CONFIDENTIAL~~

OPTIONAL FORM NO. 10
MAY 1962 EDITION
GSA FPMR (41 CFR) 101-11.6

UNITED STATES GOVERNMENT UNCLASSIFIED

Memorandum

EXCISE

TO : Ambassador Barnes
THROUGH : DCM - George F. Jones
FROM : Consul General - Jayne L. Kobliska

DATE: April 15, 1986

SUBJECT: Case of Boris Weisfeiler

Chile Project (#S199900030)
U.S. Department of State
Release__ Excise X Deny__
Declassify: In Part X In Full__
Exemption(s) B-1

Boris Weisfeiler disappeared in the south of Chile over 15 months ago. The official Chilean investigation into his disappearance is closed, the verdict being that Weisfeiler is presumed to have drowned near the confluence of the Nuble and Los Sauces rivers. [ ] believes there may be another, more sinister explanation for Weisfeiler's disappearance. So does the Embassy. In September the Acting Chief of Mission George Jones approached Carabinero General Alegria and asked him to look into the Weisfeiler case. He gave him an aide memoire. Alegria promised to investigate the matter and get back to Jones, but nothing more was said. In January Chilean criminal lawyer Alfredo Etcheberry, acting on behalf of the embassy, called on his personal friend General Stange and asked him about the case. Stange's initial reaction was that Weisfeiler might have been an impostor. He also agreed to look into the matter. Etcheberry has been pursuing Stange's aide relative to a promised report. This has yet to be received and Stange has not been back in touch.*

Neither of these "informal approaches" to high level GOC officials has yielded results. What can be done now? Etcheberry has advised the embassy that further legal action could be taken. If new prima facie evidence is uncovered, the Supreme Court could be petitioned to reopen the case. The embassy has quite a bit of circumstantial evidence but no hard prima facie evidence. Moreover, if Weisfeiler is still alive, petitioning the court could endanger his life. The Department's Legal Division is of the mind that the formal legal approach will not accomplish the goal we seek.

The possibility of going to a respected member of the U.S. press corps has been discussed in Washington. If Weisfeiler is still alive and is being held captive somewhere in Chile (probably Colonia Dignidad), widespread publicity could be the best means we have of saving his life. Throughout the world there are examples of publicity protecting lives. A. Schernenko of the Soviet Union and Nelson Mandela of South Africa are among the most prominent individuals whose safety has been enhanced by media attention; but also in Chile the tactic has been employed, most recently by Sonia Teitelbaum (daughter-in-law of Velodia Teitelbaum) in protecting her children from kidnapping threats, and by Maximo Pacheco, who widely publicized the abduction of his maid after Senator Kennedy's visit. Neither Teitelbaum nor Pacheco has experienced further threats since going public.

The head of CA/OCS/EMR, John Adams, agrees that something must be done on the Weisfeiler case. Inaction is damaging. Adams is open to the idea

* Etcheberry told me 4/18 that he thought he would eventually get a reply from Stange, but that it would be negative.

Buy U.S. Savings Bonds Regularly on the Payroll Savings Plan

UNCLASSIFIED

5010-108

PAGE 2 OF 2

UNCLASSIFIED ~~CONFIDENTIAL~~

of a calculated press leak, but he is uncertain whether this would be the best way to protect Boris Weisfeiler's life, if he is still alive. May I suggest that you telephone Adams while you are in the States to discuss our options on the Weisfeiler case and to hopefully reach a conclusion about what course of action should be taken. You can reach Adams at his office phone (202) 647-5225.

I have suggested to Adams that I be authorized to contact my personal friend George Will about the matter. Will has good access to the White House and solid conservative credentials. If he broke the case his credibility would not be challenged, and his report would be sure to reach the highest levels of attention which could bring strong pressure against the Chileans to act.

The real danger in this case is that we will delay action until it is too late to either save Weisfeiler's life or to determine the true circumstances of his death. The consulate has doggedly pursued a definitive resolution to the case, but one by one our options have been limited. On November 12th we forwarded copies of the entire Weisfeiler file to the Department due to a Freedom of Information Act request by an attorney probating his estate. The release date of these documents is not known but when these are sent to the lawyer, we will lose control of the case and in all probability be accused of inaction if we don't do something now. Thus, we have three remaining possible choices. We could petition the Supreme Court. This probably would not save Weisfeiler's life, nor would it lead to a confession of guilt on behalf of the GOC but would save the reputation of the Department of State and its' officers. Second, there is the option of going to the press and selectively leaking what we know. It is this option which I believe has the best chance of securing our goal of protecting his life if Weisfeiler is alive or determining the cause of his death. This is a calculated risk. Finally, the Weisfeiler case could be discussed at even higher levels of the Department in hopes that another option may be developed that could be successful in solving this matter.

jlk/

DOCUMENT 14. U.S. Embassy, Cable, "Request for Approval of Legal Services (W/W Case—Weisfeiler, Boris)," October 6, 1989.

UNCLASSIFIED
UNCLASSIFIED
n/a
Case Number: S1999000030

(JF007)
Page: 1
06 OCT 89

UNCLASSIFIED
UNCLASSIFIED

R

PAGE 01 SANTIA 10067 070000Z
ACTION L-03

INFO LOG-00 ADS-00 H-01 ARA-00 AMAD-01 OCS-06 CA-02
A-00 /013 W
------------------006554 080754Z /38

R 062244Z OCT 89
FM AMEMBASSY SANTIAGO
TO SECSTATE WASHDC 3264

Chile Project (#S199900030)
U.S. Department of State
Release X Excise____ Deny ____
Declassify: In Part____ In Full ✓
Exemption(s)____

UNCLAS SANTIAGO 10067

FOR LEGAL ADVISOR - JUDGE SOFAER

E.O. 12356: N/A
TAGS: CJAN, CASC, AMGT, CI
SUBJ: REQUEST FOR APPROVAL OF LEGAL SERVICES (W/W CASE--WEISFEILER, BORIS)

REF: A) SANTIAGO 2534 AND SUBSEQUENT, B) STATE 259147

1. EMBASSY SUBMITTED REQUEST FOR APPROVAL OF LEGAL SERVICES REFTEL A, DATED 14 MARCH 1989, IN THE CASE OF THE DISAPPEARANCE OF AMERICAN CITIZEN BORIS WEISFEILER. IN SPITE OF NUMEROUS FOLLOW-UP ATTEMPTS, INCLUDING A PERSONAL MEETING IN THE DEPARTMENT ON MAY 3 BETWEEN OUR CONSUL GENERAL AND A REPRESENTATIVE OF L/CA, WE RECEIVED NO RESPONSE UNTIL REFTEL B, DATED AUGUST 14, STATING "DEPARTMENT IS STUDYING PROPOSAL." GIVEN THE SENSITIVITY OF THIS CASE, WHICH HAS SPARKED CONGRESSIONAL INTEREST, WE CANNOT UNDERSTAND THE DELAY IN RESPONDING TO OUR REQUEST. WE WOULD APPRECIATE YOUR LOOKING INTO THE PROBLEM AND ADVISING US.

2. BORIS WEISFEILER DISAPPEARED IN JANUARY 1985, WHILE HIKING IN A REMOTE AREA OF SOUTHERN CHILE. THE CHILEAN COURT'S INVESTIGATION CONCLUDED PROBABLE DEATH BY DROWNING. NO BODY WAS EVER FOUND, AND SEVERAL UNEXPLAINED
UNCLASSIFIED

UNCLASSIFIED

PAGE 02 SANTIA 10067 070000Z

INCIDENTS HAVE LED EMBASSY TO MAINTAIN AN OPEN BOOK ON THE CASE THROUGHOUT THE PAST FOUR AND ONE-HALF YEARS. EMBASSY LEARNED THAT FOUR MEMBERS OF A CHILEAN ARMY PATROL WERE ALLEGED TO HAVE BEEN IN THE SAME AREA AT THE TIME OF WEISFEILER'S DISAPPEARANCE. AFTER CONSULTING A LOCAL ATTORNEY, EMBASSY BELIEVES THAT WE CAN REQUEST THE

n/a
UNCLASSIFIED
Page: 1

Case Number: S1999000030

COURT TO REOPEN THE INVESTIGATION IN ORDER TO QUESTION THE MEMBERS OF THE ALLEGED ARMY PATROL. THUS, OUR REQUEST FOR LEGAL SERVICES IN ORDER TO FUND ENGAGEMENT OF THE ATTORNEY TO PREPARE THE REQUEST AND FOLLOW THE CASE.

3. AMBASSADOR GILLESPIE WILL RAISE THIS MATTER WHEN HE MEETS WITH YOU DURING HIS FORTHCOMING TRIP TO WASHINGTON. WE APPRECIATE YOUR HELP. GILLESPIE

UNCLASSIFIED

NNNN

DOCUMENT 15. U.S. Embassy, Memorandum from Budget and Finance Office, February 6, 1990.

SAØ12L

UNCLASSIFIED

Chile Project (#S199900030)
U.S. Department of State
Release X Excise____ Deny____
Declassify: In Part____ In Full____
Exemption(s)____

R

8 Feb 90
Weisfeiler

MEMORANDUM

DATE: February 6, 1990

TO : William H. Barkell, CONS

THRU : Daniel A. Johnson, ADMIN

FROM : Franklin D. Emerine, B&F Office

SUBJECT: Funding for Weisfeilor case

REF : Your memo 02/01/90

At present time there are no funds available in Post S&E allotments for this project.

DOC 0392B

UNCLASSIFIED

DOCUMENT 16. U.S. Embassy, Cable, "Anonymous Report Regarding 1985 Missing Amcit Boris Weisfeiler," October 28, 1997.

UNCLASSIFIED

DEPARTMENT OF STATE
ARA/NEA REARCS

PAGE Ø1 . SANTIA Ø385Ø ØØ OF Ø2 2821Ø3Z Ø115Ø9 SØ33877
INFO: CI(Ø1) RSC(Ø1) BSC(Ø1) INT(Ø1) PPC(Ø1)
------------------------ 29/1259Z A1 RD (TOTAL COPIES: ØØ5)

ACTION OCS-Ø3

INFO LOG-ØØ ACDA-Ø8 ACDE-ØØ AMAD-Ø1 ARA-ØØ CA-Ø2 CIAE-ØØ
OASY-ØØ DODE-ØØ DS-ØØ UTED-ØØ TEDE-ØØ INR-ØØ L-ØØ
ADS-ØØ NSAE-ØØ PPT-Ø1 SSO-ØØ SS-ØØ DSCC-ØØ DRL-Ø4
/Ø21W
------------------F472FA 2821Ø4Z /38

P 2821Ø42Z OCT 97
FM AMEMBASSY SANTIAGO
TO SECSTATE WASHDC PRIORITY 4831

UNCLAS SANTIAGO ØØ385Ø

SENSITIVE

E.O. 12958: N/A
TAGS: CASC, PGOV, PHUM, CI
SUBJECT: ANONYMOUS REPORT REGARDING 1985 MISSING AMCIT BORIS WEISFEILER

REF: 89 SANTIAGO 445 AND PREVIOUS

SENSITIVE BUT UNCLASSIFIED; HANDLE ACCORDINGLY

1. (SBU) IN EARLY OCTOBER DR. RICARDO ISRAEL, HEAD OF THE AMERICAN STUDIES PROGRAM AT THE UNIVERSITY OF CHILE AND THE HOST OF A LOCAL CALL-IN RADIO TALK SHOW, RECEIVED AN ANONYMOUS CALL FROM A MAN CLAIMING TO BE A FORMER CHILEAN SOLDIER WHO WAS PERSONALLY INVOLVED IN THE APPREHENSION AND DETENTION OF AN AMERICAN CITIZEN NEAR THE "COLONIA DIGNIDAD" ENCLAVE ON JANUARY 4, 1985. AT DR. ISRAEL'S REQUEST, THE CALLER PREPARED AND PERSONALLY DELIVERED A REPORT OUTLINING THESE EVENTS. THE INFORMANT REFUSES TO DIVULGE HIS NAME, BUT HAS AGREED TO MEET WITH ISRAEL AGAIN ON OCTOBER 28. ISRAEL WILL ATTEMPT TO FACILITATE THE INFORMANT'S WISH TO SPEAK WITH AN UNIDENTIFIED MEMBER OF THE CHILEAN CONGRESS WHO IS INTERESTED IN THE MATTER.

2. (SBU) THE FOLLOWING IS THE EMBASSY'S INFORMAL TRANSLATION OF THE INFORMANT'S ENTIRE REPORT.

BEGIN TEXT:

"REPORT: ON JANUARY 3-6 OF 1985, IN THE COLONIA DIGNIDAD AREA, THE CHACABUCO REGIMENT INTENSIFIED ITS MILITARY PATROLS ON THE OUTSIDE PERIMETER OF THESE FACILITIES. MOTIVE: INFILTRATION OF AN ISRAELI INTELLIGENCE UNIT WHICH INTENDED TO SEIZE FROM COLONIA DIGNIDAD A PERSON BY THE NAME OF MENGELE WHO HAD ARRIVED BY AIR FROM RECIFE (BRAZIL). ON JANUARY 4 A FOREIGN CITIZEN WAS FOUND AT THE RIO SAUCE FORD (NEAR THE POINT WHERE IT MEETS THE NUBLE RIVER), WITH THE FOLLOWING PHYSICAL DESCRIPTION: HEIGHT 1.78 M., WIDE FOREHEAD, THIN HAIR, SEMI-ATHLETIC BUILD, SLAVIC FACIAL CHARACTERISTICS. DOCUMENTS: U.S. PASSPORT. NAME: BORIS W. (THIS IS ALL I REMEMBER SEEING BEFORE THE OFFICER IN CHARGE SNATCHED IT FROM ME), DOCUMENTS FROM A UNIVERSITY IN THE UNITED STATES, A MAP OF THE REGION WITH CERTAIN MARKS ON IT. PERSONAL EFFECTS: KNAPSACK, INDIVIDUAL TENT, BACKPACKING STOVE, CAMPING KNIFE, DARK BROWN PARKA, HIKING BOOTS, COMPASS, AND BINOCULARS. THIS PERSON ARRIVED AT THE CABLE FERRY WHICH CROSSES THE EL SAUCE RIVER. THE CARETAKER, WHO LIVES NEARBY AND IS AN EMPLOYEE OF COLONIA DIGNIDAD, WAS THE ONE WHO INFORMED US OF THIS PERSON'S PRESENCE. ALSO, CARABINEROS OF THE EL ROBLE POLICE STATION REGISTERED HIS

SANTIA Ø385Ø ØØ OF Ø2 2821Ø3Z Ø115Ø9 SØ33877

PASSAGE. THIS PERSON WAS DELIVERED TO THE AUTHORITIES OF COLONIA DIGNIDAD HEADED BY PERSONS BY THE NAMES OF SMIHT (SIC), P. SHAEFER AND STRAUSS. (IT IS APPROPRIATE TO MENTION THAT MAJOR NEKERMAN OF OUR ARMY WAS IN CHARGE OF INTERIOR SECURITY.) LATER ON WE FOUND OUT THAT THIS PERSON, AFTER BEING SAVAGELY INTERROGATED, WAS MADE TO KNEEL ON THE GROUND AND WAS MURDERED WITH A SHOT IN THE NAPE OF HIS NECK. THIS EXECUTION WAS CARRIED OUT SOLELY BY THE GERMANS, WHO TOOK ADVANTAGE OF THE ABSENCE OF THE CHILEAN AUTHORITIES. TWO UNITED STATES CONSULAR DELEGATIONS WENT OUT TO SEARCH FOR THIS U.S. CITIZEN. THE SECOND DELEGATION HEADED BY A WOMAN OF LATIN ORIGIN WAS MORE PERSISTENT, RESULTING IN THE DISAPPEARANCE OF THE CARABINEROS AT THE EL ROBLE POLICE STATION AND OF THEIR LOGBOOK WHERE THE PASSAGE OF THIS PERSON HAD BEEN REGISTERED. AT THE SAME TIME, ALL MILITARY PERSONNEL WERE WITHDRAWN FROM THE AREA. IT IS APPROPRIATE TO MENTION THAT MEMBERS OF THE ARMY DID NOT TAKE PART IN THIS CRIMINAL ACTION. BACKGROUND: AT THE BEGINNING OF THE SEVENTIES, THE EXCELLENT INTELLIGENCE OFFICER (COLONEL) MANUEL CONTRERAS PREPARED SEVERAL DOSSIERS ON MEMBERS OF THE JUDICIARY POWER, PROVING MANY CASES OF CORRUPTION AND UNDUE APPROPRIATION OF GOODS OR PROPERTIES TO BENEFIT FRIENDS OR FAMILY MEMBERS, PERPETRATED BY PRESENT MEMBERS OF SOME COURTS OF APPEALS AND THE SUPREME COURT WHO STILL REMAIN IN OFFICE. THESE DOCUMENTS, PERHAPS DUE TO SOME MIRACLE, ARE ALSO HELD BY THE GERMANS AT COLONIA DIGNIDAD."

END TEXT

3. (SBU) A CHECK OF POST FILES RELATING TO MISSING AMCITS REVEALS THAT PENNSYLVANIA STATE UNIVERSITY MATHEMATICS PROFESSOR BORIS WEISFEILER (DPOB APRIL 19, 1941, MOSCOW, SOVIET UNION) DISAPPEARED IN JANUARY 1985 WHILE ON A SOLITARY BACKPACKING TRIP IN THE COLONIA DIGNIDAD AREA. WEISFEILER'S DISAPPEARANCE WAS THE SUBJECT OF REPEATED AND INTENSE INQUIRY BY EMBASSY OFFICERS, INCLUDING THE EXCHANGE OF A SERIES OF DIPLOMATIC NOTES. CHILEAN AUTHORITIES CONCLUDED THAT WEISFEILER DROWNED AND DISAPPEARED WHILE ATTEMPTING TO CROSS THE EL SAUCE RIVER, ALTHOUGH THERE WERE MANY CONTRADICTIONS IN THE EVIDENCE CONSIDERED AND MANY QUESTIONS REMAIN UNANSWERED. THE EMBASSY CONSIDERS THE CASE OPEN AND UNSOLVED.

4. (SBU) COMMENT: PAST AND PRESENT ABUSES AT COLONIA DIGNIDAD HAVE RECEIVED SIGNIFICANT RECENT PUBLIC ATTENTION (E.G., FBIS PYØ71Ø135297). THIS INCLUDES ALLEGATIONS OF PAST COLLABORATION BETWEEN THE COLONIA AND CHILEAN INTELLIGENCE AGENCIES AND POSSIBLE "DISAPPEARANCES" AT THE COLONIA. THESE ALLEGATIONS MAY HAVE PROMPTED THE INFORMANT TO COME FORWARD WITH NEW REVELATIONS. WE HAVE SPOKEN WITH PROFESSOR ISRAEL REGARDING THE INFORMANT, AND IT IS ISRAEL'S BELIEF THAT THE INFORMANT IS SINCERE AND THE INFORMATION IS TRUTHFUL. POST INTENDS TO PURSUE THIS REPORT FULLY WHILE AT THE SAME TIME AVOIDING UNWARRANTED PUBLICITY UNTIL THE VERACITY OF THIS INFORMATION IS FURTHER EXPLORED.

SHAPIRO

UNCLASSIFIED

6

Operation Condor:
State-Sponsored International Terrorism

Internationally, the Latin generals look like our guys. We are especially identified with Chile. It cannot do us any good.

—Secret briefing paper for Secretary Kissinger on Operation Condor, August 1976

In October 1975, the head of Chile's feared secret police, Col. Manuel Contreras, invited his counterparts in the Southern Cone to an all-expenses-paid *"Primera Reunion InterAmericana de Inteligencia Nacional"*—the first inter-American meeting on national intelligence. The meeting would be of "a strictly secret nature," according to Contreras's invitation letter: "the hope is that this reunion can provide a basis for excellent coordination and improved action to benefit the national security of our respective nations." (Doc 1) On the conference agenda: "to establish something similar to INTERPOL in Paris, but dedicated to Subversion."

This covert intelligence convention took place between November 25 and 28 in Santiago. In a formal "closing statement," the conference participants approved the concept and structure of a new cooperative security organization. "From this date onward," read the *Acta de Clausura de la Primera Reunion InterAmericana de Intelligencia Nacional* signed by the delegates from Chile, Argentina, Uruguay, Paraguay, and Bolivia, their intelligence services would initiate "bilateral or multilateral contacts to exchange information on subversives." They agreed to create a *"sede del Sistema,"* the network "coordinating office," and to further meetings in Chile the following spring to develop and expand this new "system of coordination" to combat subversion. Finally, "in honor of the host country" they unanimously approved a motion that "this organization will be designated CONDOR"—named after Chile's national bird, the large Andean vulture. "Operation Condor" was officially inaugurated. (Doc 2)

Top-secret CIA reports would casually describe Operation Condor as "a cooperative effort by the intelligence/security services of several South American countries to combat terrorism and subversion." In fact, in the mid-1970s Condor became the most sinister state-sponsored terrorist network in the Western Hemisphere, if not the world. Those targeted went far beyond members of the militant Southern Cone guerrilla movements such as the Argentine ERP, the Uruguayan Tupamaros, and the Chilean MIR; they included civilian political figures from the region, and Latin American exile leaders living in Europe and the United States. Victims numbered in the hundreds, as the Condor nations collaborated in cross-border manhunts—tracking, surveillance, kidnappings, torture, interrogation, and elimination of opponents.

Some individuals in the region simply disappeared; many victims were kidnapped and killed while living in exile in Argentina. Others were caught in one nation, interrogated under torture by multilateral teams of Condor agents, and then secretly remitted to the nation of their nationality to be further abused and murdered. Selected special targets were subject to "phase three" Condor operations. "A third and reportedly very secret phase of 'Operation Condor' involves the formation of special teams from member countries who are to carry out operations to include assassinations," the Defense Intelligence Agency recorded in a secret intelligence report:

> [A] special team would be dispatched to locate and surveil the target . . . a second team would be dispatched to carry out an operation against the target. Special teams would be issued false documentation from member countries, could be composed either of individuals from one member nation or of persons from various member nations . . . team members would not be commissioned or non-commissioned officers of the armed forces, but rather "special agents." (Doc 3)

This would be the modus operandi used by the Pinochet regime to carry out its most infamous Condor mission—the September 21, 1976, terrorist car bombing that killed Orlando Letelier and Ronni Karpen Moffitt in the capital city of the United States.

Precursor Operations

Chile's Condor Convention of November 1975 essentially formalized coordinated operations that had been conducted among the Southern Cone nations since soon after Pinochet took power. Immediately isolated by international public opinion as a pariah regime, the Junta turned to its like-minded neighbors, particularly Argentina, for support and cooperation against what Pinochet called "the international Marxist campaign." Long before Condor's formal creation, its methods of intelligence sharing, surveillance coordination, multilateral repression, and murder were all but perfected.

The Prats Assassination

The first major collaboration to eliminate a potentially prominent opponent targeted not a radical leftist guerrilla leader, but rather Pinochet's own predecessor as commander in chief of the Chilean armed forces, Gen. Carlos Prats. Following the coup, which Prats had opposed until he was forced out of the military and replaced by Pinochet, he and his wife went into voluntary exile in Buenos Aires. There they lived unobtrusively among a large and growing Chilean exile community.

Two months after taking power, Pinochet dispatched his renowned enforcer, Gen. Sergio Arellano Stark, on "a special mission" to Argentina. In Buenos Aires, according to CIA intelligence sources inside the Chilean military, Arellano would

> discuss with the Argentine military any information they have regarding the activities of General (retired) Carlos Prats. Arellano will also attempt to gain an agreement whereby the Argentines maintain scrutiny over Prats and regularly inform the Chileans of his activities.[1]

Intelligence sharing on Prats, and other Chilean exiles, was conducted through a DINA "external branch" in Buenos Aires. In the spring of 1974, Contreras assigned a former Patria y Libertad–turned-DINA agent Enrique Arancibia Clavel to covertly establish DINA's first external base. Arancibia, who had been a fugitive in Argentina during the Allende years for his role in the assassination of Gen. René Schneider, operated out of a thirteenth-floor office of the National Bank of Chile at 845 Cordoba Ave. in downtown Buenos Aries. He used an alias, Luis Felipe Alemparte, and assumed the professional cover of a bank manager. A second DINA agent, Col. Victor Hugo Barría-Barría, was posted as the military attaché at the Chilean embassy.

Arancibia established multiple contacts with counterparts in the Argentine Servicio de Inteligencia del Estado (SIDE), and the federal police department, which oversaw the terrorist death-squad activity of vicious paramilitary groups such as the AAA—the Argentine Anticommunist Alliance—as well as with intelligence officers from other Southern Cone nations, to monitor the anti-Junta activities of Chilean exiles. On Prats, however, surveillance yielded no indication of any effort to openly oppose the Pinochet regime. Prats was "living quietly in Buenos Aires," noted a subsequent CIA situation report. "He was not permitted to make any public appearances or statements and had faithfully carried out the restrictive instructions pertaining to his exile."[2]

Nevertheless, Pinochet considered Prats far more of a threat than any politician or militant guerrilla. As a respected constitutionalist member of the Chilean armed forces, the exiled general represented the only individual with potential influence within the middle and high ranks of Pinochet's own power base, the Chilean army. When DINA obtained intelligence from Argentina that Prats was writing his memoirs about the Allende era and had applied for a visa to immigrate to a safer location in Europe, the Pinochet regime designated him the first high-profile exile to be assassinated.[3]

As the first anniversary of the Chilean coup approached, Contreras ordered his Argentine branch chief to work with Argentine paramilitary groups to kill Prats. When that plan failed to progress rapidly, Contreras assigned his new recruit, American expatriate Michael Townley, to complete the first major murder mission of DINA's "External Section." In court testimony that remains sealed, Townley recalled that he received his orders from Contreras's deputy Col. Pedro Espinoza in August 1974. Prats had the potential to become part of a "government in exile," Townley remembered being told; "Prats was a danger to Chile."[4]

Townley flew to Buenos Aires for a short reconnaissance trip, and returned again on September 10, 1974, traveling on a false passport under the name of Kenneth Enyart. He spent three weeks monitoring Prats's movements and waiting for the opportunity to kill him, working at least tacitly with members of an Argentine paramilitary group and the Department of Foreign Affairs of the federal police—the agency actually in charge of the security detail assigned to protect Prats's apartment. At one point, Townley followed Prats to a park and drew a gun, he said, but did not shoot "because there were too many people around." Instead, Townley fashioned a remote-control bomb in his hotel room—using two C4 cartridges and three detonating devices—establishing his modus operandi as an international terrorist. On September 29, he managed to slip into the parking garage of Prats's apartment building and attach the bomb, unobserved, under the chassis of his small Fiat 1600.[5]

At 12:50 A.M. on September 30, Prats and his wife Sofia returned to their apartment building after a late evening visit with friends. As Prats got out of his car to open the garage door, the powerful bomb exploded, blowing him thirteen feet though the air onto the cement sidewalk and setting the car on fire.[6] The general was killed instantly. His wife, as a cable to the U.S. National Military Command Center described the horrific crime scene, "was trapped in the vehicle and carbonized."

The Pinochet regime energetically denied any connection to the crime. But Argentine press accounts, as well as broadcasts from Radio Moscow, correctly pointed the finger at DINA, suggesting that Chile's regime was afraid that Prats would attract the loyalty of military personnel disaffected with Pinochet's expanding dictatorship. Intelligence sources in Argentina, as the CIA reported, similarly believed "the assassination of General Carlos Prats to be the work of Chileans," based on "the fact that the bomb used in the assassination was considerably larger than those ordinarily used in Argentina and on the fact that the assassination was not carried out in the manner in which such terrorist acts are usually executed by Argentine groups."(Doc 4)

The U.S. embassy, however, refused to accept the possibility that Pinochet's secret police were behind the attack. "This makes no sense to us," U.S. Ambassador David Popper cabled Washington in the first of many embassy reports turning a blind eye to Chile's involvement in international terrorism. "Nor do we see significant interest in killing Prats of any other Chilean group with capability of doing so."[7] As the Pinochet regime established a precedent for transnational violence that would later reach to Washington, D.C., the United States made no serious effort to investigate or denounce, publicly or privately, an assassination that the CIA appropriately cataloged in its Weekly Situation Report on International Terrorism.[8]

Operation Colombo

The successful bilateral effort on the Prats assassination encouraged both Chilean and Argentine officials to take a broader view of multilateral cooperation. "An idea exists to form an anti-communist intelligence community on a continental level, with members of the armies of Uruguay and Argentina who are interested in talking to Chile,"[9] Arancibia cabled DINA headquarters in a report on the Argentine armed forces two weeks after the Prats assassination. General Pinochet himself promoted this idea during one of his rare trips outside of Chile in the spring of 1974 when he traveled to Brazil, Bolivia, and Paraguay. His frequent condemnation of the threat of international communism prompted widespread speculation of the creation of "an anticommunist axis of southern Latin American military governments," as the U.S. embassy in Asuncion described it. Would Chile form an "anti-

Marxist bloc," reporters asked Pinochet. "Anything is possible," he responded.

Chilean-Argentine collaboration toward enhanced repression increased significantly toward the end of 1974. In November, Argentine secret police assisted the DINA in the brazen kidnapping of British-born Chilean stockbroker William Beausire, in the middle of the Ezeiza airport in Buenos Aires as he was in transit to London.[10] In December, intelligence operatives provided Arancibia with lists of former members of Allende's Popular Unity coalition who were now enrolled in classes at the National University in Buenos Aires. In April 1975, Arancibia reported to "Luis Gutierrez"—the code name for DINA's External Section—on anti-Pinochet Chileans at the university who had been arrested through "federal coordination" and were now believed to be "RIP"—a coded but not so subtle reference to the disappeared and murdered. By the summer of 1975, DINA obtained a commitment from its contacts in the Argentine army intelligence unit known as SIE to supply immigration records on all Chileans who had entered Argentina since the 1973 coup.[11]

In addition to committing extensive bilateral acts of repression, in the summer of 1975 Chilean and Argentine intelligence officers began cooperating on covering up those crimes. This collaboration, code-named Operation Colombo, became one of the Pinochet regime's most Machiavellian, and macabre, efforts to hide ongoing human rights abuses.

Operation Colombo grew out of increasingly forceful international condemnation of atrocities committed by Pinochet's security forces—particularly on *los desaparecidos.* The practice of disappearing hundreds of Chileans without a trace appeared to escalate in the fall of 1974 and spring of 1975 as the Chilean secret police systematically hunted down, detained, and disappeared members of the MIR and the Chilean Communist Party (PCCH). In response to habeas corpus appeals by family members, and legal demands for an accounting by Chile's leading human rights group, the Committee for Peace, as well as international agencies such as the United Nations Human Rights Commission (UNHRC), the Chilean government claimed that the missing were all leftist militants who had fled the country. Allegations that they were victims of repression, the Junta stated, were the result of a concerted Marxist campaign to mislead the world about the Pinochet regime.

As the UNHRC petitioned to conduct an onsite investigation in Chile to determine the fate of the disappeared, DINA mounted a crude covert disinformation operation—with the help of Argentine officials and secret police units—to obfuscate accountability for their deaths. In the spring of 1975, DINA's international division chief, Maj. Raúl Iturriaga Neumann, traveled to Buenos Aires to tell Arancibia to initiate "Operation Colombo." Arancibia's first assignment was to arrange the supposed appearance of the body of a disappeared Chilean, David Silberman, in Argentina. In May, a headless and handless corpse appeared on a sidewalk in Buenos Aires. A semi-destroyed photo identification card with a number that corresponded to Silberman's Chilean national registration card was in a pocket.[12] A note attached to the remains read: *Brought down by the MIR.*

The reappearance of the disappeared, through the placement of unrecognizable, supposedly Chilean corpses on Argentine soil[13] was one component of Colombo; the second component was generating press coverage indicating that these Chileans had been killed while operating outside of Chile—by their leftist brethren or in armed conflicts. But the propaganda failed to materialize in the Silberman case. Arancibia's cables back to headquarters reflected complaints that his contacts in the Argentine media hadn't followed through. But he requested additional identification papers to continue the operation.

On July 12, two more mutilated and burned bodies—hands and faces disfigured beyond recognition—were discovered by police in the town of Ciudad Pilar outside of Buenos Aires. Identification papers on the bodies named them as two disappeared Chileans: Luis Alberto Guendelman Wisniak,[14] and Jaime Robotham Bravo. A third body was also found in Buenos Aires, identified as a missing Chilean, Juan Carlos Perelman. Each body was tagged with a sign that read *Executed by the MIR.* The implication, as the *New York Times* reported, was that "they had been members of the Revolutionary Left Movement," and "had been killed as a result of an internal struggle."[15]

This time, DINA abandoned efforts to obtain mainstream media coverage and simply manufactured the initial propaganda with the help of its Argentine collaborators. Three days after the bodies appeared, an article appeared in an unknown Buenos Aires magazine called *LEA* containing a list of sixty Chileans who, according to the unnamed author, "have been eliminated during the last three months by their own comrades in arms as part of a vast and implacable program of vengeance and political purification." The article insinuated that the sixty had been executed for disputes over political differences "and money," and that the internecine killings had taken place in Argentina, Colombia, Venezuela, Panama, Mexico, and France.

A week later, the Chilean press reported on a second list of Chileans published in an obscure newsletter in Curitiba, Brazil called *Novo O Dia.* The *Novo O Dia* article, unsigned and undated, stated that fifty-nine "Chilean Marxist agitators" had been killed in a clash with Argentine security forces in the northern province of Salta.

Chile's leading newspapers dutifully reprinted the stories on what came to be known as "the list of 119." *La Segunda* republished the *Novo O Dia* list under the headline MIRISTAS EXTERMINATED LIKE RATS. *El Mercurio* ran a lengthy editorial that read as if DINA officials had drafted it themselves:

> The politicians and foreign newsmen who asked themselves so many times about the fate of these members of the MIR and blamed the Chilean government for the disappearance of many of them, now have the explanation that they refused to accept. Victims of their own methods, exterminated by their own comrades, every one of them demonstrates with tragic eloquence that violent people end up falling victims to the blind and implacable terror that they provoke.[16]

But DINA's perverse efforts to cover the tracks of its atrocities quickly unraveled. Within days, the Chilean church-sponsored Committee for Peace published a comprehensive report detailing direct evidence that seventy-seven individuals on the lists were known to have been detained in Chile by security personnel before they disappeared and providing indirect evidence of official detention on another twenty-seven individuals. In four cases of names on the *LEA* and *Novo O Dia* lists, the Committee report noted, Pinochet's authorities had, in writing, officially acknowledged arresting those individuals. Reporters from the *Washington Post, New York Times*, the *Wall Street Journal, Newsweek*, and *Time*, easily determined that *LEA* did not exist as a magazine before, or after, the July 15 edition mysteriously showed up on newsstands in Buenos Aires; the copies had been published through an industrial print shop controlled by the right-wing Argentine government minister, Jose López Rega. Similarly, *Novo O Dia*, was an unofficial and irregular publication, a mimeo published by a single individual; journalists noted that the *Novo O Dia* list had been distributed to Chilean papers by a media advisor to the Junta—identified by American journalist John Dinges as right-wing columnist Alvaro Puga[17]—several days before the newsletter actually appeared in Brazil. Finally, there existed not a shred of evidence that any military confrontation had occurred in Salta, Argentina as the *Novo O Dia* story alleged. No casualties had been reported; no bodies or graves could be located.

Nor were the mutilated bodies "discovered" in Argentina actually those of the three disappeared Chileans. When the families of Perelman and Robotham, who both appeared on the *Novo O Dia* list, and Guendelman went to Buenos Aires to retrieve the charred remains of their loved ones, they discovered that the identification cards were crude forgeries, and that the dead individuals bore physical traits quite distinct from the individuals they were purported to be.[18]

As the U.S. press descended on Chile, the embassy could no longer ignore the magnitude of what it called the "fast moving story of deaths and disappearances." Initially, Ambassador Popper waffled on whether to believe the official line that "the extremist movements themselves" had fabricated evidence of detention and disappearance, or accept the obvious. "There appears to be ground for suspicion that GOC and/or its security organs are attempting to close book on those who have died while in custody," the embassy cabled Washington on July 26. "Embassy has independent evidence that GOC security forces have detained and held persons without accounting for them, and that some have died in custody. We can believe in addition that some 'disappeared' persons indeed went underground. Whatever the facts, stories expected to emerge in foreign press are likely to put GOC in very bad light."[19]

In early August, however, after examining multiple theories on who was behind creating the lists, the embassy surmised that the Pinochet regime "might well have been impelled to plant lists." In his summary of an August 8 cable, "Analysis of Deaths and Disappearances of Chilean Extremists," Popper wrote:

> Most plausible explanation we can piece together for what will probably remain something of a mystery is that GOC security forces acted directly or through third party, planted reports in obscure publications to provide some means of accounting for disappearance of numerous violent leftists. GOC security forces may have killed some or all of them. (Doc 5)

"Additionally," the embassy wrote in its first acknowledgement of covert collaboration in the region, "it would be plausible to assume that Argentine security forces and/or right-wing groups such as AAA and López Rega elements extended at least tacit cooperation to GOC in this matter."

Chile: Base for International Terrorism

During the Allende era, the U.S. intelligence community searched for evidence on the potential for Chile to become a platform for international terrorism. It was the Pinochet regime, however, that transformed Chile into an active base and sponsor of violent terrorist groups around the world. Under the auspices of DINA, in the mid-1970s Chile created covert alliances with a number of the most notorious terrorist organizations in the United States and Europe, offering refuge, training, financing, as well as missions that ranged from photo reconnaissance, to bank robberies, to assassination of political exiles. These operations defined state-sponsored international terrorism.

DINA established its most energetic alliance with the violent anti-Castro Cuban exile groups in the United States. In December 1974 three leaders of these groups, Orlando Bosch, Guillermo Novo, and Dionesio Suárez, traveled to Santiago to offer services to, and seek support from, the Pinochet regime. Bosch, then and now the most famous exile terrorist, already had a long record of shooting bazookas at Cuban ships and sending package bombs to Cuban embassies; he would collaborate with the Chileans on one assassination attempt in Costa Rica and move on to mastermind the bombing of a Cubana airliner over Barbados in October 1976, killing all seventy-three passengers and crew.[20] Novo headed New Jersey wing of the Cuban Nationalist Movement (CNM), "an anti-Castro terrorist group," according to declassified FBI reports.

DINA took the anti-Castro Cubans up on their offer. In early February 1975 Contreras dispatched Michael Townley to Miami to recruit CNM assistance for another major mission of international terrorism. Townley carried with him the names of major Chilean exile leaders expected to attend a meeting in Mexico of the International Commission of Inquiry into the Crimes of the Military Junta in Chile, and orders "to do away with anyone on the list."[21] Under the cover of taking a camping trip, Townley, his wife, and a CNM member named Virgilio Paz, drove 4,000 miles from New Jersey to Mexico City in a recreational vehicle filled with plastique explosives.[22] But they arrived well after the conference had ended. Townley and Paz then flew to Madrid to continue tracking leading members of the Chilean exile community living in Europe.

The first name on their list was that of Carlos Altamirano. For months, agents of the Pinochet regime had been trying to assassinate the secretary-general of Chile's Socialist Party. "General Contreras had an illogical obsession with accomplishing Altamirano's demise," one informant told the FBI. "To that end Contreras had issued standing orders that all DINA agents operating abroad were to assassinate Altamirano on sight." On August 3, 1974, the chief of Chile's naval mission in London, Capt. Raul Lopez, organized a meeting of all Chilean military attachés in Europe and ordered them to report on the movements of Altamirano, and "any anti-Junta activities" in their host countries. "Elements in the Chilean government are attempting to locate and assassinate major leftist leaders such as Carlos Altamirano," as the CIA reported on the manhunt. "It is believed that the Junta wants Altamirano either assassinated or kidnapped." (Doc 6)[23]

Townley's orders were to "eliminate" the socialist leader and to make contacts with as many European-based anticommunist groups as possible to establish DINA as a principal benefactor in an international war against

Marxism. "Townley began to make the rounds of the European fascist circuit," as Dinges and Landau described this effort in their book *Assassination on Embassy Row*. The groups and individuals he contacted included the newly formed Fascist International, the Corsican Brotherhood, the famous French terrorist Albert Spaggiari (who had once tried to assassinate Charles de Gaulle) and the neo-fascist Italian Avanguardia Nazionale, led by Stefano Delle Chiaie, aka "the black bomber."

While in Frankfurt in July, Townley met and recruited Delle Chiaie—code-named "Alfa" in communications with DINA—to be a partner and participant in Chile's violent, clandestine campaign against the left. The Pinochet regime would offer a safe haven, a base and training; Avanguardia Nazionale would spy on the activities of Chilean exiles in Italy and other parts of Europe. With support from his superiors, Townley also arranged for "Alfa" to undertake a deadly operation: the assassination of Bernardo Leighton, a popular and active Chilean Christian Democrat living in exile in Rome.

On the evening of October 6, as they walked home after dinner along a narrow neighborhood street, a lone hitman wielding a nine-millimeter Beretta shot both Leighton and his wife, Anita, at close range from behind. One bullet hit Leighton in the back of the head; another tore through his wife's spine. Both survived, albeit with severe and permanent brain and paralysis injuries.

DINA considered the operation a success; Leighton was effectively silenced and a dire warning sent through the Chilean exile community in Europe. In the aftermath of the assassination attempt, Townley traveled to New Jersey and Miami, met with Novo and Paz, and agreed to let CNM take credit for the Rome operation. Using its nom de guerre "ZERO," the CNM then published a communiqué with the initials *B.L.* imposed on a large zero.[24] Several weeks later in a communiqué distributed to the Associated Press, "ZERO" described the shooting using unpublished details that Townley had provided. This deception not only diverted attention away from DINA, Townley explained in a debriefing with the FBI on the Leighton shooting in 1978; it advanced DINA's goal of fostering strong alliances. He conveyed the details to Paz "in order to allow the CNM . . . to take credit for the attempted assassination," Townley stated, "so that the CNM would gain stature as a viable international terrorist organization." (Doc 7)

The Leighton operation cemented DINA's ties with both CNM and with Avanguardia Nazionale. DINA offered CNM members safe haven in Santiago, and a special training course in intelligence operations. Contreras agreed to provide protection and support for Avanguardia Nazionale, in return for Delle Chiaie's agreement to conduct espionage operations against Peru and

Argentina. In November 1975, when both Contreras and Pinochet traveled to Madrid to attend the funeral of Spanish dictator Francisco Franco, Contreras met personally with Delle Chiaie and received a full briefing on the Italian organization's capabilities to conduct spying, sabotage, and terrorist operations on both the European and Latin American continents.

To seal this collaboration, Contreras arranged for Delle Chiaie to have a private meeting with General Pinochet. "For your knowledge, Pinochet had a meeting with Mamo [a nickname for Contreras] and Alfa in Spain," Townley would later write in a prison letter that revealed Pinochet's personal involvement.[25] "The problem of the Italians is very serious, very serious. Mamo married them a long time go . . . in a much less dissolvable way than even the Cubans," Townley wrote to a DINA collaborator, alluding to still unknown clandestine operations Avanguardia Nazionale carried out on DINA's behalf. "Alfa can be much more embarrassing for Mamo and the government in the long run. . . ."

Creating the Condor Consortium

In the spring of 1975, a leftist pamphlet began circulating in Europe announcing the formation of a Revolutionary Coordinating Junta (JCR) by militant groups in the Southern Cone. The MIR in Chile and ERP in Argentina, along with the ELN in Bolivia and the Tupamaros in Uruguay planned to merge efforts to overthrow the military regimes in the Southern Cone.

This announcement garnered little international attention; and proved to be more talk than action. In its first year of existence, U.S. intelligence recorded no major paramilitary, insurgency, or terrorist activities sponsored by the JCR. "JCR representatives in Western Europe provide assistance to cohorts temporarily residing there and publish propaganda against Southern Cone governments," the State Department's INR reported in June 1976. "According to available information, it has not sponsored any major Southern Cone operations."[26] Nevertheless, the JCR's creation generated concern among DINA officials in Chile and SIDE officials in Argentina. The subsequent capture of a courier for the JCR, a Chilean sociologist and member of the MIR named Jorge Fuentes Alarcón, provided the immediate catalyst to formally create Operation Condor.

Fuentes was detained, along with Amilcar Santucho, the brother of the head of the Argentine ERP, on May 16, 1975, as he attempted to cross into Paraguay from Argentina using a false Costa Rican passport. His fate reflected the high degree of collaboration that had already evolved among the

Southern Cone security organizations. "Various agencies were involved in capturing this MIR leader," as the *Chilean National Commission on Truth and Reconciliation* described the multinational methods of repression:

> The Paraguayan police arrested them both and took them to Asuncion. . . . Argentine intelligence services provided information on Jorge Fuentes' false passport, the U.S. Embassy staff in Buenos Aires kept the investigative police in Chile advised of the results of his interrogation, and the Paraguayan police allowed him to be transferred secretly [to the DINA in Chile].[27]

"Paraguay picked up a Mirista, Fuentes, and turned him over to Contreras," the FBI attaché in Buenos Aires, Robert Scherrer, subsequently confirmed to journalist John Dinges. "He was tortured and killed."[28]

It was Scherrer who advised the Chilean military police of the intelligence on the JCR obtained from Fuentes. Three weeks after his capture, the FBI special agent conveyed the initial results of Fuentes's brutal interrogation by the Paraguayan secret police to the head of Pinochet's "Office of Investigations." In an official letter to Chilean Gen. Ernesto Baeza, dated June 6, Scherrer wrote that the FBI had "discovered that the aforementioned subject is a citizen of Chile and a member of the MIR." The letter, on U.S. embassy stationery, continued:

> According to the information supplied by the subject during various interrogations by the capital police in Asuncion, he admitted that he is a member of the Coordinating Junta and was acting as a courier for said group. (Doc 8)

Fuentes's address book, which his Paraguayan interrogators showed to Scherrer, listed the names and addresses of three individuals living in Texas, New York City, and Puerto Rico. On the same day he wrote to General Baeza, Scherrer cabled FBI headquarters in Washington with a report. "The Bureau is requested to instruct the Dallas, New York and San Juan to conduct appropriate investigation," concluded the heavily redacted cable. Scherrer also passed the names and addresses to the Chileans. In an offer that demonstrated an active U.S. collaboration in the Pinochet regime's violent campaign against its opponents, Scherrer wrote: "The FBI [has] initiated an investigation in the United States concerning the aforementioned people and addresses. I will inform you of the results of the investigation as soon as I have them in-hand."

Intelligence on the JCR, gleaned from Fuentes's tortured confessions in

Paraguay, apparently galvanized Colonel Contreras's decision to formalize a regional anticommunist security network. In the late summer of 1975, he set out on an multi-nation tour designed to lay the groundwork for Condor. His first stop was in Washington where he met with CIA Deputy Director Vernon Walters—for the second time in less than two months. On August 27, Contreras arrived in Caracas to meet with officials from the Venezuelan intelligence service DISIP. "He said he had been making some goodwill trips to get the support of different Latin American intelligence services," DISIP deputy director Rafael Rivas Vásquez later testified to a grand jury in Washington, D.C. "He said he was building up this grandiose scheme of a very big and powerful service that could have information—worldwide information."[29] In similar meetings throughout the Southern Cone, Contreras issued an invitation to his counterparts to come to Santiago in the fall.

On November 25, 1975, Contreras convened the first Condor conference to discuss expanding, formalizing, and modernizing mutual cooperation among their secret police services. At morning and afternoon working sessions, the intelligence chieftains from Chile, Argentina, Paraguay, Uruguay, and Bolivia reported on the "situation of subversion" in their respective nations, and the structures and mechanisms each of their security agencies used to combat the left. The delegates, according to the agenda, then turned to a discussion of the creation of a coordinated regional security system built around what Colonel Contreras identified as "three basic elements": (1) a central database of information on opponents of their military regimes; (2) "a modern and agile communications system" with special codes and cryptology machines for the rapid and secure exchange of intelligence; and (3) multilateral "work meetings" on a systematic basis to enhance regional counter-subversion capability and coordination.[30]

At the conclusion of the conference, according to the minutes, the delegates agreed to phase in an advanced system of coordination through a series of future actions:

- The posting of "national intelligence personnel or similar agents in the Embassies of our countries for direct and personal liaison."
- Creation of a coded communication system known as CONDORTEL, using with cryptographic machines, and the eventual creation of a high-speed communications system for information exchange.
- Swift and immediate contact when suspicious individuals are either expelled from the country or travel outside the country so as to alert intelligence services.
- Publishing propaganda aimed at attacking subversion.

- Providing information to a technical team to create a central, modernized database on subversives.
- And conducting a "feasibility project" on advancing intelligence coordination. (See Doc 2)

They agreed that the directors of their respective military regimes would ratify this Condor accord, and it would take affect on January 30, 1976. Another Condor meeting would be scheduled in Chile later that year.

The second Condor convention convened in Santiago at the beginning of June 1976. Representatives of the five original Condor nations, joined by officials from Brazil, reviewed what they had accomplished, and discussed how to further their long-range cooperation. This meeting, monitored by U.S. intelligence, produced several decisions: Condor nations would receive numerical designations, with Chile holding the distinction of being "Condor One"; Brazil would officially join, becoming the sixth full-fledged member of the Condor organization; DINA would house a computerized databank on known and suspected subversives; and Chile, Argentina, and Uruguay would undertake covert operations against members of the JCR living in Western Europe.

Those covert operations, the CIA quickly learned, would include assassination missions against militants and civilians living in France and Portugal. Paris, where the majority of Latin American refugees from the Southern Cone military regimes resided in the mid-1970s, would be Condor's main stalking ground. Targets included the leadership of the JCR, Chilean journalists, as well as the famous Venezuelan-born master terrorist Ilich Ramirez Sanchez, aka Carlos the Jackal.

In late September 1976, a special two-month-long "Condor training course" opened at an operations center of the Argentine State Secretariat for Intelligence (SIDE) in Buenos Aires. Those enrolled were agents from Chile, Uruguay, and Argentina. Training covered urban search-and-destroy techniques that would be used to conduct surveillance on subjects in Western Europe and arrange for their elimination. At the conclusion of the course in December, at least two Uruguayan agents were to be detailed to Paris "to perform unspecified duties," according to one TOP SECRET intelligence summary. A report by the U.S. defense attaché in Buenos Aires noted that the Argentines had also organized their own "special team" of agents, "structured much like a U.S. special forces team with a medic, demolition expert, etc." to be "prepared for action in phase three." (See Doc 3)

Two factors impeded Condor's plans to expand their murderous operations onto the European continent. First, the newest member of the organization, Brazil, objected, which delayed implementation. Brazilian military intelligence preferred to confine its participation to Southern Cone activities, particularly intelligence input and exchange on subversion; subsequently, Brazil provided equipment for the communications network CONDORTEL, and collaborated with other Condor nations in tracking down and abducting foreigners living in exile in Brazil.

The second factor was CIA interference. The Agency intercepted information on a joint Chilean-Argentine covert mission to kill Carlos the Jackal and two Chilean journalists working in Europe and took active steps to thwart Condor's plot. "The CIA warned the governments of the countries in which the assassinations were likely to occur," a CIA briefer later told a special Senate Subcommittee on International Operations. In turn, those governments—France and Portugal—"warned possible targets and called in representatives of Condor countries to warn them off the action."[31] Indeed, in September, French security officials alerted the Chilean embassy in Paris that France was aware of "the existence and some objectives of Operation Condor," as the CIA later reported. In response, the assassination mission, made up of two Chilean and two Argentine agents, as well as DINA's leading international hitman Michael Townley and his wife, Mariana Callejas, was cancelled.[32] According to a top-secret INR summary in late November, Argentine and/or Chilean security officials "informed their French counterparts that Condor would function in Europe, but not in France."[33]

This breach of security coincided with the aftermath of the assassination of Orlando Letelier and Ronni Moffitt in Washington, D.C. But neither appeared to diminish Condor's pursuit of dramatic "phase three" operations. In December 1976, DINA deputy chief Colonel Espinosa directed Townley to go to Madrid, infiltrate a major international Socialist Party congress and attempt—again—to assassinate Carlos Altamirano. "*Matalo, matalo,*"—kill him, kill him—Colonel Espinoza ordered, when Townley called to report on the heavy security surrounding the conference.[34] Along with Uruguay and Argentina, the Chilean secret police continued to plot missions of murder against selected targets around the world—including in the United States.

Despite substantial evidence of continued plotting for state-sponsored terrorist attacks, there is no record that the Ford or Carter administrations pressed for Operation Condor to be dismantled. Indeed, the Condor nations continued to meet, expanding their membership and advancing their dirty war of coordinated repression. Between December 13 and 16, member countries reconvened again, this time in Buenos Aires, to weigh future plans. Principal on the agenda, as a member of the Paraguayan intelligence later informed the CIA, was "the discussion and planning of coordinated psychological warfare operations directed against leftist and radical groups in various member countries."[35] Yet another Condor meeting was planned in Paraguay to discuss "Psychological Warfare Techniques against Terrorists and Leftist Extremists" in 1977.

In early 1978, Condor added two new members. In January, Ecuador became Condor Seven. The Chilean CNI invited four Ecuadorian officers to attend an intelligence training school in Santiago, free of charge. In March, Peru also joined. According to an internal CNI memorandum, stamped SECRETO, the Chilean intelligence service requested permission to post an undercover Condor operative as a "civilian attaché" in Chile's embassy in Lima. "The Peruvian Director of Intelligence telephoned the Director of CNI," according to the memorandum, "to inform him that there would be no difficulties for the appointment of a Chilean representative in Peru."[36]

By then, internal Chilean documents suggest, Argentina had become the network "secretariat" and the base of the inter-state communications system known as "Sistema Condor." In October 1978, however, a Paraguayan official informed U.S. ambassador Robert White that the hub of this system was located the U.S. military base in the Panama Canal Zone. The Condor nations, White wrote in a "Roger Channel" cable,

> keep in touch with one another through a U.S. communications installation in the Panama Canal Zone. . . . This U.S. communications facility . . . is also employed to co-ordinate intelligence information among the Southern Cone countries. They maintain the confidentiality of their communications through the U.S. facility in Panama by using bilateral codes.

"I have no knowledge that this is true," Ambassador White concluded. But if so, "it would seem advisable to review this arrangement."[37]

When Condor officially disbanded remains unclear, as does the total number of Condor casualties. Between 1975 and 1977, the heyday of their state-sponsored acts of serial terrorism, the Southern Cone regimes coordinated the deaths of dozens of victims—many of them in Argentina. After the Argentine military coup in March 1976, some 15,000 exiles from other Southern Cone nations who had sought refuge from repression in Argentina found themselves trapped by the increasingly coordinated, regional collaboration in abductions, torture, disappearances, and murders. Examples of the scope of Condor's atrocities in Argentina included:

- April 10, 1976: Chilean and Argentine security personnel kidnapped and disappeared a ranking member of the MIR, Edgardo Enriquez in Buenos Aires, along with a number of other Chilean militants, and a Brazilian woman, Maria Regina Marcondes. After being held in Argentina, Enriquez was turned over the DINA and transported to Villa Grimaldi, tortured and disappeared.

- May 21, 1976: two prominent Uruguayan congressmen, exiled in Argentina, Zelmar Michelini, and Luis Hector Gutierrez were gunned down in the street in Buenos Aires.
- June 4, 1976: the former president of Bolivia, Juan Jose Torres, was found shot to death in his Buenos Aires apartment.
- June 11, 1976: twenty-three Chilean refugees and one Uruguayan under United Nations protection in Buenos Aires were kidnapped by forty armed and hooded men and held for more than a day at an undisclosed installation. They were interrogated and tortured by a team of Argentine, Uruguayan, and Chilean security agents and warned to "leave Argentina within 48 hours or be killed," as the U.S. embassy in Buenos Aires reported. The operation indicated "close coordination of Southern Cone security forces to eradicate what they consider to be subversion and to terrorize refugees."[38]
- September 24–27, 1976: SIDE agents and members of the Uruguayan Military Intelligence Service participated in what one DIA report called "a joint operation" against members of OPR-33, a militant Uruguayan group in Buenos Aires. More than thirty people were reportedly killed during the sweep.
- May 16, 1977: three exiled members of the Chilean Communist Party, and five Argentine members of a Chile Solidarity Committee based in Buenos Aires were arrested in a joint Argentine-Chilean operation. They subsequently disappeared.

Condor actions took place in other member nations as well. In Paraguay, JCR courier Jorge Fuentes Alarcón was the first of numerous Chileans, Uruguayans, and Argentines to fall victim to this "multinational Murder Inc." Documents discovered in the Paraguayan "archives of terror" provide ample evidence of torture sessions conducted by teams of Paraguayan, Uruguayan, and Argentine security agents—and the secret transfer of individuals kidnapped in Asuncion into the hands of the secret police agencies of their native countries.[39] One Paraguayan report described the "good work of the Brazilians" in the disappearance of several Argentine citizens detained in Brazil. In Bolivia during the Condor years, three Chileans were detained and turned over to Chilean authorities, while six Argentine exiles were kidnapped and repatriated. And after Peru joined Condor, victims began to disappear there.

Indeed, one of the last recorded cases of a Condor operation took place in Lima on June 12, 1980. Members of an Argentine death squad unit known as 601, collaborating with Peruvian military intelligence, abducted four alleged Montonero leaders. "The present situation is that the four Argentines will be held in Peru and then expelled to Bolivia where they will be expelled to Argentina," a member of 601 advised a U.S. embassy official in Buenos Aires on June 16. "Once in Argentina they will be interrogated and then permanently disappeared."[40] The declassified documents do not record any major effort on the part the embassy to save the four from this fate. Three were never seen again. In a grotesque reincarnation of Operation Colombo, the corpse of one of the victims, Noemi Esther Gianetti, was later found in an apartment in Madrid. This was proof, Argentina's Foreign Ministry declared, of the "the falseness of the campaign [regarding the four disappeared] against Argentina and Peru."

The Letelier-Moffitt Assassination

Of all of Condor's atrocities, one stands out as the most infamous and egregious—the September 21, 1976 car bombing that took the lives of former Chilean diplomat Orlando Letelier and his twenty-six-year old American colleague, Ronni Karpen Moffitt. Until Osama bin Laden's hijackers flew American Airlines flight 77 into the Pentagon on September 11, 2001, the Letelier-Moffitt assassinations constituted the most brazen act of international terrorism ever committed in the capital of the United States.

The target was Orlando Letelier—at the time of his murder the most respected and effective spokesman in the international campaign to condemn and isolate the Pinochet dictatorship. A longtime friend of Salvador Allende, Letelier had been named the Popular Unity government's first ambassador to Washington. In May 1973 he returned to Santiago to become foreign minister. As social and political turmoil escalated, Allende appointed him minister of defense in August, a position nominally in charge of Pinochet and the other Chilean officer corps. "Pinochet used to carry Orlando's briefcase," Letelier's widow, Isabel Morell, recalled.

Following the coup, Pinochet ordered Letelier, along with dozens of other VIP officials from the Allende government, locked up in a desolate, cold concentration camp on Dawson Island off the south Pacific coast. A concerted campaign of international pressure forced the Junta to free Letelier after a year in detention. He was expelled from the country and subsequently came to Washington to work at the distinguished progressive think tank, the Institute for Policy Studies.

In Washington political circles, Letelier was already well-known; he had spent the 1960s as a high-level economist at the Inter-American Development

Bank, and was considered connected, sophisticated, and extremely energetic. "Orlando was all over the place," Senator James Abourezk recalled in an interview. His efforts to press for Congressional human-rights sanctions aimed at Chile, as well as to lobby the UN and European nations to condemn the military regime, established Letelier as Pinochet's most formidable political opponent in exile. Those activities also put him on the radar screen of both Chilean and U.S. intelligence.

The CIA first began tracking Letelier's movements in May 1960, when he accompanied Salvador Allende to a conference in Havana. Over the next sixteen years, agents filled his "201" intelligence file—number 0881118—with biographic sketches, personality profiles, surveillance reports, and secret source material. The files regarding his appointment as Allende's ambassador to Washington describe him as "a personable, socially pleasant man," "a reasonable, mature democrat" with a "constructive and precise knowledge of the United States." Agency reporting covered the activities and health of his wife, their four sons, their lifestyle and interests; CIA agents even gathered intelligence on "their English sheepdog, Alfie."[41] After Letelier returned to Washington in exile, CIA agents spied on his involvement in the international organizing efforts against the Pinochet dictatorship. Letelier, the CIA reported, has been "quite successful in the United States in gaining important political support for the anti-Junta cause."[42]

That success outraged members of the Junta, particularly General Pinochet himself. Indeed, when Pinochet met with Henry Kissinger on June 8, 1976, he pointedly accused Letelier of spreading misinformation about the regime's human rights record in Washington. "We are constantly being attacked by the Christian Democrats," Pinochet told Kissinger, according to the declassified transcript of their conversation. "They have a strong voice in Washington . . . also Letelier. Letelier has access to the Congress," Pinochet complained. "We know they are giving false information."[43] Within several weeks of this meeting, Pinochet and Contreras set in motion the mission to permanently silence Letelier.

In late June, Contreras ordered his chief deputy, Col. Pedro Espinoza, to organize the Letelier operation. Espinoza instructed Townley that he and another DINA agent, Lt. Col. Armando Fernández Larios, would travel to Asunción, Paraguay, in keeping with Condor procedures, to obtain false passports and U.S. visas, and then on to Washington "to execute the assassination."[44] On July 17, Colonel Contreras sent a cable to his counterpart in the Paraguayan secret police, Benito Guanes, through the encrypted teletype system set up for Condor communications. Two DINA agents would be arriving with a request for mission support, it read. "I would appreciate assistance in the performance of the mission," Contreras wrote. The cable was signed "Condor One."[45]

Townley and Fernández arrived in Asuncion several days later. When Paraguayan intelligence officials inquired about the purpose of their mission they presented a cover story—they were traveling to conduct surveillance on suspected leftist employees of the Chilean state copper company, CODELCO, in New York. The CIA Station chief in Santiago, they claimed, had cleared this activity. Eventually they were provided false Paraguayan passports under the fake names they had chosen—Alejandro Romeral Jara (Fernández Larios) and Juan Williams Rose (Townley).

The American consulate, however, delayed issuing U.S. visas to the Chileans for eight days. Ambassador George Landau agreed to provide the paperwork only after repeated phone calls and face-to-face cajoling by President Alfredo Stroessner's right-hand "fixer," Conrado Pappalardo. Pappalardo informed Landau that Stroessner had received a call from Pinochet himself requesting the favor of providing the passports and visas. Pappalardo claimed that the two DINA officials would meet with CIA deputy director Gen. Vernon Walters when they arrived. Landau faced a diplomatic dilemma: on the one hand, knowingly issuing visas to two Chilean agents using false identities, false nationalities, and false passports seemed risky and illegal; on the other hand, he did not want to inadvertently disrupt some type of CIA-sanctioned covert mission. He ordered the consulate to issue the visas, but copied the passports, along with the photo pages and, on July 27, pouched them to General Walters at CIA.

On August 4, Walters responded that he was unaware of the Chilean operatives, fueling intense suspicion about the true nature of their mission. Landau then cabled Assistant Secretary Shlaudeman to alert him to the so-called "Paraguayan caper" which, he stated, "in my view has troublesome aspects." Landau urged that the Chileans using those visas be barred from entering the country.[46] "If there is still time, and if there is a possibility of turning off this harebrained scheme," states a Roger Channel cable that Shlaudeman immediately sent back, "you are authorized to go back [to Paraguayan officials] to urge that the Chileans be persuaded not repeat not to travel." By then, however, DINA had aborted the effort to have Townley and Fernandez travel through Paraguay to the U.S. and recalled them to Chile.

DINA waited three weeks to see if the mission had been blown; then on August 26, sent an advance team—Fernández using the alias "Armando Faundez Lyon," along with a female DINA agent, Liliana Walker—to Washington. Their assignment: conduct preliminary surveillance on Letelier's movements. On September 9, Townley arrived, entering the country under a false Chilean official passport issued to a Hans Petersen Silva. He met Fernández at Kennedy Airport in New York and received an immediate briefing on Letelier's whereabouts, home address and make of car. Townley then drove to Union City, New Jersey, a bastion of hard-line anti-Castro Cuban exiles, to meet with the Cuban National Movement leader Guillermo Novo and recruit CNM assistance.

The assassination team gathered in Washington in the early morning hours of September 15, when Townley and Virgilio Paz arrived from New Jersey; they were later joined by CNM operative Dionisio Suarez. They spent two days conducting surveillance on Letelier—monitoring the time he left for work, the route he took, his daytime and evening routine. From Radio Shack and Sears, Townley purchased final components for making a remote-control bomb, and constructed it in his Econo-Lodge motel room. In the late evening of September 18 the three drove to Letelier's Bethesda home. Under cover of darkness, Townley quietly affixed the device to the chassis under the driver's seat of Letelier's Chevrolet Chevelle as it sat in the driveway.

On the morning of September 21, as Letelier drove his colleagues Michael and Ronni Moffitt to work, his automobile was tailed down Massachusetts Avenue by Paz and Suarez. As the Chevelle rounded Sheridan Circle, passing the residence of Pinochet's ambassador and the Turkish embassy, Suarez pressed the button on an electronic paging device, detonating the bomb. Sitting in the back, Michael Moffitt was spared the power of the explosion and survived. But a piece of shrapnel pierced his wife's jugular vein and she drowned from internal bleeding into her lungs on the curb next to the car. Letelier, his legs blown off, died a short time later at George Washington University Hospital.

This unprecedented terrorist attack took place fourteen city blocks from the White House; indeed the blast could be heard at the State Department just a half-mile away. Public and political reaction was swift and spontaneous. Within minutes of the assassinations, friends and colleagues gathered in front of the Chilean residency across Sheridan Circle shouting "Pinochet. Assassin." As news of murder reached Capitol Hill, numerous Congressmen and Senators, among them Congressman Tom Harkin and Senator Edward Kennedy stood up to eulogize Letelier. "The tragedy goes beyond the cold-blooded murder of Orlando Letelier and Ronni Moffitt," stated Senator James Abourezk. "It means that the tyranny of the dictatorship has now been extended . . . to the United States."[47]

The Pinochet regime immediately went on the offensive to portray itself as the victim of this crime—rather than its perpetrator. Chile's ambassador, Manuel Trucco, arrived at the State Department for a late afternoon meeting on September 21 with Deputy Assistant Secretary William Luers, to express his government's "repulsion for this ghastly outrageous act of terrorism." He asked the State Department to "make no statements which would cast doubt on anybody."[48] In Chile, the Foreign Ministry issued a statement implying the left was responsible: "The Chilean government has taken a consistent and open stance against terrorism." This criminal act demonstrated a "cold and cruel planning of a type only instigators of hate, imbued with savage fanaticism, could carry on." At DINA headquarters, Colonel Espinoza informed his operative Armando Fernández Larios "that the assassination had been carried out by the 'opposition' to the Pinochet government to discredit the regime before the Chilean Foreign Minister was scheduled to speak at the UN that week." As Fernández recalls being told, "that is what you will say."[49]

In his first post-assassination cable to Washington, Ambassador Popper noted that the assassination "could not have been better timed to attract the attention of the UN General Assembly," and predicted that the regime "would hasten to deny all responsibility" and claim "that the affair is a leftist provocation designed to hurt the GOC." "This is not inconceivable," Popper concluded. Based on obvious motivation, however

> suspicion will fall first of all on the GOC directorate of national intelligence (DINA). Letelier was a first-rank political foe of the Junta. He was politically active in exile. Silencing him will tend to inhibit some other exiles from speaking, writing or plotting against the Junta.

Reflecting the turn-a-blind-eye gullibility that marked previous embassy reporting on the Prats assassination and Operation Colombo, the cable continued: "But we have never had any indication that DINA was in any way operational in the U.S. territory, and it is difficult for us to believe that even its rather fanatical leaders would expose themselves to the consequences of being implicated in a terrorist act in Washington." (Doc 9)

Key sectors of the intelligence community took the same position. The CIA leaked multiple stories to the press suggesting that DINA was not involved. The Defense Intelligence Agency, usually known for strong, accurate assessments, produced an initial report written by DIA Chile desk officer, R. Denk, discounting the likelihood that the Pinochet regime was behind the Washington car bombing:

> It is difficult to pin the blame on Santiago at this point for several reasons. The reach of the Chilean directorate of National Intelligence (DINA)—cited as responsible—almost certainly does not (80 percent)

> extend to the U.S. Chilean image-building received a severe setback by the killing, something that planners of the attempt would have foreknown and considered. Moreover, the event occurred, as had two previous attempts, during the convening of the UNGA in New York—poor timing for a Chilean attempt. (Doc 10)

But the FBI provided far more accurate intelligence. One week after the bombing, FBI legal attaché in Buenos Aires, Robert Scherrer, sent a secret four-page report to Washington, drawing on a source high inside the Argentine military. His cable, designated "CHILBOM," stated that the assassination was likely the work of Operation Condor. "Chile was the center of Operation Condor," Scherrer wrote. "A third and most secret phase of Operation Condor involves the formation of special teams from member countries to carry out sanctions up to assassination." As Scherrer concluded: "It is not beyond the realm of possibility that the recent assassination of Orlando Letelier in Washington D.C. may have been carried out as a third phase of Operation Condor." (Doc 11)

Condor: A Chronicle of Terrorism Foretold

For twenty years, Scherrer's September 28, 1976, CHILBOM cable was the only declassified document on Operation Condor, suggesting that the U.S. intelligence community had not discovered this international terrorist network until a week after the car bombing in Washington.[50] In truth, the Ford administration—particularly Henry Kissinger's office and the CIA—had extensive knowledge of Condor and its terrorist activities well *prior* to the Letelier-Moffitt assassination. But the complex record of U.S. action, or lack of action, in response to that knowledge was deliberately hidden from the victims' families and the public, and even withheld from Justice Department officials investigating this terrorist crime.

As early as the fall of 1974, when DINA assassinated Gen. Carlos Prats in Buenos Aires, the U.S. intelligence community knew of terrorist collaboration among U.S. allies in the Southern Cone—"the precursor to Operation Condor"—as the CIA later conceded. According to the special report to Congress, *CIA Activities in Chile,* "within a year after the coup, the CIA and other U.S. government agencies were aware of bilateral cooperation among regional intelligence services to track the activities of and in at least a few cases kill political opponents." CIA reporting also tracked Chilean military efforts in 1974 to locate and assassinate political opponents as far away as Europe. Even before the Pinochet regime formally created Condor, U.S. intelligence had documented Chile's capability—and intent—to commit atrocities beyond its borders.

CIA records acknowledge an initial awareness of "Plan Condor" in March 1976, when intelligence agents reported that DINA chieftain Manuel Contreras had "initiated a program of cooperation" among the Southern Cone intelligence agencies. The Agency obtained detailed information about the second Santiago Condor convention, held two months later at the end of May. "The basic theme of the meeting was long-range cooperation among the services of the participating countries," stated a later CIA report, "but went well beyond information exchange."

By the time of the second Condor meeting, there was ample evidence of the nature of that cooperation. The kidnapping in Argentina, transfer to Chile and murder of MIR leader Edgardo Enríquez in April 1976; the May murders of the Uruguayan parliamentarians; the slaying of the former president of Bolivia in June, along with the mass abduction, interrogation, and torture of Chilean and Uruguayan refugees by a multinational team of torturers—all indicated ongoing, increasingly brazen, joint transnational operations.

This spate of atrocities in Argentina prompted expressions of outrage on Capitol Hill, and raised concerns among a number of high State Department officials who remained unaware of CIA information on Operation Condor. There was speculation that the Southern Cone nations were "cooperating in some sort of international 'Murder Inc.' "—a possible "intergovernmental assassination program" according to an Intelligence and Research report prepared for Henry Kissinger on June 4. That same day, under Kissinger's signature, the Latin American Bureau sent an "immediate action" cable to the Southern Cone embassies, subject "possible international implications of violent deaths of political figures abroad." The cable posed two basic questions:

> Do you believe that the deaths of political refugees or asylees from your country abroad could have been arranged by your host government through institutional ties to groups, governmental or other, in the country where the deaths took place?
>
> Do you have evidence to support or deny allegations of international arrangements among governments to carry out such assassinations or executions? (Doc 12)

From Buenos Aires, Ambassador Charles Hill promptly responded that the embassy believed the Argentine security forces were involved in most of the killings, some of which may have been undertaken "as a favor" to other security forces in the region, but had no concrete evidence of a conspiracy.

The U.S. embassy in Santiago cabled back that it had no evidence of formal collaboration but "we believe these arrangements are possible, and that it is also possible Chilean agents have been involved in killings abroad, possibly in cooperation with foreign governments."[51]

Traveling in Latin America following the OAS conference in Santiago, Kissinger was informed that embassy reporting supported the following conclusion: "there is no evidence available suggesting the existence of a conspiracy among the governments of the Southern Cone to track down and [assassinate] prominent asylees resident in those countries." In two analytical reports, the Bureau of Intelligence and Research offered the same, incorrect, assessment. The June 4 report to Kissinger, drafted by INR analyst James Buchanan, acknowledged that the Southern Cone security forces "undoubtedly coordinate their anti-subversive efforts insofar as information exchanges are concerned," but attributed the assassinations to "the work of right-wingers, some of who are security personnel" in Argentina. A second, similar report, dated July 18, contained far more detail about secret police collaboration in the Southern Cone. Yet INR concluded: "the evidence does not conclusively establish the existence of formal, high-level coordination among Southern Cone security forces for the express purpose of eliminating exiles."

The CIA, however, did possess concrete evidence of a formal coordinated conspiracy for the express purpose of eliminating exiles through political assassinations around the world. Covert agents, drawing on Latin American intelligence sources who had attended the second Condor meeting, reported back in June that the Southern Cone regimes were expanding their operations and now "planned to engage in 'executive action' outside the territory of member countries." Not until the end of July, however, after the State Department had spent almost two months trying to determine if its Latin allies were indeed coordinating assassination operations, did the CIA share this intelligence. On July 30, during the weekly CIA/ARA meeting, an Agency official briefed the State Department on what he termed "disturbing developments in [Condor's] operational attitudes." Chile and the other Condor nations had assumed an "activist role," he said, that included "identifying, locating, and 'hitting' guerrilla leaders" wherever they could be found. (Doc 13)

Secretary of State Kissinger received this dramatic information on August 3. In a detailed fourteen-page report, classified SECRET and titled "The 'Third World War' and South America," Assistant Secretary for Latin America Harry Shlaudeman informed Kissinger of the existence of Operation Condor and its mission:

> There is extensive cooperation between the security/intelligence operations of six governments: Argentina, Brazil, Bolivia, Chile, Paraguay

> and Uruguay. Their intelligence services hold formal meetings to plan " 'Operation Condor.' " It will include extensive FBI-type exchanges of information on shady characters. There are plans for a special communications network. These details are still secret, but broad security cooperation is not. (Doc 14)

The Southern Cone military regimes were "joining forces to eradicate 'subversion', a word which increasingly translates into non-violent dissent from the left and center left," Shlaudeman wrote, suggesting that Condor targets were not limited to leftist insurgents. They "now coordinate intelligence activities closely" and operate in each other's countries in "pursuit of 'subversives.'" They "have established Operation Condor to find and kill terrorists . . . in their own countries and in Europe."

The Shlaudeman report identified a number of foreign policy considerations for Kissinger to evaluate. The first was the potential for terrorist violence to spread beyond the region to Western Europe and even the United States—"a chance of serious world-scale trouble," as Shlaudeman described it. If Condor undertook "counterterror operations in Europe," their targets might respond by attacking embassies and interests of the Southern Cone regimes. "The industrial democracies would be the battlefield," Shlaudeman predicted, much like in the case of the PLO-Israeli conflict.

Of even greater concern was the possibility that "police-type cooperation" could evolve "into formation of a political bloc."[52] In the Cold War context, the United States would be "an apparent beneficiary" of a right-wing Southern Cone alliance. But Washington had an image problem, Shlaudeman explained. "Internationally, the Latin generals look like our guys. We are especially identified with Chile. It cannot do us any good." Over the long term, these nations would become less responsive to U.S. influence, deeply divide the Western Hemisphere, and be even more prone to international violence then they already were.

The report to Kissinger recommended a "long-term strategic view" to undercut formation of a right-wing regional bloc. Shlaudeman offered several vague options, among them to depoliticize human rights by blunting U.S. pressure, and attempting to "bring the potential bloc-members back into our cognitive universe through systematic exchanges," among them exchanges of intelligence on subversion in the region.

Surprisingly, the Shlaudeman report contained no immediate action recommendations for thwarting Condor assassination ambitions. But over the next three weeks in August, high State Department officials, among them Kissinger, Under Secretary of State for Political Affairs Philip Habib, Shlaudeman, his deputies William Luers and Hewson Ryan, and unidentified CIA officials, deliberated what, if any, concrete policy response Washington should take to the threat of Southern Cone terrorism. Both Luers and Ryan lobbied for aggressive U.S. action to stop Condor operations. In an interview, Ryan recalled efforts "to get a cable cleared with the seventh floor [Kissinger's office] instructing our ambassadors to go in to the chiefs of state . . . and to warn them that this was a violation of the very basic fundamentals of civilized society."

At the very time those discussions were being held, the same U.S. officials unwittingly confronted evidence of the Condor mission to kill Orlando Letelier. On August 5, Shlaudeman received the alarming cable from Ambassador George Landau in Paraguay regarding the surreptitious efforts of two Chilean secret police agents to travel to Washington on false Paraguayan passports. Shortly thereafter, the CIA transferred to Shlaudeman's office the copied passports that deputy CIA director Vernon Walters had received from Landau.

While U.S. officials took steps to abort this highly suspicious mission, the declassified record does not indicate that they linked the murky actions of the Chilean secret police trying to gain illicit entry into the United States with CIA intelligence on planned Condor assassination operations. There appear to be no requests from Kissinger's office to the CIA to investigate; no instructions from CIA headquarters to the Santiago Station to obtain an explanation; and no State Department queries to the embassy about what operations Pinochet's regime might be planning in the United States.

On August 23, the State Department finally decided to register U.S. displeasure with the Southern Cone military regimes regarding their coordinated state-sponsored terrorism. Secretary Kissinger approved and signed a carefully worded Roger Channel cable—"Subject: Operation Condor"—to the U.S. ambassadors in all Condor nations. (Doc 15)

"You are aware of [a series of CIA] reports on 'Operation Condor,' " the cable began. "The coordination of security and intelligence information is probably understandable. However, government planned and directed assassinations within and outside the territory of Condor members has most serious implications which we must face squarely and rapidly."

The cable instructed the U.S. ambassador in Chile, Argentina, and Uruguay—the "front burner cases" identified by the CIA to be most actively involved in plotting assassinations—to approach "the highest appropriate official, preferably the chief of state" in their respective countries and issue a carefully worded démarche along the following lines: The United States was aware of

> information exchange and coordination . . . with regard to subversive activities. This we consider useful. There are in addition, however, rumors that this cooperation may extend beyond information exchange

> to include plans for the assassination of subversives, politicians and prominent figures both within the national borders of certain Southern Cone countries and abroad. . . . [W]e feel impelled to bring to your attention our deep concern. If these rumors were to have any shred of truth, they would create a most serious moral and political problem.

The main problem cited: that "activity of this type would further exacerbate public world criticism of the governments involved."

In the rank of Condor nations, Chile was "Condor one"—the operational command center of these plots. Therefore, issuing the diplomatic démarche to General Pinochet appeared to be the most immediate action to counter Condor. Chile was so important, in fact, that Kissinger also instructed Ambassador David Popper to "discuss [with CIA Station chief Stuart Burton] the possibility of a parallel approach by him" to his counterpart in the Chilean secret police, DINA.

After the cable arrived in Santiago, Popper met immediately with Burton and deputy chief of mission Thomas Boyatt. But they rejected the idea of speaking directly to Pinochet on the grounds that he would take such offense as to render the warning ineffective. "I seriously doubt that an approach to President Pinochet is the best way," Popper responded to the State Department in a cable on August 24. "In my judgment, given Pinochet's sensitivity regarding pressures by the USG [US government], he might well take as an insult any inference that he was connected with such assassination plots."

Instead, Popper endorsed the idea of sending the CIA Station chief to talk with Col. Manuel Contreras; Burton, he wrote, believed this would be the "most effective way of getting the message across without undesirable complications." But the ambassador questioned the urgency of any approach. "Has department received any word that would indicate that assassination activities are imminent," he asked, unaware that Contreras had already set the Letelier operation in motion. The cable ended with Popper's request to "please advise" on his suggested course of action. (Doc 16)

Popper's response generated a discussion at high levels of the State Department about whether to overrule his objections or support them. On August 27, at the weekly meeting between CIA and State Department officials on Latin America, Assistant Secretary Shlaudeman declared "that we are not making a representation to Pinochet as it would be futile to do so." According to heavily censored minutes, the group appeared to debate the CIA approach to DINA but it is not clear that any decision was made to order the chief of Station to do so.

Indeed, over the next four weeks no additional instructions are recorded—

to Ambassador Popper or the CIA Station in Santiago, or any other Southern Cone embassy. On or around September 19, deputy assistant secretary for Latin America Luers cabled a query to Shlaudeman who was traveling in Central America. The cable, no. 231654, has not been recovered but, in an interview Luers said he must have asked "how should we proceed?" U.S. ambassador to Buenos Aires, Charles Hill had a meeting scheduled for September 21 with Argentine Junta leader Gen. Jorge Videla. It is likely Luers requested instructions on whether Hill should present the Condor démarche mandated in Kissinger's August 23 instructions.

Late afternoon on September 20, Shlaudeman cabled back a short, negative, response. He ordered Luers to "simply instruct the Ambassadors to take no further action, noting that there have been no reports in some weeks indicating an intention to activate the Condor scheme." (Doc 17)[53]

In fact, the "Condor scheme" had already been activated. Two DINA agents—the same ones who had attempted to travel through Paraguay—had already arrived in Washington in late August and early September. DINA's leading terrorist operative, Michael Townley, had already taped the bomb underneath Letelier's car on the evening of September 18. Less than sixteen hours after Shlaudeman cancelled any "further action" to counter Condor terrorism, Orlando Letelier and Ronni Moffitt were killed by a terrorist attack only a few blocks from the White House.

This unprecedented act of terrorism in America's capital city shook Washington officialdom—particularly those officials knowledgeable of Operation Condor and the department's abject failure to have taken prior action to deter such assassinations. But even then, the State Department hesitated and obfuscated. On the afternoon of the assassination, the INR afternoon summary—the top-secret intelligence paper sent over to the White House for the National Security Adviser to help prepare the president's daily briefing—reported on Condor, but only in the context of Chile's promotion of a regional political and economic bloc in the Southern Cone. The report, prepared for General Scowcroft, described Operation Condor as "the Southern Cone counterterrorist network inspired by Chile and designed to promote information exchanges and the covert elimination of subversives." The Letelier-Moffitt assassination wasn't mentioned.[54]

On October 4, twelve days *after* the Letelier-Moffitt murders and almost six weeks after Ambassador Popper's August 24 request for further instructions on the démarche to Chile, Shlaudeman finally drafted a Roger Channel response. It read:

> We agree that our purpose can best be served through [CIA Station] approach to Contreras, and that the issue should not repeat not be

> raised with Pinochet. [CIA chief of Station] is receiving instructions to consult with you on manner and timing of approach. (Doc 18)

In a peculiar cover memo to INR's deputy director for operations, William McAfee, Shlaudeman wrote that "I have authority from above for this"—which McAfee interpreted to mean Secretary Kissinger—and "would appreciate NO clearances shown." This was a highly unusual request, McAfee recalled, which effectively protected the officials who had authorized Shlaudeman to send the cable. His orders also kept the cable from being shown to anyone else in the department.[55]

Two days after the Shlaudeman instructions arrived, the CIA Station obtained intelligence on the car bombing from an informant pointing the finger of responsibility at the Pinochet regime. General Pinochet himself, according to the CIA informant, had stated that Letelier's vocal criticism of the regime was "unacceptable." The source, according to the October 6 field report, "believes that the Chilean Government is directly involved in Letelier's death and feels that investigation into the incident will so indicate." (Doc 19)[56]

When the Station chief approached Contreras, however, he disavowed Chile's role in any assassination. According to a CIA summary of this meeting, the DINA chief "confirmed Condor's existence but denied it had a role in extra-judicial killings."[57]

Even in the early stages of the investigation, the CIA had substantive evidence to show that Contreras was lying. The Agency had concrete knowledge that DINA had murdered other political opponents abroad, using the same modus operandi as the Letelier case. The Agency had substantive intelligence on Condor, and Chile's involvement in planning murders of political opponents in Europe; indeed, around the time of the Letelier-Moffitt assassination, the Agency had alerted French authorities to thwart a Condor mission in Paris. Moreover, the CIA, along with the State Department, possessed the names and even the photographs of two DINA agents who had attempted to travel through Paraguay to Washington just weeks before the murders.

Neither the Agency nor the State Department expeditiously turned over what it knew to Justice Department investigators. The CIA suggested to Deputy Assistant Secretary Luers that he "review" the file on the Paraguayan caper. But the Latin America bureau waited a full month to provide the cable traffic, xeroxed passports, and photos to the FBI. During that time, State Department officials, in apparent consultation with CIA counterparts, debated "editing them" in order to "withhold information" in the cables relating to the CIA, according to declassified memoranda. "If the fact that we had intentionally withheld information on the Letelier investigation became public, we would be subject to a storm of criticism," wrote Chile desk officer Robert Driscoll on October 15, recommending that the full file be turned over to the FBI.[58] Justice Department prosecutors were not fully briefed on what the CIA and State had known about Condor until some time after the murders took place.

Instead of actively seeking to help the investigation, as John Dinges and Saul Landau recorded in *Assassination on Embassy Row*, unnamed intelligence officials attempted to shift attention away from Chile and promote the so-called "martyr theory"—Pinochet's stock argument that leftists committed the crime to create a martyr and embarrass the regime. On October 11, shortly after CIA officials spoke to Contreras, *Newsweek* magazine reported, "the CIA has concluded that the Chilean secret police were not involved in the death of Orlando Letelier. The agency reached its decision because the bomb was too crude to be the work of experts and because the murder, coming while Chile's rulers were wooing U.S. support, could only damage the Santiago regime." The next day, the *New York Times* cited "intelligence officials" as saying that the FBI and CIA has "virtually ruled out the idea that Mr. Letelier was killed by agents of the Chilean military Junta," and were "pursuing the possibility that Mr. Letelier had been assassinated by left-wing extremists." According to CIA officials, the *Washington Post* reported on November 1, "operatives of the present Chilean military Junta did not take part in Letelier's killing . . . CIA director Bush expressed this view in a conversation late last week with Secretary of State Kissinger."[59]

With their intelligence on Condor's capabilities and intentions, CIA officials along with Kissinger and his staff had ample reason to believe otherwise. The leaks to the press served to divert attention away from the true terrorists and to cover up a simple and shameful fact: official actions that could have, and should have, averted the Letelier-Moffitt assassinations had not been taken. Indeed, the same questions raised by the terrorist attack of September 11, 2001—was there enough intelligence to have taken steps to deter those acts of terrorism, and if so, why weren't preventative actions taken?—could more readily be answered regarding the terrorist bombing of September 21, 1976. Hidden for years, the documentation showed that U.S. officials knew enough—and were concerned enough about what they knew—to initiate counterterrorism actions that were, in the end, never implemented. A U.S. policy of support and sympathy for Pinochet, a blind eye toward his real and intended repression, concerns about alienating his and the other Southern Cone military regimes, and bureaucratic aversion to proactive diplomatic postures all seemed to play a role in the Ford administration's failure to deter a crime it had generally foreseen. "We were remiss," Deputy Assistant Secretary Hewson Ryan concluded:

> We were extremely reticent about taking a strong forward public posture, and even a private posture in certain cases, as was this case in the Chilean assassination. We knew fairly early on that the governments of the Southern Cone countries were planning . . . some assassinations abroad in the summer of 1976. Whether if we had gone in, we might have prevented this, I don't know. But we didn't.[60]

DOCUMENT 1. DINA, [Invitation Letter from Col. Manuel Contreras for the First Operation Condor Meeting in Santiago], October 1975.

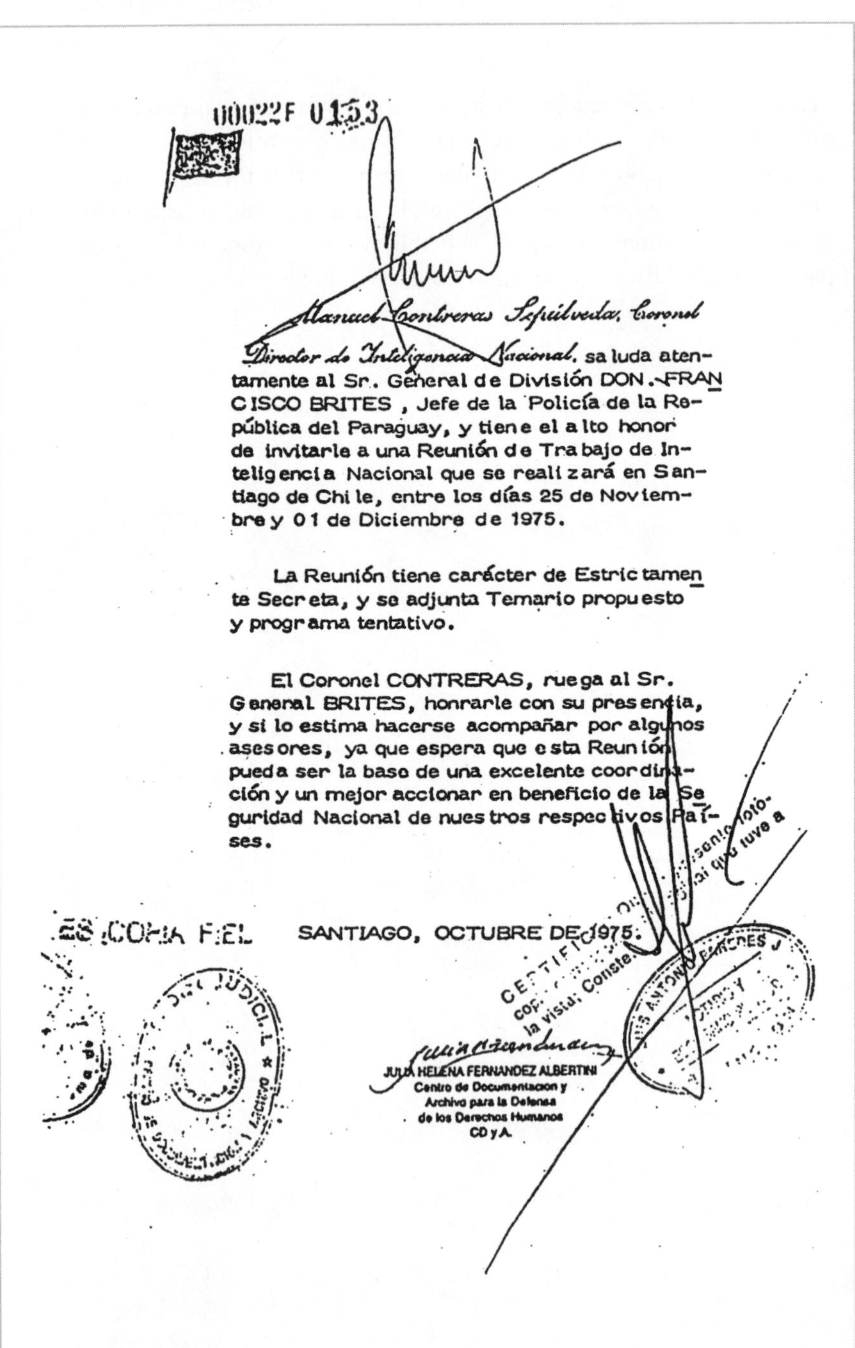

00022F 0153

Manuel Contreras Sepúlveda, Coronel
Director de Inteligencia Nacional, saluda atentamente al Sr. General de División DON FRANCISCO BRITES, Jefe de la Policía de la República del Paraguay, y tiene el alto honor de invitarle a una Reunión de Trabajo de Inteligencia Nacional que se realizará en Santiago de Chile, entre los días 25 de Noviembre y 01 de Diciembre de 1975.

La Reunión tiene carácter de Estrictamente Secreta, y se adjunta Temario propuesto y programa tentativo.

El Coronel CONTRERAS, ruega al Sr. General BRITES, honrarle con su presencia, y si lo estima hacerse acompañar por algunos asesores, ya que espera que esta Reunión pueda ser la base de una excelente coordinación y un mejor accionar en beneficio de la Seguridad Nacional de nuestros respectivos Países.

ES COPIA FIEL

SANTIAGO, OCTUBRE DE 1975.

JULIA HELENA FERNANDEZ ALBERTINI
Centro de Documentacion y
Archivo para la Defensa
de los Derechos Humanos
CD y A.

DOCUMENT 2. DINA, **SECRET** Summary, "Closing Statement of the First Inter-American Meeting of National Intelligence," November 28, 1975 (first and last page of original Spanish Document; English translation of complete document).

SECRETO

- 193 -

F.- ACTA DE CLAUSURA DE LA PRIMERA REUNION INTERAMERICANA DE INTELIGENCIA NACIONAL

En Santiago de Chile a veintiocho días del mes de Noviembre de mil novecientos setenta y cinco, se procede a clausurar la PRIMERA REUNION INTERAMERICANA DE INTELIGENCIA NACIONAL, con la participación de las Delegaciones de los Países de ARGENTINA, BOLIVIA, CHILE, PARAGUAY y URUGUAY, quienes acuerdan efectuar las siguientes recomendaciones para su accionar futuro.

RECOMENDACIONES.

1.- Iniciar a partir desde esta fecha los contactos bilateral o multilateral, a voluntad de los respectivos países aquí participantes, para el intercambio de información subversiva, abriendo propios o nuevos Kardex de antecedentes de los respectivos Servicios.

2.- Recomendamos, la formación de una Oficina Coordinadora, destinada a proporcionar antecedentes de personas y organizaciones conectadas con la Subversión.

3.- Recomendamos, se estudie la proposición de establecer un Sistema de contacto periódico entre los Servicios de Inteligencia mediante la aprobación o modificación de lo propuesto para normalizar este tipo de encuentros.

4.- Recomendamos, establecer el Sistema de Coordinación mediante tres etapas para su activación

5.- LA PRIMERA ETAPA: Que recomendamos es la siguiente:

a.- Establecer un Directorio completo con los nom

//..

SECRETO

- 196 -

intercambio de información, tanto bilateral como multinacional.

c.- Presentación del Proyecto de Factibilidad del Sistema de Coordinación de Inteligencia.

7.- Para la Tercera Fase, se recomienda:

a.- Aprobación del Proyecto de Factibilidad del Sistema y otorgamiento de los fondos que permitan su materialización.

8.- La inclusión de cualquier otro país al Sistema CONDOR, deberá contar con la aprobación del total de los países participantes a la Primera Conferencia.

9.- La presente Acta de Clausura, con las recomendaciones estampadas, será ratificada con la firma de los respectivos Jefes de Servicio de los países participantes en un plazo no superior a sesenta días a contar de esta fecha y que se materializa el 30 de ENERO de 1976.

Para Constancia Firman.

JORGE CASAS
Capitán de Navío
Jefe Delegación
ARGENTINA.

CARLOS MENA
Mayor de Ejército
Jefe Delegación
BOLIVIA

MANUEL CONTRERAS SEPULVEDA
Coronel de Ejército
Director de Inteligencia Nacional
CHILE.

JOSE A. FONS
Coronel de Ejército
Jefe Delegación
URUGUAY.

BENITO GUANES SERRANO
Coronel de Ejército
Jefe 2º Departamento del E.M. FF.AA.
PARAGUAY.

SECRET

F. **MINUTES OF THE CONCLUSIONS OF THE FIRST INTERAMERICAN MEETING ON NATIONAL INTELLIGENCE**

In Santiago, Chile, November 28, 1975, the FIRST INTERAMERICAN MEETING ON NATIONAL INTELLIGENCE concluded with the participation of delegates from ARGENTINA, BOLIVIA, CHILE, PARAGUAY and URUGUAY, who agreed to implement the following recommendations for future actions.

RECOMMENDATIONS.

1.- From this date forward, initiate bilateral or multilateral contacts, upon the will of countries participating here, for the exchange of subversive information, opening their own, or new, information files in their respective Services.

2.- We recommend the creation of a Coordinating Office, with the purpose of providing information on people and organizations linked to Subversion.

3.- We recommend carrying out a study on the proposal of establishing a System for periodic contacts among the Intelligence Services through the approval or modification of the proposal to normalize (regularize?) these type of meetings.

4.- We recommend establishing a Coordination System through three phases of implementation.

5.- The FIRST PHASE we recommend is the following:

a.- The establishment of a complete Directory (Register) with the names and addresses of those persons working in Intelligence so as to be able to request directly from them any information on people and organizations directly or indirectly linked to Marxism

b.- We recommend that the Security Services give priority to the requests for information filed by the Services involved in the System

c.- We recommend swift and immediate contact when suspicious individuals are either expelled from the country or travel outside the country, so as to alert the Intelligence Services.

d.- We recommend the use of a Cryptography System that will be available to member countries within the next 30 days, with the understanding that it may be vulnerable; it will be replaced in the future with cryptographic machines to be selected by common agreement.

e.- We recommend studying the proposed models of personal information files ("fichas"), informing each other of any needed changes.

f.- We recommend making available the information held by the Intelligence Services to the Technical Team regarding Telex; Microfilm; Computers; Cryptography, in order to complete what is lacking, make use of what is available and propose new elements.

g.- We recommend facilitating the presence of National Intelligence personnel or similar agents in the Embassies of our countries for direct and personal liaisons; they will be fully registered by their Service.

h.- We recommend receiving the people who studied the theoretical aspects of the System regarding a Data Base and Transmission of Information.

We recommend using the means of liaison of countries outside the System, especially countries outside the continent, to obtain information on Subversion.

We recommend facilitating the means to publish information aimed at attacking subversion related to our countries.

We recommend holding the next Conference a week before the Meeting of Commanders in Chief of the Armies, with Chile as the host country, where each country will be represented by no more than three delegates.

i.- This Organization will be called CONDOR, by the unanymous approval of a motion presented by the Uruguayan Delegation in honor of the host country.

6.- For the Second Phase, we recommend the following:

a.- Evaluation of the results of the First Phase and proposing information to facilitate the drafting of a feasibility project of the System being discussed.

b.- Increasing Communications Systems and links to allow for speeding up information exchange, both bilateral and multinational.

c.- Presenting the Feasibility Project of the Intelligence Coordination System

7.- For the Third Phase, we recommend:

a.- Approving the Feasibility Project of the System and assigning the funds needed for its implementation.

8.- The inclusion of any other country in the CONDOR System must be approved by the totality of the countries participating in the First Conference.

9.- These Minutes of the Conclusions, with the recommendations established, will be ratified with the signatures of the respective heads of the Intelligence Services of the participating countries within a time period of up to sixty days from this date, and will come into effect on January 30, 1976.

For the record, signed by:

JORGE CASAS	CARLOS MENA
Navy Captain	Army Major
Head of Delegation	Head of Delegation
ARGENTINA	BOLIVIA
MANUEL CONTRERAS SEPULVEDA	JOSE A. FONS
Army Colonel	Army Colonel
Director of National Intelligence	Head of Delegation
CHILE	URUGUAY

BENITO GUANES SERRANO Army Colonel Head of the Second Department of the Armed Forces High Command PARAGUAY

DOCUMENT 3. Defense Intelligence Agency, **SECRET** Report on Operation Condor, "Special Operations Forces," October 1, 1976.

UNCLASSIFIED

DEPARTMENT OF DEFENSE INTELLIGENCE INFORMATION REPORT

NOTE: This document contains information affecting the national defense of the United States within the meaning of the espionage laws, Title 18, U.S.C., Sec. 793 and 794. The transmission or the revelation of its contents in any manner to an unauthorized person is prohibited by law.

~~SECRET/WNINTEL/NOFORN~~ ~~SECRET NOFORN~~

(Classification and Control Markings)

This report contains unprocessed information. Plans and/or policies should not be evolved or modified solely on the basis of this report.

1. COUNTRY: Argentina
2. SUBJECT: (U) Special Operations Forces (U)
3. IIC NUMBER: N/A
4. DATE OF INFORMATION: 1976, SEP 28
5. PLACE AND DATE OF ACQ: 1976, SEP 28, Buenos Aires
6. EVALUATION: SOURCE A INFORMATION 1
7. SOURCE: Legal Attache, AMEMB
8. REPORT NUMBER: 6 804 0334 76
9. DATE OF REPORT: 1976, OCT 1
10. NO. OF PAGES: 2
11. REFERENCES: PG1200 PG1100 ICR A-TAC-44396 PG2200 PG1300 PG2220 PG2240
12. ORIGINATOR: USDAO BUENOS AIRES
13. PREPARED BY: LTC JOHN L. BOHACH, JR, USA, AARMA
14. APPROVING AUTHORITY: COL PAUL A. COUGHLIN, USA, ARMA, DATT

15. SUMMARY: ~~(S/WNINTEL/NOFORN)~~ This IR provides information on joint counterinsurgency operations by several countries in South America. Information was provided by US Embassy Legal Attache who has excellent contacts within the State Secretariat for Information and Federal Police Force.

This IR partially fulfills requirement of ICR A-TAC-44396.

REC'D DS-4B 13 OCT'76

1613

WARNING NOTICE-SENSITIVE INTELLIGENCE SOURCES AND METHODS INVOLVED

1. ~~(S/WNINTEL/NOFORN)~~ "Operation Condor" is the code name given for intelligence collection on "leftists," Communists and Marxists in the Southern Cone Area. It was recently established between cooperating intelligence services in South America in order to eliminate Marxist terrorist activities in member countries with Chile reportedly being the center of operations. Other participating members include: Argentina, Paraguay, Uruguay and Bolivia. In addition, Brazil has apparently tentatively agreed to provide intelligence input for Operation Condor. Members showing the most enthusiasm to date have been Argentina, Uruguay and Chile. These three countries have engaged in joint operations, primarily in Argentina, against terrorists targets. During the week of 20 September 1976, the Director of the Argentine Army Intelligence Service traveled to Santiago to consult with

(Continuation Block): 302310? AR, CI, UY, BR, BL 332080? AR 332610 SAR 306303 AR, CI, UY 306354 202160? 202130? 203156 AR, UY

16. DISTRIBUTION BY ORIGINATOR: USCINCSO; TAC/INOA, Langley AFB, Va 23665; 1st Special Operations Wing Eglin AFB Aux Field, Fl 32544; USDAO SANTIAGO; USDAO BOGOTA; USDAO MONTEVIDEO; USDAO ASUNCION; USDAO BRAZILIA

17. DOWNGRADING DATA: CLASSIFIED BY DATT EXEMPT FROM GENERAL DECLASSIFICATION SCHEDULE OF EXECUTIVE ORDER 11652. EXEMPTION CATEGORY TWO. DECLASSIFY ON 31 DEC 2006

18. ATTACHMENT DATA: NONE

Declassified by DIA in accordance with EO 12958

~~SECRET/WNINTEL/NOFORN~~ ~~SECRET-NOFORN~~

(Classification and Control Markings)

DD FORM 1396

UNCLASSIFIED

DEPARTMENT OF DEFENSE INTELLIGENCE INFORMATION REPORT

CONTINUATION SHEET

~~SECRET/WNINTEL/NOFORN~~
SECRET-NOFORN
(Classification and Control Markings)

REPORT NO. 6 804 0334 76
PAGE 2 OF 2 PAGES
ORIGINATOR
USDAO BUENOS AIRES

(Leave Blank)

his Chilean counterparts on Operation Condor (This travel is similar to trip reported in IR 6 804 0309 76.)

2. ~~(S/WNINTEL/NOFORN)~~ During the period 24-27 September 1976, members of the Argentine State Secretariat for Information (SIDE), operating with officers of the Uruguayan Military Intelligence Service carried out operations against the Uruguayan Terrorist organization, the OPR-33 in Buenos Aires. As a result of this joint operation, SIDE officials claimed that the entire OPR-33 infrastructure in Argentina has been eliminated. A large volume of US currency was seized during the combined operation.

3. ~~(S/WNINTEL/NOFORN)~~ A third and reportedly very secret phase of "Operation Condor" involves the formation of special teams from member countries who are to carry out operations to include assassinations against terrorist or supporters of terrorist organizations. For example, should a terrorist or a supporter of a terrorist organization from a member country be identified, a special team would be dispatched to locate and surveil the target. When the location and surveillance operation has terminated, a second team would be dispatched to carry out an operation against the target. Special teams would be issued false documentation from member countries, could be composed either of individuals from one member nation or of persons from various member nations. Source stated that team members would not be commissioned or non-commissioned officers of the armed forces, but rather "special agents." Two European countries, specifically mentioned for possible operations under the third phase were France and Portugal.

4. ~~(S/WNINTEL/NOFORN)~~ A special team has apparently been organized in Argentina for use in "Operation Condor." They are members of the Argentine Army Intelligence Service and the State Secretariat for Information. They are reportedly structured much like a US Special Forces Team with a medic (doctor), demolition expert, etc,. They are apparently being prepared for action in phase three.

COMMENT: ~~(S/WNINTEL/NOFORN)~~ More and more is being heard about "Operation Condor" in the southern cone. Military officers who, heretofore, had been mum on the subject have begun to talk openly about it. A favorite remark is that, "one of their colleagues is out of country because he is flying like a condor."

SECRET-NOFORN

DOCUMENT 4. CIA, **SECRET** Intelligence Report [Assassination of General Carlos Prats], October 25, 1974.

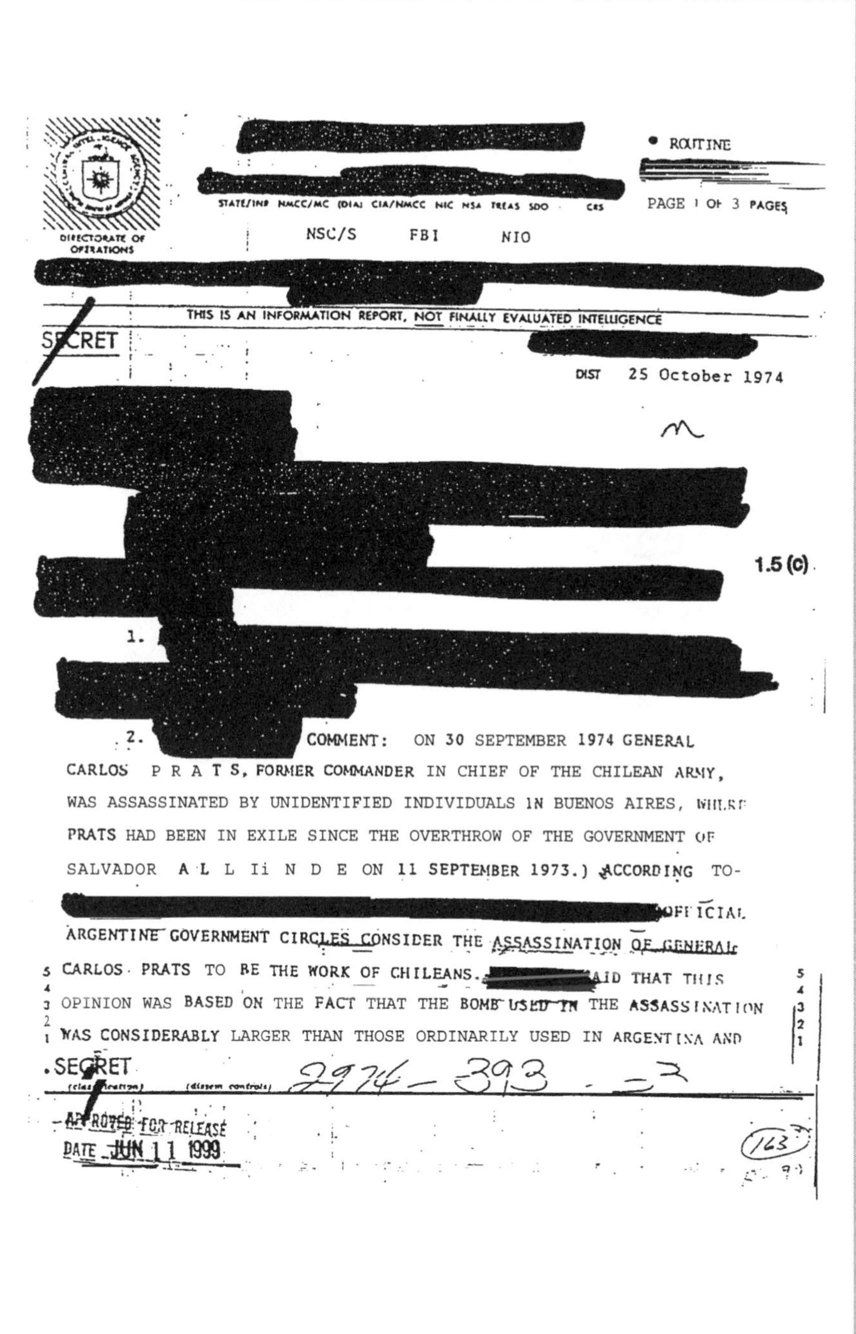

DIRECTORATE OF OPERATIONS

• ROUTINE

STATE/INR NMCC/MC (DIA) CIA/NMCC NIC NSA TREAS SDO CRS

PAGE 1 OF 3 PAGES

NSC/S FBI NIO

THIS IS AN INFORMATION REPORT, NOT FINALLY EVALUATED INTELLIGENCE

SECRET

DIST 25 October 1974

1.5 (c)

1.

2. COMMENT: ON 30 SEPTEMBER 1974 GENERAL CARLOS PRATS, FORMER COMMANDER IN CHIEF OF THE CHILEAN ARMY, WAS ASSASSINATED BY UNIDENTIFIED INDIVIDUALS IN BUENOS AIRES, WHERE PRATS HAD BEEN IN EXILE SINCE THE OVERTHROW OF THE GOVERNMENT OF SALVADOR ALLENDE ON 11 SEPTEMBER 1973.) ACCORDING TO OFFICIAL ARGENTINE GOVERNMENT CIRCLES CONSIDER THE ASSASSINATION OF GENERAL CARLOS PRATS TO BE THE WORK OF CHILEANS. SAID THAT THIS OPINION WAS BASED ON THE FACT THAT THE BOMB USED IN THE ASSASSINATION WAS CONSIDERABLY LARGER THAN THOSE ORDINARILY USED IN ARGENTINA AND

SECRET
(classification) (dissem controls)

2974-393 - 2

APPROVED FOR RELEASE
DATE JUN 11 1999

(163)

PAGE 2 of 3 PAGES

SECRET (classification) (dissem controls)

ON THE FACT THAT THE ASSASSINATION WAS NOT CARRIED OUT IN THE MANNER IN WHICH SUCH TERRORIST ACTS ARE USUALLY EXECUTED BY ARGENTINE GROUPS. IN ADDITION, NO GROUP HAS TAKEN CREDIT FOR THE ASSASSINATION, WHICH IS UNLIKE ARGENTINE EXTREMIST ORGANIZATIONS, AND PRATS HAD NO IMPORTANCE ON THE ARGENTINE POLITICAL SCENE. COMMENT: THERE WAS NO CONSENSUS AMONG OFFICIAL ARGENTINE GOVERNMENT CIRCLES REGARDING WHETHER THE ASSASSINATION WAS THE WORK OF A CHILEAN LEFT-WING OR RIGHT-WING GROUP.)

3.

1.5 (c)

4. HE HAD SEEN GENERAL PRATS IN LATE SEPTEMBER AND THAT PRATS HAD TOLD HIM THAT HE HAD RECEIVED A PHONE CALL FROM A CHILEAN ATTEMPTING TO ASSUME AN ARGENTINE ACCENT. THE CALLER WARNED PRATS THAT A TEAM WAS PREPARING TO ASSASSINATE HIM, THE CALLER ADDING THAT HE OPPOSED THE ASSASSINATION. ACCORDING TO PRATS, THE CALLER SUGGESTED THAT PRATS HOLD A PRESS CONFERENCE TO ANNOUNCE THIS THREAT, EXPLAINING THAT THE ANNOUNCEMENT WOULD LIKELY CAUSE THE TEAM TO CANCEL THE ASSASSINATION ATTEMPT. THE CALLER ALSO SUGGESTED THAT PRATS SHOULD CARRY OUT HIS PLANNED TRIP TO BRAZIL. PRATS TOLD THAT HE HAD NOT CONTEMPLATED SUCH

SECRET (classification) (dissem controls)

PAGE 3 OF 3 PAGES

SECRET (classification) (dissem controls)

A TRIP BUT THAT HE HAD USED ALLEGED TRAVEL TO BRAZIL AS A PRETEXT WITH CHILEAN CONSUL GENERAL ALVARO D R O G U E T T TO OBTAIN A PASSPORT. 1.5 (C)

5.

INSISTS THAT PRATS WAS NOT POLITICALLY ACTIVE IN BUENOS AIRES. HOWEVER, PRATS HAD NEARLY COMPLETED HIS MEMOIRS WHICH STRONGLY CONDEMNED MANY NON-POPULAR UNITY POLITICIANS AND MILITARY OFFICERS. AFTER PRATS' ASSASSINATION, HIS DAUGHTER TOOK THE MANUSCRIPT OF THE MEMOIRS BACK TO SANTIAGO. 1.5 (C)

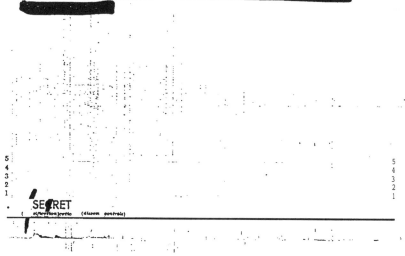

6.

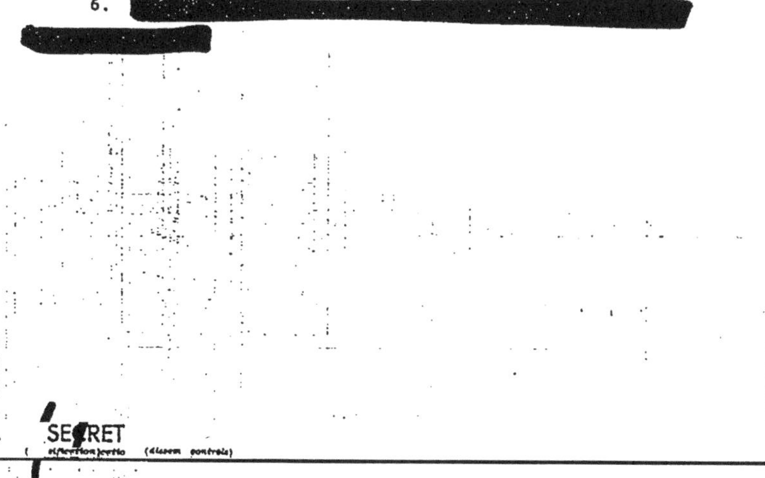

SECRET (classification) (dissem controls)

DOCUMENT 5. U.S. Embassy, **SECRET** Cable, "Analysis of Deaths and Disappearances of Chilean Extremists," August 8, 1975 (page 1).

EXCISE

E1205

PAGE 01 SANTIA 05483 01 OF 02 082108Z

63
ACTION ARA-04

INFO OCT-01 SS-14 ISO-00 NSC-05 NSCE-00 PM-01 INR-05
CIAE-00 IO-03 L-01 SY-02 SCCT-01 PRS-01 DHA-02 ORM-01
OMB-01 /042 W
--------------------- 004583

R 082005Z AUG 75
FM AMEMBASSY SANTIAGO
TO SECSTATE WASHDC 4305
AMEMBASSY BUENOS AIRES
AMCONSUL SAO PAULO
AMEMBASSY BRASILIA
USMISSION USUN
USCINCSO
DIA

Chile Project (#S199900006)
U.S. Department of State
__ Release ✓ Excise __ Deny __ Declass
Exemption(s) B1, B3

SECTION 1 OF 2 SANTIAGO 5483

LIMDIS

NOFORN

Dept of State, RPS/IPS, Margaret P. Grafeld, Dir.
( ) Classify as (✓) Extend as (S) Downgrade to
Date 1/23/01 Declassify on ____ Reason 25X1

EO 11652: XGDS-2
TAGS: CI, PINS, SHUM
SUBJECT: ANALYSIS OF DEATHS AND DISAPPEARANCES OF CHILEAN EXTREMISTS

REFS: (A) STATE 183642 (B) STATE 184296

1. SUMMARY: WE CONCLUDE THAT REPORTS DESCRIBING DEATHS OR DISAPPEARANCES OF 119 CHILEAN EXTREMISTS OUTSIDE OF CHILE ARE PROBABLY UNTRUE, THOUGH MOST OR ALL CONCERNED ARE PROBABLY DEAD. MOST PLAUSIBLE EXPLANATION WE CAN PIECE TOGETHER FOR WHAT WILL PROBABLY REMAIN SOMETHING OF A MYSTERY IS THAT GOC SECURITY FORCES ACTED DIRECTLY OR THROUGH THIRD PARTY, PLANTED REPORTS IN OBSCURE PUBLICATIONS TO PROVIDE SOME MEANS OF ACCOUNTING FOR DISAPPEARANCE OF NUMEROUS VIOLENT LEFTISTS. GOC SECURITY FORCES MAY HAVE

PAGE 02 SANTIA 05483 01 OF 02 082108Z

KILLED SOME OR ALL OF THEM. END SUMMARY.

UNCLASSIFIED SECRET

ate Printed: 01/17/1999 DOC_NUMBER: 1975SANTIA05483 CHANNEL: n/a
Page - 1

9862.

DOCUMENT 6. CIA, **SECRET** Intelligence Report [Assassination Efforts Against Chilean Political Exiles in Europe], August 20, 1974 (pages 1, 2).

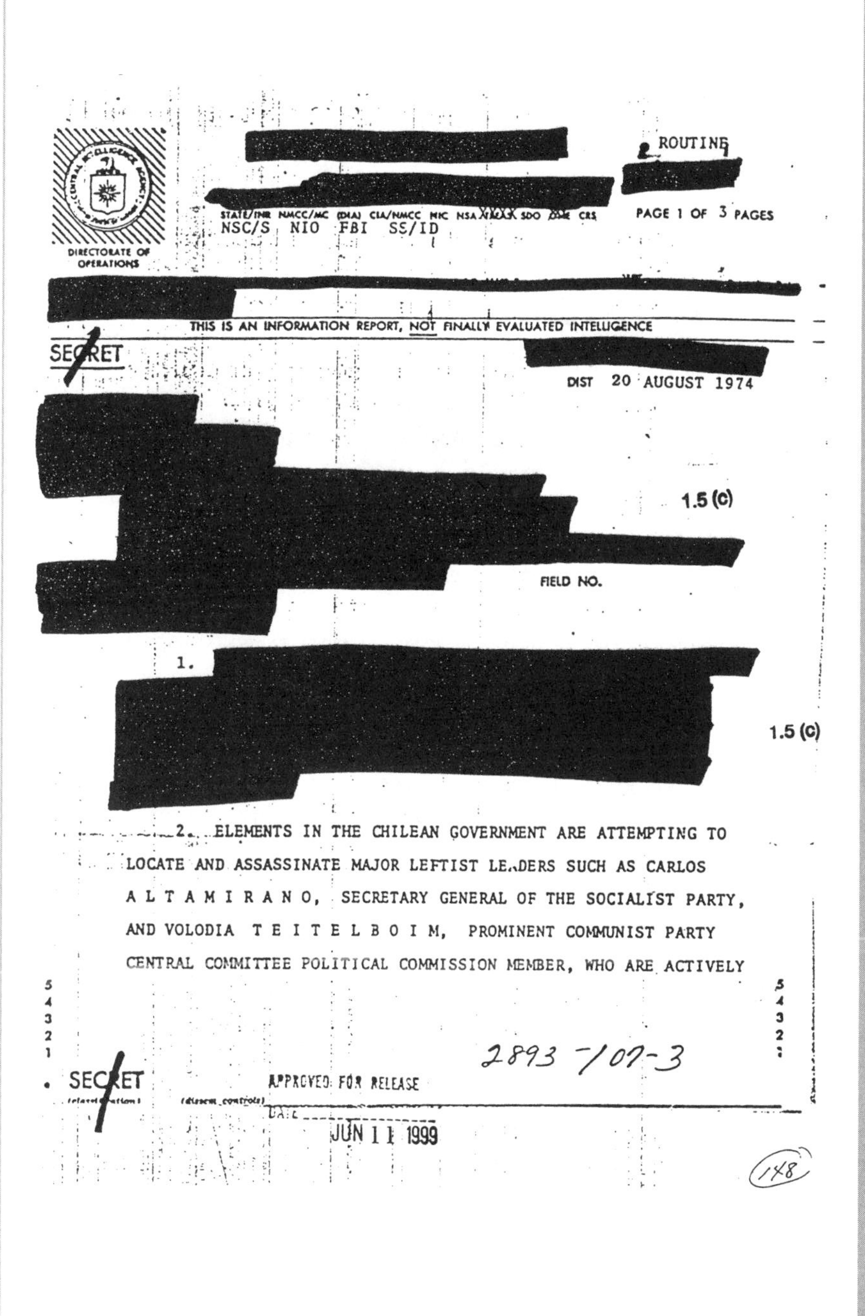

ROUTINE

STATE/INR NMCC/MC (DIA) CIA/NMCC NIC NSA SDO CRS
NSC/S NIO FBI SS/ID

PAGE 1 OF 3 PAGES

DIRECTORATE OF OPERATIONS

THIS IS AN INFORMATION REPORT, NOT FINALLY EVALUATED INTELLIGENCE

SECRET

DIST 20 AUGUST 1974

1.5 (c)

FIELD NO.

1\.

1.5 (c)

2\. ELEMENTS IN THE CHILEAN GOVERNMENT ARE ATTEMPTING TO LOCATE AND ASSASSINATE MAJOR LEFTIST LEADERS SUCH AS CARLOS A L T A M I R A N O, SECRETARY GENERAL OF THE SOCIALIST PARTY, AND VOLODIA T E I T E L B O I M, PROMINENT COMMUNIST PARTY CENTRAL COMMITTEE POLITICAL COMMISSION MEMBER, WHO ARE ACTIVELY

2893 / 07-3

SECRET

APPROVED FOR RELEASE
DATE JUN 11 1999

148

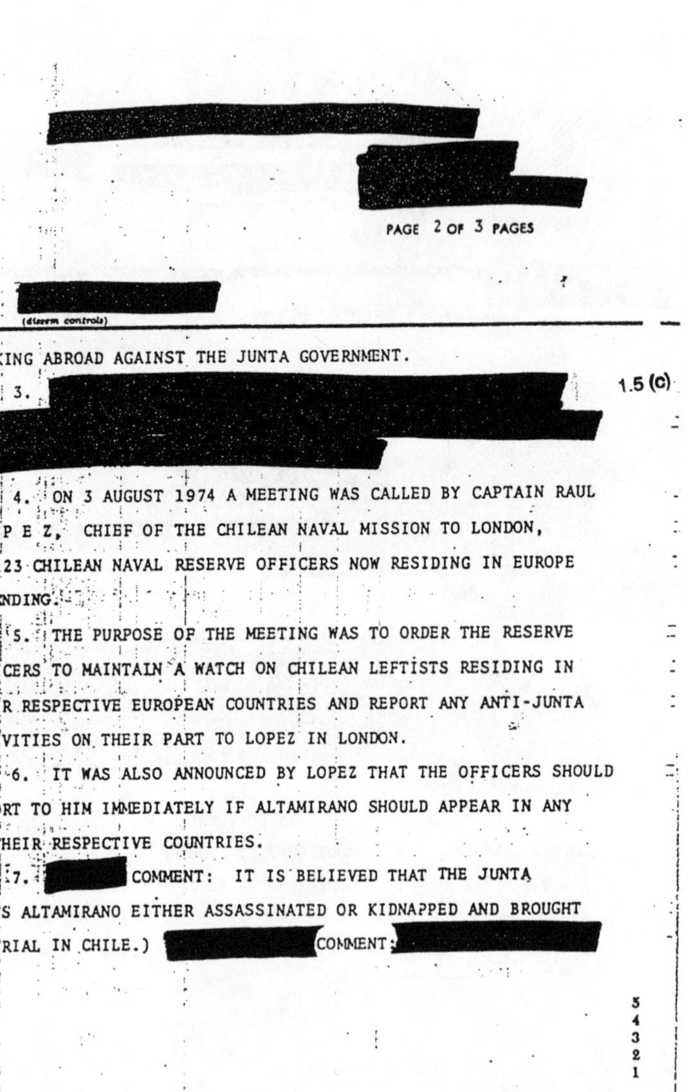

PAGE 2 OF 3 PAGES

SECRET (classification) (dissem controls)

WORKING ABROAD AGAINST THE JUNTA GOVERNMENT.

3. [redacted] 1.5 (c)

4. ON 3 AUGUST 1974 A MEETING WAS CALLED BY CAPTAIN RAUL L O P E Z, CHIEF OF THE CHILEAN NAVAL MISSION TO LONDON, WITH 23 CHILEAN NAVAL RESERVE OFFICERS NOW RESIDING IN EUROPE ATTENDING.

5. THE PURPOSE OF THE MEETING WAS TO ORDER THE RESERVE OFFICERS TO MAINTAIN A WATCH ON CHILEAN LEFTISTS RESIDING IN THEIR RESPECTIVE EUROPEAN COUNTRIES AND REPORT ANY ANTI-JUNTA ACTIVITIES ON THEIR PART TO LOPEZ IN LONDON.

6. IT WAS ALSO ANNOUNCED BY LOPEZ THAT THE OFFICERS SHOULD REPORT TO HIM IMMEDIATELY IF ALTAMIRANO SHOULD APPEAR IN ANY OF THEIR RESPECTIVE COUNTRIES.

7. [redacted] COMMENT: IT IS BELIEVED THAT THE JUNTA WANTS ALTAMIRANO EITHER ASSASSINATED OR KIDNAPPED AND BROUGHT TO TRIAL IN CHILE.) [redacted] COMMENT: [redacted]

SECRET (classification) (dissem controls)

DOCUMENT 7. FBI, Interrogation Report, "Attempted Assassination of Bernardo Leighton, October 6, 1975, Rome, Italy," April 9, 1980 (page 1).

UNITED STATES DEPARTMENT OF JUSTICE

FEDERAL BUREAU OF INVESTIGATION

In Reply, Please Refer to File No.

Washington, D.C. 20535
April 9, 1980

SECRET

DECLASSIFIED BY SP5JC/JBL ON 2-2-99 #99-107

ATTEMPTED ASSASSINATION OF
BERNARDO LEIGHTON,
OCTOBER 6, 1975, ROME, ITALY

On April 17, 1978, Michael Vernon Townley, self admitted officer for the National Directorate of Intelligence (DINA), advised Special Agents (SAs) of the Federal Bureau of Investigation (FBI) that during the late summer and early fall of 1975, he, his wife, Mariana Callejas Townley, and Virgilio Pablo Paz Romero, member of the anti-Castro Cuban exile terrorist organization, the Cuban Nationalist Movement (CNM), traveled extensively throughout Europe. Townley advised that he, Paz, and his wife visited Rome, Italy, during the early fall of 1975 and were in contact with various members of an Italian fascist organization. Townley advised that members of this Italian fascist organization indicated that former Chilean Vice President Bernardo Leighton had been identified as a dangerous catalyst that would be the basis of the formation of a coalition between the Christian Democratic Party (PCD) and the Socialist Party (PS) in Italy during the forthcoming elections. Townley advised that members of the Italian fascist organization advised that Leighton was accepted as a prominent spokesman for the PCD in Italy, and that Leighton had excellent contacts among members of the PS in Italy. Townley identified one of the principal members of the Italian fascist organization as Alfredo Di Stefano, who was also known by the nickname Topogigio (The Doll). Townley advised that after visiting Italy, he and his wife returned to Chile, while Paz returned to the United States in order to renew his activities with the CNM. (S) (U)

Virgilio Pablo Paz Romero, supra, is a Federal fugitive being sought by the FBI for his participation in the September 21, 1976, assassination of former Chilean Ambassador Orlando Letelier and his assistant, Ronnie Moffitt, in Washington, D.C.

SECRET
Classified and Extended by 7679
Reason for Extension FCIM, II, 1-2.4.2 (2)
Date of Review for Declassification April 9, 2000

ALL INFORMATION CONTAINED
HEREIN IS UNCLASSIFIED EXCEPT
WHERE SHOWN OTHERWISE

2-2-99 CLASSIFIED BY: SP5JC/JBL
REASON: 1.5 (C)
DECL: X1

109-12-233-1556X #99-107

ENCLOSURE

FBI/DOJ

0005067

DOCUMENT 8. FBI, Robert Scherrer letter to General Baeza, June 6, 1975 (with translation).

EMBASSY OF THE
UNITED STATES OF AMERICA
Buenos Aires, Argentina

Oficina del Agregado de Asuntos
Legales
6 de junio de 1975

MI CARTA #3

General Ernesto Baeza Michaelsen
Director General de Investigaciones
Dirección General de Investigaciones
Santiago de Chile

Atención: Inspector Jaime Vázquez Alcaíno

Asunto: Jorge Isaac Fuentes (a) Auriel Nodarse Ledesma

De mi mayor consideración:

Me he enterado que el sujeto citado es ciudadano Chileno y miembro de la MIR. El fué detenido el día 17 de mayo de 1975 en Asunción, Paraguay luego de entrar al país ilegalmente de Argentina portando un pasaporte Costarricense, número 142302/74 bajo la identidad de Auriel Nodarse Ledesma. El sujeto fué acompañado por Amilcar Santucho, hermano del máximo líder del ERP, Mario Roberto Santucho.

Según información suministrada por el sujeto durante various interrogatorios por parte de la policía de la capital en Asunción, él admitió que es miembro de la Junta Coordinadora y estuvo actuando como correo para dicha agrupación.

En su libro de direcciones, el sujeto tenía las siguientes anotaciones de individuos y direcciones en los EE.UU.:

-2-

1. Margaret Sun
   c/o Maria Brandao
   440 West End Avenue
   Apartment 16-E
   New York, New York 10024

2. Sonia Bacicalupe
   8024 Rothington Road
   Apartment #1071
   Dallas, Texas 75227

3. Calle Padre Colón #256
   Río Piedras, Puerto Rico

Se informó que Bacicalupe es la hermana del sujeto. El FBI inició una investigación en los Estados Unidos concerniente a las personas y direcciones mencionadas arriba. Le informaré los resultados de la misma tan pronto los tenga en mi poder.

Aprovecho esta ocasión para saludarle muy atentamente,

Robert W. Scherrer
Agregado de Asuntos
Legales

[Seal of the United States of America]

EMBASSY OF THE UNITED
STATES OF AMERICA Buenos
Aires, Argentina

Office of the Attache of Legal Affairs
June 6, 1975

MY LETTER #3

General Ernesto Baeza Michaelsen Director-General of Investigations General Office of Investigations
Santiago, Chile

Attention: Inspector Jaime Vazquez Alcaino

Regarding: Jorge Isaac Fuentes (a)
Auriel Nodarse Ledesma

With great consideration:

I have discovered that the aforementioned subject is a citizen of Chile and a member of the MIR. He was detained on May 17, 1975 in Asuncion, Paraguay after entering the country illegally from Argentina carrying a Costa Rican passport, number 1423021/74 under the identity of Auriel Nodarse Ledesma. The subject was accompanied by Amilcar Santucho, brother of the chief leader of the ERP, Mario Roberto Santucho.

According to the information supplied by the subject during various interrogations by the capital police in Asuncion, he admitted that he is a member of the Coordinating Junta and was acting as a courier for said group.

In his address book, the subject had the following listings of individuals and addresses in the USA:

1. Margaret Sun

   c/o Maria Brandao 440
   West End Avenue
   Apartment 16-E
   New York, New York 10024

2. Sonia Bacicalupe 8024
   Rothington Road
   Apartment #1071 Dallas,
   Texas 75227

3. Calle Padre Colón #256 Río
   Piedras, Puerto Rico

Apparently Bacicalupe is the subject's sister. The FBI initiated an investigation in the United States concerning the aforementioned people and addresses. I will inform you of the results of the investigation as soon as I have them in-hand.

I take advantage of this occasion to send you my sincere greetings,

[signature]

Robert W. Scherrer
Attaché of Legal Affairs

DOCUMENT 9. U.S. Embassy, Cable, "Assassination of Orlando Letelier," September 21, 1976.

3

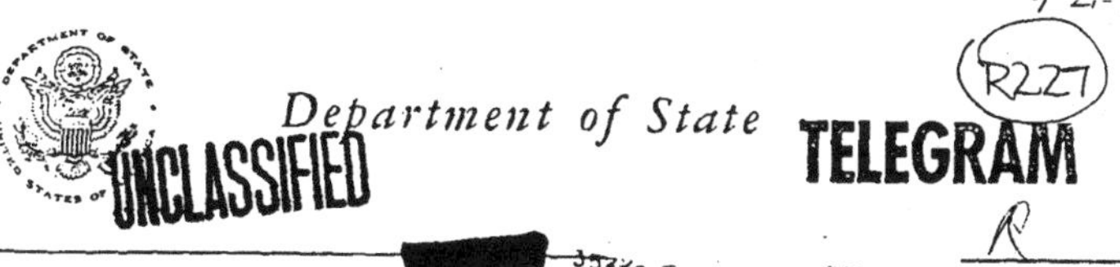

PAGE 01 SANTIA 09212 212038Z

70
ACTION ARA-10

INFO OCT-01 ISO-00 ARAE-00 DHA-02 MCT-01 CIAE-00 DODE-00
PM-04 H-02 INR-07 L-03 NSAE-00 NSC-05 PA-01 PRS-01
SP-02 SS-15 NSCE-00 SSO-00 USIE-00 INRE-00 SY-05 IO-13
USSS-00 /072 W

------------------ 124639

O 211958Z SEP 76
FM AMEMBASSY SANTIAGO
TO SECSTATE WASHDC IMMEDIATE 1467

Chile Project (#S199900030)
U.S. Department of State
Release X Excise ___ Deny ___
Declassify: In Part ___ In Full X
Exemption(s) ___

[redacted] SANTIAGO 9212

EO 11652: XGDS-3
TAGS: PINR, PINS, PINT, CI
SUBJECT: ASSASSINATION OF ORLANDO LETELIER

REF: LUERS-POPPER TELCON, SEPTEMBER 21

1. I APPRECIATE PROMPT ADVICE TO US CONCERNING BOMBING OF EX-GOC FONMIN LETELIER AND HIS TWO COMPANIONS. DETAILS ARE FILTERING IN FROM WASHINGTON, INCLUDING SENATOR ABOUREZK'S STATEMENT ATTRIBUTING RESPONSIBILITY TO "CHILEAN TYRANNY". AS OF 1500 HOURS LOCAL, GOC HAS MAINTAINED PUBLIC SILENCE.

2. DEPARTMENT WILL BE BETTER ABLE THAN WE ARE TO ESTIMATE THE EXTENT OF THE ADVERSE EFFECT OF THIS OUTRAGE ON THE JUNTA'S POSITION IN THE UNITED STATES. WE ARE SURE THERE WILL BE A VERBAL OUTBURST, AND NOTE THAT THE ASSASSINATION COULD NOT HAVE BEEN BETTER TIMED TO ATTRACT THE ATTENTION OF THE UNITED NATIONS GENERAL ASEMBLY NOW CONVENING IN NEW YORK. WE WOULD GUESS THAT THE GOC WOULD HASTEN TO DENY ALL RESPONSIBILITY. IT MAY WELL SUGGEST THE AFFAIR IS A LEFTIST PROVOCATION DESIGNED TO HURT THE GOC. THIS IS NOT INCONCEIVABLE, BUT IS UNLIKELY TO BE WIDELY ACCEPTED IN THE ABSENCE OF ANY CONFIRMING EVIDENCE.

Department of State TELEGRAM

UNCLASSIFIED

PAGE 02 SANTIA 09212 212038Z

3. WE RECALL TWO PREVIOUS INSTANCES IN WHICH JUNTA OPPONENTS WERE MYSTERIOUSLY ATTACKED: THE CASE OF GENERAL CARLOS PRATS, KILLED IN BUENOS AIRES IN SEPTEMBER 1974, AND THE CASE OF BERNARDO LEIGHTON, SERIOUSLY WOUNDED IN ROME IN OCTOBER 1975. IN BOTH CASES, TO OUR KNOWLEDGE, INVESTIGATION AS TO THE PERPETRATORS PROVED FRUITLESS. THE ATTACK ON GENERAL ALFREDO CANALES, THE JUNTA'S AMBASSADOR IN BEIRUT IN JULY 1974 HAS REMAINED EQUALLY MYSTERIOUS.

4. BASED ON OBVIOUS MOTIVIATION, SUSPICION WILL FALL FIRST OF ALL ON THE GOC DIRECTORATE OF NATIONAL INTELLIGENCE (DINA). LETELIER WAS A FIRST-RANK POLITICAL FOE OF THE JUNTA. HE WAS POLITICALLY ACTIVE IN EXILE. SILENCING HIM WILL TEND TO INHIBIT SOME OTHER EXILES FROM SPEAKING, WRITING OR PLOTTING AGAINST THE JUNTA.

5. BUT WE HAVE NEVER HAD ANY INDICATION THAT DINA WAS IN ANY WAY OPERATIONAL IN U.S. TERRITORY, AND IT IS DIFFICULT FOR US TO BELIEVE THAT EVEN ITS RATHER FANATICAL LEADERS WOULD EXPOSE THEMSELVES TO THE CONSEQUENCES OF BEING IMPLICATED IN A TERRORIST ACT IN WASHINGTON. FURTHER, IF DINA HAD BEEN PLANNING TO KILL LETELIER AND IF PRESIDENT PINOCHET KNEW OF SUCH PLANS, IT SEEMS TO US UNLIKELY THAT THE CHILEANS WOULD HAVE PROMULGATED SO SHORTLY BEFORE THE CRIME THE DECREE DEPRIVING LETELIER OF HIS CHILEAN CITIZENSHIP.

6. ANOTHER POSSIBILITY IS THAT DINA OR OTHER GOC SOURCES COULD HAVE STIMULATED ACTION BY SOME RIGHTIST GROUP LOCATED OUTSIDE CHILE. WE HAVE IN MIND POSSIBLE COOPERATION BY SOUTHERN CONE GOVERNMENT SECURITY AUTHORITIES TO ELIMINATE ENEMIES ABROAD. WE HOPE OUR INTELLIGENCE EFFORTS IN OTHER CAPITALS WILL FOLLOW UP ON ANY INDICATIONS THAT SOUTHERN CONE GOVERNMENT INTELLIGENCE AGENCIES ARE ORGANIZING FOR TERRORISM OUTSIDE THE REGION.

7. HERE IN THE EMBASSY WE ARE CONFINING OURSELVES TO REFERRING ALL INQUIRIES TO USG SPOKESMEN IN WASHINGTON. WE WILL BEEF UP OUR LOCAL SECURITY PRECAUTIONS AGAINST THE POSSIBILITY THAT AN ACTION-REACTION SYNDROME COULD TEMPORARILY MAKE US A TARGET FOR CHILEAN RESPONSE TO EMOTIONAL STATEMENTS FROM THE U.S.

POPPER

UNCLASSIFIED

DOCUMENT 10. Defense Intelligence Agency, **SECRET** Intelligence Assessment, "Letelier Assassination Aftermath," September 28, 1976.

UNCLASSIFIED

DEPARTMENT OF DEFENSE

JOINT CHIEFS OF STAFF

MESSAGE CENTER

VZCZCMLT9435CP490 ~~SECRET~~

MULT 2591

~~ACTION~~

ACTION

DIA(210)

DISTR

JCS:MC OPR IADB(01) USRMCLO(01) CJCS(04) DJS(03) SJCS(01) J3(14

J4(08) J5(07) SAGA(04) NMCC(03) JRC(01) SECDEF(10) WSEG(01)

ARPA(06) ASD:IL(03) ASD:M&RA(01) ASD:ISA(10) ATSD:AE(01) ASD:PA

ASD:PA(03) ASD:I(01) DDRE(02) STATEOP NSA(01) NSC(01) PACS FILE

(301)

( )

TRANSIT/281738Z/281742Z/000104ORP0389

DE RUEKJCS #3982 2721742

ZNY SSSSS

RUHGIIW T COMCARGRU SEVEN

P 281738Z SEP 76 ZEX

FM DIA WASH DC

TO RUCRDIB/DIACURINTEL

AIG 7011

BT

~~SECRET~~ [redacted] 2591

FROM DN-1B

SUBJ: DIA DEFENSE INTELLIGENCE NOTICE (DIN) (U)

DIADIN 272-7A (AS OF: 0900 EDT 28 SEP 76)

CHILE: LETELIER ASSASSINATION AFTERMATH. (U)

1. [redacted] THE SEPTEMBER BOMBING DEATH OF ALLENDE CABINET MEMBER AND FORMER AMBASSADOR TO THE US, ORLANDO LETELIER, PROVOKED IMMEDIATE REACTION FROM MODERATE AND LEFTIST MEDIA IN WESTERN NATIONS. SANTIAGO HAD TAKEN AWAY THE FORMER AMBASSADOR'S CITIZENSHIP ON 17 SEPTEMBER AND WAS KNOWN TO BE MAKING INQUIRIES INTO THE NATURE OF HIS ACTIVITIES AND THOSE OF HIS INTEREST GROUP. AS AN OUTSPOKEN CRITIC OF THE PINOCHET REGIME, LETELIER ADDED HIS VOICE TO THE CHORUS OF DISSENTERS ABOUT THE CONDUCT OF THE ADMINISTRATION IN CHILE SINCE THE ALLENDE ERA WAS ABRUPTLY TERMINATED THREE YEARS AGO.

2. [redacted] IT IS DIFFICULT TO PIN

PAGE 1 ~~SECRET~~ 00000001

UNCLASSIFIED

Declassified with redactions by DIA

UNCLASSIFIED DEPARTMENT OF DEFENSE
JOINT CHIEFS OF STAFF
MESSAGE CENTER

PAGE 2 ~~SECRET~~ 2591
THE BLAME ON SANTIAGO AT THIS POINT FOR SEVERAL REASONS.
THE REACH OF THE CHILEAN DIRECTORATE OF NATIONAL INTELLIGENCE
(DINA) -- CITED AS RESPONSIBLE -- ALMOST CERTAINLY DOES NOT
(80 PERCENT) EXTEND TO THE US. CHILEAN IMAGE-BUILDING RECEIVED
A SEVERE SETBACK BY THE KILLING, SOMETHING THAT PLANNERS OF THE
ATTEMPT WOULD HAVE FOREKNOWN AND CONSIDERED. MOREOVER, THE
EVENT OCCURRED, AS HAD TWO PREVIOUS ATTEMPTS, DURING THE
CONVENING OF THE UNGA IN NEW YORK -- POOR TIMING FOR A CHILEAN
ATTEMPT.

3. [redacted] CHILE WILL ATTEMPT TO RIDE OUT THE STORM
OF PROTEST, BUT ITS POSITION IN THE UN HAS LIKELY BEEN
DAMAGED. THE INCIDENT MAY NEVER BE FULLY EXPLAINED, OR
THE CULPRITS IDENTIFIED, TO THE SATISFACTION OF CHILE'S
CRITICS.

PREPARED BY: [redacted]
(XGDS-2 DECLASSIFY UPON NOTIFICATION BY THE ORIGINATOR)
BT
#3982
ANNOTES
TJ

PAGE 2 ~~SECRET~~ 00000001

NNNN
281742Z

UNCLASSIFIED

DOCUMENT 11. FBI, Intelligence Report from Attache Robert Scherrer [Letelier-Moffitt Assassination and Operation Condor], September 28, 1976.

APPENDIX 6

CLASSIFIED AND EXTENDED BY
REASON FOR EXTENSION
FCIM, II, 1-2.4.2
DATE OF REVIEW FOR DECLASSIFICATION 9/28/96

P 281830 SEP 76

FM BUENOS AIRES (109-2)(109-9)

TO DIRECTOR (109-12-201)(109-12-207) PRIORITY 204-28

BRASILIA PRIORITY 026-28

MADRID PRIORITY 007-28

PARIS PRIORITY 001-28

BT

SECRET

CHILBOM

CONDOR

FOREIGN POLITICAL MATTERS - ARGENTINA; IS - ARGENTINA;

FOREIGN POLITICAL MATTERS - CHILE; IS - CHILE.

ON SEPTEMBER 28, 1976, A CONFIDENTIAL SOURCE ABROAD [redacted] PROVIDED THE FOLLOWING INFORMATION: U

"OPERATION CONDOR" IS THE CODE NAME FOR THE COLLECTION, EXCHANGE AND STORAGE OF INTELLIGENCE DATA CONCERNING SOCALLED "LEFTISTS," COMMUNISTS AND MARXISTS, WHICH WAS RECENTLY ESTABLISHED BETWEEN COOPERATING INTELLIGENCE SERVICES IN SOUTH AMERICA IN ORDER TO ELIMINATE MARXIST TERRORIST ACTIVITIES IN THE AREA. IN ADDITION, "OPERATION CONDOR" PROVIDES FOR JOINT OPERATIONS AGAINST TERRORIST

105-307319-9

REC 90

OCT 20 1976

185-789

NOT RECORDED

APR 17 1980

UNRECORDED COPY FILED IN

SECRET

-175-

PAGE TWO BUE 109-2 109-9 SECRET

TARGETS IN MEMBER COUNTRIES OF "OPERATION CONDOR." CHILE IS THE CENTER FOR "OPERATION CONDOR" AND IN ADDITION TO CHILE ITS MEMBERS INCLUDE ARGENTINA, BOLIVIA, PARAGUAY, AND URUGUAY. BRAZIL ALSO HAS TENTATIVELY AGREED TO SUPPLY INTELLIGENCE INPUT FOR "OPERATION CONDOR." MEMBERS OF "OPERATION CONDOR" SHOWING THE MOST ENTHUSIASM TO DATE HAVE BEEN ARGENTINA, URUGUAY AND CHILE. THE LATTER THREE COUNTRIES HAVE ENGAGED IN JOINT OPERATIONS, PRIMARILY IN ARGENTINA, AGAINST THE TERRORIST TARGET. DURING THE WEEK OF SEPTEMBER 20, 1976, THE [redacted] WITH RESPECT TO "OPERATION CONDOR." 4

b1

5 A THIRD AND MOST SECRET PHASE OF "OPERATION CONDOR" INVOLVES THE FORMATION OF SPECIAL TEAMS FROM MEMBER COUNTRIES WHO ARE TO TRAVEL ANYWHERE IN THE WORLD TO NON-MEMBER COUNTRIES TO CARRY OUT SANCTIONS UP TO ASSASSINATION AGAINST TERRORISTS OR SUPPORTERS OF TERRORIST ORGANIZATIONS FROM "OPERATION CONDOR" MEMBER COUNTRIES. FOR EXAMPLE, SHOULD A TERRORIST OR A SUPPORTER OF A TERRORIST ORGANIZATION FROM A MEMBER COUNTRY OF "OPERATION CONDOR" BE LOCATED IN A EUROPEAN COUNTRY, A SPECIAL TEAM FROM "OPERATION CONDOR"

SECRET

THREE BUE 109-2 109-9 SECRET

ULD BE DISPATCHED TO LOCATE AND SURVEIL THE TARGET. WHEN THE ICATION AND SURVEILLANCE OPERATION HAS TERMINATED, A SECOND IAM FROM "OPERATION CONDOR" WOULD BE DISPATCHED TO CARRY OUT E ACTUAL SANCTION AGAINST THE TARGET. SPECIAL TEAMS WOULD BE SUED FALSE DOCUMENTATION FROM MEMBER COUNTRIES OF "OPERATION IDOR" AND MAY BE COMPOSED EXCLUSIVELY OF INDIVIDUALS FROM ONE MBER NATION OF "OPERATION CONDOR" OR MAY BE COMPOSED A MIXED GROUP FROM VARIOUS "OPERATION CONDOR" MEMBER NATIONS. O EUROPEAN COUNTRIES, SPECIFICALLY MENTIONED FOR POSSIBLE ERATIONS UNDER THE THIRD PHASE OF "OPERATION CONDOR" WERE ANCE AND PORTUGAL. U

A SPECIAL TEAM HAS BEEN ORGANIZED [redacted] b1

[redacted] WHICH ARE BEING EPARED FOR POSSIBLE FUTURE ACTION UNDER THE THIRD PHASE OF OPERATION CONDOR." U

~~CLASSIFIED BY 5951 XGDS-2 INDEFINITE.~~

[redacted] b1 S

SECRET

AGE FOUR BUE 109-2 109-9 SECRET

COORDINATED LOCALLY. U

IT SHOULD BE NOTED THAT NO INFORMATION HAS BEEN DEVELOPED NDICATING THAT SANCTIONS UNDER THE THIRD PHASE OF "OPERATION ONDOR" HAVE BEEN PLANNED TO BE CARRIED OUT IN THE UNITED ATES; HOWEVER, IT IS NOT BEYOND THE REALM OF POSSIBILITY THAT HE RECENT ASSASSINATION OF ORLANDO LETELIER IN WASHINGTON, C. MAY HAVE BEEN CARRIED OUT AS A THIRD PHASE ACTION OF "OPERATION CONDOR." AS NOTED ABOVE, INFORMATION AVAILABLE) THE SOURCE INDICATES THAT PARTICULAR EMPHASIS WAS PLACED ON HE THIRD PHASE ACTIONS OF "OPERATION CONDOR" IN EUROPE, SPECIFICALLY ANCE AND PORTUGAL. THIS OFFICE WILL REMAIN ALERT FOR ANY FORMATION INDICATING THAT THE ASSASSINATION OF LETELIER MAY BE RT OF "OPERATION CONDOR" ACTION. U

SECRET

DOCUMENT 12. Department of State, Action Cable, "Possible International Implications of Violent Deaths of Political Figures Abroad," June 4, 1976.

OO RUESBA
DE RUEHC 7156 1560024 976 JUN 4 AM 8 13 [redacted] R
ZNY SSSSS ZZH
O 042212Z JUN 76
FM SECSTATE WASHDC

IMMEDIATE ACTION DD015

TO RUESBA/AMEMBASSY BUENOS AIRES IMMEDIATE 3104
RUESDO/AMEMBASSY MONTEVIDEO IMMEDIATE 3250
RUESAS/AMEMBASSY ASUNCION IRXEDIATE 2586
RUEHLD/AMEMBASSY SANTIAGO IMMEDIATE 4808
RUESUZ/AMEMBASSY BRASILIA IMMEDIATE 0707
RUESLZ/AMEMBASSY LA PAZ IMMEDIATE 8917
BT

TO	ACT	INF	TO
AMB		✓	DAO
DCM		✓	L. GATT
			DEA
POL	3		FAS
ECOM		✓	AID
POL/R		✓	MILGP
CO S			PER
ADM			GSO
USIS		✓	B & F
SCI			CHRON
BY			HF

[redacted] STATE 137156

UNCLASSIFIED

E.O. 11652: GDS

TAGS: AR, UY, PA, CI, BR, BL, PFOR

SUBJECT: POSSIBLE INTERNATICONAL IMPLICATIONS OF VIOLENT DEATHS OF POLITICAL FIGURES ABROAD

ACTION COPY

1. THE RECENT SHARP INCREASE IN THE NUMBER OF ASSASSINATIONS OF FOREIGN POLITICAL FIGURES IN EXILE OR POLITICAL ASYLUM IN OR FROM YOUR COUNTRIES IS OF CONCERN TO THE DEPARTMENT. WE WOULD APPRECIATE YOUR ASSESSMENT OF THE POSSIBLE IMPLICATIONS OF THIS PHENOMENON.

2. YOUR COMMENTS ON THE FOLLOWING POINTS ARE REQUESTED:

A) DO YOU BELIEVE THAT THE DEATHS OF POLITICAL REFUGEES OR ASYLEES FROM YOUR COUNTRY ABROAD COULD HAVE BEEN ARRANGED BY YOUR HOST GOVERNMENT THROUGH INSTIUTIONAL TIES TO GROUPS, GOVERNMENTAL OR OTHER, IN THE COUNTRY WHERE DEATHS TOOK PLACE?

B) DO YOU BELIEVE THAT DEATHS OF FOREIGN POLITICAL REFUGEES OR ASYLEES IN YOUR COUNTRY COULD HAVE BEEN CARRIED OUT AT THE BEHEST OF THE HOME GOVERNMENT OF THE VICTIMS BY THE HOST GOVERNMENT OR BY OTHERS WITH HOST GOVERNMENT ACQUIESCENCE?

C) DO YOU HAVE EVIDENCE TO SUPPORT OR DENY ALLEGATIONS OF INTERNATIONAL ARRANGEMENTS AMONG GOVERNMENTS TO CARRY OUT SUCH ASSASINATIONS OR EXECUTIONS?

D) DO YOU HAVE ANY EVIDENCE OF ARRANGEMENTS AMONG THE GOVERNMENTS OF THE AREA TO RETURN POLITICAL ASYLEES AGAINST THEIR WILL TO THEIR COUNTRIES OF ORIGIN?

3. YOUR ANSWERS TO THE ABOVE AND ANY COMMENTS OR INSIGHTS YOU MAY HAVE ON THIS PROBLEM SHOULD BE SENT SO AS TO ARRIVE IN THE DEPARTMENT BY COB, MONDAY, JUNE 7. KISSINGER
BT
7156

ARGENTINA PROJECT (S200000044)
U.S. DEPT. OF STATE, A/RPS/IPS
Margaret P. Grafeld, Director
(X) Release ( ) Excise ( ) Deny
Exemption(s):
Declassify: ( ) In Part (X) In Full
( ) Classify as __ ( ) Extend as __ ( ) Downgrade to __
Date ___ Declassify on ___ Reason

UNCLASSIFIED

80F178
22/185

DOCUMENT 13. Department of State, **SECRET** Minutes, "ARA-CIA Weekly Meeting—30 July 1976, Operation Condor," August 3, 1976.

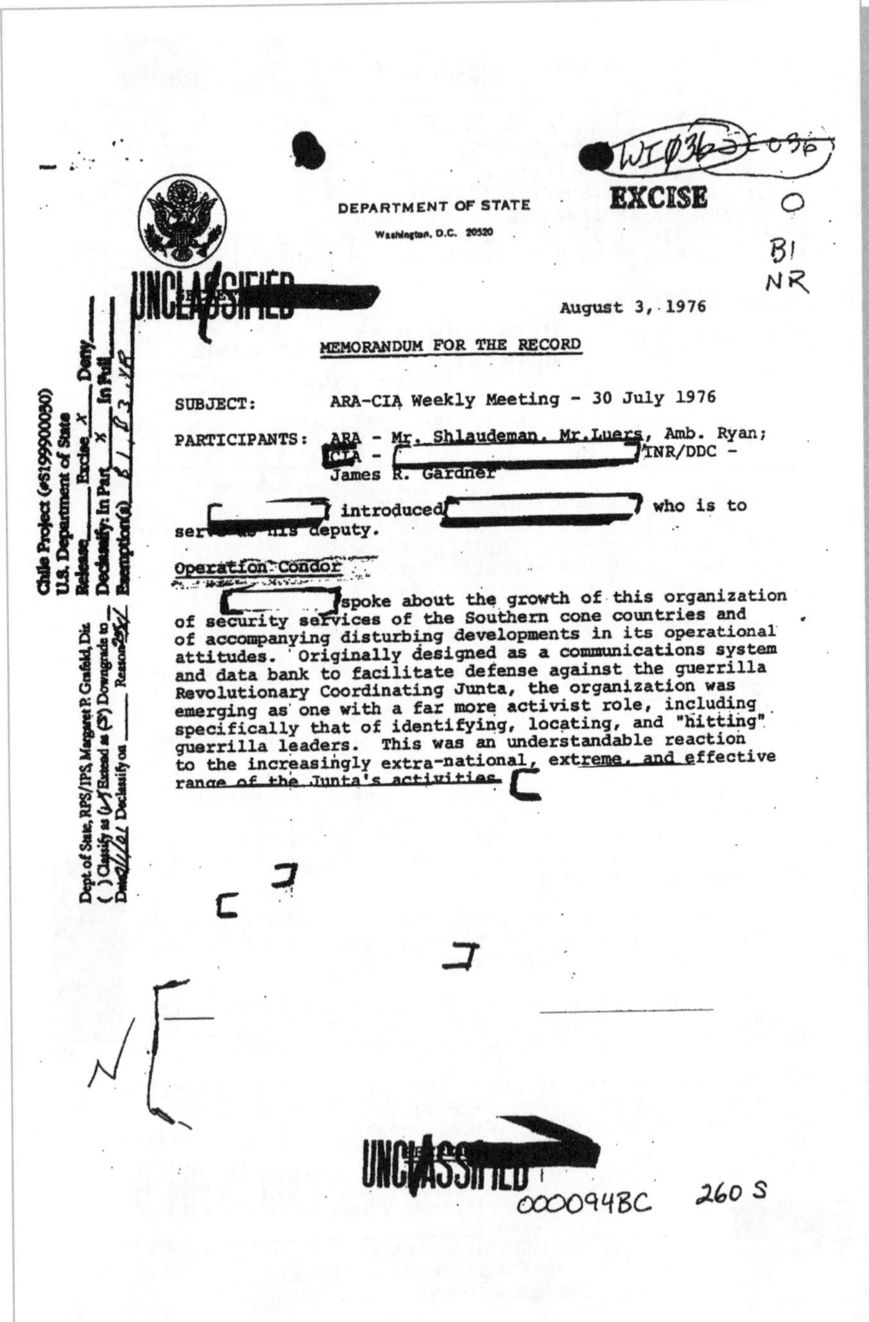

WI036 036

DEPARTMENT OF STATE

Washington, D.C. 20520

EXCISE

O

B1

NR

UNCLASSIFIED

August 3, 1976

MEMORANDUM FOR THE RECORD

SUBJECT: ARA-CIA Weekly Meeting - 30 July 1976

PARTICIPANTS: ARA - Mr. Shlaudeman, Mr.Luers, Amb. Ryan; CIA - [redacted] INR/DDC - James R. Gardner

[redacted] introduced [redacted] who is to serve as his deputy.

Operation Condor

[redacted] spoke about the growth of this organization of security services of the Southern cone countries and of accompanying disturbing developments in its operational attitudes. Originally designed as a communications system and data bank to facilitate defense against the guerrilla Revolutionary Coordinating Junta, the organization was emerging as one with a far more activist role, including specifically that of identifying, locating, and "hitting" guerrilla leaders. This was an understandable reaction to the increasingly extra-national, extreme, and effective range of the Junta's activities.

UNCLASSIFIED

000094BC 260 S

Chile Project (#S199900030)
U.S. Department of State
Release ___ Excise X Deny ___
Declassify: In Part X In Full ___
Exemption(s) B1, B3, XR
Dept of State, RPS/IPS, Margaret P. Grafeld, Dir.
( ) Classify as (U) Extend as (S) Downgrade to ___
Date 2/1/01 Declassify on ___ Reason 25X1

DOCUMENT 14. Department of State, **SECRET** Report on Operation Condor to Henry Kissinger, "ARA Monthly Report (July): The 'Third World War' and South America," August 3, 1976 (pages 1, 2)

7616677 ARA R

AUG 3 1976

AO ØØ3A

TO: The Secretary

FROM: ARA - Harry W. Shlaudeman

ARA Monthly Report (July)
The "Third World War" and South America

The military regimes of the southern cone of South America see themselves as embattled:

-- on one side by international Marxism and its terrorist exponents, and

-- on the other by the hostility of the uncomprehending industrial democracies misled by Marxist propaganda.

In response they are banding together in what may well become a political bloc of some cohesiveness. But, more significantly, they are joining forces to eradicate "subversion", a word which increasingly translates into non-violent dissent from the left and center left. The security forces of the southern cone

-- now coordinate intelligence activities closely;

-- operate in the territory of one another's countries in pursuit of "subversives";

-- have established Operation Condor to find and kill terrorists of the "Revolutionary Coordinating Committee" in their own countries and in Europe. Brazil is cooperating short of murder operations.

This siege mentality shading into paranoia is perhaps the natural result of the convulsions of recent years in which the societies of Chile, Uruguay and Argentina have been badly shaken by assault from the extreme left. But the military leaders, despite near decimation of the Marxist left in Chile and Uruguay, along with accelerating progress toward that goal in Argentina, insist that the threat remains and the war must go on. Some talk of the "Third World War", with the countries of the southern cone as the last bastion of Christian civilization.

[redacted]/XGDS-2

WARNING NOTICE: SENSITIVE INTELLIGENCE SOURCES AND METHODS INVOLVED. DISSEMINATION AND EXTRACTION OF INFORMATION CONTROLLED BY ORIGINATOR.

80D177
Box 4859

UNCLASSIFIED

DECAPTIONED

UNCLASSIFIED

-2-

Somewhat more rationally,

- -- they consider their counter-terrorism every bit as justified as Israeli actions against Palestinian terrorists; and

- -- they believe that the criticism from democracies of their war on terrorism reflects a double standard.

The result of this mentality, internally, is to magnify the isolation of the military institutions from the civilian sector, thus narrowing the range of political and economic options.

The broader implications for us and for future trends in the hemisphere are disturbing. The use of bloody counter-terrorism by these regimes threatens their increasing isolation from the West and the opening of deep ideological divisions among the countries of the hemisphere. An outbreak of PLO-type terrorism on a worldwide scale in response is also a possibility. The industrial democracies would be the battlefield.

This month's trends paper attempts for the first time to focus on long-term dangers of a right-wing bloc. Our initial policy recommendations are:

- -- To emphasize the differences between the six countries at every opportunity.

- -- To depoliticize human rights.

- -- To oppose rhetorical exaggerations of the "Third-World-War" type.

- -- To bring the potential bloc-members back into our cognitive universe through systematic exchanges.

DOCUMENT 15. Department of State, **SECRET** Roger Channel Cable, "Operation Condor," August 23, 1976.

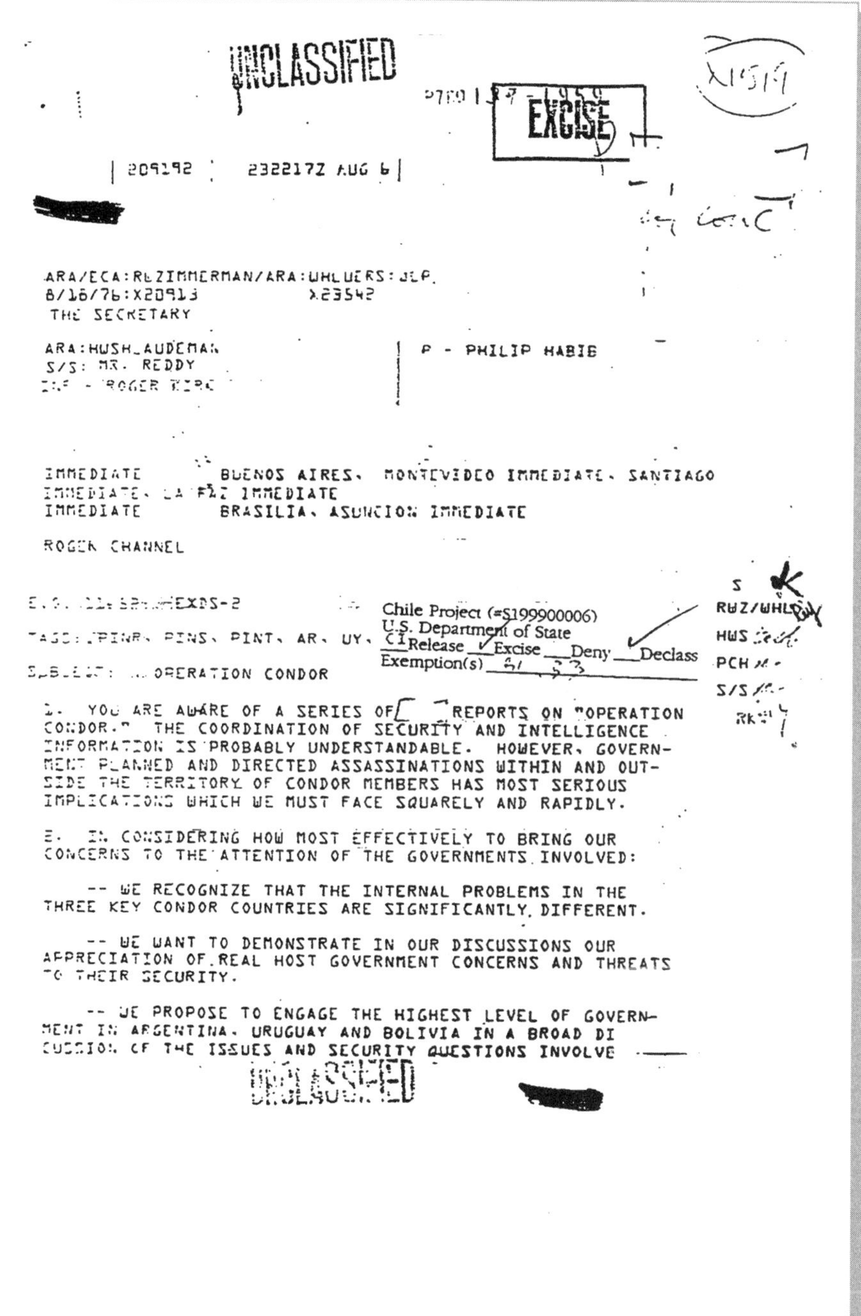

UNCLASSIFIED

EXCISE

209192 2322172 AUG 6

ARA/ECA:REZIMMERMAN/ARA:WHLUERS:JLP
8/16/76:X20913 X23542
THE SECRETARY

ARA:HUSH_AUDEMAN
S/S: MR. REDDY
INR - ROGER KIRK

P - PHILIP HABIB

IMMEDIATE BUENOS AIRES, MONTEVIDEO IMMEDIATE, SANTIAGO
IMMEDIATE, LA PAZ IMMEDIATE
IMMEDIATE BRASILIA, ASUNCION IMMEDIATE

ROGER CHANNEL

E.O. 11652: XGDS-2

TAGS: PINR, PINS, PINT, AR, UY, CI

SUBJECT: OPERATION CONDOR

Chile Project (#S199900006)
U.S. Department of State
Release ✓ Excise ___ Deny ___ Declass
Exemption(s) B1 B3

RWZ/WHL
HWS
PCH
S/S
RK

1. YOU ARE AWARE OF A SERIES OF [ ] REPORTS ON "OPERATION CONDOR." THE COORDINATION OF SECURITY AND INTELLIGENCE INFORMATION IS PROBABLY UNDERSTANDABLE. HOWEVER, GOVERNMENT PLANNED AND DIRECTED ASSASSINATIONS WITHIN AND OUTSIDE THE TERRITORY OF CONDOR MEMBERS HAS MOST SERIOUS IMPLICATIONS WHICH WE MUST FACE SQUARELY AND RAPIDLY.

2. IN CONSIDERING HOW MOST EFFECTIVELY TO BRING OUR CONCERNS TO THE ATTENTION OF THE GOVERNMENTS INVOLVED:

-- WE RECOGNIZE THAT THE INTERNAL PROBLEMS IN THE THREE KEY CONDOR COUNTRIES ARE SIGNIFICANTLY DIFFERENT.

-- WE WANT TO DEMONSTRATE IN OUR DISCUSSIONS OUR APPRECIATION OF REAL HOST GOVERNMENT CONCERNS AND THREATS TO THEIR SECURITY.

-- WE PROPOSE TO ENGAGE THE HIGHEST LEVEL OF GOVERNMENT IN ARGENTINA, URUGUAY AND BOLIVIA IN A BROAD DISCUSSION OF THE ISSUES AND SECURITY QUESTIONS INVOLVE

UNCLASSIFIED

UNCLASSIFIED

2

3. FOR BUENOS AIRES, MONTEVIDEO AND SANTIAGO: YOU SHOULD SEEK APPOINTMENT AS SOON AS POSSIBLE WITH HIGHEST APPROPRIATE OFFICIAL, PREFERABLY THE CHIEF OF STATE, TO MAKE REPRESENTATIONS DRAWING ON THE FOLLOWING POINTS:

A. THE USG IS AWARE FROM VARIOUS SOURCES, INCLUDING HIGH GOVERNMENT OFFICIALS, THAT THERE IS A DEGREE OF INFORMATION EXCHANGE AND COORDINATION AMONG VARIOUS COUNTRIES OF THE SOUTHERN CONE WITH REGARD TO SUBVERSIVE ACTIVITIES WITHIN THE AREA. THIS WE CONSIDER USEFUL.

B. THERE ARE IN ADDITION, HOWEVER, RUMORS THAT THIS COOPERATION MAY EXTEND BEYOND INFORMATION EXCHANGE TO INCLUDE PLANS FOR THE ASSASSINATION OF SUBVERSIVES, POLITICIANS AND PROMINENT FIGURES BOTH WITHIN THE NATIONAL BORDERS OF CERTAIN SOUTHERN CONE COUNTRIES AND ABROAD.

C. WHILE WE CANNOT SUBSTANTIATE THE ASSASSINATION RUMORS, WE FEEL IMPELLED TO BRING TO YOUR ATTENTION OUR DEEP CONCERN. IF THESE RUMORS WERE TO HAVE ANY SHRED OF TRUTH, THEY WOULD CREATE A MOST SERIOUS MORAL AND POLITICAL PROBLEM.

D. COUNTER-TERRORIST ACTIVITY OF THIS TYPE WOULD FURTHER EXACERBATE PUBLIC WORLD CRITICISM OF GOVERNMENTS INVOLVED.

E. WE ARE MAKING SIMILAR REPRESENTATIONS IN CERTAIN OTHER CAPITALS (WITHOUT SPECIFYING).

4. FOR BUENOS AIRES: YOU ARE AUTHORIZED TO ADD TO YOUR APPROACH THE FOLLOWING POINTS IF YOU DEEM IT APPROPRIATE:

A. WE ARE FULLY AWARE OF SECURITY THREATS CREATED BY TERRORIST ACTIVITIES WITHIN ARGENTINA. IT IS NOT THE INTENTION OF THE U.S. GOVERNMENT TO ATTEMPT TO ADVISE THE GOVERNMENT OF ARGENTINA ON HOW BEST TO GET ITS INTERNAL SECURITY PROBLEM UNDER CONTROL.

B. ACTIVITY ALONG LINES OF 3-B. WOULD HAVE SERIOUS NEGATIVE IMPACT ON ARGENTINE IMAGE ABROAD IN GENERAL AND FOREIGN REFINANCING EFFORTS OF MARTINEZ DE HOZ, IN PARTICULAR.

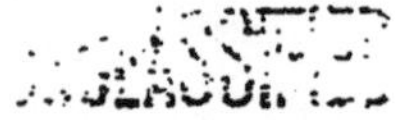

UNCLASSIFIED

FORM DS 322A(OCR)

3

C. IN CONNECTION WITH PARA 2.D., YOU SHOULD INCLUDE STATEMENT OF OUR PROFOUND CONCERN REGARDING ATTACKS ON REFUGEES FROM WHATEVER QUARTER IN ARGENTINA AND MAKE SPECIFIC REFERENCE TO SOME 30 URUGUAYANS WHO HAVE DISAPPEARED AND ABOUT WHOM WE MADE REPRESENTATIONS TO AMBASSADOR MUSICH IN WASHINGTON.

D. WE ARE PREPARED TO UNDERTAKE PERIODIC EXCHANGES WITH THE GOVERNMENT OF ARGENTINA OF INFORMATION ON THE GENERAL LEVEL AND MODE OF COMMUNIST AND OTHER TERRORIST ACTIVITY IN THE HEMISPHERE AND ELSEWHERE IF THE GOA WOULD BE INTERESTED. (FYI: WE WOULD PLAN TO PROVIDE BACKGROUND MATERIAL TO YOU LATER TO SERVE AS A BASIS FOR ORAL EXCHANGES AT A LEVEL AGREED UPON JOINTLY WITH THE GOA.)

5. FOR MONTEVIDEO: WE ASSUME YOUR BEST APPROACH IS TO GENERAL VADORA RATHER THAN TO EITHER ACTING PRESIDENT OR PRESIDENT DESIGNATE WHO APPARENTLY KNOW NOTHING ABOUT OPERATION CONDOR AND, IN ANY EVENT, WOULD PROBABLY HAVE LITTLE INFLUENCE ON SITUATION. YOU MAY USE TALKING POINT D. IN PARAGRAPH 4 ON EXCHANGE OF INFORMATION IF YOU CONSIDER IT APPROPRIATE.

6. FOR SANTIAGO: DISCUSS [ ] THE POSSIBILITY OF A PARALLEL APPROACH BY HIM.

7. FOR LA PAZ: WE AGREE WITH YOUR SUGGESTION (LA PAZ 3657), AS YOU SEE. WHILE WE ARE NOT REPEAT NOT INSTRUCTING YOU TO MAKE THE SPECIFIC DEMARCHE ON CONDOR, YOU MAY WISH TO TAKE AN APPROPRIATE OCCASION WITH BANZER OR OTHER SENIOR GOB OFFICIAL TO PROPOSE PERIODIC EXCHANGES OF INFORMATION SUCH AS CONTAINED IN PARA 4.D. ABOVE.

8. YOU WILL BE AWARE OF EXTREME SENSITIVITY OF POINTS 4.B. AND 4.C. GREAT CARE MUST BE TAKEN NOT TO GO BEYOND PHRASING USED.

10. FOR ALL ACTION AND INFO ADDRESSEES: YOU SHOULD OF COURSE BE CERTAIN THAT NO AGENCY OF THE U.S. GOVERNMENT IS INVOLVED IN ANY WAY IN EXCHANGING INFORMATION OR DATA ON INDIVIDUAL SUBVERSIVES WITH HOST GOVERNMENT. EVEN IN THOSE COUNTRIES WHERE WE PROPOSE TO EXPAND OUR EXCHANGE OF INFORMATION, IT IS ESSENTIAL THAT WE IN NO WAY FINGER INDIVIDUALS WHO MIGHT BE CANDIDATES FOR ASSASSINATION ATTEMPTS.

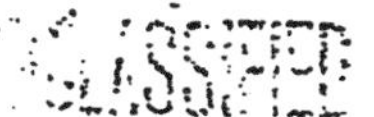

DOCUMENT 16. U.S. Embassy, **SECRET** Roger Channel Cable from Ambassador David Popper, August 24, 1976.

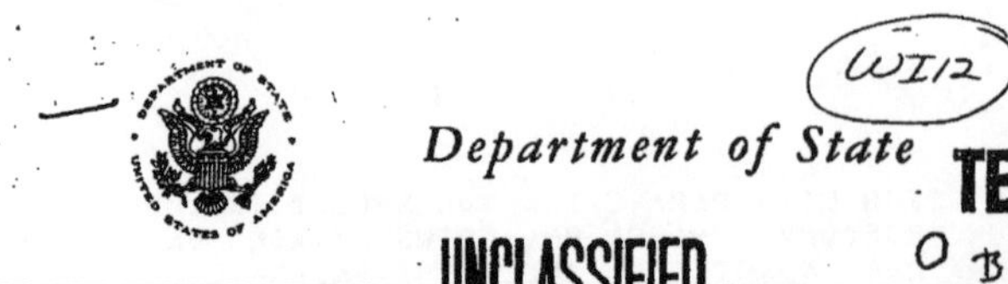

WI/2 SE 012

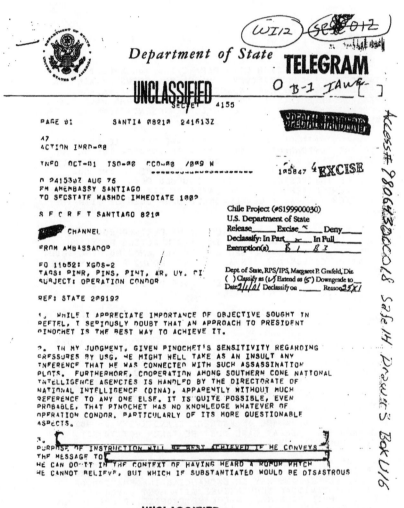

Department of State TELEGRAM

O B-1 IAW [ ]

UNCLASSIFIED

SECRET 4155

SPECIAL HANDLING

PAGE 01 SANTIA 08210 241613Z

47
ACTION INRD-08

INFO OCT-01 ISO-00 CCO-00 /009 W
------------------------- 105847 EXCISE

O 241530Z AUG 76
FM AMEMBASSY SANTIAGO
TO SECSTATE WASHDC IMMEDIATE 1002

S E C R E T SANTIAGO 8210

Chile Project (#S199900030)
U.S. Department of State
Release___ Excise X Deny___
Declassify: In Part X In Full___
Exemption(s) B1, B3

Dept of State, RPS/IPS, Margaret P. Grafeld, Dir.
( ) Classify as (✓) Extend as (S) Downgrade to___
Date 2/1/01 Declassify on ____ Reason 25X1

[redacted] CHANNEL

FROM AMBASSADOR

EO 11652: XGDS-2
TAGS: PINR, PINS, PINT, AR, UY, CI
SUBJECT: OPERATION CONDOR

REF: STATE 209192

1. WHILE I APPRECIATE IMPORTANCE OF OBJECTIVE SOUGHT IN REFTEL, I SERIOUSLY DOUBT THAT AN APPROACH TO PRESIDENT PINOCHET IS THE BEST WAY TO ACHIEVE IT.

2. IN MY JUDGMENT, GIVEN PINOCHET'S SENSITIVITY REGARDING PRESSURES BY USG, HE MIGHT WELL TAKE AS AN INSULT ANY INFERENCE THAT HE WAS CONNECTED WITH SUCH ASSASSINATION PLOTS. FURTHERMORE, COOPERATION AMONG SOUTHERN CONE NATIONAL INTELLIGENCE AGENCIES IS HANDLED BY THE DIRECTORATE OF NATIONAL INTELLIGENCE (DINA), APPARENTLY WITHOUT MUCH REFERENCE TO ANY ONE ELSE. IT IS QUITE POSSIBLE, EVEN PROBABLE, THAT PINOCHET HAS NO KNOWLEDGE WHATEVER OF OPERATION CONDOR, PARTICULARLY OF ITS MORE QUESTIONABLE ASPECTS.

3. [redacted] PURPOSE OF INSTRUCTION WILL BE BEST ACHIEVED IF HE CONVEYS THE MESSAGE TO [redacted] HE CAN DO IT IN THE CONTEXT OF HAVING HEARD A RUMOR WHICH HE CANNOT BELIEVE, BUT WHICH IF SUBSTANTIATED WOULD BE DISASTROUS

Access# 980643000018 Safe 14 Drawer 3 Box U/16

UNCLASSIFIED

262 S

000094■B5

Department of State **TELEGRAM**

~~SECRET~~ UNCLASSIFIED

PAGE 02 SANTIA 08210 241613Z

FOR THE PERPETRATORS. [redacted] BELIEVE THIS WOULD BE THE MOST EFFECTIVE WAY OF GETTING THE MESSAGE ACROSS WITHOUT UNDESIRABLE COMPLICATIONS.

4. I NOTE THAT THE INSTRUCTION IS CAST IN URGENT TERMS. HAS DEPARTMENT RECEIVED ANY WORD THAT WOULD INDICATE THAT ASSASSINATION ACTIVITIES ARE IMMINENT? THE ONLY SUCH INFO WE HAVE SEEN IS ONE REPORT FROM [redacted] UNCONFIRMED BY OTHER SOURCES.

5. PLEASE ADVISE.
POPPER

~~SECRET~~

UNCLASSIFIED

DOCUMENT 17. Department of State, **SECRET** Cable from Assistant Secretary Harry Shlaudeman, "Operation Condor," September 20, 1976.

Department of State TELEGRAM

SECRET

AN: D760356-0146

SECRET

PAGE 01 SAN JO 04526 201838Z

43
ACTION SS-25

INFO OCT-01 ISO-00 SSO-00 /026 W
------------------------ 102949

O 201818Z SEP 76
FM AMEMBASSY SAN JOSE
TO SECSTATE WASHDC IMMEDIATE 5110

S E C R E T SAN JOSE 4526

EXDIS

FOR ARA-LUERS FROM SHLAUDEMAN

E.O. 11652: XGDS-2
TAGS: PINR, PINS, PINT, AR, CL, UY
SUBJECT: OPERATION CONDOR

REF: STATE 231654 - NO RECORD

UNLESS THERE IS SOME COMPLICATION I AM UNAWARE OF, THERE WOULD SEEM TO BE NO REASON TO WAIT MY RETURN. YOU CAN SIMPLY INSTRUCT THE AMBASSADORS TO TAKE NO FURTHER ACTION, NOTING THAT THERE HAVE BEEN NO REPORTS IN SOME WEEKS INDICATING AN INTENTION TO ACTIVATE THE CONDOR SCHEME. TODMAN

SECRET

EXDIS REVIEW
Cat. A - Caption removed; transferred to O/FADRC
Cat. B - Transferred to O/FADRC with additional access controlled by S/S
Cat. C - Caption and custody retained by S/S
2/4/91

DEPARTMENT OF STATE A/CDC/MR
DATE 7/25/91

SECRET

DOCUMENT 18. Department of State, **SECRET** Cable from Assistant Secretary Harry Shlaudeman, with Cover Memo, "Operation Condor," October 4, 1976.

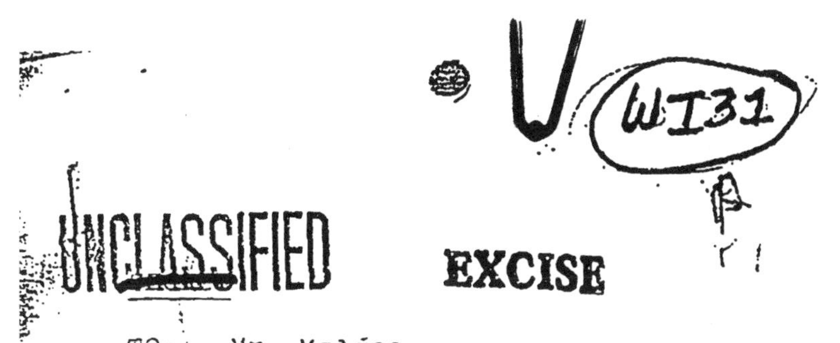

UNCLASSIFIED EXCISE

TO: Mr. McAfee

Bill:

I have authority from above for this. Would appreciate no clearances shown and distribution confined to S, P, M, you and me.

Harry W. Shlaudeman
Assistant Secretary for
Inter-American Affairs

UNCLASSIFIED

Chile Project (#S199900030)
U.S. Department of State
Release_____ Excise X Deny_____
Declassify: In Part X In Full_____
Exemption(s) B1

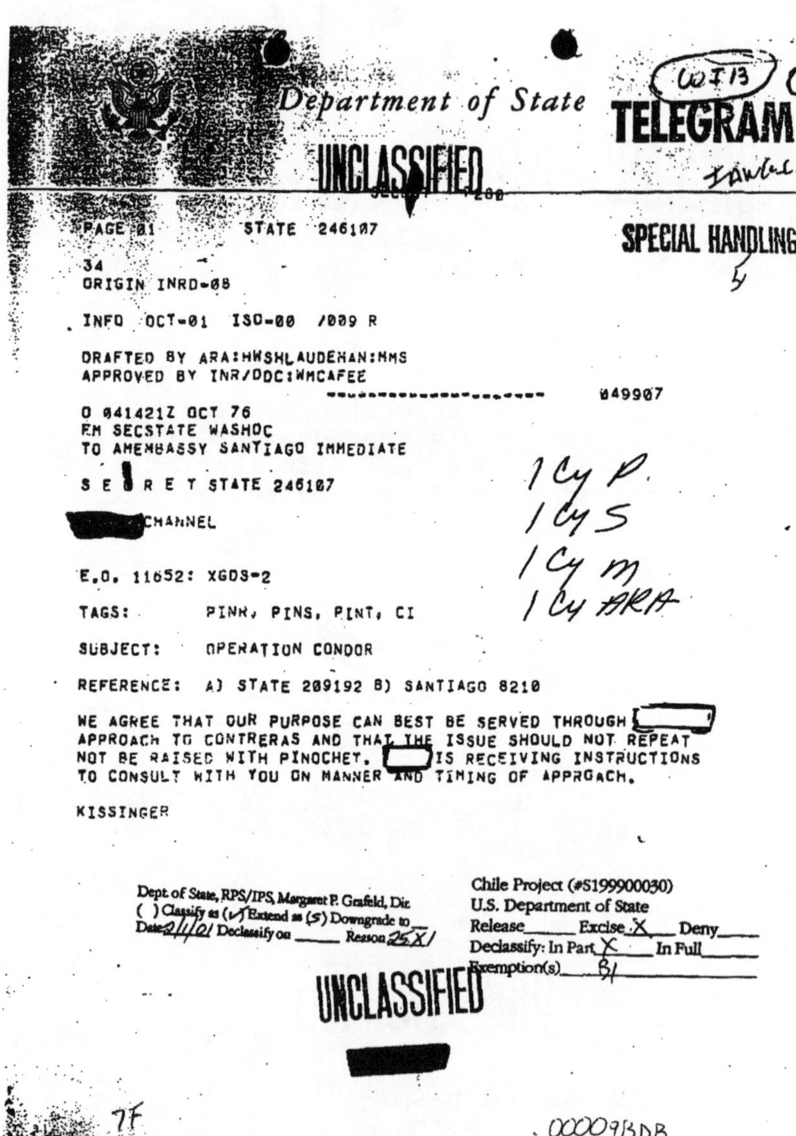

Department of State TELEGRAM

UNCLASSIFIED

PAGE 01 STATE 246107

SPECIAL HANDLING

34
ORIGIN INRD-08

INFO OCT-01 ISO-00 /009 R

DRAFTED BY ARA:HWSHLAUDEMAN:MMS
APPROVED BY INR/DDC:WMCAFEE

049907

O 041421Z OCT 76
FM SECSTATE WASHDC
TO AMEMBASSY SANTIAGO IMMEDIATE

S E [redacted] R E T STATE 246107

[redacted] CHANNEL

E.O. 11652: XGDS-2

TAGS: PINR, PINS, PINT, CI

SUBJECT: OPERATION CONDOR

REFERENCE: A) STATE 209192 B) SANTIAGO 8210

WE AGREE THAT OUR PURPOSE CAN BEST BE SERVED THROUGH [redacted] APPROACH TO CONTRERAS AND THAT THE ISSUE SHOULD NOT REPEAT NOT BE RAISED WITH PINOCHET. [redacted] IS RECEIVING INSTRUCTIONS TO CONSULT WITH YOU ON MANNER AND TIMING OF APPROACH.

KISSINGER

Dept. of State, RPS/IPS, Margaret P. Grafeld, Dir.
( ) Classify as (✓) Extend as (S) Downgrade to ___
Date 2/1/01 Declassify on ___ Reason 25X1

Chile Project (#S199900030)
U.S. Department of State
Release___ Excise X Deny___
Declassify: In Part X In Full___
Exemption(s) B1

UNCLASSIFIED

7F

000098DB

DOCUMENT 19. CIA, **SECRET** Intelligence Information Cable [Assassination of Orlando Letelier], October 6, 1976 (pages 1, 2).

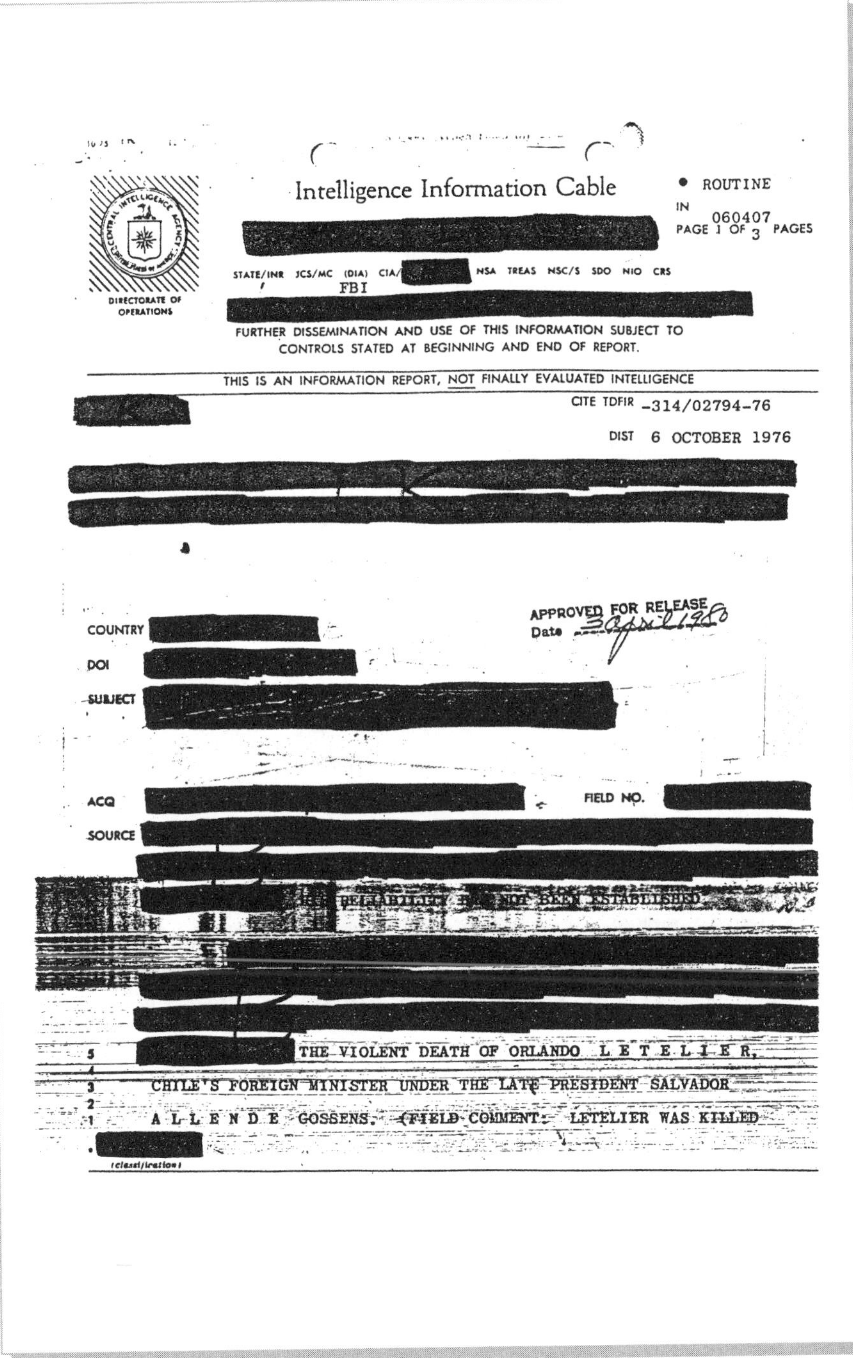

DIRECTORATE OF OPERATIONS

Intelligence Information Cable

• ROUTINE

IN 060407

PAGE 1 OF 3 PAGES

STATE/INR JCS/MC (DIA) CIA/[redacted] NSA TREAS NSC/S SDO NIO CRS

FBI

FURTHER DISSEMINATION AND USE OF THIS INFORMATION SUBJECT TO CONTROLS STATED AT BEGINNING AND END OF REPORT.

THIS IS AN INFORMATION REPORT, NOT FINALLY EVALUATED INTELLIGENCE

CITE TDFIR -314/02794-76

DIST 6 OCTOBER 1976

APPROVED FOR RELEASE
Date 3 April 1980

COUNTRY [redacted]

DOI [redacted]

SUBJECT [redacted]

ACQ [redacted] FIELD NO. [redacted]

SOURCE [redacted]

[redacted] HIS RELIABILITY HAS NOT BEEN ESTABLISHED.

[redacted] THE VIOLENT DEATH OF ORLANDO L E T E L I E R, CHILE'S FOREIGN MINISTER UNDER THE LATE PRESIDENT SALVADOR A L L E N D E GOSSENS. (FIELD COMMENT: LETELIER WAS KILLED

(classification)

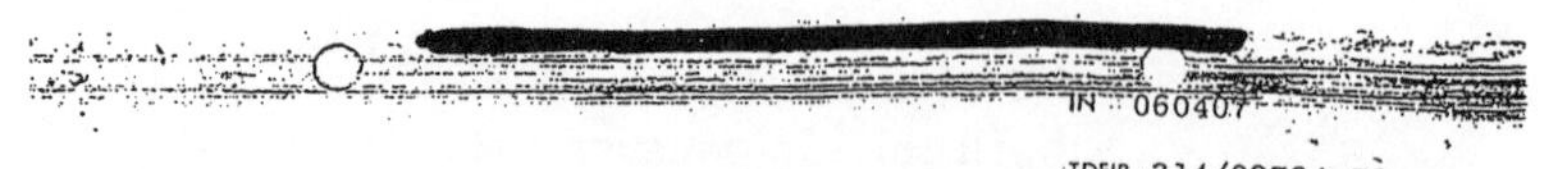
IN 060407

TDFIR-314/02794-76

PAGE 2 OF 3 PAGES

SECRET (classification) FURTHER DISSEMINATION AND USE OF THIS INFORMATION SUBJECT TO CONTROLS STATED AT BEGINNING AND END OF REPORT (dissem controls)

IN THE UNITED STATES ON 21 SEPTEMBER 1976 WHEN A BOMB EXPLODED IN HIS CAR. HE WAS BURIED IN CARACAS ON 29 SEPTEMBER WITH VENEZUELAN PRESIDENT CARLOS ANDRES P E R E Z IN ATTENDANCE AT THE FUNERAL.)

2. [redacted] BELIEVES THAT THE CHILEAN GOVERNMENT IS DIRECTLY INVOLVED IN LETELIER'S DEATH AND FEELS THAT INVESTIGATIONS INTO THE INCIDENT WILL SO INDICATE. [redacted] IN HIS CRITICISM OF THE CURRENT CHILEAN GOVERNMENT. [redacted] HAS POINTED TO COMMENTS MADE BY CHILEAN PRESIDENT AUGUSTO P I N O C H E T UGARTE TO THE EFFECT THAT LETELIER'S CRITICISM OF THE CHILEAN GOVERNMENT WAS "UNACCEPTABLE." [redacted]

3.  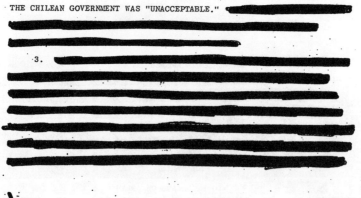

SECRET (classification) (dissem controls)

7

Denouement of the Dictator: From Terrorism to Transition

All of the Generals are very much aware that if we have sufficient evidence on Contreras, there is no way that he would have done it without informing Pinochet, with whom he had breakfast every single day.

—Top-Secret White House memorandum, June 1978

Plan to Disrupt Chile's Plebiscite*: We take seriously intelligence reports that Chilean Army elements, using violence as a pretext, may try to suspend Wednesday's scheduled plebiscite if Pinochet appears to be losing.*

—Presidential Evening Reading for Ronald Reagan, October 1988

The Letelier-Moffitt assassination would dominate U.S.-Chilean relations for more than a decade. Along with the end of the Nixon-Ford-Kissinger era and the election of a "human rights president," Jimmy Carter, the car bombing initiated a long transformation in U.S. policy toward the Pinochet regime. Carter, who blasted the Ford administration for overthrowing "an elected government and helping to establish a military dictatorship" during the campaign, gave new prominence to human rights as a criterion in U.S. foreign policy, but failed to hold the regime accountable for its atrocities in Washington. The Reagan administration attempted to reestablish cozy relations with the military government, only to find U.S. policy trapped by the reality of Pinochet's act of terrorism on U.S. soil and increasingly threatened by Pinochet's efforts to perpetuate his power. During the decade between 1978, when Chilean officials were officially indicted for the assassination, and 1988, when the military regime was peacefully voted out, Washington's posture slowly evolved into an unequivocal rejection of the still violent and bloody Chilean military dictatorship.

Pinochet's Watergate

For more than a year it appeared the Pinochet regime had actually gotten away with the most flagrant terrorist act committed in Washington in the twentieth century. Within days of the assassinations, CIA informants pointed the finger at Pinochet, and the FBI identified DINA and Operation Condor as lead suspects. Yet in September 1977 the Carter Administration actually invited General Pinochet to Washington to join other Latin American leaders at the signing of the Panama Canal treaty. During a prestigious face-to-face meeting at the White House, President Carter avoided any mention of the Letelier-Moffitt case and only mildly pressed his guest on human rights issues. According to the memorandum of conversation, "President Carter/President Pinochet Bilateral," Carter stated that he did "not want anything to stand in the way of traditional U.S.-Chilean friendship." Pinochet returned to Santiago "relieved and pleased by the entire Washington experience," deputy chief of mission Thomas Boyatt reported. "The presidential bilateral has provided Pinochet with a hefty shot in the arm. . . ."

It took U.S. authorities almost seventeen months to bring the Letelier-Moffitt investigation into Chilean territory. Cooperation from the CIA, the agency with the most evidence of Chile's international terrorist operations in its files, was ambivalent at best. In October 1976, the White House requested the CIA director George H. W. Bush to undertake "appropriate foreign intelligence and counterintelligence information collection" to support the criminal investigation. But the Agency did not provide Justice Department investigators with particularly useful information and details on the CIA's close relations with DINA chieftain Manuel Contreras appear to have been withheld from them for some time.

The CHILBOM investigation of the assassination of Orlando Letelier and Ronni Moffitt is the subject of two detailed accounts—*Assassination on Embassy Row*, authored by John Dinges and Saul Landau, and *Labyrinth*, by Taylor Branch and the lead assistant U.S. attorney in the case, Eugene Propper. To summarize: during the first year the investigation focused on the anti-Castro exile community in Miami—a community well-known to the FBI for its terrorist violence. Eventually, informants told FBI investigators that an exile group, the Cuban Nationalist Movement (CNM) had committed the crime at the behest of the Pinochet regime. The Justice Department submitted a set of questions to the Chilean government in mid-1977, and waited months while the Chilean government appointed an unwitting special investigator to pursue a response. Finally, in February 1978, the Justice Department presented an official "Letters Rogatory" to the Chilean regime, formally demanding evidence of contacts with Cuban exile terrorists, and seeking to question the two Chilean agents who had sought U.S. visas in Paraguay to travel to Washington in July 1976 before the assassinations took place. As part of the Letters Rogatory, U.S. officials submitted reproductions of the passport photos of Juan Williams and Alejandro Romeral—aliases for Michael Townley and Armando Fernández Larios—that had been copied by the then U.S. ambassador to Asuncíon, George Landau.

The break in the case came on March 3, 1978, after the FBI leaked those passport photos to reporter Jeremiah O'Leary who published them on the front page of the *Washington Star*.[1] The pictures were immediately reprinted in the Chilean press. By March 6, multiple sources had identified the photo of Williams as one Michael Vernon Townley, an American living in Santiago.

As a U.S. citizen suspected of an act of terrorism in the United States, Justice Department officials immediately demanded custody of Townley. But Pinochet's officials claimed no knowledge of him or his whereabouts, all the while secretly hiding Townley in his own home.[2] FBI agents and assistant U.S. attorney Propper flew to Santiago to force the issue. Under intense diplomatic pressure, Chilean intelligence officials conceded that Townley was a DINA agent and in their custody. After significant stalling, the regime finally agreed to expel him if the United States publicly announced that Chile was cooperating in the investigation, and signed a formal accord limiting the information provided by Townley to use only in a criminal prosecution of the Letelier-Moffitt case.[3]

On April 8, Chilean authorities put Townley on an Ecuadorian airlines plane to Miami accompanied by two FBI agents. Under questioning, he provided U.S. authorities, and Chile's special military investigator, Gen. Hector Orozco, with detailed evidence of the assassination plot. "Mr. Townley has implicated the highest officials of DINA in ordering Mr. Letelier murdered," Propper would report in a secret memorandum to Ambassador Landau on April 25. His confession led to a U.S. indictment of three high-level Chilean intelligence officers—Contreras, his deputy Pedro Espinoza, and Fernández Larios—as well as five CNM members on August 1, 1978.[4] In early September, Washington formally requested the extradition of the three DINA officials.

Revelations of the regime's complicity in the Letelier-Moffitt assassination caused a major crisis in U.S.-Chilean relations, as well as a severe scandal in Chile. "The sensational developments have evoked speculation about President Pinochet's survival," CIA analysts wrote in a secret intelligence memorandum on "Chile: Implications of the Letelier Case." (Doc 1) The threat to the regime came not from popular opposition, but rather from internal dissention within Pinochet's power base—the Chilean military. Numerous military officials inside the government, who despised Contreras for his concentration of power and damage to Chile's international image, believed that if Pinochet knew of the plot he should be ousted. A core group of military officers closely tied to DINA also opposed Pinochet—for not giving full support to Contreras, who, while no longer head of the secret police, was still the dictator's closest military adviser. For Pinochet, the scandal threatened to become a Chilean Watergate.

General Pinochet clearly understood the precarious nature of his situation. During a toast to a house full of ambassadors at a diplomatic dinner he hosted on June 23, 1978, the general openly alluded to the possibility he might be forced to resign. In a report on the dinner titled "Conversation with Pinochet—He Talks of Going," Ambassador Landau noted that during a twenty-minute private talk with the general later that evening

> Pinochet, who normally drinks very little, had two scotch and sodas. His face grew redder and redder as he talked to me. At the end he was somewhat aggressive. He appeared a deeply troubled man and his concern that he might be replaced by other military officers seems to be foremost in his mind.

Recalled to Washington several days later, Landau alerted the National Security Council staff that "we are approaching the end of the road in U.S.-Chilean relations and it is only a matter of time before the Army leadership realizes that the only way Chile will improve its relations with the rest of the world is by replacing Pinochet."[5] But his predictions of the demise of the Pinochet regime proved to be premature.

Throughout the summer and fall of 1978 General Pinochet pursued a calculated four-point strategy designed to cover up his regime's act of international terrorism and protect those who had perpetrated it. His action plan, the CIA Station learned, was to:

> A. Protect General Manuel Contreras from successful prosecution in the murder of Letelier, since Pinochet's political survival is dependent upon Contreras' fate.
> B. Stonewall any further requests from the U.S. government that would serve to build a case against Contreras and other Chileans.
> C. Continue to "lobby" the Supreme Court justices to insure that requests for extradition of Chilean citizens following anticipated indictments are rejected.
> D. Continue to exploit Chilean nationalism with a covert action campaign

> to portray the Letelier investigation as being politically motivated—another pretext for destabilizing the Pinochet regime. (Doc 2)

Key to Pinochet's survival was his ability to distance himself from Manuel Contreras—the dictator's closest advisor and the one person who could tie Pinochet directly to this act of terrorism. Only Contreras knew the details and degree of Pinochet's involvement in authorizing and instigating the Letelier assassination. Few would doubt—and most would assume—that if Contreras authorized this crime, he assuredly did so with Pinochet's explicit approval. According to the CIA's early assessment in May:

> Clouding the outlook for Pinochet is the possibility that former intelligence chief General Manuel Contreras will be linked directly to the crime. Public disclosure of Contreras' guilt—either through his own admission or in court testimony—would be almost certain to implicate Pinochet and irreparably damage his credibility within the military. None of the government's critics and few of its supporters would be willing to swallow claims that Contreras acted without presidential concurrence. The former secret police chief is known to have reported directly to the President, who had exclusive responsibility for [DINA] activities.

Loyalty to Pinochet, the CIA analysts added, was "no guarantee that Contreras would withhold sensitive details on operations authorized by the President, especially if he thought he were being tagged as a scapegoat."

Indeed, CIA sources inside the Chilean military soon reported that Contreras had taken steps to secure his own immunity—and to safeguard Pinochet's—by packing up DINA records that implicated Pinochet and clandestinely sending them out of the country. On April 20, according to one informant, Contreras shipped what was described as "a large number of suitcases" rumored to contain DINA documents on the freighter *Banndestein*, bound from Punta Arenas to an unknown European location.[6] Contreras, another source would later inform U.S. military personnel, had taken "extreme precautions to protect President Pinochet from direct involvement in the decision-making/authorization process" in Chilean acts of international terrorism. In an intelligence cable entitled "Contreras Tentacles," the DIA reported that

> All government documents pertaining to the Letelier-Moffitt assassinations in Washington in 1976 as well as the killing of Pinochet's predecessor as Army CINC, General Carlos Prats, and wife in Buenos Aires

> and the attempt on the life of regime opponent Bernardo Leighton in Rome in 1975, were removed by Contreras from DINA archives. . . . Contreras made two copies of each document, forwarding one to Germany and one to Paraguay for safe keeping while retaining the original under his control, in storage, in the south of Chile.[7]

Contreras used this evidence to protect himself, even as Pinochet tried to separate his government from the former DINA chieftain. Facing enormous pressure to mollify critics inside and outside of Chile, on March 21 Pinochet arranged the hasty resignation of Contreras from the Chilean armed forces. The Chilean army issued a perfunctory statement that Contreras had voluntarily withdrawn from active duty. But Pinochet and Contreras clearly had a secret agreement: Contreras would be protected from prosecution; in turn he would keep his knowledge of Pinochet's role to himself and help orchestrate a massive cover-up.

That cover-up began in earnest after the Chilean military investigator, Gen. Hector Orozco, returned to Santiago from debriefing Townley in Washington in the late spring of 1978. In statements to Orozco, Espinoza and Fernández Larios confirmed Townley's story. Orozco then confronted Contreras with evidence of DINA's responsibility for the car bombing. On June 23, 1978, the same day that Pinochet told Ambassador Landau that his government was making a "sincere attempt to get to the bottom of the Letelier murder," CIA sources described what happened:

> Contreras admitted his culpability, but threatened to claim that he was acting on orders from Pinochet in the event he was prosecuted. Contreras claimed he had safely secreted documentation to support his claim. This blackmail threat worked. Orozco was obviously given orders by Pinochet to accept Contreras' cover story (that he had sent Townley and Captain Armando Fernández Larios to the U.S. merely to investigate Orlando Letelier's activities—and that Townley had obviously exceeded his instructions). . . . Thus the coverup began. (Doc 2)

Thereafter, General Orozco pursued no further investigation. Instead, he became a coordinator of the cover-up. In October, he destroyed the truthful statements of Espinoza and Fernández Larios; Orozco then directed them to deceive the Chilean Supreme Court in their October 17 testimony.

Pinochet personally made sure that the Supreme Court would reject any U.S. extradition request. As early as May 31, 1978, the CIA obtained high-level intelligence on "Pinochet intercession w/Sup Crt to Prevent Extradition of Officials re: Letelier."[8] In June the CIA's Santiago Station reported, "Pinochet, acting through his legal advisor Hugo Rosende, has manipulated the Supreme Court judges and now is satisfied that the court will reject extradition of any Chileans indicted."

Pinochet's personal involvement in obstruction of justice also included witness tampering. When Fernández Larios, who had spied on Letelier to provide intelligence for the assassination mission, decided he wanted to go to Washington and confess to U.S. officials, Pinochet summoned him to the Defense Ministry and ordered him to stay silent. "I know you want to go to the U.S.," Pinochet told him. "Be a good soldier. Wait till everything's all right. A good soldier remains at his post. Tough it out and this problem will have a happy end." This order, U.S. investigators would later conclude, "directly implicates Pinochet who was directing the cover-up."[9]

Contreras's Blackmail Bid

The cover-up also included a massive nationalist propaganda campaign to convince Chilean citizens, as sources told the CIA, that Washington was "using the investigation into the Orlando Letelier assassination as a tool to destabilize the Chilean government."[10] To rally public support, Pinochet himself undertook a political tour, denouncing Washington for interfering in Chile's internal affairs. The propaganda campaign went beyond blaming the U.S. for meddling; the regime sought to blame Washington for the actual assassination.

With mounting evidence of DINA's involvement, Contreras planted the idea in the Chilean press that the CIA, not Chile, had engineered the car bombing. Throughout the summer of 1978, Contreras, his lawyers, and other Chilean officials repeatedly painted Townley as a CIA agent assigned to infiltrate DINA and embarrass the regime. Ominous hints about a "foreign ambassador" facilitating Townley's effort to go to Washington were also fed to Chilean reporters.

These arguments were bolstered by several convenient facts: Townley was a U.S. citizen who had, in fact, tried to join the CIA; the U.S. embassy in Paraguay had provided him and Armando Fernández Larios with visas to travel to Washington ostensibly to see CIA deputy director Vernon Walters.[11] Even more conveniently for Contreras's ability to confuse the Chilean public, the ambassador who had signed those visas, George Landau, was now ambassador to Santiago.[12] "Contreras plans to base his defense on the premise that Michael Townley and the Cuban exiles implicated were all under CIA control, and that the Agency ordered Letelier's assassination to throw blame on Pinochet and thus topple him. He also plans to implicate Ambassador Landau in this scheme," a CIA report warned headquarters. "While this defense is of course fabricated completely of whole cloth, it could cause us embarrassment."[13]

In Washington, U.S. officials spent considerable time discussing the Contreras problem. At an August 21 meeting between Justice, CIA, and State Department officials, U.S. Attorney Eugene Propper laid out "three basic areas of concern: Contreras' relationship [with the CIA], the issuance of U.S. visas for Paraguayan passports . . . and the relationship of 'Condor' to the case."[14] The same group of officials met the next day at the office of the CIA general counsel to review two short reports the Agency had prepared—one on Operation Condor, and the other on the top-secret history of CIA liaison relations with Contreras and collaboration with DINA.[15]

At this point, Contreras decided to supplement his public effort to implicate the CIA with a private threat to reveal his knowledge of, and involvement in, joint CIA-DINA covert operations directed at neighboring Latin American countries. On the evening of August 23, he placed a phone call to the home of Santiago Station chief Comer "Wiley" Gilstrap—or his deputy—asking to discuss an "urgent matter." The CIA official agreed to receive a Contreras "confidant," Alvaro Puga, at his house.

Puga suggested that two of Contreras's lawyers, Humberto Olavarria and Sergio Miranda, would go to Washington at the end of August and "negotiate" a settlement in the Letelier case with the CIA, State, and Justice Departments. As the Station officer related the conversation to Ambassador Landau, "a blackmail hint emerged." Puga stated that if forced to defend himself, Contreras would

> have to reveal details [two lines deleted]. It would not be in his, Chile's or the USG's, or the other countries' interest to have this information become public knowledge, but he regretfully would have no choice. Therefore, hopefully a deal can be worked out in Washington that would obviate the need for extradition requests and the subsequent public hearing. (Doc 3)

The blackmail threat, one U.S. official familiar with these communications remembered, was that if the Carter administration pursued the Letelier case, Contreras would expose previous CIA espionage operations toward a specific country in which DINA had collaborated.[16] A few weeks later, the embassy learned that Contreras's media game plan would include "revelation of close ties between the DINA and the CIA in the past, with names and supporting evidence."[17]

To their credit, neither State Department nor CIA officials were intimidated or deterred by this bald gambit. "I said 'Fuck Pinochet,' " recalled Francis McNeil, the ARA official principally responsible for the Letelier-Moffitt case in 1978.[18] With the CIA's agreement, McNeil drafted a cable to the embassy for the Station to use in responding to Contreras. "We told them in no uncertain terms that we would not submit to blackmail," McNeil informed the Defense Department, warning that Contreras might try and approach U.S. military officials in Chile, "and that no representatives or either State or CIA would meet with Contreras representatives."[19] Contreras could "say anything he wants," McNeil assured Assistant U.S. Attorney Propper. "But we're going after him."

Tepid Response to Terrorism

On September 21, 1978—the second anniversary of the car bombing—the U.S. Justice Department presented six-hundred pages of records and documents to the Chilean government as part of the formal petition, under the 1902 extradition treaty with Chile, to extradite Contreras and his subordinates. The Carter administration had overwhelming evidence of the regime's responsibility and complicity. At the same time, SECRET/SENSITIVE documents described "detailed USG knowledge" of the regime's efforts to "subvert Chilean legal procedures," obstruct justice, and block extradition of the DINA officials. To redress an act of terrorism in Washington, the United States would have to overcome the Pinochet regime's concerted effort to stonewall any investigation and cover up its involvement in this crime.

In great contrast to the forceful U.S. response to the terrorist attack of September 11, 2001, however, Washington's reaction in the CHILBOM attack was weak and equivocal. The Carter administration's counterterrorism policy fell victim to divisive bureaucratic competition, and a general lack of conviction to pursue justice and make the Pinochet regime pay a steep price for a terrorist act in Washington D.C.

Numerous mid-level officials in the State and Justice Departments did press hard for a comprehensive, forceful strategic response; as early as October 30, 1978, McNeil presented Assistant Secretary for Inter-American Affairs Viron Vaky with a continuum of measures designed, as he wrote, "to give dominant priority to the Letelier/Moffitt case in the interests of justice and deterrence of other foreign intelligence agencies from similar assassinations."[20] But senior officials chose a less activist route, preferring to wait until the case cleared the Chilean Supreme Court, with the false hopes that if Chile did not extradite its DINA officials, the Pinochet regime would at least put them on trial in Santiago.

On May 13, 1979, the president of the Chilean Supreme Court, Israel Borquez Montero, handed down a preordained decision denying the U.S. extradition request. Townley's confession was a "paid accusation," Borquez ruled, because it was part of a plea-bargain agreement—all evidence derived from it was thrown out. The ruling essentially exonerated DINA of culpability for the Letelier-Moffitt assassination, although Borquez referred suspicions regarding false testimony by the DINA officials to a Chilean military court for further study.

"That decision was much worse than any one of us had anticipated," the National Security Council's Latin America specialist Robert Pastor alerted the President's top security adviser, Zbigniew Brzezinski. U.S. policy toward Chile, he noted in a briefing memorandum, was "reaching the crunch point on Letelier."[21] Indeed, in Washington, the ruling created an immediate uproar in the executive branch, the press, and the Congress. One Congressional initiative, led by the chairman of the House Committee on Banking, Henry Reuss, called for terminating the regime's economic lifeline—private U.S. bank loans that totaled over $1 billion—until the DINA agents were extradited. To express its diplomatic dissatisfaction, on May 16 the State Department recalled Ambassador Landau—for consultations on next steps as well as to convince Congress not to prematurely legislate sanctions against the Pinochet regime.

The Carter administration, however, responded with caution and relative inaction. The State Department decided only to appeal Borquez's ruling to the entire Supreme Court and issue a diplomatic démarche warning of serious consequences for U.S.-Chilean relations if the ruling was not reversed. The internal policy debate focused on the wording and tenor of Ambassador Landau's instructions on expressing U.S. dismay. At a May 24 interagency meeting chaired by Deputy Secretary of State Warren Christopher, Assistant U.S. Attorney Propper argued for a much more forceful approach. "We understand your position," the State Department's number three-man, David Newsom, told Propper. "But you must also understand that we have to take this matter in the context of our entire range of bilateral relations with Chile." Propper's response reflected his incredulity at such a passive reaction to international terrorism: "The Letelier case," he noted, "*is* our relations with Chile."[22]

To be sure, Ambassador Landau's instructions did contain forceful language. When he returned to Santiago from Washington on June 2, Landau issued a statement at the airport rebuking the regime:

> One should not lose sight that in this case U.S. sovereignty has been violated. And not by word but by deed. We should not forget that two persons, a former foreign diplomat and an American citizen, were killed in cold blood right in the heart of our nation's capital. If this terrorist act is not a violation of our sovereignty, then I don't know what is. We cannot allow terrorist acts of this nature to go unpunished.

Relations between Chile and the United States "are approaching a crossroads," Landau warned; if the ruling stood and the DINA officials went free, the Chilean government would be held responsible for "harboring international terrorists" with all due consequences. "If these men walk the streets," the démarche concluded, "I assure you that the reaction of my government, of the U.S. Congress, and of the American people will be severe."[23]

In fact, on October 1, 1979, when the full Supreme Court not only upheld the Borquez ruling but overruled his recommendation for a military court investigation into possible perjury by Contreras and Espinoza, the Carter administration's reaction was indecisive. Far from expressing outrage that an act of state-sponsored terrorism would now go unpunished, the U.S. government agencies with military, economic, and diplomatic interests in maintaining ties with Chile all began furiously lobbying to protect their bureaucratic turfs from becoming part of any forthcoming sanctions. At the White House, Brzezinski, along with Defense Secretary Harold Brown, opposed what they called "aimless punitive actions." Even though the accumulated evidence had been used to convict the three Cuban exile terrorists in a U.S. district court earlier that year, some U.S. officials questioned the strength of the Justice Department's case against the DINA officials. The result was a set of largely symbolic sanctions that had no impact on the Pinochet regime.

At the State Department, the Office of Human Rights and Humanitarian Affairs (HA) led by Assistant Secretary Patricia Derian and her deputy Mark Schneider found itself waging a lonely battle for strong retaliatory measures. On the third anniversary of the crime, Derian sent a SECRET options memo to deputy secretary Warren Christopher laying out numerous proposals for sanctions. These ranged from the symbolic—pulling the Peace Corps out of Chile—to the substantive—"persuade private bank lenders to halt resource flows." U.S. actions, she argued, should be strong enough "to demonstrate clearly that the governments engaged in international terrorism, and those harboring its perpetrators, will suffer penalties."[24] In an October 12 follow-up memorandum to Secretary of State Cyrus Vance, Derian reiterated the need for "vigorous" sanctions "to deter further such government-supported assassinations and to reflect our outrage at this violation of our U.S. sovereignty." Failure to take such steps, she added, "would strengthen Pinochet and those opposed to an accelerated return to democracy."[25]

But State's Latin America bureau, ARA, opposed substantive sanctions. The head of ARA, Assistant Secretary for Inter-American Affairs Viron Vaky—the same official who had, eight years earlier, tried to persuade Kissinger not to pursue covert intervention against Allende—preferred not to compromise ongoing U.S.-Chilean bilateral relations. Vaky also opposed accepting the premise that the DINA agents were guilty. "I am disturbed by the too easy mindset and assumptions we get into of stating the defendants *are* guilty, *are* terrorists, and there *is* miscarriage of justice," he wrote in an October 12 cover memo to Secretary Vance, transmitting a list of nineteen potential actions against Chile. "We should *not* be so self righteous and outraged, but careful and measured. . . . [W]e should react just coldly and not as an avenging angel, however good the latter makes us feel." (Emphasis in original)

Vaky's position found an ally at the National Security Council—Robert Pastor. "I have never been comfortable with the way State has handled the Letelier case," Pastor wrote to Brzezinski after a preliminary draft list of sanctions landed on his desk on October 11. "I have been unable to comprehend the transformation of the U.S. from government to prosecutor to judge, which is where we currently are." Pastor, who was deliberately kept out of the loop by Justice and State Department officials, informed Brzezinski that the State Department had failed to justify its rejection of the Chilean Supreme Court ruling. "That case may exist," he wrote, "but I haven't seen it yet, and I have asked repeatedly for it."[26]

In an interagency meeting on October 15 to discuss sanctions against Chile, Pastor asked again, putting this question directly to Assistant U.S. Attorney Lawrence Barcella: "are we *that* confident in the evidence that we presented that we can say with assurance that the decision of the Chilean Supreme Court was in fact in error?" Barcella, who passed out autopsy photographs of the victims to remind the bureaucrats of the human nature of this crime, responded that the evidence was overwhelming.[27] "We have unequivocal proof," he told Pastor and thirty other officials, "of the most heinous act of political terrorism ever committed in the nation's capital. We have proven that it was agents of a foreign power who carried it out. That foreign power has now blatantly rejected our request to see that justice is done, and it's up to the people in this room to respond."[28]

On October 19, Secretary Vance transmitted to President Carter—via a special "Alpha Channel"—the final State Department recommendations for sanctions against Chile. Nineteen options had been whittled down to six, among them terminating $7 million of military equipment still in the foreign military sales pipeline to Chile; ending the Overseas Private Investment Program (which had not operated in Chile since 1970); suspending Export-Import Bank credits; canceling export licenses for purchases by the Chilean military, and withdrawing all four members of the U.S. MilGroup stationed in Santiago. Gone were what Vance labeled "extreme measures" such as a cutoff of private bank loans, and an indefinite recall of the U.S. ambassador to Chile. "Steps of this sort," he wrote the president, "would not serve our interests in Chile or elsewhere." (Doc 4)

The White House decided to reduce the sanctions even further. On October 26, President Carter approved four of the six recommendations,[29] and changed the proposal to withdraw the U.S. MilGroup to a simple reduction of two members.[30] (In early 1980 an additional symbolic sanction, canceling Chilean participation in the UNITAS naval maneuvers, would be added.) The president, as Brzezinski wrote in a SECRET memo to Vance titled "Letelier/Moffitt Case and U.S. Policy to Chile," had determined that these actions "would constitute a strong reaffirmation of our determination to resist international terrorism and a deterrent to those who might be tempted to commit similar acts within our borders."

But the saga of the sanctions did not end there. For almost five weeks, administration officials delayed announcement of the U.S. response. Initially the delay was intended to avoid an adverse impact on Congressional consideration of a U.S. aid package for Latin America. Then, on November 4, the U.S. experienced another act of terrorism when Iranian fundamentalists swarmed the U.S. embassy in Teheran, taking the staff hostage and demanding that the Carter administration return the Shah, who had come to the U.S. for medical treatment. Vance again delayed announcement of the Chile sanctions, fearing that they could be used to bolster Iranian demands for extradition of the Shah. "The Chilean issue will not go away, and the longer the Iranian crisis goes on, the more likely people will begin drawing parallels between the two cases," Pastor advised Brzezinski on November 19. In a SECRET/EYES ONLY memorandum titled "The Letelier Case—a Time to Reassess," Pastor recommended "you speak to the President about reconsidering the decisions on Chile in light of the crisis in Iran."

The sanctions were not reconsidered; but U.S. officials did redraft the language used to announce them. Instead of tying the measures to Chile's refusal to extradite the DINA terrorists, the administration focused on the Pinochet regime's "refusal to conduct a full and fair investigation of this crime." At a press briefing on November 30, two full months after the Chilean Supreme Court ruling, White House press secretary Hodding Carter announced the measures, stating that the regime "has, in effect, condoned this act of international terrorism." In his final comment the presidential spokesman noted that the press had made comparisons between the Letelier case and the ongoing Iranian hostage crisis. "There is only one link between those two situations," he concluded. "Both involve egregious acts of international terrorism, and in both cases our responses reflect our determination to resist such terrorist acts, wherever they occur."

Reagan and Pinochet

U.S. sanctions imposed on Chile lasted approximately one year.[31] Soon after Ronald Reagan's inauguration, in his very first policy gesture toward Latin America, his administration announced that it would rescind Jimmy Carter's limited measures against the Pinochet regime. At the same time, Reagan's new foreign policy team began working behind the scenes to restore positive U.S. relations with the regime. "You asked about our Chile policy," Reagan's secretary of state, Alexander Haig, wrote in a SECRET memo to the new president on February 16, 1981. "In the next few days I plan to lift the prohibition on Ex-Im Bank financing and approve DOD's invitation list for this year's UNITAS naval exercise, to include Chile. These are the two most annoying aspects of current policy under Executive Branch control. We will have a full inter-agency review in about one month to decide on further adjustments." (Doc 5)

Ironically, Reagan had ridden a wave of public outrage against terrorism into the Oval Office. "It is high time that the civilized countries of this world made it plain that there is no room worldwide for terrorism," he declared on the eve of his election. When it came to Chile, the White House made clear, there was a little room after all. The new president himself was a member of a small clique of right-wing ideologues who had shamelessly cast the victim as villain, and actively disseminated the regime's specious "martyr theory"—that leftists carried out the car bombing. In 1978 Reagan used his nationally broadcast radio program to accuse Letelier of being an "unregistered foreign agent" with "links to international Marxist and terrorist groups." As the future president told his listeners: "a question worth asking is whether Letelier might have been murdered by his own masters. Alive he could be compromised; dead he could become a martyr."[32] In testimony before Congress, Reagan's new ambassador-at-large, Gen. Vernon Walters, rationalized the Letelier-Moffitt car bombing as "a mistake" comparable to Napoleon's murder of the Duke of Enghien. As Walters summed up the new administration's attitude: "You can't rub their noses in it forever."[33]

In the reconfigured political priorities of President Reagan and his advisers, Pinochet's avid anticommunism far outweighed his violent atrocities. The fact that the regime had sponsored an act of terrorism on a Washington street, for these policy makers, did not make it any less pro-American. Indeed, Pinochet epitomized the "moderate autocrat friendly to American interests," as the new U.N. Ambassador Jeane Kirkpatrick characterized "authoritarian" military rulers in her famous *Commentary* article, "Dictatorships and Double Standards," which attacked Jimmy Carter's policy on human rights.[34] The Chileans could be counted on as an ideological ally in the battle against Soviet influence in the hemisphere and a supporter of a hard-line, militarist U.S. approach to revolutionary upheaval in Central America in the 1980s. In addition, Reagan officials saw Chile as a model for the free market, monetarist economic policies the administration intended to implement. "The Reagan administration," Kirkpatrick declared in the summer of 1981, "shares the same convictions as the architects of Chile's economic policy—that a free market approach will prove more effective in restoring fully the economic strength in the United States."

After four years of tense relations with the Carter administration, General Pinochet viewed Washington's renewed support as vindication and validation. The Reagan era, Chilean officials expected, portended an end to the country's international isolation as a pariah nation. "Seven years ago," Pinochet began telling Chilean audiences within two months of Reagan's election, "we found ourselves alone in the world in our firm anticommunist position in opposition to Soviet imperialism, and our firm decision in favor of a socioeconomic free enterprise system." Today, he declared, "we form part of a pronounced worldwide tendency—and I tell you, ladies and gentlemen, it is not Chile that has changed its position."

The Reagan team moved quickly to embrace the regime, and normalize bilateral relations estranged during the four years of the Carter administration. Public pronouncements of U.S. friendship became frequent; in July 1981, the administration began voting in favor of multilateral bank loans to Chile—in contemptuous violation of the 1977 International Financial Institutions Act mandating a "no" vote on loans to governments that engage in a consistent pattern of human rights violations.[35] At the United Nations, Ambassador Kirkpatrick now voted against a special human rights *rapporteur* to investigate abuses in Chile.

Diplomatic exchanges, unheard of since the days of Henry Kissinger's warm support for the Junta, also increased significantly. In late February 1981, Reagan sent his special envoy General Walters to see Pinochet. Walters conveyed a private message from Secretary Haig, and briefed the dictator on U.S. counterinsurgency operations in El Salvador. "We spoke as old friends," Walters reported back in a secret memorandum of conversation. "He was obviously very pleased to see me. He offered full support and said he would do anything we wanted to help us in the Salvadoran situation."[36] In August, Ambassador Kirkpatrick also traveled to Santiago, meeting with military and business leaders but avoiding pro-democracy and human rights groups. "We had a very pleasant tea," Kirkpatrick told reporters as she emerged from a private meeting with Pinochet. "My conversation with the president had no other fundamental purpose than for me to propose to him my government's desire to fully normalize our relations with Chile." In an overview of her visit, the Santiago embassy cabled Washington that Pinochet had "responded immediately and warmly to the basic themes of her statements on the U.S. desire to rebuild cooperative and equitable ties." In sum, the embassy reported, "Ambassador Kirkpatrick's visit was extremely valuable in accelerating the return to cooperative relations."

Repealing the Kennedy Amendment

Normalizing relations required removing the legislative bans on military and economic assistance to Chile. Through the spring and fall of 1981, the administration lobbied hard for repeal of the Kennedy amendment. Pinochet's closest ally in the U.S. Senate, Jesse Helms, led the attack, brushing away arguments that Washington should not be providing military aid to a terrorist government. Letelier, he claimed without a shred of proof, was "an agent of terrorism." On the floor of the U.S. Senate, Helms then proceeded to justify the assassination: "He who lives by the sword shall die by the sword."[37]

The bill to repeal the Kennedy amendment passed, but with significant conditions on renewing U.S. military support to Pinochet. The final legislation, influenced by human rights lobbyists in the House of Representatives, stated that any U.S. weapons or equipment sales, credits or military services would require President Reagan to certify that:

- The government of Chile has made significant progress in complying with internationally recognized human rights.
- The government of Chile is not aiding and abetting international terrorism.

- The government of Chile has taken appropriate steps to cooperate to bring to justice those indicted in connection with the murders of Orlando Letelier and Ronni Moffitt.

The Reagan administration had no problem certifying Chile on human rights grounds—despite the regime's ongoing high-profile atrocities. On February 26, 1982, CNI agents brutally murdered Chile's most famous trade union leader, Tucapel Jiménez, who was organizing a united labor front to oppose the regime's economic and political repression; he was found shot in the head and garroted to the point of decapitation. Yet, only two weeks later Assistant Secretary for Inter-American Affairs Thomas Enders traveled to Santiago to confer with Chilean officials and, according to one cable, "reiterated that the human rights question was not our immediate concern."

But the certification clause on the Letelier-Moffitt case did cause immediate concern. Both the FBI and the Justice Department actively opposed certification of Chilean cooperation, and were quite willing to say so publicly. "They haven't done spit," Assistant U.S. Attorney Barcella told the *Washington Post* about Pinochet's government. "In fact, they've been dilatory and obstructionist." Barcella and his colleagues drafted a highly classified twelve-page catalogue listing the regime's failure to cooperate and conduct its own investigation, and its multiple attempts, including the falsification of evidence, to obstruct the U.S. investigation. Privately, FBI and Justice officials warned the State Department that they would testify before Congress that any presidential certification was unfounded and false.

"You may or may not know that the DOJ seems strongly opposed to certification with respect to the Letelier case, as is the FBI," then Assistant Secretary for Human Rights and Humanitarian Affairs, Elliott Abrams warned in an EYES ONLY memo to one of Secretary Haig's deputies, Lawrence Eagleburger. "This seems to me to make it impossible to certify, for the only acceptable action on the part of the GOC might put half the [Chilean] government in jail." Pressuring the Justice Department to change its position, Abrams counseled, would be a public relations disaster. "I don't know whether there is anything the Chileans can do for us to satisfy the (foolish) demands of Congress," he advised Eagleburger. "What I am sure of is that significant opposition in the DOJ exists and that any attempt to steamroller the DOJ will be extremely damaging front-page news."[38]

Abrams joined a number of other bureaus in the State Department in recommending to Secretary Haig that the president not certify Chile along with Argentina, as Haig had planned in March 1982. A secret options memorandum—"Presidential Determinations Authorizing Security Assistance and

Arms Sales for Argentina and Chile"—presented to the secretary by seven deputies and assistant secretaries, warned that the Chile certification "will be particularly controversial." On improvements in human rights "there had been none since [1979]." The Letelier-Moffitt case posed even larger problems, the memo acknowledged. To claim Chile had cooperated in the pursuit of justice was "an extremely difficult proposition to sustain and to defend." Some bureaus worried that the certification "would also weaken our emphasis on countering international terrorism."

But there was an even larger issue for those opposing the Chile certification: compromising Reagan's top foreign policy priority of escalating U.S. counterinsurgency operations in Central America. To sustain U.S. military involvement in the region, the administration had already sent one mendacious certification on El Salvador to an increasingly skeptical Congress, and was preparing another. "The recent certification on El Salvador was even more acrimonious and difficult than we had anticipated," the authors reminded Haig. The Chile certification, particularly the clause on the Letelier-Moffitt case, would hurt the credibility of future appeals to lawmakers:

> An important question is whether sending the Chile certification will so damage our credibility on human rights as to coalesce the [Congressional] opposition, and therefore have a dangerous spillover effect on our El Salvador policy and serve to discredit the President's upcoming Caribbean Basin initiative.

This argument prevailed; the Reagan White House deferred certifying Chile. By the time the administration had finally achieved a consensus in Congress on massive intervention in Central America in 1986, however, U.S. policy interests in providing military assistance and sales to the Pinochet regime had been overtaken by events and there was a stronger policy posture against certification. As one internal State Department memorandum noted: "we do not believe Chile has met the criteria."

Iran-Contra: The Chilean Connection

Ironically, the Reagan administration sought carte blanche on military assistance to Chile, in part as a way of enlisting Pinochet's support in the Central American imbroglio. In 1980 and 1981, the Chilean regime provided substantive training and tactical advice to Salvador's cutthroat military forces. (For Chile's avid support, in May 1981 the Salvadoran high command bestowed the José Matias Delgado award on General Pinochet.) In Nicaragua, Chile was considered a potential ally in the National Security Council's illicit pro-insurgency paramilitary campaign against the Sandinista government—particularly after the U.S. Congress cut funding for CIA support of the contra war in October 1984.

In late 1984, declassified White House memoranda reveal, Lt. Col. Oliver North, the NSC official in charge of sustaining the contras after the Congressional ban on the CIA, secretly turned to the Pinochet regime for a key weapons system: the British-made Blowpipe missile. The Sandinistas were attacking contra positions with sophisticated Soviet-provided Hind helicopters; North's advisors told him that the contras needed these shoulder-held antiaircraft weapons. In a memorandum to the president's national security adviser, Robert McFarlane, dated December 20 and stamped TOP SECRET, North wrote that he had been "informed that BLOWPIPE surface-to-air missiles may be available in [Chile] for use by F.D.N. [the largest contra group] in dealing with the HIND helicopters. This information was passed through an appropriate secure and source protected means to [contra leader] Adolfo Calero who proceeded immediately to Santiago."

Entries in North's notebooks indicated that Calero and his delegation were in Chile between December 7 and 17, 1984. On December 17, North recorded the following phone conversation with Calero:

> Call from Barnaby [Calero's code name]—Returned from Chile—48 Blowpipes, free-8 launchers, 25 K ea.—Have to inform Brts—6–10 pers[ons] for training, starts 2 Jan—Will have to buy some items from Chileans which are somewhat more expensive—Deliver by sea w/trainers by end of Jan. (Doc 6)

The Chileans, as North advised McFarlane, had offered forty-eight missiles, launchers, and training "for up to ten three-man teams from the FDN on a no-cost basis." Calero, North added, "will dispatch the trainees to Chile on December 23."

There was one complication, however. In his December 20 memo, titled "Follow-up with Thatcher re: Terrorism and Central America," North noted that the Chileans had said "they would need to obtain British permission for the transfer" of the Blowpipes. North proposed having President Reagan discreetly ask British Prime Minister Margaret Thatcher to intercede on the contras' behalf.

This first initiative to get missiles from Chile ran into additional complications. On January 3, 1985, according to North's notebook entry for that day, Calero informed him that the Pinochet regime wanted to include ammunition and mortar rounds in the deal that were "too expensive." As Calero put it, the "Blow-Pipe deal is off." But additional attempts followed over the next fifteen months. Encrypted cables and secret e-mail messages between North and McFarlane's successor, Admiral John Poindexter, show that throughout the spring of 1986, NSC officials tried to obtain a British reexport license for Chile to arrange a "quick transfer of 6–10 BP." Their elaborate scheme called for Short Brothers, the Belfast-based manufacturer of the Blowpipe missile, to facilitate the transfer of the weapons from Chile to the contra forces through El Salvador, using falsified end-user certificates—a document required in major arms sales. An obscure entry under "current obligations" in the handwritten account ledger kept by North's contra arms supplier for May 1986 reads *BP $1,000,000 Chile,* suggesting that a substantial payment was expected to be made on the Blowpipe deal. "[W]e are trying to find a way to get 10 BLOW-PIPE launchers and 20 missiles from Chile thru the Short Bros. Rep," North reported to McFarlane over an encoded computer line on March 26 adding:

> The V.P. from Short Bros. sought me out several mos. Ago and I met w/ him again. . . . Short Bros., the mfgr. of the BLOWPIPE, is willing to arrange the deal, conduct the training and even send U.K. "tech. reps" fwd if we *can* close the arrangement. Dick Secord has already paid 10% down on the delivery and we have a [country deleted] EUC [end-user certificate] which is applicable to Chile.

But the issue of Pinochet's human rights atrocities came back to haunt this highly covert operation. Unaware of this secret approach to the Pinochet regime, the State Department inadvertently undermined the deal. "Unfortunately," North continued, "the week all this was going to closure we decided to go fwd [deleted reference to the State Department decision, on March 12, to sponsor a United Nations resolution condemning the regime's human rights abuses]." Pinochet's officials were furious with what they considered as the Reagan administration's betrayal.

"The arrangement is now on ice," North told McFarlane, "and we are casting about for a way to tell the Chileans that we wd be pleased if this all went thru." (Doc 7)[39]

Abandoning the Dictator

The Reagan administration's sponsorship of a U.N. resolution critical of Chile's human rights record marked a slow shift away from its early uncritical embrace of the Pinochet regime. Ironically, at the very moment North's contra representatives were secretly seeking military assistance in Santiago, the State Department initiated a major internal policy review on Chile. On December 13, 1984, Assistant Secretary for Inter-American Affairs Langhorne A. Motley held the first of three meetings with the RIG—a high-level Restricted Interagency Group made up of State, CIA, DOD, and NSC officials—to seek authorization to revamp U.S. policy toward Pinochet. On December 20th—the very same day as North submitted his request for Reagan's help in obtaining British support for the transfer of the missiles from Chile—Motley presented a draft policy proposal to the Deputy Secretary outlining "an activist but gradual approach to try to influence an orderly and peaceful transition to democracy in Chile." (Doc 8)

This reassessment was based on increasing instability in Chile, which set off alarm bells throughout a national security bureaucracy already obsessed with the upheaval in Central America. According to the policy paper:

> U.S. interests would be best served by Pinochet's leadership of a real and orderly transition to democracy. However, it is increasingly evident that Pinochet is unlikely to lead such a transition. While ostensibly serving U.S. anticommunist interests in the short run, Pinochet's intransigence on democracy is creating instability in Chile inimical to U.S. interests.

Fostering a moderate center in Chilean politics, Motley stated in a familiar refrain, would be key to protecting long-term U.S. interests. The aim of a new U.S policy approach would be "strengthening the disorganized [Chilean] moderates, specifically, weaning them away from the radical left."

Pinochet's protracted crisis of power created the catalyst for U.S. concerns. As CIA analysts summed up the situation in a succinct 1984 intelligence report, "Pinochet Under Pressure," the Chilean political scene had changed, "irreversibly we believe," over the last two years:

- Public attitudes toward the government's free market policies have been soured by a recession.
- Trade unions and political parties have undergone a revival that has brought political life back to Chile.
- Radical leftists have become more politically active—holding public

meetings and participating in informal discussions with moderate parties—and the Chilean Communist Party has developed a nationwide organizational base that is second only to the Christian Democratic Party.

- The number, sophistication, and boldness of radical leftist terrorist attacks have escalated dramatically in the last ten months, prompting . . . an increase in right-wing extremist attacks against political opposition figures.
- Military solidarity with Pinochet has suffered its first strains over differences in how to handle political dissent and the timetable for returning Chile to civilian rule.

The military regime's problems began in mid-1982 when the country suffered its worst economic recession since the Great Depression. Gross national product plummeted by 14 percent; unemployment rose to 30 percent. Chile's foreign debt reached $19 billion, then the highest per-capita debt in the world. The "economic miracle" created by the University of Chicago-trained students of free market guru and regime adviser Milton Friedman, was discredited.

The economic crisis reinvigorated the opposition to Pinochet, which increasingly included members of the conservative upper middle class hit hard by financial losses. Across the social spectrum, political parties, human rights organizations, trade unionists, and church groups all began the arduous task of mobilizing a national coalition to end military rule and restore democracy.[40] On May 11, 1983, the opposition held the first "national day of protest" that *El Mercurio* called "the most serious challenge which the government has faced in almost ten years." Thereafter, major street demonstrations and other displays of organized public discontent became frequent. At the same time, the Chilean Communist Party (PCCH) began a major campaign to regroup and revitalize its constituents. The more militant wing of the PCCH created an armed faction, the Manuel Rodriguez Patriotic Front, which carried out attacks on government installations. On September 7, 1986, the Patriotic Front boldly attempted to ambush and assassinate General Pinochet.

The regime responded to these manifestations of opposition by attempting to siphon off the moderate civilian leaders while unleashing the military's apparatus of repression. Between May and September 1983, eighty-five people were shot and killed; over 5,000 arrested. At the same time, Pinochet reshuffled his cabinet and appointed a well-known moderate conservative, Sergio Jarpa, as interior minister. He authorized Jarpa to hold a dialogue with moderate political parties regarding the 1980 constitution that the Junta had pushed through to legitimize Pinochet and gave him the opportunity to extend his personal dictatorship to the near end of the century.

Pinochet cast his 1980 constitution as providing a "protected" and "safe" transition back to democracy. Its provisions allowed for him to hold a "Yes/No" plebiscite in 1989 on a military candidate put forth by the Junta to be president until 1997—the candidate being Pinochet himself. In the extremely unlikely event that the *no* vote won, according to the constitution, Pinochet would remain in power for another seventeen months until controlled elections for a civilian president and Congress were held. Thereafter, he would remain commander-in-chief of the armed forces until 1997. The military would be given a set of seats in the new Senate and would continue to control policy through a National Security Council with widespread powers.

The opposition, including the centrist political parties, rejected the 1980 Constitution as illegitimate: it had been drafted by the military and voted on in a heavily manipulated plebiscite that was neither free nor fair. As the CIA's Directorate of Intelligence acknowledged in a comprehensive report, the regime had left "no stone unturned" in assuring the passage of the Constitution, "resorting to extensive intimidation of opposition groups, arbitrary measures to undercut the efforts of those advocating a *no* vote, and at least some fraud during the balloting and tabulation of the votes."[41] In Jarpa's dialogue with a coalition of noncommunist political parties called the Democratic Alliance, opposition leaders pressed for an accelerated timetable for the restoration of democracy, and called for Pinochet to resign and the secret police to be disbanded. The regime refused to yield on any opposition demands, and the dialogue disintegrated. In late 1984, Pinochet declared a state of siege under which the CNI escalated its brutal political assassinations of leftist leaders; in February 1985 he fired Jarpa and ended any effort at negotiations with pro-transition forces.

The Reagan administration now faced a dilemma similar to the one its predecessor confronted in Iran and Nicaragua—how to handle a stagnating, belligerent, and isolated dictatorship now an embarrassment, and increasingly a danger, to U.S. political and international interests. For Washington, the situation had implications that reached beyond Santiago, extending to Central America, Europe, and Capitol Hill.

In the administration's relations with Congress, Chile had become a major liability. The Pinochet regime had made a mockery of Reagan's claims that "quiet diplomacy," reinforced by cozy relations, would prove effective in advancing the cause of human rights. The results weakened the credibility of similar arguments administration spokesmen made virtually every week on El Salvador and Guatemala. More importantly, the Chile policy revealed the utter hypocrisy of the administration's pressure on Congress to provide tens of millions in paramilitary assistance for the contra war in the name of promoting democracy in Nicaragua, while failing to take any active steps to press Pinochet for a return to civilian rule. Numerous Congressmen, and a number of European allies troubled by U.S. policy in both Central America and Chile, cited this "double standard" in Reagan's approach to Pinochet. Not until March 1986, after the collapse of two other long-standing U.S. client regimes—Marcos in the Philippines and Duvalier in Haiti—did the president vow to "oppose tyranny in whatever form, whether of the left or the right."

Topping the list of policy concerns, however, was that Pinochet's intransigence with the centrist opposition had fostered instability and insurgency, helping to revitalize the very leftist forces in Chile that the regime, with U.S. support, had sought to brutally eradicate. In the State Department's policy review, officials underscored this point:

> the failure of pro-transition forces in the GOC, both military and civilian, and pro-negotiation forces in the opposition, to reach an understanding during the past fifteen months, has created conditions favorable to the apparent attempt by the PCCH to launch an armed, Tupamaros or Montoneros-type insurgency in Chile. Continued delay in reaching such an agreement will encourage the PCCH in its policy of violent opposition to Pinochet.

During a four-day trip to Santiago in mid-February 1985, Assistant Secretary Motley privately told the Chilean dictator that "if he [Pinochet] were writing the script for the Communists, he couldn't write it better than he was doing then."[42]

Motley's trip was supposed to be the first salvo in a new U.S. policy effort to press Pinochet to find common ground with the noncommunist opposition on negotiating a transition. But the assistant secretary's warm public endorsements of the regime overshadowed whatever private pressure he brought from Washington. In an interview with *El Mercurio*, he stated the world owed Chile "a debt of gratitude" for overthrowing Allende. At an airport press conference as he left, he noted that the "future of Chile is in Chilean hands, and from what I've seen those are good hands." The Motley visit, according to a subsequent State Department assessment, "was probably a net plus for Pinochet and resulted in no increased leverage for the U.S. on the transition."

In his own after-action report to Secretary of State George Shultz, Motley shared several superficial conclusions: Pinochet was "as formidable a head of government as we face in this hemisphere"; "Pinochet does not respond to external pressure"; "Chile and therefore our interests are headed for trouble over the long haul." He offered only vague "ideas on how maybe we can quietly help influence the situation internally." As ARA assistant secretary, his position was to continue to use "quiet diplomacy" to gently nudge Pinochet and the military. In his memorandum to Shultz, Motley complained that public criticism by Assistant Secretary for Human Rights and Humanitarian Affairs Elliott Abrams was "not in consonance with agreed-to U.S. policy," and could "only exacerbate the situation."[43]

Within a few months, however, Abrams replaced Motley as assistant secretary for inter-American affairs. Under Abrams, who also assumed a key policy role in the illegal contra resupply operations, the U.S. approach to Chile focused more aggressively on pressing elements of the military government toward a transition. To put the regime on notice, Washington began abstaining on votes on multilateral development bank loans; in internal memoranda, Abrams claimed credit for using this tactic to convince the regime to lift the state of siege in June 1985. At the same time, through stepped-up contacts and communications, Washington sought to separate the Christian Democrats from the leftist opposition, and push them into collaboration with the rightist civilian political interests. U.S. policy makers enlisted the AFL-CIO to back non-Marxist labor unions in Chile. Washington also approached the British, Germans, and the Vatican to coordinate influence and pressure on the Chilean military and centrist and center-right politicians.

In an Oval Office meeting on September 6, 1985, Secretary of State Shultz briefed President Reagan on the policy now being implemented in his name. "We are not trying to overthrow Pinochet," Shultz told the president, according to his talking points. "[B]ut there is increasing evidence that he is becoming an obstacle to the gradual evolution in Chilean politics that would favor our interest in a peaceful transition to a civilian elected government." Pinochet's intransigence would lead to Chile becoming "increasingly polarized," Shultz explained, which would "benefit the Communists." The United States would "continue to seek cooperation, dialogue and compromise," he assured Reagan, according to a memorandum prepared for the meeting, "but there is a growing tension between our national interest in orderly and peaceful transition and Pinochet's apparent desire to hang on indefinitely." (Doc 9)

In the fall of 1985, the Reagan administration used the appointment of a new ambassador to Chile, Harry Barnes, to make a stronger and more open statement about U.S. support for a return to civilian rule. When Barnes presented his credentials to Pinochet in mid-November, he pointedly remarked, "The ills of democracy can best be cured by more democracy." He then gave Pinochet a personal letter from Ronald Reagan. The letter reviewed the support and cooperation the administration had given to the regime since 1981, but noted that future cooperation would be conditioned by definable progress toward a democratic transition. "Just as in Central America the full exercise of personal and political liberties has helped the struggle against Communist subversion, progress in Chile will be similar aid," the U.S. president wrote to Pinochet. "I feel even more strongly than ever that evident progress toward full democracy in Chile is needed."

Rodrigo Rojas

The murder by immolation of a Chilean teenager, Rodrigo Rojas, drove the final wedge between Washington and the Pinochet regime. Rojas was a legal American resident; he had come to Washington D.C. in 1977 at age ten as a refugee with his younger brother and mother, Veronica De Negri, herself a torture victim and political prisoner after the coup. For eleven formative years, Rojas grew up in the activist Chilean exile community in the nation's capital, involving himself in numerous human rights and solidarity activities against the Pinochet regime. He became an avid and skilled amateur photographer, and developed a fascination for *Jane's Defense Weekly* and encyclopedias on armaments and military equipment. He was a dear friend of mine.[44] I knew him to be smart and confident, curious but cocky—and very impulsive as teenagers are wont to be. As he grew older, he became increasingly agitated about returning to his homeland.

In May 1986, Rojas dropped out of his last semester at Woodrow Wilson High School, and returned to Santiago to do freelance photography and participate in the growing opposition to the regime. On July 2, he joined a student street demonstration in the barrio of Los Nogales to photograph the protest movement. Rojas and another protester, Carmen Quintana, were intercepted by an army street patrol. As doctors who later treated them at a neighborhood clinic told U.S. embassy officials:

> Soldiers surrounded them and began to beat them. It is reported that the beating was severe and that Rojas attempted to shield Quintana. The soldiers then sprayed them with a flammable substance and set them on fire. The soldiers then wrapped blankets around them, threw them into a military vehicle, drove them to the town of Quilicura, just north of Santiago, where they threw them out of the vehicle into a ditch. They were then sighted by a passerby.[45]

Both Rojas and Quintana survived the initial beating and burning. They were taken to a small clinic, the Posta Central, where their treatment was described as "archaic and insufficient." The director of the clinic, under pressure from the military, prevented them from being transferred to a fully equipped burn unit at a major hospital. After four days of inadequate care, at 3:50 P.M. on July 6, nineteen-year-old Rodrigo Rojas died.[46]

The horrific nature of the crime, and the fact that Rojas was a resident of Washington transformed this atrocity into an international human rights scandal. The case of *Los Quemados*—the burned ones—provoked an outrage around the world, and sent a "shock wave" through Capitol Hill, as classified State Department memos admitted, reinvigorating harsh criticism of the regime. The case received so much media coverage that even President Reagan was briefed on developments. In a "Presidential Evening Reading" paper, classified SECRET/WNINTEL/NOFORN/NOCONTRACT/ORCON, Reagan was informed that Pinochet had labeled Rojas and Quintana "terrorists" and "victims of their own Molotov cocktails," even as Chile's own intelligence service "has fingered Army personnel as clearly involved." (Doc 10)[47] An internal investigation by the Chilean Carabineros quickly identified the army patrol and its commander, Lt. Pedro Fernández Dittus, as responsible, sources reported to the embassy. But Pinochet personally rejected any evidence of the military's guilt.[48] His regime soon set out to intimidate all witnesses that could identify the army personnel. "One eyewitness was briefly kidnapped, blindfolded, and threatened if he did not change his testimony," the DIA reported in a TOP SECRET RUFF UMBRA cable. "Some members of the government will quite likely continue to intimidate the witnesses in order to persuade them to change their testimony, thereby clearing the military."

In a symbolic gesture of protest against the regime, Ambassador Barnes and his wife joined Veronica De Negri in attending the Rojas funeral on July 11. During the burial procession, Barnes and 5,000 mourners were assaulted with water cannon and tear gas from military units to disperse the crowd. To add insult to injury, the government then planted accusations in the press that the Barnes's presence at the funeral had incited rioting. In the midst of the uproar, Pinochet further thumbed his nose at Washington by publicly announcing that he intended to stay in power through to the end of the century.

With the Rojas case, the breach of political relations between the U.S. and Pinochet reached a point of no return. On July 10, Assistant Secretary Abrams appeared on the ABC news program *Nightline* and issued the harshest public criticism to date from any Reagan administration official. "Fundamentally, the most important thing to say is that this is not an elected government," he told Ted Koppel. "I think there are very good grounds to be very skeptical that President Pinochet wants any kind of a transition. . . . We don't want to see it happen in the next millennium. We'd like to see it happen a little bit sooner than that." In a SECRET/SENSITIVE memo to Secretary Shultz,

Abrams reported that "I used my appearance yesterday on ABC's *Nightline* to stress our commitment to eventual free elections in Chile . . . sooner rather than later. But more than verbal volleys will be required to get Pinochet to agree to leave, or to persuade the Army to persuade him."

The "bottom line," as Abrams concluded, "is we face a worsening situation in Chile and need to use all available means of influence to protect our interests." (Doc 11)

Pinochet's Endgame: Voting Down the Regime

On February 2, 1988, fourteen of Chile's political parties announced the creation of a unified coalition—the Concertacíon de Partidos Para el NO—intended to defeat Pinochet in the upcoming plebiscite called for by the regime's 1980 constitution. The deck was stacked against the opposition; the military controlled the media and the ballot box, and held extreme coercive powers over the Chilean citizenry. Political leaders would be arrested; opposition rallies would be broken up by force; offices of the "NO" would be set on fire. But even under campaign and voting rules written, violently imposed, and controlled by the regime, the plebiscite still represented the best opportunity to peacefully rid Chile of Pinochet's fifteen-year-old dictatorship.

The effort to unite around one common goal marked a historic moment of cooperation among Chile's historically divided, and divisive, right, center, and left political leadership. The Communist Party, and several radical factions of the Socialist Party were excluded from the Concertacíon; but many Marxist leaders also called on their constituents to organize in support of what came to be called the "Command for the NO." A former Allende protégé and future Socialist Party president, Ricardo Lagos,[49] became a key campaigner for the NO; a senior Christian Democrat, Patricio Aylwin, became the command's designated spokesman, and another member of the PDC, Genero Arriagada, brilliantly managed the campaign. The opposition organized a comprehensive and extremely successful voter registration drive, registering over 92 percent of the eligible electorate by August 30, 1988. The Command for the NO also recruited poll watchers at all 22,000 voting tables and set up a secret computer system to assure that vote tallies would be rapidly transmitted to Santiago for independent tabulation and verification on October 5—D-day for the pro-democracy forces in Chile.

The Reagan administration channeled funds into the opposition campaign through the National Endowment for Democracy (NED)—a quasi-government entity set up to overtly supplement CIA covert funding of groups fighting to overthrow the Sandinista government in Nicaragua—as well as the AFL-CIO and the National Democratic Institute. Some $1.6 million went into the registration drive, voter education, opinion polling, media consultants, and organizing a rapid response parallel vote count on the day of the election. Ambassador Harry Barnes vigorously and openly supported the civic organizations that carried on much of the work to garner electoral support for the NO. The pro-Pinochet press began referring to him as "Dirty Harry." Campaigning to extend his dictatorship through 1997, General Pinochet issued repeated denounciations of "Yanqui imperialism" in Chile.

Washington's most significant actions during the plebiscite were its intelligence operations and diplomatic efforts to track and counter Pinochet's plans to nullify the plebiscite, if he lost, through acts of violence. As early as May 1988, the CIA learned, elements of the Chilean army had concluded that the NO could not be allowed to win. A chief concern, the Station reported in a heavily censored cable titled "The Increasing Resolve within the Military to Avoid a Civilian Government in Chile," was the regime's record of terrorism and human rights violations. There was a "great fear that a civilian government would cooperate with the United States Government in pursuing the case of the assassination of former foreign minister Orlando Letelier," the CIA noted, "as well as other abuses by the military, to the extreme detriment of the Chilean Army."

By late September, polls indicated that the NO campaign had surged ahead as Chileans became confident that safeguards, including hundreds of international election observers, would insure a non-fraudulent election. "Public perception of the 'NO' is increasingly that of a winner," the embassy reported on September 29. The next day, however, Ambassador Barnes sent the first "alerting" cable to Washington on information he had received regarding an "imminent possibility of government staged coup" if the vote went against Pinochet.

Both CIA and DIA intelligence provided what Ambassador Barnes characterized as "a clear sense of Pinochet's determination to use violence on whatever scale is necessary to retain power." In a secret report for Assistant Secretary Elliott Abrams, Barnes summarized Pinochet's scheme:

> Pinochet's plan is simple: A) if the "Yes" is winning, fine: B) if the race is very close rely on fraud and coersion: C) If the "NO" is likely to win clear then use violence and terror to stop the process. To help prepare the atmosphere the CNI will have the job of providing adequate violence before and on 5 October. Since we know that Pinochet's closest advisors now realize he is likely to lose, we believe the third option is the one most likely to be put into effect with probable substantial loss of life.[50]

Highly placed U.S. intelligence sources within the Chilean army command provided additional details. A Defense Intelligence Agency summary, classified TOP SECRET ZARF UMBRA, reported that

> Close supporters of President Pinochet are said to have contingency plans to derail the plebiscite by encouraging and staging acts of violence. They hope that such violence will elicit further reprisals by the radical opposition and begin a cycle of rioting and disorder. The plans call for government security forces to intervene forcefully and, citing damage to the electoral process and balloting facilities, to declare a state of emergency. At that point, the elections would be suspended, declared invalid, and postponed indefinitely. (Doc 12)

To its credit, the Reagan administration moved quickly and decisively to confront Pinochet's threat. In stark contrast to the procrastination of the Ford administration in taking steps to block the Letelier assassination, and the Carter administration's weak response to the cover-up of that crime, Reagan officials forcefully attempted to insure the sanctity of the plebiscite. Unequivocal démarches were presented to a broad range of regime officials—in the foreign and interior ministries, the army, the Junta, and to Pinochet himself—warning authorities "not to take or permit steps meant to provide pretext for canceling, suspending or otherwise nullifying the plebiscite." In their meetings with the Chileans, U.S. officials were authorized to use tough language: "I want to warn you that implementation of such a plan would seriously damage relations with the United States and utterly destroy Chile's reputation in the world," talking points read. "President Pinochet should also be informed that nothing could so permanently destroy his reputation in Chile and the world than for him to authorize or permit extreme violent and illicit steps which make a mockery of his solemn promise to conduct a free and fair plebiscite."[51]

Behind the scenes, the CIA Station chief received instructions to strongly advise Chilean secret police officials against such action; U.S. military officers at SOUTHCOMM issued similar warnings to their contacts inside the Chilean military. Washington also asked the Thatcher government—a close friend of Pinochet's—to privately pressure his regime. On October 3, the State Department raised that pressure at the noon press briefing by publicly expressing its concern that "the Chilean government has plans to cancel Wednesday's presidential plebiscite or to nullify the results."

In his evening briefing papers on October 3, President Reagan was informed of Pinochet's plan to disrupt Chile's plebiscite, and of U.S. efforts to stop him. The next day, Ambassador Barnes met with the Chilean foreign minister to discuss the sensitive U.S. intelligence on Pinochet's plan, in an effort to gain allies inside the regime. Pinochet would decide on the day of the plebiscite in the early afternoon on disrupting the vote, Barnes warned; the CNI would be called on to foment violence, if necessary. "Our information comes from senior army generals," he told Chile's foreign minister, according to a secret memorandum of conversation. This "is not a bluff by the USG."

October 5 marked a historic day for Chileans, and for U.S.-Chilean relations. The Command for the NO organized a massive turnout. Some 98 percent of eligible Chileans cast their votes. Early evening returns, according to NO campaign manager Genero Arriagada, showed the opposition ahead by 62 to 37 percent—a stunning lead. Final results had the NO winning by more than 800,000 votes, with a 54.7 percent to 43 percent victory over the vote to continue the Pinochet dictatorship.

On election day, the United States mobilized itself to track the vote and the actions of the Pinochet regime. In Santiago, the embassy established an operation center and began filing "sitreps"—situation reports—on an hourly basis. At the State Department, a special Chile Working Group gathered at a communications office designated TF1 to monitor the situation, make and take calls from the embassy over secure and dedicated lines, and respond to developments.

By 9:00 P.M., Pinochet's machinations became apparent. The government announced that the YES was ahead in the tally by 10,000 votes, at the same time as the Command for the NO, reporting far more ballots counted, claimed a lead of almost 130,000 votes. The regime then withheld scheduled hourly reports on the vote count. "The GOC is obviously sitting on voting results," the embassy cabled in "Sitrep Four." This was part of a Machiavellian plan worked out by Pinochet and his highest aides, a high-level military informant[52] would tell a CIA agent, which called for the Interior Ministry

> to delay the announcement of voting results to agitate the opposition, announce preliminary results favorable to the YES vote, and then call the YES voters to the streets to celebrate the alleged YES victory. This would then result in a strong opposition reaction, street clashes and the need to call in the Army to restore order; thereby providing a handy excuse to suspend the plebiscite.

Pinochet's attempt to orchestrate chaos and violence in the streets failed, however, when the Carabinero police refused an order to lift the cordon against street demonstrations in the capital. According to the CIA informant, Santiago garrison commander Brig. Gen. Jorge Zincke[53] also refused to permit any celebrations or protests, including for supporters of the YES. Huddled at the presidential palace with his advisers, Pinochet worked out a new, violent plan to abort the election.

At eight minutes after midnight, the Junta—air force Gen. Fernando Mattei, carabinero chief General Rodolfo Stange, CNI director Gen. Humberto Gordon, and navy Adm. José Merino—arrived at La Moneda to meet with Pinochet. In a pivotal and calculated statement, Mattei told reporters waiting outside that "it seems to me that the NO has really won" and that the "Junta would be talking about it now." This statement, the DIA would report, appeared to "be a deliberate pronouncement intended to limit General Pinochet's options."

The Junta members met with Pinochet just after 1:00 A.M. He was "nearly apoplectic" about the turn of events, one participant of the meeting noted.[54] "The Chilean President and CINC of the Army Gen. Augusto Pinochet was prepared on the night of 5 Oct to overthrow the results of the plebiscite," the DIA reported. At the meeting,

> Pinochet was described as very angry and insistent that the Junta must give him extraordinary powers to meet the crisis of the electoral defeat. He had a document prepared for their signatures authorizing this. . . . Pinochet spoke of using the extraordinary powers to have the armed forces seize the capital. At this point Mattei stood up to be counted. Mattei told Pinochet he would under no circumstances agree to such a thing . . . he had had his chance as the official candidate and lost. Pinochet then turned to the others and made the same request and was turned down. . . . (Doc 13)

According to the DIA's description of the denouement of the dictatorship, "without Junta support to overthrow the NO, Pinochet was left without alternative but to accept a NO win."

Euphoria among Pinochet's opposition, and his many victims, was instantaneous. Thousands of Chileans flooded into the streets in the dark morning hours of October 6 chanting and singing; there were reports of bystanders hugging Carabinero police. Tens of thousands made a pilgrimage a week later to Mendoza, Argentina for an Amnesty International rock concert featuring Bruce Springsteen, Sting, and Tracy Chapman held to commemorate the fortieth anniversary of the Universal Declaration of Human Rights. In a cable titled "Mendoza Human Rights Concert Sounds Sour Note for Chilean Government," a U.S. embassy officer reported that "the event was a massive NO rally" and "a repeated theme was the fact that President Pinochet had been defeated in the plebiscite and there was now hope for Chile." (Doc 14)[55]

In the aftermath of his stunning defeat, Pinochet openly toyed with violating his own Constitution and running for the presidency again in the mandated elections scheduled for December 1989. The Chilean right wing, now organized into a business-dominated coalition to compete in a post-regime political system, rejected his gambit as grotesque. "With no support from the political parties of the right," the U.S. embassy reported, "and without the army to back his candidacy it is a non-starter. He battled for and lost the chance to legitimate his power for the long term, and the very Constitution he created to perpetuate himself in power is proving to be his iron cage."

Instead, Chile's conservative forces selected Pinochet's young finance minister, Hernán Buchi, as the regime's political protégé and candidate. Another right-wing candidate, millionaire businessman Francisco Javier Errázuriz, also ran. The opposition, now organized into a coalition of centrist and leftist political parties called the Concertacíon para la Democracia agreed that a Christian Democrat would head the presidential ticket in 1989, and thereafter the parties should alternate, with the PDC supporting a Socialist candidate in 1995. Acrimony broke out when the Christian Democrats could not decide who among their elder statemen would be the candidate of the Concertacíon. Eventually, Patricio Aylwin, the spokesman for the NO, won the nomination. On December 14, 1989, Aylwin and the opposition won a definitive victory, garnering 55.2 percent of the vote against the two rightist candidates.

Between the plebiscite on October 5, 1988, and Aylwin's inauguration in March 1990, the Pinochet regime rattled its sabers to assert the impunity of the military over the transition to civilian governance. Pinochet rejected all calls to resign as commander-in-chief of the army as a gesture of national reconciliation. To safeguard the secret police, Pinochet folded the CNI into military intelligence under his army command. To protect himself and his officers from future legal challenges, Pinochet bribed six older members of the Chilean Supreme Court to resign and appointed nine new members to life terms. His generals warned the new authorities not to tamper with the Constitution that preserved Pinochet's power, lest Chile need reminding of the "example" of September 11, 1973.

To reinforce that point, in one of his last decisions as dictator, Pinochet selected the March 11 to be inauguration day for president-elect Aylwin. At the ceremony, Pinochet found himself among Chilean political figures he had tortured, imprisoned, exiled and even tried to assassinate over the past seventeen years. Pinochet expected to be hailed a savior of his country, but his was an ignoble exit. As he departed with an elaborate military escort, the

U.S. embassy reported, "Pinochet's security detail had to shield him with umbrellas and their bodies to deflect tomatoes, eggs, and other debris hurled at his open motorcade."

There would be one last confrontation with the United States. On inauguration day, Pinochet hosted a meeting at his residence with the head of the U.S. delegation, Vice President Dan Quayle, and Assistant Secretary for Inter-American Affairs Bernard Aronson. As they arrived, the general's supporters, dressed in pearls and designer jeans and angry that Washington had backed a return to civilian rule, hurled insults at the Americans and pounded on their limousine. The meeting was supposed to be a pro forma courtesy call on an outgoing leader, but Quayle carried secret diplomatic instructions to "press Pinochet in Chile to submit to the authority of the Aylwin government," and to "emphasize that the United States solidly supports the democratic process in Chile."[56] Years later, Aronson would recall the message that the U.S. officials conveyed to the general about undermining his country's attempt to rebuild a democracy: "We told him to stay the hell away. We told him to stay out of it."

DOCUMENT 1. CIA, **SECRET** Intelligence Assessment, "Chile: Implications of the Letelier Case," May 1978 (pages 1–3).

SECRET SENSITIVE
Noforn-Nocontract-Orcon

CHILE: IMPLICATIONS OF THE LETELIER CASE

Central Intelligence Agency
National Foreign Assessment Center

May 1978

Key Judgments

Recent disclosures in the investigation of the murder of Orlando Letelier, former minister in the Allende government and one-time Ambassador to the US, have raised the possibility that the crime will be linked to the highest levels of the Chilean Government. The sensational developments have evoked speculation about President Pinochet's political survival. We believe that Pinochet has a reasonable chance of riding out the storm, but if enough incriminating evidence comes to light, his support from the military could begin to slip rapidly.

Government reaction to proof of Pinochet's complicity in the Letelier slaying might take one of several courses:

-- An attempt to institute a coverup, with charges that the US is trying to destabilize the regime.

-- An effort to establish a scapegoat who would draw fire away from the President.

-- An acknowledgment of a connection with the murder, but with the explanation that the action was justified because Letelier was plotting against Pinochet.

-- A recognition that Pinochet is guilty, followed by a military decision to force his removal.

Pinochet would not be deposed unless discontent became widespread in the army and even then only after much soul-searching by its leaders. There is no easily identifiable

INTELLIGENCE MEMORANDUM

Copy No. 12

50

SECRET SENSITIVE

candidate in the wings, but an army general would most likely be named to head an interim junta. While military leaders would strive to reach a consensus on a succession formula, the present junta leaders would probably be required to step aside also.

A new president would probably attempt to heal the wounds caused by the scandal, but divisions might occur within the armed forces over the appearance of bowing to external pressures. Nevertheless, plans for a return to constitutional norms would probably be advanced. Public outrage over the revelation of transgressions by high government leaders could lead to a more rapid transition to civilian rule.

SECRET SENSITIVE

President Augusto Pinochet faces a potentially critical challenge to his continued leadership as the complex Letelier assassination probe continues to evolve. Letelier's murder in Washington raised immediate charges that Chilean intelligence agents were behind the incident. Recent developments suggesting that the death might be traced ~~to high Chilean officials have caused shock waves in~~ Santiago. Described by a junta member as "a Chilean Watergate," the controversy threatens to engulf the President along with intelligence and security officers. If the president's complicity is proved, it would have grave political implications, such as triggering military demands for Pinochet's resignation and compelling Chile's generals to find a successor.

At present, Pinochet stands a reasonable chance of holding his ground. Although there is grumbling among mid-level officers, the army does not appear to be seriously dissatisfied with the President, and most military men appear willing to accept his claim that his "hands are clean." Only if the scandal reaches considerable magnitude, with indisputable evidence of high-level conspiracy, would there be a substantial shift of sentiment against Pinochet. As long as the army remains behind him, there is little chance of his being unseated. Over the past four years, the Chilean armed forces have strived to preserve internal cohesion in the face of difficult social and economic problems and worldwide hostility. So far, dissent has been limited to low-keyed criticism of recent policy decisions. Military reluctance to move against Pinochet would be strengthened by fears of factionalism and unsettling political and economic repercussions.

Clouding the outlook for Pinochet is the possibility that former intelligence chief General Manuel Contreras will be linked directly to the crime. Public disclosure of Contreras' guilt--either through his own admission or in court testimony--would be almost certain to implicate Pinochet and irreparably damage his credibility within the military. None of the government's critics and few of its supporters would be willing to swallow claims that Contreras acted without presidential concurrence. The former secret police chief is known to have reported directly to the President, who had exclusive responsibility for the organization's activities. Some generals may already harbor suspicions about Contreras' involvement in illegal operations and probably question Pinochet's responsibility in the matter.

SECRET SENSITIVE

DOCUMENT 2. CIA, **SECRET** Intelligence Report, "[Deleted] Strategy of Chilean Government with Respect to Letelier Case, and Impact of Case on Stability of President Pinochet," June 23, 1978.

SECRET

624

PAGE 001
23 JUN 78 CIA

TO: IMMEDIATE FEDERAL BUREAU OF INVESTIGATION, DEPARTMENT OF STATE.

SUBJECT: STRATEGY OF CHILEAN GOVERNMENT WITH RESPECT TO LETELIER CASE, AND IMPACT OF CASE ON STABILITY OF PRESIDENT PINOCHET

1\.

2\. THE CHILEAN GOVERNMENT'S (AUGUSTO P I N O C H E T 'S) PRESENT STRATEGY WITH RESPECT TO THE LETELIER CASE CAN BE SUMMARIZED AS FOLLOWS:

A. PROTECT GENERAL (R) MANUEL C O N T R E R A S) FROM SUCCESSFUL PROSECUTION IN THE MURDER OF LETELIER, SINCE PINOCHET'S POLITICAL SURVIVAL IS DEPENDENT UPON CONTRERAS' FATE.

B. STONEWALL ANY FURTHER REQUESTS FROM THE U.S. GOVERNMENT THAT WOULD SERVE TO BUILD A CASE AGAINST CONTRERAS AND OTHER CHILEANS.

SECRET

Declassified and Approved for Release July 2000

SECRET

PAGE 002
23 JUN 78 CIA

C. CONTINUE TO "LOBBY" THE SUPREME COURT JUSTICES TO INSURE THAT REQUESTS FOR EXTRADITION OF CHILEAN CITIZENS FOLLOWING ANTICIPATED INDICTMENTS ARE REJECTED.

D. CONTINUE TO EXPLOIT CHILEAN NATIONALISM WITH A COVERT ACTION CAMPAIGN TO PORTRAY THE LETELIER INVESTIGATION AS BEING POLITICALLY MOTIVATED -- ANOTHER PRETEXT FOR DESTABILIZING THE PINOCHET REGIME.

E. IMPROVE THE GOC IMAGE ABROAD WITH LIBERALIZING MEASURES (E.G., ALLOWING THE VISIT OF THE UN HUMAN RIGHTS COMMISSION).

3. THE EVOLUTION OF PINOCHET'S STRATEGY FROM INITIAL GRUDGING COOPERATION TO ITS PRESENT HARDLINE POSTURE APPEARS TO BE BASED ON THE FOLLOWING FACTORS AND ASSUMPTIONS.

-- A. MICHAEL T O W N L E Y 'S DEVASTATING CONFESSION TO GENERAL HECTOR O R O Z C O, THE MILITARY PROSECUTOR, IN MID-APRIL AFTER HIS EXPULSION TO THE U.S. PUT THE ONUS FOR THE CRIME DIRECTLY ON THE DIRECTORATE OF NATIONAL INTELLIGENCE (DINA) AND ITS DIRECTOR, GENERAL CONTRERAS. WHEN OROZCO CONFRONTED CONTRERAS UPON HIS RETURN, THE LATTER ADMITTED HIS CULPABILITY, BUT THREATENED TO CLAIM THAT HE WAS ACTING ON ORDERS FROM PINOCHET IN THE EVENT HE WERE PROSECUTED. CONTRERAS CLAIMED THAT HE HAD SAFELY SECRETED DOCUMENTATION TO SUPPORT HIS CLAIM. THIS BLACKMAIL THREAT WORKED. OROZCO WAS OBVIOUSLY GIVEN ORDERS BY PINOCHET TO ACCEPT CONTRERAS' COVER STORY (THAT HE HAD SENT TOWNLEY AND CAPTAIN ARMANDO F E R N A N D E Z LARIOS TO THE U.S. MERELY TO INVESTIGATE ORLANDO L E T E L I E R 'S ACTIVITIES -- AND THAT TOWNLEY HAD OBVIOUSLY EXCEEDED HIS INSTRUCTIONS.) A SUBSEQUENT FALLBACK EFFORT BY THE GOC TO PERSUADE LT. COLONEL PEDRO E S P I N O S A, FORMER DINA CHIEF OF OPERATIONS, TO ASSUME RESPONSIBILITY FOR THE ASSASSINATION ORDER WAS THWARTED BY CONTRERAS WITH THE SAME BLACKMAIL THREAT. THUS, THE COVERUP BEGAN.

B. PINOCHET, ACTING THROUGH LEGAL ADVISOR HUGO R O S E N D E, HAS MANIPULATED THE SUPREME COURT JUDGES AND NOW IS SATISFIED THAT THE COURT WILL REJECT THE EXTRADITION OF ANY CHILEANS INDICTED.

C. PINOCHET HAS ALSO BEEN CONVINCED BY HIS LEGAL ADVISORS THAT THERE IS PROBABLY INSUFFICIENT EVIDENCE TO CONVICT CONTRERAS ET AL IN CHILEAN COURTS, SINCE THE TESTIMONY OF ONE WITNESS (TOWNLEY) WITHOUT INDEPENDENT CORROBORATION CARRIES LITTLE WEIGHT. HOWEVER, THERE IS SOME CONCERN THAT AUSA EUGENE P R O P P E R MAY HAVE SOME CARDS UP HIS SLEEVE THAT HE HAS NOT SHOWN, HENCE THE

SECRET

SECRET

PAGE 003
23 JUN 78 CIA

REPEATED CHILEAN REQUESTS TO PROPPER FOR MORE EVIDENCE.

D. THE APPEAL TO ANTI-U.S. NATIONALISM HAS FALLEN ON RECEPTIVE EARS. THE DENOUNCEMENT OF THE LETELIER CASE HAS TAKEN PLACE AMID RENEWED INTERNATIONAL EXPLOITATION OF THE "DISAPPEAREDS" IN CHILE, PRESSURE FROM ARGENTINA AND BOLIVIA, ULTIMATUMS FROM THE AFL-CIO, A MARITIME BOYCOTT AND AN INCIDENT AGAINST THE CHILEAN TRAINING SHIP "ESMERALDA" IN SAN FRANCISCO, ATTACKS BY THE U.S. MEDIA AND CONGRESSMEN, ETC., THUS IT IS EASY FOR PINOCHET'S SUPPORTERS (A MAJORITY OF THE POPULACE) TO BELIEVE THAT ALL THIS IS A CAREFULLY ORCHESTRATED PLOT BY THE CARTER ADMINISTRATION TO TOPPLE PINOCHET. IN THISCONTEXT, THE 10 JUNE EDITORIAL IN THE "WASHINGTON POST" CALLING FOR PINOCHET TO RESIGN AND TURN THE GOVERNMENT OVER TO THE CHRISTIAN DEMOCRATS PROVED TO BE A BONANZA FOR PINOCHET.

E. PINOCHET'S RESORT TO HARDLINE, STONEWALLING TACTICS HAS ALSO CALMED DOWN THE ARMY WHICH IS, AFTER ALL, HIS KEY SUPPORT BASE. WHEN THE CASE FIRST STARTED TO BREAK OPEN, PINOCHET'S HASTY RETIREMENT OF CONTRERAS IN MARCH AND THE PRECIPITOUS EXPULSION OF TOWNLEY IN EARLY APRIL UNDER PRESSURE FROM THE U.S. INDICATED EITHER GUILT OR WEAKNESS TO ARMY OFFICERS, AND HIS SERIES OF LIBERALIZING MEASURES (RELEASE OF POLITICAL PRISONERS, GENERAL AMNESTY, REPLACEMENT OF SOME MILITARY CABINET MEMBERS BY CIVILIANS, ETC.) ADDED TO THE IMPRESSION OF A DESPERATE PRESIDENT. WHEN AUSA PROPPER RETURNED TO SANTIAGO IN LATE MAY PRECEDED BY PRESS REPORTS FROM WASHINGTON THAT HE WAS COMING TO TAKE CONTRERAS TO THE U.S., THIS FURTHER ALARMED TRADITIONALLY PROUD ARMY OFFICERS ALREADY CONCERNED ABOUT THE CAVALIER TREATMENT BEING GIVEN TO SEVERAL ACTIVE DUTY ARMY SUSPECTS. IT WAS AT THAT POINT THAT PINOCHET DIRECTED GENERAL RENE V I D A L, MINISTER SECRETARY GENERAL OF GOVERNMENT, TO LAUNCH A NATIONALISTIC PROPAGANDA CAMPAIGN; ALSO PINOCHET ASSURED THE GENERALS THAT HE WOULD PROTECT THE ARMY'S INTEGRITY. THIS CAMPAIGN, AND THE GROWING THREAT FROM ARGENTINA AS PERCEIVED BY THE MILITARY HAVE SERVED TO MAKE THEM CLOSE RANKS BEHIND PINOCHET FOR THE TIME BEING, AND SPECULATION AS TO PINOCHET'S SUCCESSOR HAS DISSIPATED.

F. PINOCHET ALSO TOOK TO THE HUSTINGS THIS MONTH TO SHORE UP HIS SUPPORT. DURING A HIGHLY SUCCESSFUL VISIT TO THE SOUTH, HE USED THE OCCASION TO MOCK RUMORS THAT HE WAS STEPPING DOWN AND TO VOW THAT HE WAS REMAINING IN OFFICE UNTIL HIS NEW INSTITUTIONALITY PROGRAM IS COMPLETED.

SECRET

SECRET

PAGE 004
23 JUN 78 CIA

4. CONCLUSIONS: ALTHOUGH THE MAJORITY OF CHILEANS WOULD NOT COUNTENANCE PROVEN CHARGES THAT THEIR GOVERNMENT INSTIGATED THE MURDER OF LETELIER, THE "SHOCK" IMPACT OF THE EVIDENCE HAS LARGELY BEEN DISSIPATED BY THE MANNER IN WHICH IT HAS DRIBBLED OUT. PINOCHET NOW HAS A STRONG, NATIONALISTIC DEFENSE GOING FOR HIM, AND HE CAN PROBABLY SURVIVE INDICTMENTS AGAINST CONTRERAS AND COMPANY THAT DO NOT LEAD TO CONVICTION IN CHILEAN COURTS. MUCH WILL DEPEND ON WORLD REACTIONS; IF HIS REGIME IS "CONVICTED" BY RESPECTED WORLD OPINION AND PARTICULARLY, IF THIS LEADS TO SERIOUS REPRISALS BY THE U.S. AND WESTERN EUROPE, SUCH AS DOWNGRADING OR BREAKING RELATIONS, INTERNATIONAL TRADE AND FINANCIAL BOYCOTTS, THEN PINOCHET'S DEPARTURE WOULD ONLY BE A QUESTION OF TIME. RESPONSIBLE CHILEANS ARE ALREADY CONCERNED ABOUT CHILE'S ISOLATION; THE NATIONALISTIC FERVOR CANNOT SUBSTITUTE PERMANENTLY FOR COLD REALITIES, AND THE MILITARY REALIZE THAT CHILE WOULD BE EXTREMELY VULNERABLE TO ATTACKS FROM EITHER ARGENTINA, PERU OR BOTH. IF PINOCHET DOES FALL, IT IS LIKELY THAT ANOTHER ARMY GENERAL WITH SIMILAR IDEOLOGY WOULD SUCCEED HIM. HOWEVER, THE TRANSITION PROCESS TO CIVILIAN GOVERNMENT WOULD PROBABLY BE ACCELERATED. IF THE USG WERE DEEMED RESPONSIBLE FOR PINOCHET'S DOWNFALL, RELATIONS WOULD BE STRAINED FOR SOME TIME.

5. THE ABOVE INFORMATION WAS MADE AVAILABLE TO THE AMBASSADOR IN SANTIAGO WHO FULLY CONCURRED WITH THE APPRAISAL. IT IS REQUESTED THAT THE FBI INFORM MR. EUGENE PROPPER, ASSISTANT UNITED STATES ATTORNEY, DISTRICT OF COLUMBIA, OF THIS APPRAISAL AND RESTRICTIONS ON ITS USE. THE FBI REPRESENTATIVE IN BUENOS AIRES IS BEING INFORMED.

6.

END OF MESSAGE

SECRET

DOCUMENT 3. U.S. Embassy, **SECRET** Cable, "Letelier/Moffitt Assassination Case: Manuel Contreras," August 24, 1978.

PAGE 1 OF 2

UNCLASSIFIED

(E 4491)

PAGE 01 SANTIA 06363 241808Z
ACTION SS-25

INFO OCT-01 ISO-00 SSO-00 /026 W
------------------097857 241814Z /42

O 241613Z AUG 78
FM AMEMBASSY SANTIAGO
TO SECSTATE WASHDC IMMEDIATE 0269

Chile Project (#S199900030)
U.S. Department of State
Release___ Excise ✓ Deny___
Declassify: In Part ✓ In Full___
Exemption(s) B-1

~~S E C R E T~~ SANTIAGO 6363

EXDIS
DECAPTIONED
STADIS///////////////////////////////

FOR ARA, D, P AND L ONLY

Dept. of State, RPS/IPS, Margaret P. Grafeld, Dir.
( ) Classify as (✓) Extend as (S) Downgrade to ___
Date 1/25/11 Declassify on ___ Reason 25X1

E.O. 11652: XGDS-1
TAGS: CI PGOV SHUM
SUBJECT: LETELIER/MOFFITT ASSASSINATION CASE: MANUEL CONTRERAS

1. MANUEL CONTRERAS PHONED [ ] NIGHT OF AUGUST 23 AND SAID HE HAD TO DISCUSS URGENT MATTER. AFTER CHECKING WITH CHARGE [ ] SAID HE WOULD NOT GO SEE CONTRERAS BUT THAT HE WOULD RECEIVE A CONFIDANT AT HIS HOME. ALVARO PUGA ARRIVED A SHORT TIME LATER. HE SAID THAT CONTRERAS' LAWYERS, SERGIO MIRANDA CARRINGTON AND HUMBERTO OLAVARRIA WILL ARRIVE IN WASHINGTON AUGUST 28, AND PLAN TO REQUEST APPOINTMENTS, AUGUST 29, WITH SENIOR REPRESENTATIVES OF JUSTICE, DEPARTMENT AND CIA IN ORDER TO "NEGOTIATE" A SETTLEMENT OF THE LETELIER CASE THAT WOULD SATISFY ALL PARTIES. PUGA INDICATED THAT ALL THREE ORGANIZATIONS WOULD HAVE VESTED INTEREST IN WHAT THE LAWYERS HAD TO SAY, BUT HE NOT SURE WHETHER JOINT OR SEPARATE MEETINGS DESIRED.

2. PUGA PROFESSED NOT TO KNOW THE DETAILS OF THE LAWYERS' PROPOSAL, BUT A BLACKMAIL HINT EMERGED WHEN HE SAID THAT CONTRERAS IS CONFIDENT THAT THERE IS INSUFFICIENT EVIDENCE

~~SECRET~~

~~SECRET~~

PAGE 02 SANTIA 06363 241808Z

AGAINST HIM TO EITHER EXTRADITE HIM OR TO CONVICT HIM IN CHILEAN COURT. HOWEVER, IN DEFENDING HIMSELF, HE WOULD HAVE TO REVEAL DETAILS [ ] IT WOULD NOT BE IN HIS, CHILE'S, THE USG'S, OR THE OTHER COUNTRIES' INTEREST TO HAVE THIS INFORMATION BECOME PUBLIC KNOWLEDGE, BUT HE REGRETFULLY WOULD HAVE NO CHOICE (I.E., MORE IN SORROW THAN IN ANGER). THEREFORE, HOPEFULLY A DEAL CAN BE WORKED OUT IN WASHINGTON THAT WOULD OBVIATE THE NEED FOR EXTRADITION REQUESTS AND THE SUBSEQUENT PUBLIC HEARING.

UNCLASSIFIED

000086DD

3. PUGA ALSO CLAIMED THAT THE CASE IS FAR MORE COMPLICATED THAN MEETS THE EYE, AND LIKENED IT TO KENNEDY AND KING ASSASSINATIONS IN THAT SENSE; E.G., SUAREZ, ONE OF THE CUBANS IMPLICATED, HAS ALWAYS BEEN UNDER FIDEL CASTRO'S CONTROL, HE ASSERTED. HE ALSO ATTACKED MICHAEL TOWNLEY'S CREDIBILITY, EXPRESSING DOUBT THAT TOWNLEY HAS EVER PLACED ANY BOMBS ANYWHERE, AND HE DISMISSED TOWNLEY'S STORY THAT THE BOMB WAS UNDER LETELIER'S AUTO FOR THREE DAYS BEFORE BEING DETONATED AS PURE FANTASY, SINCE IT WOULD HAVE BEEN SET OFF ACCIDENTALLY BY TAXI RADIOS OR SOME SUCH LONG BEFORE. INTERESTINGLY, PUGA DID NOT ALLEGE ANY CIA PARTICIPATION IN THE CRIME. IN FACT, HE SAID HE KNEW TOWNLEY DURING THE ALLENDE PERIOD WHEN THEY WERE BOTH ENGAGED IN ANTI-ALLENDE PROPAGANDA ACTIVITIES, AND TOWNLEY WAS CERTAINLY NOT THE TYPE CIA WOULD EVER UTILIZE. HE DESCRIBED TOWNLEY'S WIFE AS A COMMUNIST WHO IS INTELLIGENT AND COLD-BLOODED.

4. PUGA SAID MIRANDA ALSO PLANNED TO ENGAGE A US ATTORNEY FOR CONTRERAS WHILE IN WASHINGTON.

PAGE 03 SANTIA 06363 241808Z

5. [ ] LISTENED TO THE FOREGOING WITH LITTLE COMMENT BUT [ ]

[ ]

6. COMMENT: WE HAVE BEEN INFORMED BY MIRANDA'S OFFICE THAT A VISA WILL BE REQUESTED FOR VALENTIN ROBLES LETELIER, DESCRIBED AS A LAWYER WORKING WITH MIRANDA. WE DO NOT KNOW IF HE IS IN ADDITION TO HUMBERTO OLAVARRIA. GROVER

NOTE BY OC/T: CAUTION: THIS MESSAGE APPEARS TO CONTAIN SENSITIVE INTELLIGENCE INFORMATION.

SECRET

NNN

*** Current Handling Restrictions *** ONLY STADIS
*** Current Classification *** SECRET

DOCUMENT 4. Secretary of State, Options Paper for President Carter from Cyrus Vance, "Letelier/Moffitt Case," October 19, 1979.

PAGE 1 OF 4

~~CONFIDENTIAL~~

THE SECRETARY OF STATE
WASHINGTON

VIA ALPHA CHANNEL

October 19, 1979

MEMORANDUM FOR: THE PRESIDENT

FROM: Cyrus Vance CV

RE: Letelier/Moffitt Case

As you know, the Chilean Supreme Court has denied our request for the extradition of the three Chilean intelligence officers indicted by a United States grand jury for the assassination of Orlando Letelier (a former Chilean Ambassador to the U.S.) and Ronni Moffitt. Because the Court's decision also rules out virtually any possibility that these three men will be tried in Chile, it is likely that this act of terrorism, committed on the streets of our nation's capital, will go unpunished. We therefore now face the issue of how to respond to the Government of Chile.

Background. Letelier and Moffitt were killed in September 1976 by a bomb attached to their car. On August 1, 1978, a federal grand jury handed down indictments charging Michael Townley, a member of the Chilean secret police, and two others with having carried out the crime. The same grand jury charged three high-ranking members of the Chilean secret police with having planned and directed the killings. Townley and his two accomplices were subsequently tried and convicted in a U.S. District Court. The United States sought the extradition from Chile of the other three men.

Recommendations. The Government of Chile bears a two-fold responsibility for these crimes. First, high-ranking officials of that government have been charged with having planned and directed the crimes -- and the overwhelming body of evidence that has been amassed by the Department of Justice makes it likely that those charges would be upheld if a fair trial could be held in either Chile or the U.S. Second, the Government of Chile has made no serious effort to investigate or prosecute these crimes on its own, and its judicial system has refused either to make the three Chilean officials available for trial in the U.S. or to order a thorough and effective local investigation.

~~CONFIDENTIAL~~

RDS-2/3 10/19/85 (Vance, Cyrus)

CONFIDENTIAL

- 2 -

By its actions -- and its inaction -- the Government of Chile has, in effect, condoned this act of international terrorism within the United States. We believe it is essential that we make clear, both to Chile and to others throughout the world, that such actions cannot be tolerated.

As you know, there have been suggestions from the Hill and elsewhere that we take extreme measures to demonstrate our displeasure, including enacting legislation to limit private bank lending to Chile, withdrawing our Ambassador, or even breaking relations altogether. I have considered these options, and while I share the outrage of those who have suggested them, I believe steps of this sort would not serve our interests in Chile or elsewhere. Instead, I recommend that the following steps be taken:

(1) Diplomatic Steps. During the course of the Letelier matter, Ambassador Landau has met regularly with Chilean officials to express the concern of the United States Government. In addition, we have recalled Ambassador Landau three times on consultations as a reflection of our displeasure at developments in the case, and Warren and I have made numerous demarches to Chilean officials. We will be meeting further with Chilean officials to reiterate our view that the Government of Chile's failure to investigate this crime is unacceptable, and to explain the steps we are taking. I believe we should also make a reduction in the size of our Mission in Chile as a concrete indication of our displeasure. I am prepared to make such reductions in the State Department component of the Mission staff, and I will shortly be submitting to you a proposal for personnel reductions by other agencies operating in Chile. No further diplomatic steps are possible at this time, short of recalling Ambassador Landau permanently or breaking relations, neither of which I recommend.

Approve__________ Disapprove__________

(2) Terminate the FMS Pipeline. A relatively small amount of equipment remains in the FMS pipeline (we estimate the value to be approximately $7 million). I propose to terminate the pipeline in an orderly fashion, and to attempt to minimize any termination costs that might require a Congressional appropriation. However, I believe we should complete the termination of the pipeline by January 1, 1980, even if that does entail some minimal termination costs.

Approve__________ Disapprove__________

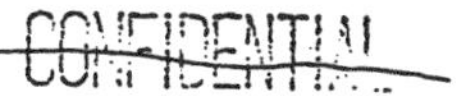

~~CONFIDENTIAL~~

(3) Withdraw the MilGroup. There are currently four U.S. officials in the MilGroup in our Embassy in Santiago. I propose to withdraw the MilGroup promptly. With the termination of the FMS pipeline by the end of the year, the Milgroup will no longer have any function to perform in Chile. I recommend, however, that our three Defense Attaches remain in Santiago.

Approve__________ Disapprove__________

(4) Suspend EX-IM Financing in Chile. The Chafee Amendment to the Export-Import Bank Act authorizes the denial of EX-IM financing in cases where the President determines that such action would be "in the national interest" and would "clearly and importantly advance U.S. policy in such areas as international terrorism...." We believe that Chile's actions in the Letelier case justify the invocation of this extraordinary remedy. While the Congress intended that this sanction should be used only sparingly, it would be difficult to conceive of a more appropriate case than the present one -- where high officials of a foreign government have been directly implicated in murders committed on United States territory, and where that government has effectively frustrated all attempts to bring the accused perpetrators of these crimes to justice.

Moreover, if the Chafee Amendment were not invoked in the present case, EX-IM activity in Chile would not simply remain at current levels; it would, instead, increase dramatically. Prior to the enactment of Chafee, EX-IM had for several years restricted financing in Chile to a maximum of $750,000 per project. Following Chafee's enactment, that restriction was informally extended pending the final outcome of the Letelier matter and a determination of whether the Amendment would be applicable. In the absence of the Presidential determination described above, EX-IM believes it would not have a legal basis for maintaining the $750,000 ceiling and would therefore resume unrestricted lending in Chile, for the first time since 1974. EX-IM loans in Chile could therefore be expected to increase sharply.

I therefore recommend that you sign the proposed Presidential determination attached at Tab 1, both as an appropriate response to Chile's actions in the Letelier matter, and to avoid the anomaly of seeming to reward those actions. Some elements of the business community will undoubtedly criticize us for taking this step, but I believe strongly that we must do so.

Approve__________ Disapprove__________

CONFIDENTIAL

CONFIDENTIAL

- 4 -

(5) Deny Validated Licenses for Exports to the Chilean Armed Forces. A number of applications for licenses to export items to Chile for the use of the Chilean armed forces have been held, pending the resolution of the Letelier matter. I believe these applications should now be denied. Under the Export Administration Act of 1979, future applications, received after October 1 of this year, may be denied only if you determine that the absence of export controls would be "detrimental to the foreign policy ... of the United States." Under this Act imposition of controls would also require us to consult with the Congress and to attempt to dissuade other countries from exporting controlled products to the Chilean armed forces. The use of export controls can be expected to draw strong opposition from the business community. I nonetheless believe that this additional Presidential determination and the other steps called for by the new Export Administration Act would be appropriate in this case. If you approve denial of these future licenses for the armed forces, we will meet with Department of Commerce officials next week to prepare specific recommendations for your review.

Approve__________ Disapprove__________

(6) Deny OPIC Guaranties. OPIC involvement in Chile is currently very limited. I propose that we not approve any future OPIC guaranties or other OPIC activities in Chile.

Approve__________ Disapprove__________

(7) Public Statement. In conjunction with the actions described above, I believe we should issue a statement reiterating our grave concern and deep disappointment at the Chilean Government's actions, including in particular its failure to investigate this crime, and outlining the actions we are taking.

Approve__________ Disapprove__________

I believe the actions I have suggested would be an appropriate and measured response to Chile's outrageous conduct in this affair. While it is unlikely that our actions will persuade Chile to alter its course and to bring the three Chilean officers to justice, our actions will constitute a strong reaffirmation of our determination to resist international terrorism, and may help to deter others who might be tempted to commit similar acts within our borders.

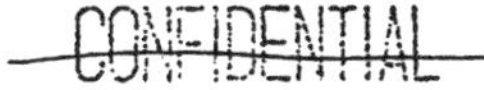

DOCUMENT 5. Secretary of State, **SECRET** Memorandum for President Reagan from Alexander Haig, "Our Policy Toward Chile," February 16, 1981.

2/16/81

P810034 - 2036

BEST COPY AVAILABLE

P810034-2036

S/S 8101855
XR 8102814

R

Chile Project (#S199900030)
U.S. Department of State
Release X Excise ___ Deny ___
Declassify: In Part ___ In Full X
Exemption(s) ___

THE SECRETARY OF STATE
WASHINGTON

SECRET
UNCLASSIFIED

February 16, 1981

MK 009a

MEMORANDUM FOR: THE PRESIDENT

From: Alexander M. Haig, Jr.

Subject: Our Policy Toward Chile

You asked about our Chile policy. In the next few days I plan to lift the prohibition on Ex-Im Bank financing and approve DOD's invitation list for this year's UNITAS naval exercise, to include Chile. These are the two most annoying aspects of current policy under Executive Branch control. We will have a full inter-agency review in about one month to decide on further adjustments. We want to maintain appropriate balance in our policies between Argentina and Chile. Both countries are now prohibited by legislation from military sales or training except under very narrow waiver authority.

Among friendly countries looking to the United States for leadership, our relations with Chile are uniquely encumbered by congressional and executive sanctions. Most were imposed because of the repressive policies of the Pinochet regime after it overthrew Allende in 1973. Although there were significant human rights improvements over the past four years, U.S. policy hardened.

In late 1979, the Chilean Supreme Court denied a request for extradition of three Chilean Army officers involved in the 1976 assassinations of Orlando Letelier and Ronni Moffit in Washington, D. C. Because the Chilean Government had failed to investigate fully or prosecute the three men, the Carter Administration then imposed a series of additional sanctions, most important of these were the suspension of all Ex-Im financing and denying an invitation to Chile for the 1980 UNITAS exercise. The suspension of Ex-Im financing puts U.S. exporters at a competitive disadvantage with other industrialized countries. Because of Chile's strategic location and naval tradition, it is in our interest to maintain military cooperation for hemispheric defense.

SECRET / UNCLASSIFIED

GDS 2/9/87

MICROFILMED BY S/S

DOCUMENT 6. NSC, Oliver North's Notes [Chilean Missiles for the Nicaraguan Contras], December 17, 1984.

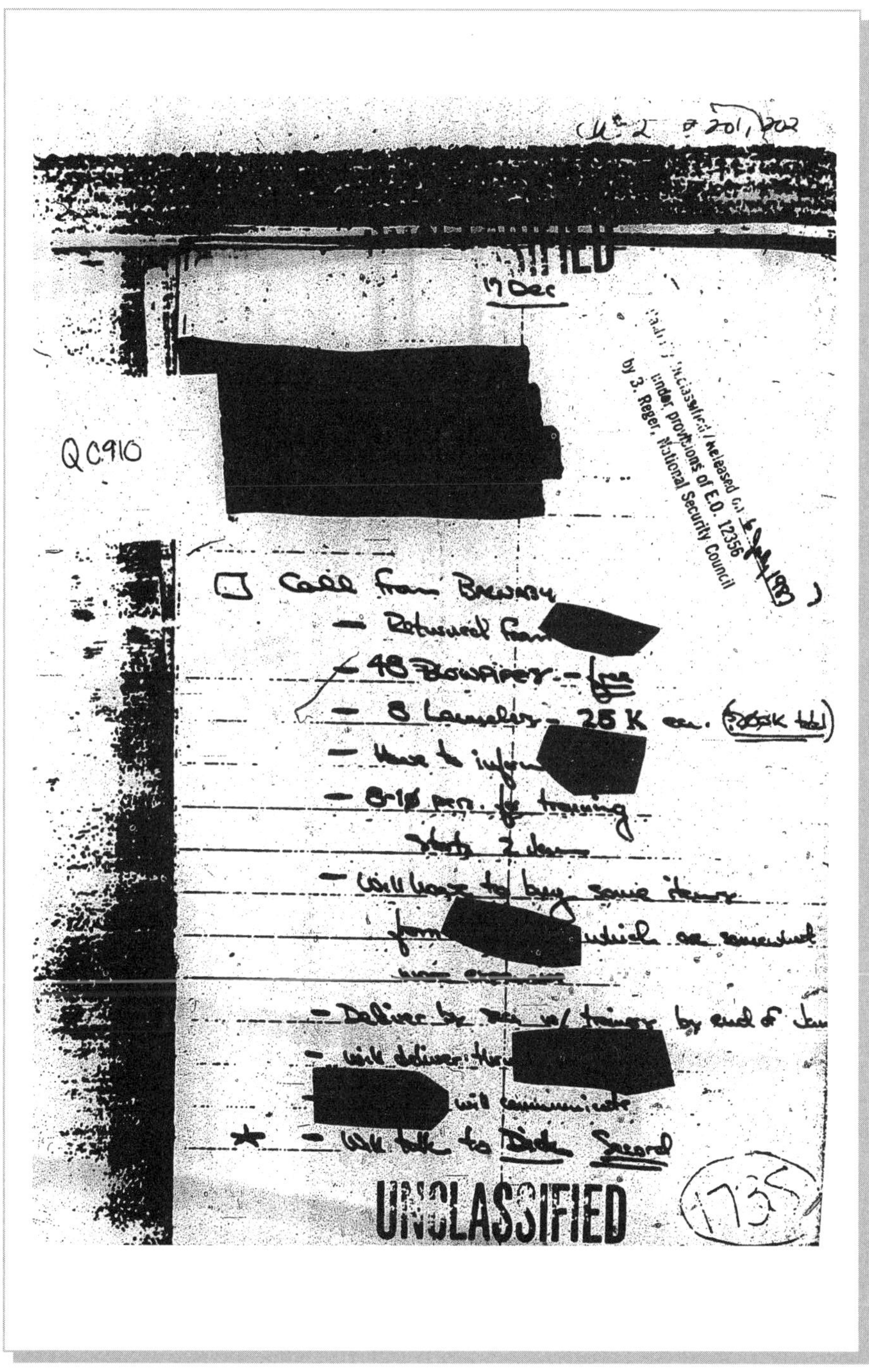

17 Dec

QC910

Declassified/Released on [illegible] under provisions of E.O. 12356 by J. Reger, National Security Council

☐ Call from [illegible]
— Returned from
— 48 Blowpipes — [illegible]
— 8 Launchers — 25 K ea. ([illegible]K total)
— Have to inform
— 8-10 pers. for training
Starts 2 Jan
— Will have to buy some items
from which are somewhat
[illegible]
— Deliver by sea w/ trainers by end of Jan
— will deliver thru
will communicate
★ — Will talk to Dick Secord

UNCLASSIFIED

1735

DOCUMENT 7. NSC, Oliver North's Email Memo to Robert McFarlane on Efforts to Arrange Chilean Arms Transfer to Contra Forces, "Anything New?," March 26, 1986.

From: NSOLN --CPUA   Date and time 03/26/86 09:19:12
To: NSRCM --CPUA

*** Reply to note of 03/20/86 23:04

NOTE FROM: OLIVER NORTH
Subject: Anything New??
After the House vote on aid to the resistance, I plan to take a few days just to get re-acquainted w/ the family. Meanwhile, we are trying to find a way to get 10 BLOWPIPE launchers and 20 missiles from [a South American country] thru the Short Bros. Rep. The V.P. from Short Bros. sought me out several mos. ago and I met w/ him again in London a few weeks ago when I was there [ ]. Short Bros., the mfgr. of the BLOWPIPE, is willing to arrange the deal, conduct the training and even send U.K. "tech reps" fwd if we can close the arrangement. Dick Secord has already paid 10% down on the delivery and we have a Salvadoran EUC which is acceptable to the [South American country]. Unfortunately, the week all this was going to closure we decided to go fwd [with a diplomatic position adverse to that country]. The arrangement is now on ice and we are casting about for a way to tell the [a South American country] that we wd be pleased if this all went thru. Y. thoughts wd be appreciated.

On our other action, there are fresh developments. Yesterday, [Iranian First Channel A] called the phone drop that Dick Secord had given him. Al Hakim, who we passed off as a "White House interpreter" at the Frankfurt mtg, spoke to [Iranian First Channel A] twice yesterday. The bottom line of the calls is that [Iranian First Channel A] wd like to have us meet w/ the Iranian side next week at Kharg Island. Supposedly, during the mtg the hostages wd be released and we wd immediately start delivering the 3k TOWs and agree at the mtg to the delivery of spare parts which they desperately need. They profess to be very concerned about the nature of the Soviet threat and want all we can give them on that score. Not sure at this point how real this offer is, but he says Rafsanjani wd come as the head of the Iranian side. If this looks like a go -- and we shd know more tomorrow when the next phone call is scheduled--how are you for travel during the week of 31Mar-4Apr? Warm regards, North BT

DOCUMENT 8. Department of State, **SECRET** Action Memorandum, "U.S. Policy Toward Chile," December 20, 1984.

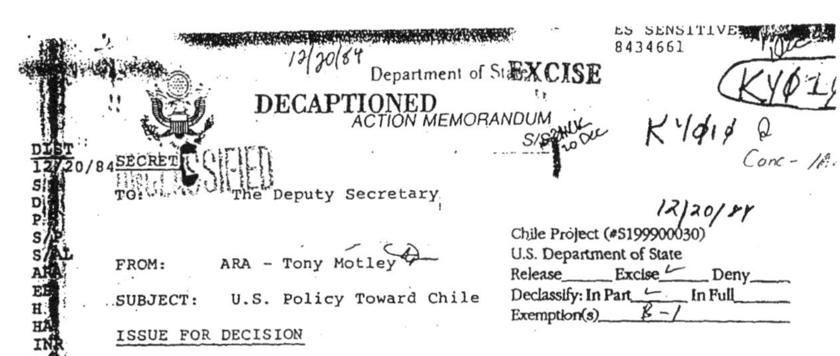

ES SENSITIVE
8434661

12/20/84

Department of State EXCISE

DECAPTIONED

ACTION MEMORANDUM

S/S

K4018 Q

Conc - ...

DIST
12/20/84

S
D
P
S/P
S/AL
ARA
EB
H
HA
INR
S/S
S/S-I

SECRET

TO: The Deputy Secretary

12/20/84

Chile Project (#S199900030)
U.S. Department of State
Release____ Excise ✓ Deny____
Declassify: In Part ✓ In Full____
Exemption(s) B-1

FROM: ARA - Tony Motley

SUBJECT: U.S. Policy Toward Chile

ISSUE FOR DECISION

Whether to approve the Chile strategy paper at Tab A.

ESSENTIAL FACTORS

REDIST
12/21

S
D
P
S/P
S/AL
ARA
EB
H
HA
INR
S/S
S/S-I

On the basis of the consensus developed at the November 23 Chile policy meeting chaired by Ken Dam, I raised our policy thinking with the members of the Restricted Inter-Agency Group (RIG) for Latin America on December 13. There was general agreement that we are on the right track. I did not ask the RIG representatives at this time to provide formal clearance to a policy guidance document, but simply to indicate whether they agreed that a more activist approach along the lines outlined in the paper at Tab A was the correct response to the Chile situation. We were encouraged, especially by DOD and CIA, on the need to move foward in addressing the transition and terrorism issues. The paper at Tab A has been revised to include the views of the RIG members.

DISCUSSION

HA and S/P have exchanged views on what to do about Chile. This exchange is at Tab C. S/P argues that the issue is whether there is a moderate center in a position to inherit the government if Pinochet is undermined (and is concerned that our policy aims at or may undermine him without assurance there is a moderate democratic alternative). ARA has made clear that this policy is not a "get Pinochet policy or a pressure Pinochet only policy." We neither want to make Pinochet fair game for the left, thereby strengthening opposition intransigence, nor act as surrogates for Pinochet, pressuring the opposition to achieve what he cannot. A tilt in either direction would make dialogue, and, therefore, the transition, more difficult. The key is to take actions which do not encourage intransigence on either side.

ARA believes that the issue is not whether Pinochet is going to depart or whether there is a moderate center -- there is, albeit disorganized, and Pinochet's term of office expires in 1989 under his own Constitution. We believe the issue,

SECRET

DECL:OADR

J99
92D52 S/45

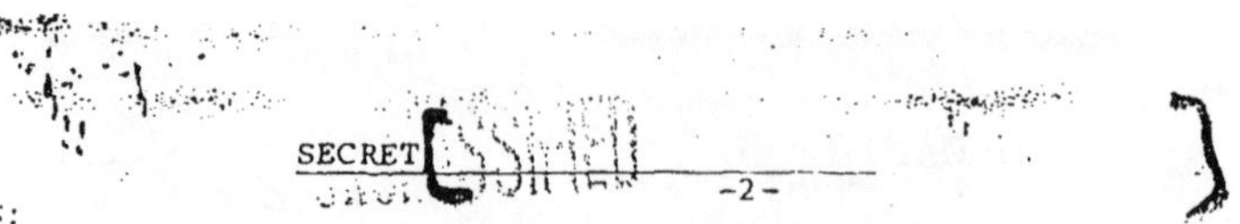

SECRET -2-

then, is when and under what circumstances Pinochet departs. We agree that whether the transition is sooner, or in 1989, the key to protecting long-term U.S. interests is strengthening the disorganized moderates, specifically, weaning them away from the radical left.

S/P also raises the question of what to do in the likely event Pinochet ignores all efforts to move him, or becomes more intransigent, e.g., that the policy outlined in this memo fails. We would be satisified if Pinochet would simply do what he said he would do when he overthrew Allende, that is, return Chile to democratic government. He is not doing this, and the opposition is not helping through its fragmentation and unwillingness to exclude the communists. Our approach is an effort to remind the military of their responsibilities under their own Constitution, and to encourage those who will govern Chile only 50 months hence (when the Presidential plebiscite is scheduled in March, 1989) of their responsibilities. This is a long-term strategy in which we will play only an indirect role in support of the process. If terrorism increases or Pinochet refuses to move, we will reassess whether a more direct involvement is warranted.

I believe we have developed a strong Departmental and inter-agency consensus on the broad outlines of a Chile policy. If you concur, we will finalize this process on an inter-agency basis and move forward with implementation.

RECOMMENDATION

That you approve the Chile policy paper at Tab A.

Approve *per KWD* Disapprove __________

Attachments:
- Tab A : Chile Strategy Paper for Approval
- Tab B : Political and Economic Assessments and Key Judgments
- Tab C : S/P - HA Exchange on Chile Policy

Drafted: ARA/SC:DBDlouhy
(1083M) 632-2575

Cleared:
- HA - EAbrams
- S/P - PRodman
- P - MArmacost
- INR - HMontgomery
- EB - RMcCormack
- H - TBennett
- S/S - BMcKinley
- S/AL - VWalters

SECRET

DOCUMENT 9. Secretary of State, Memorandum to President Reagan from George Shultz, "U.S. Policy Seeks Peaceful Transition in Chile Based on Broad National Consensus," September 3, 1985.

UNCLASSIFIED (KXØ15a)

R

THE SECRETARY OF STATE
WASHINGTON

Chile Project (#S199900030)
U.S. Department of State
Release X Excise ____ Deny ____
Declassify: In Part ____ In Full X
Exemption(s) ____

MEMORANDUM FOR: The President

FROM: George P. Shultz

SUBJECT: U.S. Policy Seeks Peaceful Transition in Chile Based on Broad National Consensus

Your policy of encouraging the growth of democracy in Latin America, on terms worked out by the people and leaders of each country, has been working, and we want it to succeed in Chile.

It is obviously not United States policy to attempt to overthrow Pinochet, but there is increasing evidence that he is becoming an obstacle to gradual evolution in Chilean politics consonant with our interest in a peaceful transition to an elected civilian government. In particular, Pinochet shows signs of wanting to remain in power after 1989, when his current term ends; he came to power in 1973.

We have tried to persuade Pinochet to take concrete steps to ease political restrictions and to establish a dialogue with non-communist, democratic political groups; we have also encouraged the democratic parties to soften their rigid opposition to Pinochet and the 1980 Constitution. The Catholic Church and its centrist leader, Cardinal Fresno, share our view and have followed this approach, as have the UK and FRG.

These joint efforts to foster greater realism within the democratic parties have begun to pay off. Cardinal Fresno has engineered wide support for a new and pragmatic transition proposal from a broad range of political groups, including ex-Pinochet supporters and non-violent marxists. Both Pinochet and the violent Communist opposition so far have rejected considering any change in the current situation, but the support Fresno's initiative is generating could cause second thoughts.

If Pinochet remains intransigent and blocks the needed transition, the country will become increasingly polarized. This policy will only benefit the Communists. We will continue to seek cooperation, dialogue and compromise, but there is a growing tension between our national interest in an orderly and peaceful process and Pinochet's apparent desire to hang on indefinitely.

UNCLASSIFIED

DOCUMENT 10. White House, **SECRET** Presidential Evening Reading, "Likely Involvement of Chilean Army in Rojas Killing," July 14, 1986.

SECRET/WNINTEL/NOFORN/NOCONTRACT/ORCON

PRESIDENTIAL EVENING READING
JULY 14, 1986

DECAPTIONED

LIKELY INVOLVEMENT OF CHILEAN ARMY IN ROJAS KILLING

The eyewitness reports of Chilean army involvement in the fatal attack on U.S. resident Rodrigo Rojas in Chile so far are holding up under closer scrutiny. According to [ ], an investigation by the Chilean intelligence service has fingered Army personnel as clearly involved. Nevertheless, the Chilean government, following Pinochet's lead, is trying publicly to brand Rojas and Carmen Quintana (the other Chilean injured) as terrorists, supposedly victims of their own Molotov cocktails. Videotapes were broadcast on government television supposedly showing Quintana carrying explosives two weeks prior to her injuries, prompting a denial by Quintana's parents that the girl shown is their critically injured daughter. Press reports say Senator Helms is returning to the U.S. carrying this videotape.

The GOC may not persist very long with such bold misrepresentations, especially if the special investigative judge requested by the GOC turns out to be honest as reported. Chilean Foreign Minister told Ambassador Barnes he was determined to work for a thorough investigation, the need for which Elliott Abrams reinforced with the Chilean Charge last week. But Pinochet is unlikely to permit Army soldiers to be tried even should the special investigator hold them responsible. If the molotov cocktail defense folds, we should expect other explanations, such as blaming communist commandos.

DOCUMENT 11. Department of State, **SECRET** Information Memorandum to Secretary Shultz, "Strategy Paper on Chile," July 11, 1986.

United States Department of State

Washington, D. C. 20520

Chile Project (#S199900030)
U.S. Department of State
Release X Excise ____ Deny ____
Declassify: In Part ____ In Full X
Exemption(s) ____

UNCLASSIFIED

INFORMATION MEMORANDUM
~~SECRET/SENSITIVE~~ S/S

TO: The Secretary

FROM: ARA - Elliott Abrams

SUBJECT: Strategy Paper on Chile

We collaborated with Harry on the paper, so it represents ARA views as well. The bottom line is we face a worsening situation in Chile and need to use all available means of influence to protect our interests.

I used my appearance yesterday on ABC's Nightline to stress our commitment to eventual free elections in Chile, making the point we want this to occur sooner rather than later. But more than verbal volleys will be required to get Pinochet to agree to leave, or to persuade the Army to persuade him. In fact, Pinochet yesterday almost entirely dropped the veil with a speech making clear he intends for the current regime to stay in power until nearly the end of the century. His choice of timing for this announcement, with furor still building over the Rojas death, suggests that he intends to ignore international criticism and tough it out at home with more repression.

Already, however, it is apparent that the shockwave sent by the Rojas death has had a major impact on Congressional attitudes. Sentiment for tough action will steadily build particularly if those responsible for this crime are not identified and prosecuted. We can expect to find our manuevering room on the MDB issue this fall even more limited. Congressman Barnes plans to introduce soon a bill requiring us to vote no on all MDB loans for Chile.

The next Chile MDB loan is still expected to come up for vote in early October. We plan to work with Treasury to produce a more detailed options paper on the MDB vote issue for interagency review. We will want to consider a NSC meeting to review our Chile policy by early September.

Bob Gelbard goes to Chile this weekend for a 6-day visit. He will meet with a wide range of people. After Bob returns we will send you further thoughts on how to handle the inceasingly worrisome situation in Chile.

Drafted: ARA/SC:JWSwigert JWS
6152B 7/11/86 x72575

Clearances: ARA:RGelbard
ARA/SC:DCox JWS

~~SECRET/SENSITIVE~~
(DECL:OADR)

Acc. # 59-96-0051
Box 6 of 8

DOCUMENT 12. Defense Intelligence Agency, **TOP SECRET ZARF UMBRA** Report, "Chile Government Contingency Plans [To Disrupt Plebiscite], October 4, 1988.

UNCLASSIFIED

~~Top Secret Zarf Umbra~~

CHILE: Government Contingency Plans. (U)

High-ranking government officials have reportedly drawn up contingency plans to sabotage the plebiscite on 5 October and to nullify the electoral process if the government is perceived as losing the referendum.

Close supporters of President Pinochet are said to have contingency plans to derail the plebiscite by encouraging and staging acts of violence. They hope that such violence will elicit further reprisals by the radical opposition and begin a cycle of rioting and disorder. The plans call for government security forces to intervene forcefully and, citing damage to the electoral process and balloting facilities, to declare a state of emergency. At that point, the elections would be suspended, declared invalid, and postponed indefinitely.

have stated that the military will not tolerate significant opposition violence or any activity recognized by the government as unconstitutional. They added that if the opposition were to challenge the government and engage in antigovernment activity, the military would take extreme, forceful measures to contain such activity. They also stated that the results would be more severe than they were in 1973, when President Allende was overthrown in a bloody coup.

COMMENT: The contingency plans, if implemented, would counter conventional logic since Pinochet would subvert the constitutional process that has thus far provided his legal basis for rule. If the opposition reacts the way the government hopes it will and plays into its hands, the probability of serious, widespread bloodshed will increase considerably.

The plans would provoke vehement international condemnation that would be enhanced by the presence of several hundred international observers. In addition, the security forces would probably face a radical left swelled by some former moderates who would view the new political situation as radical and lacking prospects for moderation or future accommodation.

Whether the commanders of the other military services represented in the junta are aware of the contingency plans is unclear. However, their personal and institutional commitments to the constitutional process would lead them to resist Pinochet if he chooses to implement plans to derail the vote. The President might ignore such protests for short-term gain if he were convinced that the army would fully back him. However, most army officers have expressed confidence in a government victory, and the majority have indicated that the military's proper reaction to a "no" victory, barring massive violence, would be to abide by the constitutional framework.

Considering the existence of extralegal contingency plans, close supporters of Pinochet have apparently considered ignoring the negative repercussions of an aborted plebiscite to ensure his continuation in power. Weighing the possible negative repercussions, the President's close supporters have evidently opted for disrupting the plebiscite and making sure that Pinochet stays in office regardless of the cost.

DIADIN 277-2B as of 2205 EDT 3 Oct 88

Not responsive

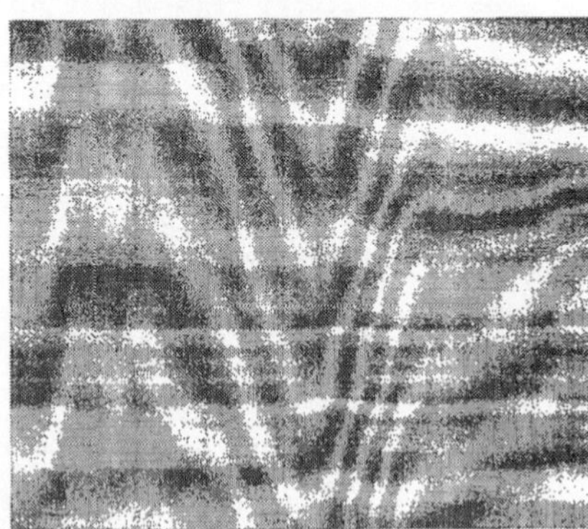

4 Oct 88 Defense Intelligence Summary Page 19

UNCLASSIFIED

~~TCS 652089/88~~
~~Handle Via TALENT-KEYHOLE-COMINT Control Channels Jointly~~

~~Top~~ Secret ~~Zarf Umbra~~

Declassified with redactions by DIA

DOCUMENT 13. Defense Intelligence Agency, Information Report, "Chilean Junta Meeting-The Night of the Plebiscite," January 1, 1989.

UNCLASSIFIED

SERIAL: (U) . IIR 6 817 0058 89.

BODY
/*********** THIS IS A COMBINED MESSAGE ************/
PASS: (U) DIA PASS TO AIG 11848.

COUNTRY: (U) CHILE (CI).

SUBJ: IIR 6 817 0058 89/CHILEAN JUNTA MEETING - THE NIGHT OF THE PLEBISCITE (U)

WARNING: THIS IS AN INFORMATION REPORT, NOT FINALLY EVALUATED INTELLIGENCE.

DEPARTMENT OF DEFENSE

DOI: (U) 881027.

SUMMARY: ~~(C/NOFORN)~~ THE CHILEAN PRESIDENT AND CINC OF THE ARMY GEN AUGUSTO PINOCHET WAS PREPARED ON THE NIGHT OF 5 OCT TO OVERTHROW THE RESULTS OF THE PLEBISCITE, ONLY THE REFUSAL OF THE JUNTA MEMBERS TO SUPPORT SUCH ACTION STOPPED HIM.
TEXT: 1. ~~(C/NOFORN)~~ REPORTS THAT THE CHILEAN MEMBERS OF THE LEGISLATIVE JUNTA, ADM MERINO, GEN MATTHEI, GEN STANGE AND GEN GORDON HAD BEEN CUT-OFF BY THE GOVERNMENT EARLY IN THE EVENING OF 5 OCT FROM RECEIVING THE GOC'S OFFICIAL PLEBISCITE RESULTS VIA THE ARMY'S NETWORK. FROM THIS TIME UNTIL THEIR JUNTA MEETING AT 0105 THE MORNING OF 6 OCT IN LA MONEDA WITH GEN PINOCHET THEY HAD TO RELY ON THE

~~CONFIDENTIAL~~

Declassified by DIA per EO 12958

UNCLASSIFIED

UNCLASSIFIED

~~CONFIDENTIAL~~

"NO" COMMAND RESULTS FOR FURTHER INFORMATION. AT AROUND MIDNIGHT ADM MERINO WAS ABOUT TO GO TO BED BUT THE OTHER JUNTA MEMBERS INSISTED ON MEETING WITH PINOCHET. GEN MATTHEI'S STATEMENT TO THE PRESS UPON ARRIVING AT LA MONEDA THAT IT APPEARED THAT THE NO HAD WON WAS A DELIBERATE PRONOUNCEMENT INTENDED TO LIMIT GENERAL PINOCHET'S OPTIONS

MATTHEI TOLD

THAT HIS MISSION WAS TO DEFUSE THE BOMB AND THAT MATTHEI DESCRIBED THE MEETING AS VERY TOUGH. MATTHEI HAD PREVIOUS GENERAL DISCUSSIONS WITH STANGE ABOUT THE POTENTIAL THAT PINOCHET MIGHT ATTEMPT TO OVERTHROW A NO WIN BUT THEY HAD NOT TALKED WITH MERINO.

2. (C/NOFORN) IN THE JUNTA MEETING, PINOCHET WAS DESCRIBED AS VERY ANGRY AND INSISTENT THAT THE JUNTA MUST GIVE HIM EXTRAORDINARY POWERS TO MEET THE CRISIS OF THE ELECTORIAL DEFEAT. HE HAD A DOCUMENT PREPARED FOR THEIR SIGNATURES AUTHORIZING THIS. THE MINISTER OF THE INTERIOR, FERNANDEZ WAS PRESENT AND TRYING TO ESTABLISH THAT 43 PERCENT WAS ACTUALLY A WIN, A POINT HE LATER PEDDLED IN PUBLIC. PINOCHET SPOKE OF USING THE EXTRAORDINARY POWERS TO HAVE THE ARMED FORCES SIEZE THE CAPITAL.

AT THIS POINT MATTHEI STOOD UP TO BE COUNTED. MATTHEI TOLD PINOCHET HE WOULD UNDER NO CIRCUMSTANCES AGREE TO SUCH A THING. PINOCHET ASKED AGAIN FOR SPECIAL POWERS AND AGAIN MATTHEI REFUSED SAYING HE HAD HIS CHANCE AS THE OFFICIAL CANDIDATE AND LOST. PINOCHET THEN TURNED TO THE OTHERS AND MADE THE SAME REQUEST AND WAS TURNED DOWN BY STANGE AND GORDON. TENSION IN THE ROOM WAS SO HIGH AT THIS MOMENT THAT BGEN SERGIO VALENZUELA, THE SECRETARY GENERAL OF THE GOVERNMENT, COLLAPSED FROM WHAT TURNED OUT TO BE THE FIRST STAGE OF A HEART ATTACK. AT THIS POINT, WITHOUT JUNTA SUPPORT TO OVERTHROW THE "NO" WIN PINOCHET WAS LEFT WITHOUT ALTERNATIVE BUT TO ACCEPT A "NO" WIN.

COMMENTS: ~~(C/NOFORN)~~ VARIOUS VERSIONS OF THE EVENTS OF THE NIGHT OF THE PLEBISCITE HAVE MADE THEIR WAY INTO THE PRESS.

DOCUMENT 14. U.S. Embassy, Cable, "Mendoza Human Rights Concert Sounds Sour Note for Chilean Government," October 24, 1988.

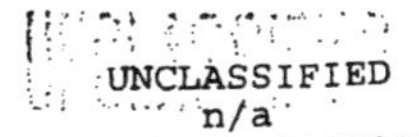

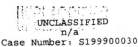

UNCLASSIFIED
n/a
Case Number: S199900030

10/24/88

Chile Project (#S199900030)
U.S. Department of State
Release X Excise _____ Deny _____
Declassify: In Part _____ In Full ✓
Exemption(s) _____

UNCLASSIFIED

PAGE 01 SANTIA 07854 241933Z
ACTION ARA-00

INFO	LOG-00	ADS-00	AID-00	INR-10	SS-00	OIC-02	CIAE-00
	DODE-00	H-01	IO-19	NSCE-00	NSAE-00	HA-09	L-03
	PA-02	INRE-00	USIE-00	SP-02	PRS-01	/049 W	

------------------206217 250456Z /21

R 241928Z OCT 88
FM AMEMBASSY SANTIAGO
TO SECSTATE WASHDC 8761
INFO AMEMBASSY BUENOS AIRES

UNCLAS SANTIAGO 07854

E.O. 12356: N/A
TAGS: PHUM, PGOV, CI
SUBJ: MENDOZA HUMAN RIGHTS CONCERT SOUNDS SOUR NOTE
\- FOR CHILEAN GOVERNMENT

1. SUMMARY: REACTION TO THE OCTOBER 14 ROCK CONCERT HELD IN MENDOZA, ARGENTINA, TO COMMEMORATE THE 40TH ANNIVERSARY OF THE UNIVERSAL DECLARATION OF HUMAN RIGHTS INDICATES HUMAN RIGHTS ABUSES CONTINUE TO BE AN EMOTIONAL ISSUE FOR CHILEANS. END SUMMARY.

2. AN EMBASSY POLITICAL OFFICER WAS ONE OF THE FEW PEOPLE OVER 30 TO ATTEND THE OCTOBER 14, 1988, AMNESTY INTERNATIONAL ROCK CONCERT IN MENDOZA, ARGENTINA, TO COMMEMORATE THE 40TH ANNIVERSARY OF THE UNIVERSAL DECLARATION OF HUMAN RIGHTS. NEWSPAPER ACCOUNTS HAVE ATTENDANCE AT THE CONCERT AT ABOUT 30 THOUSAND PEOPLE, WITH ONE PAPER ADDING THAT ONE-THIRD OF THE ATTENDEES WERE CHILEAN. EMBOFF WOULD ESTIMATE CHILEANS AT MORE LIKE TWO-THIRDS OF THE AUDIENCE. FROM ALL APPEARANCES, FROM THE BEGINNING OF THE CONCERT AROUND 1500 WITH THE CHILEAN GROUP "THE PRISONERS," TO THE END OF THE SHOW AT APPROXIMATELY 0100 WITH THE CHORAL SINGING OF "GET UP, STAND UP"
UNCLASSIFIED

UNCLASSIFIED

PAGE 02 SANTIA 07854 241933Z

n/a
UNCLASSIFIED

(STAND UP FOR YOUR RIGHTS) BY MEMBERS OF ALL THE GROUPS WHICH APPEARED, THE EVENT WAS A MASSIVE "NO" RALLY. BANNERS OF "CHILE DEMOCRATICO," THE PARTY FOR DEMOCRACY (PPD), AND THE "NO COMMAND" WERE IN EVIDENCE THROUGHOUT THE MUNICIPAL STADIUM IN MENDOZA, AS WAS THE CHILEAN FLAG.

3. ALL OF THE ARTISTS, LATIN OR FOREIGN, HAD GENERAL COMMENTS TO MAKE ON HUMAN RIGHTS AND SPECIFIC CRITICISMS TO MAKE ABOUT CHILE. A REPEATED THEME WAS THE FACT THAT PRESIDENT PINOCHET HAD BEEN DEFEATED IN THE PLEBISCITE AND THERE WAS NOW HOPE FOR CHILE. THIS THEME WAS PRESENTED IN THE OPENING SONG WHICH WAS DEDICATED TO PINOCHET: "WHY DON'T THEY LEAVE" (POR QUE NO SE VAN). THE YOUTHFUL CROWD ROARED EVERY TIME AN ANTI-GOVERNMENT SENTIMENT WAS EXPRESSED.

4. WHILE THE YOUTHFUL CROWD WAS DEFINITELY ANTI-PINOCHET AND PRO-ROCK, IT CANNOT BE SAID THAT THEY WERE PARTICULARLY COMMITTED TO HUMAN RIGHTS. CHILEAN WRITER AND POET ARIEL DORFMAN TOOK THE STAGE PRIOR TO THE PENULTIMATE ACT AND GAVE A SHORT SPEECH ON THE ATROCITIES WHICH HAVE OCCURRED IN CHILE AND ATTEMPTED TO READ A POEM ON THE SUBJECT. HE COULD NOT BE HEARD OVER THE HOOTS OF THE YOUTHS WHO ONLY WANTED TO SEE AND HEAR THE STAR ATTRACTIONS. DORFMAN PERSISTED WITH HIS PLANNED PRESENTATION AND THEN INTRODUCED THE BRITISH ROCK STAR "STING."

5. STING HAS BEEN AN ADVOCATE OF THE CHILEAN OPPOSITION FOR SEVERAL YEARS. OF ALL THE ARTISTS HE WAS BY FAR THE STRONGEST IN CONDEMNING THE CHILEAN GOVERNMENT. AT ONE JUNCTURE, HE SUGGESTED TO THE
UNCLASSIFIED

UNCLASSIFIED

PAGE 03 SANTIA 07854 241933Z

AUDIENCE (IN PASSABLE SPANISH WITH NO CUE CARD) THAT "IT HAS BEEN NINE DAYS SINCE THE PLEBISCITE AND NOTHING HAS CHANGED." THE CROWD RESPONDED WILDLY. ALSO DURING STING'S PERFORMANCE, HE CALLED A PREARRANGED GROUP OF WIDOWS AND ORPHANS OF THE MISSING IN CHILE AND ARGENTINA TO THE STAGE AND HE AND PETER GABRIEL SANG "DANCING ALONE" THE TOUCHING

SONG DEDICATED TO CHILE'S DISAPPEARED, AND THEIR RELATIVES. THE AUDIENCE WAS ALMOST PERFECTLY SILENT DURING THIS SONG (A GREAT CONTRAST TO THE NORM) AND IMPROVISED TORCHES WERE BURNED, AS THEY WERE DURING SEVERAL SONGS THROUGHOUT THE EVENING.

6. BRUCE SPRINGSTEEN, THE STAR AND CLOSING ATTRACTION, WAS ANTICLIMATIC AFTER STING. HE READ A STATEMENT IN SPANISH ABOUT HUMAN RIGHTS BUT THE MESSAGE OF HIS MUSIC IS TOO TUNED TO AMERICAN PROBLEMS TO TOUCH LATIN SENSIBILITIES. THE ONLY THING THAT SAVED THE CONCERT FROM ENDING ON A FLAT NOTE WAS THE GROUP-SINGING OF "GET UP, STAND UP" TO WHICH SPANISH LYRICS HAD BEEN ADDED -- "DERECHOS HUMANOS, PARA TODOS Y PARA SIEMPRE."

7. CHILEAN NEWSPAPERS REPORTED THAT CARS WITH CHILEAN LICENSE PLATES WERE DELIBERATELY DAMAGED BY ARGENTINE FANS, BUT EMBOFF DID NOT WITNESS SUCH VANDALISM.

8. COMMENT: THE REACTION AT THE ROCK CONCERT IN MENDOZA INDICATES THAT THE HUMAN RIGHTS SITUATION IN CHILE REMAINS AN EMOTIONAL ISSUE WHICH WILL PERSIST DESPITE POLITICAL OPENINGS. BARNES

UNCLASSIFIED

NNNN

Atrocity and Accountability:
The Long Epilogue of the Pinochet Case

The torturer, like the pirate of old, is hostis humanis generis*—the enemy of all mankind.*

—landmark 1980 U.S. Court ruling on the rights of torture victims

One who sets in motion a coup attempt can be assessed with the responsibility for the natural and probable consequences of that action.

—White House Legal Counsel Philip Buchen to the CIA, June 24, 1975

On October 16, 1998, a British judge named Nicolas Evans signed a warrant for the arrest of Augusto Pinochet. "To each and all the Constables of the Metropolitan Police Force," it read, "you are hearby required to arrest the defendant and bring [him] before a Metropolitan Magistrate sitting at Bow Street Magistrates' Court." (Doc 1) Late that evening, two detectives from Scotland Yard's organized crime division drove to the upscale private hospital where Pinochet was recuperating from back surgery. There, they served him with a "priority red warrant"—sent through INTERPOL from Spain—requesting the general's location and detention for "crimes of genocide and terrorism."

Pinochet's arrest will go down in the annals of history as a dramatic turning point for the international human rights movement—and a transcendent moment of vindication for his victims and their families. "When I read about General Pinochet being arrested," recalls Murray Karpen, father of Ronni Karpen Moffitt, "my first reaction was, 'There is a God.' " His detention empowered the principle of universal jurisdiction—the ability of the international community to pursue the prosecution of dictators, torturers, and mass murderers outside their home nations. Although the protracted saga of Pinochet's sixteen months under house arrest in London would eventually end with his return to Santiago, his case established a precedent—the Pinochet precedent—that carries implications for past and future human rights violators, as well as legal, and historical, efforts to hold them and their accomplices accountable for atrocities against humanity. In addition, his arrest led directly to a major effort in the United States to declassify the long-hidden, secret archives on Pinochet's atrocities—and the U.S. role in supporting his regime.

The Spanish Initiative

The genesis of General Pinochet's stunning arrest dates back to the day he took power. On September 11, 1973, as the Chilean military began its assault on La Moneda palace, Salvador Allende pressed one of his political advisers, a Spanish lawyer named Juan Garcés, to escape from the building and "tell the world what happened here." After two decades of writing books and articles about the Allende government and the Pinochet dictatorship, Garcés turned his attention to the pursuit of justice for the atrocities committed against Chile and Chileans. "I was witness to a crime in which an entire people was victimized, where the democratic structures of a nation were deliberately exterminated," as he explained his motivation.[1]

In the summer of 1996, Garcés launched a novel judicial effort against Pinochet and his commanders for the death of a number of Spaniards in Chile after the coup.[2] He filed a "popular action"—a criminal complaint deemed in the public interest—with a special branch of the Spanish judiciary known as the Audiencia Nacional, using legal loopholes in Spain's judicial system that recognize universal jurisdiction for offenses such as genocide, illegal detention, and terrorism. The Audiencia accepted the case, as well as a separate one filed against the Argentine military for human rights crimes, and assigned them to a pair of "superjudges"—special Spanish investigative magistrates. Judge Baltazar Garzón took the assignment to pursue atrocities in Argentina, and expanded his mandate to cover the crimes of Operation Condor; Judge Manuel García Castellon received the case against Pinochet and his military commanders.

At the initiative of Garcés, the Chile investigation expanded beyond Spanish victims into a veritable class-action human rights lawsuit for all victims of the regime. For the first time, Chileans, and the families of a number of American victims had a potential legal remedy to break the shield of impunity that Pinochet had created for himself and his generals. With Garcés's assistance, Judge Castellon took depositions from hundreds of victims and witnesses, and identified no fewer than thirty-eight regime officials who might be subject to prosecution—among them General Pinochet himself.

Pinochet's Arrest

For two years, the Spanish legal teams pursued these pioneering cases in the field of international human rights law. They faced the interference of their own government, tension in Spanish-Chilean relations, and resistance from the United States government to providing documentary evidence that could support prosecution of members of the Chilean military. Their most difficult challenge, however, was physically securing the target of their investigation. Spanish law forbids trials in absentia. Spain does have a treaty of extradition with Chile, but there was no possibility that the Chilean Supreme Court, stacked with Pinochet appointees, would expel him for trial outside the country.

In late September 1998, following twenty-fifth anniversary commemorations of his infamous putsch, Pinochet traveled to London with his wife for a vacation. While in London, he granted an interview with journalist Jon Lee Anderson for an unprecedented profile in *The New Yorker*. The profile, published four days before the general's arrest, ironically represented the beginning of a major public relations push by the former dictator to improve his international image and obtain "history's blessing."[3] It included a photo of a seemingly venerable, civilian-suited older man—"he looks like someone's genteel grandfather," reported Anderson—taken on September 25 in London's five-star Park Lane Hotel. The article implied that Pinochet would seek medical assistance there.

By the time the *New Yorker* piece appeared on the stands, officials at Amnesty International's British-based secretariat headquarters had learned that Pinochet was in England. One of Amnesty's legal advisers, Frederico Andreu, alerted Juan Garcés in Madrid. Garcés then initiated a coordinated effort through the Spanish courts to formally question, detain, and extradite the general. In order to obtain quick British cooperation, Spain invoked the European Convention on the Suppression of Terrorism—a mutual-cooperation treaty that obligates signatories to identify, locate, and hold suspected international terrorists. On October 14, Judge Baltazar Garzón sent their initial request to detain Pinochet to Scotland Yard.[4] Spain's subsequent arrest petition also focused on Pinochet's role in Operation Condor. The Chilean general, it stated, was in charge of creating an international organization that conceived, developed and carried out a systematic plan of illegal detentions, abductions, tortures, forcible transfers of persons, murders and/or disappearances of many people, including citizens from Argentina, Spain, the United Kingdom, the US, Chile and other countries. These actions were carried out in different countries . . . mainly to exterminate the political opposition."[5]

Pinochet's dramatic, unprecedented arrest began a protracted sixteen-month legal saga that commanded the rapt attention of the world community. Never before had a former head of state been detained outside his homeland for extradition to a third country; moreover, putting one of the world's most renowned human rights violators on trial carried significant legal, political, moral, and historical implications. But while Spanish prosecutors attempted to obtain his extradition, the Chilean government, still cowed by an angry military and the nationalist outrage of Chile's rabid rightwing business class, pressed the British authorities to let him go free. With Pinochet under house arrest in $16,000-a-month rented estate, his case morphed into a precedent-setting model for expanding modern human rights law, as well as the ultimate international political football.

Initially, the British courts ruled that Pinochet was "entitled to immunity as a former sovereign" from prosecution, and therefore could not be detained or extradited. Under the ancient concept of the "divine right of kings," Lord Chief Justice Thomas Bingham determined, "a former head of state is clearly entitled to immunity for criminal acts committed in the course of exercising public functions." Appearing before the House of Lords in November, Pinochet's lawyers from the prestigious firm of Kingsley Napley presented an extraordinary argument: torture, murder, and terrorism were, in fact, the official "public functions" of government, carried out by official entities of the state, under Pinochet's command. These atrocities, they argued, would have been committed "within governmental authority, under orders to the military or government forces." The language of Britain's State Immunity Act was so broad, claimed Pinochet's lead lawyer, Clive Nicholls—in the most memorable statement of the proceedings—that even "Hitler would have been protected" from prosecution in London.[6]

"Torture is conduct which no state seeks to defend," Christopher Greenwood, a prominent human rights lawyer representing Spain, responded in the appeal to the five law lords. Since it is beyond the pale of legitimate state conduct, it could not be considered an official act covered by British laws on immunity. "It is the argument of the Spanish authorities," as Alun Jones summed up the argument for extradition, "that the savage and barbarous crimes committed in Chile and the territories of other states, including the United States, Spain and Italy, are not within the functions of a head of state in English law, the law of nations or the law of Chile."

The Law Lords agreed. On November 25—Pinochet's eighty-third birthday—the Lords ruled 3-2 that genocide and torture were "not acceptable conduct on the part of anyone," particularly heads of state. But their decision that Pinochet could indeed be extradited to Spain was soon vacated when his lawyers successfully argued that one of the Lords had a conflict of interest.[7] In March 1999, a second panel of judges reaffirmed that Pinochet could be extradited—but only for human rights crimes committed after Britain signed the U.N. Convention against Torture in September 1988.

But concerted behind-the-scenes political efforts by the Chilean government—led by Foreign Minister Juan Gabriel Valdes and his top aide Alberto Vanklaveran—to convince the Blair government to allow him to return to his homeland served to sabotage both Spanish and British legal efforts to apply universal jurisdiction and bring a renowned international criminal to justice. Unable to obtain his release on the merits of the law, Chilean officials repeatedly met privately with their British counterparts to broker a deal to release Pinochet. Publicly, the administration of Eduardo Frei Jr. and the general's supporters waged a concerted media campaign to win him a pardon on humanitarian grounds. "He is ill, and about to be eighty-three," Chile's deputy foreign minister, Mariano Fernández, said after visiting the general. "We are talking about an old man, an infirm man. He has a heart pacemaker and suffers from diabetes and a chronic spine condition," former Pinochet crony Miguel Schweitzer told the press. After Pinochet gave a lengthy face-to-face interview to the *London Telegraph* in July, during which he appeared "mentally sharp and calculating," according to the article, his advisers sequestered him from the press; thereafter only photos of the general in a wheelchair appeared in the newspapers and on television. In early October, one of Pinochet's doctors announced that he had suffered a series of mini-strokes that left him "disoriented." His lawyers promptly initiated a series of legal appeals against extradition on the grounds that Pinochet's mental health prevented him from participating in his defense. British Home Secretary Jack Straw hinted that he might release him on "compassionate grounds."

On January 11, 2000, Straw announced that "following recent deterioration in the state of Senator Pinochet's health," he was "unfit to stand trial." Straw based this decision on a controversial medical report by four British specialists who conducted one examination of the former dictator. He then refused to release the medical report, citing Pinochet's "privacy rights." After another round of legal appeals, filed by Belgium—one of several nations along with Switzerland and France that also sought Pinochet's extradition—

and six human rights groups, the British government was forced to turn over the report, which recorded mild dementia commensurate with Pinochet's age, and a "memory deficit for both recent and remote events." On March 2, 2000, Straw issued his final ruling: Pinochet "would not at present be mentally capable of meaningful participation in a trial," and therefore would not be extradited to Spain.

Almost immediately, Pinochet and his entourage departed in a caravan to a military base outside of London where a private jet sat fueled and ready for takeoff. On the morning of March 3, he landed at Pudahuel airport outside Santiago, the saga of his prosecution for human rights abuses seemingly over. The Chilean military, led by Pinochet's successor as commander-in-chief, General Ricardo Izurieta, organized a red-carpet reception—in a gesture of defiance toward the international community, and in violation of an agreement with the incoming administration of Ricardo Lagos that there would be no public ceremony upon his return. As a military marching band played, Pinochet, smiling and spry, rose from his wheelchair and walked across the tarmac to shake the hands of the generals who had played such an important role in securing his release and return.

Post-Pinochet Chile 1991–2000

The country that Pinochet returned to was not the same nation he had left. Until March 1998, when he stepped down as army commander-in-chief and assumed the title of *Senador vitalica*—Senator for life—which provided him with full immunity from prosecution for his crimes, Pinochet had employed his military power to hold the civilian government hostage to the violence of the past. Under his command, the military rattled its sabers in response to any significant moves to make members of his regime legally accountable for their criminal conduct. As he warned the incoming civilian administration in 1989, "the day they touch one of my men the rule of law ends."

Such bald intimidation had the desired effect on the new civilian administration of Patricio Aylwin. Even before he took office, Aylwin confided to high U.S. officials that he was considering a pardon for regime officials who had committed atrocities. In a quiet meeting in Buenos Aires in July 1989, Aylwin told Assistant Secretary for Inter-American Affairs Bernard Aronson that the first post-Pinochet government would "need to obtain justice without a witch-hunt and without generating a conflict with the military."

In his inaugural address, given symbolically at the National Stadium where so many had died, Aylwin made it clear that his election represented only a partial return to civilian rule. "Our satisfaction this day," he stated, "cannot prevent us from issuing a clear warning about the many limitations, obstacles and forced steps which, in its zeal to remain in power, the regime dominant until just yesterday left us." The terms of the transition were strict, Aylwin admitted; the civilian government had no other choice but to accept Pinochet's conditions. "Should we, in order to avoid those limitations, have exposed our people to the risk of renewed violence, suffering, loss of life?"[8]

Under these limitations, the truth of the Pinochet regime's human rights abuses could be pursued, but justice could not. In April 1990, Aylwin established the National Commission on Truth and Reconciliation, chaired by Raul Rettig. The commission mandate was to "clarify in a comprehensive manner the truth about the most serious human rights violations" committed during the military dictatorship. A team of researchers was given less than twelve months to investigate seventeen years of massive abuses and draft a comprehensive report, but was restricted to cataloging the fates of the victims without identifying those who had tortured and killed them. "The commission named the victims," staff director José Zalaquett noted, "but not the perpetrators."[9]

Until Pinochet's arrest, Chile's political elite adopted what political scientists called a "conspiracy of consensus" to essentially bury the past and pretend that the commission report had brought the "reconciliation" of Chilean society. Monuments were built to human rights victims; ceremonies, such as an official reburial of Salvador Allende in the National Cemetery, were held; and periodically Chile experienced what Alexander Wilde characterizes as "irruptions of memory" that revealed a nation still suffering from the wounds of the past.[10] Until Pinochet stepped down as commander-in-chief of the armed forces in March 1998, however, his military acted with impunity and largely maintained its armor of immunity.

There was one notable exception: the Letelier-Moffitt case. As an act of international terrorism in the United States, the case became subject to intense political pressure from Washington. The conditionality of the Kennedy amendment—military assistance to Chile could not be restored without a presidential certification of Chilean cooperation in prosecuting the guilty—and astute lobbying by the Letelier, Moffitt, and Karpen families in Congress and the executive branch, rendered impossible the full normalization of U.S. relations with post-Pinochet Chile without justice in the murders of Orlando Letelier and Ronni Moffitt.

Washington revived its pressure on Chile to hold those responsible legally accountable in the spring of 1987, after a member of the assassination team, Armando Fernández Larios, fled Chile (with the covert help of the FBI and State Department) and agreed to plead guilty and provide testimony in return for protection in the United States. In secret debriefings, Fernández provided detailed information about the role of Manuel Contreras and Pedro Espinoza in the assassination plot, and directly implicated Pinochet in the subsequent cover-up of DINA's responsibility for the car bombing.

Using the Fernandez confession, on May 11, 1987, the United States again formally petitioned Chile to extradite Contreras and Espinoza. The Pinochet regime rejected the request. On July 17, the Reagan administration filed another diplomatic note demanding that Chile put the DINA officials on trial in Santiago. The regime refused. The only movement in the case was a ruling by a military court that the status of a purported internal investigation into the falsification of the Paraguayan passports be changed from "closed" to "suspended." Acting on that small window of opportunity, Washington supported a series of legal appeals filed by Fabiola Letelier, sister of Orlando, to move the "passports case" forward. But U.S. pressure to force Pinochet's military courts to reopen the only legal avenue to prosecute the DINA officers failed.

In addition to pressing for criminal proceedings, the Reagan administration took up the claims of the Letelier and Moffitt families for compensation for the murders. In 1979, the families had filed a civil suit for wrongful death against the Pinochet regime. After a lengthy review of the evidence, a D.C. superior court judge ruled on November 5, 1980 that the Chilean government was responsible and liable for the murders and ordered the regime to pay compensatory and punitive damages totaling $5.3 million. When the Pinochet regime ignored the ruling the families sought to execute the judgment by seizing a jetliner at Kennedy airport belonging to the state-owned LAN-Chile airlines. But a judge quickly ruled that LAN's assets were exempt from seizure, and the families were left with what the courts called "a right without a remedy."

To create a "remedy," the sole survivor of the attack, Michael Moffitt, and the vigorous lawyer for the Moffitt and Letelier families, Samuel Buffone, waged a concerted campaign in Congress to rewrite the Foreign Sovereign Immunities Act (FSIA) to facilitate seizing property from other governments. For diplomatic reasons, the Reagan administration opposed changing the law. Instead, U.S. officials offered to have the State Department "espouse the claims" of the families and present them to the Chilean government. On July 28, 1987, Assistant Secretary Elliott Abrams presented the first of several diplomatic notes to Chile's ambassador in Washington requesting that the regime pay up to $12 million in compensation for "the personal and national injury [caused by] the Chilean government's participation and cover-up of the Letelier assassination."[11] In diplomatic note no. 07731, the Chilean foreign ministry responded on August 27 that Chile "had no role in the crimes that resulted in the deaths of Mr. Letelier and Mrs. Moffitt" and "repudiates any interpretation of the facts that would seek to involve the Republic in th[ose] deaths."

Pinochet's loss in the plebiscite marked the beginning of the end of his regime's long mendacious obstruction of justice in the murders. A flurry of activity ensued. General Contreras became concerned that the incoming civilian government would turn him over to the Americans and once again tried to blackmail Washington. "One senses he may no longer feel safe hiding behind government stonewalling," the embassy informed the State Department. In a February 10, 1989, secret cable titled "Offer/Threat by Manuel Contreras," the embassy reported that Contreras claimed to have arrived at an "understanding" with four separate "gringo" officials that the U.S. would not reveal anything damaging to him and Pinochet, and, in turn, he would not reveal anything damaging about new U.S. president—who was director of CIA at the time of the assassinations—George Bush. Contreras, noted the cable, "considers this 'understanding' to have been broken by recent USG initiatives, and unless a new understanding is arrived at by the end of February, Contreras will be free to take unspecified actions prejudicial to the USG."

These actions were likely to be bombastic statements placing the blame on the CIA for the bombing. "However," the embassy concluded, "Contreras is the most dangerous man in Chile [and] is currently under extreme pressure . . . and we cannot rule out the possibility of a Contreras-initiated terrorist act." Back in Washington, however, U.S. officials remained unimpressed. "I would be mighty surprised if any USG person made any such deal with this piece of dog shit," Deputy Assistant Secretary Michael Kozak scrawled on a memo responding to Contreras's threat. "We should talk [about] how this could be used to further pressure Contreras—the best defense may be an offense."[12]

Throughout the transition period to civilian rule, Washington pursued a multitrack initiative to clear the Letelier-Moffitt case off the agenda of future U.S.-Chilean relations. Ambassador Charles Gillespie recommended back-channel approaches to key sectors of the Chilean military to convince them of their institutional interests in cutting Contreras loose. "We should encourage these sectors emphasizing that the U.S. views Letelier as one of the principal obstacles to resumption of a normal relationship," Gillespie wrote in a secret cable. "There are distinct advantages for Chile in getting our military-to-military contacts back on track, and finally, the U.S. is doggedly determined to pursue the issue. It is not going to go away, so they better face up to it."[13] The Bush administration also opened back-channel communications with Patricio Aylwin and his aides. Even before Aylwin's new civilian government was inaugurated in March 1990, emissaries had worked out a strategic timetable to establish a special commission on compensation for the families, introduce legislation in the Chilean Congress to transfer the "passport case" from a military to a civilian court, and appoint a special prosecutor to bring Contreras and Espinoza to trial.

Some sectors of the Bush administration hoped to restore full relations before Chile made concrete progress on resolving the case. "It is crucial to have a unified position," the State Department's Southern Cone desk officer noted in a May 4, 1990 memorandum, "and define precisely what we want the GOC to do before we certify." Washington's interests differed from the new civilian administration in Santiago, the desk officer Keith Smith noted in another memo:

> They want to resolve the case in order to normalize relations with the U.S., but in a manner that minimizes their financial and political cost. Aylwin wants to avoid a confrontation with the Chilean military over the Letelier case. The U.S., on the other hand, must consider a variety of factors (including the U.S. Congress and the Letelier/Moffitt families) which pressure for a complete and satisfactory resolution to both the civil and criminal sides of the case prior to normalization of relations with Chile.

The families pursued what confidential State Department documents described as a "relentless quest for justice"—for the prosecution of the responsible Chilean officials and civilian compensation. Led by Michael Moffitt and Sam Buffone, they lined up strategic support in Congress to pressure the Bush administration not to prematurely lift the Kennedy amendment before judicial proceedings of the DINA agents began, as well as to block the administration's ability to offer preferential trading status to Chile through the Generalized System of Preferences (GSP). "They want prosecution to be underway first," according to an oral report provided by phone to the embassy after State Department officials met with Moffitt and Buffone on April 19, 1990. "They said we should not underestimate their ability to screw up our plans—not only on Kennedy but on GSP. They might try and revive efforts to change Foreign Sovereign Immunities Act."[14] When Deputy Secretary of State Lawrence Eagleburger traveled to Santiago in May, he bluntly told Chilean officials that the U.S. Congress would block normalization of both economic and military relations pending a resolution of the assassinations.

In fact, Washington did not wait for resolution in the case. The administration seized on initial progress to certify Chile in December 1990, on the occasion of President Bush's state visit to Santiago. In his toast to Bush, President Aylwin committed his government to ensure that "justice is done."

Under great pressure, the Chilean government slowly fulfilled that commitment.

On June 11, 1990, the Bush and Aylwin administrations had signed a formal accord to establish an international commission to determine compensation. It took another year for both houses of the Chilean Congress to ratify the agreement, and another six months before the commission settled on a sum. In May 1992 Chile agreed to pay $2.6 million to the families of Orlando Letelier and Ronni Moffitt.

The criminal prosecution of Contreras and Espinoza proceeded on a parallel time track. On January 16, 1991, with heavy lobbying from Aylwin, the Chilean Congress finally passed a law transferring the passports case from the military courts to civilian judicial jurisdiction. Aylwin promptly asked the Chilean Supreme Court to name a special prosecutor; subsequently his first appointee to the court, Adolfo Banados, received the case. On the fifteenth anniversary of the car bombing, Banados indicted Contreras and Espinoza and ordered them bound over for trial. "This is the first time that either Contreras or Espinoza have been detained as a result of an independent Chilean judicial action," the embassy reported.

The unprecedented prosecution of Contreras and Espinoza in the fall of 1993 became the Chilean equivalent of the highly publicized O.J. Simpson trial in the United States. Day after day, the nation tuned in as the presentation of the overwhelming evidence against the DINA officials was broadcast on national television. For many in Chile, the televised trial provided their first exposure to unfiltered information on DINA's sordid and vicious operations; for DINA's victims and their families, Contreras's reckoning in a court of law, for an atrocity that occurred outside of Chile, offered a modicum of justice for the thousands of other heinous abuses he committed as Pinochet's secret police chief.

On November 12, 1993, Contreras and his DINA deputy were found guilty. Their short sentences—seven and six years respectively—reflected the limits of the Chilean judicial system's ability to hold Pinochet's military officers fully accountable for such crimes. Indeed, when their legal appeals were exhausted in May 1994, Chilean military units assisted Contreras in evading incarceration by airlifting him to the sanctuary of a military base and later to a naval hospital in Talcahuano where he and his military doctors declared that he was suffering from various infirmities that would endanger him in prison. For more than a year, the armed forces safeguarded Contreras, creating the most significant crisis in civilian-military relations since Augusto Pinochet had stepped down from power.

Finally, under intense behind-the-scenes pressure from the Clinton administration, the new president, Eduardo Frei Jr., succeeded in convincing the armed forces that harboring a convicted international terrorist was not in their institutional interest. In June 1995, Contreras joined Colonel Espinoza at Punto Peuco—a hotel-like facility constructed to house them during their short prison terms. By early 2002, both were once again free to walk the streets of Santiago—at least temporarily. Both were subsequently charged with other DINA-related crimes and once again arrested.[15]

Pinochet's Return

The twenty-fifth anniversary of the coup, September 11, 1998, became an opportunity for Chilean society to begin an open and forceful reexamination of its unresolved and still painful past. A series of books, articles, television and radio documentaries commanded widespread public attention and generated debate as never before. Ten days later, Pinochet and his family flew to London for a shopping vacation. When he was arrested in mid-October, and his abuses were thrust into headlines around the world, Chile experienced a national "eruption" of memory.

During Pinochet's dramatic 504 days under house arrest in London, debate raged in his homeland over the meaning and opportunity of his detention. Opinion polls showed that a small, but powerful minority of Chileans—about 25 percent—believed he should be set free; while 69 percent believed he should be put on trial—either in Chile or in Spain. His military railed at the civilian government of Eduardo Frei to find a way to force Pinochet's release and facilitate his return, while his most fanatical supporters financed his legal defense and living costs in London, as well as a major propaganda campaign to cast him as an innocent and his arrest as a violation of Chile's national sovereignty. In the most important reaction to his arrest, however, Chilean victims of torture, disappearance, and murder mobilized to seek legal redress against the former dictator. By the time Pinochet returned on March 3, 2000, more than seventy judicial cases had been filed against him—and accepted by a special prosecutor, Judge Juan Guzmán Tapia, for investigation.

Clearly Pinochet and his supporters believed he would return to the sanctuary of his homeland and renew his position as a "Senator for life"—immune from prosecution. But seventy-two hours after his plane landed, Judge Guzmán filed a legal request with the Chilean court of appeals to have Pinochet's immunity lifted, so that he could be prosecuted for disappearances associated with the Caravan of Death. (See Chapter 3) On May 23, the appeals court shocked the country by stripping Pinochet of his immunity. On June 5, the Chilean Supreme Court upheld that ruling by a vote of 13-9, clearing the way for a historic prosecution of the former dictator.

Unable to block Pinochet's prosecution on grounds of immunity, his lawyers adopted the same strategy they had employed in London—that the now eighty-five-year-old general was too mentally infirm to stand trial. Repeatedly they petitioned the judges to order medical tests for their client, prior to any further proceedings. Ignoring their efforts to forestall legal action, Judge Guzmán accelerated his prosecution. On December 1, 2000, in an unexpected and historic move, Guzmán indicted General Pinochet as the intellectual author of the Caravan of Death. To the surprise of the entire country, he was placed under house arrest and, for the first time, on January 24, 2001, officially interrogated by authorities about the atrocities that had been committed during his reign.

Clinton's Chile Declassification Project

Pinochet's arrest in London at the behest of Spanish authorities put an international onus on Washington. Given the long history of American involvement in Chile, the United States possessed extensive, detailed, and highly classified government archives—tens of thousands of pages of sensitive CIA reporting, DIA analysis, NSA intercepts, and State Department cables covering every aspect of the general's human rights atrocities from the Caravan of Death to Operation Condor—that could provide pivotal evidence in Spain's case against him. But at the same time the United States had the most to offer in bringing Pinochet to justice, it also had the most to hide. Prosecuting Pinochet, as one former senior intelligence official told the *New York Times*, would effectively "open up a can of worms" in the top secret record of U.S.-Chilean relations.

For almost two years, the Clinton administration had resisted Spanish efforts to obtain evidence from U.S. government archives to advance its unique case against Augusto Pinochet. In February 1997, Spanish authorities invoked a bilateral Mutual Legal Assistance Treaty (MLAT) with the United States—an accord mandating international cooperation and reciprocity in criminal investigations—and requested that the U.S. government supply records on Operation Condor and other human rights abuses by the Chilean and Argentine dictatorships. To press this request, the original judge in charge of the Chilean case, Judge García Castellon, traveled to Washington in January 1998 and received cordial treatment from U.S. officials. "I want to assure you," as President Clinton wrote to Congress in April, "that we will continue to respond as fully as we can to the request for assistance from the Government of Spain."[16]

In fact, the Clinton administration stonewalled for more than a year before producing four boxes of "files" in response to the Spanish MLAT request. One box was filled with 1,000 pages of Chilean newspaper clips, which the Spanish judge had not requested. Another held Pentagon documents on a contra operation in Honduras called "Condor" that was unrelated to Chile's Operation Condor. The other boxes contained thousands of pages of legal files on the prosecution of the anti-Castro Cubans who participated in the Letelier-Moffitt car bombing. None of these files contained any material of evidentiary value for Spain's effort to prosecute Pinochet.

The arrest on October 16, 1998, brought intense public pressure on the Clinton White House to take a stand in the Pinochet case. On October 26, the *New York Times* ran a copy of DIA biographic report on Pinochet—declassified but entirely blacked out by government censors—as a symbol of the type of documentation that Washington had to offer but continued to cover up. (Doc 2) Thirty-six members of Congress, led by Congressman George Miller, called upon Clinton to provide Spain with "material and testimony that the U.S. government has thus far withheld." Human Rights Watch executive director Kenneth Roth reminded Clinton, "Pinochet is wanted for crimes against American citizens, and even crimes on American soil" and pressed his administration "to speak out in favor of prosecuting this tyrant." And the families of Ronni Moffitt, Orlando Letelier and Charles Horman all petitioned the president and Attorney General Janet Reno to open the files and cooperate with the Spanish inquiry. "We must adhere to our policy that terrorists cannot run and hide to avoid prosecution under domestic or international law," Michael Moffitt, the sole survivor of the car bomb that killed his wife and colleague, wrote to Clinton. "The government of the United States must assist in the effort to hold Pinochet accountable for his crimes."

Inside the administration, this pressure generated an intense debate over an appropriate response. "There is a struggle going on in here," a White House aide admitted privately in the aftermath of Pinochet's arrest. "This has been an incredibly divisive issue at State and the NSC."[17] Certainly prosecuting Pinochet seemed to support the president's call for more aggressive international efforts to counter terrorism. In a major speech to the United Nations General Assembly several weeks before Pinochet's arrest—and ironically on the anniversary of the Letelier-Moffitt assassination—Clinton urged all nations to "give terrorists no support, no sanctuary . . . to act together to step up extradition and prosecution." His staff at the National Security Council's Office of Democracy, Human Rights and Humanitarian Affairs and the State Department's human rights bureau saw the benefits to U.S. policy of assisting the Spanish case. But they were stymied by two NSC officials: chief legal council Jamie Baker, who did not want to set a precedent of searching secret U.S. archives to satisfy an MLAT request, and the president's NSC adviser on Latin America, James Dobbins, who preferred to see Pinochet return to Santiago rather than stand trial in Madrid. As one official characterized Dobbins's position: "We don't want to upset Chilean democracy, we want to help [Chilean President] Frei."

In late November, Secretary of State Madeleine Albright convened a meeting of her top advisors to determine what the U.S. should do. No one at the meeting, according to participants, argued that the United States should support Spain's effort to bring Pinochet to justice. Rather, the prevailing position was that establishing a "Pinochet precedent" in international law would not benefit U.S. interests and that Washington, for the sake of stability and Chile's sovereignty, should respect the Chilean government's efforts to have Pinochet released and returned to his homeland. At the same time, Congressional demands and the position of the families of Pinochet's American victims could not be ignored. Rather than provide documents directly to Spain, the new head of the State Department's Policy Planning Office, Morton Halperin, suggested, the administration could simply undertake a major declassification review—Clinton had authorized similar projects on El Salvador, Honduras, and Guatemala during his first term—and open the files to the Americans, Chileans, and Spaniards—indeed to the world community—all at once. Secretary Albright recommended this proposal in a phone call to Clinton's National Security Advisor, Sandy Berger; they agreed to "declassify what we can so that we can say we did our share." On December 1, State Department spokesman James Rubin announced that the United States would "make public as much information as possible, consistent with U.S. laws and the national security and law enforcement interests of the United States."[18]

For the next eight weeks U.S. officials at the National Security Council, the State Department, and the CIA, hammered out the language of a presidential "tasker"—a directive establishing the guidelines and timetable for a special "Chile Declassification Project." The documents project would "shed light" on three major categories: "human rights abuses, terrorism, and other acts of political violence in Chile." The date range covered twenty-three years of history, from 1968 though 1991. Initially, policy makers intended the scope of the declassification to address only Pinochet's seventeen-year dictatorship, 1973–1990; but the Chile desk officer at the Bureau for Western Hemisphere Affairs argued that to avoid the appearance that "we were only going after the Right," as one official remembered this argument, the United States should declassify documents on alleged abuses during the Allende era as well—a decision that inadvertently opened the door to the release of records on U.S. covert intervention and efforts to foment political violence to overthrow Chilean democracy.[19] The Chile Declassification Project would be coordinated out of the National Security Council by the Senior Director of Records Management, William Leary. Leary chaired an Inter-agency Working Group (IWG) responsible for monitoring and implementing the review and declassification, which held its first meeting in February 1999 in Room 208 of the Old Executive Office Building.

"On behalf of the President," states the NSC tasker distributed on February 1, 1999 to all national security agencies, "we now ask your cooperation in undertaking a compilation and review for release of all documents that shed light on human rights abuses, terrorism and other acts of political violence during and prior to the Pinochet era in Chile." (Doc 3) To assist in computer and archival searches, the declassification directive—principally drafted by Halperin's deputy, Theodore Piccone—included a contextual narrative, a list of key human rights cases, and known perpetrators of abuses. The objective of this massive declassification effort, according to the tasker, was to "assist in encouraging a consensus within Chile on reinvigorating its truth and reconciliation process to address such questions as the fate of the disappeared." The review also would "respond to the expressed wishes of the families of American victims of human rights abuse, and to the requests of numerous members of Congress." At the recommendation of the U.S. ambassador to Chile, John O'Leary, the documents would be released simultaneously in Chile and the United States, and posted on a special State Department Web site to provide immediate international internet access.

The projected yield of declassified documents, the IWG determined, necessitated a multiphased release of records. Between June 1999 and June 2000, three so-called "tranches" were actually published:

Tranche I: 5,800 records released on June 30, 1999.[20] The declassified documents chronicled the first five years of the Pinochet regime from the September 11, 1973 coup to 1978—the most repressive period of the dictatorship. The bound volumes contained some 5,000 State Department cables, memoranda, and reports focused on the regime's abysmal human rights record. The CIA declassified, by contrast, several hundred valuable reports, intelligence assessments, and cables documenting the Pinochet regime's internal deliberations and repressive operations. Thousands of other CIA records on Agency operations to support the regime after the coup, however, were conspicuously missing.

Tranche II: Some 1,100 records released on October 8, 1999. These documents covered 1968 though 1973 and contained information on U.S. policy toward Allende's election and government. CIA papers on its covert action in Chile between 1970 and 1973, including those used by the Church Committee for its reports in the mid-1970s, should have been declassified in this tranche; none were.

Tranche III: A special release on June 30, 2000, of approximately 1,900 mostly State Department documents specific to the cases of murdered and disappeared Americans: Charles Horman, Frank Teruggi, and Boris Weisfeiler.

Originally, the Tranche III records were to be part of a massive, final release scheduled for April 2000. Claiming processing delays, the White House moved the declassification date to June. But in June only the Horman, Teruggi, and Weisfeiler records were released,[21] and IWG again postponed the declassification of 16,000 other documents until the fall. The delay resulted from a major behind-the-scenes battle between the White House and the CIA over Director George Tenet's decision to renege on declassifying operational records on Chile.

Holding History Hostage

The CIA's recalcitrant attitude toward the Chile Declassification Project threatened to transform a precedent-setting exercise in openness into another cover-up of history. From the outset, the Agency's commitment to fully participate seemed dubious. In initial meetings with State Department Policy Planning director, Morton Halperin, the CIA General Counsel's Office pledged to honor the mandate of the tasker—to release records on human rights abuses, terrorism, and political violence. At the same time, CIA lawyers insisted on inserting a sentence into the NSC directive—agencies "should retrieve and review all documents that are subject to disclosure under the Freedom of Information Act"—a veiled reference to a CIA exemption under the law from having to search certain operational files.[22] In a conversation with the author in mid-1999, one CIA official took the position that the CIA was "not legally obliged" to search its files on clandestine operations in Chile because those operations "had never been officially acknowledged."[23] At meetings of the IWG, Agency representatives, among them David Kamerling and Walter Hazlett, surprised their colleagues by arguing that documents on covert action in Chile—to undermine Allende and then in support of Pinochet—were "not relevant" to the tasker. Not even the coup itself fit the Agency's definition of "an act of political violence," the CIA officials insisted.[24] The CIA produced not a single page of documentation on its pivotal post-coup assistance to the regime and liaison relations with DINA for the release of the first tranche of documents in June 1999; and officials let it be known that Langley did not intend to produce any covert-action records for the second release in the fall, covering the 1970–1973 period of clandestine operations to bring down Allende.

CIA was joined by the National Security Agency, which also determined it would keep secret much if not all of its relevant holdings. In its initial search the NSA found over 660 records responsive to the tasker, many of them intelligence intercepts of Chilean military communications during and after the coup, as well as documents on the Horman case.[25] But in an April 6, 1999 status report, "Declassification Review of Documents Related to Human Rights Abuses in Chile," the Defense Department noted, "all the information identified as potentially responsive consists of classified signals reports, the release of which would reveal intelligence sources and methods. Therefore NSA does not anticipate recommending declassification and release of any of this material."

To the chagrin of the intelligence community, the National Archives Records Administration (NARA) discovered copies of several hundred revealing CIA and NSA documents in the classified holdings of the Nixon and Ford presidential libraries and submitted them to the IWG for final review. During a "joint declassification session" in early August 1999 at the NARA building, both CIA and NSA officials simply announced that they would have to remove the records to their headquarters for further evaluation—breaking the established IWG procedures for the Chile Declassification Project.[26] Once in their possession, the CIA and the NSA refused to review these papers for declassification.

As the CIA's obstruction of the Chile Declassification Project became publicly apparent, advocates of the project charged the Agency with whitewashing history. "The failure to release these records," the executive director of the National Security Archive, Thomas Blanton, wrote to the White House in September, "will be immediately viewed, nationally and internationally, as a cover-up of the past and an effort by Washington to shield itself from any historical accountability for events in Chile in the early 1970s."[27] "The CIA is hiding key documents," the *New York Times* editorialized on October 6. "The CIA needs to understand that full disclosure of Washington's role [in Chile] is in America's interest."[28] "We urge you to declassify without any further delay the remainder of the documents pertaining to Pinochet in the CIA files," six Congressmen wrote to CIA Director George Tenet. Prepped by his staff, even President Clinton signaled the Agency that it was time for full compliance and maximum disclosure. "I think you are entitled to know what happened back then," he responded to a question about the CIA and the Chile Declassification Project at a press conference in early October, "and how it happened."

Faced with forceful public and presidential pressure, the CIA rapidly retreated. On October 7, Agency spokesman Mark Mansfield publicly announced that the CIA "recognizes its obligation to release documents about covert action in Chile" and promised they would be declassified in the final release, then scheduled for mid-2000. Internally, Director Tenet issued a broad declassification guideline for searching Directorate of Operations files on covert actions in Chile, dating from 1962 to 1975. Over the next nine months, a team of CIA analysts compiled, reviewed, and carefully redacted close to 800 records, including cables, proposals, budgets, memcons, meeting minutes, and memoranda relating to dozens of covert programs, particularly coup plotting and destabilization operations between 1970 and 1973. Each of the documents was then actually marked with a stamp: DECLASSIFIED AND APPROVED FOR RELEASE, JULY 2000.

But as the final declassification neared, the CIA leadership reneged on its commitment to openness. In June, George Tenet ordered the new head of the Directorate of Operations, James Pavitt, to "prepare an assessment of the proposed release of the 1962–1975 material and its potential impact on current operational equities." Notwithstanding the fact that most of these documents had been identified and quoted extensively in the Senate reports on Chile twenty-five years earlier, Pavitt concluded that the records revealed too much about the basic modus operandi used by the CIA to undermine foreign governments. In July when the CIA was supposed to turn over these documents to the State Department for processing, Tenet informed the NSC that hundreds of promised operational documents would be withheld from the final release, then scheduled for September 14, 2000. "We are in no way trying to withhold information embarrassing to the United States Government," as Tenet explained his controversial decision. "It was solely made because, in their aggregate, these materials present a pattern of activity that had the effect of revealing intelligence methods that have been employed worldwide."[29]

Both inside and outside of government, everyone involved in the Chile Declassification Project—members of the IWG, families of American victims, and advocates of openness—understood that the CIA's position threatened to sabotage the credibility of the entire program. The Agency's eleventh-hour reversal cast a black shadow over the project's mission to provide a historically honest and accurate accounting of Pinochet's abuses, as well as the U.S. role in his rise and consolidation of power. The CIA's intention to cover up the most egregious aspects of U.S. intervention in Chile smelled of hypocrisy in a project designed, in large part, to assist Chile in its work on truth and reconciliation; an effort to hide the seamy, violent aspects of U.S. involvement in Chile also threatened to jeopardize the moral basis of Washington's international diplomatic initiatives toward Germany and Switzerland to fully acknowledge and redress the dark side of their own histories in the Holocaust. Finally, the CIA's mutiny constituted a direct challenge to the president's prerogative to determine and defend the public's right-to-know. The dispute over these documents represented a classic battle over the sanctity of secrecy vs. the principle of government transparency in U.S. foreign policy.

Members of the IWG who had devoted literally thousands of man-hours on the Chile project initiated a substantive behind-the-scenes effort to force the CIA to meet its commitment. At the State Department, key offices mobilized to press Secretary Albright to privately express her concerns to the White House. In addition, State Department officials quietly approached the archivist of the United States, John Carlin, to write a strong protest to National Security Advisor Sandy Berger. In a NARA letter dated July 30, Carlin warned that "such a last minute reversal will fundamentally undermine the overall integrity of the project and will result in a significantly incomplete public record of these important historical events." He urged the White House to "make every possible effort to convince the CIA to follow through on the commitments it made."

Berger met with Tenet on July 27 and insisted that the CIA agree to a rereview, conducted outside the Agency, of hundreds of Directorate of Operations records. Over the next month, an official from the NSC and an official from the State Department read through the heavily censored set of contested documents brought over from the Agency.[30] With the exception of CIA records on covert political operations between 1962 and 1968 that fell outside the defined date period of the president's tasker, and two-dozen or so highly sensitive documents on a particular covert operation, both the NSC and State Department evaluations recommended that the CIA collection could and should be declassified. On or about September 11, Berger talked to Tenet again and told him the White House was overruling the CIA's decision to withhold hundreds of revealing records. The release of the documents was postponed again for the Agency to prepare. Subsequently, the public dissemination of the fourth and final tranche was scheduled on November 13, 2000.

The Hinchey Report

Ironically, the CIA's effort to withhold history forced it to divulge far more dramatic secrets about Chile than it had intended. The decision to keep the documents secret in the summer of 2000 obligated the Agency, pursuant to an amendment to the Intelligence Authorization Act, to provide a comprehensive report to Congress on CIA involvement in Chile before and after the coup. According to the language of the law, passed in November 1999, the CIA would have nine months to

> submit a report describing all activities of officers, covert agents, and employees of all elements of the intelligence community with respect to the following events in the Republic of Chile:
>
> (1) The Assassination of President Salvador Allende in September 1973.
> (2) The accession of General Augusto Pinochet to the Presidency of the Republic of Chile.
> (3) Violations of human rights committed by officers or agents of former President Pinochet.

This amendment, sponsored by New York Congressman Maurice Hinchey, became a legal method of compelling the CIA to be forthcoming on its role in the coup and support for the Pinochet regime. His intention, Hinchey told colleagues, was to force the CIA to provide evidence that could help Spain prosecute Pinochet, as well as give the facts to the American public about the misconduct of its own government. "It is my hope that this report will shed light on what really happened in Chile in 1973 and what role was played by the United States in the overthrow of Chile's democratically elected government," Hinchey stated. "It is imperative that we have a full and public accounting of the involvement of the U.S. government in this shameful chapter of history."[31]

Initially, CIA director Tenet worked out a quiet arrangement with House Intelligence Committee chairman (and former CIA official) Porter Goss: the CIA would forgo writing an actual report and simply provide documents relating to the questions posed in the amendment that were due to be released under Clinton's Chile Declassification Project. But when the CIA decided to withhold its documents, that deal fell apart. In early August 2000, Tenet was forced to assign two National Intelligence Council (NIC) analysts to quickly draft a report, drawing on the hundreds of CIA records that had already been centralized. In the late evening of September 18, the Agency turned over to Congress a twenty-one-page, single-space study titled "CIA Activities in Chile."[32]

This report marked the first time the CIA had acknowledged the breadth and details of its long history of clandestine action in Chile. (Doc 4) The study went well beyond the three areas of inquiry posed by the Hinchey amendment; repeating information already published in the Church Committee reports, it covered the covert political operations during the 1960s in support of the Chilean Christian Democrats and the operations to block Allende's assumption of the presidency in 1970. The report provided new and damning information on the CIA's ties to the Chilean coup plotters who murdered Chilean commander-in-chief René Schneider, as well as a summary of efforts to destabilize Allende's government leading up to the coup. But on the question of helping Pinochet to power, the report hedged on the details of multiple covert operations that assisted the regime in consolidating its repressive rule. "Officers of the CIA and the Intelligence Community," the report stated, "were not involved in facilitating Pinochet's accession to President nor the consolidation of his power as Supreme Leader."[33]

The Hinchey report did, however, provide significant new information about CIA knowledge of, and ties to, Chile's apparatus of repression. "There is no doubt that some CIA contacts were actively engaged in committing and covering up serious human rights abuses," admitted the Agency authors. "The policy community and CIA recognized that the[se] relationships opened the CIA to possible identification with the liaison services' internal operations involving human rights abuses but determined that the contact was necessary for the CIA's mission."[34] In a startling section titled "Relationship with Contreras," the CIA conceded previously unknown details of its ties to the most vicious human rights violator in the Chilean military, DINA chief Manuel Contreras.

"During a period between 1974 and 1977, CIA maintained contact with Manuel Contreras Sepulveda," according to the report. Contreras was "notorious" for his atrocities and "the principle obstacle" to improving the regime's human rights record; the CIA also learned in 1974 that he was involved in acts of international assassination. Yet, in an unprecedented voluntary public acknowledgement, the report revealed that the Agency had, at least temporarily put Contreras on its payroll:[35]

> In May and June 1975, elements within the CIA recommended establishing a paid relationship with Contreras to obtain intelligence based on his unique position and access to Pinochet. This proposal was overruled, citing the US Government policy on clandestine relations with the head of an intelligence service notorious for human rights abuses. However, given miscommunications in the timing of this exchange, a one-time payment was given to Contreras.

Such revelations generated major headlines—in the United States, Chile, and around the world. Indeed, publication of the Hinchey report provided a groundswell of international attention for the final declassification of documents. On November 13, under pressure from the White House, the CIA was forced to release 1,550 heavily redacted records that at least partially chronicled its long and scandalous covert operations to undermine democracy and support dictatorship in Chile. True to form, however, many of the top secret documents used in the most controversial sections of the Hinchey report—among them cables, decision memorandum, bank deposit slips, etc. for putting Manuel Contreras on the payroll and then taking him off, and records relating to payoffs to the murderers of René Schneider—were not included.

Indicting Pinochet?

In the fourth and final release of Chile documents, the Clinton administration declassified more than 16,000 State Department, Pentagon, CIA, NSC, and Justice Department records. In total, the Chile Declassification Project resulted in the release of some 24,000 previously secret documents—over 150,000 pages of historical records—shedding substantial light on the human rights atrocities during the Pinochet era, and more than twenty years of overt and covert U.S. efforts to shape, manipulate, orchestrate, and influence Chile's future.

For all the documentation that was released, however, a countless number of records remained secret, still off-limits to public scrutiny. The CIA refused to submit hundreds of relevant records for declassification; nor would the Agency supply a list of the documents it had decided to withhold. Hundreds of documents discovered in the classified vaults of the presidential libraries and submitted to the IWG review were denied declassification and returned still sealed. Among them were dozens of National Security Agency cables dated September 11, 12, and 13, 1973, and numerous CIA reports and presidential briefing papers.[36] Declassification researchers were unable to access transcripts of Henry Kissinger's "telcons"—recorded telephone conversations between 1970 and 1976—a treasure trove of documents that Kissinger took when he left government at the end of the Ford administration.[37] Nor were Nixon tapes of meetings and phone calls from 1972 through 1974 made available. In addition, the holdings of the CIA's 201 file on Pinochet—containing the most sensitive intelligence on the dictator—were not declassified.

Perhaps the most important records from the Pinochet files excluded from declassification were several hundred documents implicating the general in the Letelier-Moffitt assassination. These documents, collected by the agencies as part of the declassification process, were then segregated and set aside at the direction of the Department of Justice as evidence in potential criminal proceedings against Pinochet. The records would be withheld, the State Department announced after the release of Tranche I in late June 1999, because "they relate to an ongoing Justice Department investigation of the murder of Ronni Moffitt and Orlando Letelier."

Like the declassification itself, this criminal investigation resulted from strong public pressure prompted by Pinochet's detention in London. In a poignant and powerful press conference organized on December 7, 1998, by the Institute for Policy Studies where Letelier and Moffitt had worked, their families publicly called on the Clinton administration to reopen the case. If Spain had standing to extradite Pinochet, the families argued, surely the United States had an even stronger case. In a sharply worded opinion piece published in the *Washington Post* on December 6, the former U.S. attorney in the case, Lawrence Barcella Jr., challenged the administration to action: the car bombing represented "the only act of state-sponsored terrorism to claim lives in the nation's capital," he wrote. "If we don't proceed, we are telling terrorists who commit murder here on our citizens there is no reason to stop." A number of politicians agreed. As thirty-six members of the House of Representatives wrote the president more than a year before the al-Qaeda attacks on the World Trade Center and the Pentagon: "We believe that this case needs to be intensified and pursued with the same vigor given to other terrorism cases such as that of [Osama] Bin Laden."

In the spring of 1999, Attorney General Janet Reno authorized a Justice Department-FBI investigation "in an effort to determine whether there is sufficient admissible, credible evidence that there are one or more persons, in addition to those previously charged, who might have been involved criminally in this act of terrorism on U.S. soil." It took until September, however, for the Justice Department to draft and transmit a "letter rogatory"—a formal request for legal assistance—to the Chilean government. The U.S. government asked for permission to send a special team of investigators to Chile, and for the Chilean Supreme Court to facilitate the interrogations of over forty witnesses and participants in the crime. In March and April 2000, a law-enforcement team led by the head of the transnational crime division of the U.S. Attorney's office, John Beasley, and consisting of FBI special agents, assistant U.S. attorneys and other Justice and State Department officials spent a month in Santiago gathering evidence of Pinochet's involvement. "We found no smoking gun," one member of investigative unit confided, "but the cumulative weight of the evidence suggested Pinochet's involvement."[38]

Under Beasley's supervision and signature, in August 2000 the FBI-DOJ team finalized a summary of the evidence, concluding with a dramatic recommendation: indict Pinochet as the ultimate author of the September 21,

1976 terrorist attack in Washington. This pivotal report, however, "fell into a black hole" inside the Justice Department's criminal division, according to one government official involved in the Pinochet investigation.[39] For the rest of the year, Pinochet's potential indictment remained bottled-up in the bureaucracy, delaying high-level consideration by the attorney general's office until after the election of George W. Bush. In January 2001, during the transition between the outgoing Clinton administration and the incoming Bush team, one of Janet Reno's deputies met with Barcella and the attorney for the Letelier and Moffitt families, Samuel Buffone, and informed them that the attorney general had decided to defer any decision on indicting Pinochet to her successor, John Ashcroft.

The new Bush administration reassured the families that the case would continue. "You may be assured that this investigation has been pursued in a vigorous, thorough, timely fashion," one of Ashcroft's deputies wrote to the Institute for Policy Studies in April 2001, "and that this department will continue to pursue this important matter further to a just conclusion."[40] But building a case against Pinochet languished, even after the Bush administration launched an aggressive U.S. war on terrorism following the September 11 terrorist attacks in New York and Washington.

Indeed, despite President Bush's resolve to "direct every resource at our command" to destroy and defeat terrorism, the indictment of General Pinochet remained on Attorney General Ashcroft's desk. The case offered the Bush administration a relatively easy way to demonstrate to the world that there is no statute of limitations on acts of terrorism on American soil and that Washington would pursue those who engaged in terror in the past as well as in the present and future. But by the spring of 2003—already four years after investigators began gathering evidence on Pinochet's role—it was clear that Washington had no intention to indict and extradite its former anticommunist ally. Under the guise of a "continuing investigation," however, the Bush administration refused to declassify the hundreds of secret documents that implicated General Pinochet in a terrorist attack in Washington.

The Riggs Bank Scandal[41]

The Letelier-Moffitt case appeared to represent the last hope that Pinochet might actually be held legally accountable for at least one of his crimes of state. In Chile, the Supreme Court had closed down the long legal process against him, ruling that he was "mentally unfit due to dementia" to stand trial for authorizing fifty-seven murders and eighteen disappearances by the

Caravan of Death in October 1973. That July 1, 2002, determination effectively ended all current judicial efforts against the former dictator.

Believing his long legal saga to be over, three days later Pinochet sent a formal, and quite intellectually coherent, letter to the Chilean Senate announcing his resignation from political life. "I have a clean conscience. I have the hope that in the future my soldierly sacrifice will be valued and recognized," he wrote. "The work of my government will be judged by history."[42]

History, as it turned out, along with the Chilean public and the courts, would judge his work and supposed "soldierly sacrifice" far sooner than Pinochet anticipated. While he settled into retirement in Santiago, in Washington a Senate investigation into the failure of American banks to safeguard against money laundering by potential terrorists after 9/11 stumbled across Pinochet's deepest secret: his illicit fortune stashed in a vast array of U.S. bank accounts. The Senate Subcommittee on Investigations, led by Senator Carl Levin, exposed Pinochet's "extensive and largely hidden network of U.S. bank and securities accounts"—more than 125 accounts containing $26 million. Their investigation revealed that Pinochet had opened the accounts fraudulently, using false passports and fake names as identification, at a number of banks, the most important of which was the Riggs National Bank. (Docs 5, 6) Officials at Riggs had aided and abetted Pinochet's corruption and conspired to circumvent a judicial order from Spain to freeze all of the former dictator's bank accounts after his arrest in London. Bank officials had withheld information from federal investigators about Pinochet's holdings; moreover, they had arranged to surreptitiously transfer some $8 million of the funds back to Pinochet after he returned to Chile in May 2000. The first of two reports by the subcommittee, *Money Laundering and Foreign Corruption: Enforcement and Effectiveness of the Patriot Act*, concluded that

> Riggs Bank assisted Augusto Pinochet, former president of Chile, to evade legal proceedings related to his Riggs bank accounts and resisted [federal] oversight of these accounts, despite red flags involving the source of Mr. Pinochet's wealth, pending legal proceedings to freeze his assets, and public allegations of serious wrongdoing by this client.[43]

The Senate reports exposed the long relationship between Riggs and the Pinochet regime, dating back to the mid-1970s when the Chilean secret police, DINA, set up clandestine bank accounts in Washington. After those accounts were exposed by the FBI investigation into the Letelier-Moffitt assassination, the regime moved its banking to Canada. But in 1986, Joseph L. Allbritton, the chairman of Riggs, traveled to Chile to meet with the dictator and appeal for the Chilean military to become a client once again. Between

1986 and 2002, senior Riggs Bank representatives met with Chilean military and government officials at least six more times—four times with Pinochet personally. "[We] called on General Pinochet in order to express our gratitude for returning the official Chilean Military's accounts from Bank of Nova Scotia to Riggs," one internal bank memo written by the senior vice president for Latin American operations reported after a trip in mid-1994. "We also offered our personal banking services to General Pinochet and stated that we would also be pleased to make our services available to officers of the Chilean military."[44]

In early 1996, Allbritton, accompanied by his wife, returned to Chile. They joined Pinochet for a luncheon at the Cavalry School in Quillota, Chile, to watch a special equestrian performance. Allbritton sent his appreciation to the general by letter: "As a horse enthusiast, your fine young cavalry officers, their horses and the superb performance they put on was excellent. . . . Chile is clearly a very impressive country with an excellent future thanks to you and the policies and reforms you instituted."[45] He then extended an invitation to the general to continue their personal and financial bonding. "I would like to thank you for the superb cufflinks you presented to me and please know that you would be most welcome to visit my wife Barby and me at our house in Middleburg, Virginia where we raise our thoroughbred race horses."[46]

Coming to the United States was out of the question for Pinochet, but the bank continued to fawn over his business. On his eighty-second birthday he received a card from Riggs president Timothy Coughlin. "All of your friends and supporters at Riggs Bank send you our appreciation and congratulations for all you have done for Chile. Please accept our best wishes for every success in your continuing service to Chile in 1998."[47]

These solicitations paid off: within a few years Pinochet's twenty-eight accounts were the fourth-largest in Riggs's exclusive Private Banking Department.[48] Pinochet established seven personal accounts, four opened under variants of his name—Augusto Ugarte and Jose Ramon Ugarte, for example—and the other three using aliases. Riggs also set up two offshore shell corporations—Ashburton Company Ltd and Althorp Investment—for Pinochet, concealing his identity by listing the beneficiary of the accounts only as a "Prominent International Private Banking Client."[49] A number of other accounts were set up in the name of his wife, Lucia Hiriart, and the names of military subordinates, who banking records identified as "front men" for the general. "Riggs appeared to take affirmative steps to hide the Pinochet relationship from bank examiners," according to Senate investigators.

After Pinochet was arrested in London and his assets ordered frozen, Riggs claimed to be unable to locate any accounts belonging to the former dictator. At the same time, the bank quietly arranged for Pinochet to withdraw $1.6 million from his holdings—monies that allowed him to pay expensive lawyers and the $16,000-a-month rental of a large home outside London while he was under house arrest. Once Pinochet returned to Chile, the bank repeatedly sent a courier to personally deliver batches of $50,000 cashier's checks, totaling $1.9 million, to his home. "Please find attached an order from client to issue 10 checks totaling $500,000," stated a memo from Riggs Vice President Carol Thompson in May 2001. "Please make each check $50,000, payable to Maria Hiriart and/or Augusto P. Ugarte." (Doc 7) In all, Riggs illicitly transferred almost $8 million dollars to Pinochet after his accounts were ordered "attached" by the courts.[50]

Among his countrymen, including many *Pinochetistas*, the Riggs Bank scandal all but ruined Pinochet's image as an honest and incorruptible military officer. Moreover, revelations that he not only had innocent blood on his hands but also presumably stolen state funds in his back pockets revived the legal proceedings against him. The fact that he had arranged to receive dozens of $50,000 checks from Riggs at the very same time he was pleading mental incompetence to stand trial was not lost on Chilean judges, lawyers, and victims, nor on officials from the Departamento de Investigación de Delitos Tributarios del Servicio de Impuestos Internos. Investigators from the Chilean equivalent of the IRS promptly launched a major inquiry into tax evasion and fraud.

Within two months, Chile's Internal Tax Service brought a formal complaint against Pinochet for filing false tax returns. The case was forwarded to Judge Sergio Muñoz, who had already initiated an investigation into fraud, embezzlement, and bribery—on charges filed by Chilean lawyers Carmen Hertz and Alfonso Insunza.[51] In November 2004, the judge uncovered an additional $4 million in hidden assets, bringing Pinochet's secret fortune to $30 million. When Judge Muñoz questioned both Pinochet and his wife about the source of the money, they claimed, but offered no proof, that the millions had been gifted by supporters of the Pinochet regime.

On June 7, 2005, the Santiago Appeals Court stripped Pinochet of his immunity from prosecution for four financial offenses related to the Riggs Bank scandal. When the Chilean Supreme Court upheld that ruling in October, it appeared likely that Pinochet would go to trial on four charges: (1) obstruction of justice; (2) use of false passports; (3) modification and use of certificates of the War Sub-secretariat; and (4) alleged perjury in a 1989 statement concerning his assets. Judge Muñoz then moved to indict other members of Pinochet's family. On August 10, 2005, the former dictator watched as police arrived at his mansion, arrested his wife, and transported her to the police station. His son Marco Antonio Pinochet Hiriart was arrested on charges of serving as an accessory to tax evasion, embezzlement, and fraud.

Shortly after those arrests, Pinochet released a statement, taking "full responsibility for the acts Judge Muñoz is investigating and [to] deny any involvement on the part of my wife, my children or my closest associates." His words proved doubly damning—first, because Pinochet confessed his responsibility for the crimes at hand, and second, because their coherence contradicted his defense attorneys' argument regarding Pinochet's mental instability. His statement also failed to stop authorities from issuing additional indictments of members of the family.

Indeed, on January 24, 2006, Pinochet's wife and son were indicted on new charges related to the Riggs accounts and placed under house arrest, along with his three daughters. Evading detention, his eldest daughter, Inés Lucía Pinochet Hiriart, fled across the border to Argentina and boarded a flight to Washington's Dulles International Airport. Once the plane landed, she requested political asylum, claiming her family was being politically persecuted in Chile. U.S. Customs and Border Protection officials took her into custody for three days while she evaluated her options: indefinite incarceration in an immigration detention center while her specious petition was being processed or immediate return to Chile.

On January 27, Ms. Pinochet gave up her bid for political asylum and flew home. Waiting at the Santiago airport was Judge Carlos Cerda, who greeted the fugitive from justice: "Ms. Lucía, how nice that you've arrived. Please come with me so that I can arraign you."[52]

Human Rights Prosecution Redux

The corruption proceedings helped to reopen legal efforts to hold Pinochet accountable for his human rights crimes. Not only did his financial deceptions suggest a high degree of mental acuity, but his legal responses and efforts to defend his family reflected a competent mind. "What has changed in this case, with the Riggs scandal, is that Pinochet was interrogated by a judge with the acquiescence of his own lawyers, implicitly admitting that their client is perfectly capable of participating in judicial proceedings," human rights lawyer Eduardo Contreras argued as he renewed efforts to prosecute Pinochet for crimes related to Operation Condor.[53]

Pinochet had undermined his own carefully crafted image of infirmity by giving an interview in November 2003 to Maria Elvira Salazar, a Cuban-American journalist for Canal 22 WDLP TV, a Spanish-language television station in Miami. The former dictator provocatively referred to himself as an "angel" while lucidly answering Salazar's questions. He smoothly shifted responsibilities for all human rights abuses onto his subordinates, claiming he was too busy as chief of state to know of, let alone oversee, such atrocities. He expressed himself clearly and even attempted to elicit sympathy from the audience. "I never complain, and I never cry. I carry my grief on the inside," the general calmly remarked.[54]

The interview generated a firestorm of protest in Chile from Pinochet's victims and their lawyers and energized efforts to revisit the Supreme Court's July 2002 ruling that the former dictator was too cognitively challenged to stand trial. Judge Juan Guzmán, whose original Caravan of Death case against the former dictator had been shut down by the Supreme Court decision, decided to pursue new charges of disappearance and murder related to Operation Condor (see Chapter 6). On August 26, 2004, the Supreme Court narrowly ruled that Pinochet was not immune from prosecution for Condor crimes, giving the green light to new human rights prosecutions.

Guzmán then moved to address the issue of mental competency. Initially, he believed Pinochet would remain beyond the reach of the law due to mental incapacity. In a handwritten draft of a decision not to pursue a legal judgment, Guzmán made sure that history would judge the general instead. A ruling not to indict, he wrote, did

> not imply that Pinochet Ugarte was not directly and indirectly responsible for the crimes described in detail in the first reflection of this verdict. . . . [H]e has reigned over a perverse and cruel system of kidnappings, of ruthless torture, of ignominious assassinations and forced disappearances, both of nationals and foreigners, using to this end state agents and dishonoring the Armed Forces previously known for their respect of the constitution and the law, and abusively utilizing an apparently legal system to cover up so much pain and so much horror.[55]

Eventually, however, Guzmán reconsidered the competency question. In an interview with the author, the judge recalled how he had assembled a team of geriatric specialists and psychiatrists to watch the Canal 22 tape and evaluate Pinochet's thought process. They determined that he showed cognitive skills related to reasoning, argument, self-defense, and self-description that belied his lawyers' portrayal of his mental deficits.

On December 13, 2004, dozens of Pinochet's victims and dozens of reporters converged on the Tribunal of Justice in downtown Santiago to await Guzmán's decision. After registering the paperwork, the judge emerged in the grand foyer of the ornate building and made a statement: "General Pinochet has been declared mentally fit for standing trial in Chile through all of the phases, investigatory statements, confrontations, etc., and this resolution has a second part: he will be prosecuted as the author of nine abductions and one qualified homicide."[56] He ordered Pinochet placed under house arrest. Pandemonium (personally witnessed by this author) ensued, as the daughters and wives of the disappeared and torture victims besieged the judge with gratitude while reporters pushed for an interview. The new indictments generated front-page headlines around the world.

The Condor indictments were only the first of many. Indeed, over the last eighteen months of his life, Pinochet faced one prosecution after another—on charges ranging from tax evasion and financial fraud to acts of disappearance and international murder. On June 7, 2005, the Santiago Appeals Court stripped the general's immunity from prosecutions related to the hidden Riggs bank accounts. One month later, Pinochet lost his immunity from prosecution for Operation Colombo, the macabre campaign that his regime implemented to cover up the murder and disappearance of some 119 Chilean citizens. On July 8, the Appeals Court determined that Pinochet was physically and mentally fit to stand trial for two killings following the 1973 coup by agents of his military regime. In November, the Supreme Court ruled he was fit to stand trial for the disappearance of six dissidents in 1974. In October 2006, Pinochet was charged with thirty-six counts of kidnapping, twenty-three counts of torture, and one count of murder for the torture and disappearances at the infamous death camp Villa Grimaldi. That same month he was indicted for the murder of one of his own former henchmen, DINA biochemist Eugenio Berrios, who was disappeared in Uruguay in 1992 to prevent him from testifying in human rights cases—his tortured body was found several years later buried on a beach—making him the last victim of Chile's era of repression.

By his ninety-first birthday on November 25, 2006, Pinochet faced no fewer than a half-dozen indictments, as well as multiple ongoing investigations into financial and human rights crimes. Old and infirm, he issued one final mea culpa. In a statement read by his wife, Lucia, the general took "full responsibility" for the atrocities committed during his seventeen-year regime: "Near the end of my days, I want to say that I harbor no rancor for anyone, that I love my country above all, and that I take responsibility for all that was done."[57] His apparent claims of remorse fell on the deaf ears of the Chilean judiciary; just two days later, Pinochet was indicted yet again and ordered placed, yet again, under house arrest on charges related to the execution of two bodyguards employed by Salvador Allende. Only the grim reaper, it appeared, could spare him a judicial accounting.

Death of the Dictator

On December 10, 2006—by ironic coincidence, International Human Rights Day—General Augusto Pinochet died from complications of a heart attack.

Outside the military hospital in Santiago, Chile, some two thousand *Pinochetistas* gathered, sharing both tears and songs. In the Plaza Italia section of downtown Santiago, an even larger crowd of Pinochet detractors celebrated in the streets shouting, "It's carnival! The general died!"[58] For many human rights activists, however, Pinochet's death represented the ultimate evasion of justice. "This criminal had departed," lamented Hugo Gutierrez, a lawyer who represented some of the general's many victims, "without ever being sentenced for all the acts he was responsible for during his dictatorship."[59]

The Chilean government denied Pinochet a state funeral, citing the atrocities committed under his regime and the criminal indictments he faced at the time of his demise. His funeral, therefore, was organized by the army and held at the Chilean Military School. Some senior politicians, businessmen, and former ministers and undersecretaries of the military regime attended, but there was no official pomp and circumstance. "It would embarrass Chile's conscience to honor somebody who was involved not only in human rights issues but even in misappropriation of public funds," stated President Michelle Bachelet, herself a victim of the abuses committed by the dictatorship.[60]

Inevitably, Pinochet's funeral became a national spectacle. The military ceremony attracted thousands of supporters, several of whom were caught on camera giving the Nazi salute to the deceased ex-dictator. But two attendees, representing opposite sides of Pinochet's bitter legacy, caused a considerable disturbance. The general's grandson Augusto Pinochet Molina (Augusto III), a military man himself, delivered a eulogy that justified his grandfather's seventeen-year regime. He lauded his grandfather's heroism as "a man who defeated, at the height of the Cold War, the Marxist model, which tried to impose its totalitarian model not by vote, but more directly by force of arms."[61] Furthermore, Augusto III chastised the judges who had been prosecuting Pinochet until the day he died, claiming that they were motivated by "notoriety, not justice."[62] Having violated government-imposed guidelines for oration at the funeral, Augusto III was dismissed from the Chilean military two days after giving his eulogy.

Another grandson also generated headlines at General Pinochet's funeral—albeit for a dramatically different form of farewell. Infiltrating the line of pro-military Chileans paying their final respects, Francisco Cuadrado Prats, the grandson of General Carlos Prats and Sofia Cuthbert, who had been assassinated by DINA agents in Buenos Aires in 1974, approached the open coffin and spit on the glass covering Pinochet's face. "It was a spontaneous act to spit at him, out of revulsion," the young Prats recalled, "because he had my grandparents murdered and because of the military honors he was given at his burial."[63] Angry *Pinochetistas* attacked and beat Prats, who was subsequently arrested for his sacrilegious conduct. But the actions of both Augusto Pinochet III and Francisco Cuadrado Prats became an emblematic coda to the Pinochet regime, reflecting the struggle over his legacy and the enduring divisions of Chilean society almost two decades after the return to democracy.

To assure no further desecration of the memory of Augusto Pinochet, his family chose to forgo a traditional burial crypt. Instead, his remains simply disappeared; at some point, he was cremated. But from the ashes, Pinochet managed to speak one last time to the Chilean people. On December 25, the Pinochet Foundation, established to promote his legacy, made public a six-page letter that the general had written before his death—a final justification for his actions. In the letter, Pinochet claimed that "it was necessary to act with maximum rigor to avoid a widening of the conflict" during his regime and that any human rights abuses had not been the result of "an institutional plan."[64] He wrote, "How I wish that the action of September 11, 1973, would not have been necessary."[65] Despite this final attempt to evade responsibility for the atrocities that would be forever associated with his name, Pinochet seemed to acknowledge that his status—in life and in death—as a world-class pariah had taken a toll on his soul. "My destiny," he lamented, "is a kind of banishment and loneliness that I would have never imagined, much less wanted."[66]

History and Accountability

In death, Pinochet had managed to evade facing his many victims in court. But history's judgment would bring the severest condemnation of Augusto Pinochet and his regime. Although the general had imposed an image of himself as a saintlike savior of his country, the saga of his detention, along with the Riggs Bank scandal, breached both the impunity of his power and the immunity of his legacy. His house arrest in England had emboldened survivors of human rights violations to break through the conspiracy of silence about Chile's dark and unresolved past. Their voices, along with the declassification of U.S. documents, established a historical record that could no longer be denied or ignored. The drama of the Pinochet case mobilized the human rights movement in Chile and around the world in pursuit of truth and justice to resolve and redress the crimes he and his subordinates had committed.

Indeed, although Pinochet managed to escape judicial reckoning, many of his once-untouchable lieutenants faced indictments, trials, and imprisonment. In Chile, a new generation of judges seemed intent on bringing charges against former and current military officers for previously unchallengeable human rights atrocities. By early 2013, the Chilean judiciary had put 62 of Pinochet's military men in prison, and convicted an additional 176 for human rights crimes. Another 549 subordinates faced ongoing legal proceedings.[67] The most notable prosecutions included cases against:

- Manuel Contreras: After serving a seven-year sentence for the Letelier-Moffitt assassination, the former head of DINA was placed under house arrest in mid-2002 while being prosecuted for the disappearances of prisoners at Villa Grimaldi. On February 25, 2003, Judge Alejandro Solis indicted Contreras for masterminding DINA's first international assassination: the September 30, 1974, car-bombing assassination of retired General Carlos Prats and his wife, Sofia, in Buenos Aires. In mid-April 2003, Contreras was convicted of atrocities at Villa Grimaldi and sentenced to fifteen years in prison. He was then arrested, convicted, and imprisoned a second time in November 2004. On June 30, 2008, Judge Alejandro Solis sentenced Contreras to life in prison after finding him guilty of murdering Carlos and Sofia Prats. He also received a twenty-year sentence for a crime of illegal association.
- Brigadier General Raúl Iturriaga Neumann: On February 25, 2003, the former head of DINA's Exterior Section and his brother Jorge Iturriaga, who served as a civilian DINA agent, were both indicted for their roles in the Prats' assassination and placed under arrest. In June 2007, Iturriaga became a fugitive to evade a five-year sentence for the disappearance of a former political militant, Luis Dagoberto San Martin. In early August of that year, he was captured in Chile's resort town of Viña del Mar.
- Brigadier General Pedro Espinoza: On February 25, 2003, DINA's deputy director was also indicted for the murder of Carlos and Sofia Prats. In June 2008, Espinoza received several sentences of fifteen to twenty years for his involvement with the assassination.
- General Sergio Arellano Stark: On June 8, 1999, Judge Juan Guzmán placed General Arellano, Pinochet's enforcer and designated representative in the Caravan of Death case, under house detention and indicted him for "qualified kidnappings" for the disappearances of eighteen victims at the hands of a military death squad he had headed; on September 25, 2000, he was also charged with "qualified murder." In October 2008, the Chilean Supreme Court ratified a six-year sentence for his involvement with the Caravan of Death. This sentence, however, was later suspended due to Arellano's poor health.
- Carlos Herrera Jiménez: Herrera was a CNI hit man tasked by his superior to kill the prominent Chilean trade union leader Tucapél Jiménez. In August 2002, Judge Sergio Muñoz sentenced Herrera to

life in prison. Twenty-seven other army, air force, and Carabinero officers, including General Fernando Torres Silva, received shorter sentences for the Tucapél Jiménez murder.

- Air Force General Patricio Campos: Campos was arrested in October 2002 for obstructing justice by destroying military evidence designated to be provided to the "Mesa Redonda"—a military-civilian commission reporting on the fates of 1,100 disappeared Chileans.
- Retired army Majors Jaime Torres and Arturo Silva: Both were indicted in October 2002 for the Condor-style execution of DINA agent Eugenio Berrios, whose body was found with two bullet holes in the back of his neck and buried on a beach in Uruguay in April 1995. Torres had served as General Pinochet's bodyguard. In June 2004, both men were charged with kidnapping and murder.
- Five pilots of the Chilean Army Air Command: In November 2003, Judge Juan Guzmán indicted the pilots for their role in disappearing an estimated four hundred to five hundred political prisoners. Guzmán's investigation uncovered the gruesome details of "Operation Puerto Montt"—the secret police system used to transport prisoners from torture camps to the coast, attaching pieces of iron girders to their bodies, putting them in canvas sacks, and dropping them from helicopters into the Pacific Ocean.
- Former Air Force intelligence agent Rafael Gonzalez: On December 10, 2003, the one-time whistle-blower in the Charles Horman case became the first person to be indicted and arrested as "an accomplice to homicide" in Horman's death. Gonzalez admitted that he had acted as an interrogator for Chile's military intelligence service after Horman was detained—not as a simple translator, as he had portrayed his role in 1976, when he first talked to reporters and revealed that Horman had been executed after the coup.

On December 6, 2009, Judge Alejandro Madrid stunned Chileans by ruling that the 1982 death of former president Eduardo Frei had been the result of poisoning by Pinochet's secret police; he issued six indictments that included an intelligence agent and a doctor associated with the DINA.[68] And in December 2012, in one of the most dramatic and emblematic of Chile's unresolved human rights cases, Chilean judge Miguel Vasquez indicted seven former military officers and a conscript for the execution of the internationally renowned Chilean troubadour Victor Jara. The indictment provided new details on how Jara was shot forty-four times in the Estadio Chile sports stadium in the days following the coup. After the return to democracy in Chile, the stadium was renamed Estadio Victor Jara.

In addition, other countries around the world filed charges against Chilean officers responsible for human rights crimes. In Spain, criminal proceedings continued against more than three dozen of Pinochet's subordinates. In Argentina, Enrique Arancibia Clavel, DINA's former Station chief in Buenos Aires, was arrested, tried, convicted, and sentenced to life in prison for his role in the September 1974 Prats car-bombing assassination. In 2007, Arancibia Clavel was quietly released. In May 2011, he was found stabbed to death in his Buenos Aires apartment.

In France, investigative magistrate Roger Le Loire issued INTERPOL arrest warrants for fourteen Chilean officers, including seven prominent DINA officials, for the disappearance of Chileans with French ancestry at the time of the coup as part of Operation Colombo and Operation Condor. Pursuant to these warrants, the former commander of the Tacna Regiment, General Luis Ramírez Piñeda, was arrested in Argentina on September 13, 2002. On January 13, 2003, General Ramírez and seven other army officers were indicted in Chile for the abduction and disappearance of twelve members of the Allende government who were seized by the military at the Moneda palace on September 11, 1973; taken to the Tacna Regiment; and never seen again. Both the Chileans and the French requested Ramirez's extradition.

The United States joined these nations by pressing for justice in the cases of the three American citizens murdered or missing in Chile. After face-to-face meetings and communications between their families and the State Department's Office of Democracy, Human Rights, and Labor, in April 2000 Secretary of State Albright issued a new démarche to the Chilean government on "Renewing Efforts to Resolve the Horman, Teruggi, and Weisfeiler Cases." (Doc 8) Ambassador John O'Leary received instructions to approach the administration of Richard Lagos "at the highest levels" and urge a new investigation. "Three American families remain these many years without full information regarding the disappearance and death in Chile of their loved ones," read his talking points. "They also remain without certain knowledge of who was responsible for these crimes."

This diplomatic initiative marked the first time the United States had identified the two murders and a disappearance of U.S. citizens in Chile as punishable offenses for which the Chilean government should be held accountable. The U.S. government, according to a diplomatic note, "requests that the appropriate authorities of the government of Chile mount a vigorous and thorough investigation aimed at uncovering the facts, and in accordance with Chilean law, prosecuting those responsible." Washington would provide newly declassified documents to assist a criminal inquiry into these cases, the diplomatic note advised. But these documents "cannot substitute for a full investigation into and accounting for the disappearance and death of these individuals"—an inquiry which "can only be carried out by the Government of Chile."

Declassified U.S. documents did play a role in moving these cases forward through Chile's complex legal system. In the fall of 2000, the Weisfeiler family used the new documentation to successfully petition for the transfer of their case from the local courts into the hands of the special prosecutor in the Pinochet case, Judge Juan Guzmán. In December of that year, Joyce Horman traveled to Chile and also petitioned Judge Guzmán to assume the Horman and Teruggi cases as part of a larger criminal investigation into the military massacre of political prisoners at the National Stadium.

Guzmán's investigations in the Weisfeiler and Horman/Teruggi cases generated headlines. In April 2002, he traveled to Colonia Dignidad with a search warrant to look for evidence concerning Boris Weisfeiler; in May of that year, he held hearings on the Horman case and the U.S. embassy's failure to protect American citizens detained in the National Stadium. Guzmán created another stir when he submitted a series of questions regarding the U.S. response to the coup to former secretary of state Henry Kissinger. When months went by without a reply, the Chilean judge suggested that Kissinger could be held in contempt of court.[69]

But after indicting the former dictator again in December 2004, Judge Guzmán retired from the bench, leaving the Pinochet prosecution, as well as the Weisfeiler and Horman/Teruggi cases, for other judges to pursue. Judge Jorge Zepeda assumed the U.S. cases, but the wheels of justice turned slowly. Almost seven years passed with little clear movement, despite pressure from the families—including yearly visits by Boris's sister Olga to Santiago—on the U.S. Embassy to push for a judicial resolution. At the behest of the families, Embassy personnel met with the judge periodically to request progress reports, particularly on the fate of Boris Weisfeiler. "In our several meetings with Judge Zepeda over the past months we have emphasized to him the importance of the Weisfeiler case to Mr. Weisfeiler's family, to this Embassy, and to the United States government," the U.S. consul general reported in a December 2005 cable.[70]

Twenty-eight years after Boris Weisfeiler was *desaparecido* at the hands of Chilean security forces, his whereabouts remained undetermined. But on August 21, 2012, Judge Zepeda finally announced a legal step forward in the investigation. Citing evidence in declassified U.S. documents, he indicted eight retired military and police officials on charges of "aggravated kidnapping" and "complicity" in Weisfeiler's disappearance. The indictment indicated that Chilean security forces had targeted Weisfeiler because the color of his hiking clothes resembled paramilitary garb that a leftist guerrilla might wear. But the court filings provided no evidence of what they had done with Weisfeiler—and consequently brought his family no nearer to a sense of closure.[71]

By then, Judge Zepeda had also issued a headline-producing indictment in the murder cases of Charles Horman and Frank Teruggi. On November 29, 2011, he charged Brigadier General Pedro Espinosa, already in prison for multiple human rights crimes committed while deputy director of DINA, with complicity in the post-coup executions of the two Americans. In a surprise move, Zepeda also indicted former head of the U.S. military group Captain Ray Davis, whose contacts with Charles Horman before he disappeared and with his wife, Joyce, after Charles was seized, are depicted in the Oscar-winning movie *Missing*. In a petition to the Chilean Supreme Court to authorize a request for extradition, Zepeda charged that Davis was responsible for a "secret intelligence-gathering investigation of US citizens" in Chile. The U.S. military group had allegedly turned over information to the Chilean military casting Horman and Teruggi as "extremists" after the coup. Such intelligence on Teruggi, including his address in Santiago, led to his detention on September 20, 1973, Zepeda argued.

As depicted in *Missing*, the conventional wisdom on Horman was that he became a target because he had inadvertently stumbled across proof of U.S. involvement in the coup. But Zepeda's investigation suggested a different scenario: the Chilean military believed that Horman was involved in "subversive" work with a government film company, Chile Films, which was under surveillance for its pro-Allende media activities. In its most chilling statement, the indictment alleged that Captain Davis was in a position to "override the will" of the Chilean military to execute Horman—but chose not to do so.

On October 18, 2012, the Chilean Supreme Court ruled that Zepeda's legal arguments were sufficient to approve a formal request to Washington for the extradition of Captain Davis. Press reports suggested that he was an Alzheimer's patient in a nursing home in Florida and thus unlikely ever to appear in a Chilean courtroom. But the dramatic indictment of an American military officer, and the evidence behind it, nevertheless refocused international attention on the role played by the U.S. government in the execution of two of its own citizens—and in the September 11, 1973, military coup itself.

United States Accountability

On September 10, 2001, more than three decades after the murder of Chilean general René Schneider, two of his sons filed a comprehensive wrongful death lawsuit against Henry Alfred Kissinger and former CIA director Richard Helms.[72] The civil complaint, drawing extensively on declassified U.S. documentation, presented a detailed summary of Track II, including the White House decisions and covert operations that led to what court papers called "General Schneider's summary execution, torture, cruel, inhuman, and degrading treatment, arbitrary detention, assault and battery, negligence, intentional infliction of emotional distress, and wrongful death." Kissinger's and Helms's activities "included the organization and instigation of a military coup d'état in Chile that required the removal of General René Schneider, father of Plaintiffs René and Raul Schneider," according to the filing. "Each of the Defendants' deliberate and designed actions were such that the Defendants knew or should have known that their acts and omissions would result in the death of General Schneider."

On November 13, 2002, eleven post-coup victims and their families filed a second civil lawsuit against Kissinger and the U.S. government. This complaint also cited recently declassified documents. According to the suit, the records showed that

> With the practical assistance and encouragement of the United States . . . the Chilean terror apparatus conducted systematic torture; cruel, inhuman or degrading treatment; false imprisonment; arbitrary detention; wrongful death; summary execution; assault and battery; forced disappearance; crimes against humanity; violence against women; intentional infliction of emotional distress; and other violations of domestic and international law of which Plaintiffs and their relatives are victims.[73]

These cases reflected a growing movement for U.S. accountability in Chile. As early as 1975, when revelations of Track II coup plotting and the CIA role in the Schneider killing first broke in the media, White House and CIA lawyers recognized the danger of legal liability for U.S. officials as high up as the president of the United States. On June 24, 1974, President Ford's White House general counsel Philip Buchen received a briefing from the CIA on Nixon's September 15, 1970, orders to foment a coup in Chile. "Buchen showed some concern that this was a documentary tie-in of the President to coup-plotting," the CIA's lead attorney reported in a secret memorandum of conversation. "As Buchen put it, *one who sets in motion a coup attempt can be assessed with the responsibility for the natural and probable consequences of that action.*" (Emphasis added.)[74]

Given the precedent set by the Pinochet case for the globalization of justice to redress human rights crimes, the effort by Chilean victims to hold the United States accountable for their actions appeared inevitable. To be sure, the Chilean military applied the electrodes, pulled the triggers, and dug the secret graves during the dictatorship; but in the eyes of many victims, and many observers around the world, the United States served as an active to tacit accomplice in the denouement of Chilean democracy and consolidation of Pinochet's dictatorship. The declassified U.S. documents revealed long-hidden details of U.S.–Chilean relations that could only reinforce this view, particularly as it pertained to the preeminent role of Henry Kissinger between 1970 and 1976.

It is, perhaps, poetic justice that the dark past of U.S. policy toward Chile would return to haunt the U.S. policy maker most responsible for the decisions and actions around which that history was made. More than any other official, Kissinger bore the burden of the unresolved and ongoing controversies relating to Chile. Along with his actions in Vietnam and Cambodia, his conduct in Chile would be the Achilles' heel of his career, dogging his movements through adverse media coverage and legal action around the world.

Indeed, Kissinger would become the first U.S. official to be "Pinocheyed"—pursued by the threat of legal proceedings from country to country.[75] During a business trip to Paris in May 2001, a French attorney served Kissinger at his hotel with a summons to testify on the disappearances of Chileans after the coup. (Kissinger immediately left the country.) In June of that year, Judge Guzmán submitted his long list of questions on the Horman case; in August, a federal judge in Argentina—a country where Kissinger traveled often—formally requested U.S. assistance in interrogating the former secretary of state about his knowledge of Operation Condor; in September, the Schneider family initiated legal proceedings against Kissinger in the United States. And in February 2002, Kissinger was forced to abandon plans to travel to São Paolo to receive a prestigious Brazilian award from President Fernando Cardoso after news of his trip sparked street protests and a threat of being held for questioning regarding U.S. and Brazilian involvement in Operation Condor.[76]

At home, the declassified U.S. documents on Chile prompted the news media to revisit U.S. policy and reexamine Kissinger's role. Major programs from CNN to PBS's *The NewsHour* and CBS's *60 Minutes* did segments on the unresolved historical questions of U.S. misconduct in Chile. In press appearances to promote the last volume of his memoirs, *Years of Renewal*, Kissinger was forced on the defensive. "What business did the U.S. have trying to overthrow the president of another country, Mr. Secretary?" he was asked on CNN's *Crossfire*.[77] On *The NewsHour*, Kissinger was pressed to answer the question "Why did you not say to him, 'You're violating human rights, you're killing people. Stop it'?" He remained unrepentant. "Human rights were not an international issue at the time, the way they have become since," he explained to *NewsHour* interviewer Elizabeth Farnsworth. Any inference that Washington had to atone for wrongdoing, he added, "assumes the policy was immoral or worse, and that I don't accept."[78]

For both the Chilean political establishment and victims of Pinochet's repression, Kissinger's attitude left a bitter resentment in bilateral relations with the United States. Those who had suffered horribly under the regime firmly believed that officials like Kissinger should be held legally accountable for policies that contributed to the wrenching repression so many Chileans had endured. Other Chileans demanded the United States acknowledge and apologize for the flagrant violations of Chilean sovereignty and indifference to the sanctity of Chilean lives. In mid-2000, a caucus of Chilean senators introduced a motion calling for the administration of President Ricardo Lagos to formally protest "violations of our sovereignty and dignity." Privately and publicly, Chilean Foreign Ministry officials let it be known that the Clinton administration should clearly acknowledge actions that contributed to changing the course of Chile's history. "I think that the reaction of my government at the time was, and still is, that we would like to see along with [declassified] papers a certain sense of remorse," Juan Gabriel Valdes, Chile's former foreign minister and then ambassador to the United Nations, told the American press. In a public appearance in Washington on September 5, 2001, Ambassador Valdes stated clearly: "An apology is appropriate."[79]

An Accounting vs. Accountability

On March 8, 1977, only a few weeks into the new human rights–oriented administration of Jimmy Carter, an obscure State Department official named Brady Tyson attempted to offer an official apology for U.S. intervention in Chile. Speaking at a meeting of the UN Human Rights Commission in Geneva in support of a resolution condemning the Pinochet regime, Tyson noted:

> We would be less than candid, and untrue to ourselves and to our people, if the delegation from the United States did not in any discussion of the situation in Chile express its profoundest regrets for the role that some U.S. government officials, agencies and private groups played in the subversion of the previous, democratically elected, Chilean government, that was overthrown by the coup of September 11, 1973. We recognize that the expression of regrets, however profound, cannot contribute significantly to undoing the suffering and terror that the people of Chile have experienced. We can only say that the great

majority of the American people have always believed in democracy, justice, and freedom for all, and that the policies and persons responsible for those acts have been rejected by the American people.[80]

Tyson's statement was honest, candid, and direct. It was also publicly repudiated and quickly retracted by his State Department superiors and the White House. Tyson was immediately recalled from Geneva and received a sharp rebuke. U.S. officials claimed his remarks were neither appropriate nor accurate and had not been cleared beforehand.

A generation later, another set of State Department officials once again considered the possibility of an official acknowledgment of U.S. culpability in Chile's tragedy. With the final release of declassified records scheduled for November 2000, the Office of Policy Planning perceived both the necessity and the opportunity to take a step toward closure of a shameful and scandal-ridden chapter of U.S. foreign policy. In October, director Morton Halperin proposed that the official statement accompanying the final release include a paragraph directly acknowledging a U.S. contribution to the coup and expressing official regret. "There were some of us who thought we owed them a straightforward apology," Halperin later stated. Theodore Piccone, deputy director of Policy Planning, recalled that he drafted simple, concise language, essentially stating that "the United States bears responsibility and expresses regrets for events contributing to the coup and the resulting human rights violations." To carry the necessary political weight, he and Halperin pushed for the statement to be issued by the White House and signed by President Bill Clinton.[81]

A presidential admission of foreign policy wrongdoing had precedent: in May 1999, following the declassification of documents revealing how Washington aided and abetted the brutal Guatemalan military, Clinton gave a speech in Guatemala City stating that Washington's "support for military forces or intelligence units which engaged in violent and widespread repression was wrong, and the United States will not repeat that mistake." But other bureaus in the State Department, as well as the intelligence community and the NSC, opposed any similar statement on Chile. The Bureau of Western Hemisphere Affairs, represented by Curt Struble, argued that the Policy Planning language went too far and would create an uproar in Chile. U.S. ambassador to Santiago John O'Leary agreed that the statement should be watered down. The State Department's legal office opposed any admission of "regret," as one official involved in the debate remembered, because this "could cause liability problems" for former U.S. policy makers.

The final crafting of a short two-sentence paragraph meant to convey U.S. government contrition while avoiding all reference to wrongdoing fell to

Arturo Valenzuela, the Chilean-born special adviser to the president on Latin America. Through a series of linguistic compromises, Valenzuela broadened and softened the phraseology. The word *undermined* in reference to Chile's democratic traditions was replaced with *affected*. Instead of admitting that Washington had "undercut" the cause of human rights, the statement left that to readers of the declassified documents to determine. After much debate and many e-mails between the White House and State Department, the final, somewhat contorted, language read:

> One goal of the project is to put original documents before the public so that it may judge for itself the extent to which U.S. actions undercut the cause of democracy and human rights in Chile. Actions approved by the U.S. government aggravated political polarization and affected Chile's long tradition of democratic elections and respect for constitutional order and the rule of law. (Doc 9)

Instead of carrying the imprimatur of the president, in the end the Office of the White House Press Secretary simply released an unsigned statement.

As the final, symbolic document in the Clinton administration's Chile Declassification Project, the press statement fell far short of acknowledging the contribution U.S. foreign policy had made to the national and human horror experienced in Chile—an acknowledgment necessary for Chileans and Americans to gain closure on a painful history. With the declassified documents, the United States had provided an accounting—but without a full acceptance of accountability.

That accounting nevertheless established a voluminous historical record—an invaluable body of evidence that would forever inform U.S. citizens; the international community; Chileans; and, even forty years after the coup, ongoing legal proceedings to judge the atrocities of Pinochet's military regime. The documentation significantly contributed to what Chilean human rights investigators called "the cleansing power of the truth," offering the accountability of a collective historical memory when judicial accountability appeared insufficient. "If, in the end, we are unable to take to trial those who were responsible, at least memory will provide a historical trial for them," one survivor of Pinochet's torture camps concluded with simple eloquence.[82] For Pinochet and those U.S. policy makers who supported his regime, there might never be a courtroom verdict; but the declassified records would help to render the damning verdict of history.

DOCUMENT 1. Bow Street Magistrates Court [Warrant for the Arrest of Augusto Pinochet], October 16, 1998.

IN THE INNER LONDON AREA

BOW STREET MAGISTRATES' COURT

To each and all of the Constables of the Metropolitan Police Force

There being evidence that

Augusto Pinochet Ugarte

(hereinafter called the defendant) is accused
~~is alleged to be unlawfully at large after conviction~~
of the offence(~~s~~) of

between the 11th September 1973 and the 31st. December 1983 within the jurisdiction of the Fifth Central Magistrates Court of the National Court of Madrid did murder Spanish Citizens in Chile.

within the jurisdiction of the Government of Spain

And there being information that the defendant is or is believed to be in or on way to the United Kingdom:

and it appears to me that the conduct alleged would constitute an extradition crime:

And I have been supplied with such information as would justify, in my opinion, the issue of a warrant for the arrest of a person accused ~~alleged to be unlawfully at large after conviction~~ of an offence within the Inner London Area:

You are hereby required to arrest the defendant and bring the defendant before a Metropolitan Magistrate sitting at Bow Street Magistrates' Court.

Date: 16th October 1998

Nicholas Evans.
Metropolitan Magistrate

EF

Provisional Warrant
Convention Countries
Section 8(1)(b)
Extradition Act 1989

DOCUMENT 2. Defense Intelligence Agency, Biographic Sketch, "General Augusto Pinochet Ugarte," February 1983.

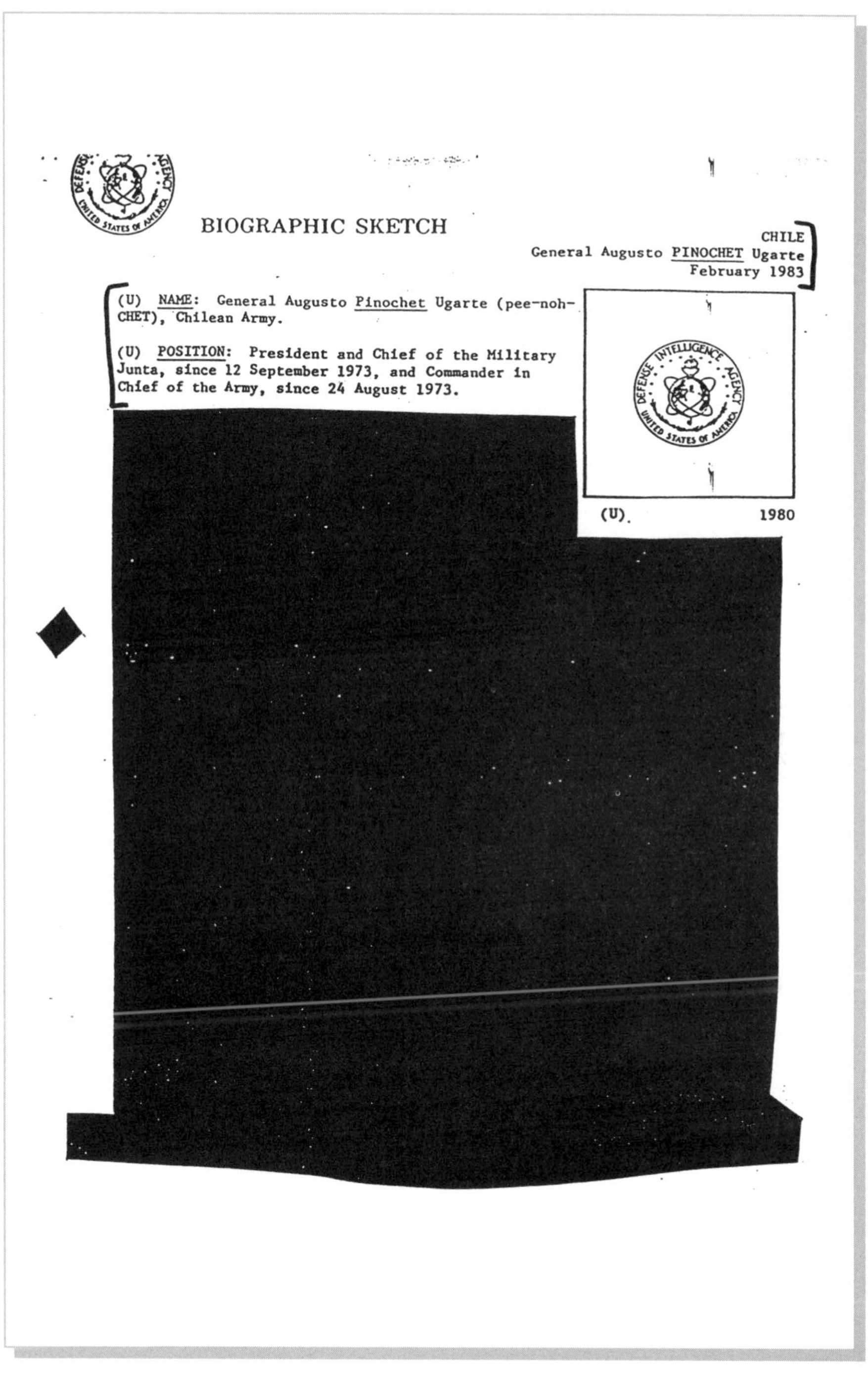

BIOGRAPHIC SKETCH

CHILE
General Augusto PINOCHET Ugarte
February 1983

(U) NAME: General Augusto Pinochet Ugarte (pee-noh-CHET), Chilean Army.

(U) POSITION: President and Chief of the Military Junta, since 12 September 1973, and Commander in Chief of the Army, since 24 August 1973.

(U). 1980

DOCUMENT 3. National Security Council, Tasker, "Declassifying Documents Related to Human Rights Abuses in Chile," February 1, 1999.

0354

NATIONAL SECURITY COUNCIL
WASHINGTON, D.C. 20504

February 1, 1999

MEMORANDUM FOR

MS. KRISTIE A. KENNEY
Executive Secretary
Department of State

COL. JOSEPH REYNES, JR.
Executive Secretary
Department of Defense

MS. ADRIENNE THOMAS
Assistant Archivist for Administrative Services
National Archives and Records Administration

MS. FRANCES F. TOWNSEND
Counsel for Intelligence Policy
Department of Justice

MS. VICKI M. HUPP
Acting Executive Secretary
Central Intelligence Agency

SUBJECT: Declassifying Documents Related to Human Rights Abuses in Chile

This Administration has consistently supported efforts, as in El Salvador, Guatemala, and Honduras, to clarify the facts surrounding human rights abuses, terrorism and other acts of political violence by releasing information from U.S. government files as appropriate. On behalf of the President, we now ask your cooperation in undertaking a compilation and review for release of all documents that shed light on human rights abuses, terrorism, and other acts of political violence during and prior to the Pinochet era in Chile.

Release of such information could assist in encouraging a consensus within Chile on reinvigorating its truth and reconciliation process to address such questions as the fate of the disappeared. A declassification review also would respond to the expressed wishes of the families of American victims of human rights abuses, and to the requests of numerous members of Congress.

Scope

As a first phase of this undertaking, you should retrieve and review for declassification documents that shed light on human rights abuses, terrorism, and other acts of political violence in Chile from 1968-78 to ensure that a balanced view of events emerges. Once this first phase has been completed, we will issue a tasker regarding documents from the period 1979-91.

You should retrieve and review all classified documents that are subject to disclosure under the Freedom of Information Act or authorities governing Presidential papers. As a point of departure in locating relevant documents, attached is a list of well-known cases, together with some events, places and alleged perpetrators associated with human rights abuses in Chile. The narrative section of the attachment provides context.

In conducting the declassification review (as distinct from searching for responsive documents), you should begin with documents from the September 1973-1978 period. Each agency is responsible for reviewing only those documents that originated with the reviewing agency.

Release Standards

In reviewing documents, the President has directed that agencies shall release all responsive information except the following: information that qualifies for continued classification under Sec. 3.4(b) of Executive Order 12958, information the release of which is prohibited by statute, information that would constitute a clearly unwarranted invasion of personal privacy, sensitive law enforcement information, and information the release of which would cause serious and identifiable harm to the deliberative process.

Deadlines and Interagency Coordination

Our goal is to complete this discretionary review and release of documents from 1968-78 by the end of the fiscal year. An initial review and release of documents -- especially from September 1973-1978 -- should be completed by May 15. Interim releases of documents are encouraged. To monitor progress toward these goals and to resolve any questions or problems of implementation, the NSC will chair an Interagency Working Group (IWG). The NSC also will chair joint declassification sessions to facilitate review of third-agency referrals as needed.

The IWG will hold its first meeting on February 3 at 2:00 p.m. in Room 208, Old Executive Office Building. Please submit the name(s) of your designated representative(s) by January 28.

DOCUMENT 4. CIA, Report, "CIA Activities in Chile," September 18, 2000 (excerpts).

SUBJECT: CIA Activities in Chile

September 18, 2000

Summary of Sources/Methodology

To respond to Section 311 of the Intelligence Authorization Act for Fiscal Year 2000 (referred to hereafter as the Hinchey Amendment), the Intelligence Community (IC), led by the National Intelligence Council, reviewed relevant CIA records of the period predominantly from recent document searches; studied extensive Congressional reports regarding US activities in Chile in the 1960s and 1970s; read the memoirs of key figures, including Richard Nixon and Henry Kissinger; reviewed CIA's oral history collection at the Center for the Study of Intelligence; and consulted with retired intelligence officers who were directly involved.

This broad information base has given us high confidence in our responses to the three questions, which are answered directly below. The body of the report, however, provides much greater detail in an effort to tell the story of CIA involvement and put the answers into their proper historical context. The Select Committee to Study Governmental Operations with Respect to Intelligence Activities—the Church Committee—conducted in 1975 a thorough document review and interviews, and produced a report that still stands as a comprehensive analysis of CIA actions in Chile during the period from 1963 to 1973.

CIA's response to the Hinchey amendment should be viewed as a good-faith effort to respond in an unclassified format to the three questions, not as a definitive history of US activities in Chile over the past 30 years.

Summary of Response to Questions

1. **Q.** All activities of officers, covert agents, and employees of all elements of the Intelligence Community with respect to the assassination of President Salvador Allende in September 1973.

   A. We find no information—nor did the Church Committee—that CIA or the Intelligence Community was involved in the death of Chilean President Salvador Allende. He is believed to have committed suicide as the coup leaders closed in on him. The major CIA effort against Allende came earlier in 1970 in the failed attempt to block his election and accession to the Presidency. Nonetheless, the US Administration's long-standing hostility to Allende and its past encouragement of a military coup against him were well known among Chilean coup plotters who eventually took action on their own to oust him.

2. **Q.** All activities of officers, covert agents, and employees of all elements of the Intelligence Community with respect to the accession of General Augusto Pinochet to the Presidency of the Republic of Chile.

A. CIA actively supported the military Junta after the overthrow of Allende but did not assist Pinochet to assume the Presidency. In fact, many CIA officers shared broader US reservations about Pinochet's single-minded pursuit of power.

3. **Q.** All activities of officers, covert agents, and employees of all elements of the Intelligence Community with respect to violations of human rights committed by officers or agents of former President Pinochet.

   A. Many of Pinochet's officers were involved in systematic and widespread human rights abuses following Allende's ouster. Some of these were contacts or agents of the CIA or US military. The IC followed then-current guidance for reporting such abuses and admonished its Chilean agents against such behavior. Today's much stricter reporting standards were not in force and, if they were, we suspect many agents would have been dropped.

Support for Coup in 1970. Under "Track II" of the strategy, CIA sought to instigate a coup to prevent Allende from taking office after he won a plurality in the 4 September election and before, as Constitutionally required because he did not win an absolute majority, the Chilean Congress reaffirmed his victory. CIA was working with three different groups of plotters. All three groups made it clear that any coup would require the kidnapping of Army Commander Rene Schneider, who felt deeply that the Constitution required that the Army allow Allende to assume power. CIA agreed with that assessment. Although CIA provided weapons to one of the groups, we have found no information that the plotters' or CIA's intention was for the general to be killed. Contact with one group of plotters was dropped early on because of its extremist tendencies. CIA provided tear gas, submachine-guns and ammunition to the second group. The third group attempted to kidnap Schneider, mortally wounding him in the attack. CIA had previously encouraged this group to launch a coup but withdrew support four days before the attack because, in CIA's assessment, the group could not carry it out successfully.

Awareness of Coup Plotting in 1973. Although CIA did not instigate the coup that ended Allende's government on 11 September 1973, it was aware of coup-plotting by the military, had ongoing intelligence collection relationships with some plotters, and—because CIA did not discourage the takeover and had sought to instigate a coup in 1970—probably appeared to condone it. There was no way that anyone, including CIA, could have known that Allende would refuse the putchists' offer of safe passage out of the country and that instead—with *La Moneda* Palace under bombardment from tanks and airplanes and in flames—would take his own life.

Knowledge of Human Rights Violations. CIA officers were aware of and reported to analysts and policymakers in 1973 that General Pinochet and the forces that overthrew the Allende Government were conducting a severe campaign against leftists and perceived political enemies in the early months after the coup. Activities of some security services portended a long-term effort to suppress opponents. In January 1974, CIA officers and assets were tasked to report on human rights violations by the Chilean government.

Liaison with Chilean Security Services. The CIA had liaison relationships in Chile with the primary purpose of securing assistance in gathering intelligence on external targets. The CIA offered these services assistance in internal organization and training to combat subversion and terrorism from abroad, not in combating internal opponents of the government. The CIA also used these relationships to admonish these services concerning human rights abuses in Chile.

The policy community and CIA recognized that the relationships opened the CIA to possible identification with the liaison services' internal operations involving human rights abuses but determined that the contact was necessary for CIA's mission.

Propaganda in Support of Pinochet Regime. After the coup in September 1973, CIA suspended new covert action funding but continued some ongoing propaganda projects, including support for news media committed to creating a positive image for the military Junta. Chilean individuals who had collaborated with the CIA but were not acting at CIA direction assisted in the preparation of the "White Book," a document intended to justify overthrowing Allende. It contained an allegation that leftists had a secret "Plan Z" to murder the high command in the months before the coup, which CIA believed was probably disinformation by the Junta.

Knowledge of "Operation Condor." Within a year after the coup, the CIA and other US Government agencies were aware of bilateral cooperation among regional intelligence services to track the activities of and, in at least a few cases, kill political opponents. This was the precursor to Operation Condor, an intelligence-sharing arrangement among Chile, Argentina, Brazil, Paraguay and Uruguay established in 1975.

Violations of Human Rights Committed by Officers or Covert Agents and Employees of the CIA

In January 1974 CIA issued a directive to all CIA staff to collect clandestine information on torture in Chile; this message directed CIA staff to work through all available agents and channels of influence to induce the Chilean Government to modify repressive measures, particularly to eliminate torture. CIA actively used its contacts, especially with members of services notorious for human rights abuses, to emphasize that human rights abuses were detrimental to the government's credibility within their own country, damaging to their international reputation, and unacceptable to the US Government. In some cases, such contacts enabled the CIA to obtain intelligence on human rights abuses that would not have otherwise been available.

Given the wide variety and nature of CIA contacts in Chile, the issue of human rights was handled in various ways over the years. Some examples:

- Before the 1973 coup, the issue of human rights was not addressed in liaison contacts and intelligence reporting.
- One CIA contact was known to be involved in an abortive coup attempt on 29 June 1973, and another was involved in the successful 11 September 1973 coup.
- In October 1973, the CIA had credible information that a high-level contact was involved in specific human rights abuses; contact was severed.
- Although the CIA had information indicating that a high-level contact was a hard-liner and therefore more likely to commit abuses, contact with him was allowed to continue in the absence of concrete information about human rights abuses.

- CIA maintained indirect contact with a source in close contact with human rights violators. There was no evidence that the source engaged in abuses, but he almost certainly knew about the practice. The intelligence value of the contact was sufficiently important that the contact was not dropped.

- In the case of an individual about whom the CIA had information concerning a corruption issue that may have been related to human rights issues, a decision was made to seek contact given his position and potential intelligence value.

- In more than one case, in light of the contacts' service affiliation and position, it seemed likely that they were involved in, knew about or covered up human rights abuses. However, because such contacts allowed the CIA to accomplish its intelligence reporting mission and maintain a channel through which to voice concerns about human rights abuses, contact was continued.

- In a few cases, although the CIA had knowledge that the contact represented a service with a known history of human rights abuses, contact was continued because refusing such contact would have had a negative impact on the CIA intelligence collection mission.

- In some cases careful checks of contacts' human rights records were not conducted, and a deliberate risk-versus-gain decision was not made. In such cases, if a contact was deemed to have intelligence value, continuing contact was authorized.

- Information concerning human rights abuses of then current and former CIA contacts was disseminated to the intelligence and policy communities.

Relationship with Contreras

During a period between 1974 and 1977, CIA maintained contact with Manuel Contreras Sepulveda, who later became notorious for his involvement in human rights abuses. The US Government policy community approved CIA's contact with Contreras, given his position as chief of the primary intelligence organization in Chile, as necessary to accomplish the CIA's mission, in spite of concerns that this relationship might lay the CIA open to charges of aiding internal political repression. From the start, the CIA made it clear to Contreras was that it would not support any of his activities or activities of his service which might be construed as "internal political repression." In its contacts with Contreras, the CIA urged him to adhere to a 17 January 1974 circular, issued by the Chilean Ministry of Defense, spelling out guidelines for handling prisoners in a manner consistent with the 1949 Geneva Convention.

The relationship, while correct, was not cordial and smooth, particularly as evidence of Contreras' role in human rights abuses emerged. In December 1974, the CIA concluded that Contreras was not going to improve his human rights performance. However, Contreras' assistance in the first quarter of 1975 in gaining the release of some PDC members who had been arrested and mistreated by another Chilean security service offered small hope that he would use his influence to end abuses. In retrospect, however, Contreras' role in this effort probably reflected inter-service rivalry and Contreras' personal efforts to control the entire Chilean intelligence apparatus.

By April 1975, intelligence reporting showed that Contreras was the principal obstacle to a reasonable human rights policy within the Junta, but an interagency committee directed the CIA to continue its relationship with Contreras. The US Ambassador to Chile urged Deputy Director of Central Intelligence Walters to receive Contreras in Washington in the interest of maintaining good relations with Pinochet. In August 1975, with interagency approval, this meeting took place.

In May and June 1975, elements within the CIA recommended establishing a paid relationship with Contreras to obtain intelligence based on his unique position and access to Pinochet. This proposal was overruled, citing the US Government policy on clandestine relations with the head of an intelligence service notorious for human rights abuses. However, given miscommunications in the timing of this exchange, a one-time payment was given to Contreras.

In addition to information concerning external threats, CIA sought from Contreras information regarding evidence that emerged in 1975 of a formal Southern Cone cooperative intelligence effort—"Operation Condor"—building on informal cooperation in tracking and, in at least a few cases, killing political opponents. By October 1976 there was sufficient information that the CIA decided to approach Contreras on the matter. Contreras confirmed Condor's existence as an intelligence-sharing network but denied that it had a role in extra-judicial killings.

Former Allende cabinet member and Ambassador to Washington Orlando Letelier and his American assistant, Ronni Moffitt, were killed in a carbombing in Washington on 21 September, 1976. Almost immediately after the assassination, rumors began circulating that the Chilean government was responsible. CIA's first intelligence report containing this allegation was dated 6 October 1976. During October 1976, the Department of Justice and the CIA worked out how the CIA would support the foreign intelligence (FI) aspects of the legal investigation. At that time, Contreras' possible role in the Letelier assassination became an issue.

By the end of 1976, contacts with Contreras were very infrequent. During 1977, CIA met with Contreras about half a dozen times; three of those contacts were to request information on the Letelier assassination. On 3 November 1977, Contreras was transferred to a function unrelated to intelligence so CIA severed all contact with him.

DOCUMENT 5. Pinochet's Falsified Passports Used to Open Secret Bank Accounts.

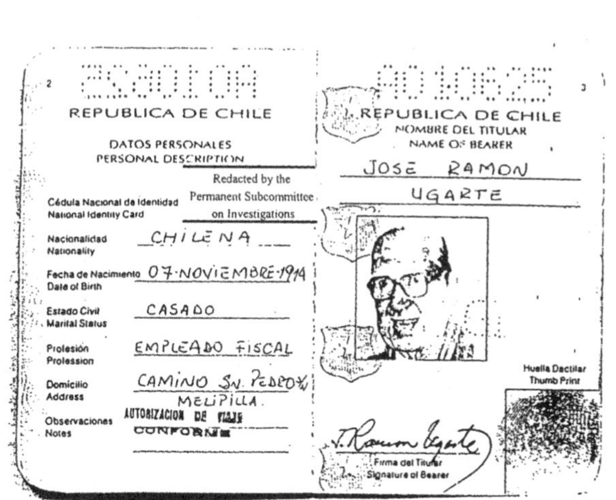

REPUBLICA DE CHILE

DATOS PERSONALES
PERSONAL DESCRIPTION

Redacted by the Permanent Subcommittee on Investigations

Cédula Nacional de Identidad / National Identity Card

Nacionalidad / Nationality: CHILENA

Fecha de Nacimiento / Date of Birth: 07-NOVIEMBRE-1914

Estado Civil / Marital Status: CASADO

Profesión / Profession: EMPLEADO FISCAL

Domicilio / Address: CAMINO SN. PEDRO MELIPILLA.

Observaciones / Notes: AUTORIZACION DE VIAJE CONFORME

REPUBLICA DE CHILE
NOMBRE DEL TITULAR
NAME OF BEARER

JOSE RAMON
UGARTE

Huella Dactilar
Thumb Print

Firma del Titular
Signature of Bearer

REPUBLICA DE CHILE
NOMBRE DEL TITULAR
NAME OF BEARER

AUGUSTO
UGARTE

Huella Dactilar
Thumb Print

Firma del Titular
Signature of Bearer

DOCUMENT 6. List of Pinochet Name Variants and Aliases Used to Open Secret Bank Accounts.

Disguised Pinochet Account Names

Given Name: Augusto Jose Ramon Pinochet Ugarte

-Augusto P. Ugarte

-A. Ugarte

-A.P. Ugarte

-Jose Pinochet

-Jose P. Ugarte

-Jose Ugarte

-Jose Ramon Ugarte

-J. Ramon Ugarte

-Jose R. Ugarte

-Daniel Lopez

Prepared by the Permanent Subcommittee
on Investigations, Minority Staff

DOCUMENT 7. Riggs Vice President Carol Thompson Order for $50,000 Cashier's Checks for Pinochet, May 14, 2001; Images of Several Checks Dated May 15, 2001.

DATE: May 14, 2001
TO: BALTAZAR PORTILLO
FROM: CAROL Thompson

RE: ALTHORP / ASHBURTON

Please find attached an ORDER from client to issue 10 checks totaling $500,000. Please make each check $50,000, payable to MARÍA HIRIART and/or Augusto P. Ugarte.

My address in Buenos Aires:

11 de Setiembre 1902, Piso 6-B
1428 Buenos Aires, Argentina
Tel (54-11) 4784-4463

Thank you,

Carol

RNB 029978

PAGE 2 OF 2

Purchaser	Daytime Phone #	Payment Method ☐ Debit Account # ☐ Cash ☐ Check	Bank Fee	Other Charges	Total Dollar Amount
			7.00		

RIGGS Cashier's Check
Riggs Bank N.A.
Debit

May 15, 2001 — Date
076 — Branch # — 1678730

Pay To The Order Of: *****Maria Hiriart &/or Augusto P. Ugarte*****
$ 50,000.00***** Amount

NON NEGOTIABLE

The Sum Of ___ Dollars

Remitter

Customer's Signature

Authorized Signature

⑈1678730⑈ ⑆051010828⑆

Purchaser	Daytime Phone #	Payment Method ☐ Debit Account # ☐ Cash ☐ Check	Bank Fee	Other Charges	Total Dollar Amount
			7.00		

RIGGS Cashier's Check
Riggs Bank N.A.
Debit

May 15, 2001 — Date
076 — Branch # — 1678731

Pay To The Order Of: *****Maria Hiriart &/or Augusto P. Ugarte*****
$ 50,000.00***** Amount

NON NEGOTIABLE

The Sum Of ___ Dollars

Remitter

Customer's Signature

Authorized Signature

⑈1678731⑈ ⑆051010828⑆

Purchaser	Daytime Phone #	Payment Method ☐ Debit Account # ☐ Cash ☐ Check	Bank Fee	Other Charges	Total Dollar Amount
			7.00		

RIGGS Cashier's Check
Riggs Bank N.A.
Debit

May 15, 2001 — Date
076 — Branch # — 1678732

Pay To The Order Of: *****Maria Hiriart &/or Augusto P. Ugarte*****
$ 50,000.00***** Amount

NON NEGOTIABLE

The Sum Of ___ Dollars

Remitter

Customer's Signature

Authorized Signature

⑈1678732⑈ ⑆051010828⑆

OCC0000045790

DOCUMENT 8. Department of State, Cable, "Renewing Efforts to Resolve the Horman, Teruggi and Weisfeiler Cases," April 1, 2000.

STATE 61812

From: DRL
Subject: RENEWING EFFORTS TO RESOLVE THE HORMAN, TERUGGI AND WEISFEILER CASES

MRN: 61812
ICNbr: TED6901

Date/Time: 010234Z APR 00
Precedence: PRIORITY

Cable Text:

```
TED6901
ORIGIN DRL-02

INFO  LOG-00   NP-00    AID-00   AMAD-01  ACQ-00   CA-02    CIAE-00
      INL-01   DODE-00  WHA-01   SRPP-00  DS-00    EB-00    UTED-00
      VC-01    H-01     TEDE-00  INR-00   IO-00    L-00     AC-01
      DCP-01   NSAE-00  NSCE-00  OCS-03   OIC-02   OMB-01   OPIC-01
      PA-00    PM-00    PRS-00   ACE-00   P-00     SP-00    SSO-00
      SS-00    STR-00   TRSE-00  T-00     USIE-00  PMB-00   DSCC-00
      PRM-01   G-00     MR-00    SAS-00   SWCI-00    /019R

061812
SOURCE:   KODAKC.001004
DRAFTED BY: DRL/BA:RWARD; WHA/BSC:DVALDERRAMA -- MAR 17 HORMAN ET AL 0
APPROVED BY: DRL:HHKOH; WHA: LHEDDLEMAN
WHA/BSC:JCSTRUBLE   WHA/BSC:MCHARLTON   WHA/BSC:WGUSSMAN
DRL:PHIGGINS        S/P:TPICCONE         L/WHA:DIROSA
L/LEI:PMASON        L/CA:KBROWN          CA/OCS:TGLOVER
NSC: BBASH          S/S: SDMULL          S/S-O: SDREW
S/WCI:TWARRICK
CA/OCS:EBETANCOURT
INR:JGIBNEY
A/RPS:FMACHAK
P: LARREAGA

                  ------------------465D92  010236Z /38
P 010234Z APR 00
FM SECSTATE WASHDC
TO AMEMBASSY SANTIAGO PRIORITY

UNCLAS STATE 061812
FOR THE AMBASSADOR

E.O. 12958: N/A
TAGS: PREL, PHUM, CASC, CI
SUBJECT: RENEWING EFFORTS TO RESOLVE THE HORMAN,
TERUGGI AND WEISFEILER CASES

REFS: (A) 2/17/00 LETTER FROM JOYCE HORMAN TO
            DRL ASSISTANT SECRETARY KOH
       (B) SANTIAGO 564,
       (C) SANTIAGO 590

1. SUMMARY AND ACTION REQUEST. JOYCE HORMAN, WIDOW OF
AMCIT CHARLES HORMAN, HAS MET WITH AND WRITTEN TO
DEPARTMENT AND NATIONAL SECURITY COUNCIL OFFICIALS TO
REQUEST RENEWED USG EFFORTS TO ENCOURAGE THE GOC TO
```

UNDERTAKE AN INVESTIGATION INTO HER HUSBAND'S EXTRAJUDICIAL EXECUTION 27 YEARS AGO. JANICE TERUGGI, THE SISTER OF AMCIT FRANK TERUGGI, WHO LIKE CHARLES HORMAN WAS EXTRAJUDICIALLY EXECUTED SHORTLY AFTER THE COUP BY CHILEAN SECURITY FORCES, REQUESTS A SIMILAR ACCOUNTING. OLGA WEISFEILER, THE SISTER OF BORIS WEISFEILER, ALSO REQUESTS AN ACCOUNTING; BORIS WEISFEILER DISAPPEARED UNDER SUSICIOUS CIRCUMSTANCES IN 1985 NEAR COLONIA DIGNIDAD AND IS PRESUMED DEAD. THE AMBASSADOR IS REQUESTED TO APPROACH

THE GOC AT THE HIGHEST LEVELS TO URGE A NEW INVESTIGATION INTO THESE DEATHS. A DIPLOMATIC NOTE AND SUGGESTED TALKING POINTS ARE PROVIDED IN PARAS 13 AND 14: TALKING POINTS MAY BE LEFT WITH INTERLOCUTORS IN THE FORM OF A NON-PAPER. THE DEPARTMENT WILL MAKE A PARALLEL APPROACH (AT THE ASSISTANT SECRETARY LEVEL) WITH THE CHILEAN EMBASSY IN WASHINGTON. END SUMMARY AND ACTION REQUEST.

BACKGROUND -- THE HORMAN CASE

2. AMCIT CHARLES HORMAN WAS DETAINED BY SECURITY FORCES IN SANTIAGO SHORTLY FOLLOWING THE SEPTEMBER 11, 1973 COUP. LIKE MANY OTHERS DETAINED IN THE IMMEDIATE AFTERMATH OF THE COUP, HE WAS HELD AT THE NATIONAL STADIUM. HIS WIFE'S INITIAL EFFORTS TO FIND HIM AND SECURE HIS RELEASE CAME TO NAUGHT; GOC OFFICIALS DENIED ANY KNOWLEDGE OF HIS DETENTION AND ULTIMATE FATE. HIS BODY WAS SUBSEQUENTLY FOUND IN A LOCAAL CEMETERY. MRS. HORMAN AND HER FATHER-IN-LAW, ED HORMAN, PRESSED THE GOC FOR AN EXPLANATION AND INVESTIGATION. NONE WAS FORTHCOMING, DESPITE EMBASSY EFFORTS AND THE ADVENT OF CONSIDERABLE CONGRESSIONAL INTEREST AND WIDESPREAD PUBLICITY. JOYCE AND ED HORMAN BELIEVED AT THE TIME THAT THE EMBASSY HAD MISHANDLED THE CASE AND WITHHELD INFORMATION FROM THEM. THEY VOICED THE FURTHER SUSPICION THAT THE USG WAS COMPLICIT IN CHARLES HORMAN'S DEATH. THE HORMANS SUED THE USG AND VARIOUS USG OFFICIALS (INCLUDING HENRY KISSINGER) FOR WRONGFUL DEATH. IN THE DISCOVERY PHASE OF THEIR CASE, NUMEROUS USG DOCUMENTS WERE PROVIDED TO THEM, THOUGH MOST WERE HEAVILY REDACTED. THE SUIT WAS EVENTUALLY DISMISSED WITH PREJUDICE.

3. AS JOYCE HORMAN EXPLAINED TO DEPARTMENT OFFICIALS IN MEETINGS WHICH FOLLOWED THE OCTOBER 1998 ARREST OF GENERAL PINOCHET IN LONDON, THE HORMAN FAMILY HAS NEVER CEASED TO SEEK AN OFFICIAL ACCOUNTING OF THE DETENTION AND DEATH OF CHARLES HORMAN. DURING PINOCHET'S 17 YEARS IN POWER, FAMILY EFFORTS WERE STYMIED. FOLLOWING PINOCHET'S OWN DETENTION, A MARKED CHANGE OF ATTITUDE APPEARS TO HAVE OCCURRED IN CHILE (REFS B AND C) AND GIVEN GROUNDS FOR RENEWED HOPE THAT AN OFFICIAL ACCOUNTING MIGHT BE POSSIBLE. THE CHILEAN JUDICIAL SYSTEM HAS BEGUN TO PROACTIVELY BRING HUMAN RIGHTS CASES AGAINST FORMER MILITARY AND POLICE OFFICIALS. FORMER DEFENSE MINISTER PEREZ YOMA CONVENED AND CHAIRED A HUMAN RIGHTS ROUNDTABLE TO ADDRESS THE ISSUE OF THE DISAPPEARED. PRESIDENT LAGOS' JANUARY 2000 ELECTION AND OFT-STATED COMMITMENT TO FULLY

BACK JUDICIAL INDEPENDENCE HAS CONTRIBUTED TO THE SENSE THAT PROSPECTS FOR GREATER JUSTICE FOR HUMAN RIGHTS VICTIMS AND ACCOUNTABILITY MAY BE AT HAND.

4. FOR THESE MANY REASONS, MRS. HORMAN ASKS THAT THE USG ENGAGE THE GOC NOW TO UNCOVER THE TRUTH REGARDING HER HUSBAND'S FATE.

-- THE TERUGGI CASE

5. LIKE CHARLES HORMAN, AMCIT FRANK TERUGGI WAS ARRESTED BY SECURITY FORCES SHORTLY AFTER THE SEPTEMBER 11 COUP. HE AND HIS AMCIT ROOMMATE DAVID HATHAWAY WERE TAKEN FROM THEIR HOME ON SEPTEMBER 23, 1973 BY SECURITY FORCES AND DETAINED AT THE NATIONAL STADIUM. HATHAWAY WAS RELEASED, WHILE TERUGGI'S CORPSE WAS IDENTIFIED IN THE MORGUE TWO WEEKS LATER. HIS THROAT HAD BEEN SLASHED, HE HAD BEEN SHOT 17 TIMES, AND HIS BODY SHOWED SIGNS OF TORTURE. CHILEAN AUTHORITTIES, AGAIN, DENIED ANY RESPONSIBILITY FOR HIS DETENTION, T'ORTURE AND MURDER.

6. THOUGH THE TERUGGI CASE RECEIVED LESS PRESS COVERAGE THAN THE HORMAN CASE, THE FAMILY HAS ALSO SOUGHT A FULL ACCOUNTING OF THE CIRCUMSTANCES LEADING TO FRANK TERUGGI'S DEATH. FRANK TERUGGI, SENIOR TRAVELED TO CHILE TO TRY TO UNCOVER THE FACTS. HE NEVER LEARNED THOSE FACTS AND REMAINED BITTER UNTIL HIS DEATH IN 1995 ABOUT THE MURDER OF HIS SON BY CHILEAN SECURITY FORCES AND A PERCEIVED LACK OF USG ASSISTANCE WITH THE CASE. FRANK'S SISTER, JANICE, CONFIRMED TO THE DEPARTMENT MARCH 13 THE FAMILY'S ONGOING INTEREST IN A FULL ACCOUNTING.

-- THE WEISFEILER CASE

7. AMCIT BORIS WEISFEILER, A MOSCOW-BORN MATHEMATICS PROFESSOR AT PENNSYLVANIA STATE UNIVERSITY, DISAPPEARED ON JANUARY 4, 1985, WHILE HIKING IN THE VICINITY OF THE GERMAN IMMIGRANT ENCLAVE, COLONIA DIGNIDAD. HIS BACKPACK WAS SUBSEQUENTLY FOUND NEAR A RIVER; THE OFFICIAL GOC POSITION AT THE TIME WAS THAT HE HAD FALLEN INTO THE WATER AND DROWNED, THOUGH HIS BODY WAS NEVER RECOVERED. THERE ARE INDICATIONS THAT WEISFEILER MAY HAVE BEEN DETAINED BY CHILEAN AUTHORITIES AND POSSIBLY TAKEN TO COLONIA DIGNIDAD. HIS SISTER OLGA WEISFEILER OF NEWTON, MASSACHUSETTS HAS ALWAYS REJECTED THE DROWNING THEORY, POINTING TO THE FACT HE WAS AN EXPERIENCED ALPINIST WHO

HAD HIKED EXTENSIVELY IN DIFFICULT TERRAIN IN SEVERAL PARTS OF THE WORLD, INCLUDING ALASKA, CANADA AND SIBERIA.

8. MS. WEISFEILER HAS BEEN CONTACTED BY THE DEPARTMENT AND HAS CONFIRMED HER INTEREST IN A FULL ACCOUNTING OF HER BROTHER'S DEATH. SHE HAS RETAINED A LOCAL ATTORNEY; AT HIS URGING, THE CHILEAN INVESTIGATIVE POLICE MAY REINITIATE EFFORTS TO GET TO THE BOTTOM OF WEISFEILER'S DISAPPEARANCE AND DEATH.

CURRENT CONSIDERATIONS

9. THE FINAL, FEBRUARY 1991 REPORT OF THE CHILEAN NATIONAL TRUTH AND RECONCILIATION COMMISSION (RETTIG COMMISSION), EXPRESSED THE "CONVICTION" THAT HORMAN AND TERUGGI WERE THE VICTIMS OF EXXTRAJUDICIAL EXECUTION "BY AGENTS OF THE STATE" IN VIOLATION OF THEIR HUMAN RIGHTS. IN THE CASE OF BORIS WEISFEILER, THE COMMISSION WAS UNABLE TO FORM A FIRM VIEW THAT HIS DIISSAPPEARANCE CONSTITUTED A VIOLATION OF HUMAN RIGHTS.

10. WHILE ACKNOWLEDGING THAT THE RETTIG COMMISSION'S LANDMARK WORK AND ASSESSMENT OF CULPABILITY IN THE DEATHS OF CHARLES HORMAN AND FRANK TERUGGI PROVIDES AN IMPORTANT MEASURE OF ACCOUNTABILITY, IT STILL FALLS SHORT OF THE FULL ACCOUNTING WHICH THE FAMILIES SEEK AND SHOULD HAVE.

DEPARTMENT BELIEVES IT REASONABLE TO ASK THAT THE GOC MAKE A GOOD FAITH EFFORT AT THIS TIME TO PROVIDE SUCH AN ACCOUNTING. OURR RESPONSIBILITY TO PROTECT AMERICAN LIVES ABROAD AND TO SEEK THE ASSISTANCE OF HOST GOVERNMENTS TO THAT END DOES NOT DIMINISH WITH THE PASSAGE OF TIME. WHEN AN AMERICAN IS THE VICTIM OF GROSS HUMAN RIGHTS VIOLATIONS -- AS CERTAINLY OCCURRED IN THE HORMAN AND TERUGGI CASES, AND MAY HAVE OCCURRED IN THE WEISFEILER CASE -- THEN WE HAVE AN OBLIGATION TO PRESS THE GOVERNMENT UNTIL ACCOUNTABILITY IS PROVIDED.

11. THESE CASES WERE EXTREMELY HIGH PROFILE AND HAD SERIOUS IMPLICATIONS FOR OUR BILATERAL RELATIONS WITH CHILE IN THE 1970'S. ONE OF THE PRINCIPAL REASONS THE NSC MANDATED THE CHILE DECLASSIFICATION PROJECT ON BEHALF OF THE PRESIDENT WAS TO HELP THE FAMILIES OF AMCIT VICTIMS OBTAIN ALL THE INFORMATION IN OUR FILES RELEVANT TO THEIR CASES. THIS PRESENT ACTION IS A LOGICAL EXTENSION OF THAT GOAL.

ACTION REQUEST

12. THE AMBASSADOR SHOULD CONVEY TO SENIOR GOC OFFICIALS THE DESIRE OF THE USG TO SEE A FULL ACCOUNTING GIVEN OF THE DETENTION AND DEATH OF CHARLES HORMAN AND FRANK TERUGGI, AND THE 1985 DISAPPEARANCE AND PROBABLE DEATH OF BORIS WEISFEILER. THE AMBASSADOR SHOULD SEEK TO ASCERTAIN THE CURRENT LEGAL AND INVESTIGATIVE STATUS OF THESE CASES AND IF NO ACTIVE INVESTIGATION IS UNDERWAY, SHOULD PRESS FOR SAME. HE SHOULD ALSO SEEK TO HAVE THE GOC APPOINT AN INDIVIDUAL TO COORDINATE INVESTIGATIVE EFFORTS AND SERVE AS LIAISON TO THE FAMILIES AND THEIR DESIGNATED REPRESENTATIVES. SUGGESTED TEXT OF A DIPLOMATIC NOTE TO BE DELIVERED IN THIS REGARD FOLLOWS IN PARA 13; SUGGESTED TALKING POINTS, WHICH MAY BE LEFT AS A NON-PAPER, FOLLOW IN PARA 14. DEPARTMENT WILL, TO PARALLEL EMBASSY SANTIAGO EFFORTS, ALSO AP?PROACH THE CHILEAN EMBASSY IN WASHINGTON.

13. SUGGESTED TEXT OF DIPLOMATIC NOTE.

(COMPLIMENTARY OPENING) AND HAS THE HONOR TO CONVEY THE REQUEST THAT A FULL ACCOUNTING BE MADE OF THE CIRCUMSTANCES LEADING TO THE DISAPPEARANCE AND DEATH IN CHILE OF THREE AMERICAN CITIZENS: CHARLES HORMAN, FRANK TERUGGI, AND BORRIS WEISFEILER.

MR. HORMAN WAS DETAINED BY SECURITY FORCES IN SANTIAGO SHORTLY AFTER THE SEPTEMBER 11, 1973 MILITARY COUP. HE WAS HELD FOR A PPERIOD OF TIME IN THE NATIONAL STADIUM. HIS BODY WAS SUBSEQUENTLY FOUND AND IDENTIFIED AT A LOCAL CEMETERY. THE HORMAN FAMILY HAS WORKED SINCE 1973 TO ASCERTAIN THE FUULLL DETAILS OF HIS DETENTION AND DEATH. DESPITE THE PASSAGE OF TIME, THE FAMILY STILL LOOKS TO RECEIVE A FULL ACCOUNTING OF MR. HORMAN'S DEATH.

MR. TERUGGI WAS ALSO DETAINED BY SECURITY FORCES IN THE IMMEDIATE AFTERMATH OF THE COUP AND TAKEN TO THE NATIONAL STADIUM. HIS BODY WAS FOUND TWO WEEKS LATER IN A MORGUE. HIS THROAT HAD BEEN SLASHED AND HE HAD BEEN SHOT 17 TIMES; HIS BODY ALSO SHOWED SIGNS OF TORTURE HAVING BEEN INFLICTED. THE TERUGGI FAMILY HAS SOUGHT AND CONTINUES TO SEEK A FULL ACCOUNTING OF HIS DEATH.

MR. WEISFEILER DISAPPEARED NEAR "COLONIA DIGNIDAD" ON JANUARY 4, 1985 UNDER ILL-DEFINED CIRCUMSTANCES. HIS

BACKPACK WAS FOUND ON A RIVERBANK NEAR THE COLONIA ON

JANUARY 15, BUT HIS REMAINS HAVE NEVER BEEN FOUND. THERE ARE INDICATIONS THAT HE MAY HAVE BEEN DETAINED BY CHILEAN AUTHORITIES AND POSSIBLY TAKEN TO COLONIA DIGNIDAD. THE WEISFEILER FAMILY ALSO SEEKS TO ASCERTAIN WITH CERTAINTY THE DETAILS OF MR. WEISFEILER'S DISAPPEARANCE AND PRESUMED DEATH.

THE UNITED STATES GOVERNMENT SHARES WITH THE HORMAN, TERUGGI AND WEISFEILER FAMILIES THE DESIRE FOR A FULL ACCOUNTING OF THE CIRCUMSTANCES OF THE AFOREMENTIONED DISAPPEARANCES//DEATHS. AT THE TIME OF THESE DISAPPEARANCES//DEATHS, UNITED STATES CONSULAR OFFICERS ATTEMPTED, CONSIISTENT WITH THE VIENNA CONVENTION ON CONSULAR RELATIONS (INCLUDING ARTICLE 5(G) AND ARTICLE 37 THEREOF), TO OBTTAIN RELEVANT INFORMATION. BECAUSE MANY QUESTIONS AT THAT TIME WERE LEFT UNANSWERED, AND PURSUANT TO THE UNITED STTATES GOVERNMENT'S RIGHTS UNDER THE CONVENTION TO ASSIST THE SURVIVING FAMILY MEMBERS WHO ARE NATIONALS OF THE] UNITED STATES, THE EMBASSY, ON BEHALF OF THE UNITED STATEES GOVERNMENT, REQUESTS THAT THE APPROPRIATE AUTHORITIES OF THE GOVERNMENT OF CHILE MOUNT A VIGOROUS AND THOROUGH INVESTIGATION AIMED AT UNCOVERING THE FACTS, AND IN ACCORDANCE WITH CHILEAN LAW, PROSECUTING THOSE RESPONSIBLE.

THE UNITED STATES REQUESTS THAT, AS PART OF RENEWED INVESTIGATIVE EFFFORTS, A POINT OF CONTACT BE NAMED BY THE GOVERNMENT OF CHILE TO COORDINATE SAID EFFORTS AND TO SERVE AS LIAISON TO THE HORMAN, TERUGGI AND WEISFEILER FAMILIES AND/OR THEIR DESIGNATED REPRESENTATIVES. (COMPLIMENTARY CLOSE). END TEXT DIPLOMATIC NOTE.

14. SUGGESTED TALKING POINTS

THE CONSIDERABLE EFFORTS OF THE CHILEAN GOVERNMENT TO COME TO TERMS WITH THE LEGACY OF HUMAN RIGHTS ABUSES LEFT BY THE PINOCHET ERA IN A MANNER WHICH FOSTERS BOTH ACCOUNTABILITY AND NATIONAL RECONCILIATION HAVE DESERVEDLY ENGENDERED INTERNATIONAL RECOGNITION.

THE RETTIG COMMISSION AND ROUNDTABLE DIALOGUE STAND OUT AS NOTEWORTHY EXAMPLES OF EFFORTS UNDERTAKEN BY THE GOVERNMENT OF CHILE TO SHED LIGHT ON THE TERRIBLE EXCESSES OF THE PAST.

DESPITE SUCH EFFORTS, THREE AMERICAN FAMILIES REMAIN THESE MANY YEARS WITHOUT FULL INFORMATION REGARDING THE DISAPPEARANCE AND DEATH IN CHILE OF THEIR LOVED ONES. THEY ALSO REMAIN WITHOUT CERTAIN KNOWLEDGE OF WHO WAS RESPONSIBLE FOR THESE CRIMES.

THEY ARE THE HORMAN, TERUGGI AND WEISFEILER FAMILIES.

ONE OF THE PRIMARY GOALS OF AMERICAN FOREIGN POLICY HAS LONG BEEN THE PROTECTION OF AMERICAN CITIZENS TRAVELING OR LIVING ABROAD.

THAT FUNDAMENTAL GOAL HAS NOT ALTERED WITH TIME. THOUGH THE HORMAN, TERUUGGI AND WEISFEILER CASES ARE ALL QUITE OLD, INTEREST IN THEIR RESOLUTION REMAINS STRONG. INFORMATION AVAILABLE TO THE UNITED STATES GOVERNMENT ON THE HORMAN AND TERUGGI CASES WAS RELEASED IN THE CONTEXT OF TRANCHES I AND II OF THE CHILE DECLASSIFICATION PROJECT. ADDITIONAL INFORMATION WILL BE MADE AVAILABLE ON THE HORMAN AND TERUGGI CASES, AS WELL AS THE WEISFEILER CASE, WHEN A THIRD AND FINAL TRANCHE IS RELEASED LATER THIS YEAR.

THE RELEASE OF INFORMATION HELD BY THE UNITED STATES ON THESE CASES, WHILE HELPFUL, CANNOT SUBSITUTE FOR A FULL INVESTIGATION INTO AND ACCOUNTING FOR THE DISAPPEARANCE AND DEATH OF THESE INDIVIDUALS.

THAT INVESTIGATION AND ACCOUNTING CAN ONLY BE CARRIED OUT BY THE GOVERNMENT OF CHILE.

THE USG FULLY SHARES THE DESIRE OF THE THREE FAMILIES FOR A FULL ACCOUNTING OF THE FATE OF CHARLES HORMAN, FRANK TERUGGI AND BORIS WEISFEILER, AND REQUESTS RENEWED AND VIGOROUS EFFORTS BY THE GOC TO PROVIDE SUCH AN ACCOUNTING.

THE USG REQUESTS THAT THE GOC NAME A COORDINATOR(S) TO SERVE AS THE POINT OF CONTACT FOR THE THREE FAMILIES.

END TALKING POINTS.
ALBRIGHT
NNNN

End Cable Text

DOCUMENT 9. White House, Press Release, "Statement by the Press Secretary [on Final Chile Declassification Release]," November 13, 2000.

THE WHITE HOUSE

Office of the Press Secretary

For Immediate Release **November 13, 2000**

STATEMENT BY THE PRESS SECRETARY

Today the Department of State, the Central Intelligence Agency, the Department of Defense, the Federal Bureau of Investigation, the National Archives and Records Administration, and the Department of Justice are releasing newly declassified and other documents related to events in Chile from 1968-91. These documents are part of a discretionary review of U.S. government files related to human rights abuses, terrorism, and other acts of political violence prior to and during the Pinochet era in Chile. National Security Council staff coordinated this interagency effort on behalf of the President.

Agencies made an initial release of approximately 5,800 documents on June 30, 1999, concentrating on the period from 1973-78, which corresponds to the period of the most flagrant human rights abuses in Chile. A second release of over 1,100 documents concentrating on the years 1968-73 followed on October 8, 1999. While the focus for this final release was on documents dated from 1978-91, additional documents from the earlier periods also are being released today.

This third and final release consists of more than 16,000 documents, including approximately 13,050 from the Department of State, 1,550 from the CIA, 620 from the Federal Bureau of Investigation, 370 from the Department of Defense, 310 from the National Archives, 110 from the National Security Council, and 50 from the Department of Justice. Information has been withheld from some of the released documents to protect the privacy of individuals, sensitive law enforcement information, and intelligence sources and methods; or to prevent serious harm to ongoing diplomatic activities of the United States.

One goal of the project is to put original documents before the public so that it may judge for itself the extent to which U.S. actions undercut the cause of democracy and human rights in Chile. Actions approved by the U.S. government during this period aggravated political polarization and affected Chile's long tradition of democratic elections and respect for the constitutional order and the rule of law.

The Chilean people deserve our praise and respect for courageously reclaiming their proud history as one of the world's oldest democracies. Healing the painful wounds of the past, Chileans from across the political spectrum have rededicated themselves to rebuilding representative institutions and the rule of law. The United States will continue to work closely with the people of Chile -- as their friend and partner -- to strengthen the cause of democracy in Latin America and around the world.

A complete set of the released documents is available for public review at the National Archives in College Park, Maryland. They also are being released simultaneously in Chile. Copies of the documents will be available on the Internet at http://foia.state.gov. Also available at this website are copies of the September 2000 Hinchey Report on "CIA Activities in Chile" and the relevant 1975 Church Committee reports on Chile.

30-30-30

Afterword: Kissinger's Response

In the fall of 2003, just a few weeks after the first edition of this book was published, an article titled "Kissinger and Chile: The Myth That Will Not Die," appeared in a conservative magazine, *Commentary*. Written by American Enterprise Institute analyst Mark Falcoff, the article was an open defense of Henry Kissinger's role in Chile and an effort to debunk the "myth," supposedly perpetuated by this book and others, about the contribution of his policies to the overthrow of Salvador Allende's government. Falcoff drew on special access to still classified "telcons"—transcripts of Kissinger's telephone conversations that he secretly recorded during his tenure in office, and then took with him into retirement—that the former secretary of state "kindly let me review," Falcoff wrote. Since there were not that many transcripts related to Chile, Falcoff concluded that "Chile was not an important part" of Kissinger's agenda between 1970 and 1973. Nevertheless, he argued, these documents helped "reconstruct the true course of events."

The article highlighted Kissinger's phone conversation with Nixon on September 16, 1973, five days after the coup, which supposedly disproved the most important "myth"—that the United States was complicit in the military coup that overthrew Allende. In that conversation, Falcoff asserted, the president "exhibited no sense of complicity with the coup-makers themselves" when he suggested to Kissinger that "we didn't—as you know—our hand doesn't show on this one, though." To which Kissinger replied, as Falcoff reconstructed the "true course" of these events, "We didn't do it."

Readers of this edition of *The Pinochet File*, published on the fortieth anniversary of the coup, will know that Kissinger actually said much more than that to Nixon. The transcript of the Kissinger–Nixon conversation was declassified in May 2004, pursuant to a lawsuit prepared by my organization, the National Security Archive, against the State Department for allowing Kissinger to walk away with 30,000 pages of official government records that were not his to take. The "telcon" revealed the context of Nixon's remark that "our hand doesn't show on this one, though." He and Kissinger were commiserating over the fact that they couldn't openly take, and receive, credit in the media as "heroes" for Allende's overthrow, as the Eisenhower administration had after the CIA-sponsored military coup against the Arbenz government in Guatemala in 1954. The "telcon" also revealed Kissinger's full response to Nixon: "We didn't do it. I mean we helped them. [Omitted word] created the conditions as great as possible." To which the President of the United States replied, "That's right." (Doc 1)

By deliberate omission, Falcoff misrepresented the historical record on U.S. intervention in Chile. U.S. operatives did not command the tanks or pilot the fighter jets that assaulted La Moneda Palace on September 11, 1973—hence Kissinger's statement that "we didn't do it." But Washington "helped" the coup plotters, before and after Chile's bloody 9/11. Kissinger's policies, and CIA operations designed to destabilize Allende's ability to govern, overtly and covertly contributed to creating "the conditions as great as possible" in which a coup would likely take place—and succeed. These inconvenient truths could not be part of Kissinger's message as he sought to manipulate the debate over the true history of U.S. involvement in Chile. On the thirtieth anniversary of the coup, the effort his office made to obfuscate and deny the facts reflected just how important Chile was, and remains, in the controversial annals of U.S. foreign policy.

Facilitating the Falcoff article was part of Henry Kissinger's larger effort to confront the problems created by the historical record that began to emerge in the aftermath of Pinochet's arrest and the Clinton administration's special Chile Declassification Project. Kissinger's lawyer, William D. Rogers, a distinguished and respected former State Department official, first became concerned when the CBS News show *60 Minutes* ran a hard-hitting segment—based on a draft of Chapter 1 of this book—on Kissinger's role in the CIA plot that led to the assassination of Chilean General René Schneider in October 1970. Broadcast on September 9, 2001, the program drew on recently declassified CIA documents and on a civil lawsuit for "wrongful death" that the Schneider family filed against Kissinger on September 10, 2001. The critical publicity generated by the CBS program and the lawsuit was immediately overtaken by the catastrophic events on September 11, 2001.

But the issue of Chile's legacy and Kissinger's reputation did not go away. Rogers was further "outraged" by Secretary of State Colin Powell's statement in February 2003 that Chile was "not part of American history that we are proud of." Powell was "implying that the U.S. was morally responsible for what happened in Chile," Rogers later told the *Washington Post*. "He bought the myth."

With the thirtieth anniversary of the coup approaching, as well as the publication of this book—Rogers had obtained an advance galley copy in preparation for a public debate with me—the Falcoff article would address that "myth" and aggressively defend Kissinger's image. The plan was for the article to be published in the prestigious Council on Foreign Relations journal, *Foreign Affairs*. But the journal's then editor, James Hoge, rejected it as "too narrow a defense of Kissinger." Instead, he tasked the Council's renowned Latin America specialist Kenneth Maxwell to address the larger issues of the debate over Chile in a lengthy review of *The Pinochet File*.

That review, titled "The Other 9/11: The United States and Chile, 1973," appeared in the November–December 2003 issue of *Foreign Affairs*. It did not attract much attention. Maxwell barely referred to the book; instead, he wrote an essay drawing on the contents of *The Pinochet File* that highlighted the new evidence in the Schneider case and Washington's efforts to undermine Allende. From information in the first two chapters of the book, Maxwell concluded that "there is no doubt that the United States did all that it could" to bring Allende down.

His review also delved into Kissinger's knowledge of Operation Condor and the implications of that knowledge on the assassination in Washington of Orlando Letelier and Ronni Moffitt in 1976. As I wrote in Chapter 6, Kissinger had learned of Operation Condor—the Southern Cone rendition and assassination program led by the Chilean secret police—in early August 1976; three weeks later his top aides had pressed him to approve a secret démarche to Pinochet and other leaders of Condor nations to desist from international murder operations, but the U.S. ambassadors in those countries never actually delivered the warning. Instead, Kissinger appeared to withdraw the démarche. On September 20, his deputy, Harry Shlaudeman, instructed the U.S. ambassadors to "take no further action" on delivering the démarche because "there have been no reports in some weeks indicating an intention to activate the Condor scheme." The very next morning, Letelier and Moffitt were assassinated by a car bomb. Maxwell's review bolstered my contention that Condor's bald act of terrorism in downtown Washington, D.C., could have and should have been detected and deterred.

Kissinger read the review and "was not pleased," as the *Washington Post* later reported. Indeed, he phoned the chairman of the Council on Foreign Relations, Peter Peterson, to complain. Peterson then called Hoge at *Foreign Affairs* and passed on Kissinger's objections. William Rogers then penned a forcefully worded response, which appeared in the next issue of the journal.

In his letter, Rogers blamed both Maxwell and me for promoting the "myth" that the United States was involved in Schneider's death and the coup itself. This "myth" was "lovingly nurtured by the Latin American left and refreshed from time to time by contributions to the literature like Peter Kornbluh's *The Pinochet File* and Kenneth Maxwell's review of that book," he noted. With a bit of tongue-in-cheek, Rogers dismissed Maxwell's assertion that the United States had "done all it could" to overthrow Allende as "an injustice to regime-changers in the U.S. government, past and present."

What really bothered Kissinger's lawyer, however, was Maxwell's assessment of the new evidence on Kissinger's knowledge of Operation Condor and the implications for the Letelier-Moffitt assassination. Rogers disputed the assertion that Kissinger's Condor démarche had never been delivered. "Kissinger's warning was delivered in robust fashion to the Argentine president—there are cables to prove it . . . and probably to Pinochet's underlings in Santiago." For Kissinger's office, it was important to win the historical debate on whether a terrorist attack in the nation's capital could have been thwarted.

Along with Roger's letter, Maxwell's rebuttal ran in the January–February 2004 issue of *Foreign Affairs*. He responded that the declassified documents published in *The Pinochet File* "cut very close to home" for Kissinger as well as Rogers, who had served as Kissinger's assistant secretary of state for Latin America in the mid 1970s when Operation Condor was formed. Drawing on my book and *The Condor Years* by John Dinges, the world's leading expert on Condor, Maxwell made clear that the Letelier-Moffitt assassination was "a tragedy that might have been prevented." The debate over this history was so important, he suggested dramatically, that a truth commission on Chile should be established to divulge the full historical record on the outstanding questions, rather than answers being "extracted painfully like rotten teeth."

When I read William Rogers's letter, I considered it a challenge to the book as well as the review; he had cited "Kornbluh and Maxwell" in virtually every paragraph. Moreover, his letter contained factual inaccuracies in a number of places, particularly on the Letelier-Moffitt case. I placed a call to *Foreign Affairs* and spoke with one of Hoge's deputy editors, saying that I wanted to provide my own response to Rogers's letter in the March–April issue. What I was told surprised and, to be honest, angered me: another letter would appear in the next issue—from Rogers. I would not be allowed to respond, but lest I feel bad about that, neither would *Foreign Affairs*' own reviewer, Ken Maxwell. Rogers (and Kissinger) would have the final word.

Roger's second letter forcefully attacked not only Maxwell's arguments but also his integrity. Rogers accused Maxwell of "bias and distortions." He objected to the "outrageous" implication that he, Shlaudeman, or Kissinger could have prevented the Condor terrorist attack in Washington, D.C. Maxwell had misread Shlaudeman's September 20 cable, he claimed; the cable instructed that "no further action" should be taken to warn Pinochet and the Condor nations to halt international assassination operations. That meant, according to Rogers, that action had already been taken to warn them. Shlaudeman was responding to another message which is "nowhere to be found," Rogers wrote, implying that the missing message contained information on how the démarche had already been distributed. Maxwell was dishonoring Shlaudeman by implying he "had the temerity to countermand a direct, personal instruction from Kissinger [to deliver the démarche], and do it behind his back" while Kissinger was out of the country. (Rogers pointed out that he and Kissinger had been together in Africa at that time, asserting U.S. influence to end white rule in Rhodesia.) Maxwell didn't understand Kissinger's stewardship at the State Department, Rogers asserted. "Such are the absurdities of this myth," he wrote, "but they are absurdities that strike at the heart of character and reputation."

William Rogers was correct: Shlaudeman would not have countermanded Kissinger's instructions. To the contrary, he would have faithfully implemented them. The important gap in the heartbreaking historical record on the Letelier-Moffitt assassination was why the démarche was not delivered when it should have been, when it could have halted a terrorist attack, and when and why Kissinger had clearly instructed Shlaudeman to rescind it. A full understanding of what had happened was imperative not only for the families of victims but also for the United States as a country. Agents had come to our nation's capital and committed an act of international terrorism. For the sake of national security, it was important to know exactly how that had occurred and whether it could have been prevented.

I knew, liked, and respected William Rogers, who died of a heart attack in September 2007; we had worked closely together on a historical project on his secret diplomacy to establish better relations with Cuba. I initiated an e-mail exchange with him at this point to suggest that his interpretation of these events could not be correct. For the sake of truth and historical justice, I urged him to assign Kissinger's private archivist to review his papers day by day from late August to September 20, 1976, to locate the records that would explain what Maxwell called the "cruel coincidence" of the démarche being withdrawn just hours before an egregious act of terrorism occurred in downtown Washington, D.C.

At the same time, my organization, the National Security Archive, redoubled efforts to obtain the declassification of the relevant records. I filed a series of FOIAs for cables and memos from that time period relating to communications between Shlaudeman and the U.S. ambassadors in the Condor nations. And eventually, we obtained a handful of documents that shed considerable light on what had happened.

It turns out that the ambassador in Uruguay, Ernest Siracusa, had joined the ambassador in Chile, David Popper, in objecting to delivering the démarche. In Chile, we already knew that Popper had responded that Pinochet would take "as an insult" any suggestion that he was involved in assassination plots. The new records showed that Siracusa also resisted; he feared for his personal safety if he issued such a warning to Uruguay's generals. Instead, he suggested that Kissinger's office deliver the démarche to the Uruguayan ambassador in Washington. The new documents I obtained revealed that on August 30, 1976, Shlaudeman wrote a secret memo to Kissinger, titled "Operation Condor," seeking authorization to instruct Siracusa that he should proceed to deliver the démarche in Montevideo. "What we are trying to head off is a series of international murders that could do serious damage to the international status and reputation of the countries involved," Shlaudeman advised Kissinger. (Doc 2)

On September 16, 1976, Kissinger responded to the "Operation Condor" memo via a cable from Lusaka, where he and Rogers were traveling. The secretary of state "declined to approve message to Montevideo," the cable stated, "and instructed that no further action be taken on this matter." This was the "missing message" that Rogers referred to in his *Foreign Affairs* letter. This was Kissinger's instruction to Shlaudeman, which he faithfully reiterated, word for word, in his September 20 cable, rescinding the démarche. If Kissinger had been seriously interested in establishing the true historical record during the bitter debate in *Foreign Affairs*, he could have easily retrieved this document. Instead, the missing cable was discovered by my intrepid colleague Carlos Osorio in an electronic database of thousands of recently declassified State Department records. When we posted it on the archive's website (www.nsarchive.org) in April 2010, the cable generated headlines around the world. (Doc 3)

Through e-mails and meetings, Ken Maxwell tried to convince the powers-that-be at *Foreign Affairs* to allow him to respond to Rogers's attack on his integrity. On January 30, 2004, he met with Hoge to discuss the issue. According to Maxwell, Hoge told him that Kissinger's powerful friend Maurice Greenberg, honorary vice chairman of the Council on Foreign Relations and chairman of AIG, had called and yelled at him for thirty minutes. Hoge said he was under intense pressure from Kissinger to terminate the debate in the pages of the journal. Maxwell wrote a response to Rogers's second letter anyway. When Hoge refused to print it, Maxwell took an unusual step of protest for a high official in a leading establishment think tank: in May 2004, he resigned.

Maxwell not only resigned, he wrote a thirty-page tell-all history of the behind-the-scenes saga of Kissinger's effort to pressure *Foreign Affairs* into limiting a full and free debate on Chile. His report, "The Case of the Missing Letter in *Foreign Affairs*: Kissinger, Pinochet and Operation Condor," was based on e-mails, memos of conversation, and information from colleagues that Maxwell had meticulously collected as the controversy evolved. It included his rebuttal to Rogers that his editor had refused to publish.

Both Maxwell's resignation and the publication of his monograph on the website of the prestigious David Rockefeller Center at Harvard University generated an extraordinary amount of publicity. On June 5, 2004, the *New York Times* ran the first of two stories on the controversy, "Kissinger Assailed in Debate on Chile," quoting Maxwell's leaked resignation letter, which accused the Council of Foreign Relations of "stifling debate on American intervention in Chile during the 1970's as a result of pressure from former Secretary of State Henry A. Kissinger." *The Nation* ran a long story as well, titled "The Maxwell Affair." The scandal endured into early 2005, when the *Washington Post* published a dramatic two-and-a-half page spread titled "The Plot Thickens," with a huge photograph of Kissinger shaking General Pinochet's hand on the front page of the "Style" section, along with an image of the cover of *The Pinochet File*.

Indeed, as the Kissinger controversy spread, the book and Maxwell's review of it received significant free and positive media coverage. Ironically, in an effort to stifle discussion of the book, Kissinger actually generated it—a lot of it! Most important, his ill-conceived actions fueled the debate over the U.S. role in Chile and brought national attention to the need to declassify all of the still-classified files on this important, but still bitterly contested, history.

"I am not the issue here; Chile, Condor and Kissinger are," Maxwell wrote in his letter that *Foreign Affairs* refused to print. "The way to clarify the record is to release it in full, not to close off debate by accusations of myth-making [and] accusations of bias." As Kissinger's reaction to *The Pinochet File* shows, Chile remains a battleground over the dark abuses of power, enabled by the dark abuses of secrecy. But forty years after the military coup, the effort to declassify, debate, and understand these troubling events of history must continue—precisely because the issues of atrocity and accountability remain immediately relevant to the global discourse over U.S. foreign policy and human rights in the present day. Inevitably, the struggle to uncover the past is a struggle to enlighten the future.

DOCUMENT 1. Department of State, Telephone Transcript, Kissinger Conversation with Nixon, September 16, 1973.

*

TelCon:9/16/73 (Home) 11:50
Mr. Kissinger/
The President:

K: Hello.

P: Hi, Henry.

K: Mr. President.

P: Where are you. In New York?

K: No, I am in Washington. I am working. I may go to the football game this afternoon if I get through.

P: Good. Good. Well it is the opener. It is better than television. Nothing new of any importance of is there?

K: Nothing of very great consequence. The Chilean thing is getting consolidated and of course the newspapers and bleeding because a pro-Communist government has been overthrown.

P: Isn't that something. Isn't that something.

K: I mean instead of celebrating - in the Eisenhower period we would be heros.

P: Well we didn't - as you know - our hand doesn't show on this one though.

K: We didn't do it. I mean we helped them. _______ created the conditions as great as possible(? ?)

P: That is right. And that is the way it is going to be played. But listen, as far as people are concerned let me say they aren't going to buy this crap from the Liberals on this one.

K: Absolutely not.

P: They know it is a pro-Communist government and that is the way it is.

K: Exactly. And pro-Castro.

P: Well the main thing was. Let's forget the pro-Communist. It was an anti-American government all the ~~wxkxk~~ way.

DOCUMENT 2. Department of State, **SECRET** Memorandum, "Operation Condor," August 1, 1976.

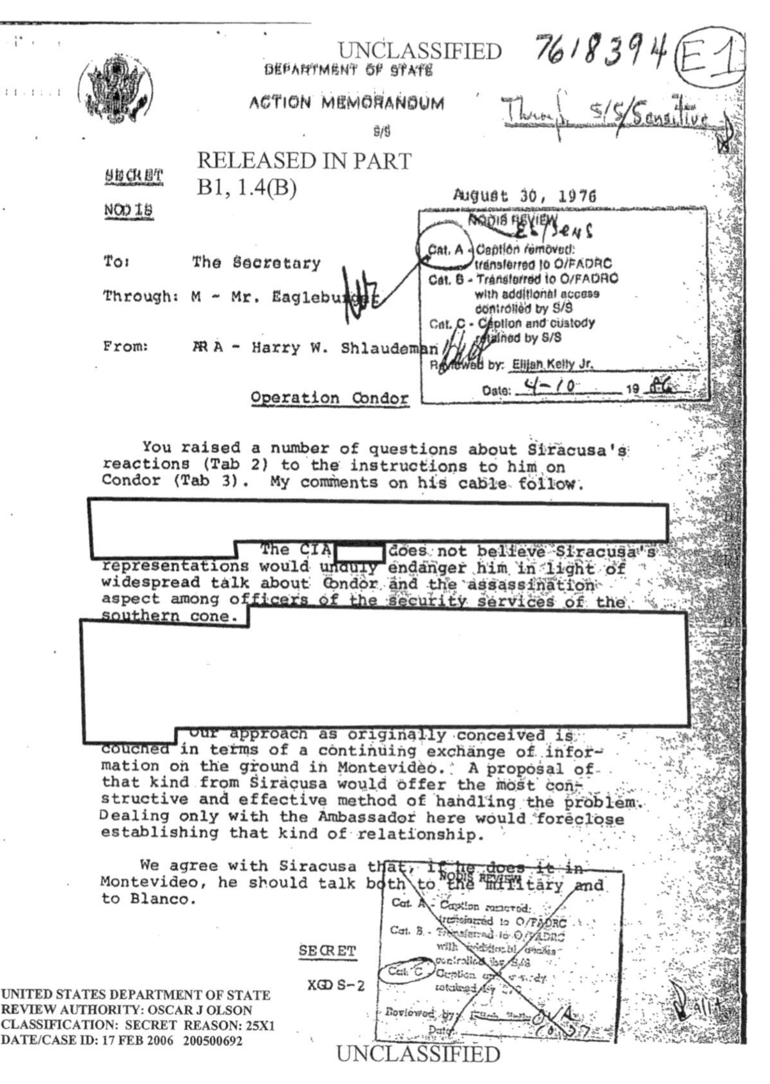

UNCLASSIFIED 7618394 E1

DEPARTMENT OF STATE

ACTION MEMORANDUM

S/S

Through S/S Sensitive

RELEASED IN PART
B1, 1.4(B)

SECRET
NODIS

August 30, 1976

NODIS REVIEW
Cat. A - Caption removed; transferred to O/FADRC
Cat. B - Transferred to O/FADRC with additional access controlled by S/S
Cat. C - Caption and custody retained by S/S
Reviewed by: Elijah Kelly Jr.
Date: 4-10 19 86

To: The Secretary

Through: M - Mr. Eagleburger

From: ARA - Harry W. Shlaudeman

Operation Condor

You raised a number of questions about Siracusa's reactions (Tab 2) to the instructions to him on Condor (Tab 3). My comments on his cable follow.

[redacted] The CIA [redacted] does not believe Siracusa's representations would unduly endanger him in light of widespread talk about Condor and the assassination aspect among officers of the security services of the southern cone.

[redacted] Our approach as originally conceived is couched in terms of a continuing exchange of information on the ground in Montevideo. A proposal of that kind from Siracusa would offer the most constructive and effective method of handling the problem. Dealing only with the Ambassador here would foreclose establishing that kind of relationship.

We agree with Siracusa that, if he does it in Montevideo, he should talk both to the military and to Blanco.

SECRET

XGDS-2

UNITED STATES DEPARTMENT OF STATE
REVIEW AUTHORITY: OSCAR J OLSON
CLASSIFICATION: SECRET REASON: 25X1
DATE/CASE ID: 17 FEB 2006 200500692

UNCLASSIFIED

SECRET

-2-

A parallel approach here, as Siracusa suggests, is acceptable to me and would help to preserve his position with the government there. But it is not my sense that this demarche is being made for domestic U.S. political considerations. What we are trying to head off is a series of international murders that could do serious damage to the international status and reputation of the countries involved.

We agree with Siracusa that he should add that the Condor targets have their own lists of Uruguayan Government officials targeted for assassination. It is precisely for that reason we propose to engage the Government of Uruguay in an exchange of views on the security situation so that we can demonstrate our appreciation of the problems they face.

Options:

We have three options in the Uruguayan case. We could do it:

-- by Siracusa to General Vadora and to Blanco, supported by a demarche to the Ambassador here and [redacted]

[redacted]

-- by me to the Ambassador here only.

Recommendation:

That you authorize the attached telegram to Siracusa instructing him to talk to both Blanco and Vadora, informing him of a parallel approach by me here and referring to a communication he will receive [redacted] on additional protection for the [redacted] (Tab I) Phil Habib has concurred in the attached suggested telegram.

ALTERNATIVELY, that we ask Siracusa to have the message [redacted] if in his judgment that can be done.

Approve_________ Disapprove______

SECRET

UNCLASSIFIED
SECRET

-3-

ALTERNATIVELY, that I make the demarche here, with no action to be taken in Montevideo for the time being.

Approve________ Disapprove________

Attachments:
 Tab 1 - Telegram to Siracusa
 Tab 2 - Montevideo 3123
 Tab 3 - State 209192

Drafted: ARA:HWShlaudeman/WHLuers:jn
 x29210 8-30-76

Clearance: P:DO'Donohue

SECRET
UNCLASSIFIED

DOCUMENT 3. Department of State, **CONFIDENTIAL** Cable, "Actions Taken [on Response to August 1 Condor Memo]," September 16, 1976.

Message Text

CONFIDENTIAL

PAGE 01 SECTO 27128 162152Z

66
ACTION SS-25

INFO OCT-01 ISO-00 SSO-00 CCO-00 /026 W
--------------------- 026821
O 162145Z SEP 76
FM USDEL SECRETARY IN LUSAKA
TO SECSTATE WASHDC IMMEDIATE

C O N F I D E N T I A L SECTO 27128

EXDIS

FOR S AND S/S ONLY

E.O. 11652: GDS
TAGS: OVIP (KISSINGER, HENRY A.)
SUBJECT: ACTIONS TAKEN

1. UNNUMBERED ARA MEMO DATED AUGUST 30, "OPERATION CONDOR". SECRETARY DECLINED TO APPROVE MESSAGE TO MONTEVIDEO AND HAS INSTRUCTED THAT NO FURTHER ACTION BE TAKEN ON THIS MATTER.

2. 7619068/9, VISIT OF MEXICAN PRESIDENT ELECT JOSE LOPEZ PORTILLO, FROM ARA. SECRETARY APPROVED TRANSMISSION OF THE BORG/SCOWCROFT MEMO WITH THE SUGGESTED GUEST LIST.
KISSINGER

CONFIDENTIAL

NNN

Acknowledgments

On September 12, 1973, a Chilean schoolmate of mine at Pioneer High in Ann Arbor, Michigan, came to first hour class in tears. She had been up all night with her family trying to reach relatives in Santiago by phone and listening to reports of the *coup d’etat* on shortwave radio. The teacher asked her what she had heard about events in her homeland and she gave a grave and desperate report: the president, Salvador Allende, was dead; the military had taken over; people were being shot in the streets; the future of her beautiful country shattered.

That girl, Eliana Loveluck, deserves much credit for my interest and work on Chile over the ensuing thirty years. She provided my first insight into the personal pain and suffering, the sense of human and national loss for Chileans, as well as the hope and political tenacity to fight against General Pinochet and his atrocities. It was through her experience and our close friendship that I first understood my own responsibility, and that of my country, in addressing and redressing what our government had done in Chile.

Along the way there have been many others whose dedication, courage, and commitment have inspired and informed my pursuit of the full history of the U.S. role in Chile. They form part of a broad, international community of activists, political figures, and victims of the Pinochet regime who coalesced around the issues of human rights and the restoration of democracy in Chile.

Those who suffered directly at the hands of Pinochet's repression and terrorism, but stood up to lead the fight for justice, peace, and dignity in Chile have been both my heroes and teachers. Michael Moffitt took me under his wing at the Institute for Policy Studies and taught me about research, writing, and the purpose of being a public scholar; Isabel Letelier provided me with a dignified model of grace and fortitude in her dedication to the cause of human rights; Murray and Hilda Karpen were tutors of the compassion and commitment that their daughter, Ronni, shared with the world; Veronica de Negri demonstrated the courage of raw emotional dedication to the memory of her son, my young friend Rodrigo Rojas; Joyce Horman taught me the true meaning of dedication, stamina, and love in her thirty-year effort to resolve the case of her murdered husband, Charles; similarly, Olga Weisfeiler redefined the meaning of tenacity in her quest to find her missing brother, Boris. It has been a great honor to have learned from, and worked with, these remarkable individuals over the years.

Along the long road to writing this book, I am fortunate to have had many mentors. At the Institute for Policy Studies, a remarkable organization that raised me and so many other young people politically and professionally, the one-and-only Saul Landau gave me my first writing assignment on Chile and made sure I understood the need to, as he would say, "stir the waters." Robert Borosage demonstrated, again and again, the patience of strategic politicking to effectively speak truth to power; Richard Barnet quite simply taught me how to reduce complicated history to a readable, written page. Others who took the time to educate me through collaborations, assignments, and the sharing of wisdom and experience, or authored pivotal works on Chile that guided my thinking, include John Dinges, Joseph Eldridge, Seymour Hersh, Sam Buffone, Michael Tigar, Lynn Bernabei, Lawrence Barcella Jr., Taylor Branch, Patricia Derian, Mark Schneider, Robert Scherrer, George Lister, Abraham Lowenthal, James Petras, Morris Morley, Richard Fagen, Patricia Fagen, Richard Feinberg, Roger Burbach, Patricia Flynn, Steve Volk, Naul Ojeda, Ariel Dorfman, Enrique Kirberg, Sofia and Maria Angélica Prats, Juan Pablo Letelier, Sergio Bitar, Carlos Portales, Alicia Frohmann, and José Pepe Zalaquett. They and so many others (who will forgive me for not identifying them) are the true pioneers of work on human rights in Chile and U.S. policy toward Pinochet in whose steps I've tried to follow. I will always be grateful to them and the power of their work.

There are two special people who, in their own way, truly made this book possible. The first is Juan Garcés, a Spanish lawyer, former aide to Salvador Allende, and tenacious advocate of justice whose singular efforts to hold Augusto Pinochet accountable for his crimes brought about his stunning arrest in October 1998. Garces has set the standard for the pursuit of memory and justice; without his quest to hold the perpetrators of crimes against humanity in Chile accountable, Pinochet would never have been arrested in London, and the Clinton administration would never have been forced to declassify the U.S. documents on Chile. The second person is the executive director of the National Security Archive, Tom Blanton. Tom graciously gave me the extended time necessary to complete this book, and remained extraordinarily supportive as the project was delayed by the terminal illness of my father. I will always be appreciative of his infinite patience, and his continuing faith in the outcome long before the manuscript was completed.

Founded by the creative genius of Scott Armstrong, under Tom's astute direction the National Security Archive has developed into an extraordinary group of forensic historians dedicated to exhuming the hidden history of U.S. foreign policy and making it available as evidence in the court of public opinion and debate. It is one hell of a great place. For their fine work, all of my colleagues at the Archive deserve the fullest acknowledgment for building this marvelous organization. My utmost gratitude goes to those who have contributed to this work: Bill Burr, who shared his Kissinger documents with me; Carlos Osorio, who has made a major contribution to uncovering the secrets of Operation Condor; Kate Martin, who played a behind the scenes role in getting the documents declassified; Rafael Cohen and Carla Humud, who helped with research; and Sue Bechtel, who always knew where everything was.

In addition, I owe thanks to many other people who have helped me over the last several years. From Chile, Pascale Bonnefoy made a major contribution through research, translations, and advice. William LeoGrande graciously spent time reading and commenting on the manuscript. Stacie Jonas and Sarah Anderson at the Institute for Policy Studies guided me to key records, clips, and files. Reed Brody, David Sugerman, and Richard Wilson provided documents and interpretation on international law and the Pinochet case. Katrina vanden Heuvel sent me to London to cover the Pinochet case for the *Nation*. David Corn also let me raid his files for documents on the CIA and Chile and then prodded me to finally finish.

Any acknowledgments would be incomplete without giving credit to the Clinton administration for the vast amount of work that went into the Chile Declassification Project. The President, his national security advisor, Sandy Berger, and his secretary of state, Madeleine Albright, deserve significant credit, as does Morton Halperin at Policy Planning, who pushed the idea of the special release, and his deputy Ted Piccone, who drafted the White House tasker. All the members of the Inter-Agency Working Group that implemented the President's directive should be hailed for the thousands of hours of work that went into finding, reviewing, and processing these records for declassification. A very, very special thanks to IWG director William Leary, Arturo Valenzuela, Peter Higgins, Hal Eisner, Robert Ward, Milton Charlton, Brad Weigmann, Carol Keeley, Nancy Smith, Gary Stern, Diana Valderrama, Curtis Struble, David Kamerling, Paolo DiRosa, John Bellinger, Frank Machak, Normon Bouton, Lee Strickland, and John Hamilton. Others whose names I don't know served on the IWG, and retired officials such as Robert Steven and Frederick Smith returned on a temporary basis to review documents for declassification. Ambassador John O'Leary gets kudos for recommending the documents be posted on a special State Department website, and Congressman Maurice Hinchey also deserves major credit for his role in pressing for the CIA to release new information on covert action in Chile. Each and every one of them, along with the still secret authors of the CIA's Hinchey report, deserve high praise for the patriotic contribution they have made to the history of U.S. foreign policy and Pinochet's atrocities in Chile.

The Ford Foundation deserves my deep appreciation for the support and encouragement they have given the Archive's Chile Documentation project over the years. Just a few weeks before Pinochet's arrest, the then-head of Ford's Santiago office, Alexander Wilde, gave our project a grant to do a website of declassified documents; Augusto Varas and Martin Abregu funded our campaign to get the documents declassified and to process them once they were. Along with Ford, the Arca Foundation has provided us with the ongoing support that made this work possible.

I tip my hat to the professionals at The New Press who literally make these books possible. André Schiffrin and my editor Diane Wachtell were tremendously patient in waiting for the manuscript; Beth Slovic and Sarah Fan walked the book through the production process. Jay Crowley and Kelly Too made the reproduction of the documents possible, and Brian Lipofsky and Andrew Hudak at Westchester Book Composition finalized the text. I am also grateful to Julie McCarroll for handling the marketing aspects of this book.

Finally, let me give a written embrace to my family for their unique support over the last several years. My dear and special compañera, Cathy Silverstein, turned her dining room and kitchen table over to this book for longer than any life partner should have to endure; she gave me all the support, encouragement, diversion, and love necessary for my mind and body to go forward. Thank you so much for putting up with me and with thousands of pages of documents scattered everywhere! Much thanks also to my mom, Joyce Kornbluh, in whose deep footsteps as a historian I have followed, and my sisters, Jane and Kathe; to my uncle and aunt Sol and Betty Kornbluh, who have been so kind and generous as this work has progressed, and to my cousin Martin for his curiosity and interest in my work.

In many ways this book is inspired by, and really written for, my wonderful son, Gabriel Kornbluh, who is half-Chilean and thus carries a heritage from both countries that dominate this work. Gabe, consider this my personal contribution to your education and understanding of the history of the two nations you are a part of and that are a part of you. You will play a role in the future of both—a future that is hopefully far more positive than the past.

In the end, however, this book is dedicated to my father, Hyman Kornbluh, who died on May 25, 2001, as it was being written. It is difficult to put into words the meaning of his contribution to guiding me, in both my formative and adult years, to a place where this work became possible. Without him, there would have been no conscience, no commitment, no outrage, nor a sense of injustice. From him I learned what goodness in a man, in a community, and in a world could conceivably be. I am so sorry, Dad, you are not here to read these pages; but I know you knew what they would say.

Washington, D.C.
May 25, 2003

Notes

1: Project FUBELT: "Formula for Chaos"

1. Establishing an "action task force," Kissinger informed Nixon, was a top priority to overcome the handicap of "bureaucratic resistance," particularly from a timid State Department. See Memorandum for the President, "Chile," September 17, 1970.
2. FU was the CIA's designated cryptonym for Chile; BELT appeared to infer the political and economic strangulation operations the CIA intended to conduct to assure Allende never reached Chile's presidential office. In 1975, when this document was shown to the Church Committee, the code name remained classified.
3. Abigail McCarthy describes arrangements for this secret meeting in her book, *Private Faces, Public Places* (New York: Doubleday, 1972).
4. *CIA Activities in Chile*, p. 3.
5. See the U.S. Congress, Senate, Select Committee to Study Government Operations with Respect to Intelligence Activities, *Covert Action in Chile, 1963–1973*, G.P.O. December 4, 1975, p. 15.
6. House Committee on Foreign Affairs, Subcommittee on National Security Policy and Scientific Development, *Report of the Special Study Mission to Latin America*. Washington, D.C, 1970, p. 31.
7. Korry's letter is reprinted in the U.S. Congress, Senate, Select Committee to Study Government Operations with Respect to Intelligence Activities, p. 118.
8. Select Committee to Study Governmental Operations, *Alleged Assassination Plots involving Foreign Leaders*, GPO, November 20, 1975. p. 228.
9. This cable has not been declassified. Ambassador Korry provided the text to me in 1978.
10. Korry's cable is dated August 11, 1970 and was sent to John Crimmins.
11. The conclusions of NSSM 97 are quoted in *Alleged Assassination Plots Involving Foreign Leaders*, p. 229.
12. This Secret Annex is undated, but was drafted around August 9 or 10, 1970.
13. Citing the "grave" disadvantages of this "extreme option," Bureau of Inter-American Affairs officials recommended to Assistant Secretary U. Alexis Johnson

that he "opposed adoption [deleted] on the ground that its prospects of success are poor and its risks prohibitively high." See Charles Meyer to U. Alexis Johnson, "NSSM 97: Extreme Option—Overthrow Allende," August 17, 1970.

14. Hecksher was soon told to keep his opinions on coup plotting to himself; in late September, he was recalled to CIA headquarters and told to cease any objections. On October 7, he received a notice from Task Force chief David Atlee Phillips stating that the Santiago Station cables "should not contain analysis and argumentation but simply report on action taken."
15. This memorandum, sent to William Broe, demonstrates that at least one CIA analyst understood the nuances of the political realities in Chile and Latin America, and made those views known to high-ranking officials. See "Chilean Crisis," September 29, 1970.
16. Vaky to Kissinger, NSC Action Memo [Non Log], "Chile—40 Committee Meeting, Monday—September 14," September 14, 1970.
17. The Assistant Secretary for Inter-American Affairs, John Crimmins, opposed this idea as risky and unnecessary, according to a CIA chronology of "Policy Decisions Related to Our Covert Action Involvement in the September 1970 Chilean Presidential Election." Korry insisted, cabling the State Department on June 22 that "If (Allende) were to gain power, what would be our response to those who asked what we did?"
18. Korry saw grave diplomatic risks for the U.S. in directly fomenting a coup. If the military was going to move, he preferred the U.S. "to be surprised." But keeping him out of the loop on Track II plotting created its own set of problems. When Hecksher sought Korry's help in passing a message to Frei about a military solution, headquarters admonished him that such action "would be tantamount to having Korry act as unwitting agent in implementing Track II of which he is not aware and is not to be made aware."
19. The Task Force logs and "Sitreps" remained classified for thirty years. A number of them were finally released as part of the Chile Declassification Project in November 2000, albeit in heavily redacted form.
20. CIA Cable, September 29, 1970.
21. See the CIA's "Special Military Situation/Analysis Report," October 7, 1970.
22. See State Department memorandum, "Suggestions that require action. Made by Ambassador Korry on September 24." Undated.
23. See the Report of the Subcommittee on Multinational Corporations, *The International Telephone and Telegraph Company in Chile, 1970–1971*, p. 9.
24. This document is one of dozens that were leaked to columnist Jack Anderson in 1972, records that first revealed CIA covert operations against Allende, in collaboration with ITT. The revelations generated the first U.S. Congressional investigation into covert U.S. intervention in Chile, conducted by Senator Frank Church's Subcommittee on Multinational Corporations. The subcommittee produced a comprehensive staff report, *The International Telephone and Telegraph Company and Chile*, in 1973. The ITT papers were published in full in *The ITT Memos, Subversion in Chile: A Case Study of U.S. Corporate Intrigue in the Third World* (London: Spokesman Books, 1972).
25. See "Memcons of Meetings between the President and Heath, Brosio," a memorandum from Winston Lord to Henry Kissinger. Lord's memo makes it clear that the transcript of this conversation is "taken from your tapes"—a reference

to Dictaphone recordings Kissinger would make following meetings he and the president held.

26. These steps were reported in an "eyes only" October 10, 1970 cable from U. Alexis Johnson to Ambassador Korry.
27. This directive sparked an incredulous response from the chief of Station. "We find it impossible to agree with Hqs reasoning that public climate in any way approximating pre-coup situation can be engineered in press [deleted], or by rumors, whatever their method of propagation." Despite these protests, Phillips ordered Hecksher to proceed.
28. Hecksher to Headquarters, "[Viaux Solution]," October 10, 1970. In a long meeting with a high-ranking member of Chile's national police force on October 8, Hecksher was told that once the military abandoned its constitutionalist stand, "all hell would break loose, with soldiers fighting soldiers." "Was that desirable?" the officer asked the CIA chief of Station. Hecksher responded that "the U.S.G. [U.S. government] did not really care as long as resulting chaos denied Allende the presidency."
29. CIA cable 628, October 8, 1970, as cited in the Senate report on *Alleged Assassination Plots*, p. 241.
30. CIA cable from Broe to Hecksher, October 10, 1970.
31. Philips and Broe to Station, October 13, 1970.
32. Until now, the date of this meeting was not publicly known. When the Church Committee report was written in 1975, Senate investigators were denied access to Nixon's Oval Office logs and Karamessines did not remember, and could not produce documentation on the date when he met the president. For the purposes of this book, I was able to obtain President Nixon's daily diary and office logs.
33. Ambassador Korry first told me this story of his dramatic meeting with President Nixon in May 1978, when I interviewed him for a college honors thesis. He also told the story to Seymour Hersh who published it in *The Price of Power: Kissinger in the Nixon White House* (New York: Summit Books, 1983). More recently, in August 2001, he repeated a version of the story in a lengthy interview for *60 Minutes* and with German documentary filmmaker Willi Huisman.
34. Kissinger had a secretary listen in and take notes on—and then transcribe—each of his telephone conversations. When he left office in early 1977, he took all the "telcons" recording his work as national security adviser and secretary of state with him, claiming they were his private papers. In 2001, my organization, the National Security Archive, threatened to sue the State Department and the National Archives for breach of responsibility for failing to recover executive branch records in Kissinger's personal possession. The lawsuit threat forced the State Department to seek the return of these records to the government. As of June 2003, Kissinger's "telcons" had not yet been declassified. But a source with access to them described to me the content of Kissinger's October 15 conversation with Nixon, and Kissinger quoted this language in his memoirs.
35. This document, which became the initial paperwork for U.S. strategy to destabilize Allende's Popular Unity government, is further described in Chapter Two.
36. At headquarters, the CIA clearly believed a coup was imminent. On October 19, Broe and Phillips cabled Hecksher with orders not, "repeat not," to advise Wimert or Ambassador Korry of "impending coup." "Should it occur," they instructed, "COS Hecksher should appear surprised and stonewall any and all queries."

37. The description of Schneider's shooting is based on Chilean police reports, and was first published by Seymour Hersh in *The Price of Power: Kissinger in the Nixon White House*, p. 290.
38. "With this incident the die has been cast," the first special CIA report on the Schneider shooting proclaimed. "For their own personal safety Valenzuela's group will have to go ahead with their plan even if Frei resists their efforts." The second report, written the next day, noted that the plotters could not now allow Allende to become president because that would ultimately lead to their arrest. "Thus far, assassination [of Allende] has not been a serious consideration, but the shooting of Schneider has raised the stakes. The plotters are now desperate and may attempt such a move even though they do not have the expertise." See "Machine Gun Assault on General Schneider," October 22, 1970 and "A Miscellaneous Thought," October 23, 1970.
39. The existence of these lists was unknown before their declassification on November 13, 2000. They remain heavily redacted, with the names of virtually all American agents and Chilean military officials blacked out. Should they ever be declassified in full, they will provide the complete record of CIA contacts with Chilean coup plotters in the fall of 1970.
40. Wimert told Seymour Hersh that he went to General Valenzuela's house to recover the $50,000 he had provided for the kidnapping. When the general refused to return the funds, according to an extraordinary scene that Hersh revealed in his book, *The Price of Power: Kissinger in the Nixon White House*, Wimert pulled out his pistol and "just hit him once and he went and got it." See *The Price of Power*, pp. 289 and 293.
41. Korry did, in fact, ask Hecksher if the CIA had been "engaged in activities of any kind" which would support "charges that [Wimert] was involved in Schneider assassination." Pursuant to his instructions to deceive the U.S. ambassador, Hecksher, according to his October 26 report to Langley, replied that "charges could obviously be made. Since Station not involved, COS doubted that charges could be substantiated."
42. As he reviewed documents after the Track II scandal broke, Kissinger seemed well-aware that his mandate to the CIA had been specific to shutting down the Viaux plot, rather than all of Track II. According to a recently declassified SECRET/NODIS White House memorandum of conversation dated July 9, 1975, Kissinger privately assured President Gerald Ford that "We are okay on this Chile thing. There is a document which shows that I turned off contact with the group which was tied to the kidnapping."
43. Kissinger's still secret deposition is quoted in *Alleged Assassination Plots*, pp. 247, 252.
44. White House, Memorandum of Conversation between President Ford and Kissinger, June 5, 1975. On assassination, Kissinger pointed out, "This is sort of a phenomenon of the Kennedys."
45. During his secret deposition before the Church Committee on August 15, 1975, Haig made it clear that he was obliged to share all CIA information on Track II with Kissinger. "At that time," he told the Committee, "I would consider I had no degree of latitude, other than to convey to him what had been given to me." See *Alleged Assassination Plots*, p. 250.
46. An early Track II log entry, dated October 7, 1970 noted that Viaux "has been

in contact with and has allegedly received support from a number of officers in the Army, Navy, Air Force, and Carabineros."

47. The actual CIA documents recording this payoff—requests, authorizations, financial transfer records, and identities of the assassins who were paid—continue to be classified.

2: Destabilizing Democracy: The United States and the Allende Government.

1. "HAK Talking Points on Chile, NSC Meeting—Thursday, November 6," p. 5.
2. Kissinger actually arranged for the NSC meeting to be postponed from November 5, when it was originally scheduled, to November 6 so he would have time to lobby the president. The original draft of Kissinger's briefing paper for Nixon, written by Viron Vaky, did not include the language pressing Nixon to make sure the National Security Council understood that coexistence was unacceptable. In a rewrite, Kissinger had Vaky add the emphatic passages on the importance of the decision Nixon faced, and the need to prevent a "drift" toward a modus vivendi. See Vaky's original transmission of the "text of memo for the President's book for the NSC Meeting" to Kissinger, November 3, 1970.
3. "HAK Talking Points on Chile, NSC Meeting—Thursday, November 6," p. 4.
4. See Briefing Memorandum, for the NSC Meeting on Chile, Thursday, November 5, 1970, written by ARA acting director Robert Hurwitch and Arthur Hartman of the Policy Coordination Office.
5. The Director of the Office of Emergency Preparedness, Gen. George Lincoln, pointed out to the president that it would be against the law to dump stockpiled U.S. copper unless it was to stabilize, as opposed to destabilize, the market price.
6. Memorandum from Haig to Tom Huston, October 22, 1970.
7. See Kissinger's Secret/Sensitive Memorandum for the President, "Status Report on Chile" that transmitted NSDM 93 as an attachment. The document is undated, but written shortly after November 9, when NSDM was finalized.
8. See *Covert Action in Chile, 1963–1973*, p. 35.
9. Economic statistics on the drop in loans and assistance to Chile are provided in *Covert Action in Chile, 1963–1973*, pp. 33, 34.
10. "Status Report on Chile," ca. November 9, 1970, p. 4.
11. CIA, "Covert Action Program in Chile," November 17, 1970.
12. This two-page analysis from the covert division of the CIA is dated October 21, the day before the Schneider shooting. It made two other key points: first, Allende would not seek "to make Chile a Soviet vassal . . . or submit to Soviet domination." Second, Allende's election would have a salient and arguably positive impact on revolutionary insurrection in Latin America, undercutting the feared influence of Castro's Cuba. "Allende's election will probably repudiate the Cuban and Chinese revolutionary approach to gaining power," the analyst observed.
13. See "Minutes of the Meeting of the 40 Committee, 13 November 1970," dated November 17, 1970. Broe responded that "such acquisition has commenced."
14. In the CIA's version of these 40 Committee meeting minutes, the majority of section d. is deleted. But in an identical State Department version, this passage was left uncensored except for the amount of escudos in the contingency fund.

15. See Korry's special cable, designated for the CIA's Western Hemisphere chief, William Broe, and Assistant Secretary Meyer, based on talks with "key officers" of the PDC, dated December 4, 1970.
16. The dates and descriptions of 40 Committee approvals can be found in "Chronology of 40 Committee Action on Chile," undated, that was declassified as part of the NARA papers on November 13, 2000.
17. *Covert Action in Chile, 1963–1973*, p. 31.
18. The discussion on *El Mercurio* funding is contained in Chronology of 40 Committee Action on Chile, under the entry for September 9, 1971.
19. A close reading of declassified White House records shows that a second 40 Committee appropriation for *El Mercurio* was made in October 1971. For unexplained reasons, the amount and details of this allotment have been completely censored. It is possible that covert funding for the paper reached closer to $2 million.
20. See Shackley's memo to Helms, "Request for Additional Funds for *El Mercurio*," April 10, 1972. Shackley replaced William Broe who was promoted to, of all posts, CIA inspector general. For a comprehensive biography of Shackley's legendary CIA career, including his involvement in this period of covert operations in Chile, see David Corn's *Blond Ghost: Ted Shackley and the CIA's Crusades* (New York: Simon & Schuster, 1994).
21. The budget breakdown of what $965,000 would pay for is entirely blacked out from CIA records and one NSC memo to Kissinger dated April 10, 1972; but in a second Top Secret memo from aide Peter Jessup dated the same day, "Chile—Request for Additional Funds for *El Mercurio*," describes how the funds would be allocated.
22. NSC Action Memorandum, "40 Committee Meeting—Chile," April 10, 1972. This secret/sensitive/eyes only memo from Jorden to Kissinger is marked "outside system" to prevent it from being distributed to files other than Kissinger's.
23. See Document X, in Chapter 4.
24. See Chief of Station Cable to Chief, Western Hemisphere Division, "Limitations in Military Effort," November 12, 1971. Headquarters made it clear that, given the Schneider debacle, the Station did not have yet have the green light to attempt to directly stimulate a military coup.
25. See "Foreign Political Matters—Chile" from the FBI director, attn. Dr. Henry A. Kissinger, March 29, 1972.
26. One of the State Department's Bureau of Intelligence and Research officials who attended this meeting, James Gardner, wrote a detailed memorandum for the record that reveals the information censored from this section. U.S. officials, he noted, considered it unlikely that the United States would be "asked to help in preparing or delivering a coup." But "it is more likely that we would be asked for assurances in advance of a planned coup that the United States would provide assistance to the new regime after it came to power." During the meeting, as Gardner recorded, CIA officials argued that "the anticipated degree and quality of U.S. support would be so important to [the Chilean military] that it would regard as essential generous and specific promises of U.S. support." See "U.S. Reaction to Possible Approach by Chilean Coup Plotters," October 30, 1972.
27. See Jack Anderson, "Memos Bare ITT Try for Chile Coup," in the *Washington Post*, March 21, 1972, p. B13.

28. A former staff member of the committee provided internal documents from the Senate Foreign Relations Committee to me.
29. See the U.S. Congress, Senate, Committee on Foreign Relations, Subcommittee on Multinational Corporations, The International Telephone and Telegraph Company and Chile, 1970–71, Committee Print, Washington D.C.: GPO, 1973.
30. The fourteen-page transcript of the March 23 State Department press conference was circulated as a cable titled "Noon Briefing Session re Chile-ITT Allegations."
31. This exchange was discovered on the declassified Nixon tapes at the National Archives in College Park, Md., and provided to me by archivist John Powers. By the time of the ITT revelations, Kissinger's staff had become extremely concerned about keeping Korry from spilling the beans after he left the Santiago embassy in mid-1971. In a secret memo for Kissinger, Haig advised that Secretary of State William Rogers was considering firing Korry and forcing him to retire from the foreign service. This might create a problem, Haig warned. "He holds a great many secrets, including the fact that the President both directly and through you communicated to him some extremely sensitive guidance. I can think of nothing more embarrassing to the Administration than thrusting a former columnist who is totally alienated from the President and yourself . . . out into the world without a means of livelihood. This can only lead to revelations which could be exploited by a hungry Democratic opposition to a degree that we might not have heretofore imagined." Haig advised Kissinger to intercede to assure that Korry was offered another post to "insure" Korry's loyalty. See Haig to Kissinger, "Ambassador Korry," March 10, 1971.
32. In April 1972, OPIC president Bradford Mills asked the CIA whether ITT activities had been carried out in Chile at the behest of the CIA and whether the CIA knew what ITT had done in Chile "to prevent the Allende government from taking office or from coming into being in 1970." These questions were discussed with CIA director Richard Helms who authorized a set of blatantly false answers: "ITT did nothing at our request. We do not know what activities ITT has [undertaken to block Allende]." This deception is recorded in a declassified memorandum for CIA general counsel titled "CIA's Replies to Queries from the Overseas Private Investment Corporation in Connection with the International Telephone and Telegraph Insurance Claim," October 31, 1974.
33. See Hanke's Memorandum of Conversation, "Meeting with Hal Hendrix," 11 May 1972. David Corn discovered this document and first revealed it in his book, *Blond Ghost: Ted Shackley and the CIA's Crusades*, p. 245.
34. The Justice Department would later indict both Gerrity and Berellez on charges of perjury, conspiracy, and obstruction of government proceedings. Prior to trial, however, both resorted to "graymail"—threatening to reveal covert secrets about CIA operations in Chile if they were prosecuted. The Carter administration's Attorney General Griffin Bell then decided to drop all charges.
35. At the end of his appearance before the committee, Senator Church suspected that Meyer had not been truthful. "I don't want you to take personal offense," the chairman told Meyer to his face. "But it is obvious, based upon the sworn testimony that we have received to date, that somebody is lying. We must take a very serious view of perjury under oath." For Meyer's complete testimony see the U.S. Congress, Senate, Committee on Foreign Relations, Subcommittee on

Multinational Corporations, *Multinational Corporations and United States Foreign Policy,* Part 1, 93rd Congress, March 20–April 4, 1973, (GPO: Washington D.C., 1973), pp. 398–428.

36. Helms understood that the Anderson columns would create serious problems for the CIA. When he learned their publication was imminent, he arranged for a secret meeting with Jack Anderson on March 17, "to try to dissuade Mr. Anderson from publishing certain classified information," according to an overview of the perjury case against Helms written by Justice Department lawyer Robert Andary.
37. Helms apparently incurred Nixon's wrath by not being sufficiently cooperative in using the CIA to obstruct the Watergate investigation.
38. Levison to Fulbright, "Helms Executive Session, 2/7/73."
39. For a comprehensive story on Helms and the perjury case against him see Richard Harris, "Secrets," in *The New Yorker*, April 10, 1978.
40. See minutes of ARA-CIA Meeting, 14 September 1973, 11:00.
41. Station to Headquarters, cable on Election Results and Aftermath, March 14, 1973.
42. See CIA memorandum, "Policy Objectives for Chile," April 17, 1973.
43. At a CIA-ARA meeting on May 30, 1973, State Department officials raised this question: "do we want to continue to involve ourselves in this kind of business, especially in view of the domestic atmosphere in the US and the alertness of the Chilean Government to the possibility that we were engaged in activities of this sort." Referring to the Church Committee hearings on ITT, Deputy Assistant Secretary John Crimmins advocated continued covert support for Chile's political parties but "said that we must however admit that there were now more vulnerabilities affecting our assistance then there had been, especially in the US and Chile. It was necessary that we be clear about the risk we are taking." The new Assistant Secretary for Inter-American Affairs, Jack Kubisch, voiced his "inclination" to "let the [CIA] program come to an end, and not to recommend its continuation."
44. CIA cable, May 2, 1973.
45. See the Station's "[Deleted] Progress Report—1 April–30 June 1973."
46. On September 16, 1973, a source high in the Chilean military supplied the CIA with a detailed account of how the takeover plan evolved. On Pinochet's role, the account is at odds with other histories that suggest that one of the leading coup plotters, Col. Arellano Stark, briefed Pinochet for the first time on coup plotting on September 8.
47. Winters was interviewed by Vernon Loeb of the *Washington Post* for a profile on Jack Devine, "Spook Story," which appeared in the Style section on September 17, 2000.
48. See minutes of the ARA/CIA Meeting, 7 September 1973, 11:00 dated September 11, 1973.
49. For years, the circumstances of Allende's death remained a point of political and historical contention. In his situation report, Lt. Col. Patrick Ryan claimed "he had killed himself by placing a submachine gun under his chin and pulling the trigger. Messy, but efficient." Michael Townley, the fugitive Patria y Libertad operative, told State Department official David Stebbing after the coup that "Allende did not commit suicide," but suffered "fatal wounds" to the chest and

stomach that might have come from the shelling of the Moneda. The Chilean military attaché to Venezuela told the Defense Intelligence Agency that Allende had agreed to surrender, only to be executed by his own guards for being a coward. For years, conventional wisdom among those who opposed the coup was that Allende had been shot by troops storming his office. After civilian governance was reinstated in 1990, Allende's family agreed to resolve the controversy by allowing a forensic examination of his remains. The scientific conclusion was that, rather than surrender, he had indeed committed suicide as Chilean military forces surrounded his office.

50. See Karamessines testimony quoted in U.S. Congress, Senate, Select Committee to Study Government Operations with Respect to Intelligence Activities, *Alleged Assassination Plots Involving Foreign Leaders* (Washington, D.C.: 1975), p. 254.
51. Kissinger Telcon transcript, September 16, 1973. Nixon remained convinced that the "people" would not be persuaded by "this crap from the Liberals" about the immorality of U.S. support for Allende's overthrow. "They know it is a pro-Communist government and that is the way it is," he told Kissinger. "Exactly. And pro-Castro," Kissinger agreed. "Let's forget the pro-Communist," Nixon suggested, citing Allende's ultimate sin. "It was an anti-American government all the way."

3: Pinochet in Power: Building a Regime of Repression.

1. There was no complete tally of post-coup victims until after Pinochet stepped down in 1990 and the new civilian government appointed a National Commission on Truth and Reconciliation (known as the Rettig Commission) to record the names and circumstances of all victims of his regime.
2. Chinese Premier Zhou Enlai prompted this report. In a private meeting in Peking on November 13, 1973, according to a TOP SECRET/SENSITIVE/EXCLUSIVELY EYES ONLY memcon, Zhou protested to Kissinger about Pinochet's ongoing bloodshed. "Could you exercise some influence on Chile?" Zhou asked. "They shouldn't go in for slaughtering that way. It was terrible . . . hundreds of bodies were thrown out of the stadium." Kissinger responded that: "We have exercised considerable influence, and we believe that after the first phase when they seized power there have been no executions with which we are familiar going on now. I will look into the matter again when we return [to Washington] and I will inform you." Kissinger then ordered his deputy, Winston Lord to "get [assistant secretary Jack] Kubisch to check on this."
3. CIA cable, October 27, 1973.
4. Ibid. The CIA noted that the regime had decided to clear the stadium camp of prisoners "to allow time for preparations for the World Cup soccer match between Chile and the USSR to be held there in late November."
5. See the Report of the National Commission on Truth and Reconciliation, known as the Rettig Commission Report, p. 140. (English Ed.: Notre Dame, Indiana: University of Notre Dame Press, 1993).
6. For a full discussion of the Horman and Teruggi cases, see Chapter 5, "American Casualties."
7. The Report of the Chilean National Commission on Truth and Reconciliation provided a detailed tally and analysis of human rights atrocities committed during the dictatorship.

8. Quoted in Genaro Arriagada, *Pinochet: the Politics of Power* (Boston: Unwin Hyman), p. 9.
9. In a March 21, 1974 secret analysis, "Aspects of the Situation in Chile," the CIA reported on how Pinochet and his army decided not to share the leadership of the Junta with the other services.
10. During the Chile Declassification Project, the CIA pointedly refused to declassify Pinochet's "201" file, where the highest-level intelligence reporting on his personality and actions, as well as the U.S. relationship with him, would be found.
11. Davis left Chile shortly after this meeting. He was replaced as ambassador by David Popper.
12. The members of General Arellano's squad involved in the executions were: Lt. Col. Sergio Arredondo; Maj. Pedro Espinoza; Capt. Marcelo Moren Brito; Lt. Armando Fernández Larios; and Lt. Juan Chiminelli Fullerton. The Puma helicopter was piloted by Capt. Sergio de la Mahotier.
13. A chapter on each massacre is provided by Chilean investigative reporter Patricia Verdugo in her book *Chile, Pinochet and the Caravan of Death*, (Miami, North-South Center Press, 2001).
14. Lagos kept the original report he had written, and thirteen years later emerged as a principal witness in the Caravan of Death cases. He provided an affidavit in July 1986 in the first legal efforts to hold Pinochet accountable for these atrocities. He also provided a deposition to the Spanish investigation into these crimes in 1998. Because fourteen of the victims of the Caravan were never found, their families were able to file suit against General Stark and Pinochet, drawing on evidence that Lagos provided, on the grounds that disappearances were not covered by the amnesty laws Pinochet had decreed for the military to provide immunity for human rights crimes committed between 1973–1978. Rather they should be treated as unresolved kidnappings and ongoing crimes. Under this reinterpretation of the amnesty decree, Stark became the first prominent Chilean general to be indicted and arrested for human rights crimes in Chile.
15. Report of the National Commission on Truth and Reconciliation, p. 146.
16. This information is contained in Stark's DIA biographic data report dated January 5, 1975.
17. DIA, Official Decree on the Creation of the National Intelligence Directorate (DINA), July 2, 1974.
18. For an insider's description of the initial reaction to Contreras's proposal, see Mary Helen Spooner, *Soldiers in a Narrow Land: The Pinochet Regime in Chile* (Berkeley: University of California Press, 1999) p. 115.
19. SENDET was officially established at the end of December 1973; the DIA reported on it a several weeks later. See DIA report, "National Executive Secretariat for Detainees, Establishment of," January 21, 1974.
20. See Hon's report to DIA, "DINA and CECIFA, Internal and the Treatment of Detainees," February 5, 1974.
21. See Hon's DIA report, "DINA, Its Operations and Power," February 8, 1974.
22. Ibid.
23. See Chapter 4 for a full discussion of the CIA's relations with DINA.
24. This assessment was written after Contreras was removed as DINA chieftain. See Department of Defense Intelligence Information Report, "Brigadier General

Juan Manuel Contreras Sepúlveda, Chilean Army—Biographic Report," February 28, 1978.

25. The gruesome, ruthless procedures at Tejas Verdes became a model for other detention-torture camps created by DINA. Prisoners were transported, and often left in locked refrigerated trucks that the military had expropriated from the fish industry. Hooded doctors supervised torture sessions to assure that the prisoner would not expire before his or her interrogation was completed. "Many people died there," the Rettig Commission noted, "or were taken from there to meet their death." For an extensive description of the Tejas Verdes camp, see the Report of the Chilean National Commission on Truth and Reconciliation, p. 134.
26. Descriptions of these facilities are drawn from ibid, pp. 483–490.
27. The Villa Grimaldi property was transformed into a "park for peace" after Pinochet stepped down. Its buildings were torn down; pieces of them were used to create monuments to the atrocities committed there. In April 1999, the author was given a private tour of the facility by a former political prisoner held there, Pedro Alejandro Matta. In an effort to "transform history into memory" and assure that what happened at Villa Grimaldi will not be forgotten, Matta has written and published a visitors' guide, *Villa Grimaldi: A Walk Through a 20th Century Torture Center.*
28. See Pedro Matta's description of this technique in ibid, p. 14.
29. Disappearances became a grotesque form of repression in every military regime in the Southern Cone during the mid and late 1970s. One Argentine woman, whose husband, four daughters, and two son-in-laws were all disappeared, captured the unique suffering such methods inflicted. "The disappearance of a person leaves those who loved him [or her] with a sensation of permanent and irreversible anguish," Elsa Oesterheld told the *New York Times.* "Even though you have the conviction that they are dead, they're not really dead to you because you have no proof. To this day, I do not have any death certificates." See "Argentine Default Reopens 'Dirty War' Wounds," *New York Times,* March 12, 2002.
30. See the CIA's Top Secret "Latin American Trends, Annex, Staff Notes," February 11, 1976, p. 2.
31. Rogers made this remark after a briefing on Contreras's visit to the CIA. See ARA/CIA Weekly Meeting, July 11, 1975, Memorandum for the Record, July 14, 1975.
32. See London's *Sunday Telegraph,* July 18, 1999.
33. When Col. Hon, the Defense Attaché, asked his source why DINA reported only to Pinochet when it originally was supposed to answer to the entire Junta, the informant replied: "That's too sensitive to discuss, even with you." See DIA Information Report, "DINA & CECIFA," February 5, 1974.
34. See the Embassy report, "Chile's Government After Two Years: Political Appraisal," October 14, 1975.
35. On September 30, 1975, the CIA Station filed a comprehensive report on the meetings and decisions that led to Pinochet's decrees to expand DINA's powers.
36. In 1979, the CIA briefed a special Senate Subcommittee on International Operations on DINA's activities and shared intelligence on Chile's efforts to establish bases abroad, and in Miami. The SECRET/SENSITIVE report of the Subcommittee, titled "Staff Report on Activities of Certain Intelligence Agencies in the United States," remains classified, but I was able to obtain a typed transcript of the section on Chile.

37. For an extraordinarily detailed overview of Townley's life leading up to his enrollment in the DINA, see Chapter 4, "Condor's Jackal," of John Dinges and Saul Landau's book, *Assassination on Embassy Row.*
38. The director of the CIA's Office of Security, Robert Gambino, provided a sworn affidavit in the Letelier-Moffitt case relating to the history of the CIA's interest in Townley. See his Affidavit, November 9, 1978.
39. See Embassy cable, "DINA, Human Rights in Chile, and Chile's Image Abroad," April 7, 1976.
40. See Dinges and Landau, *Assassination on Embassy Row*, p. 132.
41. John Dinges and Saul Landau obtained Ines Callejas's 60-page handwritten manuscript and used it extensively in Chapters 4 and 5 of their book, *Assassination on Embassy Row.* For this quote see page 130.
42. In his prison letters, Townley referred to "Andrea" and voiced fears that investigators would come to "know of a bacteriological lab." In one letter, dated September 2, 1979, Townley wrote to his DINA contact that an investigator had "asked me if I knew of a girl named Andrea." "I shrugged my shoulders," Townley reported. "It was going to happen; I always knew. Since so much time had passed I thought maybe [Andrea] would have passed without notice. But it seems there was not that level of luck." See *Labyrinth*, pp. 317, 318.
43. Townley told the FBI that he turned down this request because of the "unstable nature" of the CNM representatives, Guillermo Novo and Virgilio Paz.
44. The shipment of this deadly nerve gas aboard two LANCHILE flights put hundreds of passengers at risk. In 1982 the FAA launched an investigation into DINA's use of the airline to transport hazardous materials in violation of international aviation regulations. No penalties were ever levied against the carrier, even though LANCHILE pilots knowingly facilitated DINA's overseas operations by ferrying bomb components abroad.
45. See the DIA report, "Covert Countersubversive Activities in Chile," November 29, 1977.
46. CIA, [deleted title], November 9, 1977.
47. See the Commission's detailed assessment of the CNI, pp. 635–645.

4: Consolidating Dictatorship: The United States and the Pinochet Regime.

1. Pinochet's request for this meeting was conveyed to Washington by the CIA on the morning of September 12 as part of a "situation report" on the progress of the coup. For Davis's memcon on the Pinochet-Urrutia meeting, see "Gen. Pinochet's Request for Meeting with MILGP Officer," September 12, 1973.
2. Secret cable to the White House Situation Room, "FMS Sales to FACH," September 15, 1973.
3. Ibid.
4. "Chilean Request for Detention Center Advisor and Equipment," September 28, 1973.
5. See "Secretary's Staff Meeting," October 1, 1973. The next day, according to the transcript for October 2, Kissinger and his staff joked about how other Latin American diplomats would perceive the presence of the Junta's new foreign min-

ister, Admiral Ismael Huerta, at a Washington lunch Kissinger was hosting for Latin American diplomats. Assistant Secretary Kubisch warned Kissinger that "your behavior with him will be watched very closely by the others to see whether or not you are blessing the new regime in Chile, or whether it is just protocol." The conversation then continued: Kissinger: "What will be the test? How will they judge?" Kubisch: "I suppose if you give him warm *abrazos* [hugs], sitting next to you, and huddling in the corner, that will all be reported back to their governments." [Laughter] Kissinger: "What the secretary of state has to do for the national interest!"

6. See the secret memorandum of conversation on "Secretary's Meeting with Foreign Minister Carvajal," September 29, 1975, p. 8.
7. Analysis of U.S. economic support for Pinochet can be found in the seminal work by Lars Schoultz, *Human Rights and United States Policy toward Latin America* (Princeton, N.J.: Princeton University Press, 1981), pp. 185, 186.
8. "Secretary's Meeting with Foreign Minister Carvajal," p. 5.
9. Popper's twenty-six-page policy review is titled "The Situation in Chile and the Prospects for US Policy." See pp. 19,20.
10. The Chilean military requests for lethal weapons are described in a memorandum from ARA Assistant Secretary Jack Kubisch, "Supply of Lethal Military Items to Chile," December 5, 1973.
11. See Schoultz, p. 186. See also the *New York Times*, October 16, 1977.
12. CIA cable from headquarters, September 18, 1973.
13. The addresses of CIA officials posing as embassy officers were obtained from the telephone directory, Embassy of United States of America, Santiago, Chile; October 1971 edition.
14. CIA cable, October 3, 1973. Phillips advised Warren to "concoct some plausible story why materials not available" at this time.
15. The purchase of these media outlets, probably a chain of radio Stations, is discussed in several declassified CIA and State Department documents dated October 1973.
16. The Church Committee report, p. 40.
17. See the memo for the chief, Western Hemisphere Division, "[Deleted] Project," January 9, 1974.
18. Enrique Krauss, a congressman at the time of the coup, later became the first Interior Minister under the first post-Pinochet president, Patricio Aylwin. Hamilton was a senator from Valparaiso; Pedro Jesus Rodriguez was Frei's former minister of justice.
19. CIA memorandum, "Project [Deleted] Amendment No. 1 for FY 1973 and Renewal for FY 1974," November 29, 1973.
20. See "Request for [$160,000] for Chilean Christian Democratic Party (PDC)." Undated.
21. Gardner's memo, classified SECRET/SENSITIVE., is titled "Covert Assistance to the PDC in Chile," and shows a handwritten date of February 1974.
22. "Request for [$160,000] for Chilean Christian Democratic Party, January 7, 1974, p. 6.
23. See Popper's cable, "Assistance to the Christian Democratic Party," February 27, 1974. Popper did stress, however, that if a breach developed between the PDC and Pinochet, the U.S. would stand on Pinochet's side. "The chance exists that

the relationship may become openly antagonistic at some point in the future. *In these circumstances we would not want to be linked to the PDC, even as to past actions, at any point in the post-coup period.*" (Emphasis added)

24. Davis to Kubisch via CIA channel, May 3, 1974.
25. According to a "termination" memorandum from David Atlee Phillips to the CIA's associate deputy director for operations, the final payment to the Christian Democrats was not actually made until August 20, 1974. See "Project [deleted] Amendment No. 1 for FY 1974 and Termination," April 25, 1975.
26. Author interview.
27. See John Dinges and Saul Landau, *Assassination on Embassy Row*, p. 126. A former DINA official told Dinges that he had seen CIA manuals of instruction and procedure being used for operations. "I thought he [Contreras] was some kind of genius to have built up such a large, complicated apparatus in such a short time," this source said. "Then I found out how much help he got from the CIA in organizing it."
28. Covert Operations in Chile, 1963–1973, p. 40.
29. See Lucy Komisar, "Into the Murky Depths of Operation Condor," *Los Angeles Times*, November 1, 1998.
30. The CIA briefer to the ARA meetings provided State Department officials with a lengthy description of the Contreras-Walters meeting at the ARA-CIA weekly meeting on July 11, 1975.
31. The CIA continues to hide details of this meeting. A one-page attachment to this memo was withheld from declassification in its entirety.
32. Fimbres recorded the meeting in a comprehensive memorandum of conversation, titled after all the subjects they discussed, "UNGA, Economic Situation; the Disappeared 119; the GOC's Image Abroad; Willoughby," August 24, 1975.
33. State Department memo, "Contreras-Salzberg Conversation," August 26, 1975. Contreras told Salzberg that DINA "now makes only a few arrests each day, and is the sole agency arresting and interrogating political prisoners," as if that represented an achievement in improving human rights abuses in Chile.
34. In a 1979 FBI interview, Walters shared little information about the purpose of the meetings. He said that "part of his function as deputy director of the CIA was to coordinate and conduct foreign liaison for the CIA and within that framework he had received General Contreras in 1975." In an interview given while in prison in 1999 to Chilean journalist Rodrigo Frey, Contreras was far more verbose. He claimed that Walters had proposed placing CIA agents within DINA, similar to the deployment of CIA Cuban-American agents working in DISIP, the Venezuelan intelligence service. This, according to Contreras, explained why he traveled from Washington to Caracas at the end of August 1975. He also claimed that Walters had recommended recruiting five presumably retired senators as lobbyists for Chile in the Congress, at the cost of $2 million a year. Until the meeting memcons are declassified there is no way to fully evaluate these seemingly dubious claims.
35. Author interviews. Over the course of several meetings, this source repeated that Burton had one particular project in which Contreras's collaboration was deemed critical.
36. Townley letter to Gustavo Echavere, June 29, 1979. Townley wrote this letter to his DINA handler from a U.S. prison after being turned over to the FBI by Chilean authorities for his role in the Letelier-Moffitt assassination. All of his

letters were copied by the secretary of his lawyer before being sent, and eventually were obtained by authors Taylor Branch and Eugene Propper for the book on the Letelier case, *Labyrinth.*

37. Author interviews.
38. The timing of this deposit makes it likely that it was, in fact, the CIA payment to Contreras. The July 21, 1975 deposit was the only substantive transaction to the account in almost ten years. After the U.S. identified Contreras in the Letelier assassination, and arrested the Cuban exile terrorists who collaborated with DINA, however, he transferred $20,000 from a mysterious Panamanian brokerage account in the name of Sudhi S.A. in New York to his private account in Washington. Two months later, in December 1978, he arranged for the husband of a Lan-Chile employee based in Florida to withdraw $25,000 in cash from the account. FBI investigators later told John Dinges and Saul Landau that they believed the money was used to pay the defense lawyers for the Cuban coconspirators.
39. Author interview. The source for this account did not reveal Warren's identity, which was obtained independently. The CIA has refused to declassify any of the cable traffic, or administrative records relating to putting Contreras on the payroll, taking him off the payroll, and making the one payment to him in the summer of 1975.
40. See the *Washington Post,* "CIA had Covert Tie to Letelier Plotter; Contreras Masterminded Bombing," September 20, 2000.
41. Memorandum for the Record, July 29, 1975. "ARA/CIA Weekly Meeting, 25 July 1975."
42. Colby's actual testimony has never been declassified. See U.S. Congress, House, Special Subcommittee on Intelligence, *Inquiry into Matters Regarding Classified Testimony taken on April 22, 1974 Regarding the CIA and Chile,* 93rd Cong., 2nd sess., September 25, 1974, pp. 31–37.
43. The memorandum on official perjury, titled "Subcommittee Hearings—ITT & Chile and Report of Colby Testimony before the Nedzi House Subcommittee," was written early September 1974. It circulated through the Senate Foreign Relations Committee and was subsequently leaked to Lawrence Stern of the *Washington Post,* causing a huge public uproar, and behind-the-scenes controversy on Capitol Hill. In a phone call to Levinson, Senator Church told him that Secretary Kissinger had contacted the Senate minority leader, Hugh Scott, and demanded Levinson be fired. Until the publication of the Hersh article, "nobody wanted to touch it. Nobody!," Levinson recalls. "I never understood why Congress appeared to be more concerned over leaks than lying," he said, "just as they are today."
44. See *Years of Renewal,* pp. 313, 320.
45. In an October 31, 1975, memo titled "Background on Covert Operations in Chile," Marsh attached a transcript of Ford's September 16 press conference, highlighting his denial of any U.S. involvement in the coup and directing him to review Tab A. But when the Gerald Ford Library submitted Tab A to the CIA for review as part of the Chile Declassification Project in 1999, the document was withheld in its entirety from release.
46. The report Kissinger refers to was the CIA's "family jewels" report—a seventy-page compilation of 693 episodes of covert illegal and illicit operations—put together at the request of Colby's predecessor, James Schlesinger. This report was

leaked to Hersh and served as the basis for much of his extraordinary reporting on CIA domestic spying and assassination operations. The Schneider plot was not in the family jewels report, although one CIA official in Mexico had submitted several memos regarding CIA ties to that plot to headquarters in response to Schlesinger's request.

47. *Years of Renewal*, p. 313.
48. "What counts is official acknowledgement," Rogers wrote Kissinger. "We can live, although uncomfortably, with unsubstantiated revelations. . . . Latin Americans have had a full dose of such stories from the Marxists in any case. But when past intervention is confirmed by Congressional expose or Executive admission the Latins can do no less than respond with shock and suspicion." See Rogers to Kissinger, "CIA Investigations and Latin America," February 28, 1975.
49. See "The Secretary's Principals' and Regionals' Staff Meeting, Monday, July 14, 1975, 8:00 A.M.." p. 36. During the meeting Kissinger was adamant that "We cannot turn over all cables on a subject to any Congressional committee" because "it's going to set the most awful precedent."
50. See Johnson's comprehensive account, *A Season of Inquiry: The Senate Intelligence Investigation* (Lexington: University of Kentucky Press, 1985), pp. 46, 47.
51. White House Decision Memorandum, "Senate Select Committee Plans for Open Hearing on Covert Actions in Chile," November 1, 1975.
52. See Hearings before the Select Committee to Study Government Operations with Respect to Intelligence Activities of the United States Senate, 94th Cong., 1st sess; *Covert Action*, December 4, 5, 1975, pp. 1,2.
53. See *Years of Upheaval*, p. 411.
54. Conversation with President Pinochet, January 3, 1975.
55. The first of these publications, "Chile: Key Target of Soviet Diplomacy," was written by James Theberge, whom Ronald Reagan would name U.S. Ambassador to Chile in 1982.
56. Information on the history and illegal practices of the ACC is drawn from the submission of evidence seized by Justice Department agents from Liebman's office and submitted in court proceedings on December 18, 1978. See also the *Washington Post*, "Justice Department Says Group Illegally Lobbies for Chile Dictator," December 19, 1978.
57. Lars Schoultz attributes this attitude to Kissinger in his detailed discussion of the Ford administration's resistance to limits on military aid to Chile. See his *Human Rights and United States Policy toward Latin America*, p. 255.
58. The Gerald Ford presidential library declassified the notes of this meeting, written by Scowcroft, on February 20, 2002 pursuant to a request by the author. The notes bear the heading, *P/K*—reference to President and Kissinger. In the margins, Scowcroft recorded a question "Can we do anything on Chile," and then the answer, presumably from Kissinger: "Do *all* we can." (Emphasis in original)
59. "The Secretary's Principals' and Regionals' Staff Meeting," Friday, December 20, 1974, 8:00 A.M.., p. 31.
60. "The Secretary's Principals' and Regionals' Staff Meeting," Monday, December 23, 1974, 8:00 A.M.., p. 30,31.
61. Ibid.
62. See Popper's cable, "Conversation with President Pinochet," January 3, 1975.

63. See the memcon of "Secretary's Meeting with Foreign Minister Carvajal," September 29, 1975, p. 1.
64. See the transcript of Kissinger's breakfast meeting with Carvajal, May 8, 1975.
65. See the embassy's "Country Analysis and Strategy Paper, Chile 1976, 77," May 18, 1975, p. 5.
66. NSC action memorandum, "Disarray in Chile Policy," July 1, 1975.
67. See Boyatt's cable, "Secretary's Travel to OASGA," April 21, 1976.
68. See Popper's SECRET, EXDIS Cable, Biographic Sketch—General Augusto Pinochet Ugarte, May 27, 1976.
69. Rogers to Kissinger, "Overall Objectives for Your Visit to Santiago," May 26, 1976.
70. Henry Kissinger, *Years of Renewal* (New York: Simon & Schuster, 1999), p. 758.

5: American Casualties.

1. CBS News reporter Frank Manitzas, accompanied by the *Washington Post*'s Southern Cone correspondent, Joanne Omang, taped their interviews with Gonzalez; in August, Manitzas provided the tape to the State Department where it was transcribed as "The Second Interview, Tuesday, June 8, 1976, in the Italian Embassy." Omang's story on the interview appeared in the *Washington Post* on June 10, 1976; a follow-up *Post* story titled "The Man who Knew too Much," appeared on June 20. Gonzalez's taped comments were also cited by Thomas Hauser in his comprehensive book on the Horman case, *The Execution of Charles Horman: An American Sacrifice* published by Harcourt, Brace, Jovanovich in 1978, reissued in paperback under the title *Missing.*
2. *Missing*, based on the Hauser book and directed by Costa-Gavras, premiered in February 1982. The movie received an Academy Award nomination for best picture and won the Oscar for best screenplay. In January 1983, former ambassador Nathaniel Davis, U.S. consul Fred Purdy and U.S. naval attaché Ray Davis sued Hauser, Costa-Gavras and Universal Pictures for $150 million for defamation of character. In July 1987 the libel claim was dropped after the judge in the case ruled that there were no legal grounds to bring it, and Universal and Costa-Gavras agreed to a joint statement saying that *Missing* was "not intended to suggest that Nathaniel Davis, Ray Davis or Frederick Purdy ordered or approved the order for the murder of Charles Horman—and would not wish viewers of the film to interpret it this way."
3. "He was shot in the stadium. I'm sorry. Things like this should not happen," a Chilean officer told Ed Horman on October 19. See "Victim's Father is Bitter at U.S. Handling of Case," *New York Times*, November 19, 1973. Pinochet's Defense and Foreign Ministries later denied they had ever admitted murdering Charles Horman.
4. Rudy Fimbres to Harry Shlaudeman, "The Charles Horman Case," July 15, 1976.
5. An October 26, 1978, memorandum from McNeil to Assistant Secretary Viron Vaky indicates that State Department lawyers wanted to keep secret the conclusion that the Chilean military had executed Horman to assist the legal defense of former U.S. officials being sued by the Horman family for wrongful death.

McNeil forcefully recommended that the U.S. government "discharge our responsibility to be more responsive to these American citizens" and issue an official statement that "there is evidence to suggest that they died while in custody" of the Chilean military. Such a statement was never issued. The lawyers also objected to declassifying the suggestion that CIA and/or DOD intelligence agents might have played a role in Horman's death on the grounds that it was speculative opinion. In a December 28, 1978 memorandum, McNeil suggested "the Department of State is better off releasing everything it possibly can now, rather than be forced to release later and so appear to be 'covering up.' Lastly, the material in question is natural speculation that has occurred to almost everyone who has contact with the case," he added. "It may indeed anger some in the CIA and the military, but the speculation exists and is very much in public print. (Moreover, keeping the CIA and DOD happy is not grounds for FOI [Freedom of Information Act] refusals)." McNeil was overruled and the passage was deleted and kept hidden from the families for another twenty-one years.

6. See Washington Special Action Group Meeting, Subject: Chile, September 20, 1973.
7. Father Doherty's journal, which he later provided to State Department officials, recording the graphic details of abuse and torture inside the stadium, for Chileans and numerous foreigners from at least twenty-five different nations jailed with him. Soldiers, he wrote, formed a gauntlet outside his cell. "Men were made to run this gauntlet and as they did so they were beaten by soldiers with rifle butts. One man fell down from a blow he received and was shot in the chest by a soldier . . . he died five minutes later. The soldier who shot the man blew off the end of his rifle and laughed." He also recorded hearing an hour of machine-gun and pistol fire at the far end of the stadium between 4:00 and 5:00 A.M. on the morning of September 20. "I guessed that people were being executed and that those who had not died were being [given] the coup d' grace."
8. Horman interpreted Creter's comment as an admission of U.S. involvement in the coup. Terry Simon recalled that he told her that night that "We've stumbled upon something very important." But the U.S. embassy and Creter insisted he was referring to his naval engineering assignment in Chile, which, if real, was far more mundane. A cable from the commander of the U.S. military group in Chile, Captain Ray Davis, dated August 21, 1973 to Fort Amador in the Panana Canal Zone, requested the Creter be prepared to "assist Chilean Navy in following areas" among them: "producing their own CO_2 for recharging shipboard fire extinguishers" and "recommendations concerning installation of fluorescent lighting in living spaces aboard all Chilean ships." In an interview with author Thomas Hauser several years later Creter conceded that those jobs had not been accomplished when he met Charles and Terry in Vina del Mar. Hauser also obtained through a FOIA request a consulate file card on Charles Horman that indicated that Creter had sought and provided intelligence to the embassy on Horman's visit to Vina. The card noted: "Art Creeter—15 ND [Naval Division]/ 2 checked into Miramar Hotel, Rm. 315, 2300 on 10 Sept./ used 425 Paul Harris address/ said 'escritor' left 15 Sept." Hauser interviewed Creter about this strange document and noted: "One would not normally expect to find a 'naval engineer' leafing through hotel records, and Creter has no explanation for his conduct." See *The Execution of Charles Horman*, p. 234.

9. See "Resume of Naval Mission Contacts with Charles Horman and Terry Simon during the Period 11 September–15 September 1973 Valparaiso, Chile" signed by Patrick J. Ryan, LTCOL, USMC.
10. Simon recounted this episode to author Thomas Hauser as well as wrote about it in a short memoir in the magazine *Senior Scholastic.* See *The Execution of Charles Horman*, p. 94; and *Senior Scholastic*, "American Girl in Chile's Revolution," December 6, 1973.
11. One of the peculiar aspects of the Horman case is the fact that Joyce and Charles had moved to this home on September 7, only four days before the coup—too recently for their new address to be available to Chilean or U.S. authorities. (For reasons that are unclear, Charles used his prior address when registering at the Hotel Miramar in Vina.) None of their old neighbors reported anyone looking for them prior to September 17. It is possible, as in the case of other Americans arrested, that their move on September 7 attracted the attention of coup supporters in the neighborhood who denounced them as foreigners to the new military authorities and resulted in the house being targeted for a military raid.
12. The daughter of one of Horman's neighbors happened to be leaving after visiting her mother at the time he was taken by the military. Her car followed the truck all the way to the National Stadium and she later told Joyce Horman that she saw the truck go through the stadium gates.
13. Frederick Smith, Jr., "Death in Chile of Charles Horman," p. 3. The former neighbor was a courageous woman named Isabella Carvajal. In a Spanish-language statement her husband, Mario Carvajal, stated that the military official had referred to Horman as a *Norteamericano.* According to the statement, the SIM officer ended the telephone conversation by threatening her with death if what she had told him on the phone about Horman turned out not to be true.
14. Carlotta Manosa, a close friend of the Hormans at whose home Joyce stayed on September 18 after she found her own house ransacked and Charles missing, asked a relative who worked at the embassy to inform Purdy about the SIM phone call.
15. See "Victim's Father is Bitter at U.S. Handling of Case," *New York Times*, November 29, 1973.
16. Hall was one of several vice-consuls at the embassy. His meeting with Joyce is recorded in Hauser's *The Execution of Charles Horman*, pp. 117, 118. When she asked to stay at the consulate he told her, "we have no accommodations."
17. Captain Ray Davis, head of the MilGroup, took notes on the meeting and included them in a six-page draft chronology of his contacts with Charles and Terry, and his ostensible efforts to help Joyce
18. *The Execution of Charles Horman*, p. 133. Joyce told Hauser that the ambassador had asked: "Just what do you want us to do—look under all the bleachers?" She recalls responding, "That's exactly what I want you to do, and I see nothing wrong with it."
19. See Kessler's memorandum to Rudy Fimbres, "Diuguid Article on Horman Case," July 19, 1976, and his undated letter to Frederick Purdy, written soon after.
20. *The Execution of Charles Horman*, p. 217.
21. After Horman's body was found on October 18, and the regime concocted the story that he had been shot in the street on September 18, the Foreign Ministry withdrew its October 3 statement as "an error."

22. In a rebuttal cable to Washington, Davis wrote that Purdy, and the U.S. military attaché, Colonel Hon, had a different recollection of his remarks. "According to their recollection, the Ambassador certainly never said 'that the Embassy feeling was that Charles probably was in hiding.' He may have mentioned this as a possibility." Davis himself did not offer an opinion on what he said.
23. Anderson wrote this "memorandum to the files" on October 17.
24. Dolguin lived next door to the Ford Foundation's Lowell Jarvis. Jarvis identified him to Horman only as an official from an English-speaking embassy with whom Jarvis played tennis.
25. Purdy made this statement in an unvarnished draft response to the letter Edmund Horman wrote to Congress in late October, complaining about how the embassy handled his son's case. The draft, dated November 17, 1973, was subsequently rewritten and sent as a rebuttal to the Horman letter signed by deputy chief of mission Herbert Thompson. See "Senator Javits' Interest in Horman Case," November 18, 1973.
26. State Department cable, confidential, "Approach to Foreign Office on Missing American Citizens Horman and Teruggi," October 3, 1973.
27. Ambassador Davis cabled a summary of this conversation to Washington. See "Kubisch Meeting with Minister Huerta," February 24, 1974.
28. Quoted from Horman's letter to Charles Anderson at the Office of Special Consular Services, March 27, 1974.
29. In an October 27, 1973, cable on "Disposition of Remains," the embassy reported that Sanitation officials "advises embassy that it cannot authorize shipment in present state, and that alternatives are cremation (and shipment of ashes) or reduction to skeleton (and shipment of bones). Sanitation says there is no possibility of exemptions." After two months of that argument, the minister of interior, General Bonilla, told the embassy he had "delayed authorization to ship Horman remains out of concern that release be so timed as to minimize use of event to detriment of Chile in U.S. media and public opinion."
30. "Death in Chile of Charles Horman," p. 6.
31. Quoted from Ed Horman's letter to Charles Anderson at the Office of Special Consular Services, March 27, 1974. In a follow-up letter to Charles Horman's widow on April 4, the chief of the State Department's Division of Property Claims, Estates and Legal Documents, Larry Lane, advised her that "Congress has not appropriated funds for payment of these expenses for private American citizens who die abroad and they must necessarily be met by the estate or relatives of the deceased."
32. State Department, "Chronology of Information Relevant to Frank Randall Teruggi," October 5, 1973. The Chilean medical examiner was apparently able to match fingerprints from Teruggi's application for Chilean identification card to the fingers on the body.
33. Hathaway called Volk as he was leaving Chile to ask him to look again at the body at the morgue and see if he could identify it. When Volk, now a history professor at Oberlin College, went to the consulate, he spoke with James Anderson. "I don't care what Hathaway told Volk. He told me that it wasn't Teruggi and that's the end of it," Puddy yelled. Anderson returned to tell Volk that they would not visit the morgue again because "we don't want to pressure the new government by asking for too many favors." The next day Purdy changed his mind.

34. Defense Department, Memorandum for the Records, from Colonel W.M. Hon, Defense Attaché, October 16, 1973.
35. Ibid.
36. *The Execution of Charles Horman*, p. 244. Sandoval presumed, as he told Hauser, that this file "came from your CIA or Department of State."
37. CIA letter to Edna Selan Epstein, "Re: Freedom of Information Act Request of Frank F. Teruggi for Information Concerning his Son Frank Randall Teruggi," May 7, 1976.
38. FBI memorandum from Legat Bonn to Acting Director, [deleted] SM-Subversive, November 28, 1972.
39. Quoted in *The Execution of Charles Horman*, pp. 192, 195.
40. Rudy Fimbres to Harry Shlaudeman, "The Charles Horman Case," July 15, 1976.
41. See Document 3. When the August 25, 1976, Fimbres, Driscoll, and Robertson memo was released to the Horman family in 1979, this paragraph on the CIA's lack of candor was also censored.
42. I interviewed Smith in October 1999 and arranged for him to meet Joyce Horman for the first time. He made it clear that he did not consider his report to be a substantive investigation of the Horman case. His report is undated but was prepared in November-December 1976 and given to Shlaudeman near the end of the year.
43. This paragraph was deleted when the Smith report was first released to the Horman family in early 1980 on the grounds that it contained "thoughts intended for internal State Department deliberations," according to court records.
44. Years later, when Joyce Horman told Sandoval about the State Department's conclusions, he claimed that he didn't have a brother. Col. Sandoval Velasquez, who was tracked down by a researcher for U.S. television network in 2000, also denied he was Sandoval's brother—or his source. In 2003, Sandoval finally admitted that his source was his brother, a former military attorney.
45. Fimbres letter to Ambassador David Popper, August 4, 1976.
46. Hauser, *The Execution of Charles Horman*, p. 217.
47. See Smith's cover memo of his report to Shlaudeman, "Further Steps in the Case of Charles Horman," ca. December 26, 1976.
48. See Popper's letter to Fimbres on further investigation of the Horman case, August 17, 1976.
49. David Dreher, "Subject: Charles Horman case," March 11, 1987.
50. See Dreher's memo to the DCM, subject [deleted], April 20, 1987
51. Col. Pedro Espinoza, convicted as a DINA co-conspirator in the Letelier-Moffitt assassination, has never been linked to the atrocities at the National Stadium. While it is possible he played a role, it is also possible his name has been confused with that of the top military commander at the Stadium, Jorge Espinosa Ulloa. It is possible that the informant confused the two in his comments or that Dreher himself simply assumed the Espinosa he referred to was Pedro and put that in his memorandum of conversation.
52. See Dreher's memo to the DCM, subject [deleted], April 20, 1987.
53. See Dreher's memo to the DCM, subject [deleted], April 24, 1987.
54. This information is reported in a secret Embassy cable, "Horman Case: Embassy Views on Credibility of Source," June 15, 1987. The cable also reports that

during a trip to the Embassy the informant left "a written document" with the Consul General, Jayne Kobliska, a typed four-page overview of events in September-October 1973 detailing his knowledge of Horman's fate. This important record was not included in the declassified files on the Horman case.

55. At that point the Department decided to inform Joyce Horman of this new development. In a brief phone call, an official named Peter DeShazo told her that the validity of the information the informant had shared "was difficult to ascertain," and "the informant was seeking certain monetary favors from the USG, a fact which also colors his motives for providing more information if not the story itself."

56. The Sociedad Benefactora y Educacional Dignidad, popularly known as Colonia Dignidad, was founded in 1962 by a fugitive named Paul Schafer. In 1961, Schafer left Germany to evade multiple charges of child sexual abuse. The enclave has been characterized as a German Jonestown with allegations of mistreatment of its residents—especially children—for years. "Rumors of forced labor, torture, murder and complicity in these acts with elements of the Chilean armed forces have circulated with tantalizing frequency," according to declassified documents. For the most recent coverage of the Colony and its power to evade legal scrutiny see "Chile Sect Thrives Despite Criminal Charges," *New York Times*, December 30, 2002.

57. Embassy cable, "Case of Boris Weisfeiler, Colonia Dignidad—New Information," July 23, 1987.

58. Interview with Jayne Kobliska, April 30, 2002. Kobliska remembered that her predecessor in the Consulate, Fred Purdy, had been accused of mishandling the Horman case and believed it had ruined his career. "It had an impact on everyone," she recalled. "No one wanted to get hung out to dry."

59. Embassy report, "Review of w/w case of Boris Weisfeiler," June 30, 1987.

60. The Carabineros told the Embassy that Lopez had committed suicide. He was despondent, they said, over being abandoned by his girlfriend for another man.

61. One of Kobliska's preoccupations was that the lawyer hired by Penn State to handle Weisfeiler's estate had filed a FOIA request for documents in the case. Her fear regarding declassification was twofold: "we will lose control of the case and in all probability be accused of inaction if we don't do something now."

62. Embassy report, "Review of w/w case of Boris Weisfeiler," June 30, 1987.

63. "Daniel" refused to give his real name or any identification. He had gone first to the Church-run human rights agency, the Vicariate of Solidaridad, with his story; social workers there had introduced him to a leading human rights official, Max Pacheco, who taped his confession and brought it to the U.S. Embassy. Eventually, "Daniel" allowed U.S. embassy officials to interview him several times at Pacheco's office. His last meeting, with Consular official Larry Huffman, took place on August 19, 1987, in a car and a public plaza. At that point, the informant provided a list of the names of the Carabinero unit that had, along with his patrol, searched for and found Weisfeiler on January 5, 1985. He also claimed to have access to CNI's Weisfeiler "case file" and that the file indicated that Boris had been hired by a Nazi hunter in Israel to track Nazi fugitives using the Colonia as a safehaven.

64. As in the case of the Horman informant, the Embassy considered the possibility that Daniel was a plant, "some kind of elaborate, extremely detailed set-up to entrap and embarrass the Embassy." Unlike the Horman case, in this one the Embassy personnel noted, "we can [not] imagine what the Chilean government,

or anyone else, might hope to gain." See Embassy cable, "Case of Boris Weisfeiler, Colonia Dignidad—New Information," July 23, 1987.

65. State Department Action cable, "Case of Missing American in Chile," July 31, 1987.
66. See Diplomatic Note No. 250, dated August 5, 1988.
67. Bill Barkell to George Jones, "Recommendation to Request Court to Re-open Weisfeiler Case," January 3, 1989.

6: Operation Condor: State Sponsored International Terrorism.

1. See CIA Information Report, November 27, 1973.
2. See CIA, *Weekly Situation Report on International Terrorism*, "Assassination of Former Chilean General Carlos Prats," October 2, 1974.
3. After the assassination, the CIA reported, Prats's daughters took the manuscript of the memoirs back to Chile. Eleven years after his murder, the book was published under the title *Memorias: Testimonio de Un Soldado* (Santiago, Chile: Pehuen Editores LTDA, 1985.)
4. Through a petition to the U.S. Justice Department in 1998, Argentine judge Servini de Cubria obtained permission to come to Washington and secretly interview Townley in the Prats case. His full deposition, which remains under seal in Buenos Aires, was selectively quoted in open court proceedings during the trial of Arancibia.
5. See "*Testimonio Secreto de Michael Townley*," *La Tercera* Web site.
6. According to Townley's secret testimony, he and his wife, Mariana Callejas—also a DINA agent—detonated the bomb using a remote-control device as they sat in a car near the driveway of the Prats apartment building.
7. See State Department cable, "Assassination of General Prats," October 24, 1974.
8. CIA, *Weekly Situation Report on International Terrorism*, "Assassination of Former Chilean General Carlos Prats," October 2, 1974.
9. Arancibia's cables to DINA, written under the name of Luis Felipe Alemparte are summarized in a lengthy Argentine court document called "*Poder Judicial de la Nacion*."
10. A well-to-do British-born stockbroker, Beausire was uninvolved in politics. DINA sought him for the sole purpose forcing his sister, Mary Ann who was married to MIR leader Andres Pascale Allende, to turn herself in. When Beausire learned that his mother and other relatives had been detained, he decided to leave Chile and return to Britain. At DINA's request, Argentine officials paged Beausire at the airport claiming he had a phone call. They then threw him in a wooden box and put it on the next plane to Santiago. Beausire was believed to have been brutally tortured at Villa Grimaldi about his sister's whereabouts, of which he was unaware, and subsequently disappeared.
11. Arancibia's cables, dated April 11 and August 27, are drawn from the summary Argentine court document, "*Poder Judicial de la Nacion*."
12. Silberman was disappeared in Chile on October 4, 1974. The former general manager of the Cobre-Chuqui copper company had been incarcerated by the Pinochet regime. DINA agents actually abducted him from prison and tortured him to death in an apparent effort to find copper company funds it falsely believed

he had taken after the coup. When DINA agents were accused of kidnapping him from prison, they concocted an elaborate story that the MIR, impersonating military officers, had taken him.

13. The corpses, who have never been identified, were presumed to be victims of Argentine paramilitary death squads, particularly the AAA.
14. DINA agents seized Guendelman at his home in Santiago on September 2, 1974. Fellow prisoners reported that he was last seen alive at a DINA camp known as Cuatro Alamos.
15. See *New York Times*, "Chile's Version of Leftists' Fate Doubted," August 3, 1975.
16. *El Mercurio*'s editorial ran on July 25, 1975.
17. Dinges was the first foreign journalist to break the Operation Colombo story, providing the details of the list of 119 to *Time* magazine. He wrote about the human rights scandal for the *National Catholic Reporter* under a pseudonym, Ramon Marsano. See *National Catholic Reporter*, "Anatomy of a Cover-up," October 3, 10, 1975.
18. The actual Luis Alberto Guendelman had had one hip removed in a childhood operation; the corpse had both hips intact. The body identified as Jaime Robotham was two and one half inches shorter than the real Robotham. Moreover, the photo on the identification card found with the body was one of him as an adolescent that his mother had provided to a supposed military investigator after he was abducted by armed agents on New Year's eve, 1974.
19. Department of State, Cable, "Chilean Extremists Reported Killed or Disappeared Abroad," July 26, 1975.
20. After providing him with safe haven for months, in early 1976 DINA would sent Bosch on a mission to Costa Rica to attempt to kill socialist leader Pascal Allende. He failed. Eventually Bosch went to Venezuela and masterminded the October 6, 1976, terrorist attack on the Cubana airliner, killing seventy-three people, including Cuba's twenty-four-member Olympic fencing team.
21. See Branch and Propper, p. 243.
22. Ibid, p. 244. According to Taylor Branch and Eugene Propper, the explosives were hidden in waffle containers and kept in the freezer in the camper.
23. This intelligence report, dated August 30, 1974, represents the earliest evidence of CIA awareness of Chile's international assassination efforts.
24. See Branch and Propper, *Labyrinth,* p. 310.
25. After his arrest for the Letelier-Moffitt assassination, Townley wrote a series of typed and handwritten letters to a DINA intermediary, Gustavo, from prison. These letters were copied by his lawyer's secretary and then obtained by former prosecutor Eugene Propper and Taylor Branch for their book, *Labyrinth.*
26. State Department, Bureau of Intelligence and Research, "South America: Southern Cone Security Practices," July 19, 1976, p. 3.
27. See Report of the Chilean National Commission on Truth and Reconciliation, Vol 2; p. 614.
28. Dinges discovered the Fuentes connection to the creation of Condor in documents at the Paraguayan "Archives of Terror." See his comprehensive book, *The Condor Years* (New York: The New Press, 2004).
29. Rivas Vasquez related the details of Contreras's visit to a U.S. federal grand jury on June 29, 1978 as part of the investigation into the Letelier-Moffitt assassination. This scene is described in Dinges and Landau, *Assassination on Embassy Row*, pp. 156,157.

30. A comprehensive agenda for the *"Primera Reunion de Trabajo de Inteligencia Nacional"* dated October 29, 1975, was discovered in military archives in Paraguay.
31. The Subcommittee, chaired by George McGovern, issued a still top-secret-sensitive 1979 report titled "Staff Report on Activities of Certain Intelligence Agencies in the United States" that contained a section on the operations of the Chilean DINA. Parts of the report were leaked to columnist Jack Anderson in August 1979, who published the first article on Condor activities, "Condor: South American Assassins," *Washington Post*, August 2, 1979.
32. Townley's participation in this operation is revealed in *Labyrinth,* p. 324. The targets of the mission were two Chilean journalists, one with possible ties to Carlos the Jackal, who were setting up a pan-European newspaper for a leftist coalition. Condor's intent appeared to be to disrupt a Socialist Party congress being held in Portugal, and undermine any effort to establish a broad unified front in Europe that could bring further international pressure against the Southern Cone regimes. As Townley related this story, the mission took place in late November. But the U.S. intelligence community dated the warning to France on Condor in September, suggesting that the mission took place earlier in the fall.
33. Department of State, INR Afternoon Summary, November 23, 1976.
34. A number of major luminaries, including Chancellor Willy Brandt from West Germany, and French socialist leader François Mitterrand attended the Congress. Townley's mission is detailed in *Labyrinth*, pp. 324,325.
35. See, CIA intelligence cable, April 17, 1977.
36. This memo, written by a high CNI officer, Col. Jeronimo Pantoja to the deputy foreign minister, reviews the communications with Peruvian officials over the Stationing of a Chilean intelligence officer in Lima. It is dated April 14, 1978 and was obtained from Chilean sources.
37. In an interview with the author, White said he never received a reply from the State Department about this stunning information. See his cable on his meeting with one of General Stroessner's top aides, chief of staff Gen. Alejandro Fretes Davalos, "Second Meeting with Chief of Staff re: Letelier Case," October 13, 1978.
38. See U.S. State Department, "Aftermath of Kidnapping of Refugees in Buenos Aires," June 15, 1976.
39. See Stella Calloni, *Los Anos Del Lobo: Operacion Condor* (Argentina: Ediciones Continente, 1999), Chapter 10. Calloni was the first analyst to sift through the Paraguayan documents for evidence of Operation Condor activities.
40. See a memcon filed by James Blystone, "Meeting with Argentine Intelligence Service," June 19, 1980. The memo represents the only known documentation of advance U.S. knowledge of a planned disappearance.
41. One biographic sketch, prepared by the CIA's Central Reference Service in coordination with the Office of Current Intelligence, Office of Economic Research and Clandestine Service reported on Letelier after he was named to be Chile's ambassador to Washington. The document noted that "the family has an English sheepdog, Alfie, which they will give up upon moving to the embassy residence." The CIA's source for this critical information remains a historical mystery.
42. CIA Intelligence Information Report, "Subject: Plans of Chilean Leftists in Exile to Hold another Joint Meeting to Discuss Anti-Junta Strategy," November 18,

1975. The last CIA report in Letelier's 201 intelligence file is dated September 16, 1976, only four days before the assassination. Released to the Letelier and Moffitt families in 1980, the document is too heavily redacted to determine why the CIA was reporting on Letelier's activity at that time.

43. Kissinger did not respond to Pinochet's complaints about Letelier. The transcript of the conversation is reproduced in Chapter 4.
44. See the State Department's January 1989 history, "The Letelier Case: Background and Factual Summary," p. 3. This twenty-four-page memorandum was prepared in anticipation of pursuing the perpetrators of the Letelier-Moffitt assassination after Pinochet turned power over to a civilian government.
45. Ibid.
46. Shlaudeman acted on Landau's recommendation immediately. He sent a memo to the Immigration and Naturalization Service, with attached photocopies of the passport pages, asking that Romeral and Williams be stopped and questioned if they attempted to enter the country. Nevertheless, on August 22, two Chilean officers using the names Romeral and Williams, traveling on official Chilean passports, did enter the country through Miami. Although their names were on the watch list, they were not stopped. The two were decoys, sent by DINA to confuse U.S. officials who, Contreras believed, were looking for Townley and Fernandez. At the time of the assassination the decoys were detailed to the Chilean military mission in Washington.
47. Abourezk is quoted from the *Congressional Record*, September 21, 1976, p. 31464.
48. Luers prepared a briefing summary of the meeting for Kissinger, who was out of town. See "Briefing Memorandum: Ambassador Trucco and Orlando Letelier," September 22, 1976.
49. Fernández related this conversation with his superior officer in a proffer of evidence made to the U.S. Justice Department when he fled Chile and pleaded guilty in 1987. It is cited in the State Department's January 1989 history, "The Letelier Case: Background and Factual Summary," p. 7.
50. The Scherrer cable was attached to a Letters Rogatory request for information that the U.S. Justice Department sent to Chile in 1978. It was first obtained and cited by Dinges and Landau in their book *Assassination on Embassy Row*. Subsequently it was declassified and remained the only available document on U.S. knowledge of Condor until 1999. Doc 2, the DIA cable from Buenos Aires, is drawn virtually word-for-word from Scherrer's cable.
51. Embassy cable, "Possible International Implications of Violent Deaths of Political Figures Abroad," June 7, 1976.
52. Beyond their compatible military ideologies, Shlaudeman reported to Kissinger, the Southern Cone regimes shared a "suspicion that even the U.S. has lost its will to stand firm against communism because of Viet-Nam, détente, and social decay." They also held a common "resentment of human-rights criticism," Shlaudeman noted, "which is often taken as just one more sign of the commie encirclement." See ARA Monthly Report (July) "The 'Third World War' and South America," p. 10.
53. This explosive document was declassified in 1991, but lay unnoticed for a decade in a batch of microfiched documents on Argentina at the State Department FOIA reading room. It was discovered by National Security Archive analyst Carlos Osorio.

54. See INR Afternoon Summary, September 21, 1976, "Latin America: Political and Economic Cooperation in the Southern Cone."
55. "Ninety-nine percent of Roger Channels weren't like this one," McAfee said in an interview with the author. Shlaudeman's language, he said, "meant that the top command of State was behind this." Since INR was responsible for transmitting all Roger Channel cables, the only clearance shown was that of McAfee himself. Per Shlaudeman's request, copies of the cable were restricted to a handful of offices—Kissinger's, Habib's, Shlaudeman's, McAfee's, and administration. Interview with William McAfee, December 15, 2001.
56. When this document was first declassified and given to the Letelier and Moffitt families in 1980 pursuant to FOIA suit they had filed, all references to Pinochet and the informant's belief that he was responsible for the crime were blacked out. The document was declassified again in November 2000, but remains heavily excised.
57. This summary of the Station's reporting on the meeting is cited in the Hinchey report, *CIA Activities in Chile*, section on "Relationship with Contreras."
58. At issue was the information in the records that indicated the two DINA agents intended to travel to Washington to meet CIA deputy director Gen. Vernon Walters. "The General is an old hand. He can take care of himself," Robert Driscoll wrote. See "The Paraguayan Caper," October 15, 1976.
59. These articles are cited in Dinges and Landau, *Assassination on Embassy Row*, p. 243, 244.
60. Hewson Ryan was interviewed on April 27, 1988, by Richard Nethercut for the Association for Diplomatic Studies and Training, Foreign Affairs Oral History Project.

7: Denouement of the Dictator: From Terrorism to Transition.

1. See Jeremiah O'Leary's banner headline story, "U.S. Threatening to Sever Chilean Relations," *Washington Star*, March 3, 1978.
2. The Chilean military repeatedly faked searches for Townley. They would alert him in advance before arriving at his home; usually he hid in an empty water tank on the roof. See *Labyrinth,* p. 464.
3. This accord, signed on April 7, 1978, is known as the Silbert-Montero accord, because it was signed by Earl Silbert, the U.S. attorney for Washington, D.C. and Chilean Interior Ministry official Enrique Montero.
4. The five Cubans were Guillermo Novo, his brother Ignacio Novo, Alvin Ross, Virgilio Paz, and Dionesio Suarez, who is believed to have pressed the pager button that actually triggered the bomb. The Novos and Ross were quickly arrested. Paz and Suarez escaped and remained fugitives for more than a decade before they were finally arrested.
5. After meeting with Landau, NSC Latin America specialist Robert Pastor reported to Zbigniew Brzezinski on the conversation in a memo titled "Conversation with our Ambassador to Chile, George Landau—June 28, 1978." The memorandum demonstrates that the highest U.S. officials were aware that if Contreras was responsible for the terrorist bombing, Pinochet would likely have authorized it.
6. CIA intelligence report, untitled, May 24, 1978.
7. DIA Information Report, "Contreras Tentacles," ca. January 1, 1989.

8. This CIA cable document is cited in a long list of documents the Agency compiled for the Chile Declassification Project. Next to the entry of the subject title are the words *FBI Requests Withhold.* The document, which contains evidence of Pinochet's personal involvement in obstructing justice in the Letelier case, was one of hundreds pulled by FBI and Justice Department officials for their investigation into Pinochet's role in the assassination. See the Epilogue for a full discussion of these records.
9. In 1987, eleven years after the assassination, Fernández Larios fled Chile with the secret help of the FBI. He was interrogated for more then ten hours and revealed Pinochet's efforts to block his testimony after the murders. See the State Department's secret report on the Letelier case, January 26, 1987.
10. CIA Intelligence cable, "Government Sponsored Propaganda Campaign Re US Interference in Chile," May 26, 1978.
11. See Chapter 6 for a description of Contreras's effort to obtain U.S. visas in Asuncion to disguise Chile's role in the assassination mission, and Ambassador Landau's role in copying the passports and the photos.
12. In a telephone interview with the author from his office in Florida, Ambassador Landau said that he and the State Department had not connected the effort by the Chilean agents to obtain visas from Paraguay to the Letelier-Moffitt assassination before early 1978. "If we had," he said, "I never would have been transferred to Chile after my posting in Paraguay."
13. Untitled CIA memorandum, August 24, 1978.
14. See CIA Memorandum for the Record, Meeting with State Department and Justice Department Officials Regarding Letelier Case, 21 August, 1978.
15. This CIA report, perhaps the most comprehensive summary of the Agency's connections to Contreras, has been withheld in its entirety from declassification. Even its title remains secret.
16. Author interview.
17. Author interview. See also an untitled September 22, 1978 confidential memorandum of conversation written by embassy officer Felix Vargas, based on a conversation with the reporter who spoke to Miranda.
18. Author interview. See also *Labyrinth,* p. 584. Branch and Propper's account places the date of this episode between August 28 and September 1, 1978. But it is clear from the declassified cables that Contreras made his blackmail bid on August 23, using Puga as an emissary with CIA officials in Santiago.
19. See McNeil's memo to Michael Armacost, "Possible Approach by Chilean representatives of General Contreras to DOD Officials," Aug. 29, 1978.
20. See McNeil's memorandum, "Letelier Case," October 30, 1978.
21. Pastor to Brzezinski, "U.S. Policy to Chile—Reaching the Crunch Point on Letelier," May 25, 1979.
22. This exchange is described in *Labyrinth,* p. 594.
23. Landau's démarche is recorded in the State Department cable, "Instructions re U.S. Reaction to Outcome of Letelier Case," June 1, 1978.
24. Derian to Christopher, SECRET, "Letelier Case," September 21, 1979.
25. Derian to Vance, SECRET, "Letelier-Moffitt—ARA Memorandum of October 12, 1979," October 12, 1979.
26. Former State and Justice Department officials interviewed for this book acknowledged that the White House in general, and Pastor in particular, were kept in

the dark about the investigation into the assassinations. The reluctance to share information derived from Assistant U.S. Attorney Eugene Propper's concern about keeping the criminal case free from any taint of politicization, and the potential for leaks. "Over his dead body would the White House be informed," one State Department officer recalled Propper's position. Nevertheless, Pastor's own memoranda record that he was informed in May 1979 that "there is strong evidence of tampering with the court by Pinochet." In his May 25, 1979 memorandum to Brzezinski, Pastor noted, "I have not been following this case closely but [deputy secretary of state] Christopher has, and I am surprised at how strongly he and others in State feel about this case and about how illegitimate is the Chilean decision." By October 11, however, he felt that three fundamental questions had to be addressed and answered before the U.S. could proceed with sanctions: (1) "By what justification can we be displeased with the Chilean Supreme Court decision?"; (2) "By what right can the U.S. State Department judge another government's laws and court?"; and (3) "What are our objectives in the Letelier case, in U.S. Chilean relations, and overall?" See Pastor to Brzezinski, "Reaction to Chile's Decision on Letelier," October 11, 1979.

27. To address both Pastor's and Vaky's skepticism, the Department of Justice drafted a memo on October 15 reviewing the overwhelming evidence of Chile's guilt in the assassination. "The United States Department of Justice persuasively maintains that any future course of action should not be based upon any suggestion that the evidence presented by the United States is anything less than conclusive."
28. Barcella described to me how appalled he was by this question, and the whole direction of this meeting when he realized that the sanctions would not be commensurate with the crime. For quotations, see *Labyrinth*, p. 598.
29. Carter overruled recommendation number 5—"Deny validated Licenses for Exports to the Chilean Armed Forces." This would have meant employing export controls to deny millions of dollars of purchases by the Pinochet regime from U.S. businesses. A seventh option focused not on the sanctions, but on the official statement that would announce them.
30. Secretary of Defense Harold Brown lobbied hard to keep the MilGroup from being withdrawn. In a confidential memo to Vance and Brzezinski dated October 9, 1979, he argued that the situation in Nicaragua and El Salvador, poor relations with Argentina, and the possibility that the Soviets would be given "new opportunities in Chile" mitigated against closing the U.S. military liaison office in Chile. Pastor rejected Brown's concerns as "bureaucratically self-serving" and "nonsense," but Brzezinski compromised by reducing but not closing the MilGroup office.
31. It took only two months for the bureaucracy to initiate an effort to rescind or limit the sanctions, starting with the UNITAS exercises. In February 1980, one of Brzezinski's aides, Thomas Thorton, wrote to him about the sanctions. "The question arises as to whether we want to continue punishment of the Chileans on this issue. Do we want this to be a time-limited action or is it supposed to remain a semi-permanent factor in U.S.-Chilean relations? My preference is to put the issue behind us—the UNITAS decision would be our last one under its influence—and judge future issues in U.S.-Chilean relations on the basis of their merits and overall Chilean behavior." To his credit, Robert Pastor forcefully argued against this position. In a February 20, 1980 memo to Brzezinski com-

menting on Thorton's points, Pastor stated that it would "be a terrible embarrassment to the president if we proceeded with 'business as usual,' such as suggested by the UNITAS exercise, four months after he announces a strong and firm policy." Pastor also noted that Patricia Derian's former deputy, Mark Schneider, was now running Edward Kennedy's presidential primary campaign against Jimmy Carter for the Democratic Party nomination. "Kennedy is hungry for issues," he observed. "You can be absolutely certain that a decision to put the 'Letelier phase' behind us and proceed with UNITAS will be noticed."

32. Undated radio broadcast transcript. Reagan based his comments on a report by the extreme right-wing Council for Inter-American Security. He appeared to discount evidence compiled by the FBI of the Pinochet regime's responsibility, blaming "the efforts of leftist groups to get our government to pin it on the current government of Chile."
33. Walters made this statement at a March 10, 1981 hearing on lifting the Chile sanctions before the House Subcommittee on Inter-American Affairs, and Subcommittee on International Economic Policy.
34. Kirkpatrick's article provided the theoretical basis for Ronald Reagan's campaign denunciations of the Carter administration's approach to human rights. Once president, Reagan promptly appointed her ambassador to the United Nations. See *Commentary*, Vol. 68, No. 5, November 1979. For a rebuttal of Kirkpatrick's article as it applied to Pinochet's Chile, see Robert Kaufman and Arturo Valenzuela, "Authoritarian Chile: Implications for American Foreign Policy," in Richard Newhouse, ed., *Gunboats and Diplomacy* (Washington, D.C.: Democratic Policy Committee, 1982).
35. Under the law, the Carter administration voted against MDB loans to Chile eight consecutive times. The Reagan administration simply asserted that the Pinochet regime did not engage in a pattern of rights violations and therefore, "did not now fall within the standard that would require a 'no' vote."
36. Walters "eyes only" cable to Haig, "Chile/El Salvador," February 27, 1981.
37. Helms made these remarks during the Senate debate over lifting the Kennedy amendment on October 22, 1981. The author was sitting in the Senate gallery listening. For a full record of the debate see *Congressional Record*, October 22, 1982, pp. 11894–11917.
38. Abrams to Eagleburger, March 13, 1982.
39. Efforts to obtain secret arms from Chile continued until the Iran-Contra scandal broke in November 1986 and North was removed from his position. For the complete story of Chile's role in the Iran-Contra operations, see Peter Kornbluh, "The Chilean Missile Caper," *The Nation*, May 18, 1988.
40. For a comprehensive treatment of the opposition's efforts to organize against the regime see Mark Ensalaco, *Chile Under Pinochet: Recovering the Truth* (Philadelphia: University of Pennsylvania Press), chapters 6, 7.
41. See the CIA's "Chile: How Authoritarian is Pinochet's Constitution?," May 17, 1988.
42. Quoted in Mary Helen Spooner, *Soldiers in a Narrow Land* (Berkeley: University of California Press, 1999), p. 202. See also the *New York Times*, May 16, 1986.
43. Motley to Shultz, "Chile and My Visit," February 21, 1985. Abrams opposed Motley's "no public criticism" position, which was shared by the NSC. In a December 27, 1984 memo to Deputy Secretary Kenneth Dam, he argued that "if we desist from public criticism of Chilean repression . . . we are virtually beg-

ging for congressional initiatives which will tie our hands and destroy our policy. I do not believe the NSC's proposal of 'no public criticism' is wise, because I think we must make our position on human rights clear to the people of Chile and, even more important, the people of the United States."

44. I knew Rodrigo and his family and spent considerable time with him while he was growing up in Washington. At one point, Rodrigo arranged for me to come speak to his civics class at Wilson High School about the U.S. role in the Chilean coup and human rights abuses by the Pinochet regime. But he also spent considerable time playing hooky and hanging out in my office. Several months before his senior graduation, he decided to drop out and return to Chile. With my then wife, Eliana Loveluck, we took him out to lunch and tried to convince him that just a few more weeks of school would benefit him for the rest of his life; and he could then return to Chile with a high school diploma. A stubborn, rebellious teenager, he listened to us but decided to leave nonetheless. If we had managed to convince him to finish school and delay returning until the summer of 1986, I've often wondered, perhaps he might not have made it to that particular street protest in Santiago on that truly tragic day in July.
45. State Department cable, "W/W: Case of Rodrigo Rojas De Negri," July 8, 1986.
46. Carmen Quintana miraculously survived. The forceful complaints of inadequate care by an American doctor from Massachusetts General Hospital, John Constable, and Rojas's mother, Veronica De Negri, who had both flown to Santiago, resulted in Quintana's transfer to the burn unit of the Workers Hospital within a few hours of Rodrigo's death. Eventually she was flown to Canada where she underwent multiple skin graft and facial reconstruction surgeries over the course of several years. She eventually returned to Chile after civilian rule was restored.
47. Reagan was also informed that Senator Jesse Helms, who was in Santiago at the time, was assisting the regime's effort to smear the victims and exonerate the regime. Helms met privately with Pinochet for two hours and then became a American shill for the regime's cover-up of the crime. "You have screwed it up—you and the people in Washington," Helms told Barnes during a private meeting at the Crowne Plaza Hotel in Santiago. According to a declassified memcon, the senator "said he wasn't a complete apologist for Pinochet; but Pinochet, warts and all, was a lot better than what was likely to come after." Publicly, the senator denounced Rojas as "a communist terrorist" and accused Barnes of "planting the American flag in the midst of a communist activity" and urged Reagan to recall him. For the comprehensive story of Helms's effort to assist those responsible for this crime, see Jon Elliston, "Deadly Alliance," *The Independent Weekly*, May 23, 2001.
48. A reliable source reported to the Embassy that on July 10, the head of the Carabineros—and member of the Junta—Gen. Rodolfo Strange wrote a one-page report identifying the Army personnel involved in burning Rojas and Quintana and dumping their bodies and provided it to President Pinochet. "President Pinochet told General Strange that he did not believe the report, and he refused to receive the report," according to the source. See the Embassy's cable, "Information Regarding the Rodrigo Rojas Investigation," July 22, 1986.
49. Lagos helped energize the campaign by appearing on television in April 1988 and boldly addressing Pinochet: "You promise the country eight more years of torture, assassination, and human rights violations." See Constable and Valenzuela, *A Nation of Enemies*, p. 306.

50. For Assistant Secretary Abrams from Barnes, October 1, 1988.
51. State Department cable to Santiago, "Chile—Trying to Deter Possible Government Action to Suspend or Nullify Plebiscite," October 1, 1988.
52. The informant's name is blacked out but DIA records indicate it was Air Force General and Junta member Fernando Mattei who took the strongest position against Pinochet's overturning the plebiscite.
53. Gen. Zincke is, perhaps, the unsung hero of efforts to blow the whistle on Pinochet's plans. On September 30, during a meeting with the head of the Civitas Civic Education Crusade, one of the voter education groups receiving U.S. support for the plebiscite, Zincke began describing a Communist plot to foment violence to disrupt the election. "The persons with whom Zincke spoke," Amb. Barnes cabled Assistant Secretary Abrams at the State Department that day, "are convinced he, for unknown reasons, was warning them of what the Army, not the Communists, were planning to do to disrupt the plebiscite." It is not known whether Gen. Zincke later provided key details of this plot to U.S. intelligence agents, but, at minimum, he set in motion U.S. intelligence gathering efforts to ascertain the nature of Pinochet's plan to keep power.
54. This CIA intelligence report is dated November 18, 1988.
55. The Embassy officer reported that the first song of the ten hour-long concert, "Por Que No Se Van"—Why Don't They Go—was dedicated to Pinochet with tremendous approval from the crowd. The highlight of the concert for the diplomat-turned rock critic was Sting and Peter Gabriel singing a song called "La Cueca Sola"—Dancing Alone—with women from Chile and Argentina who had lost loved ones. Among the women who danced with Sting on stage was Veronica de Negri, the mother of Rodrigo Rojas. In an obvious but important conclusion, the cable noted, "The reaction at the rock concert in Mendoza indicates that the human rights situation in Chile remains an emotional issue which will persist despite political openings." (I am grateful to Sarah Anderson and Stacie Jonas of the Institute for Policy Studies for bringing this document to my attention.)
56. See Scope Paper, "Vice President Trip to Barbados, Venezuela, Chile, Paraguay, Argentina, and Brazil, March 9-16, 1990." In a confidential briefing paper prepared for Quayle to use in his meeting with Pinochet, Quayle was warned that Pinochet has "vowed to confront the civilian government if it attempts to prosecute military officers accused of human rights violations or change the status of the military." Quayle's talking points included urging Pinochet "to support our efforts to seek justice for those responsible for . . . an act of terrorism committed on the streets of the capital of the United States." "The United States insists on the resolution of this case," Quayle was to say. "We will not normalize relations until this is done."

Atrocity and Accountability: The Long Epilogue of the Pinochet Case.

1. Author interview.
2. In particular, Garces used the case of Spanish citizen Carmelo Soria to trigger Madrid's quest to bring Pinochet to justice. A Spanish economist working in Chile for the U.N. on a diplomatic passport, Soria was picked up by agents of the

DINA, on July 15, 1976. According to human rights investigators, his captors dragged Soria into the basement of a DINA safe house and, during a torture session, broke his neck. Then Pinochet's agents doused him with liquor and forged a suicide note. The next day his car and body were discovered in an irrigation canal.

3. Pinochet's daughter had talked him into doing an unprecedented interview with a U.S. magazine because, wrote author Jon Lee Anderson, "if people understand her father better he will be maligned less."
4. See "Spanish Request to Question General Pinochet," October 14, 1998, reprinted in Reed Brody and Michael Ratner, *The Pinochet Papers: The Case of Augusto Pinochet in Spain and Britain* (The Hague: Kluwar Law International, 2000), p. 55.
5. Quoted in Peter Kornbluh, "Prisoner Pinochet," *The Nation*, November 29, 1998.
6. I attended these hearings in the House of Lords between November 3 and 13, 1998. Quotes can be found in the article, "Prisoner Pinochet."
7. Pinochet's lawyers successfully argued that the swing vote on the five-member panel, Lord Hoffmann, had failed to disclose that he was a fund-raiser for Amnesty International and had a bias in the case. A second set of legal hearings was held in mid-January 1999.
8. For a detailed discussion of how the civilian government handled the human rights issue in Chile, see Marc Ensalaco, *Chile Under Pinochet: Recovering the Truth* (Philadelphia: University of Pennsylvania Press, 2000), chapter 8.
9. See Zalaquett's introduction to the English edition of the *Report of the Chilean National Commission on Truth and Reconciliation* (Notre Dame, In.: University of Notre Dame Press, 1993), p. xxxii.
10. See Wilde's provocative article, "Irruptions of Memory: Expressive Politics in Chile's Transition to Democracy," in the *Journal of Latin American Studies*, Vol. 31, Part 2, May 1999.
11. When Chile refused the request for compensation, the new Bush administration invoked a treaty from 1914 known as the Treaty for the Settlement of Disputes that May Occur Between the U.S. and Chile, also known as the Bryan Accord. The treaty provided a foundation for bilateral negotiations to settle the compensation issue. For a comprehensive chronology of the evolution of the case in the late 1980s, see the State Department's twenty-four-page report, "The Letelier Case: Background and Factual Summary," January 1989.
12. Kozak recommended going to Pinochet's foreign minister and stating that the U.S. would hold the government responsible for anything Contreras did. His handwritten memo is undated but clearly is a response to the February 10 embassy cable.
13. See Embassy Cable "Letelier-Moffitt Case: Pursuing it with the Armed Forces," May 30 1989.
14. The concern of the families, as voiced by Moffitt and Buffone at this meeting, and members of the Letelier family in Santiago, was that the Bush administration would prematurely certify that the Chilean government was cooperating in the Letelier-Moffitt case before legal proceedings had been initiated or an agreement on compensation reached. According to a memorandum of conversation, both Moffitt and Buffone wanted to see a timetable for Chilean government action; as pressure they believed the U.S. government should once again initiate extradition proceedings against the DINA officers. Although the families were repeatedly

assured that justice in the case remained a precondition for lifting the Kennedy amendment, secret State Department documents show that U.S. officials had concluded the president could certify Chile if Aylwin moved to transfer of the case from a military to a civilian court and planned to have President Bush announce the certification during his December 1990 trip to Santiago.

15. The pursuit of justice also advanced in the Letelier case in the U.S. In 1990 and 1991, the two Cuban exile fugitives, Dionisio Suarez and Virgilio Paz were captured and imprisoned. Suarez was arrested in April and convicted in July; Paz, who pushed the button on the car bomb, was captured on the day after *America's Most Wanted* aired a segment on his role in the assassinations. On July 30, 1991 he plea-bargained to a charge of conspiracy to murder a foreign official and was sentenced to twelve years in prison.
16. See Peter Kornbluh, "Prisoner Pinochet," *The Nation*, December 11, 1998.
17. Author interview.
18. For Rubin's announcement, see the *Washington Post*, December 2, 1998.
19. The official I interviewed recalled the argument advanced by the Chile desk officer: "If it was just the Pinochet years it would look unbalanced to the Chileans. It would look like we were just going after the right. So it should cover Allende also."
20. Tranche 1 was delayed several days because Henry Kissinger learned of the scheduled release and had his office call National Security Adviser Sandy Berger and request an entire set of documents to review prior to publication.
21. The NSC repeatedly promised Joyce Horman that the final declassification would take place in April, and that all remaining records, among them CIA and Pentagon documents long sought by the family, would be released. In April the date was postponed to June. After they informed her that the final release would be postponed again until the fall, she petitioned the chairman of the IWG, William Leary, to release the records relating to her case as scheduled. "The Horman family, and many others have waited patiently for these records. The CIA, NSC, NSA and Pentagon all should have released records on our case last June or last October. That they did not comply with the president's request at that time is most unfortunate," she wrote in May 2000. The White House agreed, and released the documents on the Teruggi and Weisfeiler case at the same time.
22. The CIA counted on a 1984 modification to the FOIA law known as the CIA Information Act, which exempted operational files from being searched in response to FOIA requests. But the Chile Information Act explicitly stated that operational files that had previously been searched subject to law-enforcement proceedings or Congressional inquiries were eligible under the FOIA. Since the Agency had been forced to share almost all of its Chile files with the Department of Justice for legal proceedings in the Helms case and the Horman case, and show many of its Directorate of Operations records to the Senate Select Committee in the mid-1970s, the law offered no shield from search and review during the Chile declassification project.
23. I reported this conversation in the *Washington Post* Outlook section, "Still Hidden: A Full Record of What the U.S. did in Chile," October 24, 1999.
24. Interview with a member of the Inter-Agency Working Group.
25. The National Security Agency continues to keep secret six documents on the Horman case. In a December 1, 1999, letter to the author, the agency stated,

"the documents date from September 1973 through February 1974 and do not contain information which identifies who may have been responsible for Mr. Horman's death or the circumstances surrounding his death. The documents suggest that Mr. Horman was detained and released on or about 20 September 1973, but that his whereabouts were unknown."

26. In one of his first internal memos on the declassification process, "IWG on Chile Documents," William Leary wrote to the CIA, DOJ, DOD, FBI, and State Department that the "NSC would chair joint declassification sessions to facilitate such review by 3rd agencies." The idea was to quickly, and jointly evaluate documents that involved more than one agency—presidential records generated by the CIA for example—to determine what portions needed to be censored.
27. The Archive's letter is dated September 16, 1999. It noted that "as the U.S. presses countries like Germany, Switzerland, and Guatemala among others, to acknowledge and rectify their mistakes of the past, the CIA's position that we must hide our own can only undermine the credibility of our policy." In a response to Blanton dated November 30, 1999, Berger wrote: "I have received assurances that CIA material reviewed and released in the final phase . . . will include relevant operational records, such as documents related to covert action, documents associated with the Church Committee hearings in 1975, and operational files disseminated outside the Directorate of Operations."
28. *New York Times* editorial, "Exposing America's Role in Chile," October 6, 1999.
29. Tenet made this statement in a lengthy letter to Congressman George Miller, responding to a call from Miller protesting the withholding of documents on Chile. The letter is dated August 11, 2000.
30. At the NSC, William Leary reviewed the CIA records, Adolf "Hal" Eisner read them at the State Department. The CIA records were heavily redacted leading to complaints that it was impossible to ascertain the actual sensitivity of the documentation.
31. See Hinchey's press release, "CIA Finally Responds to Hinchey Legislation, Report on U.S. Involvement in Pinochet Coup Due," September 14, 2000.
32. On September 7, the CIA provided a classified version of the report to the House Intelligence Committee. According to sources who have read both versions, the main difference is that the classified version cited the actual amount of CIA funding for DINA chieftain Manuel Contreras, and named the two NIC officers who authored the report.
33. "CIA Activities in Chile," September 18, 2000, p. 15. The Hinchey amendment clearly intended the CIA to address its broader actions in support of the military regime's consolidation of power. But the CIA chose to interpret the question as whether the agency had assisted Pinochet in outmaneuvering other members of the military to become head of the Junta and "President" of Chile.
34. Ibid, p. 5.
35. See Chapter 4 for a comprehensive discussion of the CIA's interaction with Contreras and DINA.
36. In early 2000 I filed a FOIA with NARA for administrative records on what the Nixon, Ford, Carter, and Reagan presidential libraries had submitted to the Chile Declassification Project, and what had been denied declassification. The lists I received of denied documents contained over three hundred documents.

37. The National Security Archive successfully threatened to sue the U.S. government to recover the Telcons; the first set, from Kissinger's tenure as National Security Advisor, were scheduled for declassification in mid-2004. State Department historians also gained access to these papers for their work on the *Foreign Relations of the United States* (FRUS) series.
38. Author interview. One aspect that investigators focused on was evidence of Pinochet's motivation to assassinate Letelier. Top-secret CIA and DIA documents seen by the FBI recorded his involvement in a decision to strip Letelier of his Chilean citizenship ten days before the murders took place. U.S. investigators pursued several witnesses in Chile on this aspect of events leading up to the car bombing and concluded that Pinochet was "obsessed" with Letelier. See the *Washington Post*, May 28, 2000.
39. This source spoke to a Chilean journalist, Pascale Bonnefoy. See her story "FBI Requests Prosecution of Pinochet, But No One Lifts a Finger," in the Chilean newspaper *El Periodista*, April 15, 2002. I also interviewed, on background, a source who had been a member of the investigation team that traveled to Santiago and participated in the drafting of the recommendation to indict. He told the same story. The report went to the criminal division for review and stayed there, despite multiple efforts to get it cleared and submitted to the attorney general. According to my source, the report was never actually sent up to Janet Reno's office. But it appears she was briefed before the Clinton administration left office.
40. The letter to Marcus Raskin, who had written to the Justice Department on behalf of Murray Karpen, was signed by Ashcroft's deputy, Bruce Swartz. It was reprinted in the IPS electronic newsletter, Pinochet Watch 35, April 11, 2001.
41. The author appreciates the contribution of Joshua Frenz-String and Carly Ackerman for research, crafting, and drafting support on this section.
42. La Tercera, "La Carta de Pinochet al Senado, July 4, 2002.
43. Permanent Subcommittee on Investigations of the Committee on Governmental Affairs, United States Senate, 109th Cong., 2nd sess., S. HRG. 108-633. *Money Laundering and Foreign Corruption: Enforcement and Effectiveness of the Patriot Act*, July 15, 2004 (Washington, D.C.: U.S. Government Printing Office, 2004), p. 21 (hereafter referred to as *Senate Report 2004*). While the first report focused on Riggs Bank's noncompliance with anti–money laundering laws, a second May 16, 2005, study by the subcommittee examined all U.S. accounts used by Augusto Pinochet specifically—a network spread across ten financial institutions, of which Riggs was the most extensive (hereafter referred to as *Senate Report 2005*).
44. See Riggs memorandum, "RE: Business Meetings During Trip to Chile and Ecuador," *Senate Report 2005*, p. 20.
45. *Senate Report 2005*, p. 21.
46. Ibid., p. 22. Pinochet received further praise in additional letters sent from Riggs personnel. For example, in a letter dated November 10, 1997, Timothy Coughlin wrote, "Of the books that you have given me, I am just finishing my reading of 'The Crucial Day.' The factual objectivity with which you tell the story of Chile in the early 1970s is both fascinating and instructive. History provides for fair and proper judgment only when the true facts are known." Also, a November 14, 1997, letter from Joseph Allbritton glowingly remarks "you [Pinochet] have rid Chile from the threat of totalitarian government and an archaic economic system based on state-owned property and centralized planning. We in the United States and the

rest of the Western hemisphere owe you a tremendous debt of gratitude and I am confident your legacy will have been to provide a more prosperous and safer world for your children and grandchildren." (See *Senate Report 2005*, pp. 23–25.)

47. Ibid., p. 25.
48. *Senate Report 2004*, p. 21.
49. *Senate Report 2005*, p. 28.
50. For its misconduct, Riggs was fined $16 million by the U.S. Justice Department in January 2005. In February 2005, Riggs settled a complaint brought by Spanish lawyer Joan Garces to recover the funds given to Pinochet by providing $8 million to Garces's Allende Foundation in Madrid; Albritton paid an additional $1 million out of his personal funds. Garces pledged to redistribute the $9 million to Chilean victims of Pinochet's repression.
51. Shortly thereafter, on September 16, 2004, Spanish magistrate Baltasar Garzón followed suit, adding to the charges of genocide, terrorism, and torture against Pinochet the offenses of concealment of assets and money laundering in connection with the Pinochet accounts at Riggs Bank.
52. Quoted in "Pinochet Daughter Is in Custody in Chile," *New York Times*, January 29, 2006, sec. 1, Foreign Desk, p. 4.
53. "New Spotlight on Pinochet: Probe Renews Push to Prosecute Ex-Dictator," *Washington Post*, August 25, 2004.
54. "Entrevista de Pinochet a canal de Miami desata pugna en familia del general (R)," *La Tercera*, November 25, 2003, available at www.icarito.cl/medio/articulo/0,0,3255_5664_44959735,00.html (accessed March 12, 2009).
55. Interview with Judge Guzmán, December 10, 2004.
56. Carolina Valenzuela, "Caso Cóndor: Juez Guzmán procesa a Pinochet," *El Mercurio Electrónica*, December 13, 2004.
57. "Pinochet Takes Responsibility for His Regime's Actions," EFE News Services, November 26, 2006.
58. Ibid.
59. "Former Chilean Dictator Augusto Pinochet Dies—News Sparks Violent Clashes Between Opponents, Police," *Guelph Mercury* (Ontario, Canada), December 11, 2006.
60. "Pinochet to Be Buried Without State Funeral, Mourning," Agence France-Presse, December 11, 2006.
61. "Bachelet Calls on Army to Punish Pinochet Grandson for Remarks," Agence France-Presse, December 13, 2006.
62. Associated Press, "Army Ousts Pinochet's Kin," *New York Times*, December 14, 2006, sec. A, p. 27, col. 6.
63. "Pinochet Grandson Kicked Out of Military over Funeral," Deutsche Press-Agentur, December 14, 2006.
64. "Pinochet's Plea from the Grave," *Herald Sun* (Melbourne, Australia), December 26, 2006.
65. "Pinochet's Posthumous Letter Fails to Impress," EFE News Service, December 26, 2006.
66. "Pinochet Justifies Coup from Grave," *Yorkshire Post* (UK), December 26, 2006.
67. These statistics are taken from the Web site of the leading database on legal accountability in Chile, Observatorio Derechos Humanos, in March 2013. See www.icso.cl/observatorio-derechos-humanos/cifras-causas-case-statistics.

68. Alexei Barrionuevo, "6 Accused in 1982 Poisoning Death of Chilean Leader," *New York Times*, December 7, 2009.
69. After more than a year, in October 2002, the State Department finally submitted a lengthy diplomatic note that answered the questions Guzmán had posed to Kissinger.
70. U.S. Embassy, cable, "Consul General's Meeting with Judge Investigating Weisfeiler Case," December 5, 2005.
71. For comprehensive information on the Weisfeiler case, see the Web site created by Olga Weisfeiler: www.boris.weisfeiler.com.
72. In November 2002, Helms died at the age of eighty-nine. The suit was amended and refiled by the attorney for the Schneider family, Michael Tigar Esq., on November 12, 2002, as Civil Action No. 1: 01-CV-01902. Quotes are drawn from the second filing.
73. This suit was brought by ten Chilean survivors and families of victims of torture, disappearance, and murder, as well as the family of Spanish economist Carmelo Soria, tortured to death by DINA agents in the house of Michael Townley. Along with Kissinger, Townley was named as a defendant. See U.S. District Court for the District of Colombia, case number 1:02CV02240, p.3. This legal action was also filed by Michael Tigar Esq.
74. See CIA general counsel John Warner's memo to the CIA assistant director, "Discussions with Phil Buchen and James Wilderotter and Resulting Requests," June 25, 1975.
75. Sarah Anderson, a senior fellow at the Institute for Policy Studies, deserves credit for coining this new verb as part of the language of the human rights movement.
76. See the article "Barrado no Brasil" in the April 2002 issue of the Brazilian magazine *Revista Epoca.*
77. Bill Press, then cohost of *Crossfire*, with Robert Novak, posed this question to Kissinger. He responded by declaring that "it never happened" and then proceeded to blame the idea to block Allende's inauguration on former ambassador Edward Korry. As Kissinger knew, both in cables and in a personal meeting between Korry, Kissinger, and Nixon, the ambassador had adamantly opposed U.S. support for military coup plotting and had been kept in the dark about Track II, which Kissinger oversaw. See Chapter 1.
78. See *The News Hour with Jim Lehrer* transcript, "Pursuing the Past," February 20, 2001.
79. Valdes spoke on a Latin American Studies Association panel, hosted by this author, on the Clinton administration's Chile Declassification project.
80. Tyson's remarks were reported in a State Department cable, "Human Rights Commission: Agenda Item 5, Chile," March 9, 1977.
81. Interview with Theodore Piccone, June 9, 2002.
82. "Gabriella" was interviewed by Patricio Guzmán for his movie *The Pinochet Case.* In the final moment of the film, she states: "I believe that the strength of memory will help us heal. That's why it is so important to establish a collective memory, in order to live now and build the future."

Index

Page numbers in **bold** refer to documents

Publishing in the Public Interest

Thank you for reading this book published by The New Press. The New Press is a nonprofit, public interest publisher. New Press books and authors play a crucial role in sparking conversations about the key political and social issues of our day.

We hope you enjoyed this book and that you will stay in touch with The New Press. Here are a few ways to stay up to date with our books, events, and the issues we cover:

- Sign up at www.thenewpress.com/subscribe to receive updates on New Press authors and issues and to be notified about local events
- Like us on Facebook: www.facebook.com/newpressbooks
- Follow us on Twitter: www.twitter.com/thenewpress

Please consider buying New Press books for yourself; for friends and family; or to donate to schools, libraries, community centers, prison libraries, and other organizations involved with the issues our authors write about.

The New Press is a 501(c)(3) nonprofit organization. You can also support our work with a tax-deductible gift by visiting www.thenewpress.com/donate.